Scale 1:250,000 or 3.95 miles to 1 inch (2.5km to 1cm) Some islands are shown at smaller scales and Ireland at 1:1,000,000 scale

Motoring information

M4	Motorway with number	1	Primary route junction with and without number		Roundabout	or	Vehicle ferry	H	24-hour Accident & Emergency hospital

Motorway with number — M4

Toll motorway with toll station — Toll T4

Motorway junction with and without number — 8

Restricted motorway junctions — 5

Motorway service area — Fleet

Motorway and junction under construction

Primary route single/dual carriageway — A3

Primary route junction with and without number — 1

Restricted primary route junctions — 3

Primary route service area

Primary route destination — BATH

Other A road single/dual carriageway — A1123

B road single/dual carriageway — B2070

Minor road more than 4 metres wide, less than 4 metres wide

Roundabout

Interchange/junction

Narrow primary/other A/B road with passing places (Scotland)

Road under construction/approved

Road tunnel

Road toll, steep gradient (arrows point downhill) — Toll

Distance in miles between symbols — 5

Vehicle ferry — or

Fast vehicle ferry or catamaran

Railway line, in tunnel

Railway station and level crossing

Tourist railway

City, town, village or other built-up area

Airport, heliport, international freight terminal — (H) (P) (F)

24-hour Accident & Emergency hospital — H

Crematorium — C

Sandy beach

Park and Ride (at least 6 days per week) — P·R

Height in metres, mountain pass — 628 637 Lecht Summit

National boundary

County, administrative boundary

Touring information To avoid disappointment, check opening times before visiting

Scenic route

Tourist Information Centre

Tourist Information Centre (seasonal)

Visitor or heritage centre

Picnic site

Caravan site (AA inspected)

Camping site (AA inspected)

Caravan & camping site (AA inspected)

Abbey, cathedral or priory

Ruined abbey, cathedral or priory

Castle

Historic house or building

Museum or art gallery

Industrial interest

Aqueduct or viaduct

Garden

Arboretum

Vineyard

Brewery or distillery

Country park

Agricultural showground

Theme park

Farm or animal centre

Zoological or wildlife collection

Bird collection

Aquarium

RSPB site

National Nature Reserve (England, Scotland, Wales)

Wildlife Trust reserve

Local nature reserve

Forest drive

National trail

Waterfall

Viewpoint

Hill-fort

Roman antiquity

Prehistoric monument

Battle site with year — 1066

Steam railway centre

Cave

Windmill, monument

Beach (award winning)

Lighthouse

Golf course (AA listed)

Football stadium

County cricket ground

Rugby Union national stadium

International athletics stadium

Horse racing, show jumping

Motor-racing circuit

Air show venue

Ski slope (natural, artificial)

National Trust property

National Trust for Scotland property

English Heritage site

Historic Scotland site

Cadw (Welsh heritage) site

Other place of interest — ★

Boxed symbols indicate attractions within urban areas

World Heritage Site (UNESCO)

National Park

National Scenic Area (Scotland)

Forest Park

Heritage coast

Major shopping centre

37th edition June 2017

© AA Media Limited 2017

Revised version of the atlas formerly known as *AA Big Road Atlas*. Original edition printed 1981.

Cartography: All cartography in this atlas edited, designed and produced by the Mapping Services Department of AA Publishing (A05514).

This atlas contains Ordnance Survey data © Crown copyright and database right 2017.

This is based upon Crown Copyright and is reproduced with the permission of Land & Property Services under delegated authority from the Controller of Her Majesty's Stationery Office, © Crown copyright and database right 2017. PMLPA No. 100497.

© Ordnance Survey Ireland/Government of Ireland Copyright Permit No. MP000717.

Publisher's notes: Published by AA Publishing (a trading name of AA Media Limited, whose registered office is Fanum House, Basing View, Basingstoke, Hampshire RG21 4EA, UK. Registered number 06112600).
All rights reserved. No part of this publication may be reproduced, stored in a retrieval system, or transmitted in any form or by any means – electronic, mechanical, photocopying, recording or otherwise – unless the permission of the publisher has been given beforehand.

A CIP catalogue record for this book is available from The British Library.

Disclaimer: The contents of this atlas are believed to be correct at the time of the latest revision, it will not include any subsequent amended, new or temporary information including diversions and traffic control or enforcement systems. The publishers cannot be held responsible or liable for any loss or damage occasioned to any person acting or refraining from action as a result of any use or reliance on material in this atlas, nor for any errors, omissions or changes in such material. This does not affect your statutory rights.

The publishers would welcome information to correct any errors or omissions and to keep this atlas up to date. Please write to the Atlas Editor, AA Publishing, The Automobile Association, Fanum House, Basing View, Basingstoke, Hampshire RG21 4EA, UK.
E-mail: roadatlasfeedback@theaa.com

Acknowledgements: AA Publishing would like to thank the following for their assistance in producing this atlas: Crematoria data provided by the Cremation Society of Great Britain. Cadw, English Heritage, Forestry Commission, Historic Scotland, Johnsons, National Trust and National Trust for Scotland, RSPB, The Wildlife Trust, Scottish Natural Heritage, Natural England, The Countryside Council for Wales (road maps). Award winning beaches from 'Blue Flag' and 'Keep Scotland Beautiful' (summer 2016 data): for latest information visit www.blueflag.org and www.keepscotlandbeautiful.org

Printer: Wyndeham Peterborough Ltd, UK

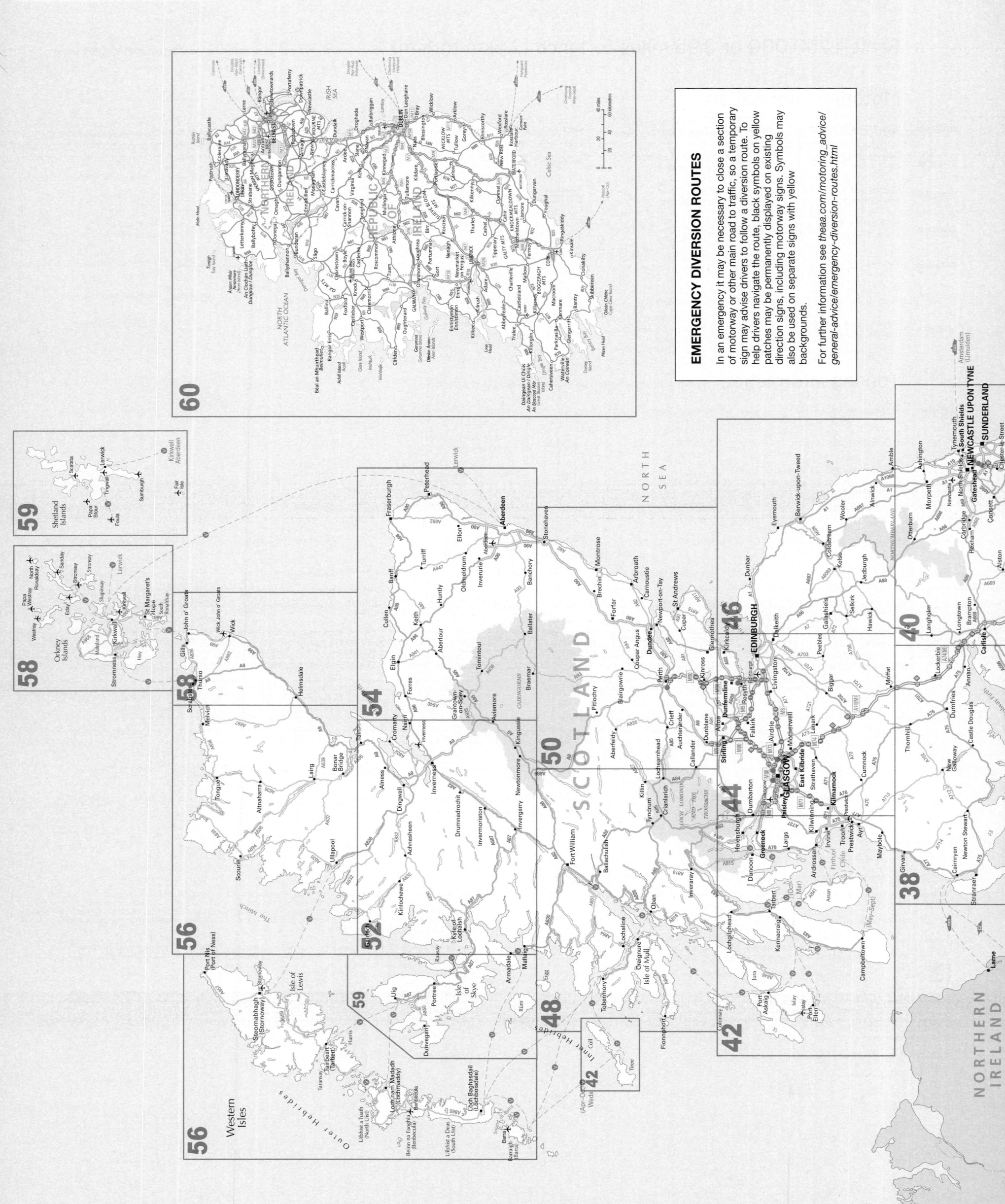

EMERGENCY DIVERSION ROUTES

In an emergency it may be necessary to close a section of motorway or other main road to traffic, so a temporary sign may advise drivers to follow a diversion route. To help drivers navigate the route, black symbols on yellow patches may be permanently displayed on existing direction signs, including motorway signs. Symbols may also be used on separate signs with yellow backgrounds.

For further information see *theaa.com/motoring_advice/general-advice/emergency-diversion-routes.html*

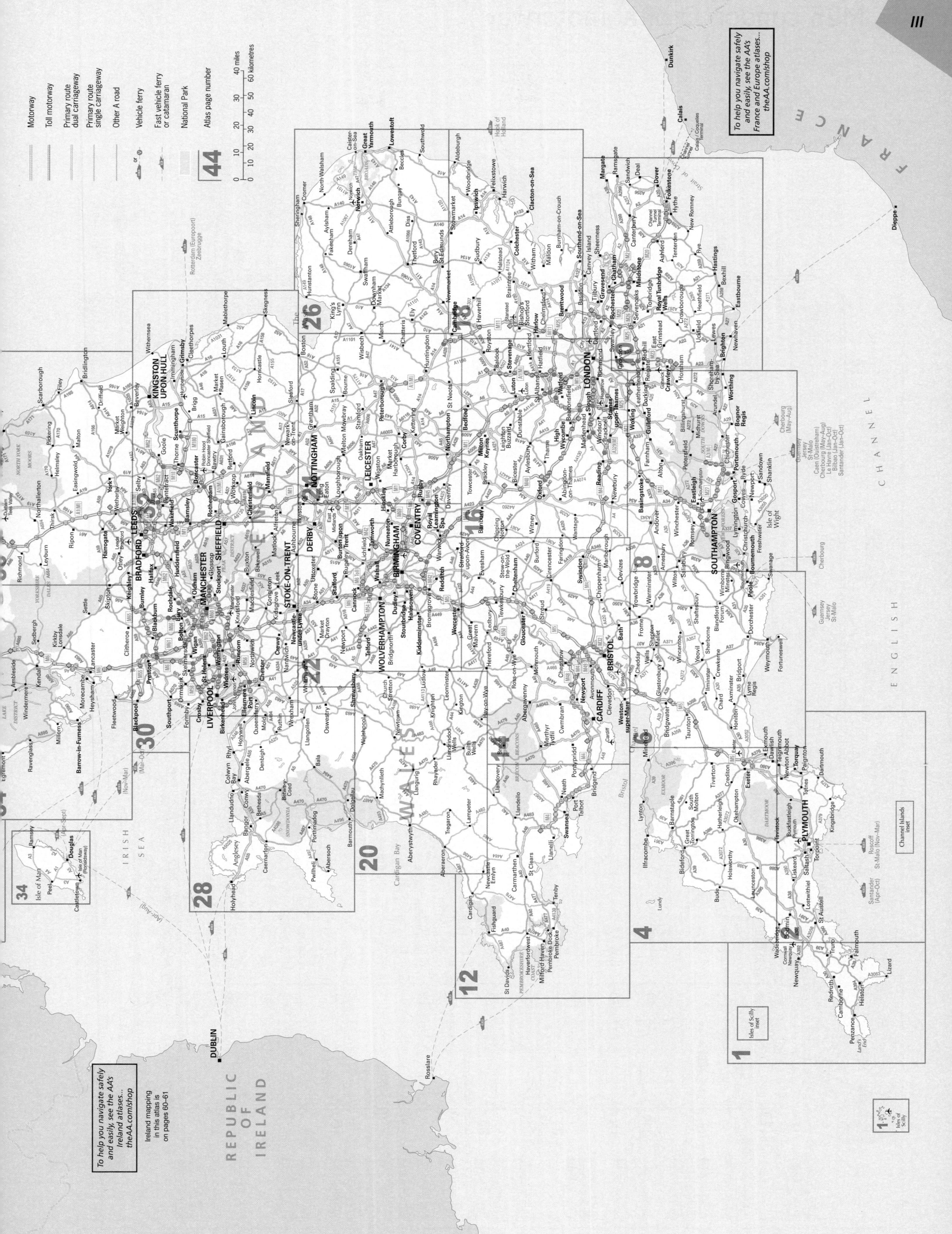

Motorway
Toll motorway
Primary route dual carriageway
Primary route single carriageway
Other A road
Vehicle ferry
Fast vehicle ferry or catamaran
National Park
44 Atlas page number

0 10 20 30 40 miles
0 10 20 30 40 50 60 kilometres

To help you navigate safely and easily, see the AA's France and Europe atlases... theAA.com/shop

To help you navigate safely and easily, see the AA's Ireland atlases... theAA.com/shop

Ireland mapping in this atlas is on pages 60–61

Refer also to atlas pages 9–10 and 17–18

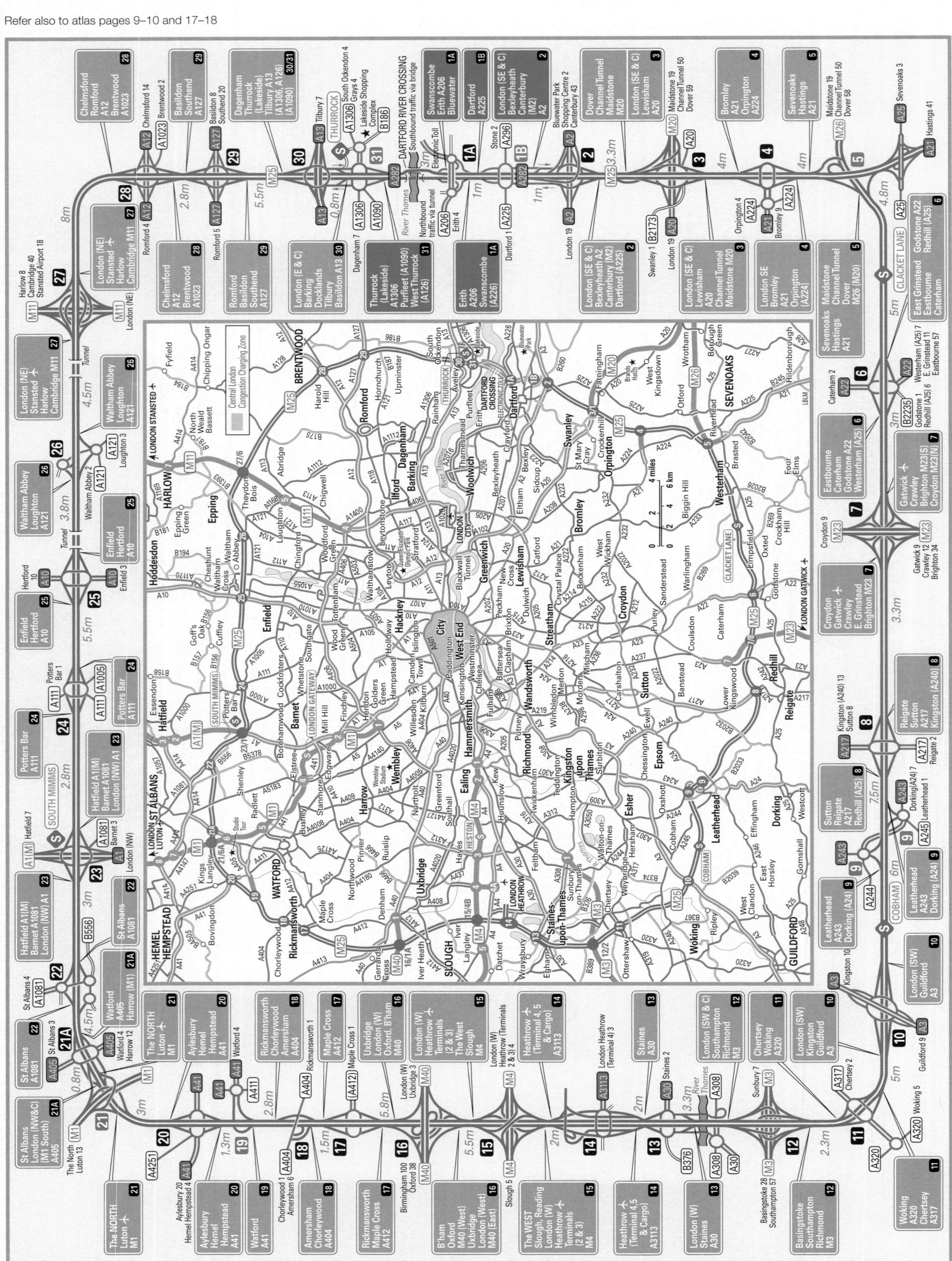

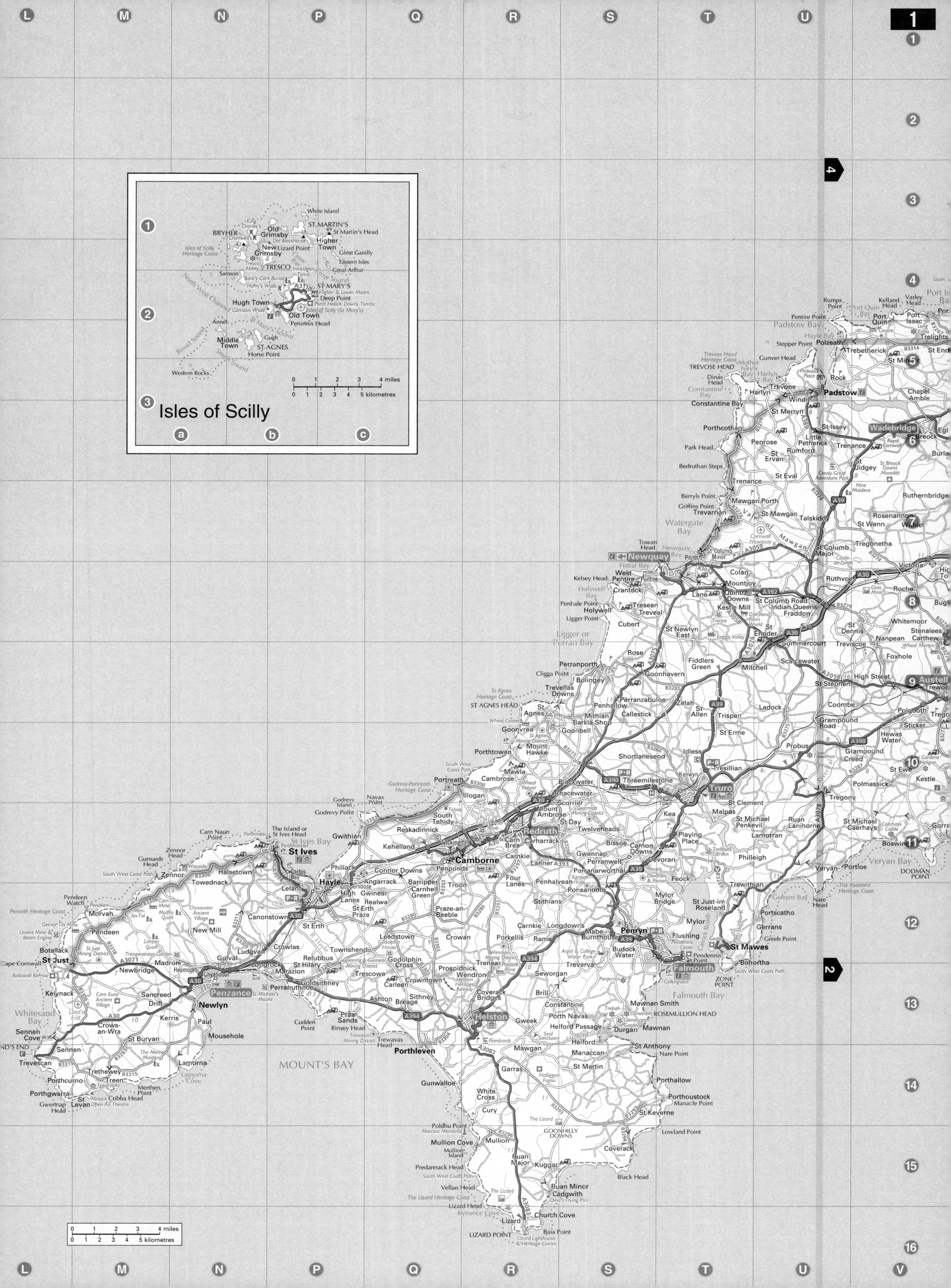
Isles of Scilly
White Island
ST. MARTIN'S
St Martin's Head
BRYHER
Old Grimsby
Higher Town
New Grimsby
Lizard Point
Isles of Scilly Heritage Coast
TRESCO
Great Ganilly
Eastern Isles
Great Arthur
Samson
Crow Sound
ST. MARY'S
North West Channel
Hugh Town
Deep Point
Old Town
Peninnis Head
St Mary's Sound
Annet
Middle Town
Gugh
ST. AGNES
Horse Point
Broad Sound
Smith Sound
Western Rocks
0 1 2 3 4 miles
0 1 2 3 4 5 kilometres
Padstow Bay
Pentire Point
Rumps Point
Port Quin
Kelland Head
Varley Head
Port Isaac
Stepper Point
Polzeath
Trebetherick
St Minver
Trevose Head Heritage Coast
TREVOSE HEAD
Gunver Head
Dinas Head
Harlyn
Trevone
Padstow
Rock
Chapel Amble
Constantine Bay
Windmill
St Merryn
Porthcothan
Little Petherick
St Issey
Wadebridge
Trenance
Egloshayle
Park Head
Penrose
St Ervan
Rumford
Bedruthan Steps
St Jidgey
Burlawn
St Eval
Berryls Point
Griffins Point
Trevarrian
Mawgan Porth
St Mawgan
Talskiddy
Rutherbridge
Watergate Bay
Rosenannon
St Wenn
Withiel
Towan Head
Newquay Bay
Newquay
Fistral Bay
St Columb Minor
St Columb Major
Tregonetha
West Pentire
Kelsey Head
Crantock
Colan
Ruthvoes
Victoria
Holywell Bay
Holywell
Penhale Point
Ligger Point
Tresean
Treveal
Lane
Quintrell Downs
Kestle Mill
St Columb Road
Indian Queens
Fraddon
Roche
Cubert
Ligger or Perran Bay
St Newlyn East
St Enoder
Summercourt
St Dennis
Whitemoor
Nanpean
Stenalees
Carthew
Treviscoe
Rose
Fiddlers Green
Mitchell
Scarcewater
Foxhole
Perranporth
Bolingey
Goonhavern
Cligga Point
Trevellas Downs
High Street
St Stephen
St Austell
Trewoon
St Agnes Heritage Coast
ST AGNES HEAD
Penhallow
Perranzabuloe
Zelah
St Allen
Ladock
Coombe
Polgooth
St Agnes
Mithian
Callestick
Trispen
Grampound Road
Sticker
Goonvrea
Barkla Shop
Goonbell
St Erme
Hewas Water
Porthtowan
Mount Hawke
Shortlanesend
Idless
Probus
Grampound
Creed
St Ewe
Mawla
Threemilestone
Tresillian
Kestle
Portreath
Godrevy-Portreath Heritage Coast
Cambrose
Blackwater
Truro
Polmassick
Navax Point
Godrevy Island
Godrevy Point
Illogan
Chacewater
Scorrier
Tregony
St Clement
South Tehidy
Mount Ambrose
St Day
Kea
Malpas
St Michael Penkevil
Ruan Lanihorne
St Michael Caerhays
Gwithian
Reskadinnick
Twelveheads
Carn Naun Point
The Island or St Ives Head
St Ives Bay
St Ives
Kehelland
Carn Brea
Redruth
Carharrack
Bissoe
Playing Place
Lamorran
Zennor Head
Gurnards Head
Zennor
Halsetown
Camborne
Carnkie
Lanner
Gwennap
Perranwell
Carnon Downs
Devoran
Philleigh
Boswinger
Veryan Bay
South West Coast Path
Towednack
Carbis Bay
Lelant
Phillack
Hayle
Connor Downs
Penponds
Perranarworthal
Feock
Veryan
Portloe
DODMAN POINT
Pendeen Watch
Angarrack
Barripper
Carnhell Green
Troon
Four Lanes
Penhalvean
Ponsanooth
Trewithian
The Roseland Heritage Coast
Penwith Heritage Coast
Morvah
Copperhouse
High Lanes
Gwinear
Realwa
St Erth Praze
Stithians
Mylor Bridge
St Just-in-Roseland
Gerrans Bay
Nare Head
Levant Mine & Beam Engine
Pendeen
Chysauster Ancient Village
New Mill
Canonstown
St Erth
Praze-an-Beeble
Carnkie
Longdowns
Mylor
Portscatho
Gerrans
Greeb Point
Botallack
St Just
Cape Cornwall
Ballowall Barrow
Crowlas
Townshend
Leedstown
Crowan
Porkellis
Rame
Mabe Burnthouse
Penryn
Flushing
St Mawes
Gulval
Ludgvan
Madron
Newbridge
Longrock
Relubbus
St Hilary
Godolphin Cross
Marazion
Trescowe
Prospidnick
Trenear
Wendron
Treverva
Budock Water
Pendennis Point
Falmouth
Bohortha
ZONE POINT
Kelynack
Heamoor
Chyandour
Penzance
Perranuthnoe
Goldsithney
Carleen
Crowntown
Sithney
Sancreed
Drift
Newlyn
St Michael's Mount
Ashton
Breage
Coverack Bridges
Seworgan
Brill
Constantine
Mawnan Smith
Falmouth Bay
Whitesand Bay
Crows-an-Wra
Kerris
Paul
Cudden Point
Praa Sands
Rinsey Head
Helston
Gweek
Porth Navas
Helford Passage
ROSEMULLION HEAD
Durgan
Mawnan
Sennen Cove
LAND'S END
Mousehole
St Buryan
Trewavas Head
Porthleven
Helford
St Anthony
Nare Point
Sennen
Trevescan
MOUNT'S BAY
Mawgan
Manaccan
Lamorna
Lamorna Cove
St Martin
Trethewey
Treen
Porthcurno
Garras
Porthallow
Porthgwarra
Gwennap Head
St Levan
Merthen Point
Minack Open Air Theatre
Cribba Head
Gunwalloe
White Cross
Porthoustock
Manacle Point
Cury
St Keverne
Poldhu Point
GOONHILLY DOWNS
Lowland Point
Mullion Cove
Mullion
Mullion Island
Coverack
Predannack Head
Ruan Major
Kuggar
Black Head
Vellan Head
Ruan Minor
Cadgwith
The Lizard Heritage Coast
Lizard Head
Kynance Cove
Lizard
Church Cove
LIZARD POINT
Bass Point
A30
A39
A390
A394
A3083
A3078
A3058
A3075
A3076
B3314
B3276
B3274
B3279
B3284
B3285
B3277
B3300
B3301
B3311
B3306
B3318
B3315
B3283
B3280
B3302
B3303
B3297
B3298
B3304
B3296
B3293
B3294
0 1 2 3 4 miles
0 1 2 3 4 5 kilometres
L M N P Q R S T U V
1 2 3 4 5 6 7 8 9 10 11 12 13 14 15 16
4
2

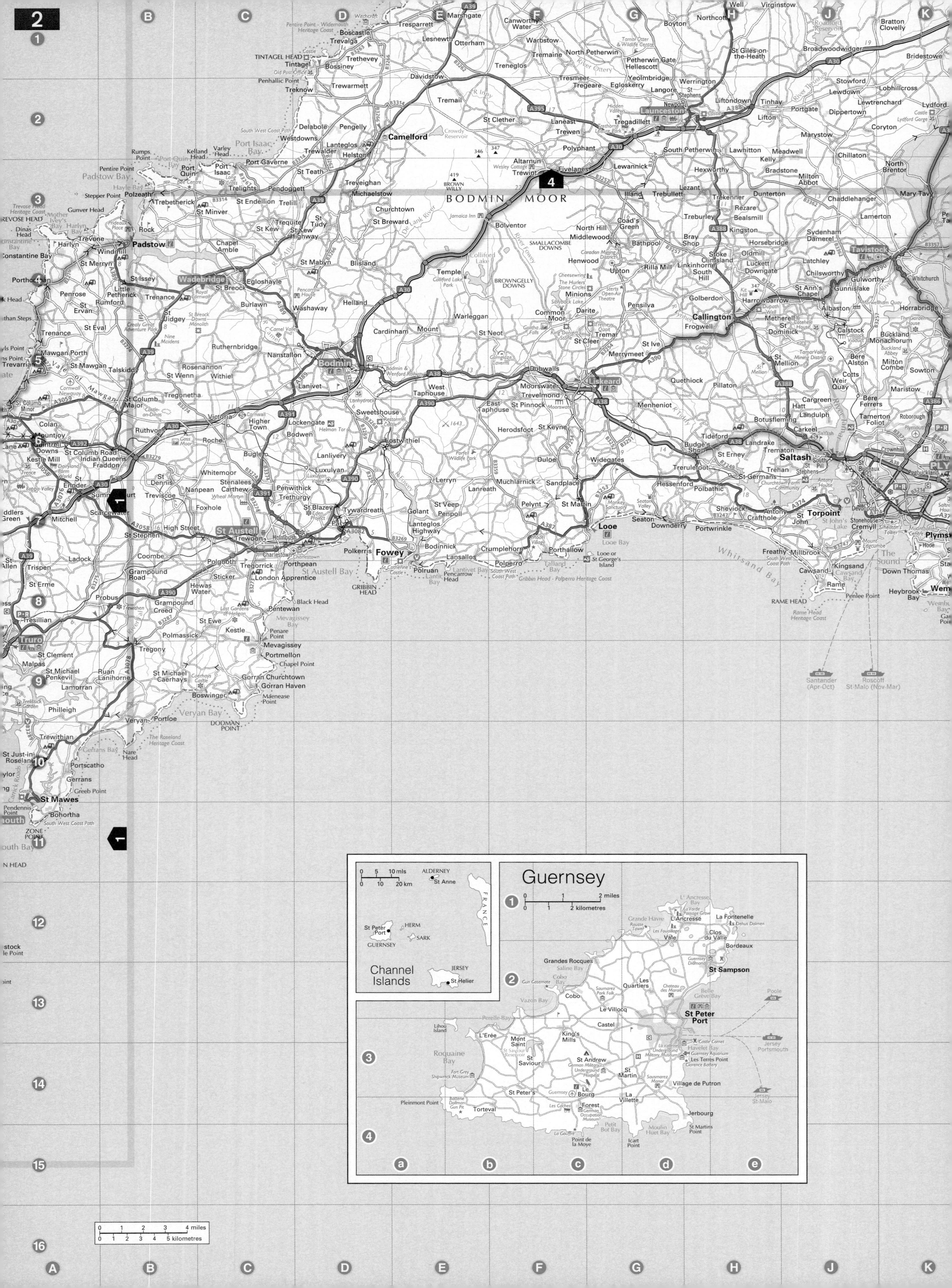
BODMIN MOOR
Boscastle
Tintagel
Camelford
Launceston
Padstow
Wadebridge
Bodmin
Liskeard
Callington
Tavistock
Saltash
Torpoint
Looe
Fowey
Lostwithiel
St Austell
Mevagissey
Truro
St Mawes
Polzeath
Port Isaac
Padstow Bay
St Austell Bay
Veryan Bay
Whitsand Bay
Gerrans Bay
Looe Bay
Lantic Bay
Mevagissey Bay
DODMAN POINT
GRIBBIN HEAD
RAME HEAD
Black Head
Nare Head
Pentire Point
Stepper Point
TINTAGEL HEAD
Penhallic Point
Trevose Head
Brown Willy
Colliford Lake
Crowdy Reservoir
Siblyback Lake
Santander (Apr-Oct)
Roscoff
St Malo (Nov-Mar)
Guernsey
Channel Islands
ALDERNEY
St Anne
HERM
SARK
GUERNSEY
JERSEY
St Helier
FRANCE
St Peter Port
St Sampson
Vale
L'Ancresse
Bordeaux
Grandes Rocques
Cobo
Vazon Bay
Castel
King's Mills
St Andrew
St Martin
Le Bourg
Forest
Torteval
St Peter's
St Saviour
L'Erée
Lihou Island
Rocquaine Bay
Pleinmont Point
Petit Bot Bay
Icart Point
Moulin Huet Bay
Jerbourg
Village de Putron
La Villette
Le Villocq
Les Quartiers
Belle Grève Bay
Havelet Bay
Poole
Jersey
Portsmouth
St Malo
0 1 2 3 4 miles
0 1 2 3 4 5 kilometres

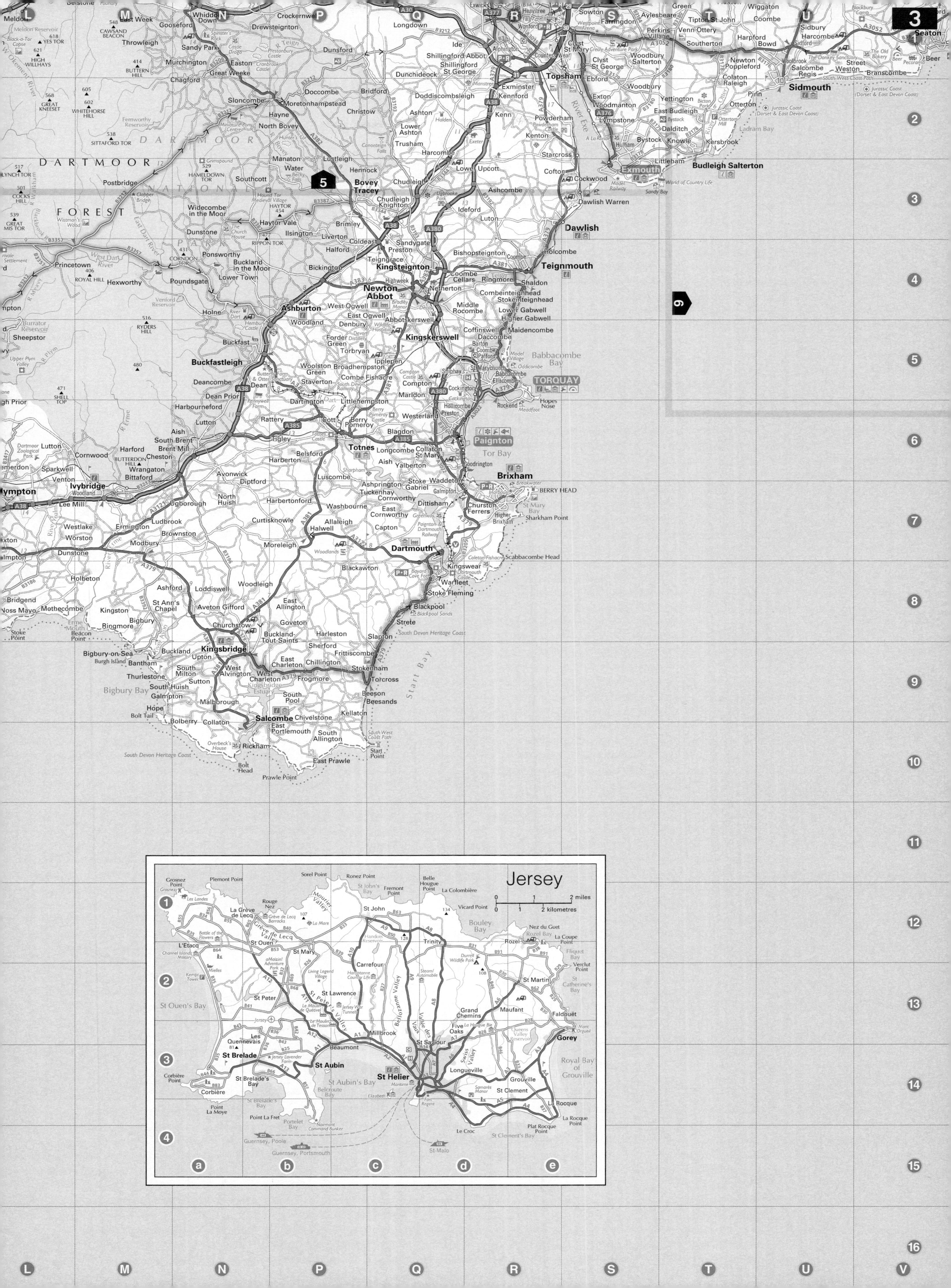
DARTMOOR
FOREST
DARTMOOR NATIONAL PARK
Okehampton
Moretonhampstead
Bovey Tracey
Chudleigh
Exeter
Topsham
Exmouth
Budleigh Salterton
Sidmouth
Seaton
Beer
Dawlish
Teignmouth
Kingsteignton
Newton Abbot
Ashburton
Buckfastleigh
Kingskerswell
TORQUAY
Babbacombe Bay
Paignton
Tor Bay
Brixham
BERRY HEAD
Totnes
Dartmouth
Kingswear
Ivybridge
Plympton
Kingsbridge
Salcombe
Bigbury Bay
Start Bay
Start Point
Prawle Point
Bolt Head
South Devon Heritage Coast
Jurassic Coast (Dorset & East Devon Coast)
Ladram Bay
Princetown
Widecombe in the Moor
Jersey
Grosnez Point
Plemont Point
Sorel Point
Ronez Point
St John
Bouley Bay
Rozel
La Coupe Point
St Martin
St Catherine's Bay
Gorey
Royal Bay of Grouville
Grouville
La Rocque
Le Croc
St Clement's Bay
St Clement
St Helier
Elizabeth Castle
St Aubin's Bay
St Aubin
Beaumont
St Brelade
St Brelade's Bay
Corbière
Point La Moye
Quennevais
St Ouen's Bay
L'Etacq
St Ouen
St Mary
St Peter
St Lawrence
Carrefour
Trinity
Millbrook
St Saviour
Longueville
Five Oaks
Grand Chemins
Maufant
Faldouet
Guernsey, Poole
Guernsey, Portsmouth
St-Malo
0 1 2 miles
0 1 2 kilometres
L M N P Q R S T U V
1 2 3 4 5 6 7 8 9 10 11 12 13 14 15 16

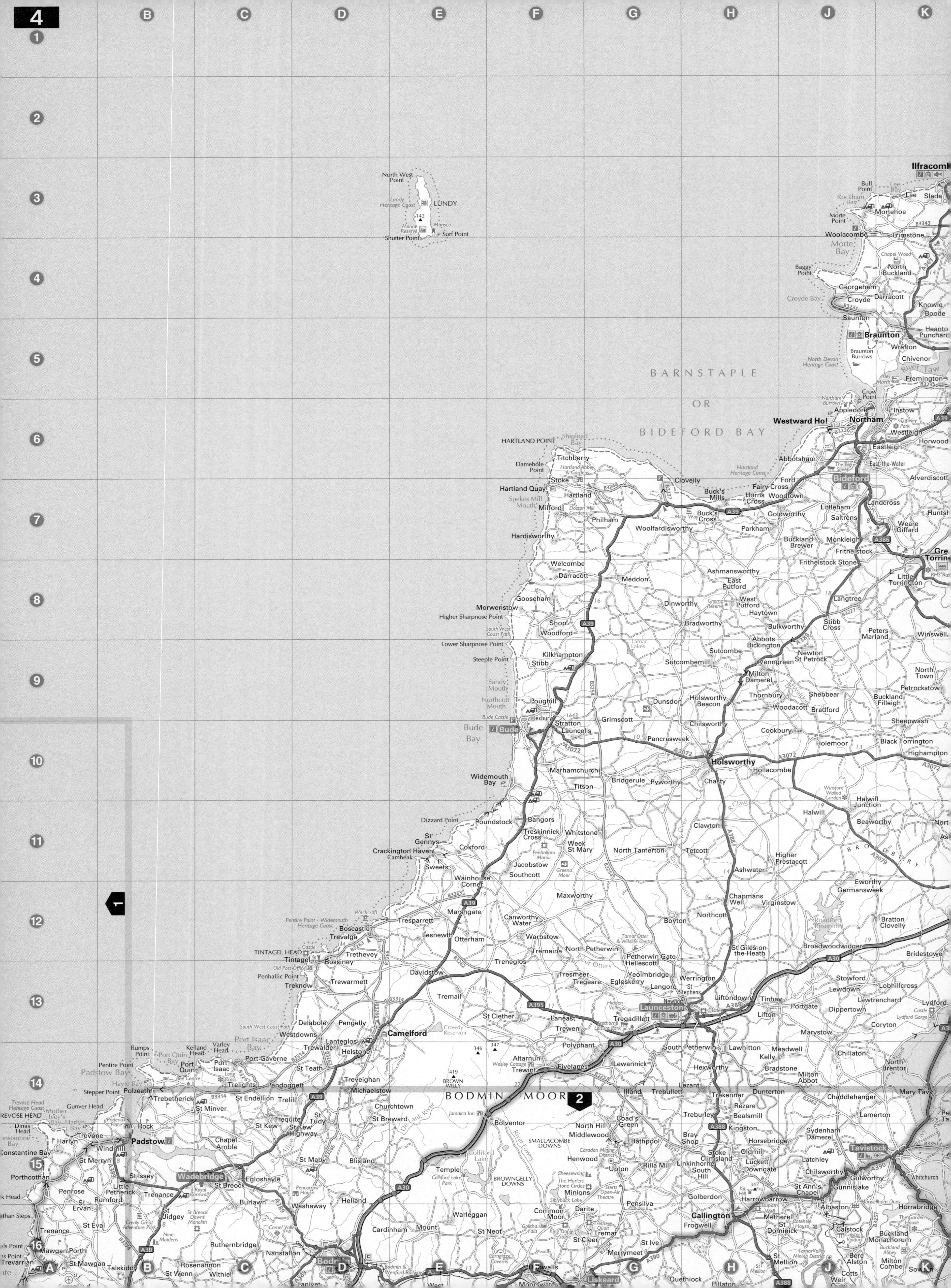
LUNDY
North West Point
Shutter Point
Surf Point
Lundy Heritage Coast
Marine Reserve
Marisco
142
BARNSTAPLE
OR
BIDEFORD BAY
Ilfracombe
Bull Point
Lee
Slade
Morte Point
Mortehoe
Woolacombe
Trimstone
Morte Bay
Baggy Point
North Buckland
Georgeham
Croyde
Croyde Bay
Darracott
Saunton
Knowle
Braunton
Braunton Burrows
Wrafton
Chivenor
North Devon Heritage Coast
Fremington
Crow Point
Appledore
Instow
Westward Ho!
Northam
Westleigh
Eastleigh
Horwood
Abbotsham
Bideford
East-the-Water
Alverdiscott
HARTLAND POINT
Shipload Bay
Titchberry
Dameholc Point
Stoke
Hartland
Hartland Quay
Spekes Mill Mouth
Milford
Philham
Clovelly
Buck's Mills
Fairy Cross
Ford
Horns Cross
Woodtown
Buck's Cross
Woolfardisworthy
Parkham
Goldworthy
Littleham
Landcross
Saltrens
Weare Giffard
Hardisworthy
Buckland Brewer
Monkleigh
Frithelstock
Frithelstock Stone
Great Torrington
Little Torrington
Welcombe
Darracott
Meddon
Ashmansworthy
East Putford
West Putford
Gooseham
Morwenstow
Higher Sharpnose Point
Dinworthy
Langtree
Haytown
Shop
Woodford
Bradworthy
Bulkworthy
Stibb Cross
Peters Marland
Lower Sharpnose Point
Steeple Point
Kilkhampton
Stibb
Abbots Bickington
Sutcombe
Sutcombemill
Venngreen
Newton St Petrock
Milton Damerel
North Town
Sandy Mouth
Northcott Mouth
Poughill
Flexbury
Bude
Bude Bay
Stratton
Launcells
Grimscott
Dunsdon
Holsworthy Beacon
Thornbury
Woodacott
Shebbear
Bradford
Buckland Filleigh
Chilsworthy
Pancrasweek
Cookbury
Sheepwash
Holemoor
Black Torrington
Highampton
Holsworthy
Hollacombe
Marhamchurch
Bridgerule
Pyworthy
Chasty
Titson
Widemouth Bay
Halwill Junction
Halwill
Beaworthy
Dizzard Point
Poundstock
Bangors
Treskinnick Cross
Whitstone
Clawton
St Gennys
Crackington Haven
Cambeak
Coxford
Week St Mary
North Tamerton
Tetcott
Higher Prestacott
Sweets
Jacobstow
Southcott
Ashwater
Wainhouse Corner
Maxworthy
Eworthy
Germansweek
Chapmans Well
Virginstow
Marshgate
Tresparrett
Boscastle
Canworthy Water
Northcott
Boyton
Bratton Clovelly
Trevalga
Lesnewth
Otterham
Warbstow
St Giles-on-the-Heath
Broadwoodwidger
Bridestowe
TINTAGEL HEAD
Tintagel
Trethevey
Bossiney
Tremaine
North Petherwin
Petherwin Gate
Hellescott
Penhallic Point
Treknow
Trewarmett
Davidstow
Treneglos
Tresmeer
Tregeare
Egloskerry
Yeolmbridge
Werrington
Langore
Stowford
Lewdown
Lobhillcross
Lewtrenchard
Tremail
Launceston
Liftondown
Tinhay
Lifton
Portgate
Dippertown
Lydford
St Clether
Laneast
Tregadillett
Coryton
Delabole
Pengelly
Camelford
Trewen
Westdowns
Lanteglos
Helstone
Trewalder
Polyphant
South Petherwin
Lawhitton
Marystow
Meadwell
Kelly
Chillaton
Rumps Point
Port Quin Bay
Kelland Head
Varley Head
Port Isaac Bay
Port Gaverne
Port Quin
Port Isaac
Pentire Point
Padstow Bay
St Teath
Altarnun
Trewint
Fivelanes
Lewannick
Hexworthy
Bradstone
North Brentor
Milton Abbot
Hayle Bay
Stepper Point
Polzeath
Trelights
Pendoggett
Treveighan
Michaelstow
BROWN WILLY
BODMIN MOOR
Illand
Trebullett
Lezant
Trekenner
Dunterton
Mary Tavy
Trevose Head
Mother Ivey's Bay
Gunver Head
Trebetherick
St Minver
St Endellion
Trelill
Churchtown
Bolventor
Jamaica Inn
Coad's Green
Rezare
Bealsmill
Chaddlehanger
Dinas Head
Harlyn
Trevone
Rock
St Kew
Treguite
St Tudy
St Kew Highway
St Breward
North Hill
Middlewood
Treburley
Kingston
Lamerton
Constantine Bay
Windmill
Padstow
Chapel Amble
SMALLACOMBE DOWNS
Bathpool
Bray Shop
Horsebridge
Sydenham Damerel
St Merryn
Wadebridge
St Mabyn
Blisland
Temple
Henwood
Upton
Rilla Mill
Stoke Climsland
Oldmill
Luckett
Tavistock
Porthcothan
St Issey
Little Petherick
St Breock
Egloshayle
Trenance
Penrose
St Ervan
Rumford
St Jidgey
Burlawn
Washaway
Helland
BROWNGELLY DOWNS
Minions
Linkinhorne
South Hill
Downgate
Latchley
Chilsworthy
Gulworthy
Whitchurch
Gunnislake
St Ann's Chapel
Harrowbarrow
Pensilva
Golberdon
Callington
Albaston
Horrabridge
St Eval
Cardinham
Mount
Warleggan
Common Moor
Darite
Tremar
Frogwell
Metherell
St Dominick
Calstock
Buckland Monachorum
Trenance
Mawgan Porth
Nine Maidens
Rutherbridge
Nanstallon
St Neot
St Cleer
St Ive
Merrymeet
Bere Alston
Milton Combe
Trevarrian
St Mawgan
Talskiddy
Rosenannon
St Wenn
Withiel
Bodmin
Lanivet
Fowalls
Liskeard
Quethiock
Pillaton
St Mellion
Weir
Cotts
Sowton
A39
A30
A388
A386
A3072
A390
A395
B3263
B3314
B3266
B3248
B3237
B3254
B3257
B3362
B3227
A B C D E F G H J K
1 2 3 4 5 6 7 8 9 10 11 12 13 14 15 16

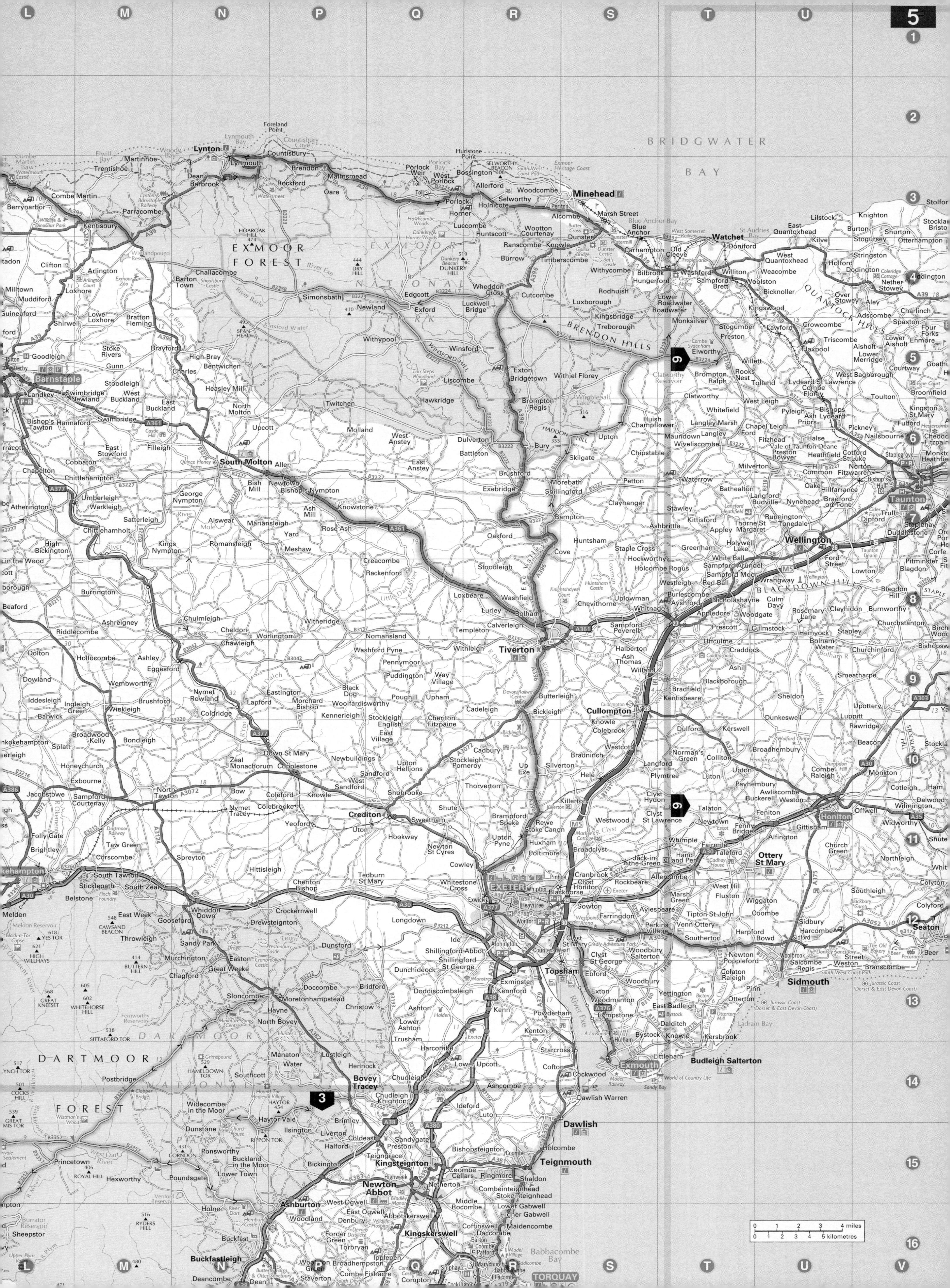
BRIDGWATER BAY
EXMOOR FOREST
EXMOOR NATIONAL PARK
BRENDON HILLS
QUANTOCK HILLS
BLACKDOWN HILLS
DARTMOOR FOREST
DARTMOOR NATIONAL PARK
Lynton
Lynmouth
Countisbury
Foreland Point
Hurlstone Point
Porlock
Porlock Weir
Minehead
Dunster
Blue Anchor
Watchet
Doniford
Combe Martin
Berrynarbor
Barnstaple
South Molton
Dulverton
Wiveliscombe
Bampton
Tiverton
Wellington
Taunton
Cullompton
Crediton
Exeter
Honiton
Ottery St Mary
Sidmouth
Seaton
Budleigh Salterton
Exmouth
Topsham
Dawlish
Teignmouth
Kingsteignton
Newton Abbot
Bovey Tracey
Chudleigh
Ashburton
Buckfastleigh
Kingskerswell
Torquay
Okehampton
Chagford
Moretonhampstead
Babbacombe Bay
Lyme Bay
Ladram Bay
Sandy Bay
Dawlish Warren
Simonsbath
Exford
Winsford
Wimbleball Lake
Clatworthy Reservoir
Dunkery Beacon 519
River Exe
River Barle
Wheddon Cross
Exton
Exebridge
Hatherleigh
Chulmleigh
Witheridge
Bradninch
Silverton
Stoke Canon
Whimple
Clyst Honiton
Feniton
Dunkeswell
Hemyock
Culmstock
Uffculme
Willand
Halberton
Sampford Peverell
Burlescombe
Milverton
Bishops Lydeard
Stogumber
Williton
Crowcombe
Kilve
East Quantoxhead
Holford
Norton Fitzwarren
Staplehay
Trull
Churchinford
Sheldon
Luppitt
Upottery
Combe Raleigh
Gittisham
Offwell
Widworthy
Colyton
Colyford
Beer
Branscombe
Salcombe Regis
Sidford
Newton Poppleford
Colaton Raleigh
East Budleigh
Otterton
Lympstone
Woodbury
Exton
Ebford
Clyst St Mary
Clyst St George
Exminster
Kenton
Kennford
Powderham
Starcross
Cockwood
Kenn
Ide
Alphington
Dunsford
Christow
Doddiscombsleigh
Ashton
Trusham
Ideford
Luton
Bishopsteignton
Shaldon
Combeinteignhead
Stokeinteignhead
Maidencombe
Coffinswell
Abbotskerswell
Ipplepen
Denbury
Broadhempston
Staverton
Dean Prior
Holne
Poundsgate
Widecombe in the Moor
Haytor Vale
Ilsington
Liverton
Lustleigh
Manaton
North Bovey
Postbridge
Princetown
Hexworthy
Sheepstor
South Zeal
Sticklepath
Belstone
South Tawton
Whiddon Down
Drewsteignton
Throwleigh
Gidleigh
Spreyton
Bow
North Tawton
Sampford Courtenay
Winkleigh
Dolton
Iddesleigh
Lapford
Morchard Bishop
Cheriton Fitzpaine
Thorverton
Shobrooke
Sandford
Copplestone
Yeoford
Cheriton Bishop
Tedburn St Mary
Whitestone
Newton St Cyres
Brampford Speke
Upton Pyne
Rewe
Poltimore
Broadclyst
Pinhoe
Rockbeare
Aylesbeare
Farringdon
Woodbury Salterton
Tipton St John
Harpford
Bowd
Venn Ottery
Southerton
Talaton
Clyst Hydon
Plymtree
Payhembury
Awliscombe
Buckerell
Weston
Kentisbeare
Blackborough
Bradfield
Ashill
Craddock
Clayhidon
Burnworthy
Bolham Water
Holcombe Rogus
Ashbrittle
Stawley
Kittisford
Greenham
Appley
Thorne St Margaret
Langford Budville
Runnington
Nynehead
Bradford on Tone
Oake
Hillfarrance
Bathealton
Waterrow
Chipstable
Upton
Skilgate
Morebath
Shillingford
Clayhanger
Petton
Huntsham
Hockworthy
Staple Cross
Uplowman
Chevithorne
Sampford Arundel
Sampford Moor
Ford Street
Pitminster
Blagdon
Lowton
Knighton
Stogursey
Otterhampton
Nether Stowey
Over Stowey
Aisholt
Enmore
Spaxton
Charlinch
Broomfield
Kingston St Mary
Cheddon Fitzpaine
Monkton Heathfield
Creech St Michael
Nailsbourne
Pickney
Pyleigh
Lydeard St Lawrence
Tolland
Brompton Ralph
Elworthy
Monksilver
Nettlecombe
Sampford Brett
Bicknoller
Roadwater
Luxborough
Treborough
Kingsbridge
Cutcombe
Timberscombe
Withycombe
Carhampton
Old Cleeve
Washford
Rodhuish
Withiel Florey
Brompton Regis
Bury
Haddon Hill
Winsford Hill
Withypool
Hawkridge
Liscombe
Twitchen
Molland
West Anstey
East Anstey
Knowstone
Bishop's Nympton
Rose Ash
Meshaw
Romansleigh
Kings Nympton
Chittlehamholt
Chittlehampton
Umberleigh
Atherington
High Bickington
Burrington
Ashreigney
Riddlecombe
Chawleigh
Cheldon
Worlington
Eggesford
Wembworthy
Brushford
Nymet Rowland
Coldridge
Bondleigh
Zeal Monachorum
Down St Mary
Broadwood Kelly
Honeychurch
Exbourne
Jacobstowe
Folly Gate
Brightley
Taw Green
Corscombe
Hittisleigh
Crockernwell
Longdown
Holcombe Burnell
Shillingford Abbot
Shillingford St George
Dunchideock
Bridford
Doccombe
Easton
Great Weeke
Sloncombe
Murchington
Sandy Park
Gooseford
Hennock
Chudleigh Knighton
Brimley
Coldeast
Sandygate
Preston
Teigngrace
Bickington
Ogwell
Woodland
Forder Green
Torbryan
Buckland in the Moor
Lower Town
Ponsworthy
Dunstone
Great Mis Tor
High Willhays 621
Yes Tor 618
Cawsand Beacon
Great Kneeset
Whitehorse Hill
Sittaford Tor
Hameldown Tor
Haytor 454
Rippon Tor
Corndon Tor
Ryders Hill
Royal Hill
Stolford
Stockland Bristol
Burton
Shurton
Stringston
Dodington
Holford
Adscombe
Four Forks
Aley
Trull
Dipford
Cotford St Luke
Heathfield
Preston Bowyer
Halse
Ash Priors
Fitzhead
Chapel Leigh
Ford
Langley Marsh
Maundown
Huish Champflower
Clatworthy
West Leigh
Whitefield
Rooks Nest
Willett
Combe Florey
Triscombe
Crowcombe
Lawford
Kingswood
Flaxpool
Lower Aisholt
Merridge
Courtway
Fyne Court
Goathurst
Sidbury
Harcombe
Stockland
Monkton
Cotleigh
Wilmington
Dalwood
Shute
Northleigh
Southleigh
Wiggaton
Fluxton
West Hill
Fairmile
Taleford
Alfington
Church Green
Wolford Chapel
Broadhembury
Rawridge
Beacon
Newtown
Fenny Bridges
Escot
Hand and Pen
Jack-in-the-Green
Marsh Green
Perkins Village
Cranbrook
Allercombe
Sowton
Whipton
Heavitree
Wonford
Countess Wear
Exwick
Cowley
Hele
Killerton
Up Exe
Westwood
Clyst St Lawrence
Colliton
Norman's Green
Langford
Dulford
Kerswell
Westcott
Butterleigh
Bickleigh
Cadeleigh
Cadbury
Stockleigh Pomeroy
Stockleigh English
East Village
Upton Hellions
Newbuildings
Woolfardisworthy
Kennerleigh
Black Dog
Poughill
Upham
Puddington
Way Village
Pennymoor
Washford Pyne
Nomansland
Templeton
Calverleigh
Withleigh
Loxbeare
Lurley
Bolham
Washfield
Stoodleigh
Oakford
Rackenford
Creacombe
Newtown
Bish Mill
Aller
George Nympton
Alswear
Mariansleigh
Yard
Ash Mill
Kingsheanton
Swimbridge
Swimbridge Newland
Landkey
Goodleigh
Stoke Rivers
Gunn
Stoodleigh
West Buckland
East Buckland
Charles
Heasley Mill
High Bray
Bentwichen
North Molton
Filleigh
Castle Hill
Hannaford
Bishop's Tawton
Cobbaton
East Stowford
Chapelton
Warkleigh
Satterleigh
Brayford
Bratton Fleming
Lower Loxhore
Loxhore
Shirwell
Muddiford
Milltown
Arlington
Challacombe
Barton Town
Clifton
Kentisbury
Parracombe
Martinhoe
Trentishoe
Barbrook
Dean
Brendon
Rockford
Malmsmead
Oare
West Porlock
Bossington
Allerford
Selworthy
Holnicote
Luccombe
Horner
Woodcombe
Wootton Courtenay
Huntscott
Ranscombe
Knowle
Alcombe
Marsh Street
Burrow
Edgcott
Luckwell Bridge
Newland
Dry Hill
Span Head
Hoaroak Hill
Exton Bridgetown
Staplegrove
Bishopswood
Smeatharpe
Churchstanton
Stapley
Hemyock
Churchinford
Culm Davy
Rosemary Lane
Woodgate
Prescott
Appledore
Whitnage
Ayshford
Westleigh
Red Ball
Wrangway
Nicholashayne
Holywell Lake
White Ball
Chelston
Bagborough
West Bagborough
Toulton
Lydeard St Lawrence

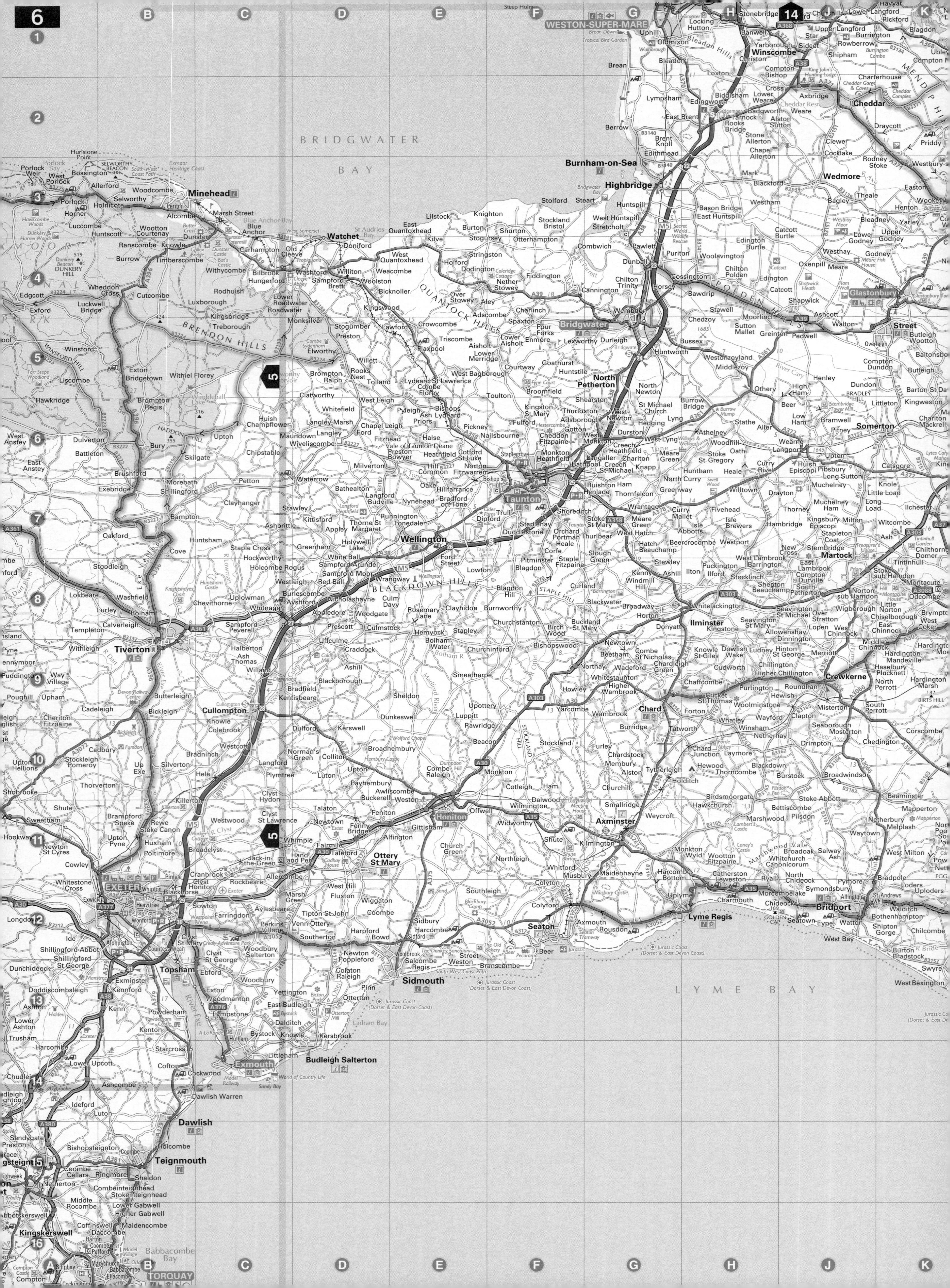
BRIDGWATER BAY
LYME BAY
WESTON-SUPER-MARE
Steep Holm
Minehead
Watchet
Burnham-on-Sea
Highbridge
Bridgwater
Taunton
Wellington
Tiverton
Cullompton
Honiton
Chard
Ilminster
Crewkerne
Axminster
Lyme Regis
Bridport
Seaton
Sidmouth
Ottery St Mary
Budleigh Salterton
Exmouth
EXETER
Topsham
Dawlish
Teignmouth
Kingskerswell
TORQUAY
Glastonbury
Street
Somerton
Martock
Cheddar
Wedmore
Winscombe
Porlock
Dulverton
Bampton
QUANTOCK HILLS
BRENDON HILLS
BLACKDOWN HILLS
POLDEN HILLS
MENDIP HILLS
North Petherton
Williton
Bishops Lydeard
Wiveliscombe
Dunster
Jurassic Coast (Dorset & East Devon Coast)
South West Coast Path
M5
A30
A35
A38
A39
A303
A358
A361
A396
A3052

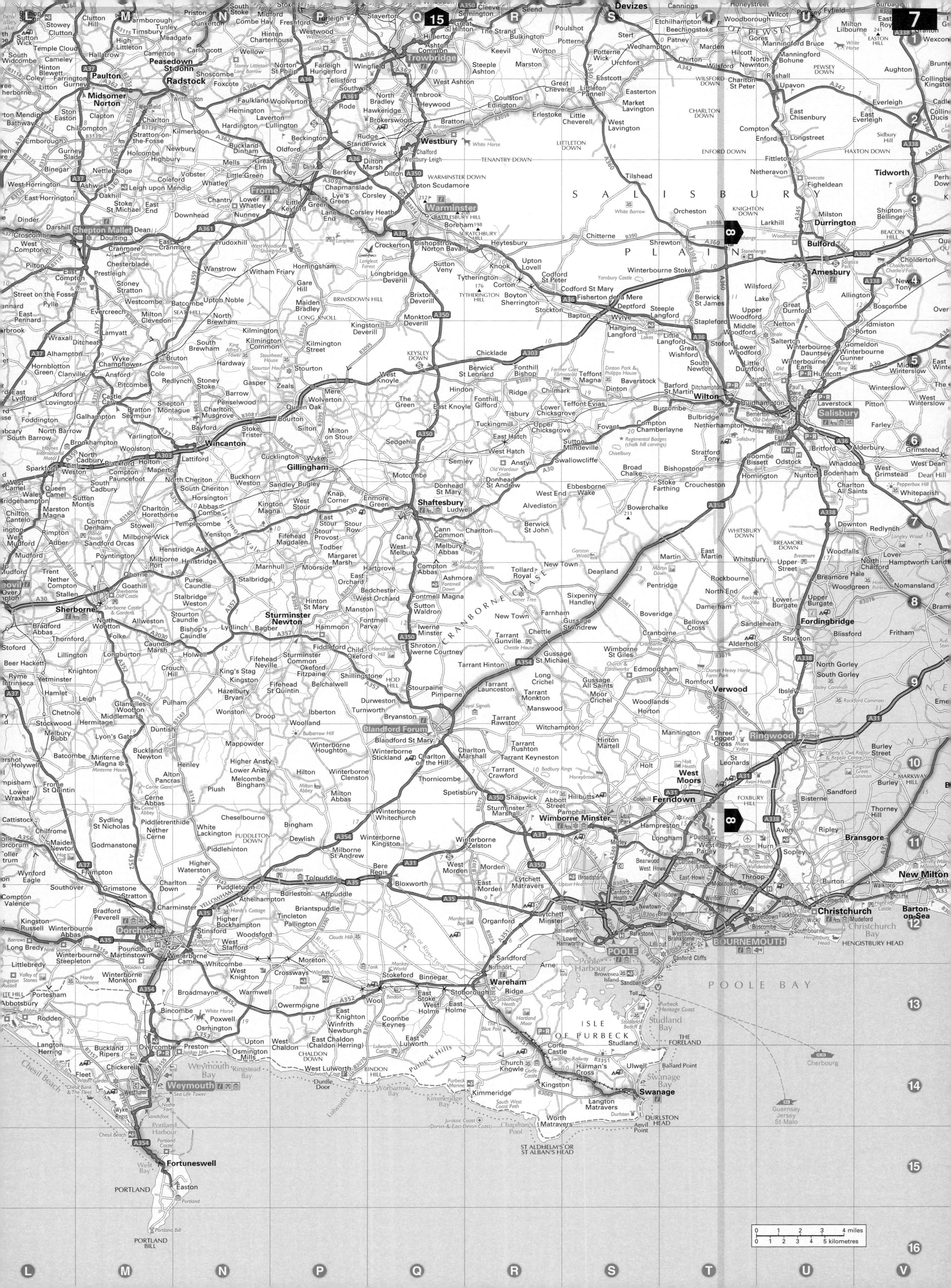
15
8
Devizes
Trowbridge
Westbury
Frome
Warminster
Shepton Mallet
Midsomer Norton
Radstock
Paulton
Peasedown St John
SALISBURY PLAIN
Amesbury
Bulford
Durrington
Tidworth
Salisbury
Wilton
Shaftesbury
Gillingham
Wincanton
Sherborne
Sturminster Newton
Blandford Forum
CRANBORNE CHASE
Fordingbridge
Verwood
Ringwood
Ferndown
Wimborne Minster
Dorchester
POOLE
BOURNEMOUTH
Christchurch
New Milton
Barton-on-Sea
Wareham
Swanage
ISLE OF PURBECK
Weymouth
Fortuneswell
PORTLAND
PORTLAND BILL
Chesil Beach
Weymouth Bay
POOLE BAY
Poole Harbour
Christchurch Bay
HENGISTBURY HEAD
DURLSTON HEAD
ST ALDHELM'S OR ST ALBAN'S HEAD
Cherbourg
Guernsey
Jersey
St Malo
A303
A350
A354
A338
A36
A37
A30
A31
A35
A352
0 1 2 3 4 miles
0 1 2 3 4 5 kilometres
L
M
N
P
Q
R
S
T
U
V
1
2
3
4
5
6
7
8
9
10
11
12
13
14
15
16

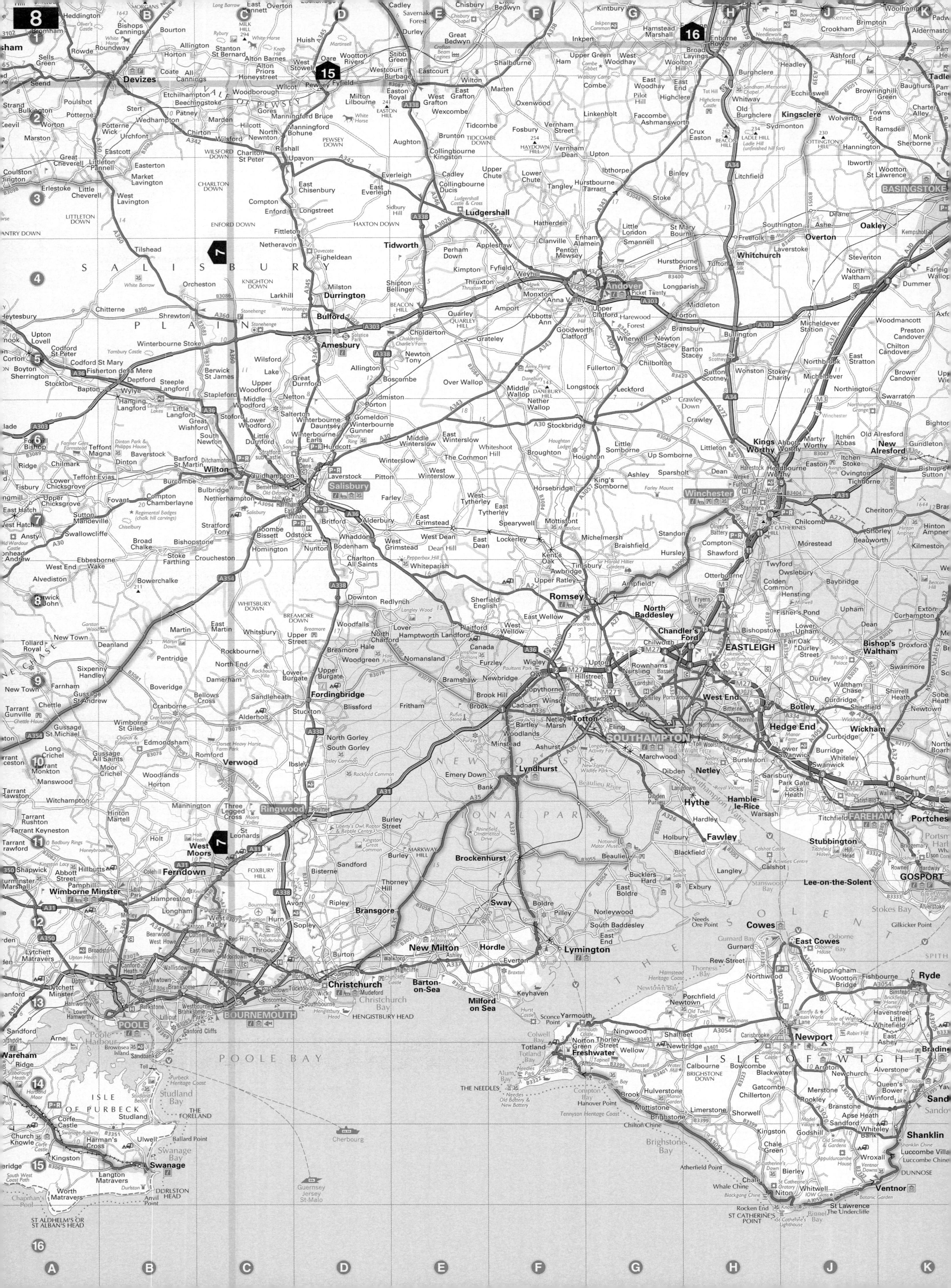
15
16
7
SALISBURY PLAIN
VALE OF PEWSEY
NEW FOREST NATIONAL PARK
POOLE BAY
ISLE OF PURBECK
ISLE OF WIGHT
THE SOLENT
Devizes
Pewsey
Upavon
Ludgershall
Tidworth
Andover
Whitchurch
Overton
Oakley
BASINGSTOKE
Kingsclere
Durrington
Bulford
Amesbury
Stockbridge
Kings Worthy
New Alresford
Winchester
Wilton
Salisbury
Romsey
North Baddesley
Chandler's Ford
EASTLEIGH
Bishop's Waltham
Fordingbridge
Ringwood
West Moors
Ferndown
Wimborne Minster
Verwood
Totton
SOUTHAMPTON
West End
Hedge End
Botley
Wickham
Netley
Hamble-le-Rice
Hythe
Fawley
Lyndhurst
Brockenhurst
FAREHAM
Portchester
GOSPORT
Lee-on-the-Solent
Stubbington
Christchurch
BOURNEMOUTH
POOLE
New Milton
Barton-on-Sea
Milford on Sea
Lymington
Sway
Bransgore
Hordle
Wareham
Swanage
Corfe Castle
Studland
Yarmouth
Freshwater
Cowes
East Cowes
Newport
Ryde
Brading
Sandown
Shanklin
Ventnor
Cherbourg
Guernsey
Jersey
St Malo
THE NEEDLES
HENGISTBURY HEAD
DURLSTON HEAD
ST ALDHELM'S OR ST ALBAN'S HEAD
ST CATHERINE'S POINT
A B C D E F G H J K
1 2 3 4 5 6 7 8 9 10 11 12 13 14 15 16

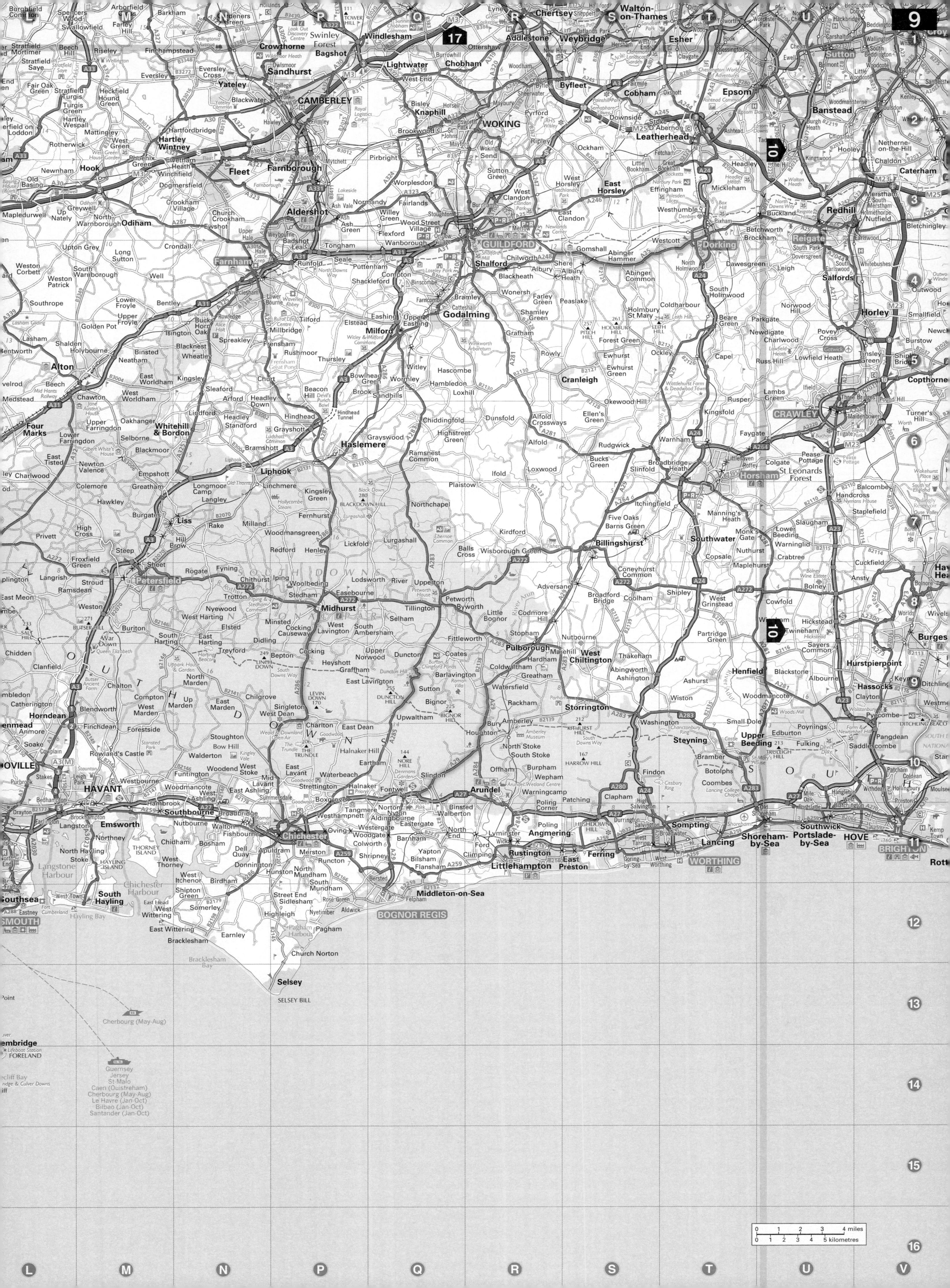

L
M
N
P
Q
R
S
T
U
V
1
2
3
4
5
6
7
8
9
10
11
12
13
14
15
16
17
10
Crowthorne
Windlesham
Chertsey
Walton-on-Thames
Addlestone
Weybridge
Esher
Bagshot
Sandhurst
Lightwater
Chobham
Yateley
Byfleet
Cobham
Epsom
CAMBERLEY
Knaphill
WOKING
Banstead
Leatherhead
Hartley Wintney
Hook
Fleet
Farnborough
Aldershot
Caterham
Redhill
Reigate
Odiham
Farnham
GUILDFORD
Dorking
Shalford
Salfords
Godalming
Milford
Horley
Alton
Cranleigh
CRAWLEY
Haslemere
Liphook
Horsham
Liss
Billingshurst
Southwater
Petersfield
Midhurst
Pulborough
West Chiltington
Henfield
Hurstpierpoint
Hassocks
Storrington
Steyning
HAVANT
Emsworth
Southbourne
Chichester
Arundel
Angmering
Rustington
Littlehampton
Lancing
Sompting
Shoreham-by-Sea
Portslade-by-Sea
HOVE
BRIGHTON
WORTHING
Middleton-on-Sea
BOGNOR REGIS
South Hayling
Selsey
SELSEY BILL
Cherbourg (May-Aug)
Guernsey
Jersey
St-Malo
Caen (Ouistreham)
Cherbourg (May-Aug)
Le Havre (Jan-Oct)
Bilbao (Jan-Oct)
Santander (Jan-Oct)
0 1 2 3 4 miles
0 1 2 3 4 5 kilometres

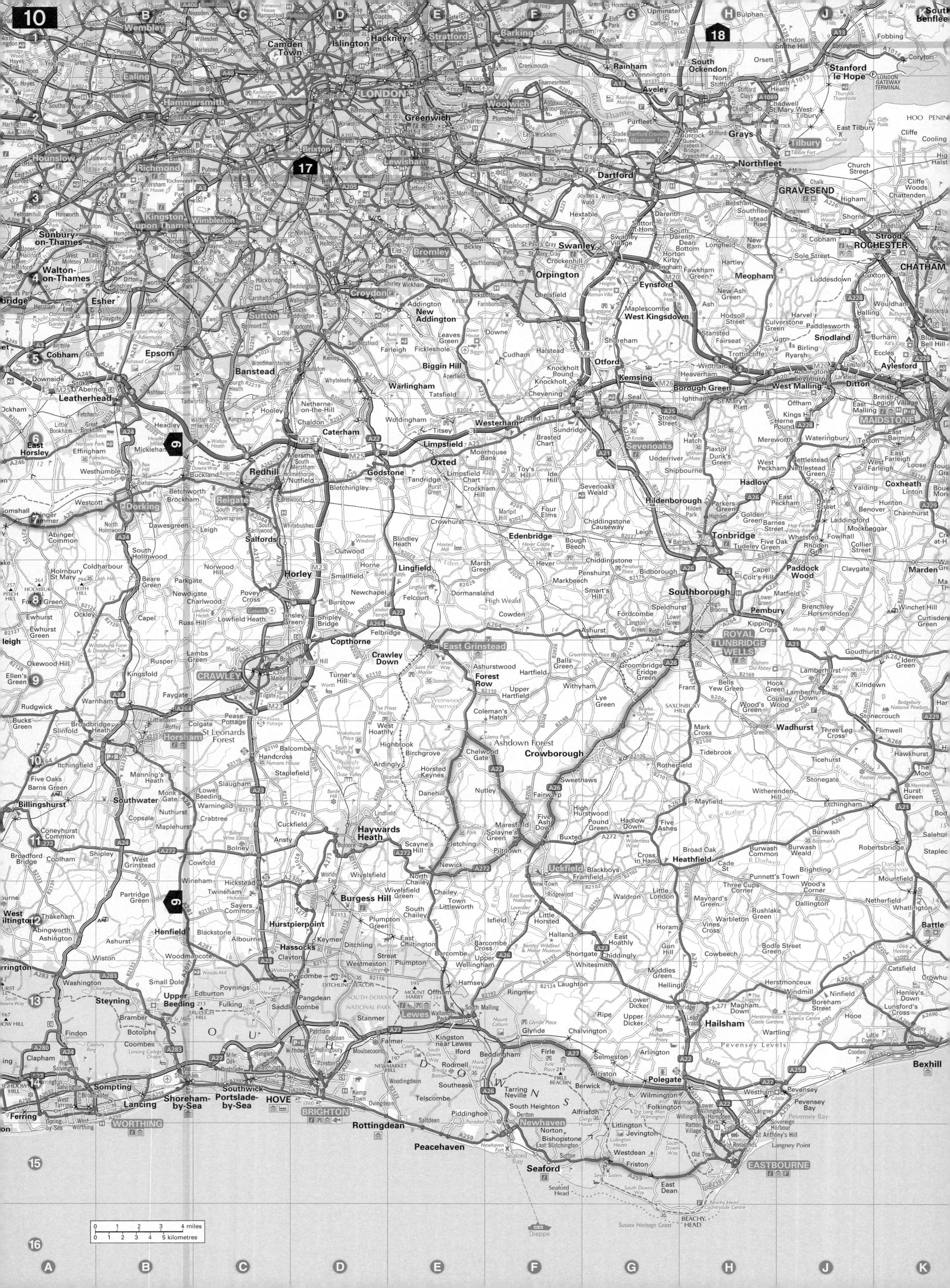
Wembley
Camden Town
Islington
Hackney
Stratford
Barking
Ealing
Hammersmith
LONDON
Woolwich
Greenwich
Brixton
Lewisham
Hounslow
Richmond
Kingston upon Thames
Wimbledon
Sunbury-on-Thames
Walton-on-Thames
Esher
Bromley
Croydon
Sutton
Epsom
Cobham
Leatherhead
Banstead
Caterham
Redhill
Reigate
Dorking
Horley
Crawley
Horsham
East Grinstead
Haywards Heath
Burgess Hill
Hurstpierpoint
Hassocks
Henfield
Steyning
Lancing
Shoreham-by-Sea
Southwick
Portslade-by-Sea
HOVE
BRIGHTON
WORTHING
Rottingdean
Peacehaven
Newhaven
Seaford
Lewes
Uckfield
Crowborough
Heathfield
Hailsham
Polegate
EASTBOURNE
Bexhill
Battle
Wadhurst
ROYAL TUNBRIDGE WELLS
Southborough
Tonbridge
Sevenoaks
Oxted
Edenbridge
Westerham
Orpington
Swanley
Dartford
Gravesend
Northfleet
Grays
Tilbury
ROCHESTER
CHATHAM
MAIDSTONE
Aylesford
West Malling
Paddock Wood
Pembury
Marden
Hadlow
Ashdown Forest
SOUTH DOWNS NATIONAL PARK
BEACHY HEAD
Seaford Head
Dieppe
0 1 2 3 4 miles
0 1 2 3 4 5 kilometres

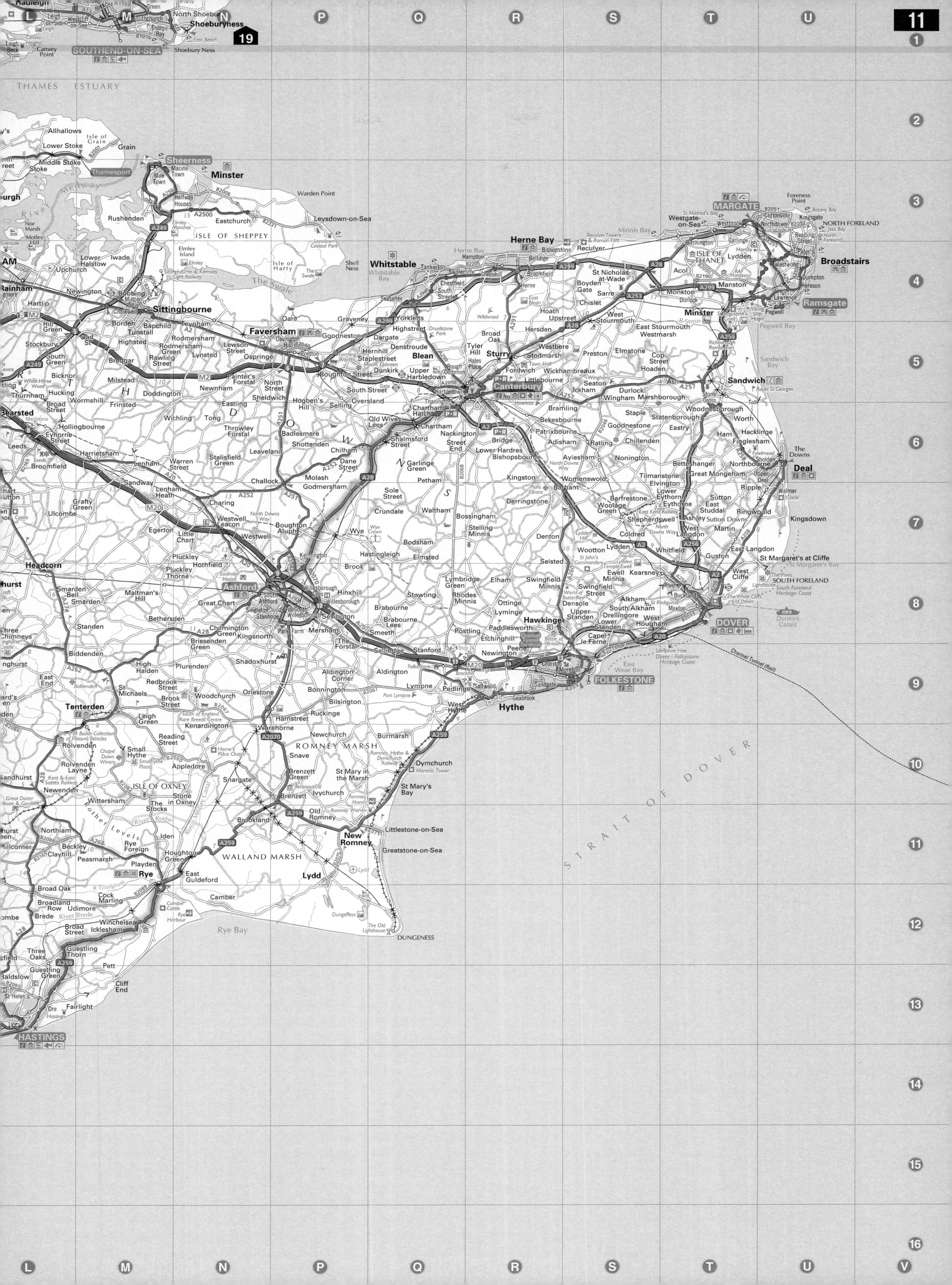

L
M
N
P
Q
R
S
T
U
V
1
2
3
4
5
6
7
8
9
10
11
12
13
14
15
16
19
SOUTHEND-ON-SEA
Shoeburyness
Shoebury Ness
Canvey Point
THAMES ESTUARY
Allhallows
Isle of Grain
Grain
Lower Stoke
Middle Stoke
Stoke
Thamesport
Sheerness
Marine Town
Mile Town
Minster
Halfway Houses
Eastchurch
Warden Point
Leysdown-on-Sea
ISLE OF SHEPPEY
Rushenden
Elmley Island
Isle of Harty
Shell Ness
River Medway
The Swale
Lower Halstow
Iwade
Upchurch
Rainham
Newington
Bobbing
Hartlip
Sittingbourne
Borden
Tunstall
Bapchild
Teynham
Rodmersham
Rodmersham Green
Highsted
Stockbury
South Green
Bredgar
Rawling Street
Lynsted
Lewson Street
Ospringe
Faversham
Goodnestone
Oare
Graveney
Whitstable
Seasalter
Yorkletts
Dargate
Highstreet
Hernhill
Staplestreet
Dunkirk
Denstroude
Blean
Upper Harbledown
Harbledown
Herne Bay
Hampton
Tankerton
Swalecliffe
Chestfield
South Street
Greenhill
Beltinge
Bishopstone
Reculver
Herne
Broomfield
Broad Oak
Tyler Hill
Hales Place
Sturry
Fordwich
Hersden
Upstreet
Hoath
St Nicholas at-Wade
Sarre
Boyden Gate
Chislet
West Stourmouth
East Stourmouth
Westmarsh
MARGATE
Westgate-on-Sea
Westbrook
Cliftonville
Northdown
Kingsgate
Foreness Point
NORTH FORELAND
Broadstairs
ISLE OF THANET
Birchington
Garlinge
Acol
Lydden
Manston
Monkton
Minster
Ramsgate
Pegwell
Pegwell Bay
Sandwich Bay
Sandwich
Canterbury
Thanington
Chartham Hatch
Chartham
Nackington
Street End
Bridge
Bekesbourne
Littlebourne
Wickhambreaux
Stodmarsh
Westbere
Preston
Elmstone
Cop Street
Hoaden
Seaton
Ickham
Wingham
Durlock
Ash
Marshborough
Staple
Goodnestone
Statenborough
Woodnesborough
Eastry
Worth
Ham
Hackling
Finglesham
Northbourne
Betteshanger
Great Mongeham
Deal
The Downs
Sholden
Upper Deal
Walmer
Ripple
Kingsdown
Sutton
East Studdal
Ringwould
Martin
West Langdon
East Langdon
St Margaret's at Cliffe
St Margaret's Bay
SOUTH FORELAND
Guston
West Cliffe
DOVER
Dunkirk
Calais
Faversham
Painter's Forstal
North Street
Sheldwich
Newnham
Doddington
Eastling
Milstead
Frinsted
Wormshill
Hucking
Bicknor
Broad Street
Thurnham
Bearsted
Hollingbourne
Eyhorne Street
Leeds
Harrietsham
Broomfield
Lenham
Warren Street
Wichling
Tong
Throwley
Throwley Forstal
Stalisfield Green
Leaveland
Badlesmere
Shottenden
Selling
Hogben's Hill
Oversland
Old Wives Lees
Shalmsford Street
Chilham
Dane Street
Molash
Godmersham
Challock
Charing
Lenham Heath
Sandway
Grafty Green
Ulcombe
Egerton
Little Chart
Westwell Leacon
Westwell
Boughton Aluph
Wye
Crundale
Sole Street
Garlinge Green
Petham
Waltham
Bossingham
Stelling Minnis
Kingston
Barham
Derringstone
Womenswold
Aylesham
Adisham
Bramling
Patrixbourne
Bishopsbourne
Lower Hardres
Nonington
Ratling
Chillenden
Tilmanstone
Elvington
Lower Eythorne
Eythorne
Barfrestone
Woolage Green
Shepherdswell
Coldred
Denton
Lydden
Wootton
Selsted
Ewell Minnis
Kearsney
Whitfield
Alkham
South Alkham
Capel-le-Ferne
Hawkinge
Swingfield Minnis
Swingfield Street
Densole
Upper Standen
Lower Standen
Drellingore
West Hougham
Maxton
Folkestone
FOLKESTONE
Cheriton
Morehall
Sandgate
Seabrook
Hythe
West Hythe
Saltwood
Pedlinge
Lympne
Stanford
Postling
Etchinghill
Peene
Newington
Paddlesworth
Lyminge
Ottinge
Elham
Rhodes Minnis
Lymbridge Green
Stowting
Brabourne
Brabourne Lees
Smeeth
Sellindge
Mersham
Sevington
Willesborough
Hinxhill
Kennington
Ashford
Brook
Hastingleigh
Bodsham
Elmsted
Headcorn
Smarden
Smarden Bell
Maltman's Hill
Pluckley
Pluckley Thorne
Hothfield
Great Chart
Bethersden
Chilmington Green
Kingsnorth
Brissenden Green
Shadoxhurst
Biddenden
Standen
High Halden
Plurenden
Redbrook Street
St Michaels
Brook Street
Woodchurch
Tenterden
Leigh Green
Kenardington
Orlestone
Aldington
Aldington Corner
Bonnington
Bilsington
Ruckinge
Hamstreet
Warehorne
Newchurch
Burmarsh
Dymchurch
ROMNEY MARSH
Snave
Brenzett Green
Brenzett
Snargate
St Mary in the Marsh
St Mary's Bay
Ivychurch
Old Romney
New Romney
Littlestone-on-Sea
Greatstone-on-Sea
Lydd
WALLAND MARSH
Brookland
Appledore
Rolvenden
Rolvenden Layne
Small Hythe
Reading Street
ISLE OF OXNEY
Stone in Oxney
Wittersham
The Stocks
Newenden
Northiam
Beckley
Iden
Rye Foreign
Peasmarsh
Playden
Houghton Green
Rye
East Guldeford
Camber
Rye Bay
DUNGENESS
Broad Oak
Cock Marling
Udimore
Broadland Row
Brede
Winchelsea
Icklesham
Broad Street
Guestling Thorn
Three Oaks
Guestling Green
Pett
Cliff End
Fairlight
Ore
HASTINGS
Baldslow
St Helen's
STRAIT OF DOVER
Channel Tunnel (Rail)

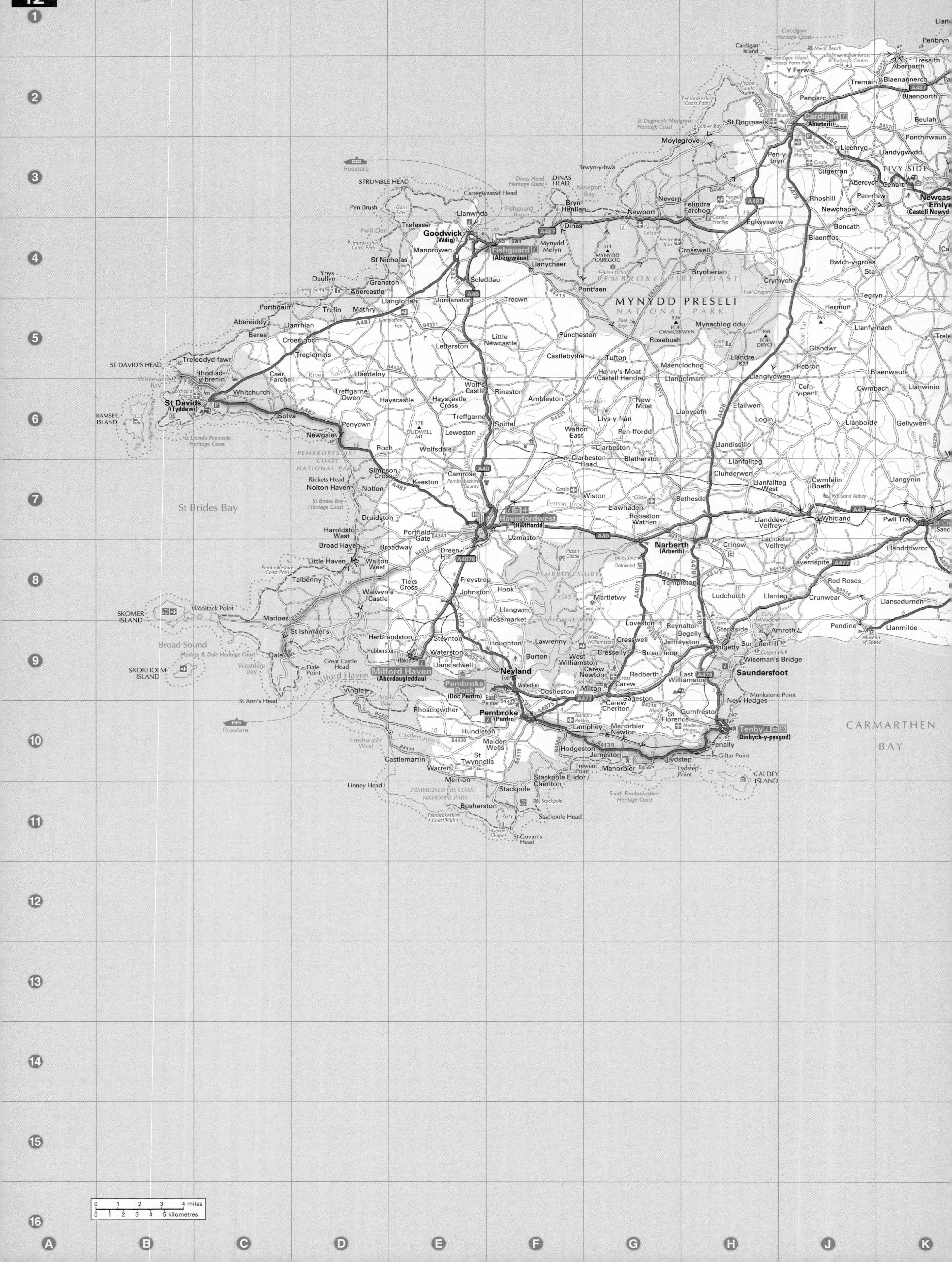
B
C
D
E
F
G
H
J
K
1
2
3
4
5
6
7
8
9
10
11
12
13
14
15
16
Ceredigion Heritage Coast
Cardigan Island
Cardigan Island Coastal Farm Park
Mwnt Beach
Felinwynt Rainforest & Butterfly Centre
Penbryn
Aberporth
Tresaith
Y Ferwig
Tremain
Blaenannerch
Poppit Sands
Pembrokeshire Coast Path
Penparc
Blaenporth
St Dogmaels Moylgrove Heritage Coast
Ceibwr Bay
St Dogmaels
Cardigan
(Aberteifi)
Beulah
Moylegrove
Pen-y-bryn
Welsh Wildlife Centre
Teifi Marshes
Llechryd
Ponthirwaun
Llandygwydd
Rosslare
STRUMBLE HEAD
Trwyn-y-bwa
Cilgerran
TIVY SIDE
Dinas Head Heritage Coast
DINAS HEAD
Newport Bay
Carregwastad Head
Abercych
Cenarth
Pen Brush
Garn Fawr
Bryn-Henllan
Nevern
Felindre Farchog
Rhoshill
Pen-rhiw
Newcastle Emlyn
(Castell Newydd
Llanwnda
Fishguard Bay
Newport
Newchapel
Pwll Deri
Trefasser
Goodwick
(Wdig)
Ocean Lab
Lower Town
Dinas
Castell Henllys
Eglwyswrw
Boncath
Pembrokeshire Coast Path
Fishguard
(Abergwaun)
Mynydd Melyn
311
MYNYDD CAREGOG
Crosswell
Blaenffos
Manorowen
St Nicholas
Llanychaer
Pentre Ifan
Bwlch-y-groes
Ynys Daullyn
Granston
Scleddau
Pontfaen
Brynberian
Star
Carreg Sampson
Abercastle
PEMBROKESHIRE COAST
Crymych
Foel Drygarn
Tegryn
Porthgain
Trefin
Mathry
Llangloffan
Jordanston
Trecwn
MYNYDD PRESELI
NATIONAL PARK
Hermon
Abereiddy
A487
Llangloffan Fen
B4331
Foel Eryr
536
FOEL CWMCERWYN
Mynachlog ddu
265
Llanfyrnach
Berea
Llanrhian
368
FOEL DRYCH
Croes-goch
Little Newcastle
Puncheston
Rosebush
Gors Fawr
Letterston
Glandwr
ST DAVID'S HEAD
Treleddyd-fawr
Treglemais
Castlebythe
Tufton
Llandre Isaf
Whitesands Bay
Rhodiad-y-brenin
Caer Farchell
River Solva
Llandeloy
Henry's Moat
(Castell Hendre)
Maenclochog
Llangolman
Hebron
Blaenwaun
Bishop's Palace
Whitchurch
Treffgarne Owen
Wolf's Castle
Rinaston
Llanglydwen
Cefn-y-pant
Cwmbach
Llanwinio
RAMSEY ISLAND
Ramsey Sound
St Davids
(Tyddewi)
Hayscastle
Hayscastle Cross
Ambleston
Llys-y-frân Reservoir
New Moat
Efailwen
Solva
Treffgarne
Spittal
Llys-y-frân
Llanycefn
Login
Llanboidy
Gellywen
Newgale
Penycwn
178
DUDWELL MT
Leweston
Walton East
Pen-ffordd
St David's Peninsula Heritage Coast
Roch
Wolfsdale
Scolton
Clarbeston
Bletherston
Llandissilio
PEMBROKESHIRE COAST
NATIONAL PARK
Simpson Cross
Camrose
Clarbeston Road
Llanfallteg
Rickets Head
Nolton Haven
Nolton
Keeston
Pembrokeshire County
Clunderwen
Cwmfelin Boeth
Llangynin
Llanfallteg West
Whitland Abbey
St Brides Bay
St Brides Bay Heritage Coast
Castle
Wiston
Llawhaden
Bethesda
Fenton Brook
Whitland
Pwll Trap
Druidston
Haverfordwest
(Hwlffordd)
Robeston Wathen
Llanddewi Velfrey
Haroldston West
Portfield Gate
B4341
Uzmaston
A40
Narberth
(Arberth)
Crinow
Lampeter Velfrey
Broad Haven
Broadway
Dreen Hill
Picton Castle
Bluestone
Oakwood
Llanddowror
Little Haven
Walton West
A4076
Tavernspite
Pembrokeshire Coast Path
Talbenny
Tiers Cross
Freystrop
Hook
Templeton
Red Roses
Walwyn's Castle
Johnston
PEMBROKESHIRE COAST NATIONAL PARK
Martletwy
Ludchurch
Llanteg
Crunwear
Llansadurnen
SKOMER ISLAND
Wooltack Point
Marloes
Llangwm
Rosemarket
Cwm Deri
Colby Woodland Garden
St Ishmael's
Herbrandston
Steynton
Loveston
Reynalton
Begelly
Stepaside
Amroth
Pendine
Llanmiloe
Broad Sound
Hubberston
Waterston
Houghton
Lawrenny
West Williamston
Cresswell
Jeffreyston
Summerhill
Museum of Speed
Marloes & Dale Heritage Coast
Dale
Hakin
Llanstadwell
Burton
Cresselly
Broadmoor
Kilgetty
Copper Hall
SKOKHOLM ISLAND
Westdale Bay
Dale Point
Great Castle Head
Milford Haven
(Aberdaugleddau)
Neyland
West Williamston
Carew Newton
Redberth
Wiseman's Bridge
Saundersfoot
Milford Haven
Pembroke Dock
(Doc Penfro)
Waterloo
Cosheston
Tidal Mill
Milton
Carew
East Williamston
St Ann's Head
Angle
Angle Bay
East Pennar
A477
Sageston
Carew Cheriton
Monkstone Point
New Hedges
Rhoscrowther
Pembroke
(Penfro)
Bishop's Palace
St Florence
Gumfreston
Rosslare
Castlemartin Brook
Hundleton
Lamphey
Manorbier Newton
Medieval House
Tenby
(Dinbych-y-pysgod)
CARMARTHEN BAY
Freshwater West
Maiden Wells
Hodgeston
Penally
Castlemartin
St Twynnells
Jameston
Lydstep
Giltar Point
Trewent Point
Manorbier
Warren
Lydstep Point
Merrion
Stackpole Elidor / Cheriton
CALDEY ISLAND
Linney Head
PEMBROKESHIRE COAST NATIONAL PARK
Stackpole
South Pembrokeshire Heritage Coast
Bosherston
Pembrokeshire Coast Path
Stackpole Head
St Govan's Chapel
St Govan's Head
0 1 2 3 4 miles
0 1 2 3 4 5 kilometres
A
B
C
D
E
F
G
H
J
K

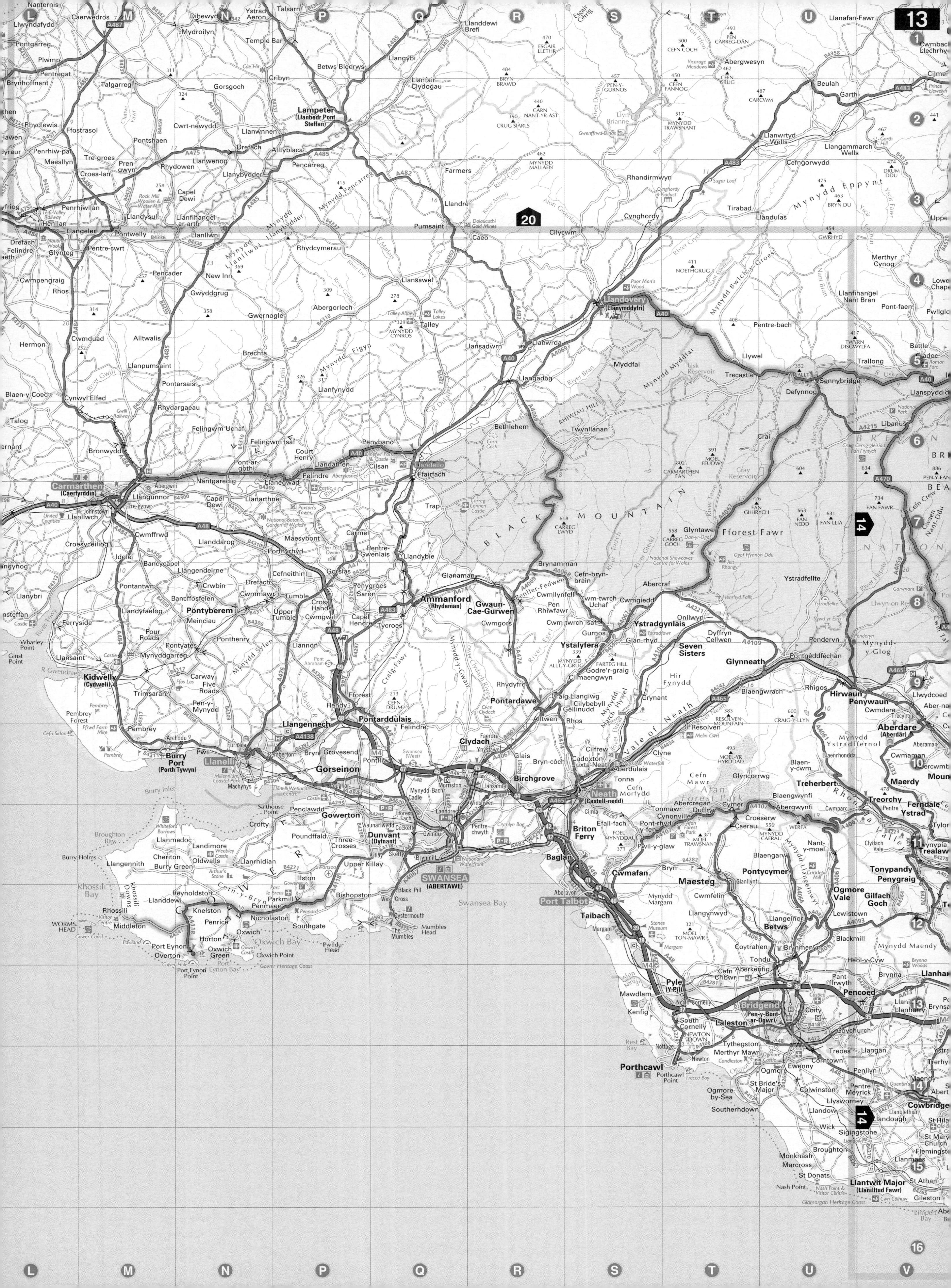
Lampeter (Llanbedr Pont Steffan)
Llandovery (Llanymddyfri)
Carmarthen (Caerfyrddin)
Llandeilo
Ammanford (Rhydaman)
Kidwelly (Cydweli)
Burry Port (Porth Tywyn)
Llanelli
Gorseinon
Pontarddulais
Gowerton
Dunvant (Dyfnant)
SWANSEA (ABERTAWE)
Neath (Castell-nedd)
Port Talbot
Briton Ferry
Baglan
Taibach
Pyle (Y Pîl)
Bridgend (Pen-y-Bont-ar-Ogwr)
Porthcawl
Maesteg
Aberdare (Aberdâr)
Hirwaun
Treorchy
Ystradgynlais
Ystalyfera
Pontardawe
Clydach
Glynneath
Llantwit Major (Llanilltud Fawr)
Cowbridge
Llandrindod Wells
Llanwrtyd Wells
Sennybridge
Black Mountain
Fforest Fawr
Mynydd Eppynt
Gower
Swansea Bay
Rhossili Bay
Oxwich Bay
Burry Inlet
Mumbles Head
Worms Head
Port Eynon Point
Vale of Neath
Rhondda Valley
20
14
16

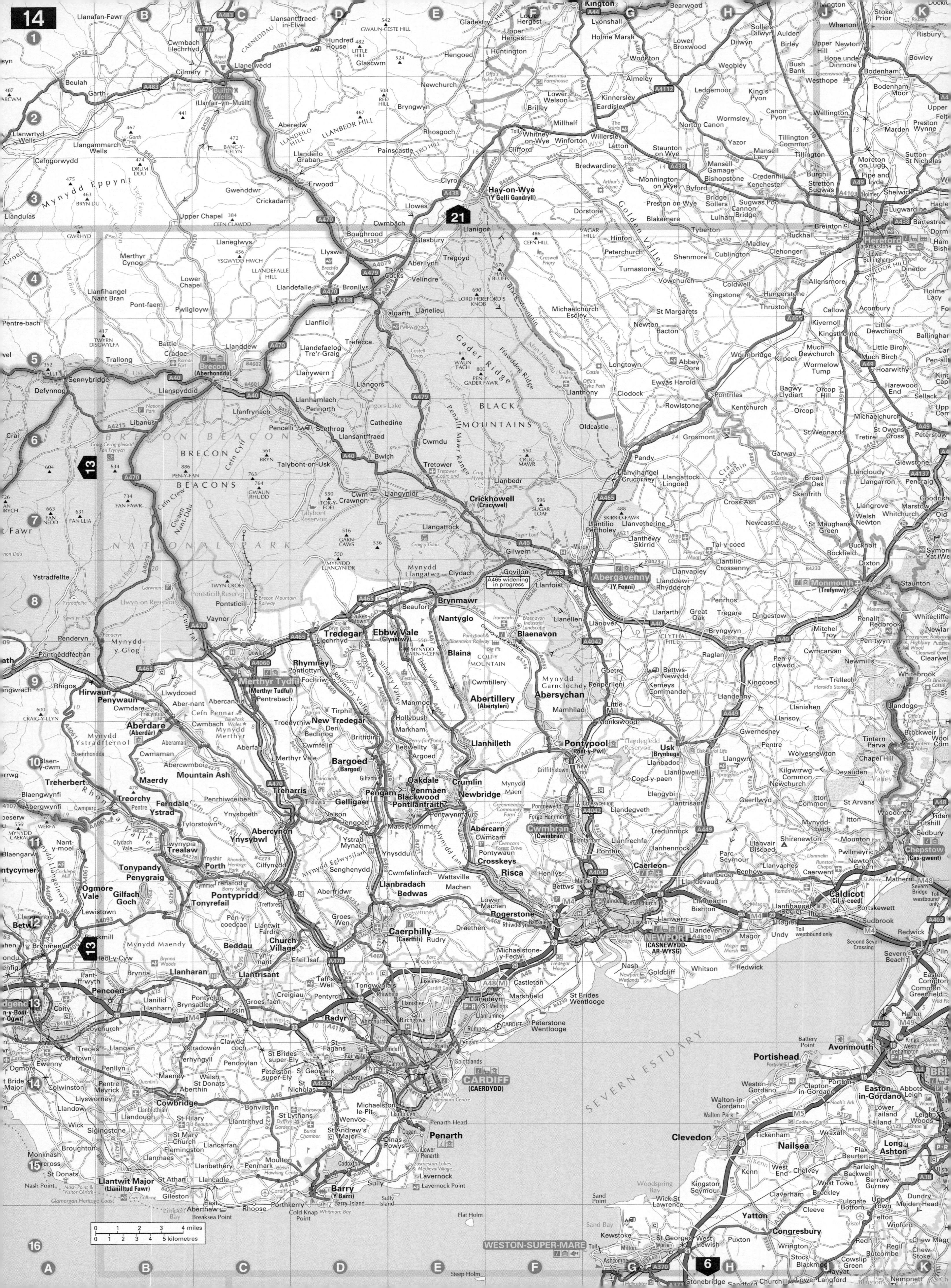
Kington
Builth Wells
(Llanfair-ym-Muallt)
Hay-on-Wye
(Y Gelli Gandryll)
21
Hereford
Brecon
(Aberhonddu)
BRECON BEACONS
BRECON BEACONS
NATIONAL PARK
BLACK MOUNTAINS
Gader Ridge
Black Mountain
Golden Valley
Mynydd Eppynt
Crickhowell
(Crucywel)
Abergavenny
(Y Fenni)
A465 widening in progress
Monmouth
(Trefynwy)
Brynmawr
Tredegar
Ebbw Vale
(Glynebwy)
Nantyglo
Blaenavon
Merthyr Tydfil
(Merthyr Tudful)
Hirwaun
Aberdare
(Aberdâr)
Abertillery
(Abertyleri)
Abersychan
Pontypool
(Pont-y-Pŵl)
Usk
(Brynbuga)
Chepstow
(Cas-gwent)
Caldicot
(Cil-y-coed)
Cwmbran
(Cwmbrân)
Caerleon
Newport
(CASNEWYDD-AR-WYSG)
Risca
Crosskeys
Caerphilly
(Caerffili)
Bargoed
(Bargod)
Treharris
Pontypridd
Porth
Tonypandy
Treorchy
Ferndale
Mountain Ash
Llantrisant
Pencoed
Cowbridge
Llantwit Major
(Llanilltud Fawr)
Barry
(Y Barri)
Penarth
Cardiff
(CAERDYDD)
Radyr
Rogerstone
SEVERN ESTUARY
Portishead
Avonmouth
Clevedon
Nailsea
Long Ashton
Yatton
Congresbury
WESTON-SUPER-MARE
Steep Holm
Flat Holm
Second Severn Crossing
Severn Bridge
Toll westbound only
6
13
0 1 2 3 4 miles
0 1 2 3 4 5 kilometres
A B C D E F G H J K
1 2 3 4 5 6 7 8 9 10 11 12 13 14 15 16

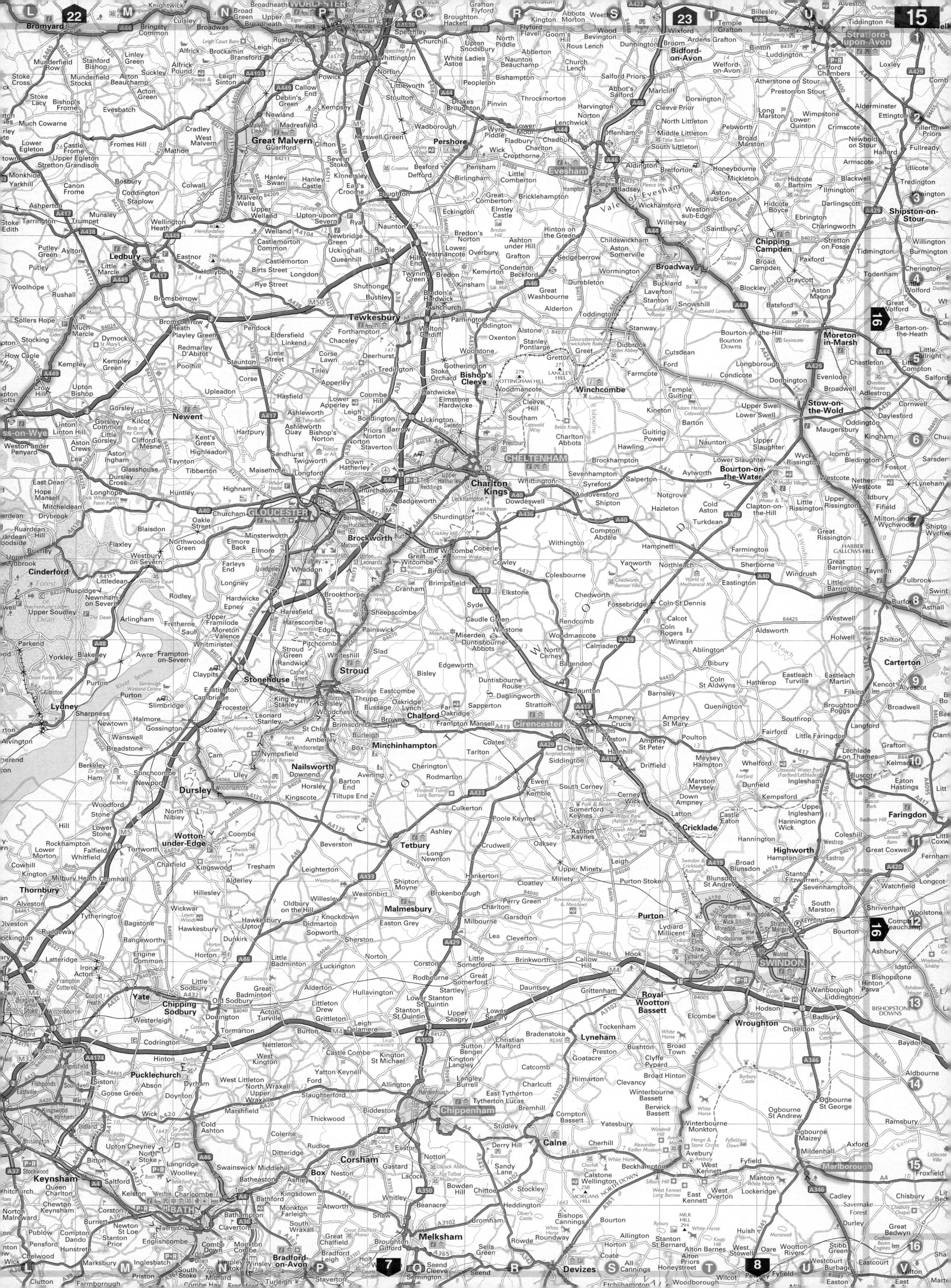
22
23
16
7
8
Bromyard
Worcester
Stratford-upon-Avon
Bidford-on-Avon
Great Malvern
Pershore
Evesham
Ledbury
Tewkesbury
Chipping Campden
Broadway
Shipston-on-Stour
Moreton-in-Marsh
Newent
Bishop's Cleeve
Winchcombe
Stow-on-the-Wold
Cheltenham
Charlton Kings
Gloucester
Brockworth
Bourton-on-the-Water
Cinderford
Burford
Stroud
Stonehouse
Lydney
Chalford
Cirencester
Carterton
Minchinhampton
Nailsworth
Dursley
Faringdon
Wotton-under-Edge
Tetbury
Cricklade
Highworth
Thornbury
Malmesbury
Purton
Swindon
Yate
Chipping Sodbury
Royal Wootton Bassett
Wroughton
Lyneham
Chippenham
Calne
Corsham
Keynsham
Bath
Marlborough
Melksham
Bradford-on-Avon
Devizes
Vale of Evesham
Cotswolds
River Severn
Forest of Dean

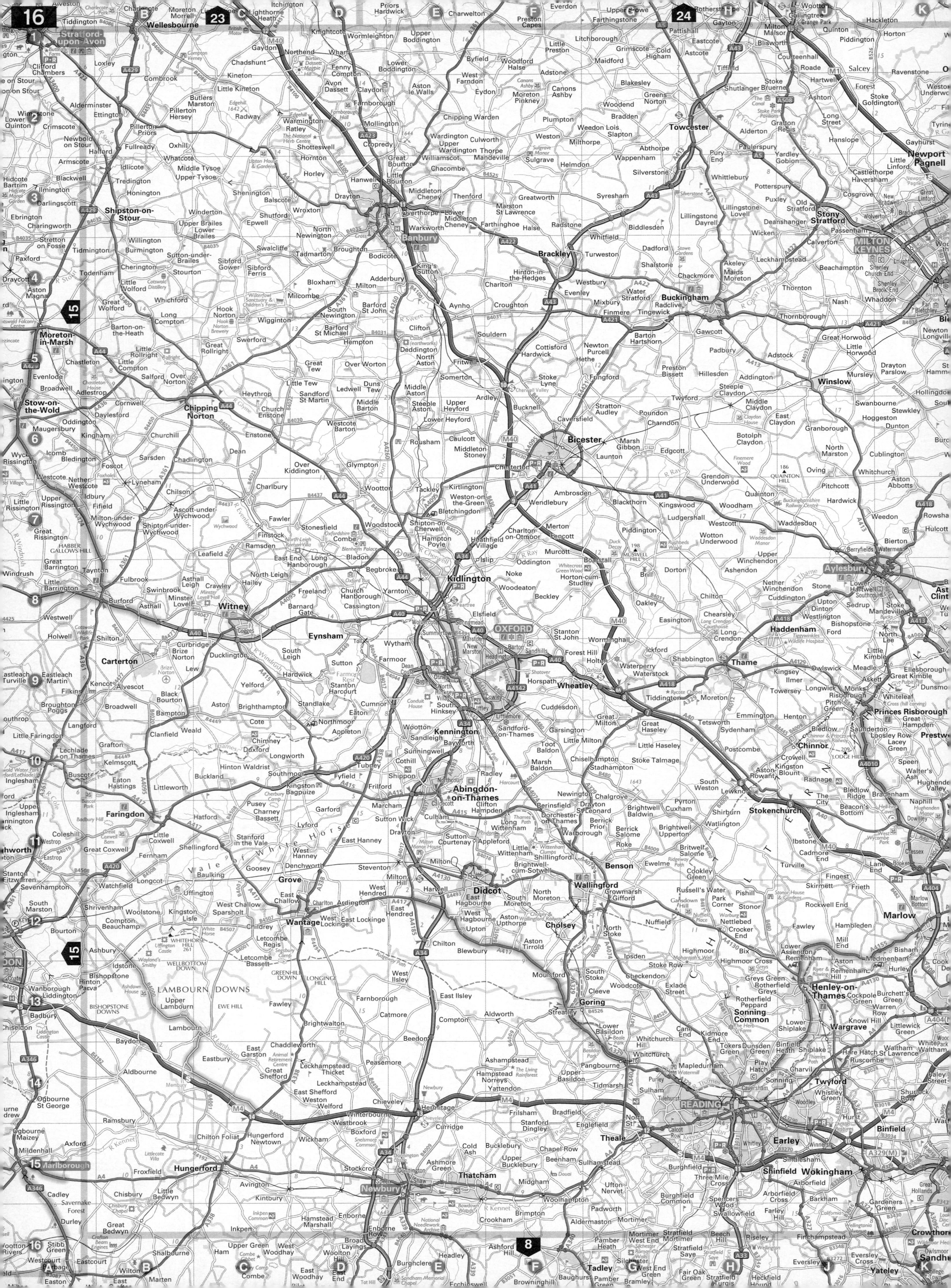
23
24
15
8
Stratford-upon-Avon
Wellesbourne
Shipston-on-Stour
Moreton-in-Marsh
Stow-on-the-Wold
Chipping Norton
Banbury
Brackley
Towcester
Buckingham
Newport Pagnell
Stony Stratford
MILTON KEYNES
Bicester
Winslow
Aylesbury
Kidlington
Witney
Burford
Carterton
Eynsham
Woodstock
OXFORD
Thame
Haddenham
Wheatley
Princes Risborough
Chinnor
Stokenchurch
Faringdon
Abingdon-on-Thames
Wantage
Didcot
Wallingford
Cholsey
Goring
Henley-on-Thames
Marlow
READING
Twyford
Earley
Wokingham
Theale
Thatcham
Newbury
Hungerford
Marlborough
Lambourn
LAMBOURN DOWNS
Vale of White Horse
Sonning Common
Tadley
Yateley

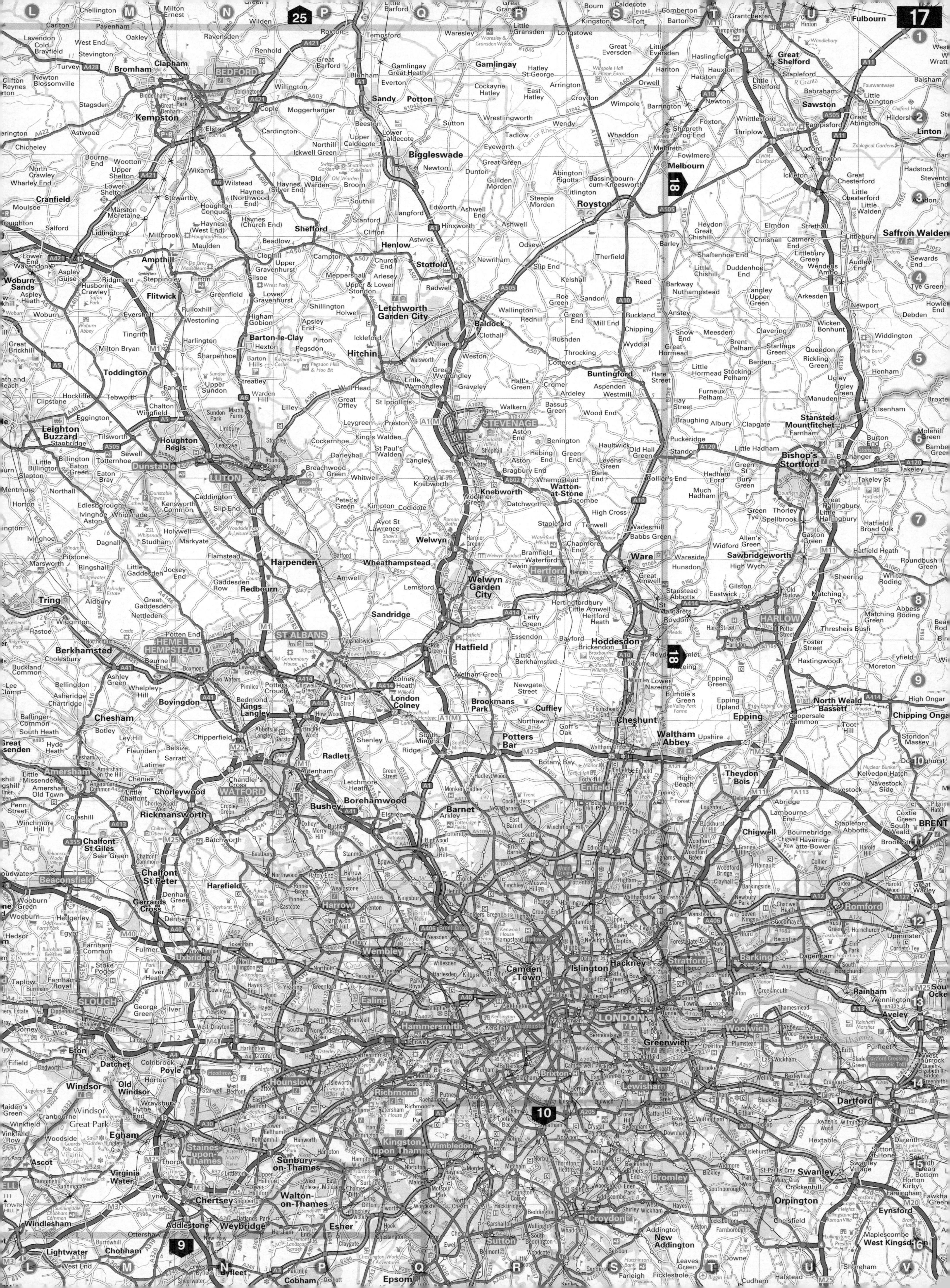

25
BEDFORD
Kempston
Bromham
Clapham
Sandy
Potton
Biggleswade
Gamlingay
Royston
Melbourn
18
Great Shelford
Sawston
Linton
Saffron Walden
Shefford
Henlow
Stotfold
Baldock
Letchworth Garden City
Hitchin
Ampthill
Flitwick
Toddington
Leighton Buzzard
Houghton Regis
Dunstable
LUTON
STEVENAGE
Buntingford
Bishop's Stortford
Stansted Mountfitchet
Harpenden
Welwyn
Welwyn Garden City
Hertford
Ware
Sawbridgeworth
HARLOW
Tring
Berkhamsted
HEMEL HEMPSTEAD
ST ALBANS
Hatfield
Hoddesdon
Cheshunt
Waltham Abbey
Epping
Chesham
Amersham
WATFORD
Rickmansworth
Borehamwood
Potters Bar
Enfield
Barnet
Beaconsfield
Harrow
Wembley
Uxbridge
Camden Town
Islington
Hackney
Stratford
Barking
Romford
SLOUGH
Ealing
Hammersmith
LONDON
Greenwich
Woolwich
Windsor
Hounslow
Richmond
Brixton
Lewisham
Dartford
10
Egham
Staines-upon-Thames
Kingston upon Thames
Wimbledon
Bromley
Swanley
Orpington
Croydon
Weybridge
Esher
Sutton
9
Epsom

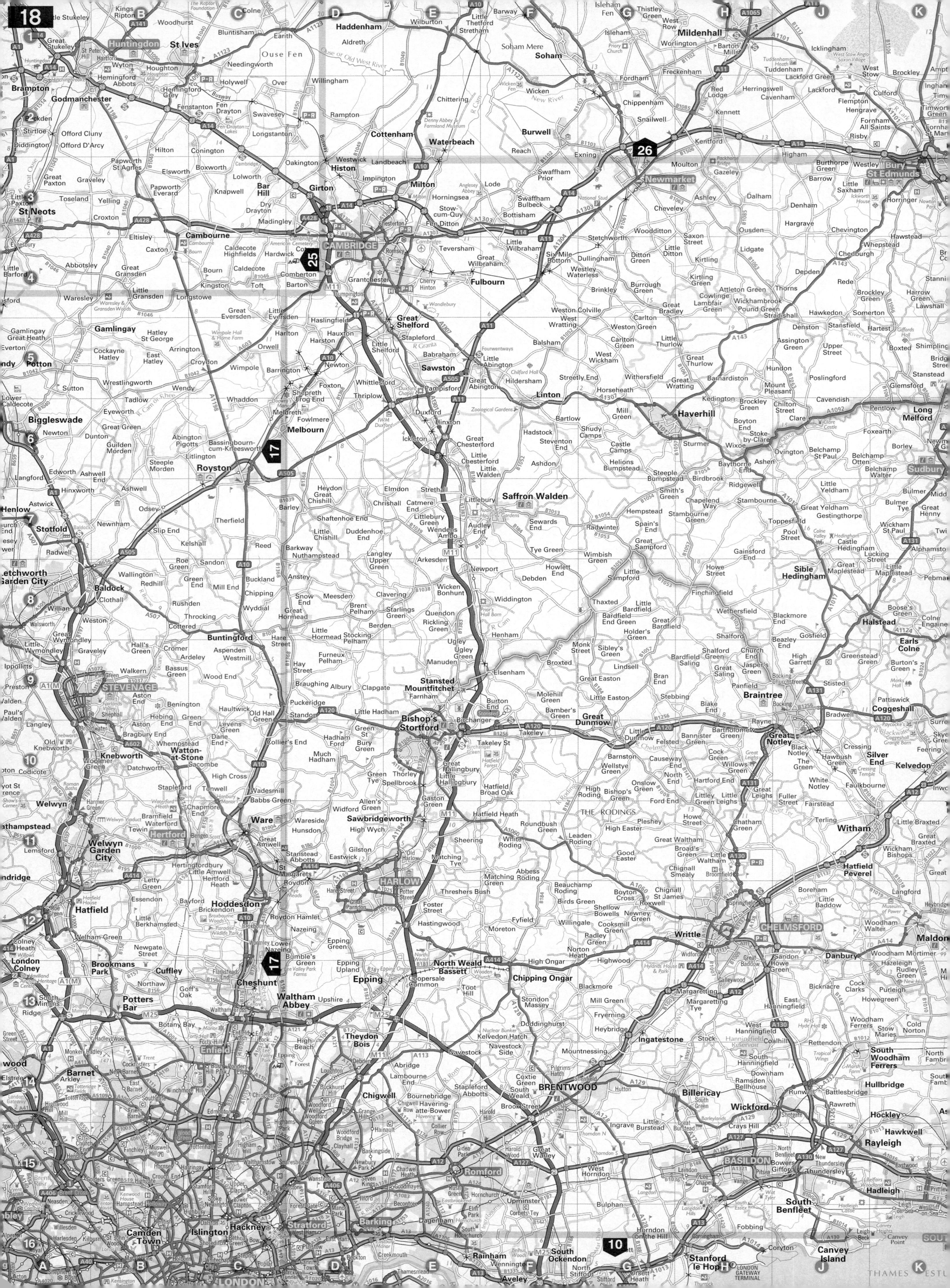
Huntingdon
St Ives
Brampton
Godmanchester
St Neots
Haddenham
Mildenhall
Soham
Newmarket
Bury St Edmunds
Cambridge
Cottenham
Waterbeach
Histon
Girton
Milton
Burwell
Cambourne
Fulbourn
Great Shelford
Sawston
Linton
Haverhill
Royston
Melbourn
Saffron Walden
Biggleswade
Potton
Gamlingay
Baldock
Letchworth Garden City
Stotfold
Stevenage
Buntingford
Knebworth
Welwyn
Welwyn Garden City
Hertford
Ware
Hatfield
Hoddesdon
Cheshunt
Waltham Abbey
Potters Bar
Enfield
Barnet
Bishop's Stortford
Stansted Mountfitchet
Sawbridgeworth
Harlow
Epping
North Weald Bassett
Chipping Ongar
Great Dunmow
Thaxted
Braintree
Halstead
Witham
Coggeshall
Kelvedon
Chelmsford
Writtle
Maldon
Danbury
Ingatestone
Billericay
Wickford
Brentwood
Romford
Basildon
Rayleigh
Hadleigh
South Benfleet
Canvey Island
Stanford le Hope
South Ockendon
Chigwell
Theydon Bois
Hackney
Islington
Camden Town
Stratford
Barking
Rainham
Upminster
Sudbury
Long Melford
Clare
Hockley
London
THE RODINGS
THAMES ESTUARY
M11
M25
A1(M)
A14
A11
A10
A120
A12
A13
A127
A130
A131
A505
17
25
26
10
A B C D E F G H J K
1 2 3 4 5 6 7 8 9 10 11 12 13 14 15 16

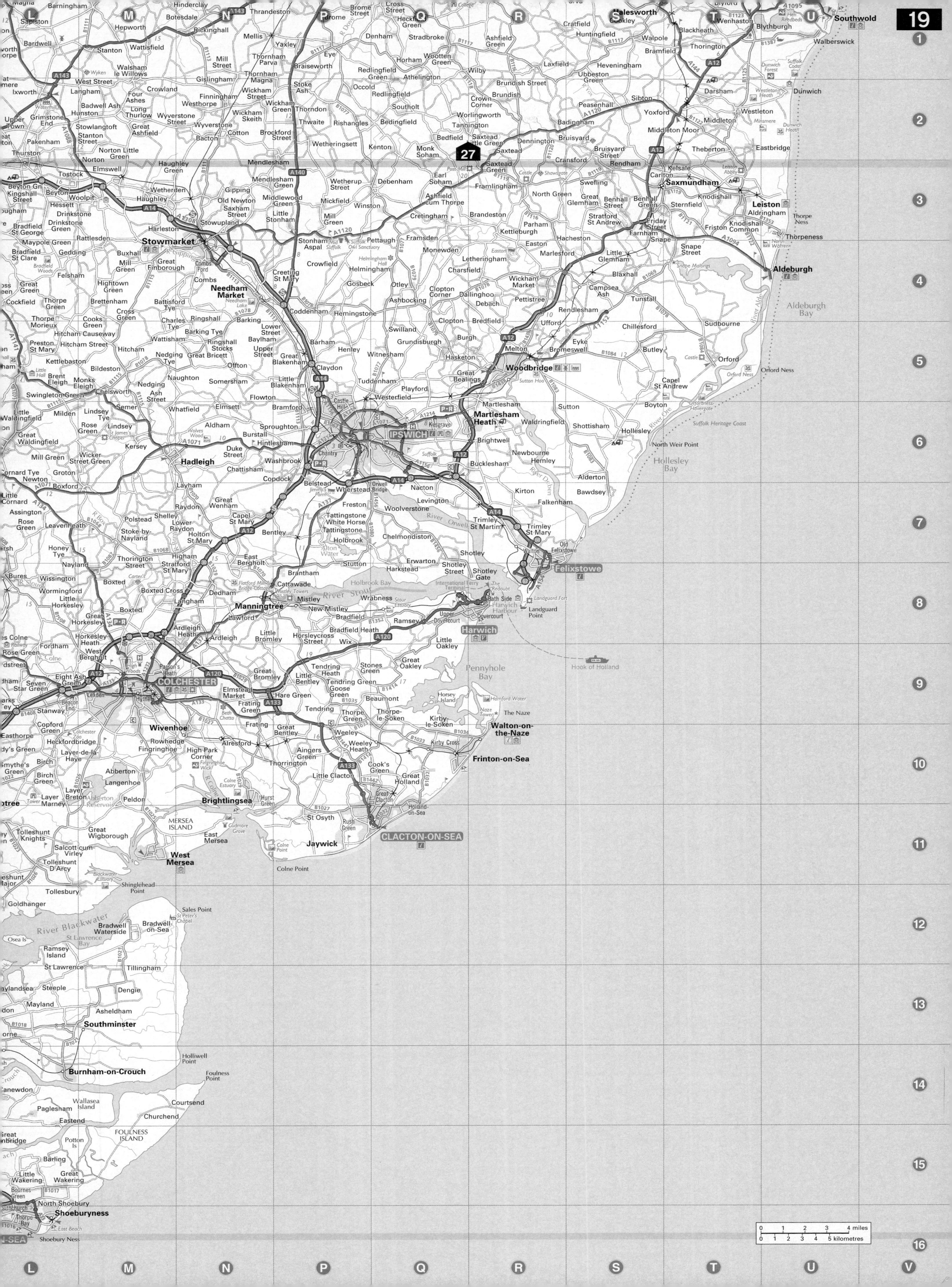
Southwold
Halesworth
Saxmundham
Leiston
Aldeburgh
Aldeburgh Bay
Orford
Orford Ness
Woodbridge
Martlesham Heath
IPSWICH
Stowmarket
Needham Market
Hadleigh
Felixstowe
Harwich
Hook of Holland
Manningtree
COLCHESTER
Wivenhoe
Walton-on-the-Naze
Frinton-on-Sea
CLACTON-ON-SEA
Brightlingsea
Jaywick
West Mersea
Southminster
Burnham-on-Crouch
Shoeburyness
Hollesley Bay
Pennyhole Bay
River Blackwater
Suffolk Heritage Coast
27
0 1 2 3 4 miles
0 1 2 3 4 5 kilometres

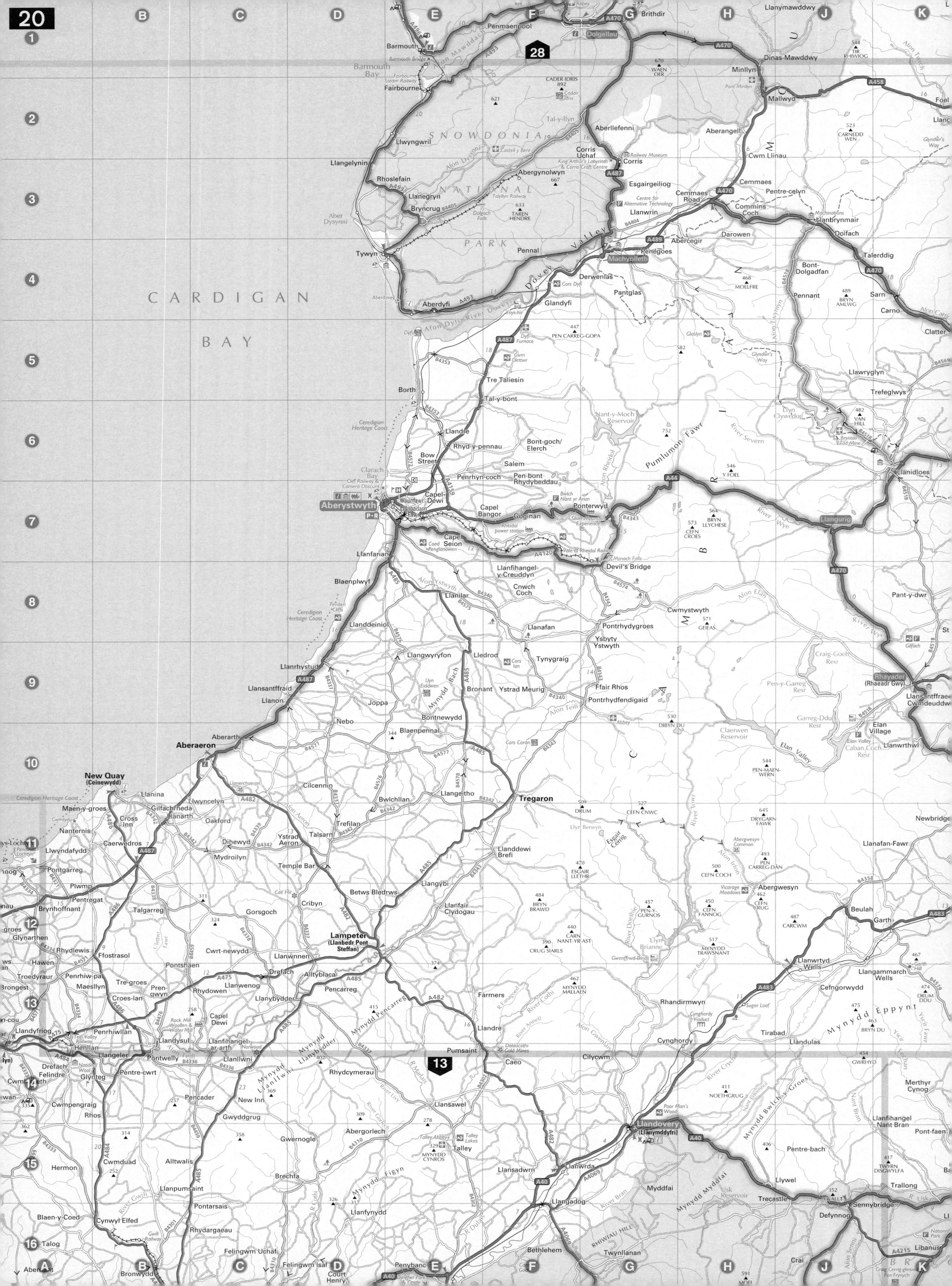
CARDIGAN
BAY
SNOWDONIA
NATIONAL
PARK
28
13
Dolgellau
Penmaenpool
Barmouth
Barmouth Bay
Fairbourne
Brithdir
Llanymawddwy
Dinas-Mawddwy
Minllyn
Mallwyd
CADER IDRIS 892
Tal-y-llyn
Llwyngwril
Llangelynin
Aberllefenni
Corris Uchaf
Corris
Aberangell
Cwm Llinau
Rhoslefain
Llanegryn
Bryncrug
Abergynolwyn
Esgairgeiliog
Cemmaes Road
Cemmaes
Pentre-celyn
Commins Coch
Llanbrynmair
Dolfach
Talerddig
Tywyn
Pennal
Llanwrin
Abercegir
Penegoes
Darowen
Machynlleth
Derwenlas
Pantglas
Dovey Valley
Aberdyfi
Glandyfi
Bont-Dolgadfan
Pennant
Sarn
Carno
Clatter
Tre Taliesin
Tal-y-bont
Borth
Llandre
Rhyd-y-pennau
Bont-goch/ Elerch
Bow Street
Salem
Penrhyn-coch
Pen-bont Rhydybeddau
Aberystwyth
Capel-Dewi
Capel Bangor
Goginan
Ponterwyd
Capel Seion
Pumlumon Fawr
River Severn
Llanidloes
Llangurig
Trefeglwys
Llawryglyn
Llanfarian
Llanfihangel-y-Creuddyn
Devil's Bridge
Blaenplwyf
Llanilar
Cnwch Coch
Cwmystwyth
Llanddeiniol
Llanafan
Pontrhydygroes
Ysbyty Ystwyth
Llangwyryfon
Lledrod
Tynygraig
Llanrhystud
Llansantffraid
Llanon
Bronant
Ystrad Meurig
Ffair Rhos
Pontrhydfendigaid
Rhayader (Rhaeadr Gwy)
Elan Village
Elan Valley
Joppa
Nebo
Bontnewydd
Blaenpennal
Aberarth
Aberaeron
New Quay (Ceinewydd)
Llanina
Cilcennin
Bwlchllan
Llangeitho
Tregaron
Gilfachreda
Llwyncelyn
Llanarth
Oakford
Cross Inn
Maen-y-groes
Nanternis
Caerwedros
Trefilan
Talsarn
Ystrad Aeron
Dihewyd
Mydroilyn
Llwyndafydd
Pontgarreg
Plwmp
Temple Bar
Llanddewi Brefi
Newbridge
Llanafan-Fawr
Abergwesyn
Pentregat
Brynhoffnant
Talgarreg
Gorsgoch
Cribyn
Betws Bledrws
Llangybi
Llanfair Clydogau
Beulah
Garth
Rhydlewis
Ffostrasol
Cwrt-newydd
Lampeter (Llanbedr Pont Steffan)
Llanwnnen
Pontshaen
Hawen
Troedyraur
Penrhiw-pal
Maesllyn
Tre-groes
Croes-lan
Pren-gwyn
Drefach
Alltyblaca
Rhydowen
Llanwenog
Llanybydder
Pencarreg
Farmers
Rhandirmwyn
Llanwrtyd Wells
Llangammarch Wells
Cefngorwydd
Capel Dewi
Llandyfriog
Penrhiwllan
Henllan
Llandysul
Llanfihangel-ar-arth
Llandre
Pumsaint
Cynghordy
Tirabad
Llandulas
Mynydd Eppynt
Llangeler
Pontwelly
Llanllwni
Drefach Felindre
Pentre-cwrt
Rhydcymerau
Caeo
Cilycwm
Glynteg
Cwmpengraig
Pencader
New Inn
Llansawel
Merthyr Cynog
Rhos
Gwyddgrug
Abergorlech
Gwernogle
Talley
Llandovery (Llanymddyfri)
Pentre-bach
Llanfihangel Nant Bran
Pont-faen
Hermon
Cwmduad
Alltwalis
Brechfa
Llansadwrn
Llanwrda
Myddfai
Llywel
Trallong
Llanpumsaint
Pontarsais
Llanfynydd
Llangadog
Trecastle
Sennybridge
Blaen-y-Coed
Cynwyl Elfed
Rhydargaeau
Defynnog
Talog
Felingwm Uchaf
Bethlehem
Twynllanan
Libanus
Bronwydd
Felingwm Isaf
Court Henry
Penybanc
Crai

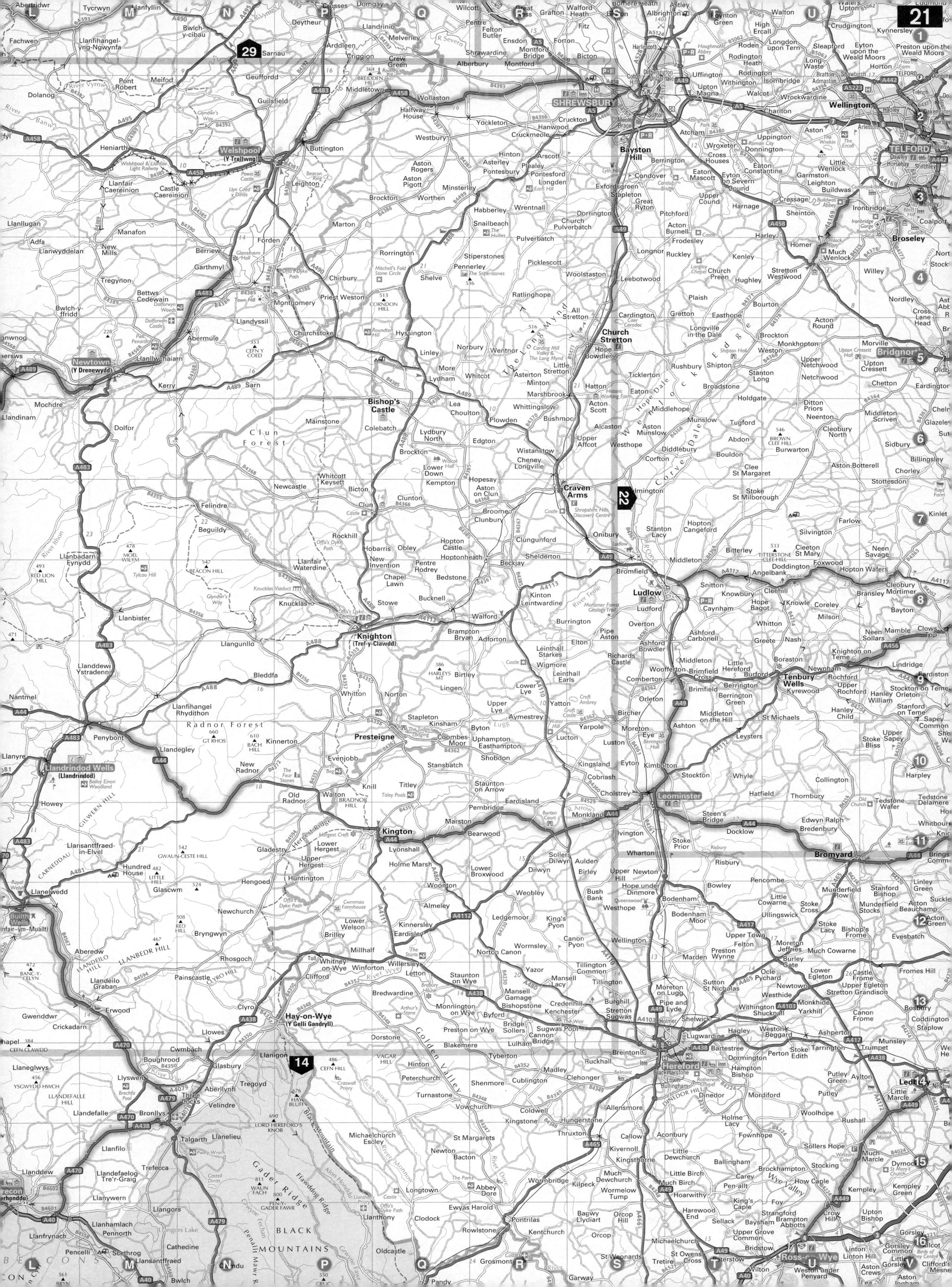
29
22
14
Shrewsbury
Telford
Wellington
Bridgnorth
Broseley
Welshpool (Y Trallwng)
Newtown (Y Drenewydd)
Montgomery
Bishop's Castle
Church Stretton
Craven Arms
Ludlow
Knighton (Tref-y-Clawdd)
Presteigne
Llandrindod Wells (Llandrindod)
Kington
Leominster
Tenbury Wells
Bromyard
Builth Wells
Hay-on-Wye (Y Gelli Gandryll)
Hereford
Ledbury
Ross-on-Wye
Brecon
Clun Forest
Radnor Forest
The Long Mynd
Wenlock Edge
Corve Dale
Golden Valley
Black Mountains
Gader Ridge

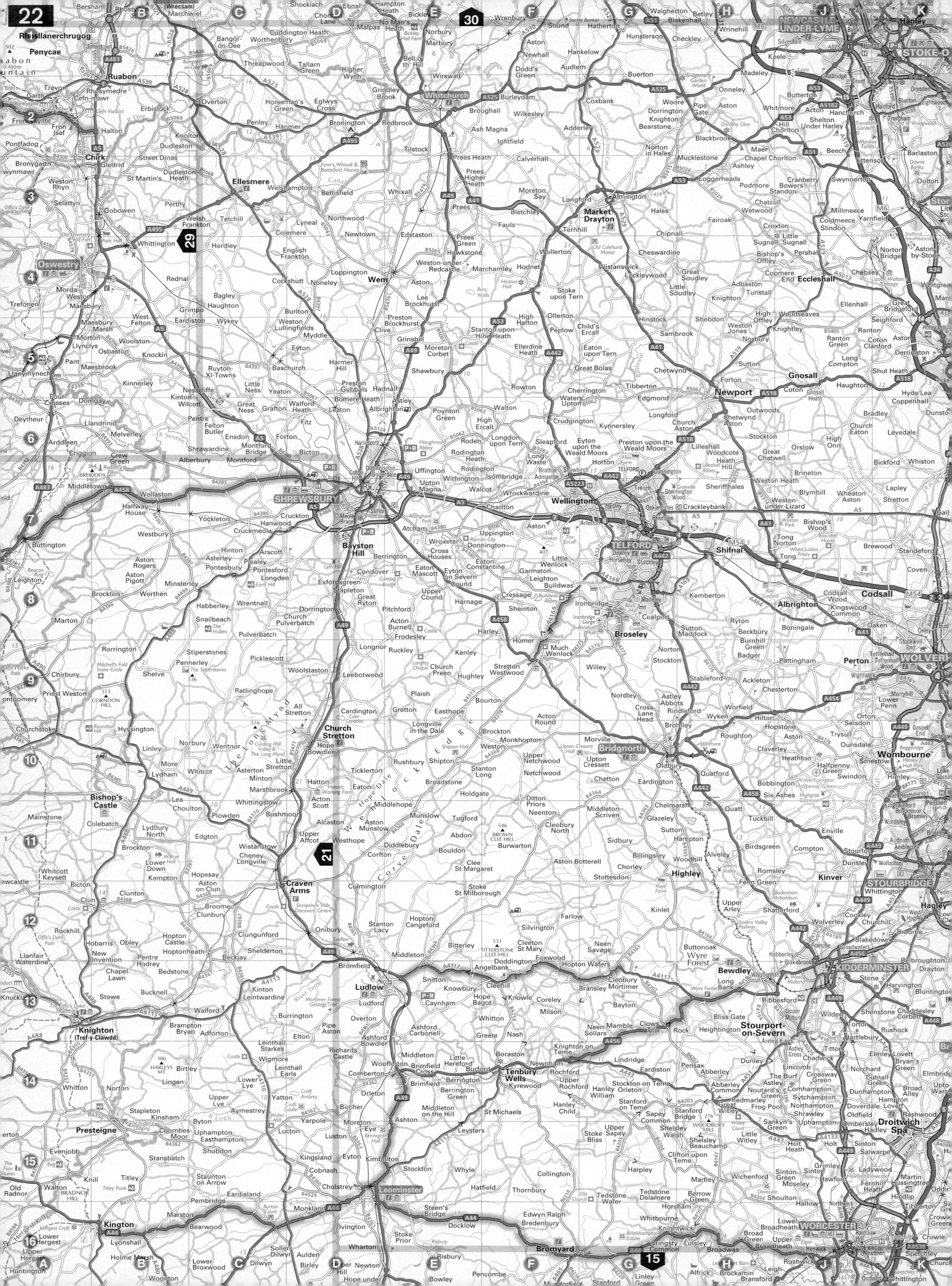
Ruabon
Chirk
Oswestry
Ellesmere
Whitchurch
Wem
Market Drayton
Newport
Eccleshall
Newcastle-under-Lyme
Stoke-on-Trent
Hanley
Shrewsbury
Wellington
Telford
Shifnal
Codsall
Albrighton
Ironbridge
Broseley
Much Wenlock
Bridgnorth
Wombourne
Church Stretton
Bishop's Castle
Craven Arms
Ludlow
Cleobury Mortimer
Bewdley
Kidderminster
Stourport-on-Severn
Stourbridge
Tenbury Wells
Knighton (Tref-y-Clawdd)
Presteigne
Kington
Leominster
Bromyard
Worcester
Droitwich Spa
Highley
Kinver
Bayston Hill
Clun
Welshpool
Long Mynd
Wenlock Edge
Corve Dale
River Severn
M54
A5
A49
A41
A442
A458
A44
29
30
21
15

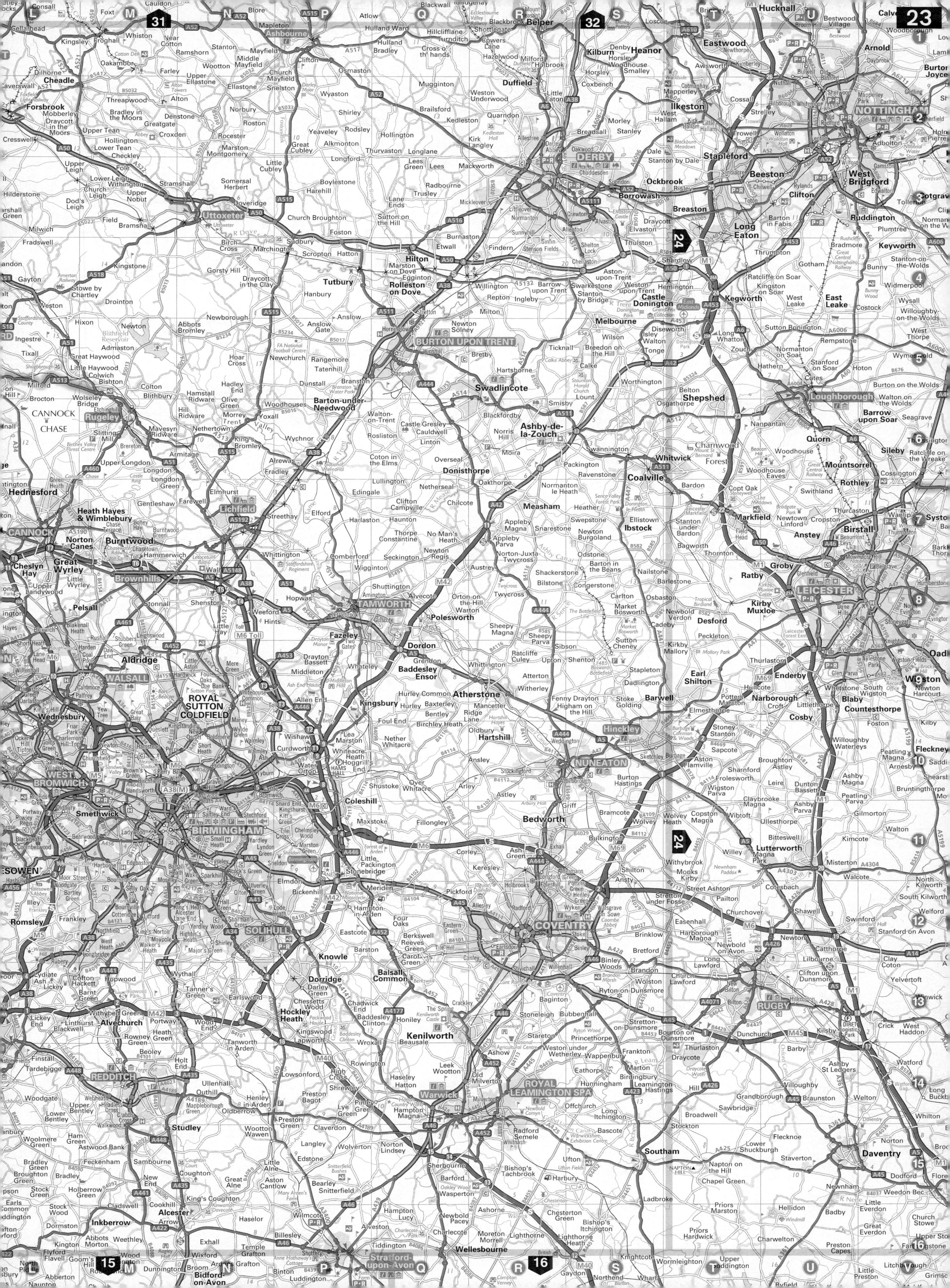
31
32
24
15
16
NOTTINGHAM
DERBY
LEICESTER
BIRMINGHAM
COVENTRY
WEST BROMWICH
WALSALL
SOLIHULL
NUNEATON
ROYAL SUTTON COLDFIELD
ROYAL LEAMINGTON SPA
BURTON UPON TRENT
TAMWORTH
Loughborough
Lichfield
Rugeley
Uttoxeter
Ashbourne
Hinckley
Rugby
Redditch
Warwick
Stratford-upon-Avon
Brownhills
CANNOCK
Belper
Heanor
Eastwood
Ilkeston
Stapleford
Beeston
West Bridgford
Long Eaton
Castle Donington
Kegworth
Shepshed
Coalville
Ashby-de-la-Zouch
Swadlincote
Melbourne
Atherstone
Bedworth
Kenilworth
Daventry
Southam
Lutterworth
Alcester
Studley
Smethwick
Wednesbury
Hednesford
Cheadle
Duffield
Hucknall
Arnold
Hilton
Tutbury
Aldridge
Coleshill
Polesworth
Measham
Ibstock
Earl Shilton
Barwell
Wellesbourne
Alvechurch
Knowle
Dorridge
Hockley Heath

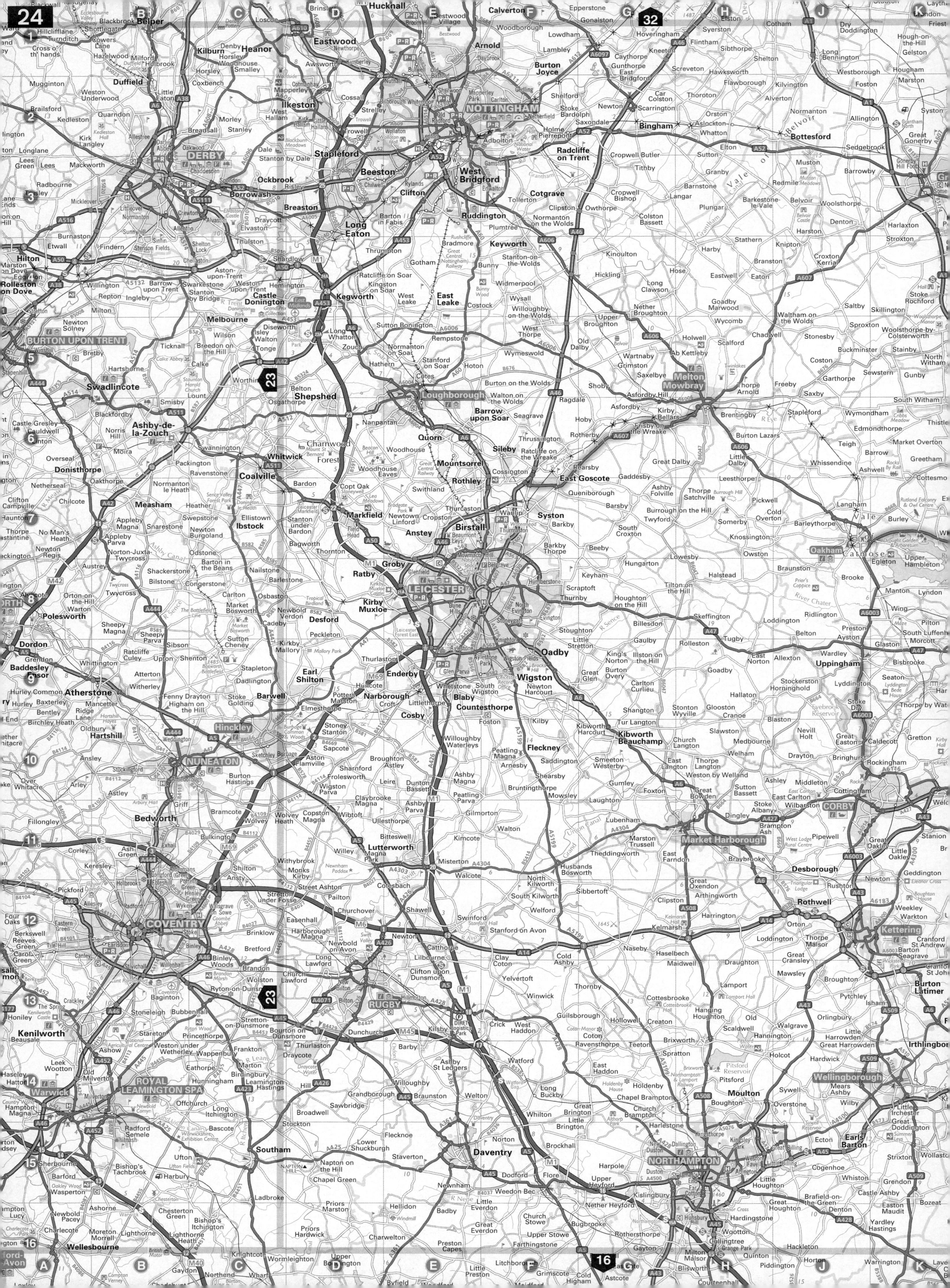
32
23
16
NOTTINGHAM
DERBY
LEICESTER
COVENTRY
NUNEATON
RUGBY
ROYAL LEAMINGTON SPA
Warwick
NORTHAMPTON
BURTON UPON TRENT
Loughborough
Melton Mowbray
Hinckley
Market Harborough
Kettering
CORBY
Wellingborough
Oakham
Belper
Heanor
Eastwood
Hucknall
Ilkeston
Arnold
Beeston
Stapleford
West Bridgford
Long Eaton
Castle Donington
Swadlincote
Ashby-de-la-Zouch
Coalville
Shepshed
Bingham
Bottesford
Syston
Oadby
Wigston
Uppingham
Lutterworth
Daventry
Kenilworth
Bedworth
Atherstone
Southam
Wellesbourne
Desborough
Rothwell
Burton Latimer
Irthlingborough
Earls Barton
Duffield
Melbourne
Kibworth Beauchamp
Countesthorpe
Market Bosworth

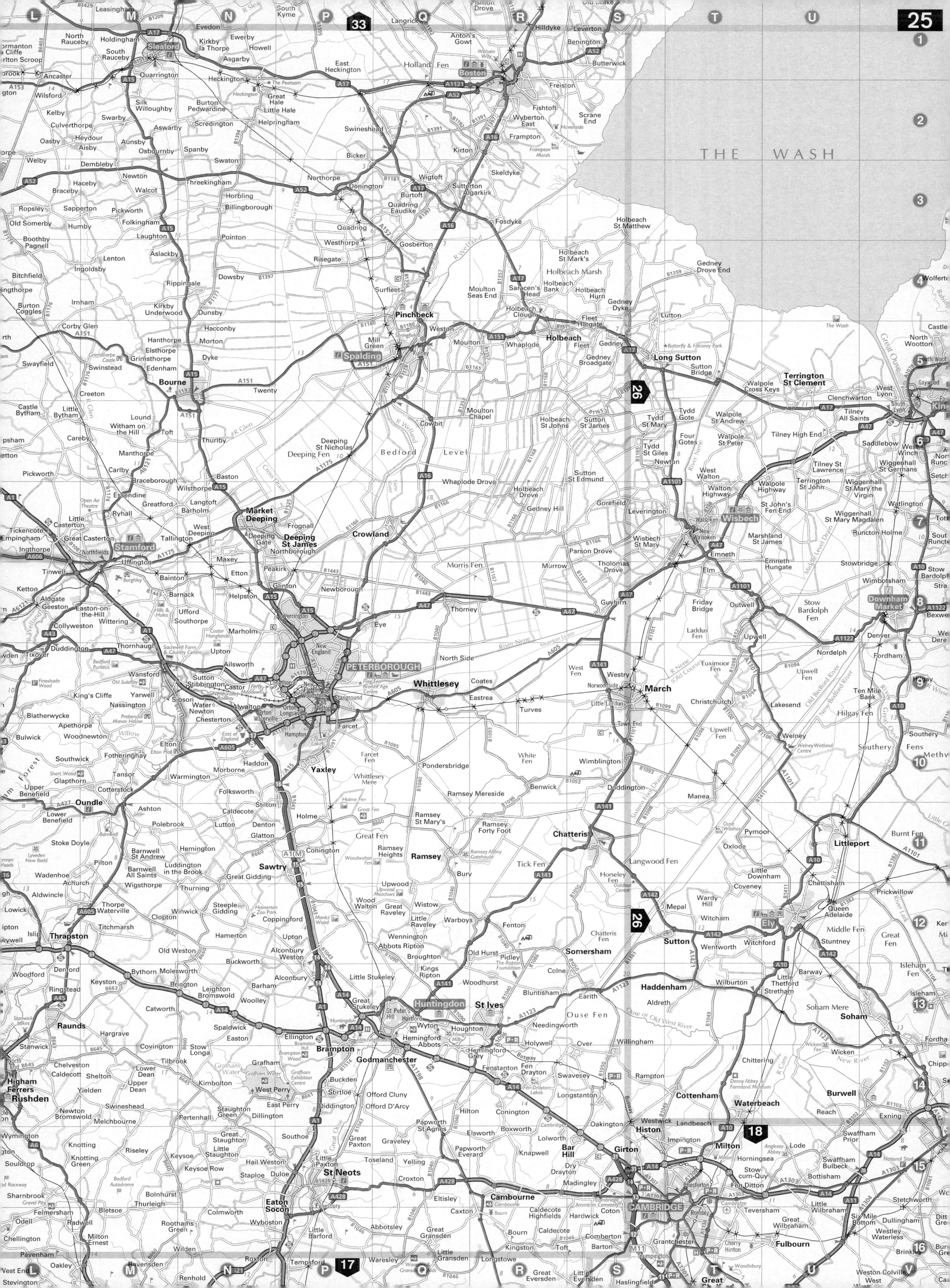
THE WASH
Leasingham
Evedon
South Kyme
Langrick
Anton's Gowt
Hilldyke
Leverton
Benington
Butterwick
North Rauceby
Holdingham
Sleaford
Kirkby la Thorpe
Ewerby
Howell
South Rauceby
Asgarby
Quarrington
Ancaster
Heckington
The Pearoom
East Heckington
Holland Fen
Boston
Freiston
Wilsford
Great Hale
Little Hale
Silk Willoughby
Burton Pedwardine
Kelby
Swarby
Culverthorpe
Scredington
Helpringham
Fishtoft
Wyberton East
Scrane End
Hovenside
Swineshead
Frampton
Frampton Marsh
The Haven
Oasby
Heydour
Aisby
Aunsby
Osbournby
Spanby
Swaton
Bicker
Kirton
Welby
Dembleby
Haceby
Newton
Walcot
Threekingham
Northorpe
Donington
Wigtoft
Sutterton
Algarkirk
Skeldyke
Braceby
Sapperton
Pickworth
Horbling
Billingborough
Burtoft
Quadring Eaudike
Ropsley
Old Somerby
Humby
Folkingham
Laughton
Pointon
Quadring
Fosdyke
Holbeach St Matthew
Boothby Pagnell
Aslackby
Westhorpe
Gosberton
Risegate
Lenton
Ingoldsby
Bitchfield
Rippingale
Dowsby
Surfleet
Holbeach St Mark's
Holbeach Marsh
Holbeach Bank
Holbeach Hurn
Saracen's Head
Moulton Seas End
Gedney Drove End
Irnham
Kirkby Underwood
Dunsby
Burton Coggles
Pinchbeck
Holbeach Clough
Gedney Dyke
Lutton
Fleet Hargate
Corby Glen
Hanthorpe
Hacconby
Morton
Weston
Moulton
Whaplode
Holbeach
Fleet
Gedney
Gedney Broadgate
Long Sutton
Sutton Bridge
Butterfly & Falconry Park
The Wash
Elsthorpe
Grimsthorpe
Grimsthorpe Castle
Swinstead
Swayfield
Edenham
Dyke
Mill Green
Spalding
Bourne
Twenty
Creeton
Castle Bytham
Little Bytham
Lound
Witham on the Hill
Toft
Cowbit
Moulton Chapel
Holbeach St Johns
Sutton St James
Tydd St Mary
Tydd Gote
Walpole St Andrew
Walpole Cross Keys
Terrington St Clement
Clenchwarton
West Lynn
North Wootton
Castle
Tilney All Saints
Tilney High End
Saddlebow
Walpole St Peter
Tydd St Giles
Four Gotes
Newton
Carlby
Careby
Thurlby
Deeping St Nicholas
Deeping Fen
Bedford Level
R. Welland
Braceborough
Baston
Whaplode Drove
Sutton St Edmund
West Walton
Tilney St Lawrence
Terrington St John
Walpole Highway
Walton Highway
Wiggenhall St Germans
Wiggenhall St Mary the Virgin
Wiggenhall St Mary Magdalen
Pickworth
Essendine
Wilsthorpe
Langtoft
Barholm
Greatford
Holbeach Drove
Gedney Hill
Gorefield
Leverington
Wisbech
St John's Fen End
Watlington
Ryhall
Market Deeping
Frognall
Deeping Gate
Deeping St James
Northborough
Crowland
Little Casterton
Tickencote
Empingham
Great Casterton
Stamford
Tallington
West Deeping
Wisbech St Mary
Parson Drove
Murrow
Tholomas Drove
Emneth
Marshland St James
Emneth Hungate
Runcton Holme
Stowbridge
Wimbotsham
Downham Market
Ingthorpe
Uffington
Maxey
Etton
Bainton
Peakirk
Morris Fen
Elm
Tinwell
Ketton
Barnack
Helpston
Glinton
Newborough
Guyhirn
Friday Bridge
Outwell
Stow Bardolph
Fen
Aldgate
Geeston
Easton-on-the-Hill
Wittering
Ufford
Southorpe
Werrington
Eye
Thorney
Laddus Fen
Upwell
Denver
Collyweston
Marholm
Castor Hanglands
Nordelph
Fordham
Duddington
Thornhaugh
Sacrewell Farm & Country Centre
Upton
New England
North Side
Westry
Euximoor Fen
Upwell Fen
Tixover
Bedford Purlieus
Wansford
Ailsworth
Sutton
Stibbington
Castor
PETERBOROUGH
Whittlesey
Coates
Eastrea
Turves
March
Norwoodside
Little London
Christchurch
Ten Mile Bank
Fineshade Wood
Old Sulehay
King's Cliffe
Yarwell
Nassington
Sibson
Water Newton
Chesterton
Alwalton
Orton Waterville
Orton Longueville
Woodston
Fletton
Stanground
Flag Fen Bronze Age Centre
Lakesend
Hilgay Fen
Blatherwycke
Prebendal Manor House
Apethorpe
Woodnewton
Elton
Elton Hall
Hampton
Farcet
Town End
Welney
Welney Wetland Centre
Southery
Bulwick
Willow Brook
Fotheringhay
East of England Showground
Farcet Fen
Upwell Fen
White Fen
Wimblington
Southwick
Haddon
Yaxley
Pondersbridge
Benwick
Doddington
Short Wood
Glapthorn
Tansor
Morborne
Warmington
Whittlesey Mere
Ramsey Mereside
Manea
Upper Benefield
Cotterstock
Folksworth
Stilton
Oundle
Ashton
Caldecote
Holme Fen
Great Fen
Holme
Ramsey St Mary's
Ramsey Forty Foot
Lower Benefield
Polebrook
Lutton
Denton
Glatton
Chatteris
Pymoor
Oxlode
Burnt Fen
Littleport
Stoke Doyle
Barnwell St Andrew
Hemington
Conington
Ramsey Heights
Ramsey
Ramsey Abbey Gatehouse
Langwood Fen
Lyveden New Bield
Pilton
Barnwell All Saints
Luddington in the Brook
Sawtry
Tick Fen
Little Downham
Chettisham
Wadenhoe
Great Gidding
Woodwalton Fen
Bury
Horseley Fen
Coveney
Prickwillow
Aldwincle
Achurch
Wigsthorpe
Thurning
Upwood
Upwood Meadows
Wardy Hill
Mepal
Queen Adelaide
Lowick
Thorpe Waterville
Winwick
Steeple Gidding
Hamerton Zoo Park
Monks Wood
Wood Walton
Great Raveley
Wistow
Witcham
Ely
Middle Fen
Titchmarsh
Clopton
Coppingford
Little Raveley
Warboys
Fenton
Chatteris Fen
Sutton
Wentworth
Witchford
Stuntney
Great Fen
Islip
Thrapston
Hamerton
Upton
Wennington
Abbots Ripton
Old Weston
Alconbury Weston
Broughton
Old Hurst
Pidley
The Raptor Foundation
Somersham
Colne
Isleham Fen
Denford
Woodford
Buckworth
Bythorn
Molesworth
Little Stukeley
Kings Ripton
Haddenham
Wilburton
Little Thetford
Stretham
Barway
Isleham
Keyston
Brington
Alconbury
Great Stukeley
Woodhurst
Bluntisham
Earith
Aldreth
Ringstead
Leighton Bromswold
Barham
Woolley
Huntingdon
St Ives
Ouse Fen
Soham Mere
Soham
Catworth
St Peter's Hill
Hartford
Wyton
Houghton
Houghton Mill
Needingworth
Old West River
Raunds
Spaldwick
Hargrave
Easton
Ellington
Brampton
Brampton Hut
Brampton Wood
Godmanchester
Hinchingbrooke
Hemingford Abbots
Hemingford Grey
Holywell
Over
Willingham
Fordham
Stanwick
Covington
Stow Longa
Grafham
Grafham Water
Grafham Exhibition Centre
Fenstanton
Fen Drayton
Swavesey
Rampton
Chittering
Wicken Fen
Wicken
New River
Chippenham
Chelveston
Caldecott
Shelton
Lower Dean
Upper Dean
Tilbrook
Kimbolton
West Perry
Buckden
Stirtloe
Offord Cluny
Offord D'Arcy
Fen Drayton Lakes
Longstanton
Cottenham
Denny Abbey & Farmland Museum
Waterbeach
Burwell
Higham Ferrers
Rushden
Yielden
Newton Bromswold
Swineshead
Melchbourne
East Perry
Staughton Green
Pertenhall
Dillington
Diddington
Hilton
Conington
Papworth St Agnes
Westwick
Oakington
Landbeach
Histon
Reach
Swaffham Prior
Exning
Wymington
Knotting
Knotting Green
Riseley
Great Staughton
Little Staughton
Southoe
Great Paxton
Graveley
Elsworth
Boxworth
Lolworth
Bar Hill
Impington
Girton
Milton
Horningsea
Anglesey Abbey
Lode
Swaffham Bulbeck
National Stud
Souldrop
Keysoe
Keysoe Row
Hail Weston
Little Paxton
Toseland
Yelling
Papworth Everard
Knapwell
Dry Drayton
Stow-cum-Quy
Bottisham
Bedford Autodrome
Bolnhurst
Staploe
Duloe
St Neots
Croxton
Madingley
Fen Ditton
Chesterton
Sharnbrook
Gravel Pits
Thurleigh
Eaton Socon
Eynesbury
Eltisley
Cambourne
Caldecote Highfields
American Cemetery
Cambridge
CAMBRIDGE
Teversham
Little Wilbraham
Stetchworth
Felmersham
Bletsoe
Colmworth
Wyboston
Caxton
Bourn
Hardwick
Coton
Romsey
Great Wilbraham
Six Mile Bottom
Dullingham
Westley Waterless
Odell
Radwell
Roothams Green
Little Barford
Abbotsley
Great Gransden
Caldecote
Bourn
Kingston
Comberton
Barton
Grantchester
Cherry Hinton
Fulbourn
Chellington
Milton Ernest
Wilden
Toft
Brinkley
Pavenham
Oakley
Ravensden
Roxton
Tempsford
Waresley
Little Gransden
Longstowe
Great Eversden
Little Eversden
Haslingfield
Trumpington
Wandlebury
Great
Weston Colville
West End
Stevington
Renhold
West

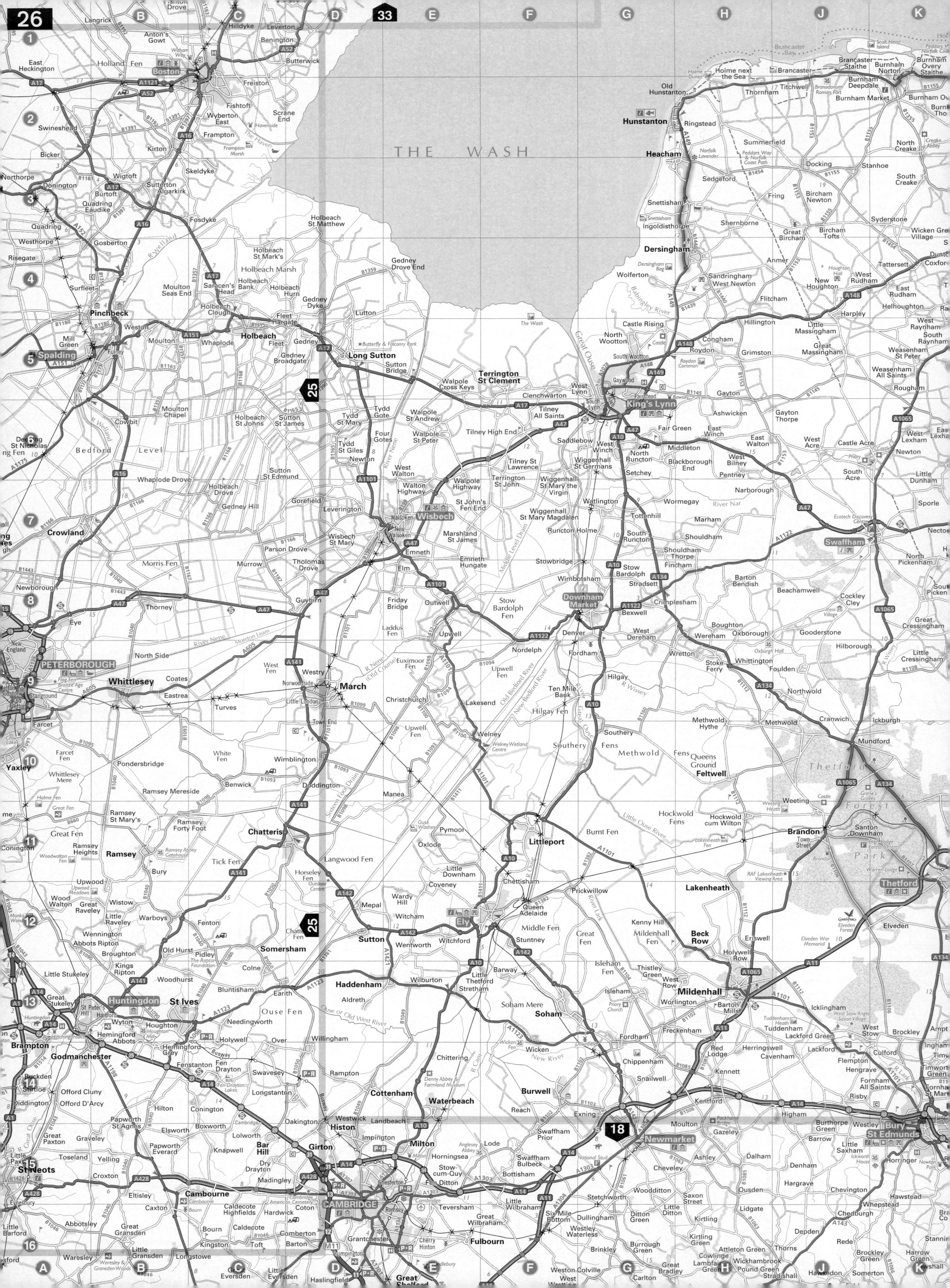
THE WASH
33
25
18
Boston
Spalding
Pinchbeck
Holbeach
Long Sutton
Sutton Bridge
Terrington St Clement
King's Lynn
Hunstanton
Heacham
Dersingham
Sandringham
Castle Rising
Gaywood
West Lynn
Wisbech
Downham Market
Swaffham
Thetford
Brandon
Mundford
Feltwell
Methwold
Littleport
Ely
March
Chatteris
Whittlesey
PETERBOROUGH
Crowland
Thorney
Eye
Yaxley
Ramsey
Huntingdon
St Ives
Godmanchester
St Neots
Cambourne
CAMBRIDGE
Histon
Girton
Milton
Waterbeach
Cottenham
Haddenham
Sutton
Soham
Burwell
Newmarket
Mildenhall
Lakenheath
Bury St Edmunds
Fulbourn
Great Shelford
Brancaster
Burnham Market
Docking
Snettisham
Sedgeford
Fakenham
Stow Bardolph
Upwell
Outwell
Emneth
Elm
Guyhirn
Doddington
Manea
Welney
Kirton
Swineshead
Donington
Gosberton
Surfleet
Fleet Hargate
Gedney
Holbeach Marsh
Moulton
Whaplode
Cowbit
Newborough
Farcet
Somersham
Warboys
Pidley
Brampton
Buckden
Offord Cluny
Papworth Everard
Bar Hill
Madingley
Comberton
Grantchester
Teversham
Six Mile Bottom
Dullingham
Cheveley
Kentford
Risby
Elveden
Icklingham
Tuddenham
Barton Mills
Worlington
Freckenham
Fordham
Isleham
Chippenham
Wicken
Stretham
Little Downham
Pymoor
Coveney
Witchford
Wentworth
Witcham
Mepal
Sutton
Wilburton
Aldreth
Willingham
Over
Swavesey
Fen Drayton
Fenstanton
Hemingford Grey
Houghton
Wyton
Thetford Forest
Middle Level Drain
River Nene
Great Ouse
New Bedford River
Old Bedford River
Little Ouse River
River Lark
River Wissey
A17
A16
A47
A10
A11
A14
A141
A142
A134
A1065
A148
A149
A1101
A1122
A1123
M11

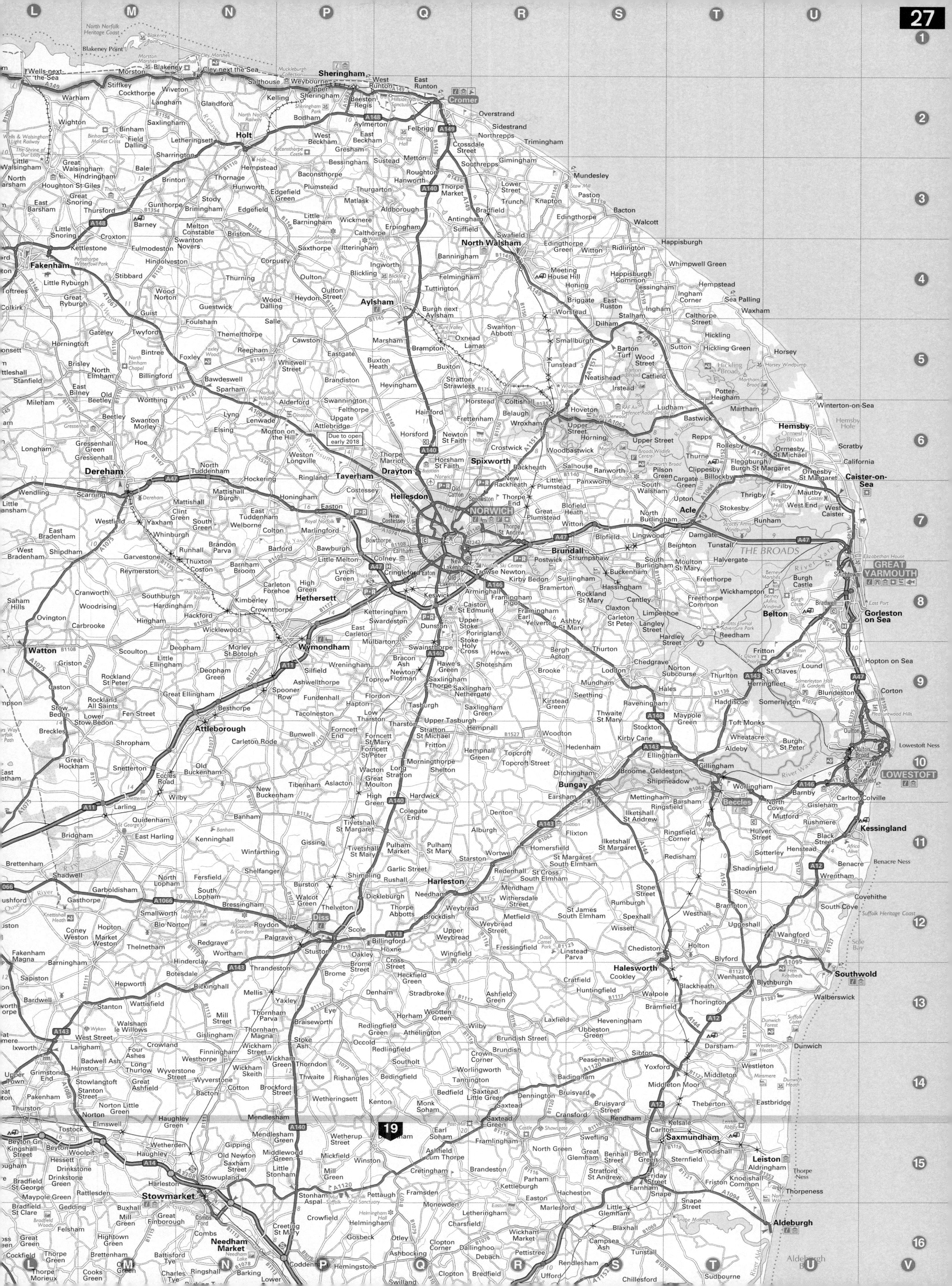
North Norfolk Heritage Coast
Blakeney Point
Wells-next-the-Sea
Blakeney
Cley next the Sea
Sheringham
Cromer
Holt
Fakenham
Dereham
Aylsham
North Walsham
Mundesley
Happisburgh
Sea Palling
Hemsby
Winterton-on-Sea
Caister-on-Sea
GREAT YARMOUTH
Gorleston on Sea
Hopton on Sea
NORWICH
Drayton
Taverham
Hellesdon
Spixworth
Wroxham
Hoveton
Acle
Brundall
THE BROADS
Wymondham
Hethersett
Attleborough
Watton
Belton
Lowestoft Ness
LOWESTOFT
Kessingland
Beccles
Bungay
Harleston
Diss
Halesworth
Southwold
Walberswick
Dunwich
Leiston
Aldeburgh
Saxmundham
Stowmarket
Needham Market
Framlingham
Eye
Benacre Ness
Thorpe Ness
Suffolk Heritage Coast
19

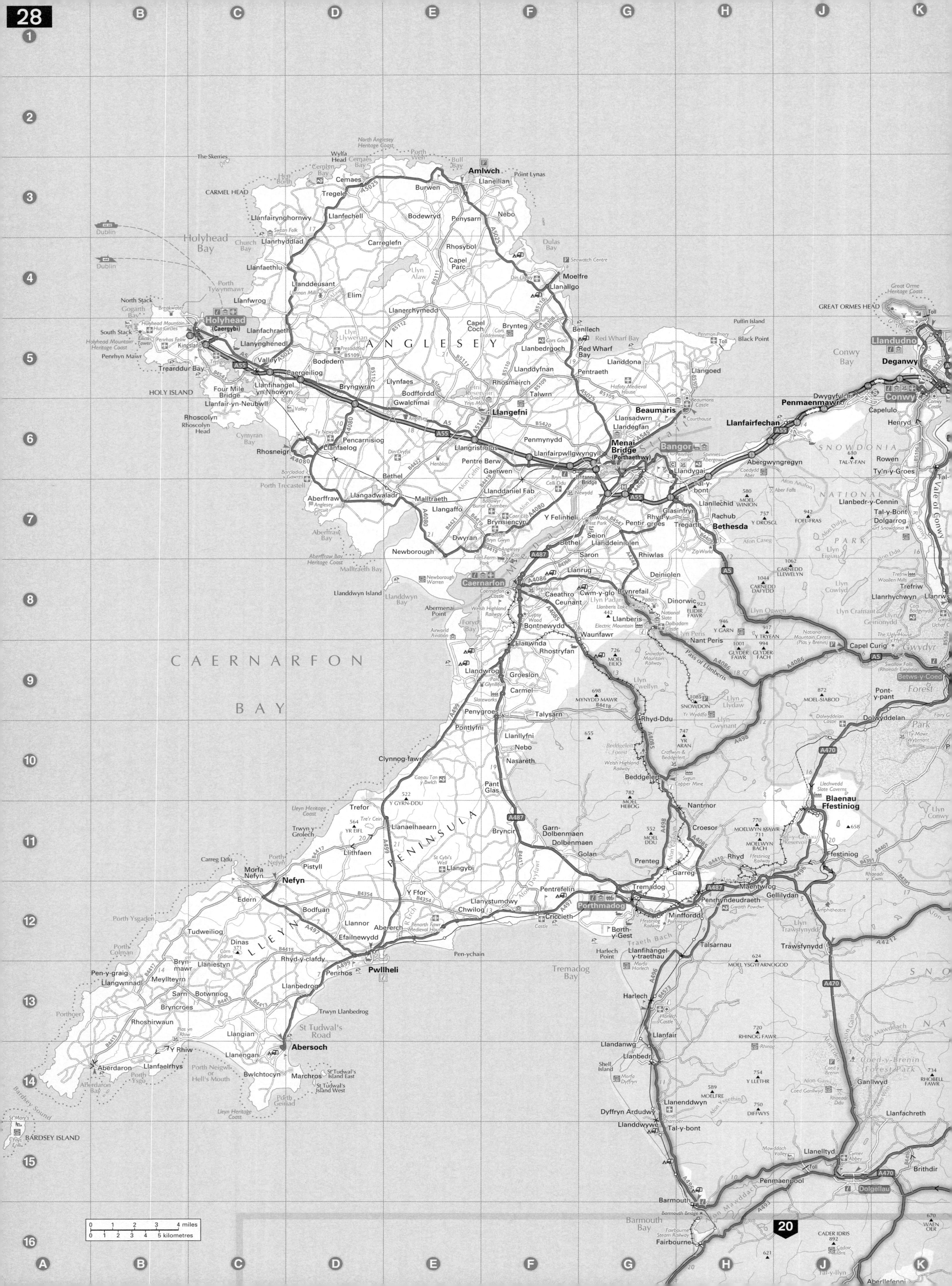

A
B
C
D
E
F
G
H
J
K
1
2
3
4
5
6
7
8
9
10
11
12
13
14
15
16
North Anglesey Heritage Coast
Wylfa Head
Cemaes Bay
Porth Wen
Bull Bay
Amlwch
Point Lynas
The Skerries
Cemlyn Bay
Cemaes
Hen Borth
CARMEL HEAD
Tregele
Burwen
Llaneilian
Llanfechell
Bodewryd
Penysarn
Nebo
Llanfairynghornwy
Dublin
Holyhead Bay
Church Bay
Llanrhyddlad
Carreglefn
Rhosybol
Dulas Bay
Seawatch Centre
Llanfaethlu
Capel Parc
Llyn Alaw
Moelfre
Llanallgo
Porth Tywynmawr
Llanddeusant
North Stack
Llanfwrog
Elim
Gogarth Bay
Holyhead
(Caergybi)
Llanerchymedd
South Stack
Holyhead Mountain Heritage Coast
Llanfachraeth
Capel Coch
Brynteg
Benllech
Puffin Island
Red Wharf Bay
Penmon Priory
Black Point
Kingsland
Llanynghenedl
ANGLESEY
Llanbedrgoch
Red Wharf Bay
Toll
Penrhyn Mawr
Valley
Trearddur Bay
Bodedern
Llanddyfnan
Llanddona
Caergeiliog
Llangoed
Four Mile Bridge
Llanfihangel yn Nhowyn
Bryngwran
Llynfaes
Bodffordd
Rhosmeirch
Pentraeth
HOLY ISLAND
Lanfair-yn-Neubwll
Gwalchmai
Talwrn
Beaumaris
Llangefni
Rhoscolyn
Rhoscolyn Head
Llansadwrn
Llandegfan
Cymyran Bay
Pencarnisiog
Penmynydd
Menai Bridge
(Porthaethwy)
Bangor
Rhosneigr
Llanfaelog
Llangristiolus
Llanfairpwllgwyngyll
Pentre Berw
Gaerwen
Britannia Bridge
Bethel
Porth Trecastell
Llangadwaladr
Malltraeth
Llanddaniel Fab
Aberffraw
Llangaffo
Aberffraw Bay
Brynsiencyn
Y Felinheli
Dwyran
Newborough
Aberffraw Bay Heritage Coast
Malltraeth Bay
Caernarfon
Llanddwyn Island
Llanddwyn Bay
Abermenai Point
Foryd Bay
Great Orme Heritage Coast
GREAT ORMES HEAD
Llandudno
Conwy Bay
Deganwy
Conwy
Penmaenmawr
Dwygyfylchi
Capelulo
Henryd
Llanfairfechan
Abergwyngregyn
Rowen
Ty'n-y-Groes
SNOWDONIA
NATIONAL
PARK
Llandygai
Tal-y-bont
Llanllechid
Rachub
Glasinfryn
Bethesda
Tregarth
Pentir
Rhyd-y-groes
Seion
Llanddeiniolen
Saron
Rhiwlas
Llanrug
Deiniolen
Caeathro
Cwm-y-glo
Brynrefail
Ceunant
Dinorwic
Llanberis
Bontnewydd
Waunfawr
Llanwnda
Rhostryfan
Nant Peris
Pass of Llanberis
Capel Curig
Llanbedr-y-Cennin
Tal-y-Bont
Dolgarrog
Trefriw
Llanrhychwyn
Vale of Conwy
Betws-y-Coed
Gwydyr
Forest
Pont-y-pant
Dolwyddelan
CAERNARFON
BAY
Llandwrog
Groeslon
Carmel
Penygroes
Talysarn
Pontllyfni
Llanllyfni
Nebo
Nasareth
Clynnog-fawr
Pant Glas
Rhyd-Ddu
Beddgelert
Nantmor
Croesor
Blaenau Ffestiniog
Ffestiniog
Trefor
Llanaelhaearn
Trwyn y Gwlech
Llithfaen
PENINSULA
LLEYN
Pistyll
Carreg Ddu
Morfa Nefyn
Nefyn
Edern
Bryncir
Garn-Dolbenmaen
Dolbenmaen
Golan
Prenteg
Garreg
Tremadog
Porthmadog
Penrhyndeudraeth
Maentwrog
Gellilydan
Rhyd
Llangybi
Y Ffor
Llanystumdwy
Pentrefelin
Chwilog
Criccieth
Minffordd
Bodfuan
Llannor
Abererch
Efailnewydd
Pwllheli
Porth Ysgaden
Tudweiliog
Porth Colman
Dinas
Llaniestyn
Rhyd-y-clafdy
Penrhos
Pen-y-chain
Borth-y-Gest
Harlech Point
Llanfihangel-y-traethau
Talsarnau
Trawsfynydd
Tremadog Bay
Pen-y-graig
Llangwnnadl
Brynmawr
Meyllteyrn
Sarn
Botwnnog
Bryncroes
Llanbedrog
Trwyn Llanbedrog
St Tudwal's Road
Harlech
Rhoshirwaun
Llangian
Abersoch
Llanfair
Y Rhiw
Llanengan
Aberdaron
Llanfaelrhys
Aberdaron Bay
Porth Ysgo
Porth Neigwl or Hell's Mouth
Bwlchtocyn
Marchros
St Tudwal's Island East
St Tudwal's Island West
Porth Ceiriad
Bardsey Sound
BARDSEY ISLAND
Llandanwg
Llanbedr
Shell Island
Llanenddwyn
Dyffryn Ardudwy
Llanddwywe
Tal-y-bont
Ganllwyd
Llanfachreth
Coed-y-Brenin Forest Park
Llanelltyd
Penmaenpool
Dolgellau
Brithdir
Barmouth
Barmouth Bay
Fairbourne
CADER IDRIS
Tal-y-llyn
Aberllefenni
20
0 1 2 3 4 miles
0 1 2 3 4 5 kilometres

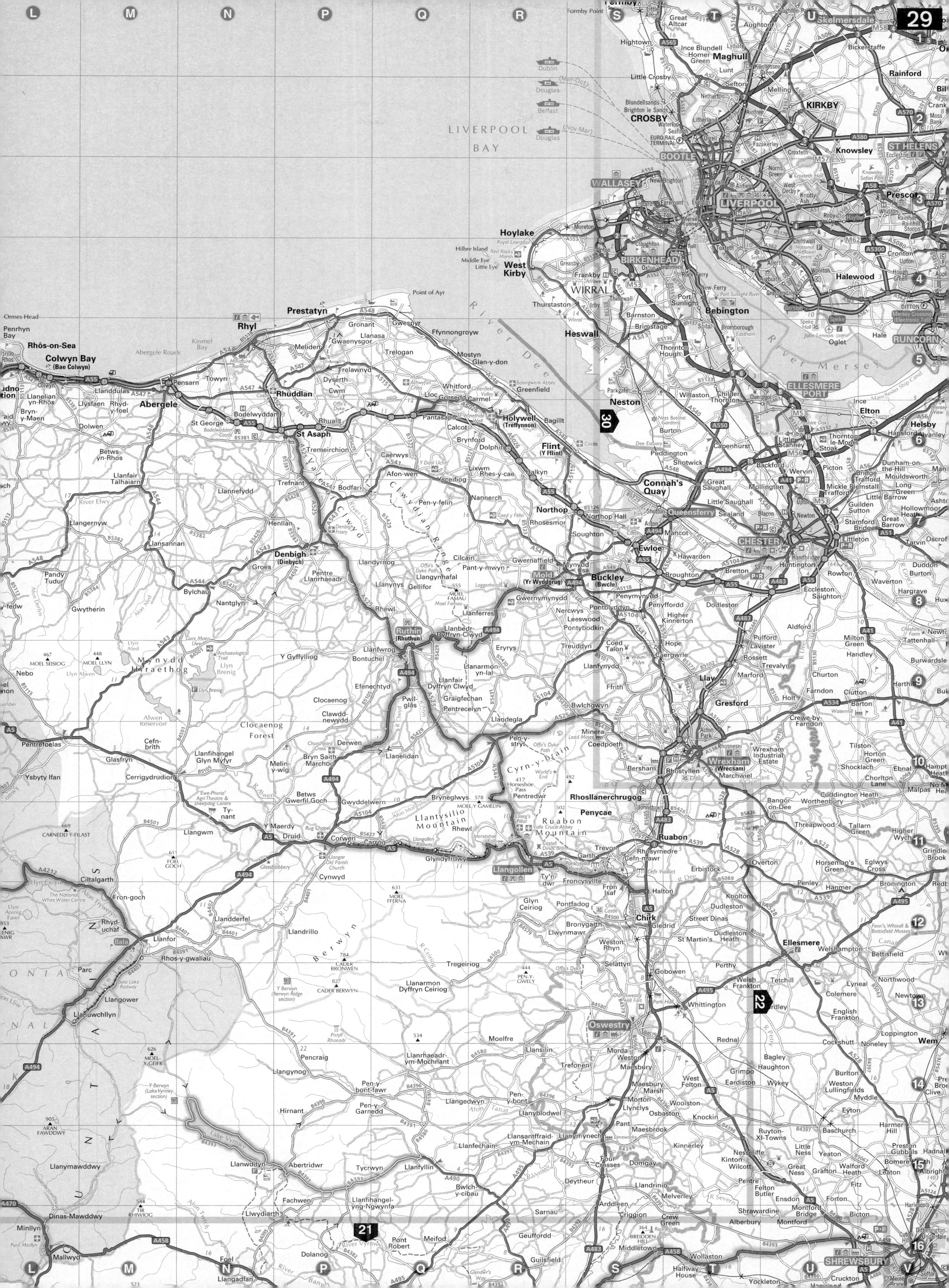
LIVERPOOL BAY
Skelmersdale
Maghull
KIRKBY
CROSBY
BOOTLE
Knowsley
ST HELENS
WALLASEY
LIVERPOOL
Prescot
BIRKENHEAD
Hoylake
West Kirby
WIRRAL
Halewood
Bebington
Heswall
RUNCORN
ELLESMERE PORT
Neston
Elton
Helsby
Prestatyn
Rhyl
Colwyn Bay
(Bae Colwyn)
Rhôs-on-Sea
Abergele
Rhuddlan
St Asaph
Holywell
(Treffynnon)
Flint
(Y Fflint)
Connah's Quay
Queensferry
Northop
CHESTER
Ewloe
Buckley
(Bwcle)
Mold
(Yr Wyddgrug)
Denbigh
(Dinbych)
Ruthin
(Rhuthun)
Clwydian Range
Mynydd Hiraethog
Clocaenog Forest
Llay
Gresford
Wrexham
(Wrecsam)
Rhosllanerchrugog
Penycae
Ruabon
Llangollen
Corwen
Chirk
Ellesmere
Oswestry
Whittington
Bala
Berwyn
Lake Vyrnwy
Llanfyllin
Welshpool
SHREWSBURY
Mallwyd
Dinas-Mawddwy
Pont Robert
Meifod
Llangadfan
21
22
30

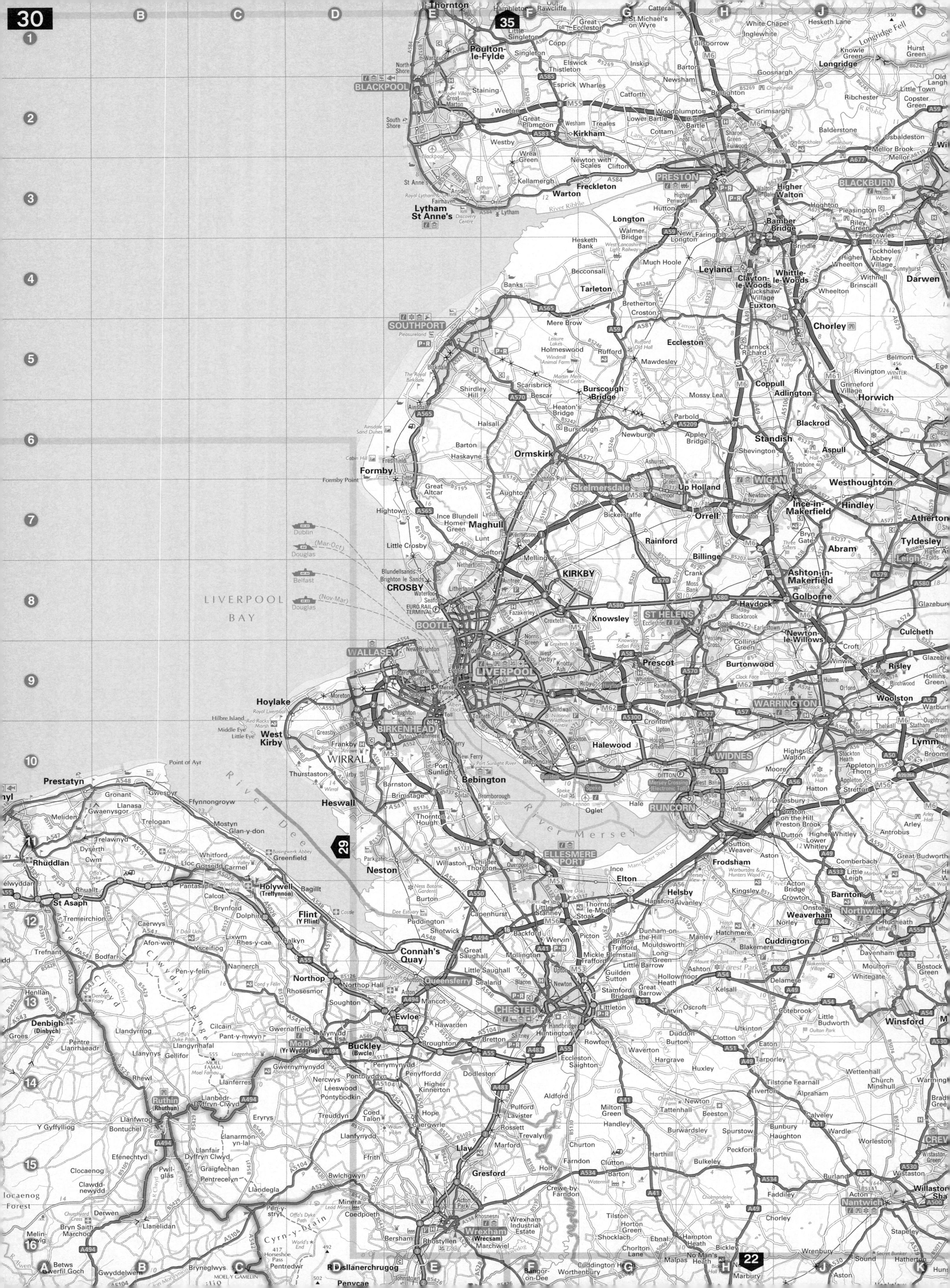
BLACKPOOL
Poulton-le-Fylde
Lytham St Anne's
PRESTON
BLACKBURN
Leyland
Chorley
SOUTHPORT
Ormskirk
Formby
WIGAN
Skelmersdale
KIRKBY
CROSBY
BOOTLE
LIVERPOOL BAY
WALLASEY
LIVERPOOL
ST HELENS
WARRINGTON
BIRKENHEAD
WIRRAL
Hoylake
West Kirby
WIDNES
RUNCORN
ELLESMERE PORT
Prestatyn
Rhuddlan
St Asaph
Holywell (Treffynnon)
Flint (Y Fflint)
Connah's Quay
Queensferry
CHESTER
Mold (Yr Wyddgrug)
Buckley (Bwcle)
Denbigh (Dinbych)
Ruthin (Rhuthun)
Wrexham (Wrecsam)
Northwich
Winsford
Nantwich
River Dee
River Mersey
Clwydian Range
Point of Ayr
Dublin
Douglas
Belfast
35
29
22

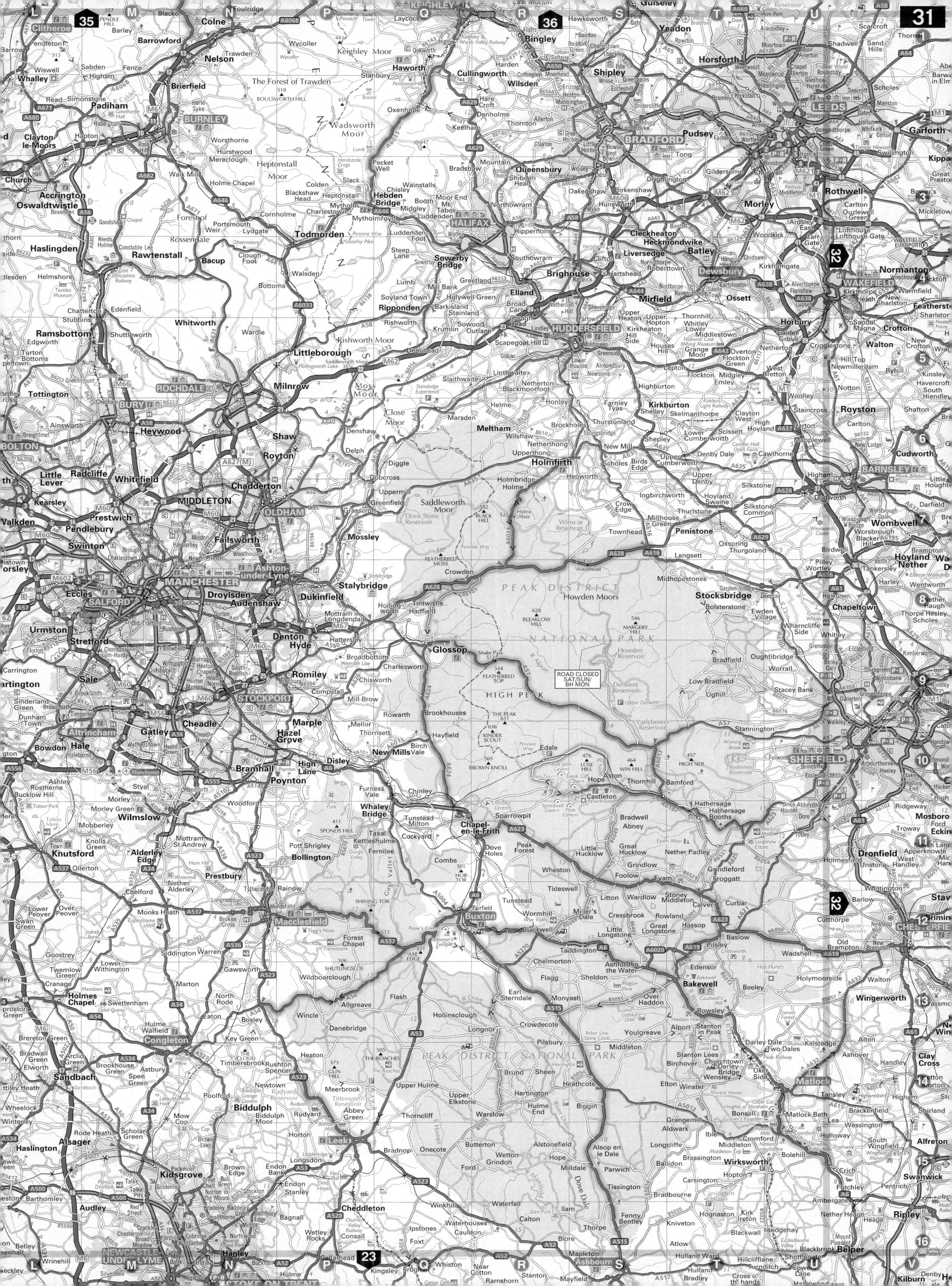
35
36
32
23
Clitheroe
Colne
Nelson
Burnley
Padiham
Accrington
Oswaldtwistle
Haslingden
Rawtenstall
Bacup
Todmorden
Hebden Bridge
Haworth
Keighley
Bingley
Shipley
Yeadon
Horsforth
Leeds
Bradford
Pudsey
Halifax
Queensbury
Brighouse
Elland
Huddersfield
Cleckheaton
Heckmondwike
Batley
Dewsbury
Liversedge
Mirfield
Ossett
Morley
Rothwell
Wakefield
Normanton
Horbury
Garforth
Ramsbottom
Bury
Rochdale
Littleborough
Milnrow
Heywood
Bolton
Shaw
Royton
Oldham
Middleton
Chadderton
Radcliffe
Whitefield
Prestwich
Swinton
Eccles
Salford
Manchester
Ashton-under-Lyne
Stalybridge
Dukinfield
Droylsden
Audenshaw
Denton
Hyde
Glossop
Stockport
Romiley
Marple
Cheadle
Gatley
Sale
Stretford
Urmston
Altrincham
Hale
Bramhall
Poynton
Disley
New Mills
Whaley Bridge
Chapel-en-le-Frith
Buxton
Macclesfield
Bollington
Wilmslow
Knutsford
Alderley Edge
Prestbury
Congleton
Sandbach
Holmes Chapel
Biddulph
Kidsgrove
Alsager
Leek
Cheddleton
Hanley
Newcastle-under-Lyme
Audley
Holmfirth
Meltham
Marsden
Kirkburton
Penistone
Barnsley
Royston
Cudworth
Wombwell
Hoyland Nether
Stocksbridge
Chapeltown
Sheffield
Dronfield
Chesterfield
Bakewell
Matlock
Wirksworth
Belper
Ripley
Alfreton
Ashbourne
Hathersage
Castleton
Tideswell
Peak District National Park
Howden Moors
High Peak
Saddleworth Moor
Road closed Sat/Sun/BH Mon
Ladybower Reservoir
Howden Reservoir
Derwent Reservoir
The Forest of Trawden
Wadsworth Moor
Snake Pass
Kinder Scout
The Roaches
Dove Dale

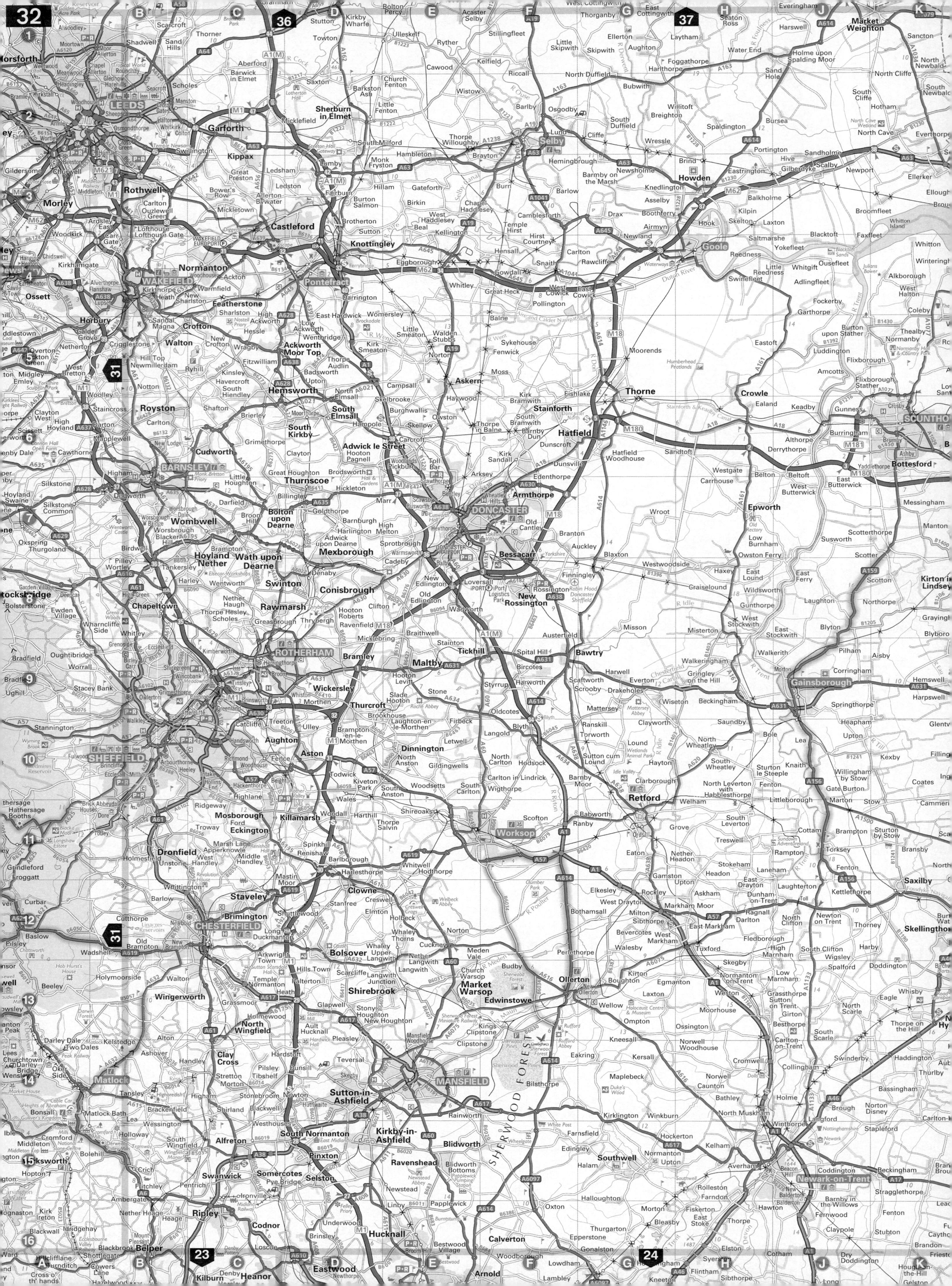
36
37
31
23
24
LEEDS
Morley
Rothwell
Garforth
Castleford
Knottingley
Pontefract
WAKEFIELD
Normanton
Featherstone
Ossett
Horbury
Selby
Sherburn in Elmet
Howden
Goole
Thorne
Hatfield
Crowle
SCUNTHORPE
Bottesford
Epworth
Royston
Hemsworth
South Elmsall
South Kirkby
Ackworth Moor Top
Askern
Stainforth
Armthorpe
DONCASTER
Adwick le Street
BARNSLEY
Cudworth
Thurnscoe
Bolton upon Dearne
Wombwell
Hoyland Nether
Wath upon Dearne
Mexborough
Conisbrough
Swinton
Rawmarsh
Chapeltown
Stocksbridge
ROTHERHAM
Bramley
Maltby
Tickhill
Bawtry
Bessacarr
New Rossington
Gainsborough
Wickersley
Thurcroft
SHEFFIELD
Aughton
Aston
Dinnington
Killamarsh
Mosborough
Eckington
Dronfield
Worksop
Retford
Staveley
Clowne
Bolsover
CHESTERFIELD
Brimington
Shirebrook
Market Warsop
Edwinstowe
Ollerton
MANSFIELD
Sutton-in-Ashfield
Kirkby-in-Ashfield
Alfreton
Ripley
Belper
Matlock
Wirksworth
Hucknall
Eastwood
Heanor
Southwell
Newark-on-Trent
Saxilby
Skellingthorpe
Market Weighton
SHERWOOD FOREST

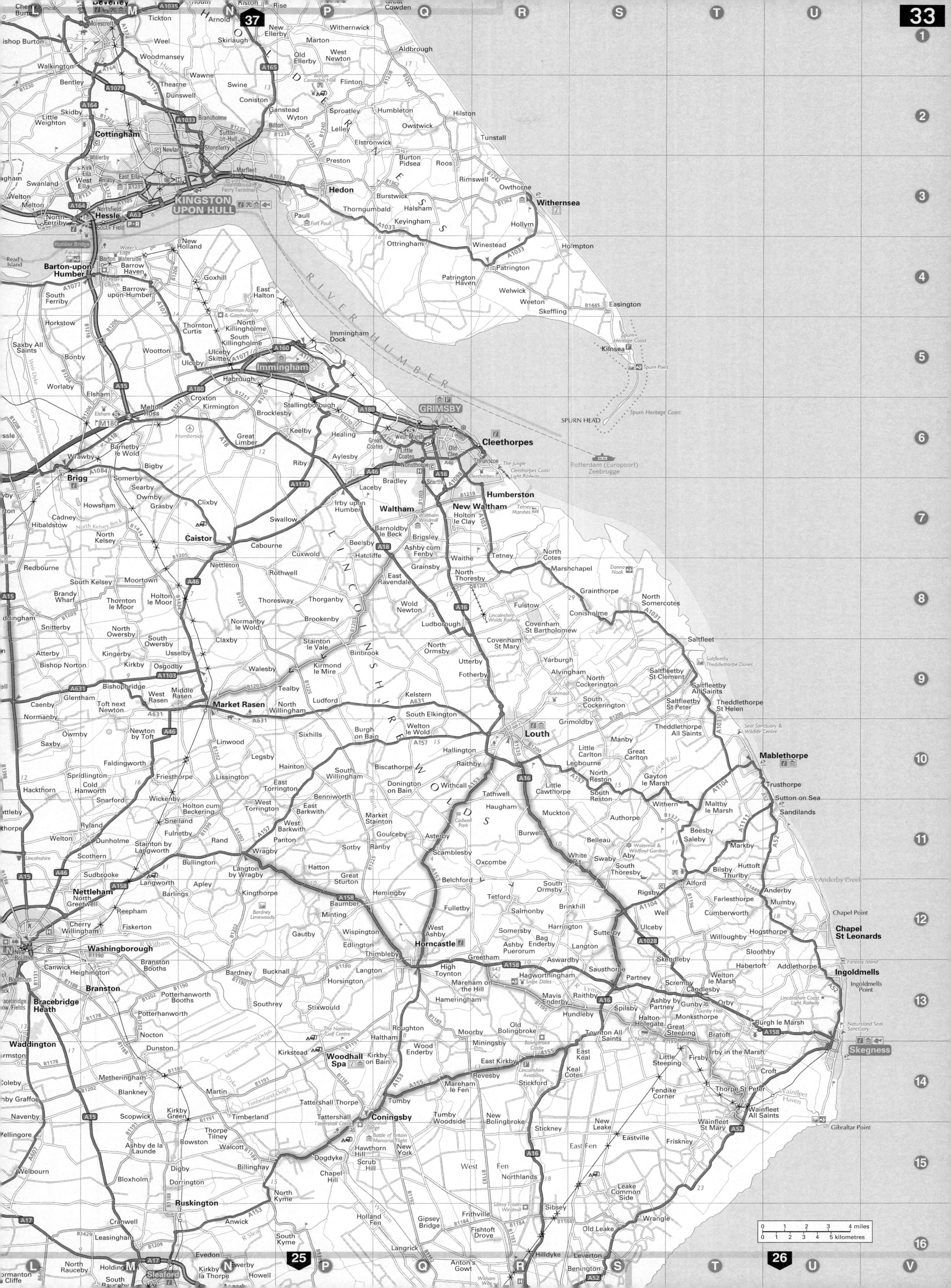

Beverley
Tickton
Arnold
Rise
Cowden
Withernwick
Aldbrough
New Ellerby
Marton
West Newton
Old Ellerby
Skirlaugh
Weel
Woodmansey
Walkington
Bentley
Wawne
Thearne
Swine
Flinton
Dunswell
Coniston
Skidby
Little Weighton
Ganstead
Wyton
Sproatley
Humbleton
Hilston
Cottingham
Bransholme
Bilton
Lelley
Owstwick
Tunstall
Willerby
Newland
Stoneferry
Elstronwick
Burton Pidsea
Roos
Swanland
East Ella
Marfleet
Preston
Rimswell
Kirk Ella
West Ella
Hedon
Owthorne
Withernsea
Welton
Melton
KINGSTON UPON HULL
Burstwick
Halsham
Thorngumbald
Hessle
North Ferriby
Paull
Keyingham
Hollym
Humber Bridge
Ottringham
Winestead
Holmpton
New Holland
Barton-upon-Humber
Barrow Haven
Patrington
Patrington Haven
Welwick
Goxhill
Barrow-upon-Humber
East Halton
South Ferriby
Weeton
Skeffling
Easington
Horkstow
Thornton Curtis
North Killingholme
South Killingholme
Immingham Dock
Kilnsea
Spurn Point
Saxby All Saints
Bonby
Wootton
Ulceby Skitter
Ulceby
Immingham
RIVER HUMBER
Worlaby
Habrough
Elsham
Croxton
Kirmington
Stallingborough
Melton Ross
Brocklesby
GRIMSBY
SPURN HEAD
Spurn Heritage Coast
Keelby
Healing
Great Coates
Cleethorpes
Barnetby le Wold
Great Limber
Aylesby
Little Coates
Old Clee
Wrawby
Riby
Brigg
Somerby
Bigby
Bradley
Scartho
Humberston
Searby
Laceby
Rotterdam (Europoort)
Zeebrugge
Howsham
Owmby
Grasby
Irby upon Humber
Waltham
New Waltham
Cadney
Clixby
Holton le Clay
Hibaldstow
Swallow
North Kelsey
Caistor
Barnoldby le Beck
Cabourne
Beelsby
Brigsley
Ashby cum Fenby
Tetney
Hatcliffe
Waithe
North Cotes
Cuxwold
Grainsby
Marshchapel
Redbourne
Nettleton
Rothwell
North Thoresby
South Kelsey
Moortown
East Ravendale
Grainthorpe
Brandy Wharf
Thornton le Moor
Holton le Moor
Thoresway
Thorganby
Wold Newton
Fulstow
North Somercotes
Conisholme
Snitterby
Normanby le Wold
Brookenby
Ludborough
Covenham St Bartholomew
North Owersby
South Owersby
Claxby
Stainton le Vale
North Ormsby
Covenham St Mary
Saltfleet
Atterby
Kingerby
Usselby
Binbrook
Utterby
Yarburgh
Bishop Norton
Kirkby
Osgodby
Walesby
Kirmond le Mire
Alvingham
Saltfleetby St Clement
Fotherby
North Cockerington
Saltfleetby All Saints
Bishopbridge
Glentham
West Rasen
Middle Rasen
Tealby
Kelstern
South Cockerington
Saltfleetby St Peter
Theddlethorpe St Helen
Caenby
Toft next Newton
Market Rasen
North Willingham
Ludford
South Elkington
Grimoldby
Normanby
Theddlethorpe All Saints
Owmby
Newton by Toft
Sixhills
Burgh on Bain
Welton le Wold
Louth
Manby
Saxby
Linwood
Hallington
Little Carlton
Great Carlton
Mablethorpe
Legsby
Raithby
Legbourne
Faldingworth
Hainton
Biscathorpe
North Reston
Gayton le Marsh
Trusthorpe
Spridlington
Friesthorpe
Lissington
South Willingham
Cold Hanworth
East Torrington
Donington on Bain
Withcall
Little Cawthorpe
South Reston
Sutton on Sea
Hackthorn
Snarford
Tathwell
Withern
Maltby le Marsh
Sandilands
Wickenby
Benniworth
Holton cum Beckering
West Torrington
Haugham
Muckton
Authorpe
Snelland
East Barkwith
Market Stainton
Ryland
West Barkwith
Beesby
Saleby
Fulnetby
Goulceby
Asterby
Burwell
Belleau
Markby
Welton
Dunholme
Stainton by Langworth
Rand
Panton
Sotby
Ranby
Scamblesby
White Pit
Swaby
Aby
Scothern
Wragby
Bullington
Oxcombe
South Thoresby
Bilsby
Huttoft
Thurlby
Sudbrooke
Langton by Wragby
Hatton
Great Sturton
Langworth
Apley
Belchford
Alford
Anderby
Nettleham
Barlings
Kingthorpe
Hemingby
South Ormsby
Rigsby
Farlesthorpe
Mumby
North Greetwell
Baumber
Tetford
Reepham
Minting
Fulletby
Salmonby
Brinkhill
Well
Cumberworth
Chapel Point
Cherry Willingham
Fiskerton
Gautby
West Ashby
Somersby
Harrington
Ulceby
Chapel St Leonards
Wispington
Horncastle
Bag Enderby
Sutterby
Willoughby
Hogsthorpe
Washingborough
Edlington
Ashby Puerorum
Langton
Sloothby
Thimbleby
Greetham
Aswardby
Skendleby
Canwick
Heighington
Branston Booths
Bardney
Bucknall
Langton
High Toynton
Hagworthingham
Sausthorpe
Partney
Habertoft
Addlethorpe
Ingoldmells
Branston
Horsington
Mareham on the Hill
Scremby
Welton le Marsh
Candlesby
Ingoldmells Point
Bracebridge Heath
Potterhanworth Booths
Mavis Enderby
Raithby
Gunby
Orby
Potterhanworth
Southrey
Stixwould
Hameringham
Hundleby
Spilsby
Ashby by Partney
Halton Holegate
Monksthorpe
Burgh le Marsh
Nocton
Roughton
Moorby
Old Bolingbroke
Great Steeping
Bratoft
Skegness
Waddington
Dunston
Haltham
Miningsby
Toynton All Saints
Kirkstead
Woodhall Spa
Kirkby on Bain
Wood Enderby
East Keal
Little Steeping
Firsby
Irby in the Marsh
East Kirkby
Metheringham
Revesby
Keal Cotes
Croft
Blankney
Martin
Mareham le Fen
Stickford
Fendike Corner
Thorpe St Peter
Wainfleet All Saints
Navenby
Scopwick
Kirkby Green
Tattershall Thorpe
Tumby
Timberland
Tattershall
Coningsby
Tumby Woodside
New Bolingbroke
Stickney
New Leake
Wainfleet St Mary
Gibraltar Point
Wellingore
Thorpe Tilney
Rowston
Walcott
Eastville
Friskney
Ashby de la Launde
Hawthorn Hill
New York
East Fen
Dogdyke
Scrub Hill
Digby
Billinghay
West Fen
Welbourn
Chapel Hill
Northlands
Bloxholm
Dorrington
Leake Commonside
North Kyme
Ruskington
Sibsey
Frithville
Wrangle
Cranwell
Anwick
Holland Fen
Gipsey Bridge
Fishtoft Drove
Old Leake
Leasingham
South Kyme
Langrick
Evedon
Hilldyke
Leverton
North Rauceby
Holdingham
Kirkby la Thorpe
Ewerby
Howell
Anton's Gowt
Benington
Sleaford
South Rauceby
0 1 2 3 4 miles
0 1 2 3 4 5 kilometres

37
25
26

Isle of Man

0 1 2 3 4 miles
0 1 2 3 4 5 kilometres

POINT OF AYRE

Rue Point

The Lhen
Ayres
Cronk y Bing
Jurby Head   Bride
                        Andreas   Point Cranstal
Jurby   Shellag Point
          Sandygate
                                  Ramsey Bay
St Jude's
          Sulby   Sulby R.   Ramsey (Rhumsaa)
Ballaugh   Churchtown   Manx Electric Railway
Orrisdale Head   Cronk   Glen
                  Sulmark   Auldyn
                                          Maughold
ISLE OF   Sartfield   NORTH   Maughold Head
Kirk Michael   488   BARRULE   Ballajora
              MAN   Cooildarry   Cashtal yn Ard
                        Sulby
                        Reservoir 620
                        SNAEFELL FELL   462
              The   545   SLIEAU LHEAN
              Bungalow
              Snaefell Mountain Railway   Dhoon
ELLAN   Bay
Knocksharry   BEINN PHOT   Great
St Patrick's Isle 487   Millennium Laxey
Peel Castle   COLDEN   Way   Wheel
Peel   VANNIN   Laxey
(Purt ny-hinshey)   SLIEAU RUY   Laxey Head
Contrary Head   R.Dhoo   479   Laxey Bay
Patrick   St John's   Ballacheannagh Clay Head
          Glen Maye   Crosby   Cloven Stones
Glen Maye   Glen   Baldrine
                Vine   Manx Electric Railway
Dalby   Strang
          Foxdale   Union Mills   Onchan
Niarbyl Bay   Dalby   Noas   (Kiondroghad)
          Round   483   House   Groudle Glen Railway
          Table   SOUTH   Onchan Head
          Mountain BARRULE
          437   Brough DOUGLAS
          CRONK NY   Fort   (DOOLISH)
          ARREY LAA   Douglas Head
Fleshwick Bay   St Marks
          Grenaby   Isle of Man Steam Railway
Bradda Head Colby   Port Soderick
Port Erin   Silverdale Gr   Santon Head
          Ballasalla
          Isle of Man (Ronaldsway)
The Sound   Castletown   Derbyhaven
Calf of   Port   Derby Fort
MAN   St Mary Close ny Hango Hill
Cregneash   Chollagh Castletown
                     Scarlett Bay
CALF OF   Spanish Point   Herring Tower
MAN   Head   Dreswick Point
Caigher
Point

▽ Manx Heritage site

0 1 2 3 4 miles
0 1 2 3 4 5 kilometres

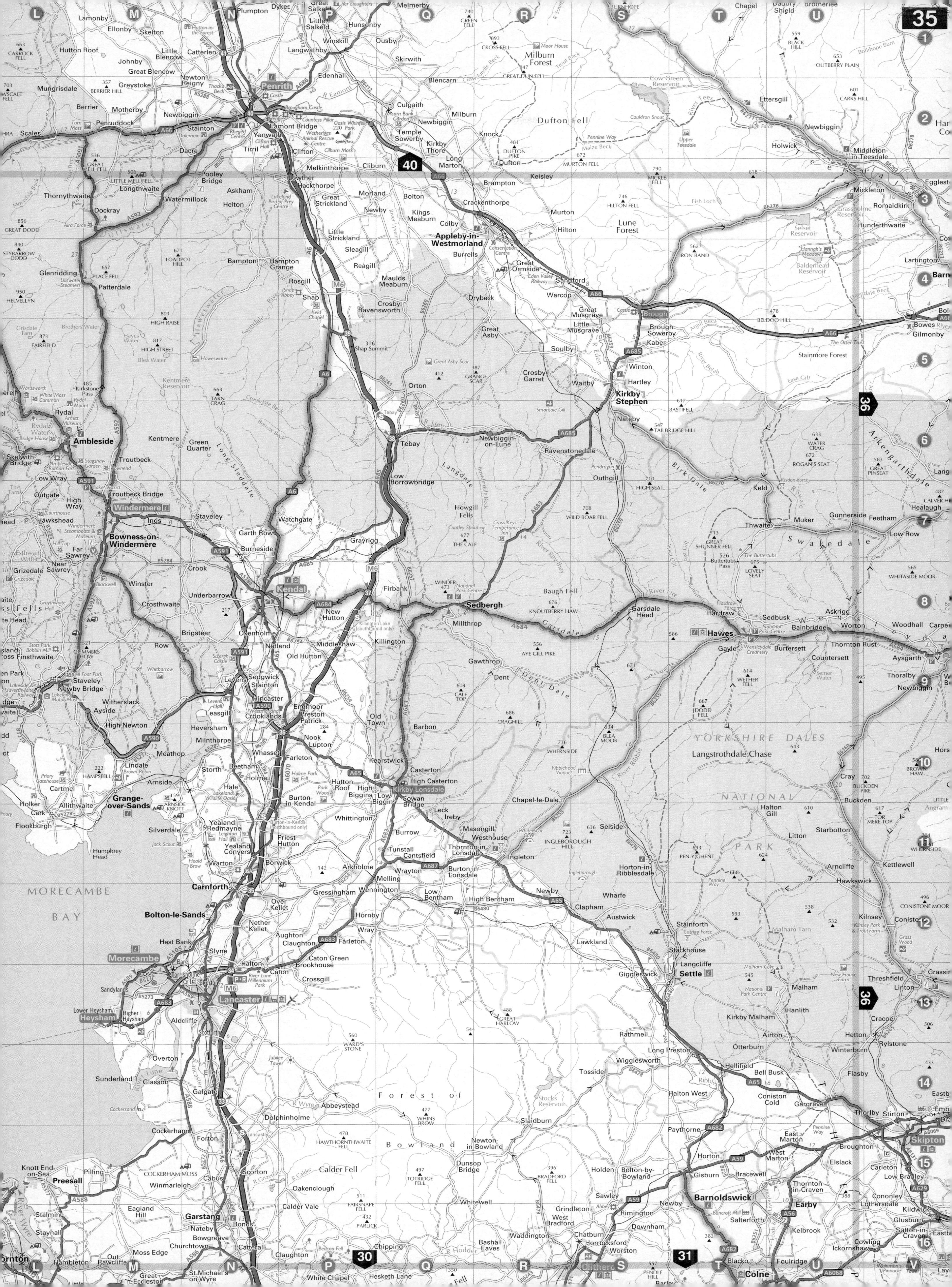
40
36
30
31
Penrith
Kendal
Windermere
Kirkby Lonsdale
Morecambe
Lancaster
Heysham
Brough
Skipton
Clitheroe
Plumpton
Lamonby
Ellonby
Skelton
Hutton Roof
Johnby
Great Blencow
Little Blencow
Catterlen
Newton Reigny
Greystoke
Mungrisdale
Berrier
Motherby
Newbiggin
Penruddock
Scales
Stainton
Eamont Bridge
Yanwath
Tirril
Dacre
Clifton
Pooley Bridge
Askham
Helton
Lowther
Hackthorpe
Great Strickland
Thornthwaite
Dockray
Watermillock
Longthwaite
Glenridding
Patterdale
Bampton
Bampton Grange
Rosgill
Shap
Little Salkeld
Salkeld
Hunsonby
Melmerby
Winskill
Langwathby
Ousby
Skirwith
Edenhall
Blencarn
Culgaith
Newbiggin
Milburn
Temple Sowerby
Kirkby Thore
Long Marton
Knock
Dufton
Dufton Fell
Milburn Forest
Cliburn
Melkinthorpe
Morland
Bolton
Newby
Kings Meaburn
Colby
Brampton
Crackenthorpe
Keisley
Appleby-in-Westmorland
Burrells
Murton
Hilton
Lune Forest
Little Strickland
Sleagill
Reagill
Maulds Meaburn
Crosby Ravensworth
Drybeck
Great Ormside
Sandford
Warcop
Great Musgrave
Little Musgrave
Great Asby
Soulby
Brough Sowerby
Kaber
Winton
Hartley
Kirkby Stephen
Nateby
Waitby
Crosby Garret
Orton
Tebay
Newbiggin-on-Lune
Ravenstonedale
Outhgill
Low Borrowbridge
Langdale
Howgill Fells
Sedbergh
Millthrop
Firbank
Grayrigg
Ambleside
Rydal
Troutbeck
Troutbeck Bridge
Kentmere
Green Quarter
Long Sleddale
Staveley
Ings
Bowness-on-Windermere
Hawkshead
Near Sawrey
Far Sawrey
Garth Row
Burneside
Watchgate
Crook
Winster
Underbarrow
Crosthwaite
New Hutton
Killington
Middleshaw
Oxenholme
Natland
Old Hutton
Brigsteer
Row
Levens
Sedgwick
Stainton
Hincaster
Endmoor
Crooklands
Preston Patrick
Old Town
Barbon
Newby Bridge
Staveley
Witherslack
Ayside
High Newton
Heversham
Milnthorpe
Leasgill
Nook
Lupton
Farleton
Meathop
Lindale
Beetham
Storth
Holme
Hale
Arnside
Cartmel
Grange-over-Sands
Allithwaite
Holker
Cark
Flookburgh
Silverdale
Yealand Redmayne
Yealand Conyers
Warton
Carnforth
Bolton-le-Sands
Hest Bank
Slyne
Halton
Caton
Brookhouse
Caton Green
Crossgill
Burton-in-Kendal
Priest Hutton
Borwick
Burrow
Whittington
Hutton Roof
High Biggins
Low Biggins
Cowan Bridge
Casterton
High Casterton
Kearstwick
Leck
Ireby
Tunstall
Cantsfield
Arkholme
Melling
Wrayton
Burton in Lonsdale
Thornton in Lonsdale
Westhouse
Masongill
Ingleton
Gressingham
Wennington
Low Bentham
High Bentham
Hornby
Wray
Over Kellet
Nether Kellet
Aughton
Claughton
Farleton
Newby
Clapham
Austwick
Lawkland
Wharfe
Giggleswick
Settle
Stackhouse
Langcliffe
Stainforth
Horton-in-Ribblesdale
Selside
Chapel-le-Dale
Dent
Gawthrop
Dent Dale
Garsdale
Garsdale Head
Hawes
Gayle
Hardraw
Sedbusk
Bainbridge
Askrigg
Worton
Burtersett
Countersett
Thornton Rust
Aysgarth
Thoralby
Newbiggin
Woodhall
Keld
Thwaite
Muker
Gunnerside
Feetham
Low Row
Healaugh
Swaledale
Arkengarthdale
Langthwaite
Yorkshire Dales National Park
Langstrothdale Chase
Cray
Buckden
Halton Gill
Litton
Starbotton
Arncliffe
Hawkswick
Kettlewell
Kilnsey
Conistone
Threshfield
Linton
Malham
Hanlith
Kirkby Malham
Airton
Otterburn
Hetton
Rylstone
Cracoe
Flasby
Winterburn
Hellifield
Long Preston
Rathmell
Wigglesworth
Tosside
Bell Busk
Coniston Cold
Gargrave
Halton West
Paythorne
Thorlby
Stirton
East Marton
West Marton
Broughton
Horton
Gisburn
Bracewell
Elslack
Carleton
Thornton-in-Craven
Earby
Barnoldswick
Salterforth
Kelbrook
Sawley
Newby
Rimington
Downham
Chatburn
Worston
Holden
Bolton-by-Bowland
Slaidburn
Grindleton
West Bradford
Waddington
Dunsop Bridge
Newton-in-Bowland
Whitewell
Bashall Eaves
Chipping
Hesketh Lane
Forest of Bowland
Calder Fell
Abbeystead
Dolphinholme
Cockerham
Forton
Scorton
Cabus
Winmarleigh
Garstang
Nateby
Bowgreave
Bonds
Catterall
Churchtown
Calder Vale
Oakenclough
Claughton
Galgate
Ellel
Scotforth
Aldcliffe
Overton
Sunderland
Glasson
Lower Heysham
Higher Heysham
Sandylands
Torrisholme
Bare
Pilling
Knott End-on-Sea
Preesall
Eagland Hill
Stalmine
Staynall
Hambleton
Out Rawcliffe
Moss Edge
Great Eccleston
St Michael's on Wyre
Poulton
Colne
Foulridge
Blacko
Cowling
Sutton-in-Craven
Glusburn
Kildwick
Lothersdale
Cononley
Low Bradley
Middleton-in-Teesdale
Mickleton
Romaldkirk
Hunderthwaite
Eggleston
Lartington
Bowes
Gilmonby
Stainmore Forest
Newbiggin
Holwick
Ettersgill
Chapel
Daddry Shield
Brotherlee
Morecambe Bay
Ullswater
Haweswater
Windermere
Cow Green Reservoir
Grassholme Reservoir
Selset Reservoir
Balderhead Reservoir
Stocks Reservoir
Kentmere Reservoir
M6
A6
A66
A65
A683
A684
A685
A590
A591
A592
A59
A682
A629
A56
A6068
A588
A586
A589
A5105
B6260
B6259
B6255
B6276
B6270
B6480
B6478
B6265
B6160
B5284
B5278
B5273
B5288
B6412
B6413
B6254
B6261

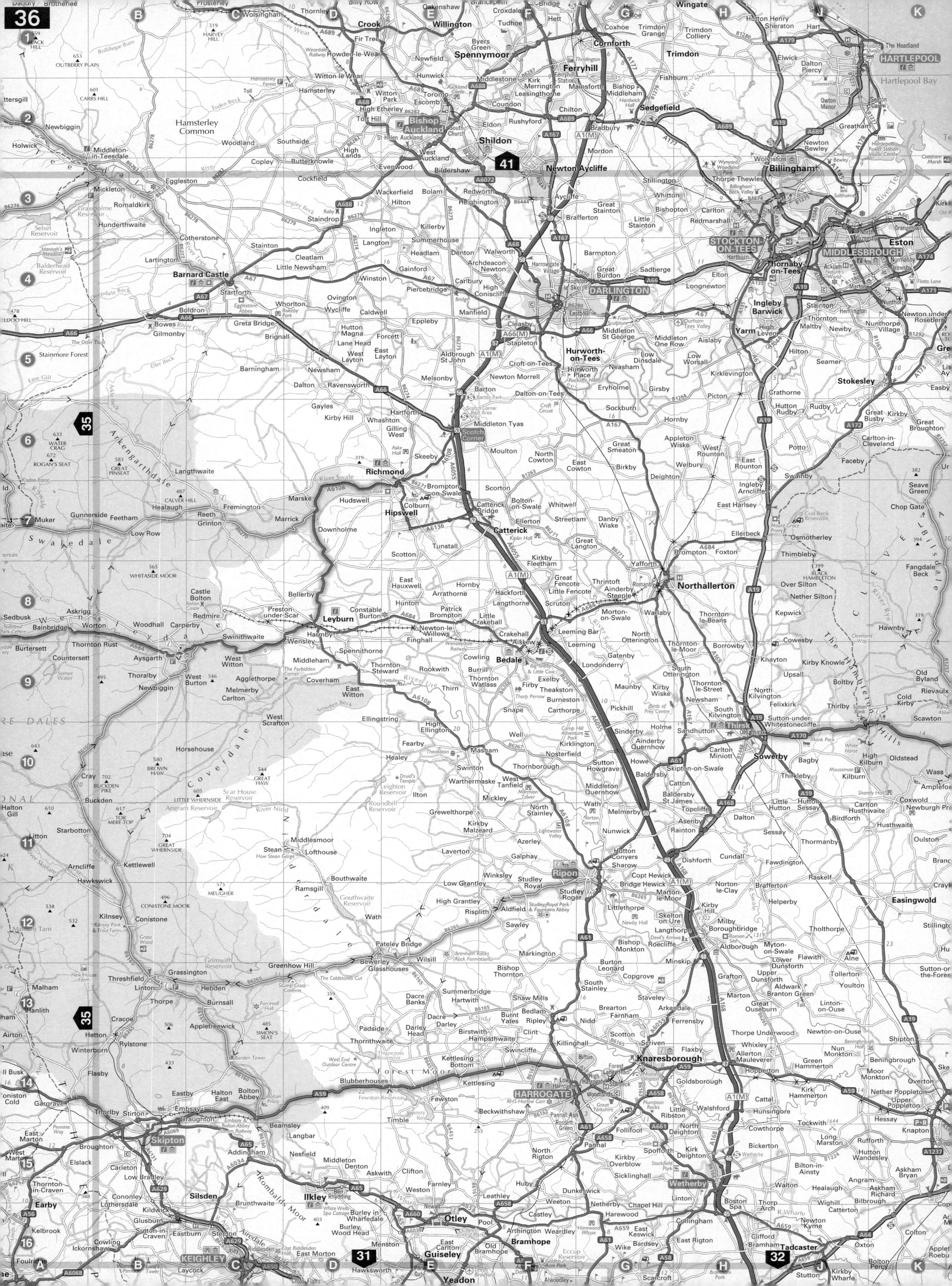

Crook
Willington
Spennymoor
Ferryhill
Cornforth
Trimdon
Sedgefield
HARTLEPOOL
Hartlepool Bay
Bishop Auckland
Shildon
Newton Aycliffe
Billingham
STOCKTON-ON-TEES
MIDDLESBROUGH
Thornaby-on-Tees
Eston
Hamsterley Common
Middleton-in-Teesdale
Barnard Castle
DARLINGTON
Ingleby Barwick
Yarm
Hurworth-on-Tees
Stokesley
Richmond
Hipswell
Scotch Corner
Catterick
Northallerton
Leyburn
Bedale
Swaledale
Arkengarthdale
Wensleydale
Coverdale
Nidderdale
Masham
Thirsk
Sowerby
Ripon
Easingwold
Pateley Bridge
Knaresborough
HARROGATE
Skipton
Wetherby
Ilkley
Otley
KEIGHLEY
Guiseley
Yeadon
Tadcaster
Forest Moor
Rombalds Moor
Cleveland Hills

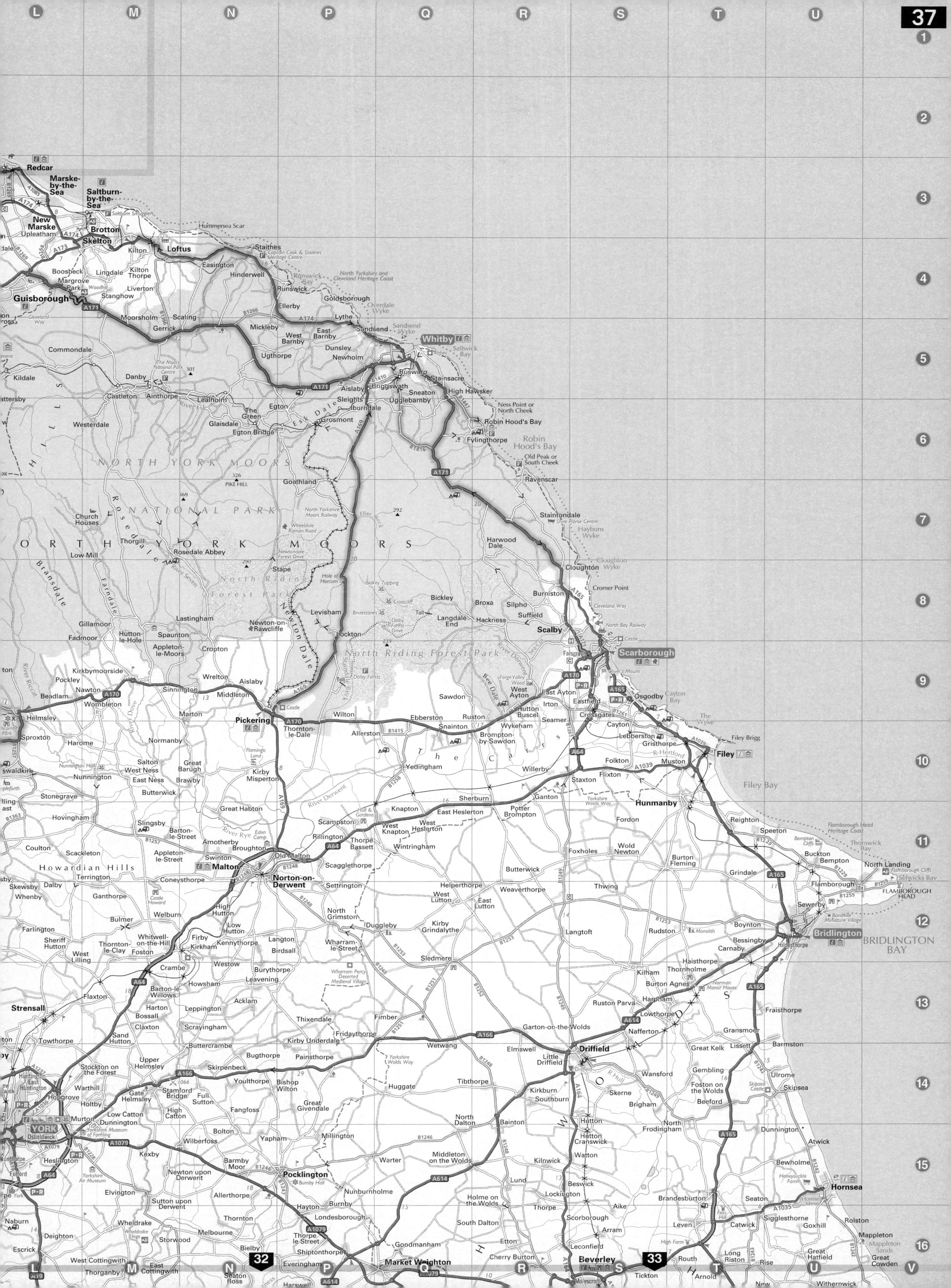
L
M
N
P
Q
R
S
T
U
V
1
2
3
4
5
6
7
8
9
10
11
12
13
14
15
16
Redcar
Marske-by-the-Sea
Saltburn-by-the-Sea
Saltburn Smugglers
New Marske
Upleatham
Brotton
Skelton
Hummersea Scar
Kilton
Loftus
Staithes
Captain Cook & Staithes Heritage Centre
Easington
Boosbeck
Lingdale
Kilton Thorpe
Margrove Park
Woodhill
Liverton
Hinderwell
Runswick
Runswick Bay
North Yorkshire and Cleveland Heritage Coast
Guisborough
Stanghow
Goldsborough
Overdale Wyke
Cleveland Way
Ellerby
Moorsholm
Scaling
Gerrick
Mickleby
Lythe
Sandsend
Sandsend Wyke
Whitby
Saltwick Bay
West Barnby
East Barnby
Dunsley
Commondale
Ugthorpe
Newholm
Ruswarp
Stainsacre
Kildale
Danby
The Moors National Park Centre
Castleton
Ainthorpe
Lealholm
River Esk
Aislaby
Briggswath
Sneaton
High Hawsker
Sleights
Ugglebarnby
Ness Point or North Cheek
Egton
The Green
Esk Dale
Iburndale
Westerdale
Glaisdale
Egton Bridge
Grosmont
Robin Hood's Bay
Fylingthorpe
NORTH YORK MOORS
Old Peak or South Cheek
Ravenscar
PIKE HILL
Goathland
NATIONAL PARK
Church Houses
North Yorkshire Moors Railway
Wheeldale Roman Road
Eller Beck
Staintondale
Shire Horse Centre
Hayburn Wyke
Rosedale
Thorgill
Harwood Dale
Low Mill
Rosedale Abbey
Newtondale Forest Drive
Cloughton Wyke
Cloughton
Bransdale
Farndale
River Seven
Stape
North Riding Forest Park
Hole of Horcum
Blakey Topping
Cromer Point
Burniston
Bickley
Crosscliff
Broxa
Silpho
Cleveland Way
Levisham
Bridestones
Dalby Forest Drive
Langdale End
Suffield
Hackness
North Bay Railway
Lastingham
Gillamoor
Newton-on-Rawcliffe
Newton Dale
Scalby
Fadmoor
Hutton-le-Hole
Spaunton
Lockton
Castle
Appleton-le-Moors
Cropton
Falsgrave
Scarborough
Oliver's Mount
Kirkbymoorside
Pockley
Wrelton
Aislaby
Dalby Forest
Forge Valley Woods
River Derwent
Bee Dale
Sea Cut
Thornton Beck
Nawton
Beadlam
Wombleton
Sinnington
Middleton
West Ayton
East Ayton
Sawdon
Osgodby
Cayton Bay
Irton
Eastfield
Helmsley
Marton
Pickering
Wilton
Ebberston
Ruston
Hutton Buscel
Seamer
Crossgates
The Wyke
Sproxton
Harome
Normanby
Thornton-le-Dale
Allerston
Snainton
Wykeham
Cayton
Lebberston
Filey Brigg
Brompton-by-Sawdon
Gristhorpe
Filey
Flamingo Land
Oswaldkirk
Nunnington Hall
Salton
West Ness
Great Barugh
Kirby Misperton
Yedingham
The Carrs
Willerby
Folkton
Muston
R. Hertford
Nunnington
East Ness
Brawby
Flixton
Filey Bay
Staxton
Stonegrave
Butterwick
River Derwent
Sherburn
Ganton
Yorkshire Wolds Way
Hunmanby
Hovingham
Great Habton
Knapton
East Heslerton
Potter Brompton
Fordon
Reighton
Slingsby
Barton-le-Street
River Rye
Eden Camp
Scampston Hall & Gardens
West Knapton
West Heslerton
Speeton
Flamborough Head Heritage Coast
Rillington
Thornwick Bay
Coulton
Scackleton
Amotherby
Broughton
Thorpe Bassett
Wintringham
Foxholes
Wold Newton
Bempton Cliffs
Buckton
Bempton
Howardian Hills
Appleton-le-Street
Swinton
Malton
Old Malton
Burton Fleming
North Landing
Flamborough Cliffs
Selwicks Bay
Terrington
Coneysthorpe
Norton-on-Derwent
Scagglethorpe
Butterwick
Grindale
Flamborough
FLAMBOROUGH HEAD
Skewsby
Dalby
Whenby
Settrington
Helperthorpe
Weaverthorpe
Thwing
Ganthorpe
Castle Howard
High Hutton
West Lutton
East Lutton
Sewerby
Bondville Miniature Village
North Grimston
Bulmer
Welburn
Low Hutton
Duggleby
Kirby Grindalythe
Langtoft
Rudston
Monolith
Boynton
Farlington
Whitwell-on-the-Hill
Langton
Bridlington
BRIDLINGTON BAY
Sheriff Hutton
Thornton-le-Clay
Foston
Firby
Kirkham
Kennythorpe
Birdsall
Wharram-le-Street
Bessingby
Hilderthorpe
Carnaby
West Lilling
Priory
Sledmere
Crambe
Westow
Burythorpe
Haisthorpe
Thornholme
Wharram Percy Deserted Medieval Village
Kilham
Flaxton
Barton-le-Willows
Howsham
Leavening
Burton Agnes
Norman Manor House
Strensall
Harton
Acklam
Harpham
Ruston Parva
Fraisthorpe
Leppington
Lowthorpe
Bossall
Thixendale
Fimber
Claxton
Scrayingham
Fridaythorpe
Garton-on-the-Wolds
Nafferton
Gransmoor
Towthorpe
Sand Hutton
Buttercrambe
Kirby Underdale
Wetwang
Elmswell
Driffield
Great Kelk
Lissett
Barmston
Bugthorpe
Painsthorpe
Yorkshire Wolds Way
Little Driffield
Upper Helmsley
Huntington
East Huntington
Stockton on the Forest
Skirpenbeck
Wansford
Gembling
Ulrome
Youlthorpe
Bishop Wilton
Tibthorpe
R. Hull
Warthill
Gate Helmsley
Stamford Bridge
Huggate
Kirkburn
Skerne
Foston on the Wolds
Skipsea Castle
Skipsea
Heworth
Hopgrove
Full Sutton
Southburn
Brigham
Holtby
High Catton
Great Givendale
Beeford
Murton
Low Catton
Dunnington
Fangfoss
North Dalton
Bainton
Hutton
North Frodingham
Osbaldwick
YORK
Yorkshire Museum of Farming
Bolton
Hutton Cranswick
Dunnington
Atwick
Yapham
Millington
Wilberfoss
Kexby
Heslington
Fulford
Middleton on the Wolds
Watton
Bewholme
Barmby Moor
Warter
Kilnwick
Yorkshire Air Museum
Newton upon Derwent
Pocklington
Burnby Hall
Honeysuckle Farm
Hornsea
Lund
Beswick
Elvington
Nunburnholme
Holme on the Wolds
Brandesburton
Seaton
Allerthorpe
Hornsea Mere
Sutton upon Derwent
Hayton
Burnby
Lockington
Aike
Thorpe
Sigglesthorne
Rolston
Naburn
Thornton
Londesborough
South Dalton
Scorborough
Foss Hill
Catwick
Goxhill
Wheldrake
Melbourne
Arram
Leven
Mappleton
Deighton
Storwood
Thorpe le Street
Etton
High Farm
Mappleton Sands
Escrick
Shiptonthorpe
Goodmanham
Leconfield
Great Hatfield
West Cottingwith
Bielby
Cherry Burton
Beverley
Routh
Long Riston
Great Cowden
Thorganby
East Cottingwith
Everingham
Market Weighton
Molescroft
Tickton
Arnold
Rise
Seaton Ross
Harswell
New
Withernwick
32
33
A174
A173
A171
A1085
B1269
B1268
B1266
B1366
A169
B1416
B1447
B1410
A165
A170
A64
B1261
A1039
B1258
B1415
B1257
B1248
B1249
B1253
B1251
B1252
A614
A166
B1229
B1255
A1237
A1036
A1079
B1228
B1246
B1247
A1035
B1242
B1243
B1244
A1079
A19
A1174
326
369
290
301
292
239

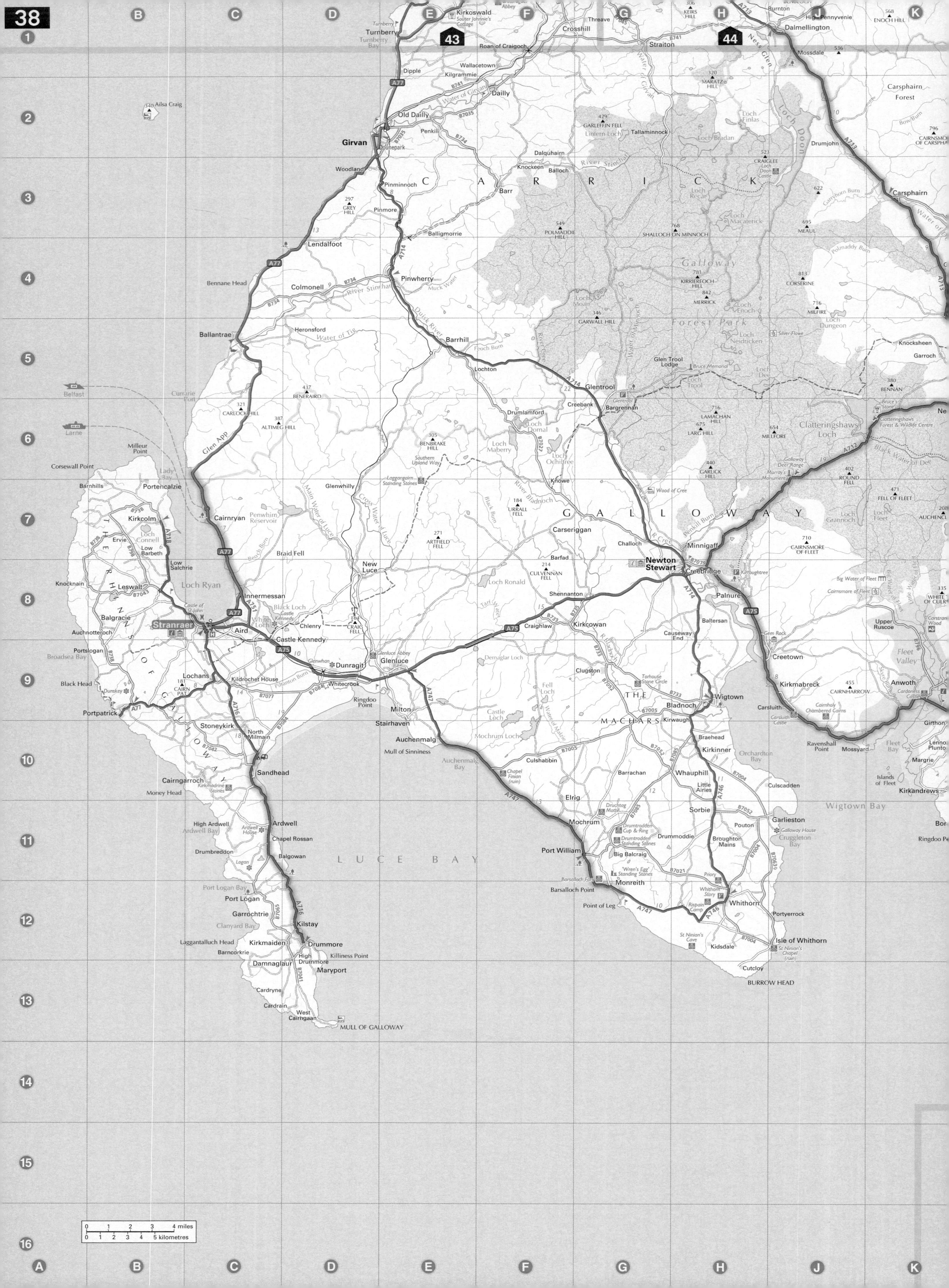
43
44
Kirkoswald
Turnberry
Turnberry Bay
Crosshill
Threave
Straiton
Dalmellington
Roan of Craigoch
Wallacetown
Dipple
Kilgrammie
Dailly
Old Dailly
Girvan
Dounepark
Penkill
Woodland
Ailsa Craig
Pinminnoch
Pinmore
GREY HILL
Barr
Dalquhairn
Knockeen
Balloch
Balligmorrie
Lendalfoot
Bennane Head
Colmonell
Pinwherry
River Stinchar
Ballantrae
Heronsford
Water of Tig
Barrhill
Lochton
Glentrool
Creebank
Bargrennan
Glen Trool Lodge
Drumlamford
Loch Dornal
Loch Maberry
BENRAIRD
CARLOCK HILL
ALTIMEG HILL
BENBRAKE HILL
Southern Upland Way
Loggangairn Standing Stones
Glenwhilly
Cross Water of Luce
Main Water of Luce
Glen App
Currarie Port
Belfast
Larne
Milleur Point
Corsewall Point
Lady Bay
Barnhills
Portencalzie
Kirkcolm
Ervie
Loch Connell
Low Barbeth
Low Salchrie
Cairnryan
Penwhirn Reservoir
Braid Fell
Knocknain
Leswalt
Loch Ryan
Innermessan
Castle of St John
Black Loch
Castle Kennedy
White Loch
Chlenry
CRAIG FELL
New Luce
Balgracie
Stranraer
Aird
Castle Kennedy
Auchnotteroch
Portslogan
Broadsea Bay
Lochans
CAIRN PAT
Kildrochet House
Dunragit
Glenluce Abbey
Glenluce
Black Head
Dunskey
Portpatrick
Whitecrook
Ringdoo Point
Piltanton Burn
Stoneykirk
North Milmain
Milton
Stairhaven
Auchenmalg
Mull of Sinniness
Auchenmalg Bay
Sandhead
Cairngarroch
Kirkmadrine Stones
Money Head
High Ardwell
Ardwell Bay
Ardwell
Ardwell House
Chapel Rossan
Drumbreddon
Logan
Balgowan
LUCE BAY
Port Logan Bay
Port Logan
Garrochtrie
Clanyard Bay
Kilstay
Laggantalluch Head
Kirkmaiden
Drummore
Barncorkrie
Damnaglaur
High Drummore
Killiness Point
Maryport
Cardryne
Cardrain
West Cairngaan
MULL OF GALLOWAY
C A R R I C K
G A L L O W A Y
THE RHINS OF GALLOWAY
THE MACHARS
Galloway Forest Park
Loch Doon
Loch Finlas
Loch Bradan
Loch Recar
Loch Macaterick
Loch Moan
Loch Enoch
Loch Neldricken
Loch Trool
Loch Dee
Loch Dungeon
Tallaminnock
GARLEFFIN FELL
Linfern Loch
CRAIGLEE
Loch Doon Castle
MARATZ HILL
POLMADDIE HILL
SHALLOCH ON MINNOCH
KIRRIEREOCH HILL
MERRICK
GARWALL HILL
LAMACHAN HILL
LARG HILL
MILLFORE
GARLICK HILL
CORSERINE
MILFIRE
MEAUL
Carsphairn Forest
Carsphairn
Drumjohn
Mossdale
Knocksheen
Garroch
BENNAN
Clatteringshaws Loch
Clatteringshaws Forest & Wildlife Centre
Black Water of Dee
Galloway Deer Range
Murray's Monument
ROUND FELL
FELL OF FLEET
Loch Grannoch
Loch Fleet
CAIRNSMORE OF FLEET
Silver Flowe
Bruce Memorial
Wood of Cree
Knowe
Loch Ochiltree
River Bladnoch
URRALL FELL
ARTFIELD FELL
Carseriggan
Challoch
Minnigaff
Newton Stewart
Creebridge
Kirroughtree
Palnure
Barfad
CULVENNAN FELL
Loch Ronald
Shennanton
Craighlaw
Kirkcowan
Baltersan
Causeway End
Dernaglar Loch
Clugston
Torhouse Stone Circle
Fell Loch
Castle Loch
Mochrum Loch
Bladnoch
Wigtown
Kirwaugh
Braehead
Kirkinner
Culshabbin
Barrachan
Whauphill
Little Airies
Chapel Finian (ruin)
Elrig
Sorbie
Mochrum
Drumtroddan Cup & Ring
Drumtroddan Standing Stones
Drummoddie
Port William
Big Balcraig
'Wren's Egg' Standing Stones
Barsalloch Fort
Barsalloch Point
Monreith
Point of Leg
Priory
Whithorn Story
Rispain Camp
Whithorn
Portyerrock
Garlieston
Galloway House
Cruggleton Bay
Pouton
Broughton Mains
Culscadden
Orchardton Bay
St Ninian's Cave
Kidsdale
Isle of Whithorn
St Ninian's Chapel (ruin)
Cutcloy
BURROW HEAD
Wigtown Bay
Creetown
Fleet Valley
Kirkmabreck
CAIRNHARROW
Cairnholy Chambered Cairns
Carsluith
Carsluith Castle
Ravenshall Point
Mossyard
Fleet Bay
Anworth
Islands of Fleet
Kirkandrews
Gem Rock
Upper Ruscoe
Big Water of Fleet
Cairnsmore of Fleet
Ringdoo Point
Girthon
Margrie
A77
A714
A75
A747
A746
A714
A713
A712
A716
A718
A751
A71
B7035
B7027
B7044
B7052
B7004
B7005
B7021
B7085
B7065
B7041
B7084
B7077
B7042
B738
B7043
B733
B735
B741
B734
0 1 2 3 4 miles
0 1 2 3 4 5 kilometres
A B C D E F G H J K
1 2 3 4 5 6 7 8 9 10 11 12 13 14 15 16

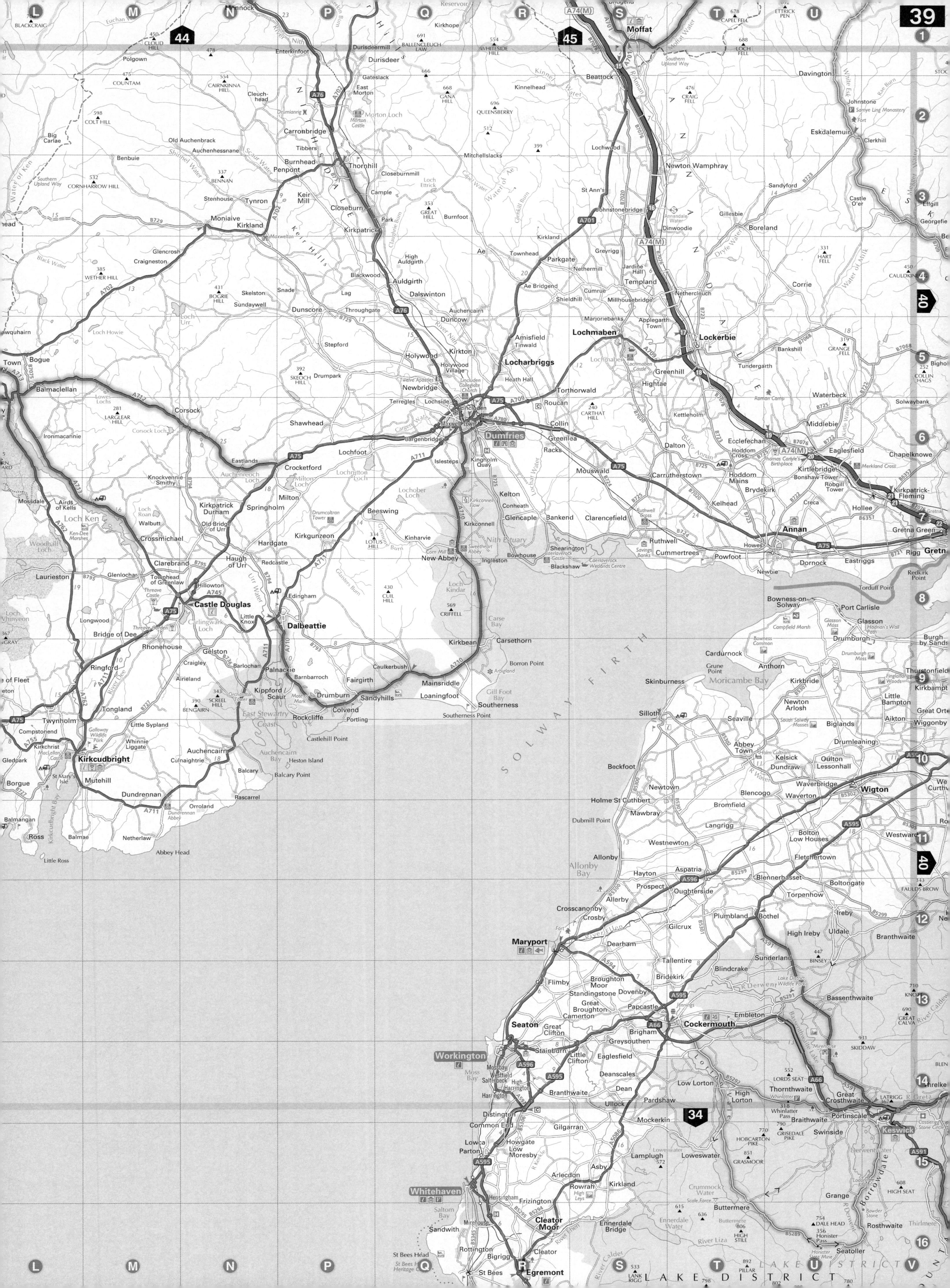

44
45
40
34
Moffat
Durisdeer
Thornhill
Penpont
Moniaive
Kirkland
Tynron
Keir Mill
Closeburn
Kirkpatrick
Auldgirth
Dalswinton
Dunscore
Holywood
Kirkton
Locharbriggs
Lochmaben
Lockerbie
Newbridge
Dumfries
Maxwelltown
Lincluden
Torthorwald
Collin
Annan
Ecclefechan
Kirtlebridge
Kirkpatrick-Fleming
Gretna Green
Eastriggs
Dornock
Powfoot
Cummertrees
Ruthwell
Clarencefield
Bankend
Glencaple
Kirkconnell
New Abbey
Kirkbean
Carsethorn
Southerness
Southerness Point
Mainsriddle
Caulkerbush
Sandyhills
Colvend
Rockcliffe
Kippford
Palnackie
Dalbeattie
Castle Douglas
Haugh of Urr
Crocketford
Springholm
Kirkpatrick Durham
Corsock
Balmaclellan
Crossmichael
Clarebrand
Laurieston
Rhonehouse
Gelston
Ringford
Tongland
Twynholm
Kirkcudbright
Dundrennan
Auchencairn
Balcary Point
Abbey Head
Little Ross
Solway Firth
Nith Estuary
Moricambe Bay
Allonby Bay
Bowness-on-Solway
Port Carlisle
Glasson
Drumburgh
Cardurnock
Anthorn
Kirkbride
Skinburness
Silloth
Seaville
Abbey Town
Newton Arlosh
Beckfoot
Newtown
Holme St Cuthbert
Mawbray
Dubmill Point
Allonby
Westnewton
Wigton
Bromfield
Waverton
Aspatria
Hayton
Crosscanonby
Crosby
Maryport
Dearham
Gilcrux
Plumbland
Bothel
Ireby
Uldale
Bassenthwaite
Cockermouth
Brigham
Papcastle
Embleton
Dovenby
Bridekirk
Tallentire
Flimby
Great Broughton
Seaton
Camerton
Great Clifton
Workington
Stainburn
Little Clifton
Eaglesfield
Harrington
Distington
Lowca
Parton
Whitehaven
Moresby
Frizington
Cleator Moor
Cleator
Egremont
St Bees
St Bees Head
Sandwith
Rowrah
Kirkland
Lamplugh
Loweswater
Buttermere
Ennerdale Bridge
Braithwaite
Portinscale
Keswick
Thornthwaite
Seatoller
Rosthwaite
Grange
Skiddaw
Lake District
A74(M)
A75
A76
A701
A702
A709
A710
A711
A712
A595
A596
A66
A591

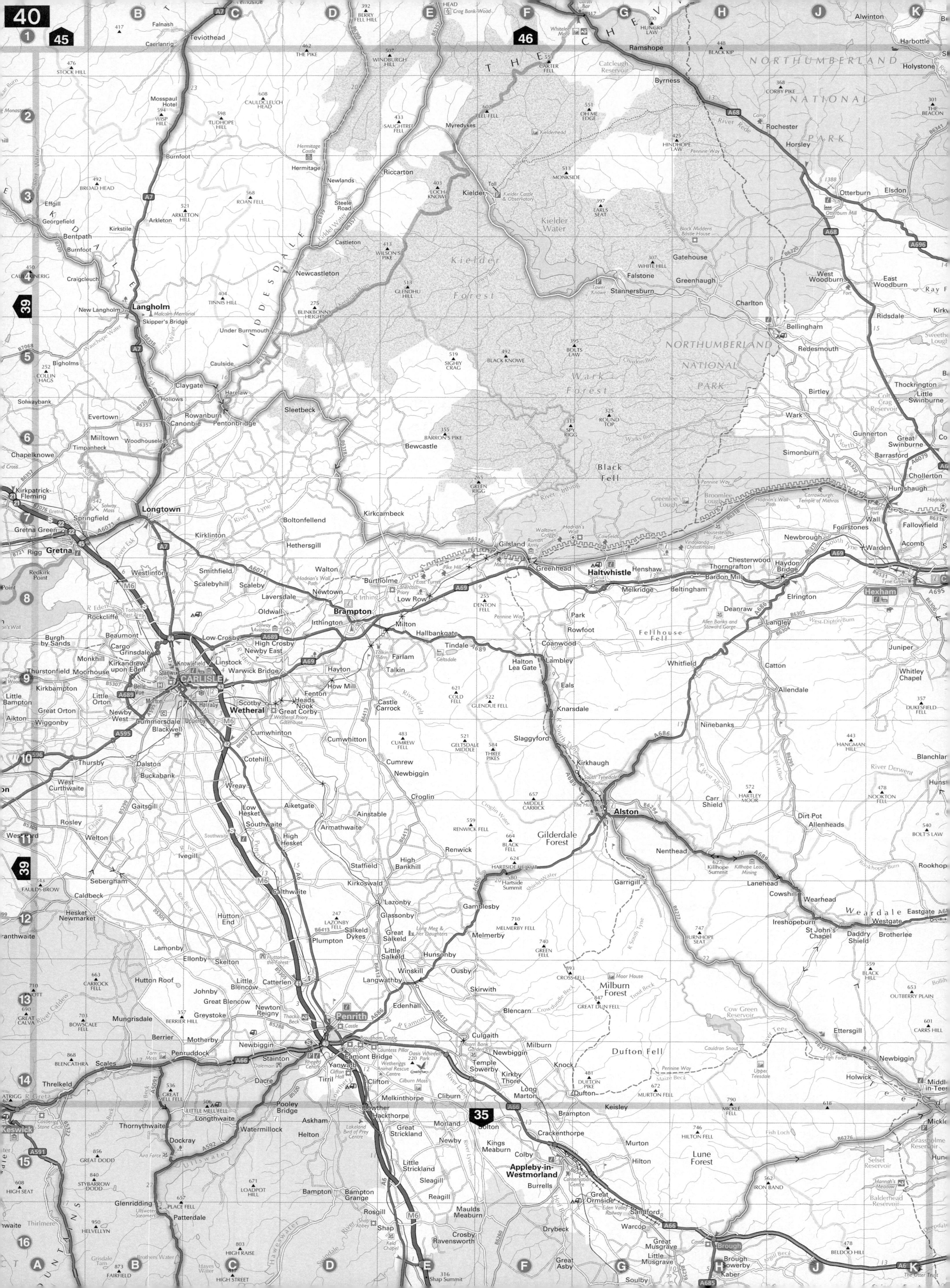

45
46
39
35
THE CHEVIOT
NORTHUMBERLAND NATIONAL PARK
Teviothead
Caerlanrig
Falnash
Stock Hill
Mosspaul Hotel
Wisp Hill
Tudhope Hill
Cauldcleuch Head
Windburgh Hill
The Pike
Berry Fell Hill
Saughtree Fell
Hermitage Castle
Hermitage
Riccarton
Myredykes
Peel Fell
Carter Fell
Catcleugh Reservoir
Ramshope
Hungry Law
Black Kip
Byrness
Corby Pike
Rochester
Horsley
Harbottle
Holystone
Alwinton
The Beacon
Hindhope Law
Pennine Way
Oh Me Edge
Kielderhead
Monkside
Kielder
Toll
Kielder Castle & Observatory
Kielder Water
Earls Seat
Loch Knowe
Newlands
Steele Road
Burnfoot
Broad Head
Roan Fell
Arkleton Hill
Arkleton
Kirkstile
Effgill
Georgefield
Bentpath
Burnfoot
Castleton
Wilson's Pike
Kielder Forest
Otterburn
Otterburn Mill
Elsdon
Black Middens Bastle House
Gatehouse
White Hill
Falstone
Tower Knowe
Stannersburn
Greenhaugh
West Woodburn
East Woodburn
Ridsdale
Charlton
Bellingham
Redesmouth
Craigcleuch
Newcastleton
Langholm
Malcolm Memorial
Skipper's Bridge
New Langholm
Tinnis Hill
Glendhu Hill
Blinkbonny Height
Under Burnmouth
LIDDESDALE
ESKDALE
Caulside
Bigholms
Collin Hags
Sighty Crag
Black Knowe
Bolts Law
Wark Forest
Birtley
Thockrington
Little Swinbourne
Colt Crag Reservoir
Wark
Gunnerton
Great Swinburne
Barrasford
Simonburn
Chollerton
Humshaugh
Solwaybank
Claygate
Harelaw
Hollows
Evertown
Sleetbeck
Rowanburn
Canonbie
Pentonbridge
Milltown
Woodhouselees
Timpanheck
Chapelknowe
Barron's Pike
Bewcastle
Round Top
Spy Rigg
Black Fell
Green Rigg
Kirkpatrick-Fleming
Springfield
Gretna Green
Gretna
Rigg
Solway Moss
Longtown
Boltonfellend
Kirkcambeck
Kirklinton
Hethersgill
Gilsland
Walltown Crags
Hadrian's Wall
Cawfields
Vindolanda (Chesterholm)
Housesteads Fort
Broomlee Lough
Greenlee Lough
Carrawburgh Temple of Mithras
Chesters Fort
Wall
Fourstones
Fallowfield
Newbrough
Acomb
Warden
Redkirk Point
Westlinton
Smithfield
Scalebyhill
Scaleby
Walton
Laversdale
Burtholme
Lanercost Priory
Newtown
Low Row
Greenhead
Haltwhistle
Henshaw
Thorngrafton
Chesterwood
Bardon Mill
Haydon Bridge
Melkridge
Beltingham
Hexham
Elrington
Rockcliffe
Oldwall
Brampton
Denton Fell
Irthington
Milton
Park
Rowfoot
Deanraw
Langley
Allen Banks and Staward Gorge
Fellhouse Fell
Burgh by Sands
Beaumont
Low Crosby
Solway Aviation Museum
Carlisle Airport
Cargo
Grinsdale
High Crosby
Newby East
Hallbankgate
Coanwood
Lambley
Monkhill
Kirkandrews upon Eden
Linstock
Warwick Bridge
Tindale
Halton Lea Gate
Whitfield
Catton
Juniper
Thurstonfield
Moorhouse
Kirkbampton
CARLISLE
Stanwix
Hayton
Farlam
Talkin
Geltsdale
How Mill
Eals
Allendale
Whitley Chapel
Little Bampton
Little Orton
Great Orton
Aikton
Wiggonby
Newby West
Scotby
Wetheral
Heads Nook
Great Corby
Wetheral Priory Gatehouse
Fenton
Castle Carrock
Cold Fell
Glendue Fell
Knarsdale
Dukesfield Fell
Harraby
Upperby
Cummersdale
Blackwell
Cumwhinton
Cumwhitton
Cumrew Fell
Geltsdale Middle
Three Pikes
Slaggyford
Ninebanks
Hangman Hill
Blanchland
Thursby
Dalston
Buckabank
Cotehill
Cumrew
Newbiggin
Kirkhaugh
South Tynedale Railway
Hartley Moor
Nookton Fell
River Derwent
West Curthwaite
Wreay
Croglin
Middle Carrick
The Hub
Alston
Carr Shield
Dirt Pot
Allenheads
Gaitsgill
Rosley
Low Hesket
Southwaite
Aiketgate
Ainstable
Armathwaite
Renwick Fell
Black Fell
Gilderdale Forest
Bolts Law
Welton
Ivegill
High Hesket
High Bankhill
Renwick
Nenthead
Killhope Summit
Killhope Lead Mining
Rookhope
Sebergham
Faulds Brow
Caldbeck
Staffield
Kirkoswald
Hartside Height
Hartside Summit
Garrigill
Lanehead
Cowshill
Wearhead
Calthwaite
Lazonby
Gamblesby
Weardale
Eastgate
Westgate
Ireshopeburn
St John's Chapel
Daddry Shield
Brotherlee
Hesket Newmarket
Hutton End
Lazonby Fell
Glassonby
Salkeld Dykes
Plumpton
Great Salkeld
Long Meg & her Daughters
Melmerby Fell
Melmerby
Burnhope Seat
Little Salkeld
Hunsonby
Green Fell
Lamonby
Ellonby
Skelton
Hutton-in-the-Forest
Cross Fell
Moor House
Black Hill
Carrock Fell
Hutton Roof
Little Blencow
Catterlen
Langwathby
Winskill
Ousby
Milburn Forest
Outberry Plain
Knott
Johnby
Great Blencow
Skirwith
Great Dun Fell
Great Calva
Bowscale Fell
Berrier Hill
Mungrisdale
Greystoke
Newton Reigny
Thacka Beck
Edenhall
Blencarn
Cow Green Reservoir
Berrier
Motherby
Penrith
Castle
Culgaith
Ettersgill
Carrs Hill
Blencathra
Scales
Penruddock
Newbiggin
Stainton
Dalemain
Rheged Centre
Eamont Bridge
Brougham Castle
Countess Pillar
Oasis Whinfell Park
Wetheriggs Animal Rescue Centre
Acorn Bank Garden
Newbiggin
Milburn
Temple Sowerby
Knock
Dufton Fell
Cauldron Snout
Newbiggin
High Force
Holwick
Threlkeld
Great Mell Fell
Dacre
Yanwath
Tirril
Clifton Hall
Clifton
Cliburn Moss
Kirkby Thore
Long Marton
Dufton Pike
Dufton
Murton Fell
Upper Teesdale
Middleton-in-Teesdale
Keswick
Castlerigg Stone Circle
Little Mell Fell
Longthwaite
Pooley Bridge
Melkinthorpe
Cliburn
Lowther
Hackthorpe
Keisley
Mickle Fell
Brampton
Thornythwaite
Askham
Morland
Bolton
Crackenthorpe
Hilton Fell
Watermillock
Helton
Lakeland Bird of Prey Centre
Great Strickland
Newby
Kings Meaburn
Murton
Lune Forest
Grassholme Reservoir
Dockray
Aira Force
Ullswater
Colby
Great Dodd
Little Strickland
Appleby-in-Westmorland
Hilton
Selset Reservoir
Stybarrow Dodd
Loadpot Hill
Sleagill
Burrells
Iron Band
Hannah's Meadow
High Seat
Glenridding
Place Fell
Bampton
Bampton Grange
Reagill
Great Ormside
Eden Valley Railway
Balderhead Reservoir
Ullswater Steamers
Rosgill
Maulds Meaburn
Sandford
Thirlmere
Patterdale
Helvellyn
Shap Abbey
Shap
Crosby Ravensworth
Drybeck
Warcop
Great Musgrave
Brough
Castle
High Raise
Keld Chapel
Little Musgrave
Beldoo Hill
Grisdale Tarn
Brothers Water
Fairfield
Haweswater
Hayes Water
High Street
Shap Summit
Great Asby
Soulby
Brough Sowerby
Kaber
The Otter Trust
A7
A68
A696
A6071
A69
A689
A686
A6
A66
M6
A595
A591
A592
A5091
A685
B6357
B6318
B6320

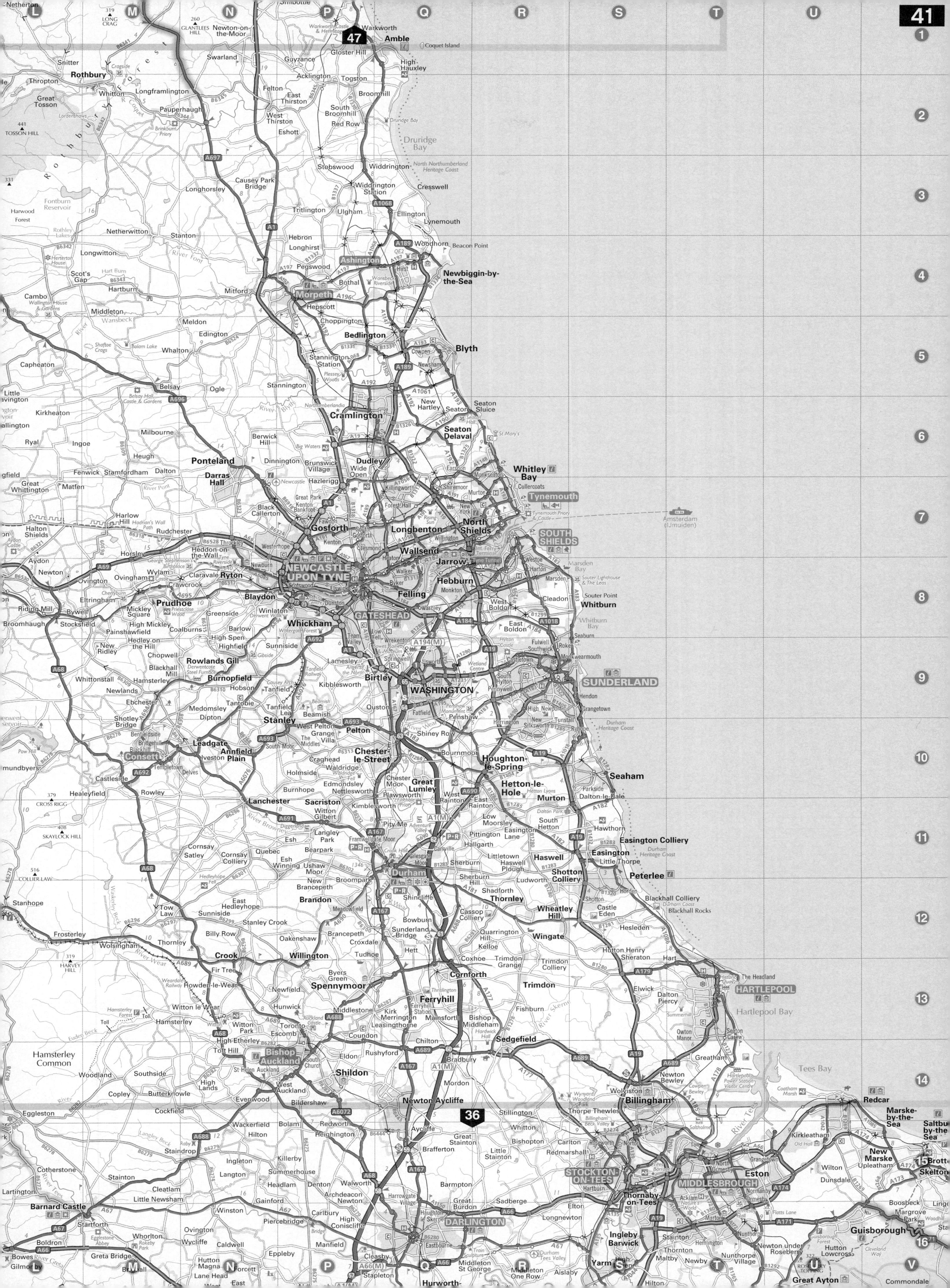
47
Amble
Warkworth
Coquet Island
Gloster Hill
High Hauxley
Swarland
Newton-on-the-Moor
Guyzance
Acklington
Togston
Rothbury
Snitter
Thropton
Great Tosson
Whitton
Longframlington
Pauperhaugh
Felton
East Thirston
Broomhill
South Broomhill
West Thirston
Red Row
Eshott
Druridge Bay
Stobswood
Widdrington
Widdrington Station
Cresswell
Causey Park Bridge
Longhorsley
Tritlington
Ulgham
Ellington
Lynemouth
Fontburn Reservoir
Harwood Forest
Netherwitton
Stanton
Hebron
Longhirst
Woodhorn
Beacon Point
Longwitton
Ashington
Pegswood
Newbiggin-by-the-Sea
Scot's Gap
Hartburn
Bothal
Cambo
Mitford
Morpeth
Hepscott
Middleton
Choppington
Meldon
Edington
Bedlington
Whalton
Blyth
Capheaton
Stannington Station
Belsay
Ogle
Stannington
Seaton Sluice
Kirkheaton
Cramlington
New Hartley
Seaton
Seaton Delaval
Ryal
Ingoe
Milbourne
Berwick Hill
Heugh
Ponteland
Dinnington
Brunswick Village
Dudley
Wide Open
Whitley Bay
Fenwick
Stamfordham
Dalton
Darras Hall
Hazlerigg
Great Whittington
Matfen
Tynemouth
Harlow Hill
Black Callerton
Halton Shields
Rudchester
Gosforth
Longbenton
North Shields
South Shields
Amsterdam (IJmuiden)
Heddon-on-the-Wall
Throckley
Horsley
Wallsend
Jarrow
Aydon
Newton
Wylam
Ovingham
Claravale
Ryton
Newcastle upon Tyne
Hebburn
Felling
Ovington
Crawcrook
Riding Mill
Bywell
Eltringham
Prudhoe
Blaydon
Whitburn
Souter Point
Cleadon
West Boldon
Stocksfield
Mickley Square
Greenside
Winlaton
Whickham
Gateshead
East Boldon
Broomhaugh
High Mickley
Painshawfield
Coalburns
Barlow
High Spen
Seaburn
New Ridley
Hedley on the Hill
Highfield
Sunniside
Chopwell
Rowlands Gill
Lamesley
Blackhall Mill
Birtley
Sunderland
Whittonstall
Hamsterley
Burnopfield
Kibblesworth
Washington
Newlands
Hobson
Tanfield
Ebchester
Medomsley
Tantobie
Tanfield Lea
Beamish
Ouston
Penshaw
Grangetown
Shotley Bridge
Dipton
Stanley
Fatfield
Tunstall
Leadgate
Annfield Plain
West Pelton
Pelton
Shiney Row
Consett
Iveston
Grange Villa
Chester-le-Street
Bournmoor
Houghton-le-Spring
Seaham
Craghead
Waldridge
Holmside
Edmondsley
Great Lumley
Hetton-le-Hole
Castleside
Chester Moor
Murton
Dalton-le-Dale
Healeyfield
Rowley
Burnhope
Nettlesworth
West Rainton
East Rainton
Lanchester
Sacriston
Kimblesworth
Witton Gilbert
Low Moorsley
South Hetton
Hawthorn
Langley Park
Pity Me
Pittington
Easington Lane
Easington Colliery
Esh
Bearpark
Hallgarth
Easington
Cornsay
Quebec
Carrville
Littletown
Haswell
Little Thorpe
Satley
Cornsay Colliery
Esh Winning
Ushaw Moor
Durham
Sherburn
Haswell Plough
Shotton Colliery
Peterlee
New Brancepeth
Broompark
Sherburn Hill
Ludworth
Stanhope
Brandon
Shincliffe
Shadforth
Thornley
Blackhall Colliery
Blackhall Rocks
East Hedleyhope
Meadowfield
Wheatley Hill
Castle Eden
Tow Law
Sunniside
Bowburn
Cassop Colliery
Stanley Crook
Quarrington Hill
Hesleden
Frosterley
Billy Row
Oakenshaw
Brancepeth
Sunderland Bridge
Croxdale
Kelloe
Wingate
Wolsingham
Thornley
Crook
Willington
Tudhoe
Hett
Coxhoe
Trimdon Grange
Trimdon Colliery
Hutton Henry
Sheraton
Hart
Fir Tree
Byers Green
Cornforth
The Headland
Howden-le-Wear
Spennymoor
Trimdon
Hartlepool
Newfield
Ferryhill
Elwick
Dalton Piercy
Witton le Wear
Hunwick
Middlestone
Kirk Merrington
Fishburn
Hartlepool Bay
Hamsterley
Witton Park
Toronto
Leasingthorne
Mainsforth
Bishop Middleham
Owton Manor
Escomb
Coundon
Seaton Carew
High Etherley
Chilton
Sedgefield
Toft Hill
Bishop Auckland
Eldon
Rushyford
Greatham
Hamsterley Common
St Helen Auckland
South Church
Shildon
Bradbury
Tees Bay
Woodland
Southside
High Lands
West Auckland
Mordon
Newton Bewley
Copley
Butterknowle
Evenwood
Wolviston
Redcar
Eggleston
Cockfield
Bildershaw
Newton Aycliffe
36
Stillington
Billingham
Thorpe Thewles
Marske-by-the-Sea
Saltburn-by-the-Sea
Wackerfield
Bolam
Redworth
Whitton
Hilton
Heighington
Aycliffe
Great Stainton
Bishopton
Carlton
Kirkleatham
Staindrop
Brafferton
Redmarshall
Little Stainton
Killerby
Ingleton
New Marske
Upleatham
Cotherstone
Langton
Summerhouse
Stockton-on-Tees
Middlesbrough
Eston
Wilton
Skelton
Stainton
Headlam
Denton
Walworth
Barmpton
Dunsdale
Lartington
Cleatlam
Archdeacon Newton
Great Burdon
Sadberge
Elton
Thornaby-on-Tees
Little Newsham
Gainford
Barnard Castle
Winston
Carlbury
Boosbeck
Margrove Park
Startforth
Piercebridge
High Coniscliffe
Darlington
Longnewton
Guisborough
Whorlton
Ovington
Ingleby Barwick
Stainton
Hemlington
Boldron
Wycliffe
Caldwell
Newton under Roseberry
Hutton Lowcross
Bowes
Thornton
Greta Bridge
Eppleby
Manfield
Eastbourne
Middleton St George
Nunthorpe Village
Maltby
Newby
Hutton Magna
Cleasby
Yarm
Gilmonby
Lane Head
Forcett
Stapleton
Middleton One Row
Aislaby
High Leven
Hilton
Great Ayton
East
Hurworth
Commondale

48

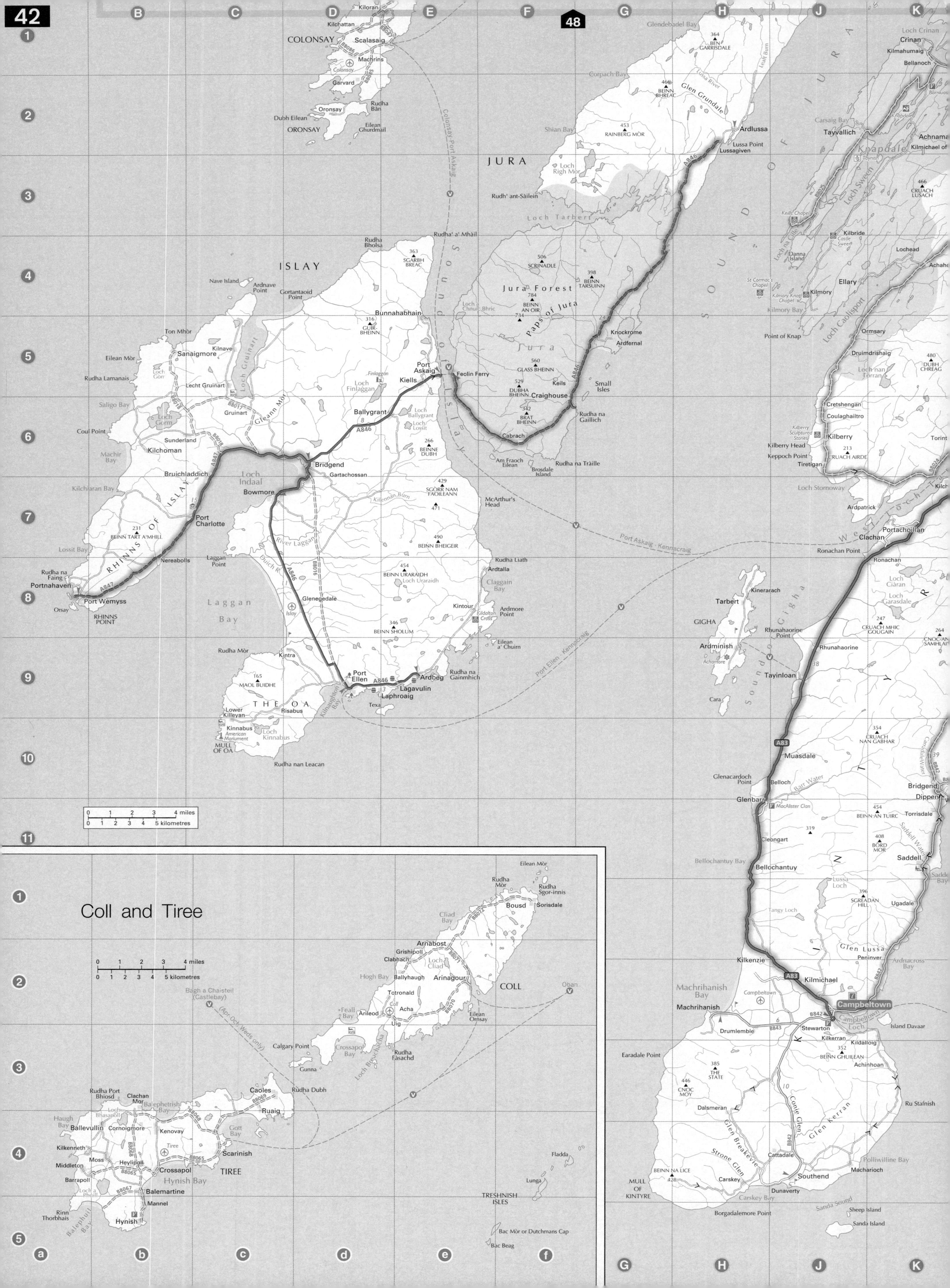
COLONSAY
Kiloran
Kilchattan
Scalasaig
Machrins
Colonsay
Garvard
Oronsay
Rudha Bàn
Dubh Eilean
ORONSAY
Eilean Ghurdmail
Colonsay-Port Askaig
JURA
Glendebadel Bay
364 BEN GARRISDALE
Corpach Bay
466 BEINN BHREAC
Glen Grundale
Lussa River
453 RAINBERG MÒR
Shian Bay
Ardlussa
Lussa Point
Lussagiven
Loch Righ Mòr
Rudh' ant-Sàilein
Loch Tarbert
506 SCRINADLE
398 BEINN TARSUINN
Jura Forest
784 BEINN AN OIR
734
Paps of Jura
Jura
560 GLASS BHEINN
529 DUBHA BHEINN
Craighouse
Keils
Small Isles
Knockrome
Ardfernal
Feolin Ferry
442 BRAT BHEINN
Rudha na Gaillich
Cabrach
Am Fraoch Eilean
Brosdale Island
Rudha na Tràille
Sound of Islay
SOUND OF JURA
ISLAY
Rudha Bholsa
Rudha' a' Mhàil
363 SGARBH BREAC
Nave Island
Ardnave Point
Gortantaoid Point
Bunnahabhain
316 GUIR-BHEINN
Ton Mhòr
Sanaigmore
Kilnave
Eilean Mòr
Rudha Lamanais
Loch Gorr
Lecht Gruinart
Loch Gruinart
Finlaggan
Loch Finlaggan
Port Askaig
Kiells
Saligo Bay
Gruinart
Loch Gorm
Gleann Mòr
Ballygrant
Loch Ballygrant
Loch Lossit
A846
Coul Point
Sunderland
266 BEINNE DUBH
Kilchoman
Machir Bay
Bridgend
Gartachossan
Bruichladdich
Loch Indaal
Bowmore
429 SGÒRR NAM FAOILEANN
Kilchiaran Bay
Kilennan Burn
471
McArthur's Head
Port Charlotte
231 BEINN TART A' MHILL
RHINNS OF ISLAY
Lossit Bay
River Laggan
490 BEINN BHEIGEIR
Nereabolls
Laggan Point
Duich R.
Rudha Liath
Ardtalla
454 BEINN URARAIDH
Loch Uaraidh
Claggain Bay
Rudha na Faing
Portnahaven
Port Wemyss
Orsay
RHINNS POINT
Laggan Bay
Islay
Glenegedale
Kintour
Kildalton Cross
Ardmore Point
346 BEINN SHOLUM
Eilean a' Chuirn
Rudha Mòr
Kintra
165 MAOL BUIDHE
Port Ellen
Ardbeg
Rudha na Gainmhich
Lagavulin
Laphroaig
Texa
THE OA
Kilnaughton Bay
Lower Killeyan
Risabus
Kinnabus
American Monument
Loch Kinnabus
MULL OF OA
Rudha nan Leacan
Port Askaig - Kennacraig
Port Ellen - Kennacraig
0 1 2 3 4 miles
0 1 2 3 4 5 kilometres
Loch Crinan
Crinan
Kilmahumaig
Bellanoch
Carsaig Bay
Tayvallich
Knapdale
Achnamara
Kilmichael of
Loch Sween
466 CRUACH LUSACH
Keils Chapel
Kilbride
Castle Sween
Danna Island
Loch na Cille
Lochead
Achahoish
St Cormac's Chapel
Kilmory Knap Chapel
Kilmory
Ellary
Kilmory Bay
Loch Caolisport
Point of Knap
Ormsary
Druimdrishaig
480 DUBH CHREAG
Loch nan Torran
Cretshengan
Coulaghailtro
Kilberry Sculptured Stones
Kilberry
Kilberry Head
Keppoch Point
Tiretigan
213 CRUACH AIRDE
Torinturk
Loch Stornoway
Ardpatrick
West Loch Tarbert
Portachoillan
Clachan
Ronachan Point
Ronachan
Loch Ciaran
Loch Garasdale
Kinerarach
Tarbert
GIGHA
Sound of Gigha
Ardminish
Achamore
Cara
247 CRUACH MHIC GOUGAIN
Rhunahaorine Point
Rhunahaorine
264 CNOC AN SAMHLAIDH
Tayinloan
A83
354 CRUACH NAN GABHAR
Muasdale
Glenacardoch Point
Belloch
Barr Water
Bridgend
Dippen
Glenbarr
MacAlister Clan
454 BEINN AN TUIRC
Torrisdale
319
408 BORD MOR
Saddell Water
Cleongart
Saddell
Bellochantuy Bay
Bellochantuy
Lussa Loch
396 SGREADAN HILL
Ugadale
Tangy Loch
Glen Lussa
Peninver
Ardnacross Bay
Kilkenzie
Kilmichael
Machrihanish Bay
Campbeltown
Machrihanish
Drumlemble
Stewarton
Campbeltown Loch
Island Davaar
Kilkerran
Kildalloig
352 BEINN GHUILEAN
Achinhoan
Earadale Point
385 THE STATE
446 CNOC MOY
Dalsmeran
Glen Breakerie
Conie Glen
Glen Kerran
Ru Stafnish
Strone Glen
Cattadale
Polliwilline Bay
Macharioch
BEINN NA LICE 428
Carskey
Southend
MULL OF KINTYRE
Dunaverty
Carskey Bay
Borgadalemore Point
Sanda Sound
Sheep Island
Sanda Island
KINTYRE
Coll and Tiree
0 1 2 3 4 miles
0 1 2 3 4 5 kilometres
Eilean Mòr
Rudha Mòr
Rudha Sgor-innis
Bousd
Sorisdale
Cliad Bay
Arnabost
Grishipoll
Clabhach
Loch Cliad
Hogh Bay
Ballyhaugh
Arinagour
COLL
Totronald
Bagh a Chaisteil (Castlebay)
(Apr-Oct Weds only)
Oban
Feall Bay
Arileod
Coll
Acha
Uig
Eilean Ornsay
Calgary Point
Crossapol Bay
Loch Breachacha
Rudha Fasachd
Gunna
Rudha Dubh
Rudha Port Bhiosd
Clachan Mor
Loch Bhasapoll
Balephetrish Bay
Caoles
Ruaig
Haugh Bay
Ballevullin
Cornaigmore
Kenovay
Gott Bay
Kilkenneth
Tiree
Scarinish
Middleton
Moss
Heylipoll
Crossapol
TIREE
Barrapoll
Hynish Bay
Loch a' Phuill
Balemartine
Mannel
Rinn Thorbhais
Balephuil Bay
Hynish
Fladda
Lunga
TRESHNISH ISLES
Bac Mòr or Dutchmans Cap
Bac Beag

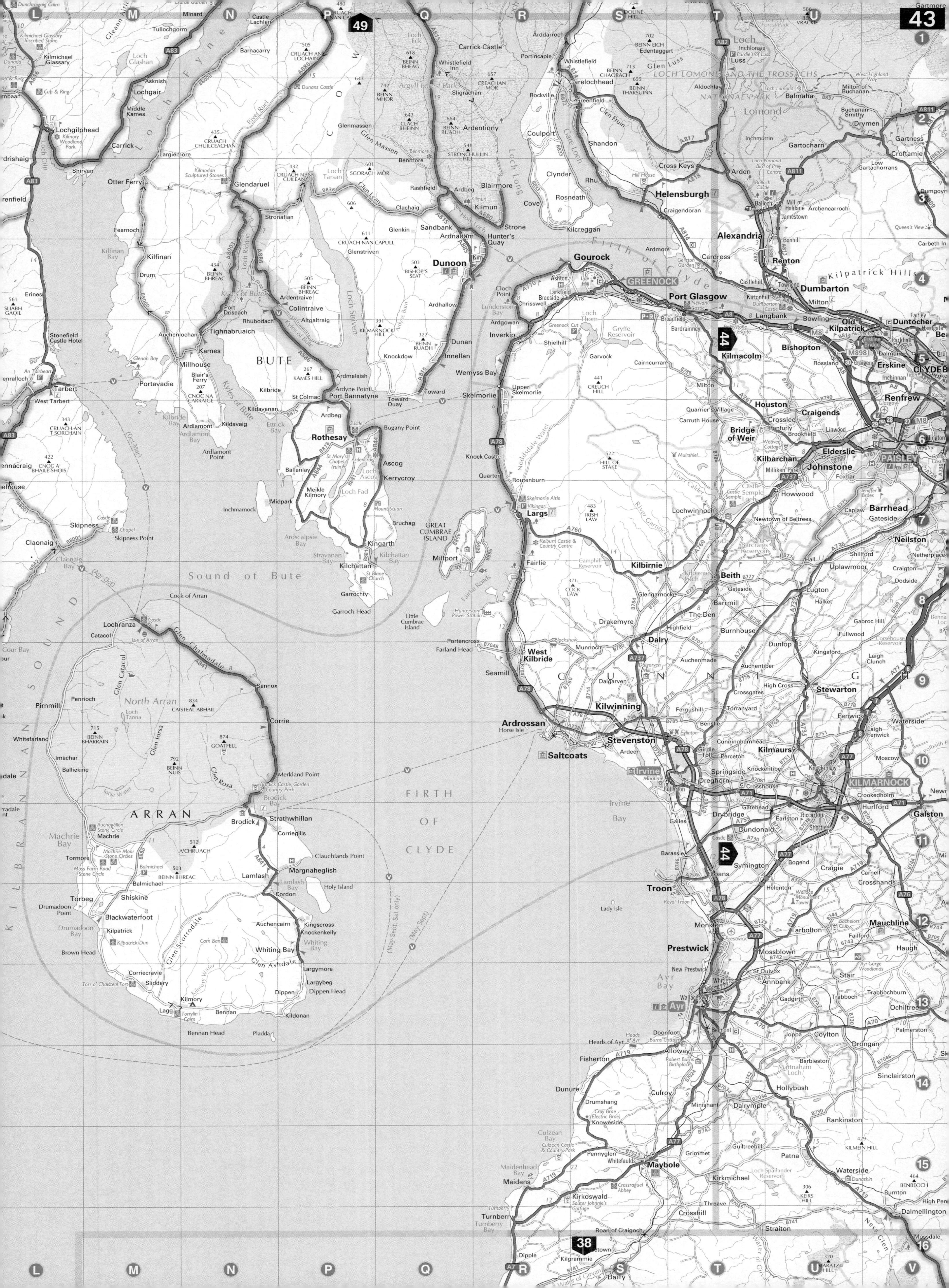
Lochgilphead
Tarbert
West Tarbert
Skipness
Claonaig
Otter Ferry
Glendaruel
Kilfinan
Tighnabruaich
Kames
Millhouse
Portavadie
BUTE
Rothesay
Port Bannatyne
Ascog
Kerrycroy
Kingarth
Kilchattan
Dunoon
Sandbank
Hunter's Quay
Innellan
Toward
Strone
Kilmun
Ardentinny
Carrick Castle
Cove
Kilcreggan
Rosneath
Garelochhead
Helensburgh
Alexandria
Balloch
Renton
Dumbarton
Gourock
GREENOCK
Port Glasgow
Inverkip
Wemyss Bay
Skelmorlie
Largs
Fairlie
Millport
GREAT CUMBRAE ISLAND
Little Cumbrae Island
West Kilbride
Seamill
Ardrossan
Saltcoats
Stevenston
Kilwinning
Irvine
Troon
Prestwick
Ayr
Dalry
Kilbirnie
Beith
Lochwinnoch
Kilmacolm
Bridge of Weir
Houston
Erskine
Renfrew
PAISLEY
Johnstone
Elderslie
Kilbarchan
Barrhead
Neilston
Lugton
Stewarton
Kilmaurs
KILMARNOCK
Galston
Mauchline
Tarbolton
Annbank
Maybole
Kirkoswald
Turnberry
Maidens
Dunure
Dalrymple
Hollybush
Patna
Dalmellington
Straiton
Crosshill
Kirkmichael
Sound of Bute
FIRTH OF CLYDE
Firth of Clyde
Loch Fyne
ARRAN
North Arran
Lochranza
Catacol
Pirnmill
Sannox
Corrie
Brodick
Lamlash
Whiting Bay
Kildonan
Lagg
Kilmory
Blackwaterfoot
Machrie
Pladda
Holy Island
Sound of Arran
KILBRANNAN SOUND
Loch Lomond
LOCH LOMOND AND THE TROSSACHS NATIONAL PARK
Kilpatrick Hills
Old Kilpatrick
Bishopton
Clydebank
49
44
38

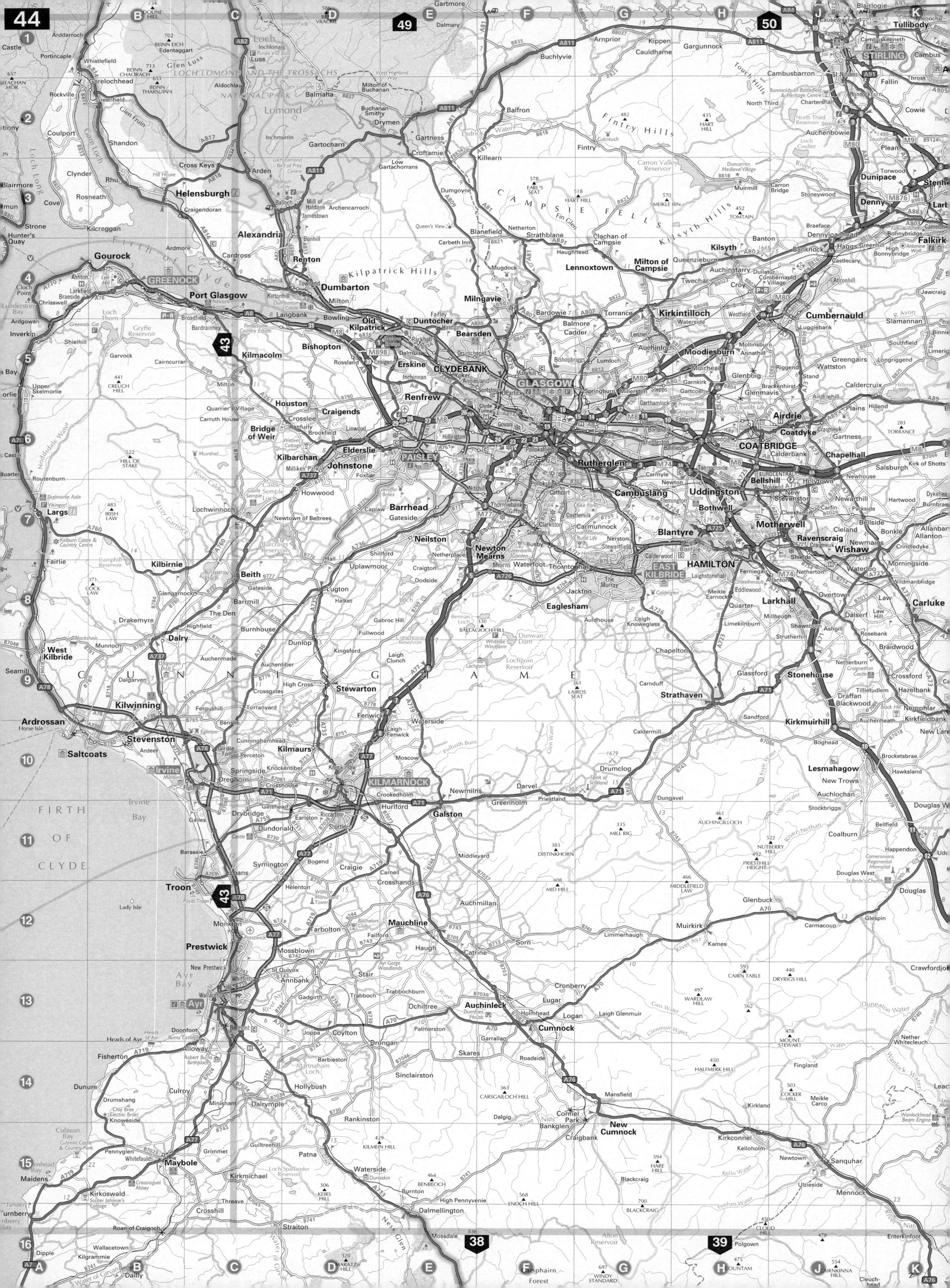
49
50
43
38
39
STIRLING
GLASGOW
GREENOCK
PAISLEY
KILMARNOCK
EAST KILBRIDE
HAMILTON
COATBRIDGE
CLYDEBANK
Irvine
Ayr
Gourock
Port Glasgow
Helensburgh
Dumbarton
Alexandria
Renton
Balloch
Milngavie
Bearsden
Kirkintilloch
Cumbernauld
Kilsyth
Falkirk
Denny
Dunipace
Airdrie
Coatdyke
Motherwell
Wishaw
Bellshill
Uddingston
Bothwell
Blantyre
Larkhall
Carluke
Rutherglen
Cambuslang
Newton Mearns
Barrhead
Neilston
Renfrew
Johnstone
Elderslie
Kilbarchan
Bridge of Weir
Houston
Kilmacolm
Largs
West Kilbride
Ardrossan
Saltcoats
Stevenston
Kilwinning
Dalry
Beith
Kilbirnie
Stewarton
Kilmaurs
Galston
Newmilns
Darvel
Strathaven
Stonehouse
Lesmahagow
Kirkmuirhill
Douglas
Muirkirk
Troon
Prestwick
Mauchline
Auchinleck
Cumnock
New Cumnock
Maybole
Dalmellington
Sanquhar
Eaglesham
Lennoxtown
Milton of Campsie
Tullibody
Campsie Fells
Kilsyth Hills
Fintry Hills
Kilpatrick Hills
Loch Lomond and The Trossachs National Park
Firth of Clyde
Cunninghame
Irvine Bay
Ayr Bay
Culzean Bay

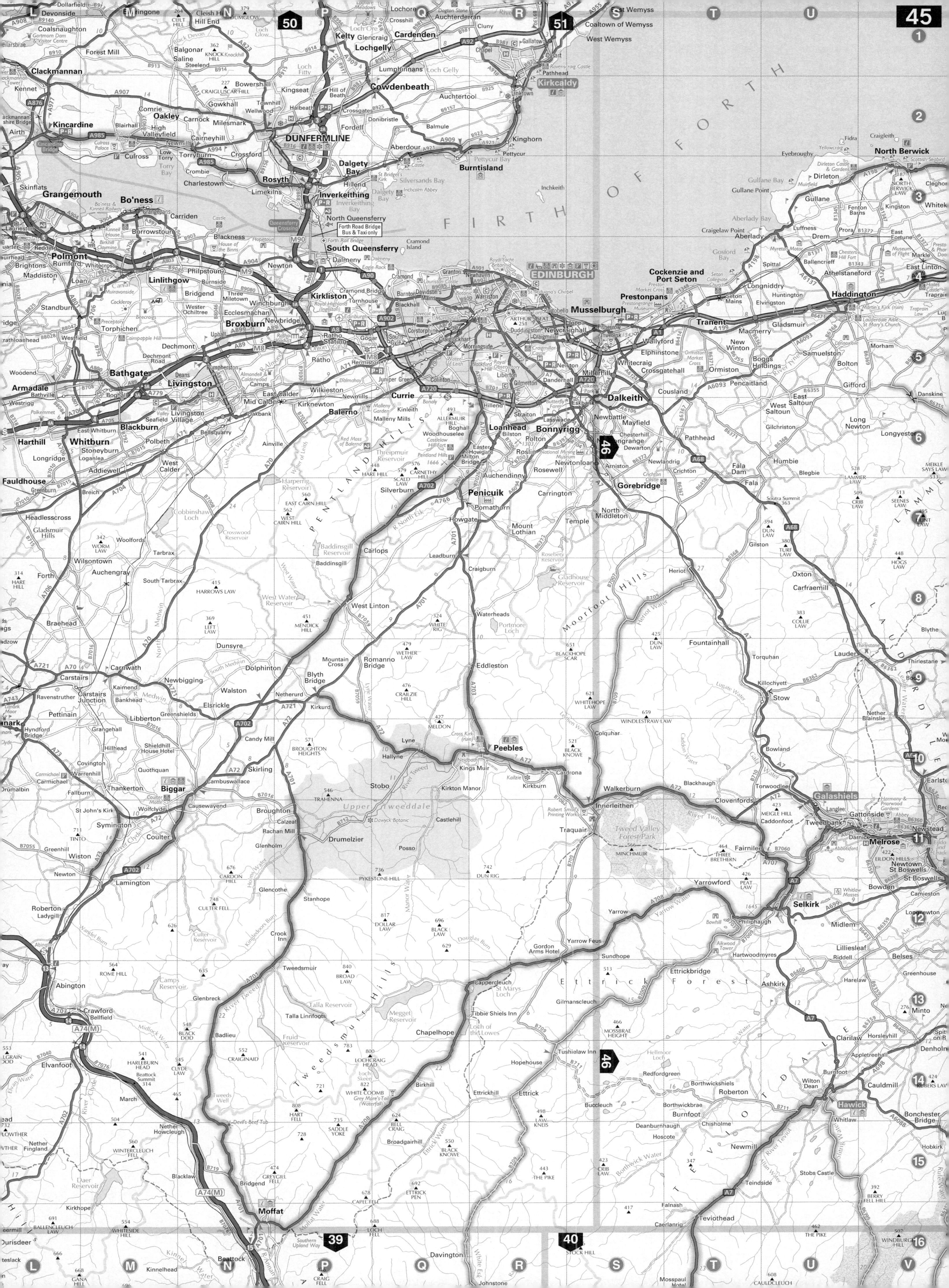

50
51
46
39
40
FIRTH OF FORTH
Kirkcaldy
Dunfermline
Cowdenbeath
Lochgelly
Kelty
Cardenden
Burntisland
Kinghorn
Aberdour
Dalgety Bay
Inverkeithing
North Queensferry
Rosyth
Limekilns
Charlestown
Crossford
Culross
Torryburn
Kincardine
Clackmannan
Oakley
Forest Mill
Saline
Grangemouth
Bo'ness
Polmont
Linlithgow
South Queensferry
Forth Road Bridge
Bus & Taxi only
Queensferry Crossing
Kirkliston
Broxburn
Uphall
Livingston
Bathgate
Armadale
Whitburn
Blackburn
West Calder
Mid Calder
East Calder
Ratho
Currie
Balerno
Juniper Green
Edinburgh
Musselburgh
Prestonpans
Cockenzie and Port Seton
Tranent
Dalkeith
Bonnyrigg
Loanhead
Penicuik
Gorebridge
Haddington
North Berwick
Gullane
Aberlady
Dirleton
East Linton
Pentland Hills
Moorfoot Hills
Lauderdale
Carlops
West Linton
Leadburn
Eddleston
Peebles
Innerleithen
Walkerburn
Traquair
Carnwath
Carstairs
Biggar
Lauder
Stow
Galashiels
Melrose
Tweedbank
Selkirk
St Boswells
Newtown St Boswells
Upper Tweeddale
Tweed Valley Forest Park
Yarrowford
Ettrick Forest
Tweedsmuir Hills
Tweedsmuir
Moffat
Abington
Crawford
Elvanfoot
Hawick
Teviotdale
Denholm
Ashkirk
Ettrickbridge
Gordon Arms Hotel
St Marys Loch
Tibbie Shiels Inn
Talla Reservoir
Megget Reservoir
Broughton
Drumelzier
Stobo
Lamington
Symington
Coulter
Roberton
Beattock
Davington
Teviothead

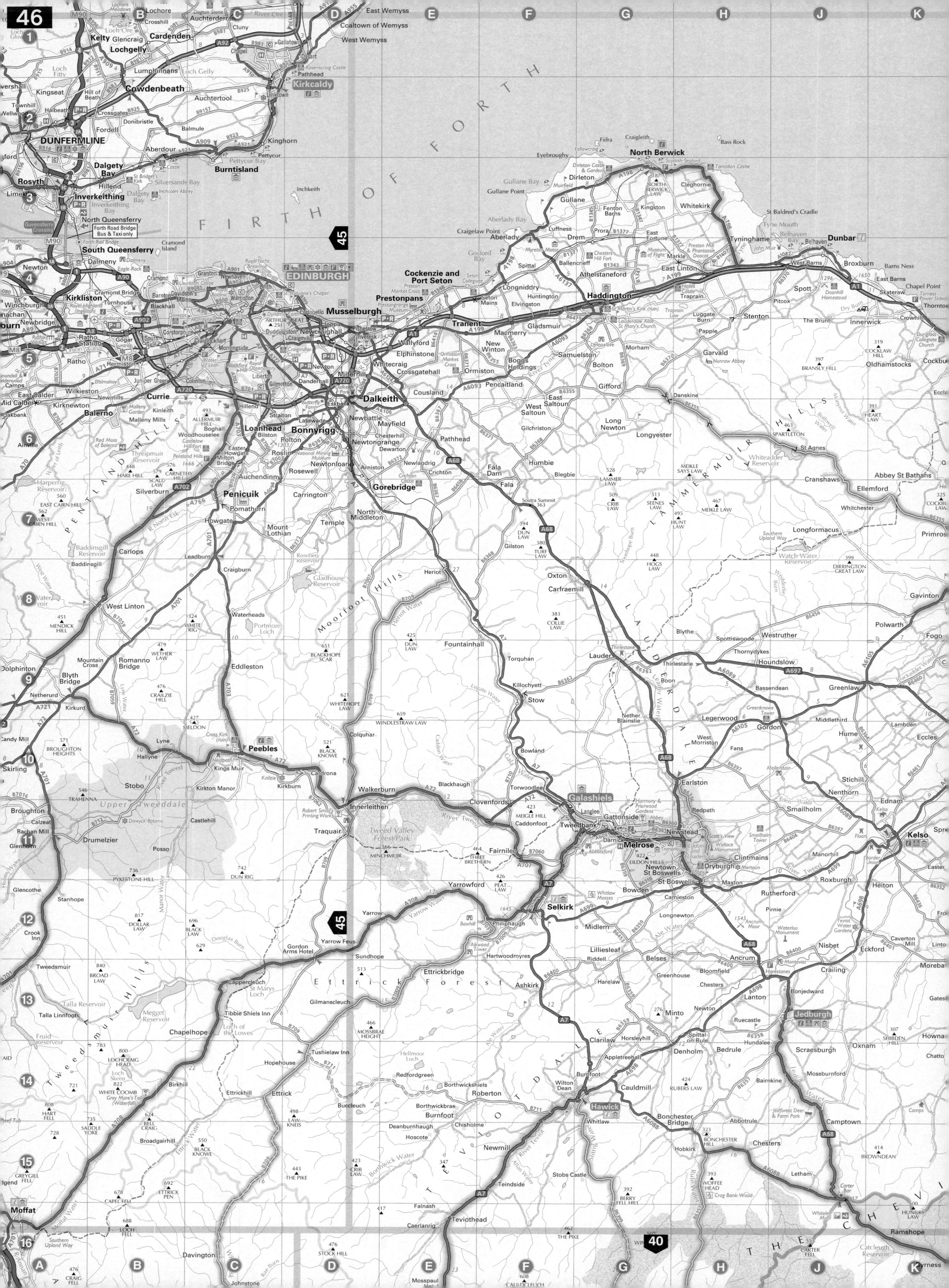
FIRTH OF FORTH
Kirkcaldy
Kelty
Lochgelly
Cardenden
Cowdenbeath
DUNFERMLINE
Rosyth
Inverkeithing
Dalgety Bay
Burntisland
Kinghorn
Aberdour
North Queensferry
South Queensferry
Forth Road Bridge Bus & Taxi only
Dalmeny
Kirkliston
EDINBURGH
Musselburgh
Prestonpans
Cockenzie and Port Seton
Tranent
Haddington
North Berwick
Dunbar
Dirleton
Gullane
Aberlady
Longniddry
East Linton
Dalkeith
Bonnyrigg
Loanhead
Penicuik
Currie
Balerno
Gorebridge
Pathhead
PENTLAND HILLS
Moorfoot Hills
LAMMERMUIR HILLS
LAUDERDALE
Lauder
Stow
Peebles
Innerleithen
Walkerburn
Galashiels
Melrose
Newtown St Boswells
St Boswells
Earlston
Selkirk
Kelso
Jedburgh
Hawick
TEVIOTDALE
Ettrick Forest
Tweedsmuir Hills
Upper Tweeddale
Moffat
Broughton
West Linton
Gifford
Duns
Greenlaw
Gordon
Yarrow
Ettrick
Teviothead
Denholm
Ancrum
Oxton
Heriot
Eddleston
THE CHEVIOT
A1
A7
A68
A72
A701
A702
A703
M8
M9
M90
45
40

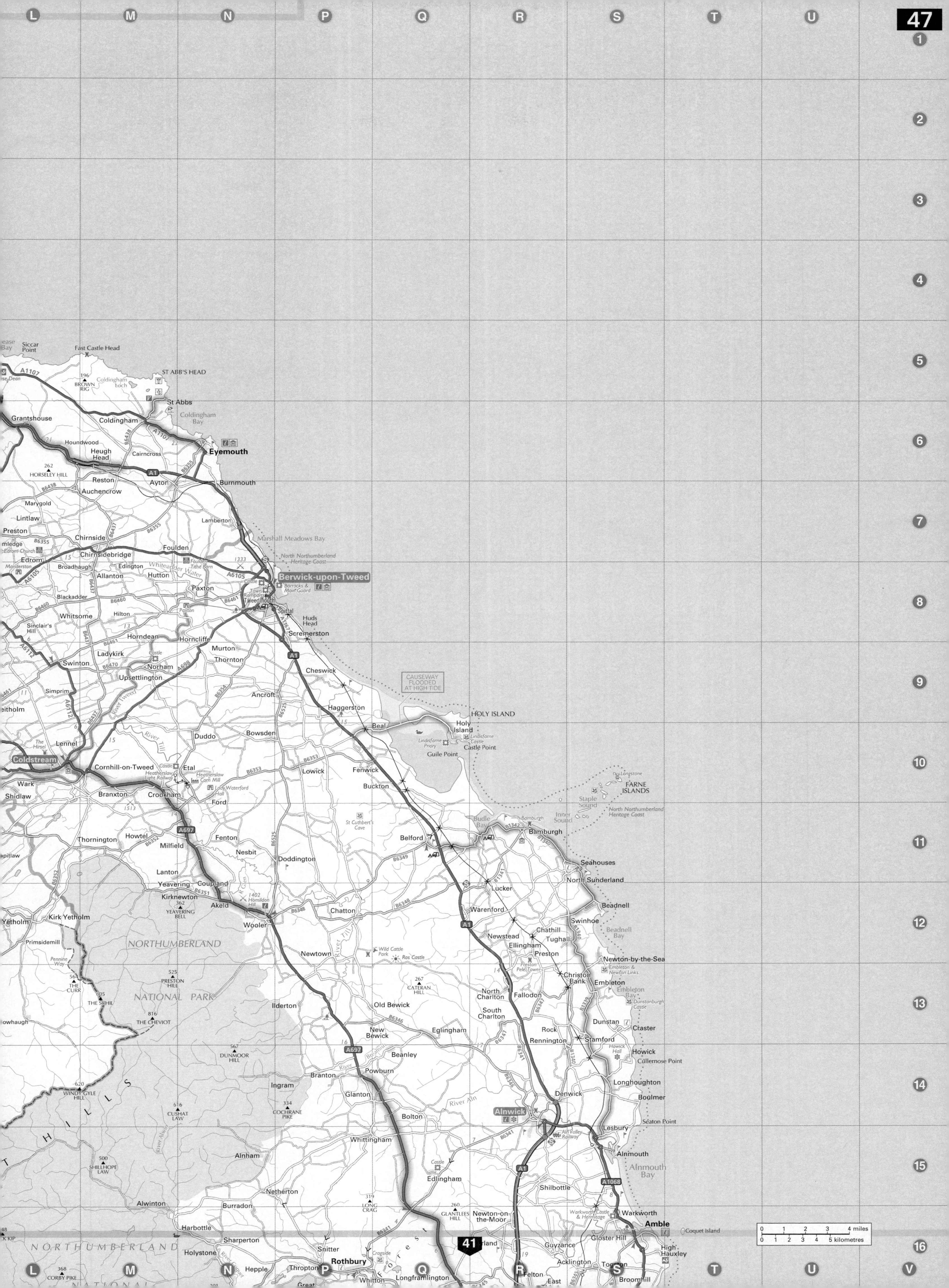
Siccar Point
Fast Castle Head
ST ABB'S HEAD
196 BROWN RIG
Coldingham Loch
St Abbs
Coldingham Bay
Grantshouse
Coldingham
Houndwood
Heugh Head
Cairncross
Eyemouth
262 HORSELEY HILL
Reston
Ayton
Burnmouth
Auchencrow
Marygold
Lintlaw
Lamberton
Preston
Chirnside
Marshall Meadows Bay
Foulden
Edrom
Chirnsidebridge
North Northumberland Heritage Coast
Broadhaugh
Edington
Whiteadder Water
Allanton
Hutton
Berwick-upon-Tweed
Paxton
Barracks & Main Guard
Blackadder
Tweedmouth
Spittal
Whitsome
Hilton
Huds Head
Sinclair's Hill
Horndean
Scremerston
Horncliffe
Ladykirk
Murton
Norham
Thornton
Swinton
Upsettlington
Cheswick
CAUSEWAY FLOODED AT HIGH TIDE
Simprim
Ancroft
Haggerston
HOLY ISLAND
Holy Island
Beal
Lindisfarne Castle
Lindisfarne Priory
Castle Point
Duddo
Bowsden
Guile Point
Lennel
The Hirsel
Coldstream
Cornhill-on-Tweed
Etal
Lowick
Fenwick
Longstone
FARNE ISLANDS
Wark
Shidlaw
Branxton
Crookham
Heatherslaw Corn Mill
Ford
Buckton
Staple Sound
North Northumberland Heritage Coast
Inner Sound
Budle Bay
Bamburgh
St Cuthbert's Cave
Thornington
Howtel
Milfield
Fenton
Belford
Nesbit
Doddington
Seahouses
Lanton
North Sunderland
Yeavering
Coupland
Lucker
Kirknewton
1402 Humildon Hill
362 YEAVERING BELL
Akeld
Chatton
Beadnell
Warenford
Kirk Yetholm
Wooler
Swinhoe
Beadnell Bay
Chathill
Primsidemill
NORTHUMBERLAND
Newstead
Tughall
Ellingham
Preston
Wild Cattle Park
Ros Castle
Newtown
Newton-by-the-Sea
Pennine Way
564 THE CURR
525 PRESTON HILL
267 CATERAN HILL
Christon Bank
Embleton
Embleton Bay
605 THE SCHIL
NATIONAL PARK
North Charlton
Fallodon
Dunstanburgh Castle
816 THE CHEVIOT
Ilderton
Old Bewick
South Charlton
Dunstan
Craster
New Bewick
Eglingham
Rock
Rennington
Stamford
Howick Hall
Howick
567 DUNMOOR HILL
Beanley
Cullernose Point
Branton
Powburn
620 WINDY GYLE HILL
Ingram
Longhoughton
Glanton
334 COCHRANE PIKE
River Aln
Denwick
Boulmer
616 CUSHAT LAW
Bolton
Alnwick
Seaton Point
Aln Valley Railway
Lesbury
Whittingham
Alnmouth
500 SHILLHOPE LAW
Alnham
Alnmouth Bay
Edlingham
Shilbottle
Netherton
Alwinton
Burradon
319 LONG CRAG
260 GLANTLEES HILL
Newton-on-the-Moor
Warkworth Castle & Hermitage
Warkworth
Amble
Coquet Island
Harbottle
Sharperton
Snitter
41
Guyzance
Gloster Hill
High Hauxley
NORTHUMBERLAND
Holystone
Thropton
Rothbury
Acklington
Togston
Hepple
Whitton
Longframlington
Felton
East
Broomhill
368 CORBY PIKE
0 1 2 3 4 miles
0 1 2 3 4 5 kilometres

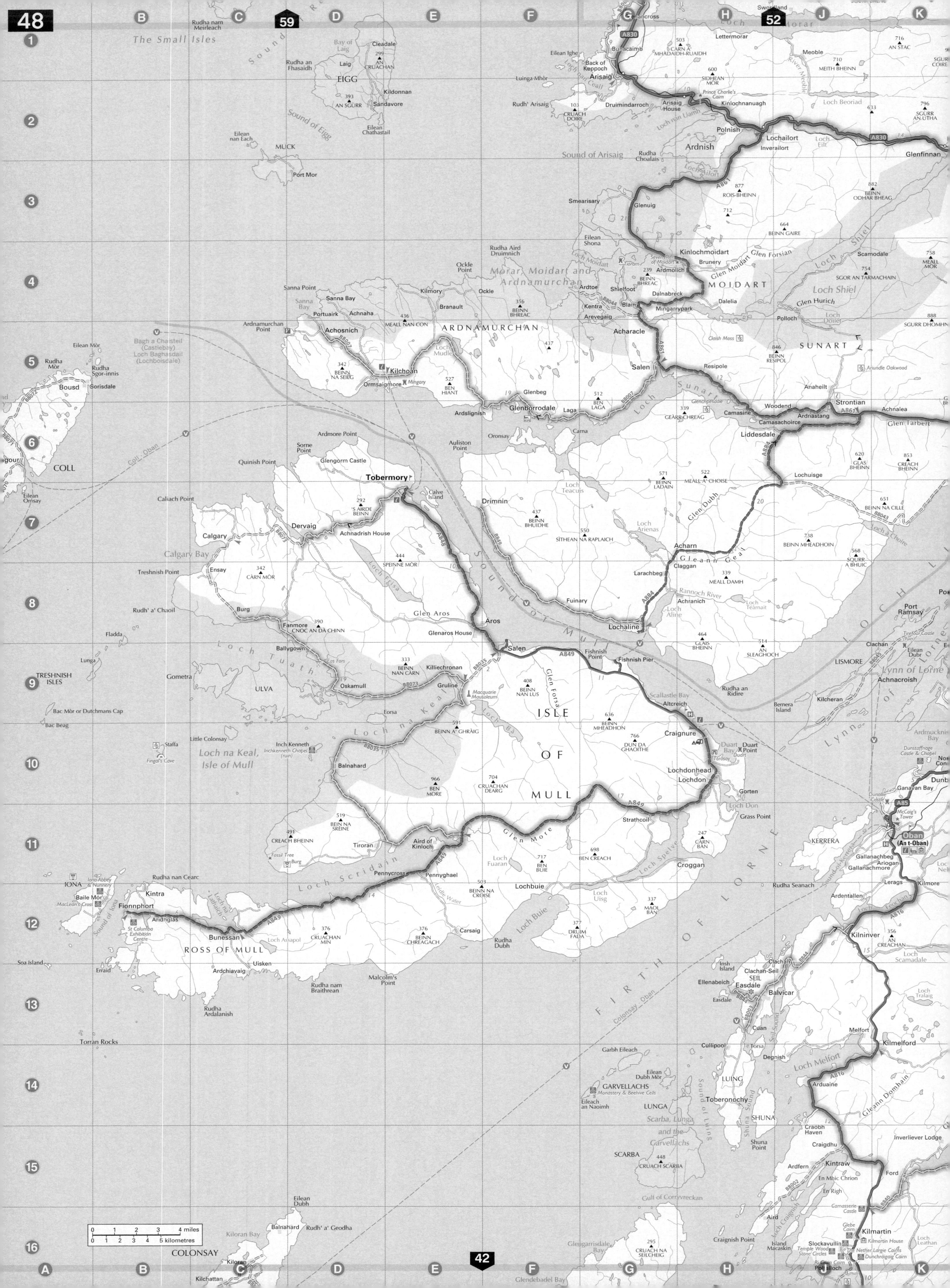
59
52
42
The Small Isles
Rudha nam Meirleach
EIGG
Bay of Laig
Laig
Cleadale
299 AN CRUACHAN
Rudha an Fhasaidh
Kildonnan
393 AN SGURR
Sandavore
Eilean Chathastail
Sound of Eigg
Eilean nan Each
MUCK
Port Mor
Mallaig
Arisaig
Back of Keppoch
Eilean Ighe
Luinga Mhòr
Rudh' Arisaig
103 CRUACH DOIRE
Druimindarroch
Arisaig House
Lettermorar
503 CARN A' MHADAIDH-RUAIDH
600 SIDHEAN MOR
Prince Charlie's Cairn
Kinlochnanuagh
Loch nan Uamh
Polnish
Ardnish
Lochailort
Inversilort
Loch Eilt
Glenfinnan
A830
Meoble
Loch Beoriad
716 AN STAC
710 MEITH BHEINN
633
796 SGURR AN UTHA
Sound of Arisaig
Rudha Chaolais
Loch Ailort
877 ROIS-BHEINN
712
882 BEINN ODHAR BHEAG
664 BEINN GAIRE
Smearisary
Glenuig
Eilean Shona
Rudha Aird Druimnich
Loch Moidart
Seven Men of Moidart
Kinlochmoidart
Brunery
Glen Forsian
Glen Moidart
MOIDART
Scamodale
754 SGOR AN TARMACHAIN
758 MEALL MOR
Loch Shiel
Glen Hurich
239 BEINN BHREAC
Ardmolich
Ardtoe
Shielfoot
Dalnabreck
Kentra
Blain
Dalelia
Arevegaig
Mingarrypark
Polloch
888 SGURR DHOMHNUILL
Acharacle
Morar, Moidart and Ardnamurchan
Ockle Point
Sanna Point
Sanna Bay
Portuairk
Achnaha
Kilmory
Ockle
Branault
436 MEALL NAN CON
356 BEINN BHREAC
Ardnamurchan Point
Achosnich
ARDNAMURCHAN
437
Claish Moss
846 BEINN RESIPOL
SUNART
Anundle Oakwood
Eilean Mòr
Rudha Mòr
Rudha Sgor-innis
Bousd
Sorisdale
Bagh a Chaisteil (Castlebay) Loch Baghasdail (Lochboisdale)
342 BEINN NA SEILG
Kilchoan
Ormsaigmore
Mingary
527 BEN HIANT
Loch Mudle
Salen
Resipole
Anaheilt
Strontian
Achnalea
Glenbeg
512 BEN LAGA
Glenborrodale
Laga
Ardslignish
Loch Sunart
339 GEARR CHREAG
Glenchreadaile
Camasine
Woodend
Ardnastang
Camasachoirce
Glen Tarbert
A861
Carna
Oronsay
Auliston Point
Liddesdale
Ardmore Point
Sorne Point
COLL
Coll - Oban
Quinish Point
Glengorm Castle
Tobermory
620 GLAS BHEINN
853 CREACH BHEINN
571 BEINN LADAIN
522 MEALL A' CHOISE
Lochuisge
Loch Teacuis
Glen Dubh
Eilean Ornsay
Caliach Point
292 'S AIRDE BEINN
Calve Island
Drimnin
437 BEINN BHUIDHE
651 BEINN NA CILLE
Dervaig
Calgary
Achnadrish House
550 SÌTHEAN NA RAPLAICH
Loch Arienas
Acharn
738 BEINN MHEADHOIN
568 SGURR A BHUIC
Calgary Bay
444 SPEINNE MÒR
Loch Frisa
Gleann Geal
Claggan
Larachbeg
339 MEALL DAMH
Treshnish Point
Ensay
342 CARN MÒR
Sound of Mull
Rannoch River
Achranich
Loch Aline
Loch Tearnait
Fuinary
Port Ramsay
Rudh' a' Chaoil
Burg
Fanmore
390 CNOC AN DÀ CHINN
Glen Aros
Aros
Lochaline
Glenaros House
464 GLAIS BHEINN
514 AN SLEAGHOCH
Fladda
Tirefour Castle
Clachan
Eilean Dubh
Loch Tuath
Ballygown
Eas Fors
Salen
A849
Fishnish Point
Fishnish Pier
LISMORE
Lynn of Lorne
Lunga
Gometra
333 BEINN NAN CÀRN
Killiechronan
408 BEINN NAN LUS
Glen Forsa
Achnacroish
TRESHNISH ISLES
ULVA
Oskamull
Gruline
Macquarie Mausoleum
Rudha an Ridire
Kilcheran
Scallastle Bay
Altcreich
Bernera Island
Bac Mòr or Dutchmans Cap
Bac Beag
Forsa
ISLE OF MULL
636 BEINN MHEADHON
Craignure
Loch na Keal
591 BEINN A' GHRÀIG
Loch Bà
766 DÙN DA GHAOITHE
Lynn of Lorne
Ardmucknish Bay
Little Colonsay
Inch Kenneth
Inchkenneth Chapel (ruin)
Staffa
Fingal's Cave
Loch na Keal, Isle of Mull
Duart Bay
Duart Point
Torosay
Dunstaffnage Castle & Chapel
Balnahard
966 BEN MORE
704 CRUACHAN DEARG
MULL
Lochdonhead
Lochdon
Ganavan Bay
Dunbeg
Gorten
Dunollie Castle
A85
Loch Don
Grass Point
McCaig's Tower
Oban (An t-Oban)
519 BEINN NA SREINE
Glen More
Strathcoil
491 CREACH BHEINN
Tiroran
Aird of Kinloch
247 CARN BAN
KERRERA
Fossil Tree
Burg
Loch Fuaran
698 BEN CREACH
Gallanachbeg
Ariogan
Gallanachmore
Loch Spelve
717 BEN BUIE
Croggan
Lerags
Kilmore
Iona Abbey & Nunnery
IONA
Rudha nan Cearc
Loch Scridain
Pennycross
Pennyghael
503 BEINN NA CROISE
Lochbuie
Rudha Seanach
Ardentallen
Baile Mòr
MacLean's Cross
Kintra
Loch Uisg
337 MAOL BAN
Fionnphort
Aridhglas
St Columba Exhibition Centre
Sound of Iona
Bunessan
Loch Assapol
376 CRUACHAN MIN
376 BEINN CHREAGACH
Carsaig
Rudha Dubh
Loch Buie
377 DRUIM FADA
FIRTH OF LORNE
Kilninver
356 AN CREACHAN
Loch Scamadale
ROSS OF MULL
Uisken
Soa Island
Erraid
Ardchiavaig
Rudha nam Braithrean
Malcolm's Point
Insh Island
Clachan
Clachan-Seil
SEIL
Easdale
Ellenabeich
Balvicar
Loch Tralaig
Rudha Ardalanish
Colonsay - Oban
Cuan
Melfort
Kilmelford
Torran Rocks
Garbh Eileach
Cullipool
Torsa
Degnish
Loch Melfort
Eilean Dubh Mòr
LUING
Arduaine
GARVELLACHS
Monastery & Beehive Cells
Eileach an Naoimh
LUNGA
Toberonochy
Shuna Sound
SHUNA
Gleann Domhain
Scarba, Lunga and the Garvellachs
Craobh Haven
Inverliever Lodge
Craigdhu
SCARBA
448 CRUACH SCARBA
Shuna Point
Kintraw
Ardfern
Ford
En Mhic Chrion
Gulf of Corryvreckan
Eilean Dubh
Camasserie Castle
Aird
Balnahard
Rudh' a' Geodha
Kilmartin
Kilmartin House
Kiloran Bay
Craignish Point
Glebe Cairn
Slockavullin
Temple Wood Stone Circles
Nether Largie Cairns
Dunchraigaig Cairn
Loch Leathan
Island Macaskin
COLONSAY
Kiloran
Glengarrisdale Bay
295 CRUACH NA SEILCHEIG
Poltalloch
Kilchattan
Glendebadel Bay
0 1 2 3 4 miles
0 1 2 3 4 5 kilometres
A B C D E F G H J K
1 2 3 4 5 6 7 8 9 10 11 12 13 14 15 16

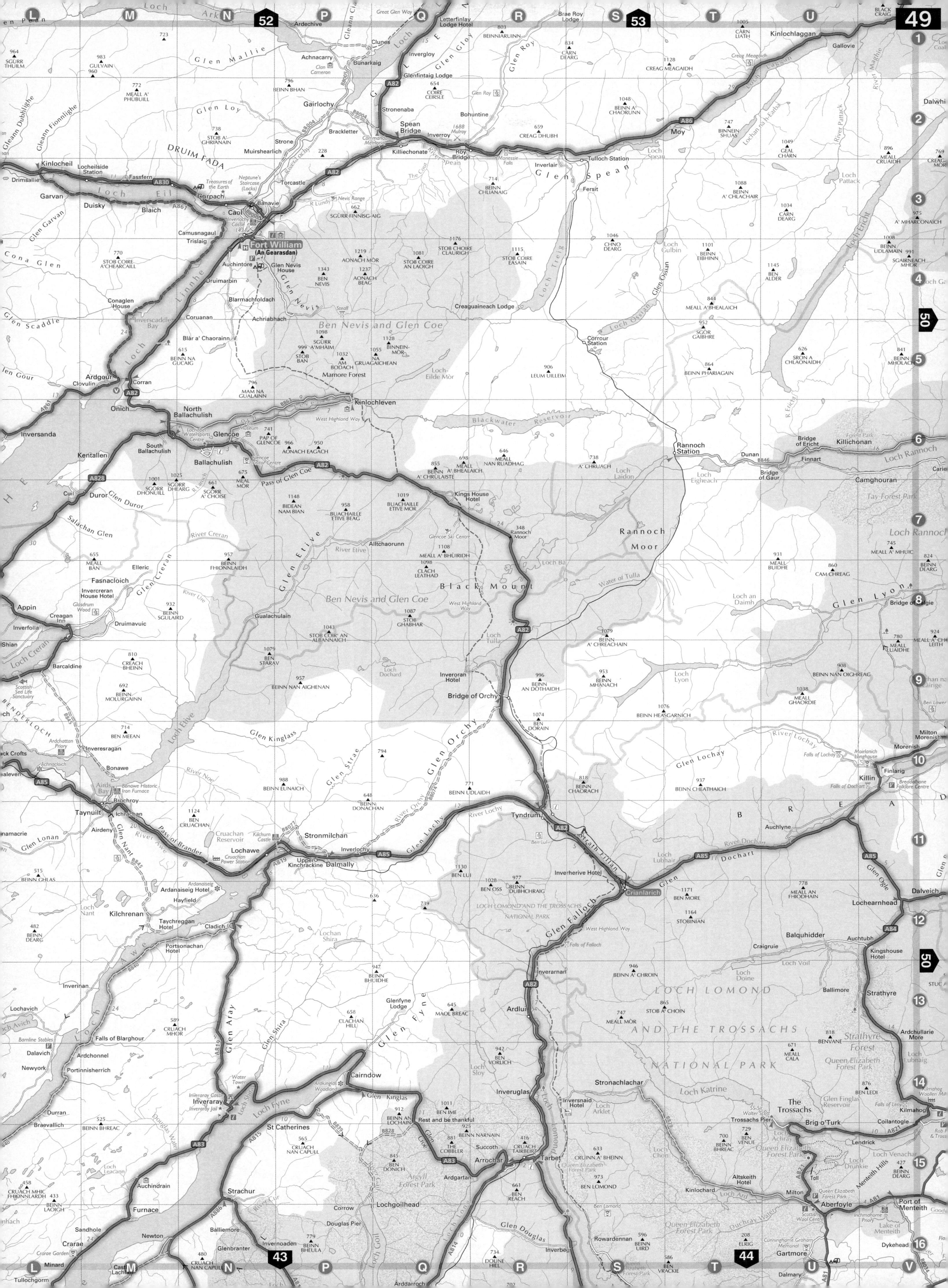

52
53
50
43
44
L
M
N
P
Q
R
S
T
U
V
1
2
3
4
5
6
7
8
9
10
11
12
13
14
15
16
Ardechive
Great Glen Way
Letterfinlay Lodge Hotel
803 BEINN IARUINN
Brae Roy Lodge
1005 CÀRN LIATH
Kinlochlaggan
BLACK CRAIG
Gallovie
723
Glen Mallie
Clunes
Achnacarry
Clan Cameron
Bunarkaig
Invergloy
Glen Gloy
Glen Roy
834 CARN DEARG
1128 CREAG MEAGAIDH
Creag Meagaidh
Loch Laggan
964 SGÙRR THUILM
983 GULVAIN
960
772 MEALL A' PHUBUILL
796 BEINN BHAN
Glenfintaig Lodge
654 COIRE CEIRSLE
Glen Roy
Gairlochy
Stronenaba
Bohuntine
1048 BEINN A' CHAORUINN
Dalwhinnie
Glen Loy
Gleann Fionnlighe
Gleann Dubhlighe
738 STOB A' GHRIANAIN
Brackletter
Spean Bridge
Commando Memorial
1688 Mulroy
Inverroy
659 CREAG DHUBH
Moy
747 BEINNEIN SHUAS
Lochan na h-Earba
River Pattack
1049 GEAL CHARN
896 MEALL CRUAIDH
769 CREAG MOR
DRUIM FADA
Strone
Muirshearlich
228
Killiechonate
Roy Bridge
Monessie Falls
Tulloch Station
Loch Spean
Kinlocheil
Locheilside Station
Fassfern
A830
Drimsallie
Neptune's Staircase (Locks)
Treasures of the Earth
Torcastle
The Cour
Inverlair
Glen Spean
Fersit
Loch Pattack
714 BEINN CHLIANAIG
1088 BEINN A' CHLACHAIR
Garvan
Duisky
Loch Eil
Corpach
Banavie
Caol
Blaich
Nevis Range
662 SGURR FINNISG-AIG
1034 CARN DEARG
975 A' MHARCONAICH
Glen Garvan
Inverlochy Castle
Camusnagaul
Trislaig
Fort William (An Gearasdan)
1176 STOB CHOIRE CLAURIGH
1115 STOB COIRE EASAIN
1046 CHNO DEARG
Loch Gulbin
1101 BEINN EIBHINN
1008 BEINN UDLAMAIN
991 SGAIRNEACH MHOR
Loch Ericht
770 STOB COIRE A' CHEARCAIL
Cona Glen
Auchintore
Glen Nevis House
1219 AONACH MÒR
1081 STOB COIRE AN LAOIGH
1343 BEN NEVIS
1237 AONACH BEAG
Loch Treig
1145 BEN ALDER
Druimarbin
Glen Nevis
Conaglen House
Blarmachfoldach
Creaguaineach Lodge
Glen Ossian
844 MEALL A' BHEALAICH
Loch Linnhe
Steall
Glen Scaddle
Inverscaddle Bay
Coruanan
Achriabhach
Ben Nevis and Glen Coe
Loch Ossian
952 SGÒR GAIBHRE
Blàr a' Chaorainn
1098 SGURR A'MHAIM
1128 BINNEIN MÒR
Corrour Station
999 STOB BAN
1032 AM BODACH
1055 NA GRUAGAICHEAN
615 BEINN NA GUCAIG
626 SRON A CHLAOINEAIDH
841 BEINN MHOLACH
Glen Gour
Ardgour
Clovulin
Corran
Mamore Forest
Loch Eilde Mòr
906 LEUM UILLEIM
864 BEINN PHARIAGAIN
796 MAM NA GUALAINN
A861
Onich
North Ballachulish
Kinlochleven
Blackwater Reservoir
R. Ericht
Inversanda
Lochaber Watersports Centre
Glencoe Museum
West Highland Way
741 PAP OF GLENCOE
966 AONACH EAGACH
950
Rannoch Station
Bridge of Ericht
Killichonan
Tay Forest Park
South Ballachulish
Glencoe
Ballachulish
Glencoe Visitor Centre
A82
698 MEALL A' BHEALAICH
646 MEALL NAN RUADHAG
738 A' CHRUACH
Dunan
B846
Finnart
Loch Rannoch
Kentallen
855 BEINN A' CHRULAISTE
Loch Laidon
Loch Eigheach
Bridge of Gaur
Camghouran
A828
1001 SGORR DHONUILL
1025 SGORR DHEARG
661 SGORR A' CHOISE
675 MEALL MOR
Pass of Glen Coe
Kings House Hotel
Cuil
Duror
Glen Duror
1148 BIDEAN NAM BIAN
958 BUACHAILLE ETIVE BEAG
1019 BUACHAILLE ETIVE MOR
Salachan Glen
River Creran
Alltchaorunn
Glencoe Ski Centre
348 Rannoch Moor
Rannoch Moor
Loch Rannoch
745 MEALL A' MHUIC
River Etive
1108 MEALL A' BHÙIRIDH
1098 CLACH LEATHAD
Loch Ba
931 MEALL BUIDHE
860 CAM CHREAG
824 BEINN DEARG
655 MEALL BAN
Elleric
Glen Creran
957 BEINN FHIONNLAIDH
Glen Etive
Black Mount
Water of Tulla
Fasnacloich
Invercreran House Hotel
River Ure
Loch an Daimh
Glen Lyon
Bridge of Balgie
Appin
Glasdrum Wood
West Highland Way
932 BEINN SGULAIRD
1087 STOB GHABHAR
Creagan Inn
Druimavuic
Gualachulain
Inverfolla
Shian
1043 STOB COIR' AN ALBANNAICH
Loch Tulla
1079 BEINN A' CHREACHAIN
780 MEALL LUAIDHE
924 MEALL A' CHR...
Loch Creran
1079 BEN STARAV
810 CREACH BHEINN
Barcaldine
Loch Dochard
Inveroran Hotel
996 BEINN AN DOTHAIDH
953 BEINN MHANACH
Loch Lyon
908 BEINN NAN OIGHREAG
Scottish Sea Life Sanctuary
692 BEINN MOLURGAINN
957 BEINN NAN AIGHENAN
Bridge of Orchy
1038 MEALL GHAORDIE
BENDERLOCH
B845
Loch Etive
1074 BEN DORAIN
1076 BEINN HEASGARNICH
Ben Lawers
714 BEN MEEAN
Glen Kinglass
Glen Orchy
River Lochay
Milton Morenish
Ardchattan Priory
Inveresragan
794
Glen Strae
Glen Lochay
Mairlonich Longhouse
Falls of Lochay
Finlarig
Achnacloich
Bonawe
River Noe
Killin
A85
988 BEINN EUNAICH
Glen Orchy
771 BEINN UDLAIDH
818 BEINN CHAORACH
937 BEINN CHEATHAICH
Breadalbane Folklore Centre
Falls of Dochart
Airds Bay
Bonawe Historic Iron Furnace
Brochroy
648 BEINN DONACHAN
River Orchy
B8074
Taynuilt
Ichrachan
1124 BEN CRUACHAN
River Lochy
Tyndrum
BREADALBANE
Airdeny
Glen Nant
Pass of Brander
Cruachan Reservoir
Kilchurn Castle
B8077
Stronmilchan
Ben Lui
Strath Fillan
Auchlyne
Glen Lonan
River Awe
Lochawe
Cruachan Power Station
Inverlochy
Glen Lochy
Loch Lubhair
A85
Dochart
River Dochart
B845
A819
Upper Kinchrackine
Dalmally
Inverherive Hotel
515 BEINN GHLAS
1130 BEN LUI
1028 BEN OSS
977 BEINN DUBHCHRAIG
Crianlarich
Glen Ogle
Glen
Ardanaiseig
Ardanaiseig Hotel
Hayfield
636
LOCH LOMOND AND THE TROSSACHS NATIONAL PARK
1171 BEN MORE
778 MEALL AN FHIODHAIN
Dalveich
Loch Nant
Kilchrenan
739
Glen Falloch
1164 STOBINIAN
Lochearnhead
482 BEINN DEARG
Taychreggan Hotel
Cladich
Lochan Shira
West Highland Way
A84
Portsonachan Hotel
Falls of Falloch
Craigruie
Balquhidder
Auchtubh
Kingshouse Hotel
B840
947 BEINN BHUIDHE
Inverarnan
946 BEINN A' CHROIN
Loch Voil
Loch Doine
Inverinan
Loch Awe
LOCH LOMOND
Ballimore
Strathyre
Glenfyne Lodge
Glen Fyne
645 MAOL BREAC
Ardlui
865 STOB A' CHOIN
Lochavich
658 CLACHAN HILL
747 MEALL MÒR
AND THE TROSSACHS
818 BENVANE
Strathyre Forest
Ardchullarie More
589 CRUACH MHOR
Glen Aray
Glen Shira
Barnline Stables
Falls of Blarghour
671 MEALL CALA
Queen Elizabeth Forest Park
Dalavich
Ardchonnel
942 BEN VORLICH
Loch Lubnaig
Newyork
Portinnisherrich
Loch Sloy
NATIONAL PARK
Cairndow
Water Tower
Ardkinglas Woodland
Stronachlachar
Loch Katrine
876 BEN LEDI
Inveraray Castle
Inveraray
Inveraray Jail
Loch Shira
Loch Fyne
Glen Kinglas
Inveruglas
Inversnaid Hotel
Loch Arklet
Falls of Leny
Kilmahog
912 BEINN AN LOCHAIN
1011 BEN IME
Rest and be thankful
The Trossachs
Glen Finglas Reservoir
Durran
B828
925 BEINN NARNAIN
B829
Sir Walter Scott
Trossachs Pier
Brig o'Turk
Coilantogle
Braevallich
525 BEINN BHREAC
St Catherines
B839
881 THE COBBLER
Succoth
416 CRUACH TAIRBEIT
700 BEINN BHREAC
729 BEN VENUE
Loch Achray
Lendrick
A821
565 CRUACH NAN CAPULL
A815
Loch Chon
Loch Venachar
A83
845 BEN DONICH
Arrochar
Tarbet
Loch Lomond
633 CRUINN A' BHEINN
Queen Elizabeth Forest Park
Loch Drunkie
Menteith Hills
427 BEINN DEARG
Loch Leacann
Argyll Forest Park
Ardgartan
A83
973 BEN LOMOND
Altskeith Hotel
Toll
Auchindrain
661 BEN REACH
458 CRUACH MHIC FHIONNLAIDH
433 BEINN LAOIGH
Strachur
River Cur
Kinlochard
Loch Ard
Milton
Queen Elizabeth Forest Park
A81
Port of Menteith
Furnace
A886
Lochgoilhead
Corrow
Ben Lomond
Aberfoyle
Scottish Wool Centre
Inchmahome Priory
Lake of Menteith
Sandhole
Newton
Douglas Pier
Glen Douglas
Loch Long
Loch Goil
Queen Elizabeth Forest Park
Duchray Water
Balliemore
Invernoaden
779 BEINN BHEULA
Cunninghame Graham Memorial
Crarae
Crarae Garden
Glenbranter
A814
734 DOUNE HILL
Inverbeg
Rowardennan
596 BEINN UIRD
208 ELRIG
Gartmore
Dykehead
480 CRUACH NAN CAPULL
Minard
Castle Lachlan
Queen Elizabeth Forest Park
586 BEN VRACKIE
Tullochgorm
Arddarroch
702
Dalmary

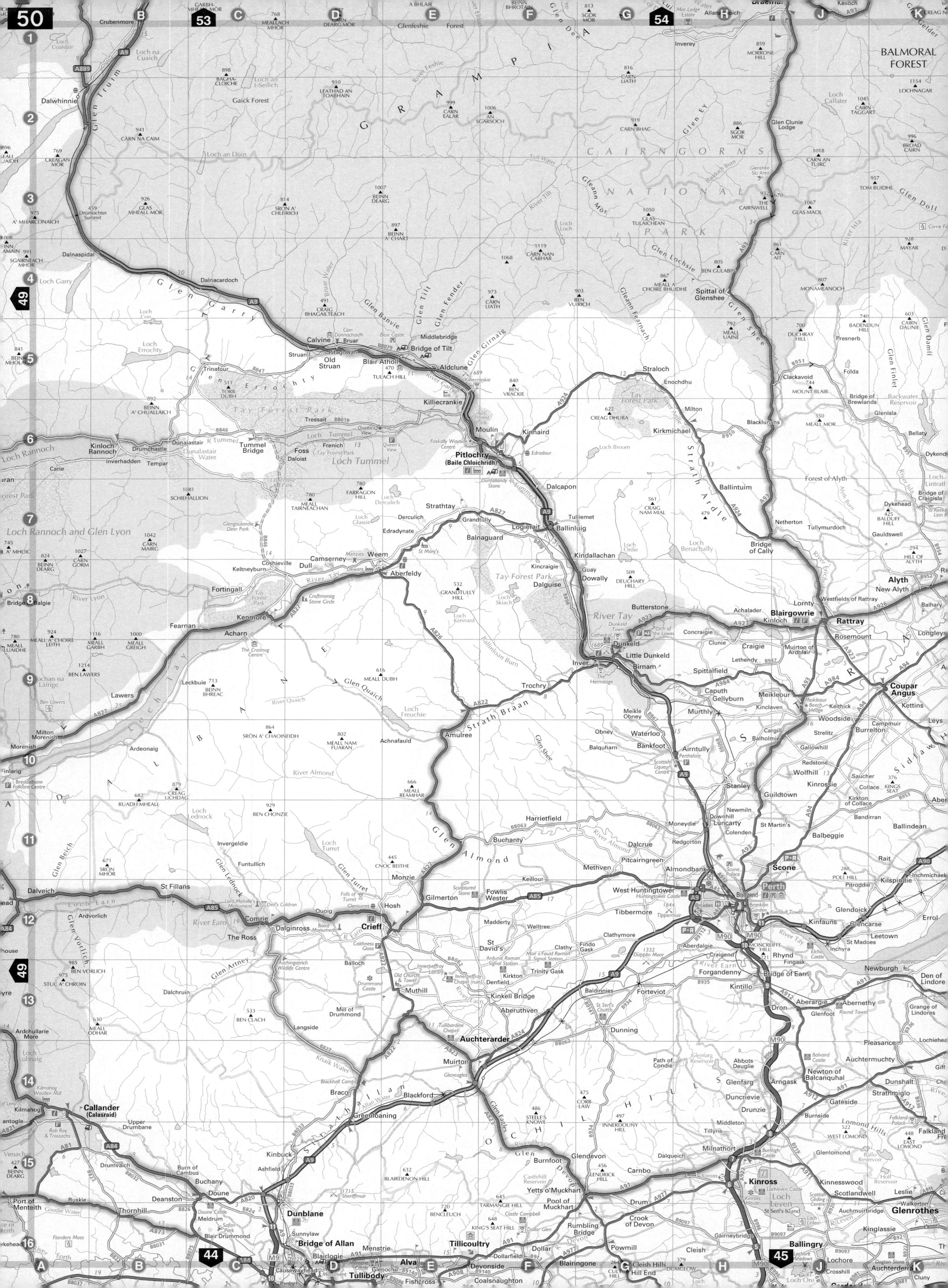
53
54
49
44
45
Crubenmore
Dalwhinnie
Glen Truim
Loch na Cuaich
Gaick Forest
Loch an t-Seilich
Loch an Dùin
G R A M P I A N
Glenfeshie
Forest
Inverey
Braemar
Mor Lodge Estate
BALMORAL FOREST
LOCHNAGAR
Loch Callater
Glen Clunie Lodge
CAIRNGORMS
NATIONAL
PARK
Glen Ey
Glen Shee
Spittal of Glenshee
Glen Lochsie
Gleann Mòr
Glen Doll
THE CAIRNWELL
GLAS MAOL
Drumochter Summit
Dalnaspidal
Loch Garry
Dalnacardoch
Glen Garry
Glen Errochty
Loch Errochty
Trinafour
Calvine
Struan
Old Struan
Pitagowan
Blair Atholl
Bridge of Tilt
Middlebridge
Glen Tilt
Glen Fender
Glen Banvie
Aldclune
Killiecrankie
Tay Forest Park
Tressait
Loch Rannoch
Kinloch Rannoch
Drumchastle
Dunalastair
Dunalastair Water
R. Tummel
Tummel Bridge
Loch Tummel
Foss
Dalcist
Frenich
Queen's View
Inverhadden
Tempar
Carie
SCHIEHALLION
Loch Rannoch and Glen Lyon
Moulin
Kinnaird
Pitlochry
(Baile Chloichridh)
Edradour
Dalcapon
Straloch
Enochdhu
Milton
Kirkmichael
Loch Broom
Strath Ardle
Ballintuim
Strathtay
Grandtully
Derculich
Edradynate
Logierait
Ballinluig
Tulliemet
Balnaguard
Kindallachan
Guay
Dowally
Dalguise
Kincraigie
Camserney
Weem
Aberfeldy
Dull
Coshieville
Keltneyburn
Fortingall
Bridge of Balgie
Kenmore
Acharn
Fearnan
Loch Tay
Lawers
BEN LAWERS
Milton Morenish
Morenish
Ardeonaig
Finlarig
Killin
Butterstone
Dunkeld
Little Dunkeld
Birnam
Inver
Trochry
Strath Braan
Amulree
Glen Quaich
Loch Freuchie
Achnafauld
River Almond
Glen Almond
Harrietfield
Buchanty
Bridge of Cally
Blairgowrie
Rattray
Kinloch
Alyth
New Alyth
Rosemount
Coupar Angus
Meikleour
Kinclaven
Caputh
Spittalfield
Murthly
Stanley
Luncarty
Redgorton
Scone
Perth
Almondbank
Methven
Pitcairngreen
Tibbermore
West Huntingtower
Crieff
Comrie
St Fillans
Dalveich
Lochearnhead
Loch Earn
Ardvorlich
Dalginross
Gilmerton
Monzie
Fowlis Wester
Madderty
Muthill
Auchterarder
Aberuthven
Kinkell Bridge
Dunning
Forteviot
Forgandenny
Bridge of Earn
Abernethy
Aberargie
Newburgh
Braco
Blackford
Greenloaning
Muirton
Gleneagles
Glen Eagles
Glen Devon
Glendevon
Yetts o'Muckhart
Pool of Muckhart
Rumbling Bridge
Crook of Devon
Kinross
Milnathort
Loch Leven
Scotlandwell
Kinnesswood
Glenrothes
Leslie
Ballingry
Lochore
Kelty
Glenfarg
Arngask
Duncrievie
Callander
(Calasraid)
Kilmahog
Doune
Deanston
Thornhill
Dunblane
Bridge of Allan
Blair Drummond
Kinbuck
Ashfield
Sheriffmuir
Menstrie
Alva
Tillicoultry
Tullibody
Dollar
Muckhart
Cleish
Kinglassie
OCHIL HILLS
SIDLAW HILLS
Inchture
Errol
St Madoes
Glencarse
Kinfauns
Balbeggie
Wolfhill
Burrelton
Woodside
Kettins
Newtyle
Longleys

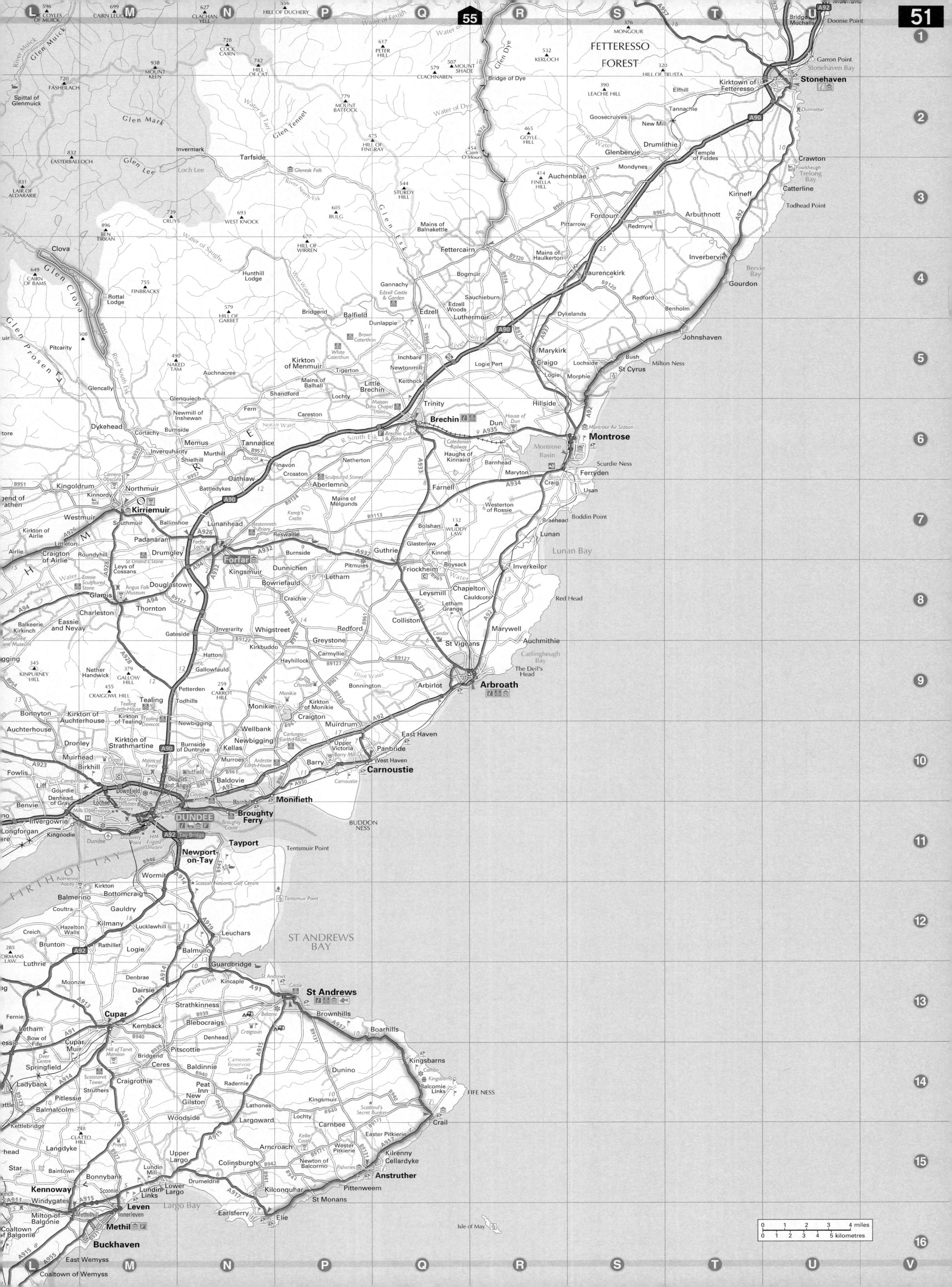
55
FETTERESSO FOREST
Stonehaven
Stonehaven Bay
Garron Point
Doonie Point
Kirktown of Fetteresso
Elfhill
Tannachie
Goosecruives
New Mill
Drumlithie
Glenbervie
Temple of Fiddes
Crawton
Mondynes
Auchenblae
Catterline
Todhead Point
Kinneff
Fordoun
Arbuthnott
Redmyre
Pittarrow
Fettercairn
Mains of Haulkerton
Inverbervie
Bervie Bay
Gourdon
Laurencekirk
Bogmuir
Sauchieburn
Redford
Benholm
Johnshaven
Edzell
Edzell Woods
Luthermuir
Dykelands
Marykirk
Craigo
Logie
Lochside
Morphie
Bush
St Cyrus
Milton Ness
Logie Pert
Hillside
Brechin
Trinity
Dun
House of Dun
Montrose
Montrose Basin
Montrose Air Station
Scurdie Ness
Ferryden
Usan
Craig
Maryton
Barnhead
Farnell
Westerton of Rossie
Boddin Point
Braehead
Lunan
Lunan Bay
Inverkeilor
Red Head
Chapelton
Cauldcots
Marywell
Auchmithie
Carlingheugh Bay
The Deil's Head
Arbroath
St Vigeans
Colliston
Letham Grange
Leysmill
Friockheim
Guthrie
Boysack
Kinnell
Glasterlaw
Bolshan
WUDDY LAW
Haughs of Kinnaird
Caledonian Railway
Arbirlot
Bonnington
East Haven
Panbride
Carnoustie
West Haven
BUDDON NESS
Muirdrum
Upper Victoria
Barry
Monifieth
Broughty Ferry
Broughty Castle
DUNDEE
Tay Bridge
Newport-on-Tay
Tayport
Tentsmuir Point
Wormit
Kirkton
Balmerino
Bottomcraig
Gauldry
Kilmany
Lucklawhill
Leuchars
ST ANDREWS BAY
Balmullo
Guardbridge
Logie
Rathillet
Brunton
Luthrie
Creich
Hazelton Walls
Coultra
Moonzie
Denbrae
Dairsie
Kincaple
St Andrews
Strathkinness
Brownhills
Boarhills
Blebocraigs
Cupar
Kemback
Denhead
Pitscottie
Ceres
Bridgend
Baldinnie
Cameron Reservoir
Kingsbarns
Dunino
Craigrothie
Peat Inn
Radernie
New Gilston
Kingsmuir
Cambo
Balcomie Links
FIFE NESS
Crail
Lathones
Largoward
Lochty
Carnbee
Scotland's Secret Bunker
Woodside
Arncroach
Wester Pitkierie
Easter Pitkierie
Kilrenny
Cellardyke
Anstruther
Pittenweem
St Monans
Kilconquhar
Colinsburgh
Newton of Balcormo
Upper Largo
Lundin Mill
Lundin Links
Lower Largo
Drumeldrie
Largo Bay
Earlsferry
Elie
Isle of May
Leven
Methil
Buckhaven
East Wemyss
Coaltown of Wemyss
Kennoway
Windygates
Milton of Balgonie
Coaltown of Balgonie
Bonnybank
Baintown
Star
Langdyke
CLATTO HILL
Kettlebridge
Balmalcolm
Pitlessie
Struthers
Ladybank
Springfield
Cupar Muir
Bow of Fife
Letham
Fernie
Forfar
Kirriemuir
Glamis
Kingsmuir
Dunnichen
Letham
Lunanhead
Padanaram
Drumgley
Douglastown
Thornton
Charleston
Eassie and Nevay
Inverarity
Whigstreet
Kirkbuddo
Greystone
Carmyllie
Redford
Hatton
Gallowfauld
Petterden
Tealing
Monikie
Craigton
Newbigging
Wellbank
Kellas
Murroes
Baldovie
Kirkton of Auchterhouse
Auchterhouse
Dronley
Muirhead
Birkhill
Fowlis
Liff
Benvie
Invergowrie
Longforgan
Kingoodie
Kirkton of Strathmartine
Brechin
Aberlemno
Finavon
Oathlaw
Tannadice
Memus
Careston
Fern
Kirkton of Menmuir
Little Brechin
Balfield
Dunlappie
Gannachy
Bridgend
Inchbare
Newtonmill
Keithock
Glen Clova
Clova
Glen Prosen
Pitcarity
Glencally
Dykehead
Cortachy
Inverquharity
Kingoldrum
Kinnordy
Northmuir
Westmuir
Southmuir
Glen Muick
Spittal of Glenmuick
Glen Mark
Glen Lee
Loch Lee
Invermark
Tarfside
Glen Esk
Glen Tennet
Water of Dye
Bridge of Dye
MOUNT BATTOCK
CLACHNABEN
KERLOCH
MONGOUR
HILL OF TRUSTA
LEACHIE HILL
GOYLE HILL
FINELLA HILL
STURDY HILL
BULG
WEST KNOCK
HILL OF WIRREN
Hunthill Lodge
Rottal Lodge
FINBRACKS
HILL OF GARBET
NAKED TAM
Auchnacree
Shandford
Glenquiech
Newmill of Inshewan
ST ANDREWS BAY
FIRTH OF TAY
0 1 2 3 4 miles
0 1 2 3 4 5 kilometres

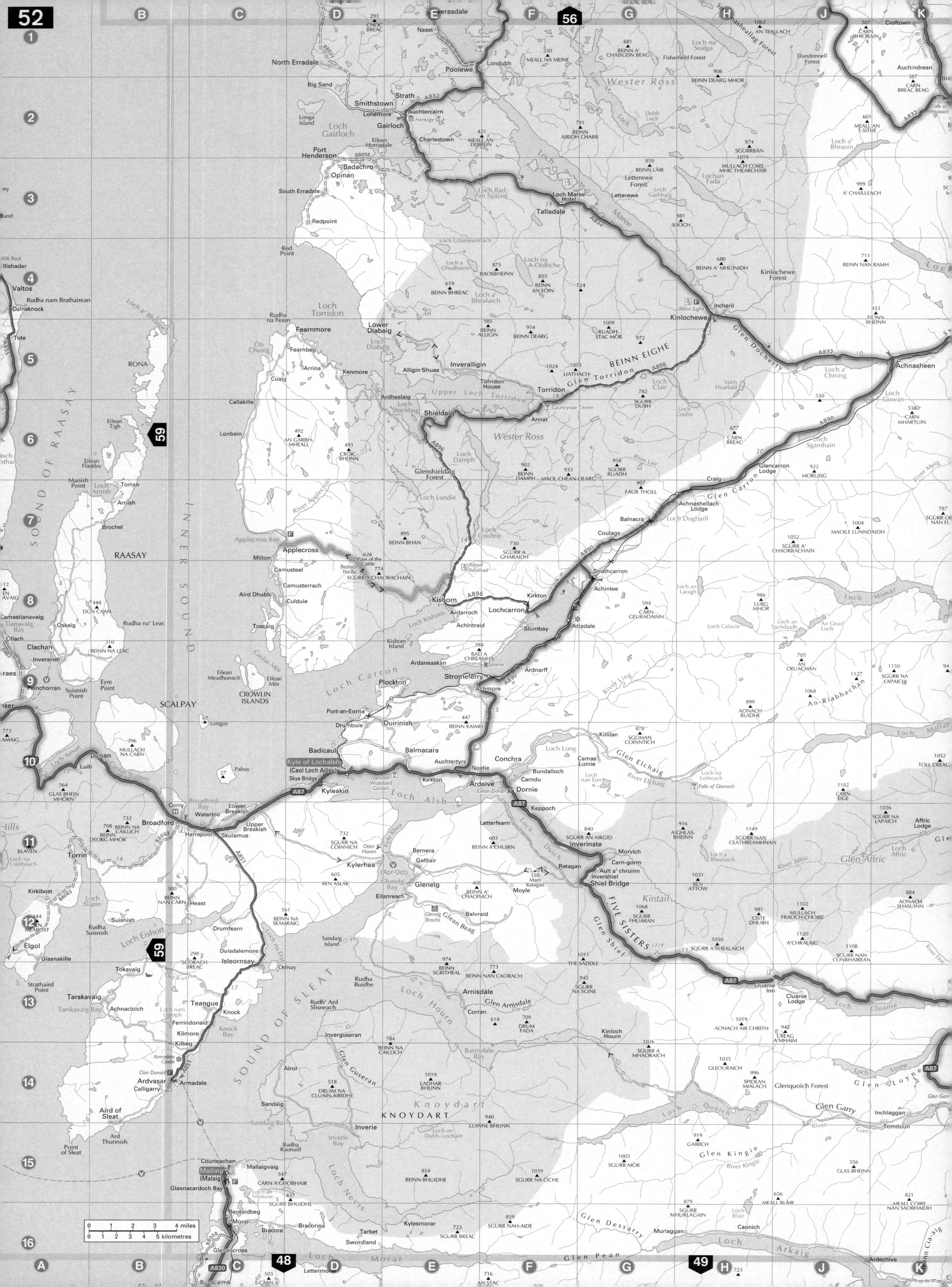
56
59
48
49
North Erradale
Poolewe
Londubh
Naast
Everasdale
Inverewe Garden
Big Sand
Strath
Smithstown
Lonemore
Auchtercairn
Heritage
Gairloch
Charlestown
Longa Island
Loch Gairloch
Eilean Horrisdale
Port Henderson
Badachro
Opinan
South Erradale
Redpoint
Red Point
Loch Torridon
Rudha na Fearn
Fearnmore
Fearnbeg
Òb Chuaig
Cuaig
Arrina
Kenmore
Lower Diabaig
Loch Diabaig
Alligin Shuas
Inveralligin
Torridon House
Upper Loch Torridon
Torridon
Annat
Countryside Centre
Glen Torridon
BEINN EIGHE
Loch Clair
Kinlochewe
Incheril
Glen Docherty
Achnasheen
Loch a' Chroisg
Loch Fhiarlaid
Loch Gowan
Loch Sgamhain
Wester Ross
Loch Maree
Loch Maree Hotel
Talladale
Letterewe
Letterewe Forest
Loch Garbhaig
Slioch
Fisherfield Forest
Loch na Sealga
Strathnasheallag Forest
Dundonnell Forest
Croftown
Auchindrean
Falls of Measach
Loch a' Bhraoin
Kinlochewe Forest
Loch Bad an Sgalaig
Loch Ghaineamhach
Loch a' Ghobhainn
Loch na h-Oidhche
Loch a' Bhealaich
Callakille
Lonbain
Ardheslaig
Loch Shieldaig
Shieldaig
Loch Damph
Glenshieldaig Forest
Loch Lundie
Loch Coultrie
Loch Coulin
Applecross Bay
Applecross
Milton
Camusteel
Camusterrach
Culduie
Aird Dhubh
Toscaig
Bealach Na Bà
Pass of the Cattle
Rassal Ashwood
Kishorn
Ardarroch
Achintraid
Loch Kishorn
Kishorn Island
Lochcarron
Kirkton
Slumbay
Strathcarron
Achintee
Attadale
Glen Carron
Craig
Glencarron Lodge
Achnashellach Lodge
Balnacra
Loch Dughaill
Coulags
Loch an Laoigh
Loch Monar
Loch Calavie
An Gead Loch
Ardaneaskan
Strome
Stromeferry
Ardnarff
Achmore
Plockton
Loch Carron
Port-an-Eorna
Drumbuie
Duirinish
Badicaul
Balmacara
Auchtertyre
Kyle of Lochalsh (Caol Loch Aillse)
Skye Bridge
Kyleakin
Lochalsh Woodland Garden
Kirkton
Nostie
Ardelve
Eilean Donan
Loch Alsh
Conchra
Dornie
Carndu
Bundalloch
Camas Luinie
Loch Long
Glen Elchaig
River Elchaig
Loch na Leitreach
Falls of Glomach
Loch Mullardoch
An Riabhachan
Keppoch
Letterfearn
Loch Duich
Inverinate
Morvich
Carn-gorm
Ratagan
Ault a' chruinn
Invershiel
Shiel Bridge
Kintail
FIVE SISTERS
Glen Shiel
Cluanie Inn
Cluanie Lodge
Loch Cluanie
Glen Affric
River Affric
Loch Affric
Affric Lodge
Bernera
Galltair
Glenelg
Glenelg Bay
Eilanreach
Glenelg Brochs
Glean Beag
Balvraid
Moyle
Mam Ratagan
Kylerhea
Kyle Rhea
Otter Haven
Sandaig Island
Rudha Buidhe
Rudh' Ard Slisneach
Loch Hourn
Arnisdale
Corran
Glen Arnisdale
Kinloch Hourn
Barrisdale Bay
Inverguseran
Glen Guseran
Airor
Sandaig
Sandaig Bay
Knoydart
KNOYDART
Inverie
Inverie Bay
Rudha Raonuill
Loch Nevis
Loch Quoich
Glen Garry
Glenquoich Forest
Inchlaggan
Tomdoun
Glen Kingie
River Kingie
Loch Loyne
Glen Loyne
Glen Dessarry
Murlaggan
Loch Arkaig
Caonich
Ardechive
Glen Pean
Loch Morar
Lettermorar
Kylesmorar
Tarbet
Swordland
Bracorina
Bracora
Morar
Beoraidbeg
Glenancross
Bunacaimb
Mallaigvaig
Mallaig
Courteachan
Glasnacardoch Bay
Loch an Nostaire
SOUND OF SLEAT
Ornsay
Isleornsay
Duisdalemore
Drumfearn
Loch na Dal
Loch Eishort
Teangue
Knock
Knock Bay
Ferrindonald
Kilmore
Kilbeg
Armadale Castle
Clan Donald
Ardvasar
Armadale
Calligarry
Aird of Sleat
Ard Thurinish
Point of Sleat
Tarskavaig
Tarskavaig Bay
Achnacloich
Tokavaig
Ord River
Strathaird Point
Elgol
Glasnakille
Suisnish
Rudha Suisnish
Loch Slapin
Kirkibost
Torrin
Heast
Broadford
Broadford Bay
Corry
Waterloo
Lower Breakish
Upper Breakish
Skulamus
Harrapool
Luib
Dunan
Loch Ainort
Caolas Scalpay
SCALPAY
Longay
Pabay
CROWLIN ISLANDS
Eilean Mòr
Eilean Meadhonach
Caolas Mòr
INNER SOUND
RAASAY
SOUND OF RAASAY
RONA
Eilean Tigh
Eilean Fladday
Manish Point
Torran
Loch Arnish
Arnish
Brochel
Oskaig
Rudha na' Leac
Clachan
Inverarish
Eyre Point
Suisnish Point
Peinchorran
Camastianavaig
Tianavaig Bay
Ollach
Kilt Rock
Valtos
Rudha nam Brathairean
Culnaknock
Tote
Loch a' Bhraige
A832
A896
A890
A87
A851
A855
B8021
B8056
B8083
B8008
A830
0 1 2 3 4 miles
0 1 2 3 4 5 kilometres

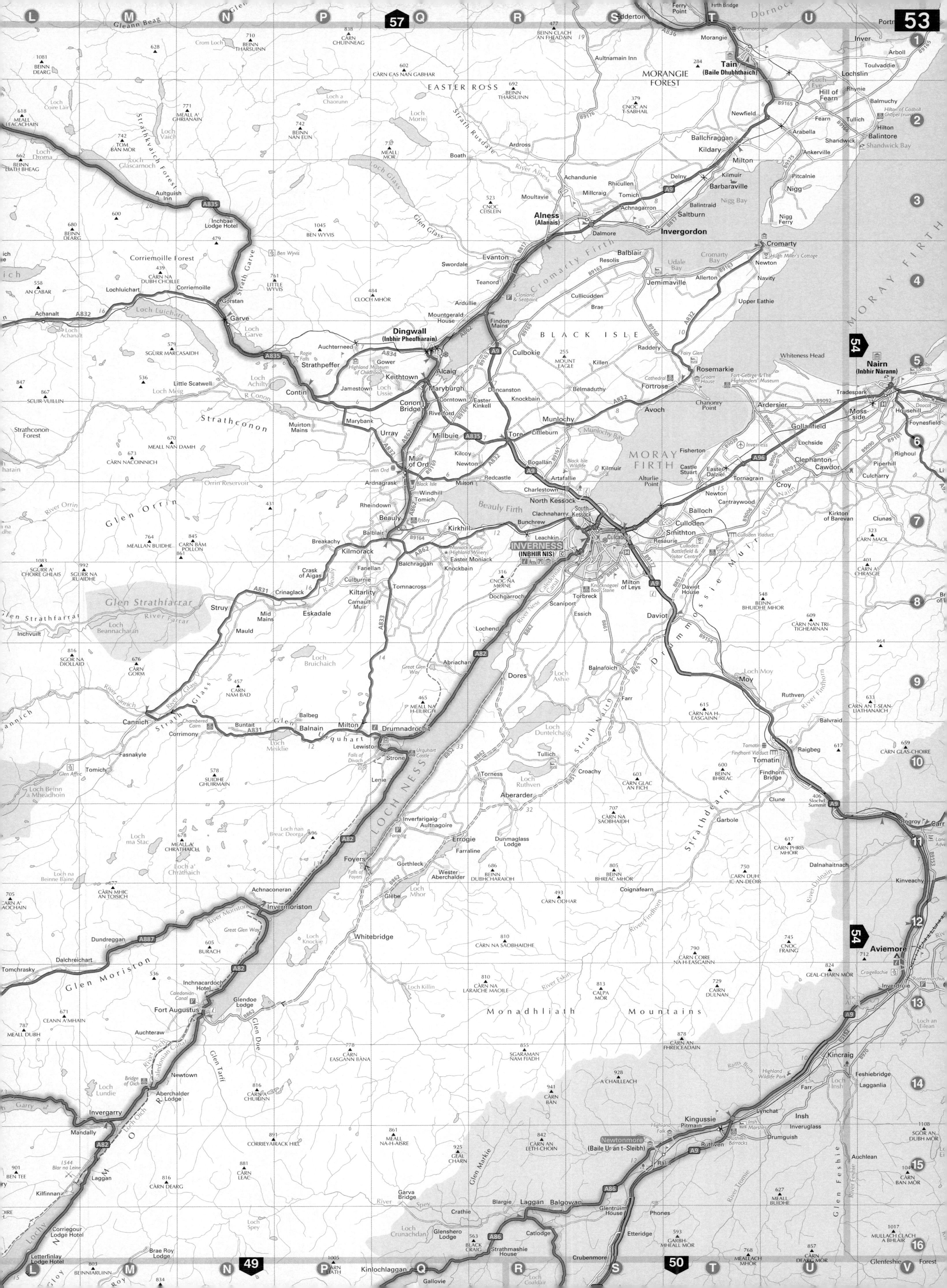

57
49
50
54
Tain (Baile Dhubhthaich)
Morangie
Glenmorangie
MORANGIE FOREST
EASTER ROSS
Inver
Arboll
Toulvaddie
Lochslin
Hill of Fearn
Rhynie
Balmuchy
Fearn
Tullich
Hilton
Arabella
Balintore
Shandwick
Shandwick Bay
Ankerville
Newfield
Ballchraggan
Kildary
Milton
Pitcalnie
Nigg
Nigg Bay
Nigg Ferry
Kilmuir
Barbaraville
Delny
Balintraid
Saltburn
Invergordon
Achnagarron
Tomich
Rhicullen
Millcraig
Achandunie
Ardross
Boath
Alness (Alanais)
Dalmore
Aultnamain Inn
Strath Rusdale
River Alness
Glen Glass
Loch Glass
Loch Morie
Loch a Chaorunn
CÀRN CAS NAN GABHAR
BEINN THARSUINN
CNOC AN T-SABHAIL
CNOC CEISLEIN
MEALL MÓR
BEINN NAN EUN
BEN WYVIS
Ben Wyvis
LITTLE WYVIS
CLOCH MHÒR
CÀRN CHUINNEAG
BEINN CLACH AN FHEADAIN
Crom Loch
Gleann Beag
BEINN DEARG
MEALL LEACACHAIN
Loch Coire Lair
Strathvaich Forest
MEALL A' GHRIANAIN
Loch Vaich
TOM BAN MÒR
Loch Droma
BEINN LIATH BHEAG
Loch Glascarnoch
Aultguish Inn
A835
Inchbae Lodge Hotel
Corriemoille Forest
CÀRN NA DUBH CHOILLE
Corriemoille
Strath Garve
Lochluichart
AN CABAR
Gorstan
Garve
Loch Luichart
Achanalt
A832
Loch Achanalt
Loch Garve
SGÙRR MARCASAIDH
Cromarty Firth
Cromarty
Hugh Miller's Cottage
Cromarty Bay
Udale Bay
Balblair
Resolis
Newton
Navity
Jemimaville
Allerton
Cullicudden
Brae
Upper Eathie
Evanton
Swordale
Teanord
Ardullie
Clanland & Seaport
Mountgerald House
Findon Mains
BLACK ISLE
Culbokie
MOUNT EAGLE
Killen
Raddery
Fairy Glen
Rosemarkie
Fort George & The Highlanders' Museum
Fortrose
Cathedral
Chanonry Point
Whitehead Head
Nairn (Inbhir Narann)
Tradespark
Ardersier
Moss-side
Househill
Fouynesfield
Gollanfield
Lochside
Clephanton
Cawdor
Piperhill
Righoul
Culcharry
Dingwall (Inbhir Pheofharain)
Auchterneed
Strathpeffer
Rogie Falls
Gower
Highland Museum of Childhood
A834
Keithtown
Alcaig
Maryburgh
Jamestown
Loch Ussie
Contin
Conon Bridge
Corntown
Duncanston
Easter Kinkell
Knockbain
Belmaduthy
Avoch
Munlochy
Munlochy Bay
Tore
Littleburn
Riverford
Marybank
Urray
Muirton Mains
Millbuie
A835
Kilcoy
Newton
Muir of Ord
Glen Ord
Black Isle
Bogallan
Artafallie
Kilmuir
Redcastle
Windhill
Tomich
Milton
Ardnagrask
Rheindown
Beauly
Priory
Beauly Firth
North Kessock
Charlestown
Clachnaharry
South Kessock
Bunchrew
Kirkhill
Balblair
MORAY FIRTH
Fisherton
Castle Stuart
Easter Dalziel
Alturlie Point
Tornagrain
A96
Croy
Newton
Cantraywood
Balloch
Culloden
Smithton
Culcabock
Resaurie
Culloden Battlefield & Visitor Centre
Clava Cairns
Culloden Viaduct
Kirkton of Barevan
Clunas
CÀRN MAOL
CÀRN A' CHRASGIE
INVERNESS (INBHIR NIS)
Leachkin
Moniack Castle (Highland Winery)
Easter Moniack
Knockbain
Balchraggan
Breakachy
Kilmorack
Crask of Aigas
Fanellan
Culburnie
Kiltarlity
Tomnacross
Camault Muir
Dochgarroch
CNOC NA MÒINE
Caledonian Canal
Knocknagael Boar Stone
Torbreck
Milton of Leys
Scaniport
Essich
Daviot
Daviot House
Drummossie Muir
BEINN BHUIDHE MHÒR
CÀRN NAN TRI-TIGHEARNAN
Strathconon
Strathconon Forest
SCUIR VUILLIN
Little Scatwell
Loch Meig
Loch Achilty
River Conon
MEALL NAN DAMH
CÀRN NA CORNICH
Orrin Reservoir
River Orrin
Glen Orrin
MEALLAN BUIDHE
CÀRN BAN POLLON
SGÙRR A' CHOIRE GHLAIS
SGÙRR NA RUAIDHE
Glen Strathfarrar
River Farrar
Strathfarrar
Loch Beannacharan
Inchvuilt
A831
Crinaglack
Struy
Mid Mains
Eskadale
Mauld
A833
SGOR NA DIOLLAID
CÀRN GORM
CÀRN NAM BAD
Loch Bruichaich
Lochend
Abriachan
A82
Great Glen Way
MEALL NA H-EILRIGH
Dores
Loch Ashie
Balnafoich
Farr
Loch Moy
Moy
Ruthven
River Findhorn
CÀRN AN T-SEAN-LIATHANAICH
Balvraid
CÀRN NA H-EASGAINN
Strath Nairn
Loch Duntelchaig
Tullich
Croachy
CÀRN GLAC AN FICH
BEINN BHREAC
Tomatin
Findhorn Viaduct
Raigbeg
Findhorn Bridge
Clune
Slochd Summit
CÀRN GLAS-CHOIRE
A9
Bogroy
River Glass
Cannich
Strath Glass
Chambered Cairn
Buntait
Glen Urquhart
Balbeg
Balnain
Milton
Drumnadrochit
Corrimony
Loch Meiklie
Lewiston
Urquhart Castle
Strone
Falls of Divach
Fasnakyle
Tomich
Glen Affric
Loch Beinn a Mheadhoin
SUIDHE GHUIRMAIN
Lenie
LOCH NESS
Torness
Loch Ruthven
Aberarder
Inverfarigaig
Aultnagoire
Errogie
Dunmaglass Lodge
Farraline
Loch nan Breac Dearga
Loch ma Stac
MEALL A' CHRATHAICH
Loch a' Chràthaich
Foyers
Falls of Foyers
Gorthleck
Wester Aberchalder
Loch Mhor
Glebe
BEINN DUBHCHARAIDH
BEINN BHREAC MHÒR
CÀRN ODHAR
Coignafearn
Strathdearn
Garbole
CÀRN NA SAOBHAIDHE
CÀRN PHRIS MHÒIR
Dalnahaitnach
River Dulnain
Kinveachy
CÀRN DUH IC-AN-DEÒIR
Loch na Beinne Baine
CÀRN MHIC AN TOISICH
CÀRN A' CHAOCHAIN
Achnaconeran
Invermoriston
River Moriston
Great Glen Way
Loch Knockie
Whitebridge
Dundreggan
A887
Dalchreichart
Glen Moriston
Tomchrasky
BURACH
Inchnacardoch Hotel
Fort Augustus
Caledonian Canal
Glendoe Lodge
Glen Doe
B862
CEANN A' MHAIM
MEALL DUBH
Auchteraw
CÀRN NA SAOBHAIDHE
CÀRN NA LARAICHE MAOILE
Loch Killin
River Eskin
CALPA MÒR
CAIRN DULNAN
CNOC FRAING
CÀRN COIRE NA H-EASGAINN
GEAL-CHÀRN MÒR
Craigellachie
Aviemore
Rothiemurchus
Inverdruie
Monadhliath Mountains
CÀRN EASGANN BANA
SGARAMAN NAM FIADH
CÀRN AN FHREICEADAIN
Kincraig
Feshiebridge
Lagganlia
Highland Wildlife Park
Loch Insh
Farr
River Oich
Bridge of Oich
Newtown
Glen Tarff
Aberchalder Lodge
Loch Oich
Loch Lundie
Invergarry
Garry
Mandally
CÀRN A' CHUILINN
A' CHAILLEACH
CÀRN BÀN
Kingussie
Pitmain
Lynchat
Insh
Inverugiass
Insh Marshes
Ruthven Barracks
Drumguish
Ruthven
Newtonmore (Baile Ur an t-Sleibh)
Highland Folk
CÀRN AN LETH-CHOIN
CORRIEYAIRACK HILL
MEALL NA-H-AISRE
GEAL CHARN
Glen Markie
Ralia
A86
River Tromie
BEN-TEE
Blar na Leine
Laggan
CÀRN DEARG
CÀRN LEAC
Kilfinnan
Garva Bridge
River Spey
Crathie
Blargie
Laggan
Balgowan
Glentruim House
Phones
MEALL BUIDHE
Glen Feshie
River Feshie
Auchlean
SGÒR AN DUBH MÒR
CÀRN BAN MÒR
Corriegour Lodge Hotel
Loch Lochy
Loch Spey
Loch Crunachdan
Glenshero Lodge
BLACK CRAIG
Catlodge
Strathmashie House
Etteridge
GARBH-MHEALL MÒR
MULLACH CLACH A BHLAIR
Letterfinlay Lodge Hotel
BEINNARUINN
Brae Roy Lodge
CÀRN DEARG MÒR
MEALL CHUAICH MÒR
Crubenmore
Kinlochlaggan
Gallovie
Loch Coaldair
Glenfeshie
Forest

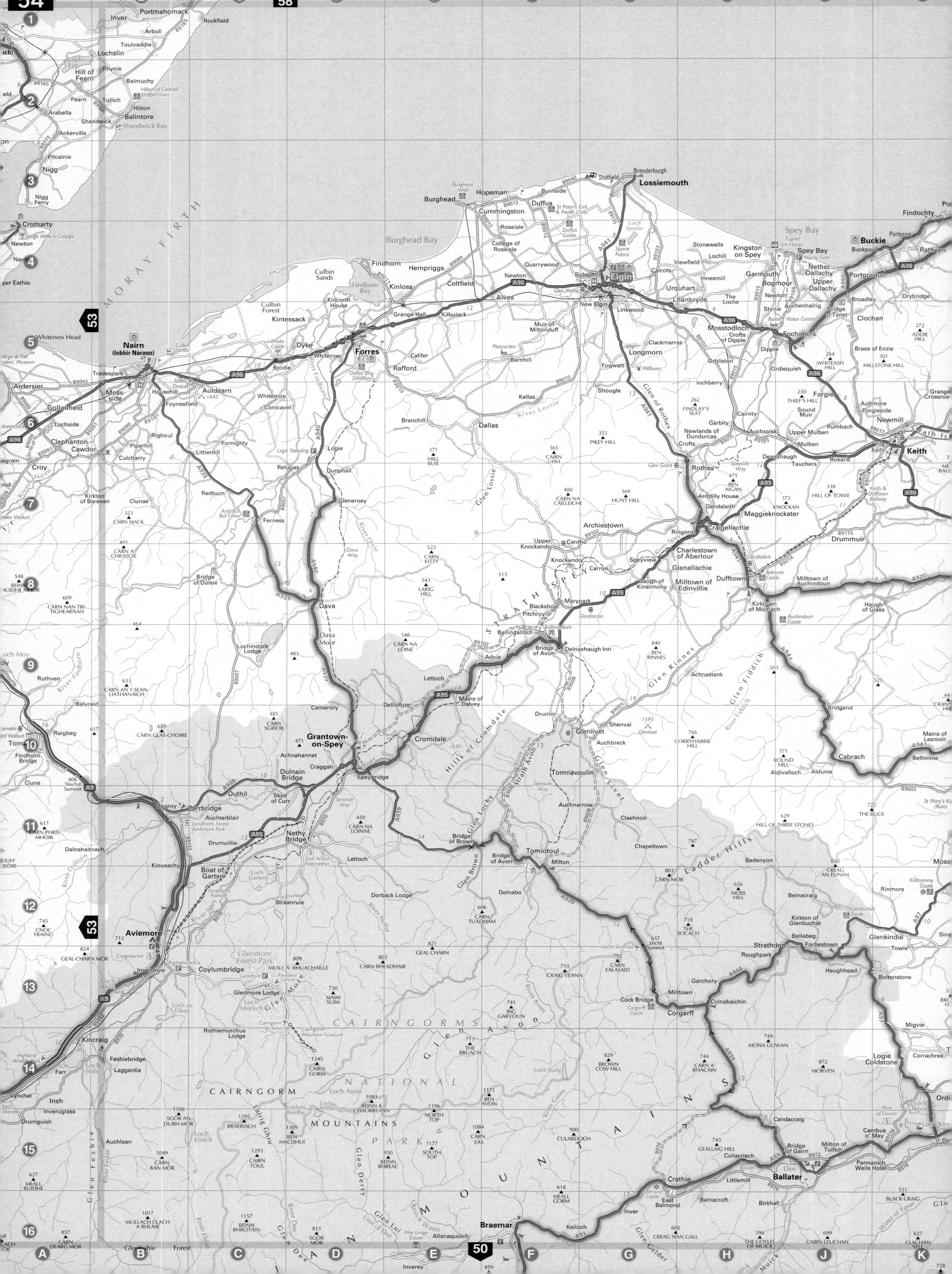
58
53
50
A
B
C
D
E
F
G
H
J
K
Portmahomack
Rockfield
Inver
Arboll
Toulvaddie
Lochslin
Rhynie
Hill of Fearn
Balmuchy
Hilton of Cadboll Chapel (ruin)
Fearn
Tullich
Hilton
Arabella
Balintore
Shandwick
Shandwick Bay
Ankerville
Pitcalnie
Nigg
Nigg Ferry
Cromarty
Hugh Miller's Cottage
Newton
Navity
MORAY FIRTH
Whiteness Head
Nairn
(Inbhir Nàrann)
Ardersier
Tradespark
Moss-side
Househill
Auldearn
Gollanfield
Lochside
Clephanton
Cawdor
Croy
Kirkton of Barevan
Culcharry
Piperhill
Righoul
Littlemill
Fornighty
Redburn
Clunas
Ferness
Ardclach Bell Tower
323 CARN MAOL
401 CARN A' CHRASGIE
Bridge of Dulsie
548 BEINN BHUIDHE MHOR
609 CARN NAN TRI-TIGHEARNAN
464
Lochindorb
Lochindorb Lodge
Loch Moy
Ruthven
River Findhorn
Balvraid
633 CARN AN T-SEAN-LIATHANAICH
659 CARN GLAS-CHOIRE
Raigbeg
Tomatin
Findhorn Bridge
Clune
406 Slochd Summit
617 CARN PHRIS MHOIR
Dalnahaitnach
Kinveachy
River Dulnain
745 CNOC FRAING
Aviemore
824 GEAL-CHARN MOR
712
Burghead
Burghead Bay
Hopeman
Cummingston
Duffus
Roseisle
College of Roseisle
Findhorn
Culbin Sands
Culbin Forest
Kintessack
Kincorth House
Findhorn Bay
Kinloss
Hempriggs
Coltfield
Newton
Alves
Kilbuiack
Grange Hall
Sueno's Stone
Dyke
Brodie Castle
Brodie
Whiterow
Forres
Califer
Rafford
Dallas Dhu Distillery
Whitemire
Conicavel
Boath Doocot
Logie Steading
Logie
Dunphail
Relugas
Glenerney
River Divie
Dava Way
Dava
Dava Moor
483
Branchill
371 MILL BUIE
Dallas
Kellas
Pluscarden
Barnhill
Muir of Miltonduff
Quarrywood
Glen Moray
Stotfield
Branderburgh
Lossiemouth
Burnside
St Peter's Kirk & Parish Cross
Duffus Castle
Loch Spynie
Spynie Palace
Bishopmill
Elgin
New Elgin
Linkwood
Calcots
Urquhart
Lhanbryde
Innesmill
Viewfield
Stonewells
Lochill
Kingston on Spey
Spey Bay
Tugnet Ice House
Garmouth
Bogmoor
Nether Dallachy
Upper Dallachy
Newton
Auchenhalrig
Stynie
Baxters Visitor Centre
Fochabers
The Lochs
Mosstodloch
Crofts of Dipple
Dipple
Clackmarras
Longmorn
Fogwatt
Millbuies
Orbliston
Inchberry
Shougle
Glen of Rothes
Ordiequish
262 FINDLAY'S SEAT
Garbity
Newlands of Dundurcas
Crofts
Cairnty
Auchroisk
Glen Grant
Rothes
Speyside Way
471 BEN AIGAN
Arndilly House
Dandaleith
Craigellachie
Maggieknockater
Ringorm
355 PIKEY HILL
365 CARN LUSH
400 CARN NA CAILLEICHE
369 HUNT HILL
Glen Lossie
River Lossie
Archiestown
Cardhu
Upper Knockando
Knockando
Carron
Charlestown of Aberlour
Speyview
Glenallachie
Daugh of Kinermony
Milltown of Edinvillie
Marypark
Blacksboat
Pitchroy
Glenfarclas
STRATH SPEY
Ballindalloch
Bridge of Avon
Delnashaugh Inn
Advie
515
522 CARN KITTY
543 LARIG HILL
548 CARN NA LOINE
Lettoch
Mains of Dalvey
Dellefure
Camerory
485 CARN SGRIOB
471
Grantown-on-Spey
Achnahannet
Cromdale
Hills of Cromdale
Craggan
Dulnain Bridge
Speybridge
Duthil
Skye of Curr
Carrbridge
Auchterblair
Landmark Forest Adventure Park
Drumuillie
Nethy Bridge
Dell Wood (Abernethy)
Lettoch
459 CARN NA LOINNE
Boat of Garten
Loch Garten
Strathspey Railway
Dorback Lodge
Straanruie
River Nethy
Bridge of Brown
Glen Brown
Bridge of Avon
Tomintoul
Milton
Delnabo
606 CARN TUADHAM
Drumin
Glenlivet
Shenval
1595 Glenlivet
Auchbreck
Tomnavoulin
Glen Livet
Strath Avon
River Avon
Glen Lochy
Auchnarrow
Clashnoir
840 BEN RINNES
Glen Rinnes
Achnastank
766 CORRYHABBIE HILL
Glen Fiddich
River Fiddich
Dufftown
Glenfiddich
Balvenie Castle
Kirktown of Mortlach
Auchindoun Castle
Milltown of Auchindoun
Haugh of Glass
Findochty
Portessie
Buckie
Buckpool
Rathven
Portgordon
Broadley
Drybridge
Bridge of Tynet
Clochan
272 ADDIE HILL
Braes of Enzie
301 MILLSTONE HILL
264 WHITEASH HILL
Forgie
250 THIEF'S HILL
Sound Muir
Aultmore
Forgieside
Newmill
Rumbach
Upper Mulben
Mulben
Deanshaugh
Tauchers
Rosarie
Keith
Strathisla
Keith & Dufftown Railway
338 HILL OF TOWIE
372 KNOCKAN
Drummuir
Grange Crossroads
503
525
Bridgend
Mains of Lesmoir
Cabrach
Belhinnie
571 ROUND HILL
Aldivalloch
Aldunie
722 THE BUCK
St Mary's Kirk (Ruin)
629 HILL OF THREE STONES
Chapeltown
787
Ladder Hills
Badenyon
803 CARN MOR
656 MOSS HILL
632 CREAG AN EUNAN
Kildrummy Castle
Rinmore
Belnacraig
Glenbuchat Castle
Kirkton of Glenbuchat
718 THE SOCACH
Bellabeg
Forbestown
Strathdon
Roughpark
Glenkindie
Towie
Heughhead
Boltenstone
Lecht Ski Area
637 Lecht Summit
792 CARN EALASAID
710 CRAIG VEANN
Garchory
Milltown
Cock Bridge
Corgarff Castle
Corgarff
Colnabaichin
Migvie
749 MONA GOWAN
744 CARN A' BHACAIN
872 MORVEN
Logie Coldstone
Corrachree
Muir of Dinnet
Loch Kinord
Cambus o' May
Candacraig
743 GEALLAIG HILL
Bridge of Gairn
Milton of Tullich
Coilacriech
Pannanich Wells Hotel
Ballater
Littlemill
River Dee
Crathie
Balmoral Castle
East Balmoral
Balnacroft
Birkhall
531 BLACK CRAIG
Water of Tanar
596 THE COYLES OF MUICK
699 CAIRN LEUCHAN
627 CLACHAN YELL
600 CREAG NAN GALL
Glen Gelder
Inver
Keiloch
Braemar
Glen Muick
900 CULARDOCH
618 MEALL GORM
Glen Gairn
Rothiemurchus
Coylumbridge
Inverdruie
Craigellachie
Glenmore Forest Park
809 MEALL A' BHUACHAILLE
Reindeer Centre
Glenmore Lodge
Glen More
Loch Morlich
730 MAIM SUIM
Loch an Eilein
Loch Alvie
Rothiemurchus Lodge
Cairngorm Ski Area
Cairngorm Mountain Funicular
1245 CAIRN GORM
821 GEAL CHARN
803 CARN BHEADHAIR
741 BIG GARVOUN
River Avon
CAIRNGORMS
Glen Avon
713 THE BRUACH
Loch Builg
829 BROWN COW HILL
Kincraig
Highland Wildlife Park
Feshiebridge
Loch Insh
Lagganlia
Farr
Lynchat
Insh
Insh Marshes
Inverglass
Drumguish
Auchlean
CAIRNGORM
NATIONAL
MOUNTAINS
PARK
Loch Avon
1083 BEINN A' CHAORRUINN
Loch Etchachan
Lochan Buidhe
1108 SGOR AN DUBH MOR
1295 BRAERIACH
Lairig Ghru
1309 BEN MACDHUI
1196 NORTH TOP
1171 BEN AVON
1084 CARN EAS
1177 SOUTH TOP
930 BEINN BHREAC
Glen Derry
Loch Einich
1049 CARN BAN MOR
1293 CAIRN TOUL
627 MEALL BUIDHE
Glen Feshie
River Feshie
1017 MULLACH CLACH A' BHLAIR
1157 BEINN BHROTAIN
River Eidart
Glen Dee
River Dee
813 SGOR MOR
Glen Lui
Linn of Dee
Quoich Water
Mar Lodge Estate
Allanaquoich
857 CARN DEARG MOR
Glenfeshie
Forest
Inverey
859
GRAMPIAN MOUNTAINS
A9
A95
A96
A939
A940
A941
A920
A97
A93
A944
B9006
B9007
B9008
B9009
B9010
B9012
B9013
B9014
B9015
B9016
B9017
B9040
B9089
B9090
B9091
B9092
B9101
B9102
B9103
B9104
B9115
B9119
B9135
B9136
B9152
B9153
B9163
B9165
B9166
B9175
B970
B972
B976
B9002
728

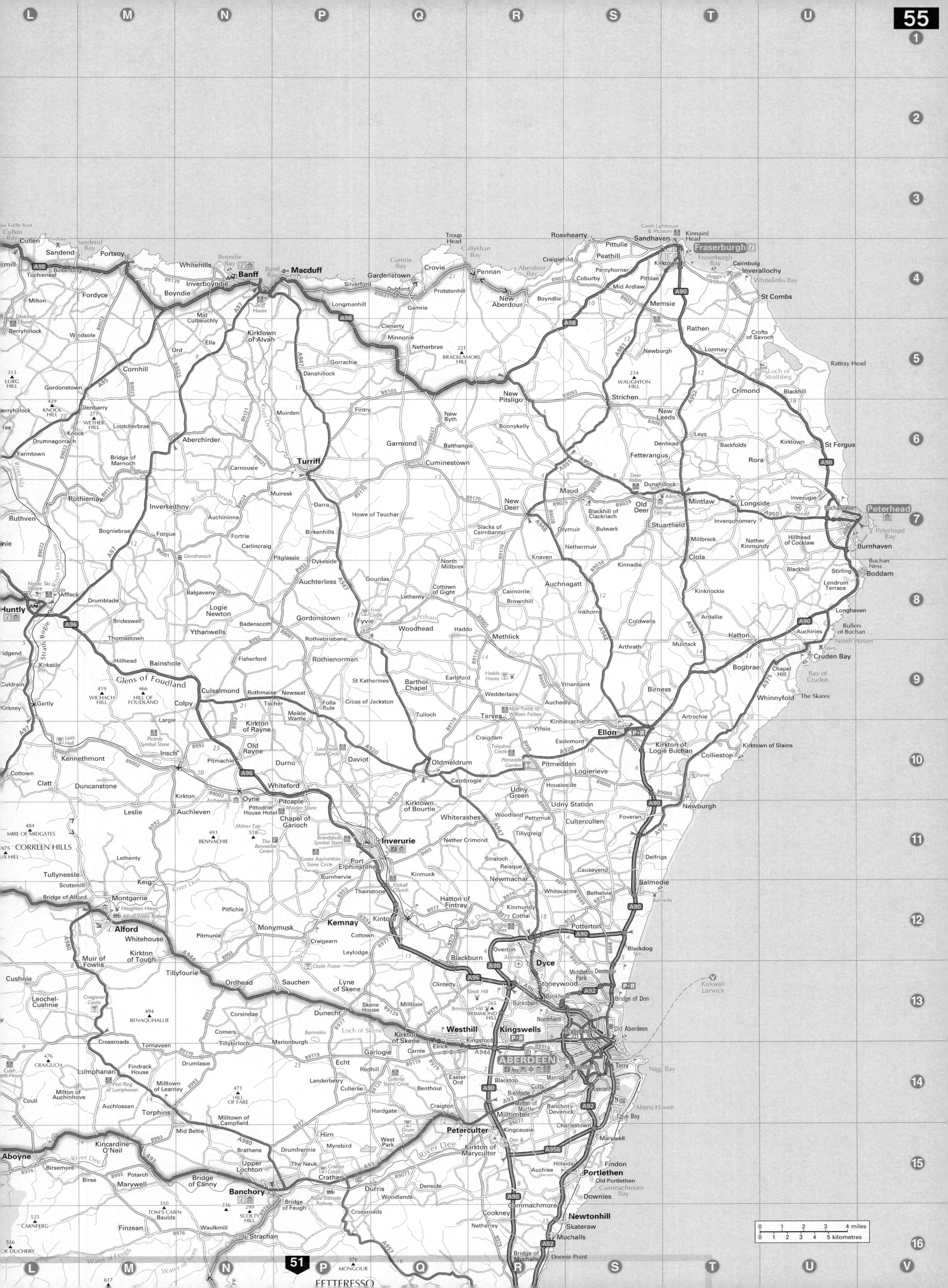
Cullen
Sandend
Portsoy
Whitehills
Banff
Macduff
Gardenstown
Crovie
Pennan
Rosehearty
Pittulie
Sandhaven
Kinnaird Head
Fraserburgh
Inverallochy
St Combs
Memsie
Rathen
New Aberdour
Boyndie
Fordyce
Kirktown of Alvah
Cornhill
Aberchirder
Turriff
Cuminestown
New Pitsligo
Strichen
New Leeds
Crimond
Rattray Head
St Fergus
Peterhead
Mintlaw
Longside
Old Deer
Maud
New Deer
Fetterangus
Stuartfield
Burnhaven
Boddam
Longhaven
Cruden Bay
Hatton
Whinnyfold
Collieston
Ellon
Methlick
Fyvie
Huntly
Drumblade
Insch
Oyne
Inverurie
Oldmeldrum
Pitmedden
Udny Green
Newburgh
Balmedie
Kintore
Kemnay
Alford
Monymusk
Dyce
Blackburn
Westhill
Kingswells
ABERDEEN
Old Aberdeen
Bridge of Don
Cults
Milltimber
Peterculter
Portlethen
Newtonhill
Muchalls
Banchory
Aboyne
Torphins
Lumphanan
Echt
Crathes
Durris
Bridge of Feugh
Strachan
Glens of Foudland
River Deveron
River Dee
River Don
River Ythan
A90
A96
A98
A947
A948
A950
A952
A93
A944
A980
A92
A956
A975
A981
A97
A95
A920
Kirkwall
Lerwick
0 1 2 3 4 miles
0 1 2 3 4 5 kilometres

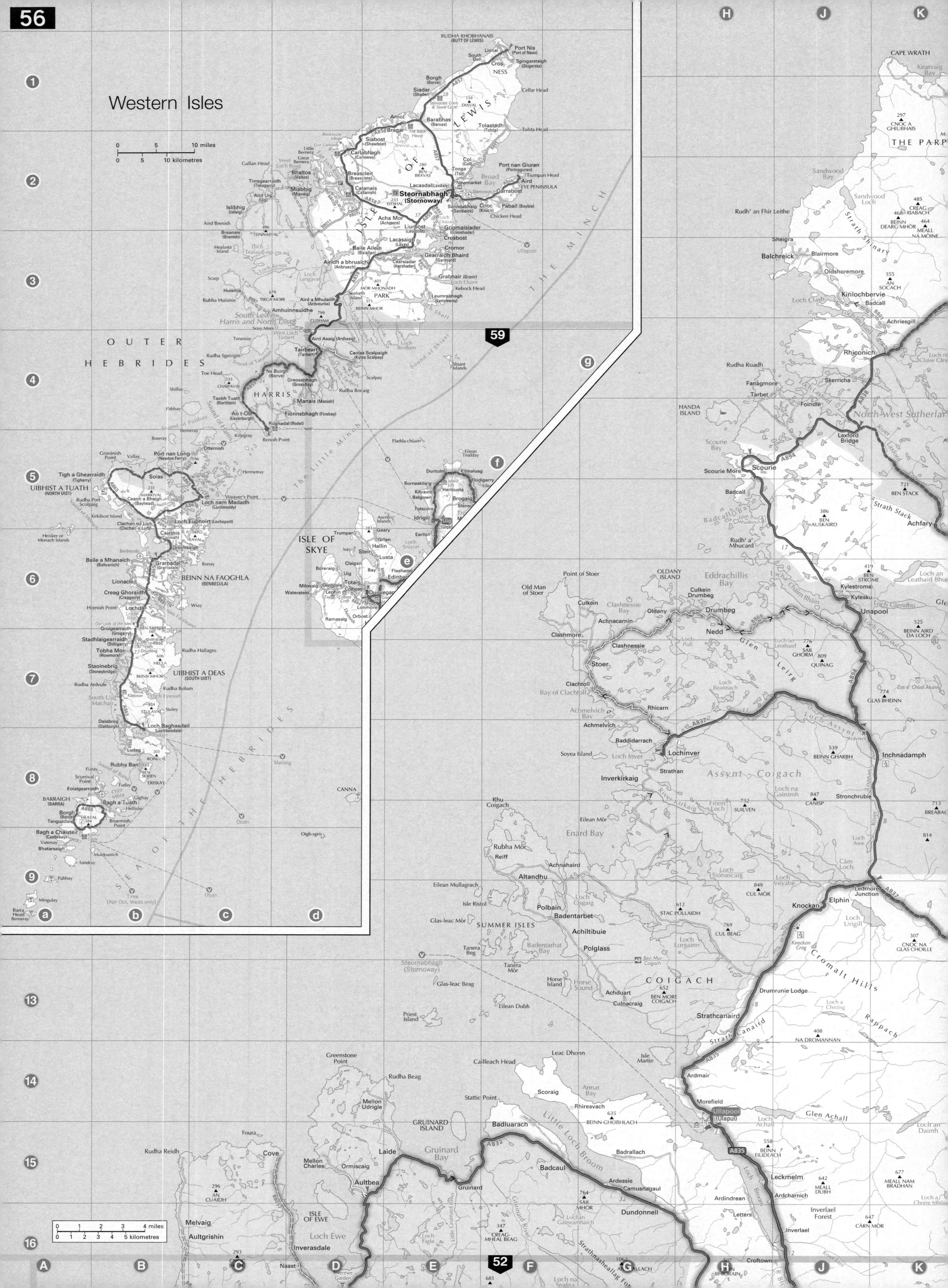
Western Isles
0 5 10 miles
0 5 10 kilometres
RUDHA RHOBHANAIS (BUTT OF LEWIS)
Port Nis (Port of Ness)
Sgiogarstaigh (Skigersta)
South Dell
Lional
Cros
NESS
Borgh (Borve)
Siadar (Shader)
Cellar Head
Arnol
Barabhas (Barvas)
ISLE OF LEWIS
Tolastadh (Tolsta)
Tolsta Head
Bragar
Siabost (Shawbost)
Carlabhagh (Carloway)
Gallan Head
Bhaltos (Valtos)
Breascleit (Breasclete)
Col (Coll)
Tonga (Tong)
Port nan Giuran (Portnaguran)
Tiumpan Head
Aird
EYE PENINSULA
Timsgearraidh (Timsgarry)
Miabhig (Miavaig)
Aird Uig (Uig)
Calanais (Callanish)
Lacasdal (Laxdale)
Steornabhagh (Stornoway)
Newmarket
Broad Bay
Garrabost
Islibhig (Islivig)
Sandwick
Cnoc (Knock)
Pabail (Bayble)
Chicken Head
Aird Brenish
Breanais (Brenish)
Mealasta Island
TEINNASVAL
Acha Mor (Achmore)
Liurbost (Leurbost)
Griomaisiader (Grimshader)
Crosbost
Lacasaigh (Laxay)
Baile Ailein (Balallan)
Cromor
Gearraidh Bhaird (Garyvard)
Airidh a bhruaich (Arnibruaich)
Cearsiadar (Kershader)
Ullapool
Scarp
Huisinis
Rubha Huisinis
TIRGA MOR
MOR MHONADH
PARK
Grabhair (Gravir)
Kebock Head
Aird a Mhulaidh (Ardvourlie)
Seaforth Island
BEINN MHOR
Leumrabhagh (Lemreway)
Amhuinnsuidhe
CLISHAM
South Lewis Harris and North Uist
THE MINCH
Taransay
Aird Asaig (Ardhasig)
Tairbeart (Tarbert)
59
OUTER HEBRIDES
Rudha Sgeirigin
Caolas Scalpaigh (Kyles Scalpay)
Scalpay
Shiant Islands
Sound of Shiant
Toe Head
CHAIPAVAL
Na Buirgh (Borve)
Greosabhagh (Grosebay)
HARRIS
Rudha Bocaig
Shillay
Taobh Tuath (Northton)
Manais (Manish)
Pabbay
An t-Ob (Leverburgh)
Fionnsbhagh (Finsbay)
Roghadal (Rodel)
Renish Point
Killegray
Boreray
Berneray
Fladda-chùain
Otternish
Griminish Point
Vallay
Port nan Long (Newton Ferry)
Eilean Trodday
Tigh a Ghearraidh (Tigharry)
Solas
Duntulm
Kilmaluag
Hermetray
UIBHIST A TUATH (NORTH UIST)
MARRIVAL
Ceann a Bhaigh (Bayhead)
Weaver's Point
Borneskitaig
Flodigarry
Heribusta
Kilvaxter
Balgown
Brogaig
Rudha Port Scolpaig
Loch nam Madadh (Lochmaddy)
Kirkibost Island
Totscore
Idrigill
Uig
Clachan na Luib (Clachan-a-Luib)
Loch Euphoirt (Locheport)
Heisker or Monach Islands
Cairinis (Carinish)
EAVAL
Ascrib Islands
Earlish
Trumpan
Geary
ISLE OF SKYE
Griomsaigh
Gillen
Hallin
Stein
Lusta
Baile a Mhanaich (Balivanich)
Gramsdal (Gramsdale)
Ronay
Claigan
Lionacleit
BEINN NA FAOGHLA (BENBECULA)
Boreraig
Glendale
Totaig
Flashader
Edinbane
Creag Ghoraidh (Creagorry)
Milovaig
Lephin
Colbost
Waterstein
Dunvegan
Hornish Point
Lochdar
Wiay
Lonmore
Orbost
Ramasaig
Groigearraidh (Grogarry)
BEN TARBERT
Stadhlaigearraidh (Stilligarry)
Tobha Mor (Howmore)
Rudha Hallagro
HECLA
Staoinebrig (Stoneybridge)
BEINN MHOR
UIBHIST A DEAS (SOUTH UIST)
Rudha Ardvule
Rudha Bolum
Loch Eynort
South Uist Machair
STULAVAL
Stuley
Dalabrog (Daliburgh)
Loch Baghasdail (Lochboisdale)
Ludag
RONEVAL
Mallaig
Rubha Ban
BEN SCRIEN
Fiaray
ERISKAY
Scurrival Point
CANNA
Eolaigearraidh
Fuday
BARRAIGH (BARRA)
Bagh a Tuath
Gighay
Hellisay
Borgh (Borve)
HEAVAL
Tangusdale
Bruernish Point
Oban
Bagh a Chaisteil (Castlebay)
Vatersay
Bhatarsaigh
Oigh-sgeir
Muldoanich
SEA OF THE HEBRIDES
Sandray
Pabbay
Mingulay
Barra Head Berneray
Tiree (Apr-Oct, Weds only)
Oban
The Little Minch
CAPE WRATH
Kearvaig Bay
CNOC A GHIUBHAIS
THE PARPH
Sandwood Bay
Sandwood Loch
CREAG RIABACH
BEINN DEARG MHOR
MEALL NA MOINE
Rudh' an Fhir Leithe
Strath Shinary
Sheigra
Balchreick
Blairmore
Oldshoremore
AN SOCACH
Kinlochbervie
Badcall
Loch Clash
Achriesgill
Rhiconich
Rudha Ruadh
Skerricha
Fanagmore
Tarbet
Foindle
HANDA ISLAND
North-west Sutherland
Laxford Bridge
Scourie Bay
Scourie
Scourie More
BEN STACK
Badcall
Strath Stack
Badcall Bay
BEN AUSKAIRD
Achfary
Rudh' a' Mhucard
BEN STROME
Loch an Leathaid Bhuain
Point of Stoer
OLDANY ISLAND
Eddrachillis Bay
Kylestrome
Old Man of Stoer
Culkein Drumbeg
Culkein
Clashnessie Bay
Oldany
Drumbeg
Kylesku
Unapool
Achnacarnin
Nedd
Clashmore
Clashnessie
Glen Leirg
SAIL GHORM
QUINAG
BEINN AIRD DA LOCH
Stoer
Clachtoll
Bay of Clachtoll
GLAS BHEINN
Achmelvich Bay
Rhicarn
Achmelvich
Baddidarrach
Loch Assynt
Ardvreck
Lochinver
Soyea Island
Loch Inver
BEINN GHARBH
Inchnadamph
Strathan
Inverkirkaig
Assynt Coigach
CANISP
Stronchrubie
Rhu Coigach
River Kirkaig
SUILVEN
BREABAG
Eilean Mòr
Enard Bay
Rubha Mòr
Reiff
Loch Awe
Achnahaird
Altandhu
Loch Sionascaig
Cam Loch
Eilean Mullagrach
CUL MOR
Ledmore Junction
Elphin
Isle Ristol
Polbain
STAC POLLAIDH
Knockan
Loch Urigill
Badentarbet
Glas-leac Mòr
SUMMER ISLES
Achiltibuie
CUL BEAG
CNOC NA GLAS CHOILLE
Tanera Beg
Badentarbat Bay
Polglass
Loch Lurgainn
Knockan Crag
Cromalt Hills
Steornabhagh (Stornoway)
Tanera Mòr
Ben Mor Coigach
Horse Island
Horse Sound
COIGACH
Glas-leac Beag
BEN MORE COIGACH
Achduart
Culnacraig
Drumrunie Lodge
Eilean Dubh
Rappach
Priest Island
Strathcanaird
Strath Canaird
NA DROMANNAN
Greenstone Point
Leac Dhonn
Isle Martin
Cailleach Head
Rudha Beag
Ardmair
Scoraig
Annat Bay
Mellon Udrigle
Stattic Point
Morefield
Rhireavach
BEINN-GHOBHLACH
Ullapool
Glen Achall
GRUINARD ISLAND
Badluarach
Little Loch Broom
Foura
Rudha Reidh
Cove
Laide
Gruinard Bay
Badrallach
BEINN EILIDEACH
Mellon Charles
Ormiscaig
Badcaul
MEALL NAM BRADHAN
Aultbea
Gruinard
Ardessie
Camusnagaul
Leckmelm
MEALL DUBH
AN CUAIDH
SAIL MHOR
Ardcharnich
ISLE OF EWE
Ardindrean
Dundonnell
Inverlael Forest
Loch Ewe
Lochan Gaineamhaich
Letters
CARN MOR
Melvaig
Aultgrishin
CREAG-MHEAL BEAG
Inverlael
0 1 2 3 4 miles
0 1 2 3 4 5 kilometres
Inverasdale
Naast
Strathnasheallag Forest
Croftown
52
Inverewe Garden

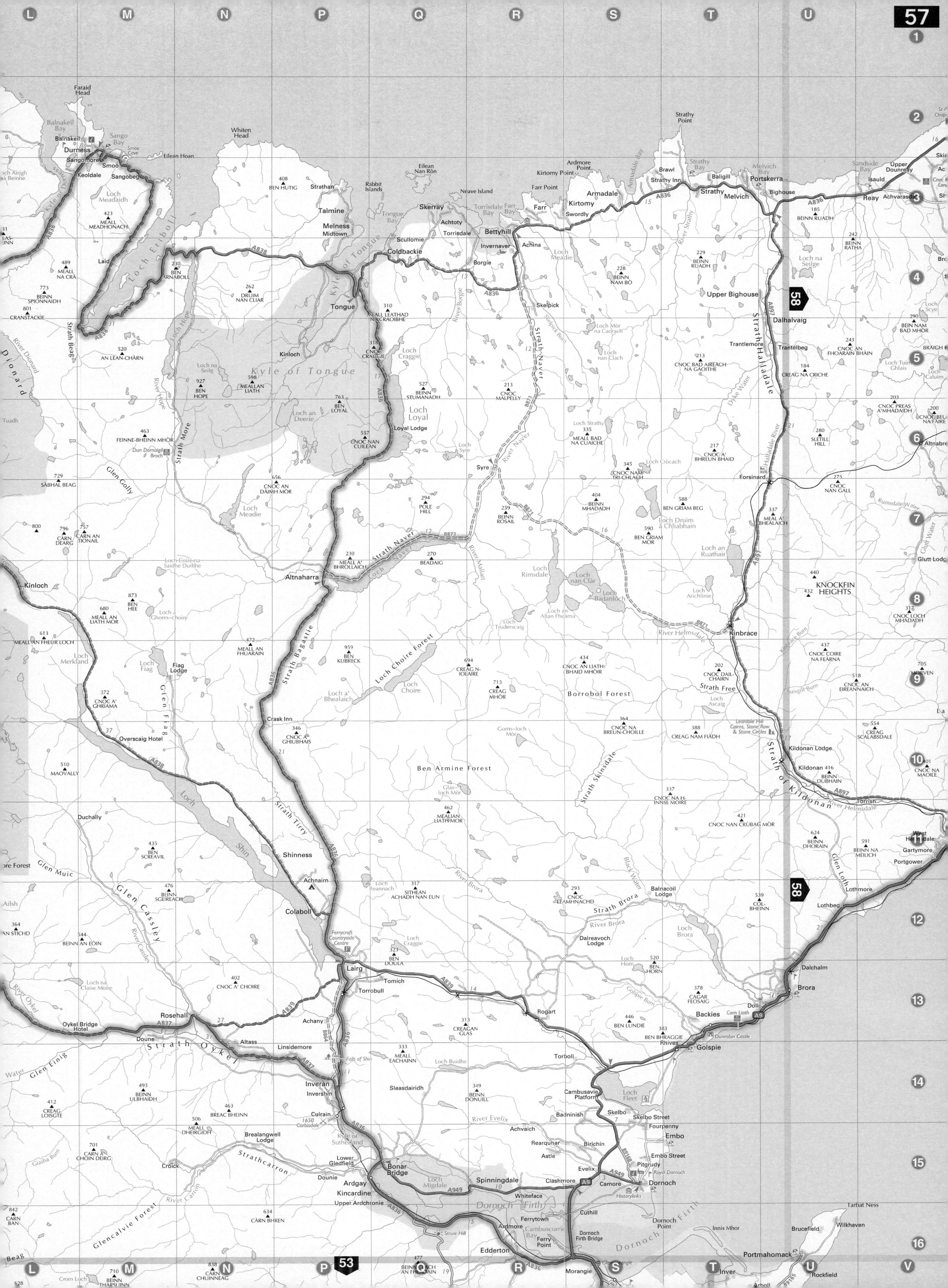
Faraid Head
Balnakeil Bay
Balnakeil
Durness
Sango Bay
Sangomore
Smoo
Keoldale
Sangobeg
Eilean Hoan
Whiten Head
Loch Meadaidh
423 MEALL MEADHONACH
Loch Eriboll
Kyle of Durness
Laid
489 MEALL NA CRÀ
773 BEINN SPIONNAIDH
801 CRANSTACKIE
Strath Beag
520 AN LEAN-CHÀRN
River Dionard
Dionard
230 BEN ARNABOLL
262 DRUIM NAN CLIAR
408 BEN HUTIG
Strathan
Talmine
Melness
Midtown
Rabbit Islands
Eilean Nan Ròn
Neave Island
Skerray
Tongue Bay
Achtoty
Torrisdale
Torrisdale Bay
Farr Bay
Scullomie
Coldbackie
Kyle of Tongue
Tongue
Kinloch
Loch na Seilg
927 BEN HOPE
598 MEALLAN LIATH
Strath More
River Hope
Loch Hope
310 MEALL LEATHAD NA CRAOIBHE
318 CNOC CRAGGIE
Loch Craggie
527 BEINN STUMANADH
763 BEN LOYAL
Loch an Deerie
Loch Loyal
Loyal Lodge
557 CNOC NAN CUILEAN
463 FEINNE-BHEINN MHÒR
Dun Dornaigil Broch
Tuadh
729 SÀBHAL BEAG
Glen Golly
656 CNOC AN DAIMH MÒR
Loch Meadie
294 POLE HILL
800
796 CARN DEARG
757 CARN AN TIONAIL
Loch Coire na Saidhe Duibhe
230 MEALL A' BHROLLAICH
Strath Naver
Loch Naver
270 BEADAIG
Altnaharra
Kinloch
873 BEN HEE
680 MEALL AN LIATH MOR
Loch a' Ghorm-choire
613 MEALL AN FHEUR LOCH
472 MEALL AN FHUARAIN
Loch Merkland
Loch Fiag
Fiag Lodge
Glen Fiag
372 CNOC A' GHRIAMA
Overscaig Hotel
510 MAOVALLY
Strath Bagastie
959 BEN KLIBRECK
Loch Choire Forest
Loch a' Bhealaich
Loch Choire
Crask Inn
346 CNOC A' GHIUBHAIS
Bettyhill
Invernaver
Borgie
River Borgie
Achina
Loch Meadie
Farr
Farr Point
Kirtomy
Kirtomy Point
Swordly
Ardmore Point
Armadale
Armadale Bay
Strathy Point
Strathy Bay
Brawl
Strathy Inn
Strathy
Baligill
Melvich
Melvich Bay
Portskerra
Bighouse
River Strathy
228 BEINN NAM BO
229 BEINN RUADH
Skelpick
Loch Mòr na Caorach
Loch nan Clach
Strath Naver
213 CNOC MALPELLY
River Naver
Loch Syre
Syre
Loch Strathy
335 MEALL BAD NA CUAICHE
345 CNOC NAM TRI-CHLACH
Loch Cròcach
217 CNOC A' BHREUN BHAID
213 CNOC BAD AIREACH NA GAOITHE
Dyke Water
Upper Bighouse
Strath Halladale
Dalhalvaig
Trantlemore
Halladale River
Forsinard
404 BEINN MHADADH
588 BEN GRIAM BEG
259 BEINN ROSAIL
590 BEN GRIAM MOR
Loch Druim a' Chliabhain
Loch an Ruathair
Loch Rimsdale
Loch nan Clàr
Loch Badanloch
Loch Arichlinie
River Mallart
Loch Truderscaig
Loch an Alltan Fhearna
River Helmsdale
Kinbrace
694 CREAG N-IOLAIRE
434 CNOC AN LIATH-BHAID MHÒIR
202 CNOC DAIL-CHAIRN
Strath Free
713 CREAG MHÒR
Borrobol Forest
Loch Ascaig
Gorm-loch Mòr
364 CNOC NA BREUN-CHOILLE
388 CREAG NAM FIADH
Learable Hill Cairns, Stone Row & Stone Circles
Ben Armine Forest
Strath Skinsdale
Glas-loch Mòr
462 MEALLAN LIATH MÒR
337 CNOC NA H-INNSE MOIRE
Strath of Kildonan
Kildonan Lodge
Kildonan
Sandside Bay
Upper Dounreay
Isauld
Reay
Achvarasdal
185 BEINN RUADH
242 BEINN RATHA
Loch na Seilge
290 BEIN NAM BAD MHÒR
243 CNOC AN FHOARAIN BHAIN
Trantlebeg
184 CREAG NA CRICHE
Loch Tuim Ghlais
Loch Calium
203 CNOC PREAS A' MHADAIDH
200 CNOC BEAG NA FAIRE
280 SLETILL HILL
Altnabreac
275 CNOC NAN GALL
Rumsdale Water
337 MEAL A' BHEALAICH
Glutt Water
Glutt Lodge
440 KNOCKFIN HEIGHTS
432
317 CNOC LOCH MHADADH
Kinbrace Burn
437 CNOC COIRE NA FEARNA
705 MORVEN
518 CNOC AN EIREANNAICH
Suisgill Burn
554 CREAG SCALABSDALE
416 BEINN DUBHAIN
401 CNOC NA MAOILE
Torrish
River Helmsdale
421 CNOC NAN CRÙBAG MÒR
624 BEINN DHORAIN
591 BEINN NA MEILICH
West Helmsdale
Gartymore
Portgower
Glen Loth
Lothmore
Lothbeg
539 COL-BHEINN
Duchally
435 BEN SCREAVIL
Loch Shin
Strath Tirry
Shinness
Achnairn
Glen Muic
Glen Cassley
476 BEINN SGEIREACH
364 AN STICHD
544 BEINN AN EOIN
River Cassley
Colaboll
Loch Beannach
317 SITHEAN ACHADH NAN EUN
River Brora
Black Water
293 CNOC LEAMHNACHD
Balnacoil Lodge
Strath Brora
Loch Brora
Dalreavoch Lodge
Ferrycroft Countryside Centre
323 BEN DOULA
Loch Craggie
Lairg
Tomich
Torrobull
Loch na Claise Moire
402 CNOC A' CHOIRE
River Oykel
Rosehall
Oykel Bridge Hotel
Achany
Doune
Strath Oykel
Altass
Linsidemore
Loch Horn
520 BEN HORN
378 CAGAR FEOSAIG
Golspie Burn
Rogart
313 CREAGAN GLAS
446 BEN LUNDIE
383 BEN BHRAGGIE
Rhives
Backies
Carn Liath
Dunrobin Castle
Golspie
Doll
Brora
Dalchalm
Glen Einig
493 BEINN ULBHAIDH
412 CREAG LOISGTE
Falls of Shin
333 MEALL EACHAINN
Loch Buidhe
Torboll
Inveran
Invershin
Sleasdairidh
349 BEINN DONUILL
Loch Fleet
Cambusavie Platform
Skelbo
Skelbo Street
Fourpenny
Embo
463 BREAC BHEINN
506 MEALL DHEIRGIDH
Culrain
1650 Carbisdale
Kyle of Sutherland
Brealangwell Lodge
River Evelix
Achvaich
Badninish
Rearquhar
Birichin
Astle
Embo Street
701 CARN A' CHOIN DEIRG
Strathcarron
Croick
Glasha Burn
Lower Gledfield
Bonar Bridge
Loch Migdale
Spinningdale
Dounie
Ardgay
Kincardine
Upper Ardchronie
Clashmore
Evelix
Camore
Pitgrudy
Royal Dornoch
Dornoch
Historylinks
River Carron
Glencalvie Forest
842 CARN BAN
634 CARN BHREN
Whiteface
Dornoch Firth
Ferrytown
Cuthill
Dornoch Point
Struie Hill
Ardmore
Cambuscurrie Bay
Dornoch Firth Bridge
Ferry Point
Edderton
Tarbat Ness
Innis Mhor
Brucefield
Wilkhaven
Portmahomack
Inver
Morangie
710 BEINN THARSUINN
838 CARN CHUINNEAG
477 BEINN NA CH AN FHEAIN
Crom Loch
628
Beag
Rockfield
Arboll
A838
A836
A897
A839
A837
A9
A949
B871
B873
B864
B9168
58
53
L
M
N
P
Q
R
S
T
U
V
1
2
3
4
5
6
7
8
9
10
11
12
13
14
15
16

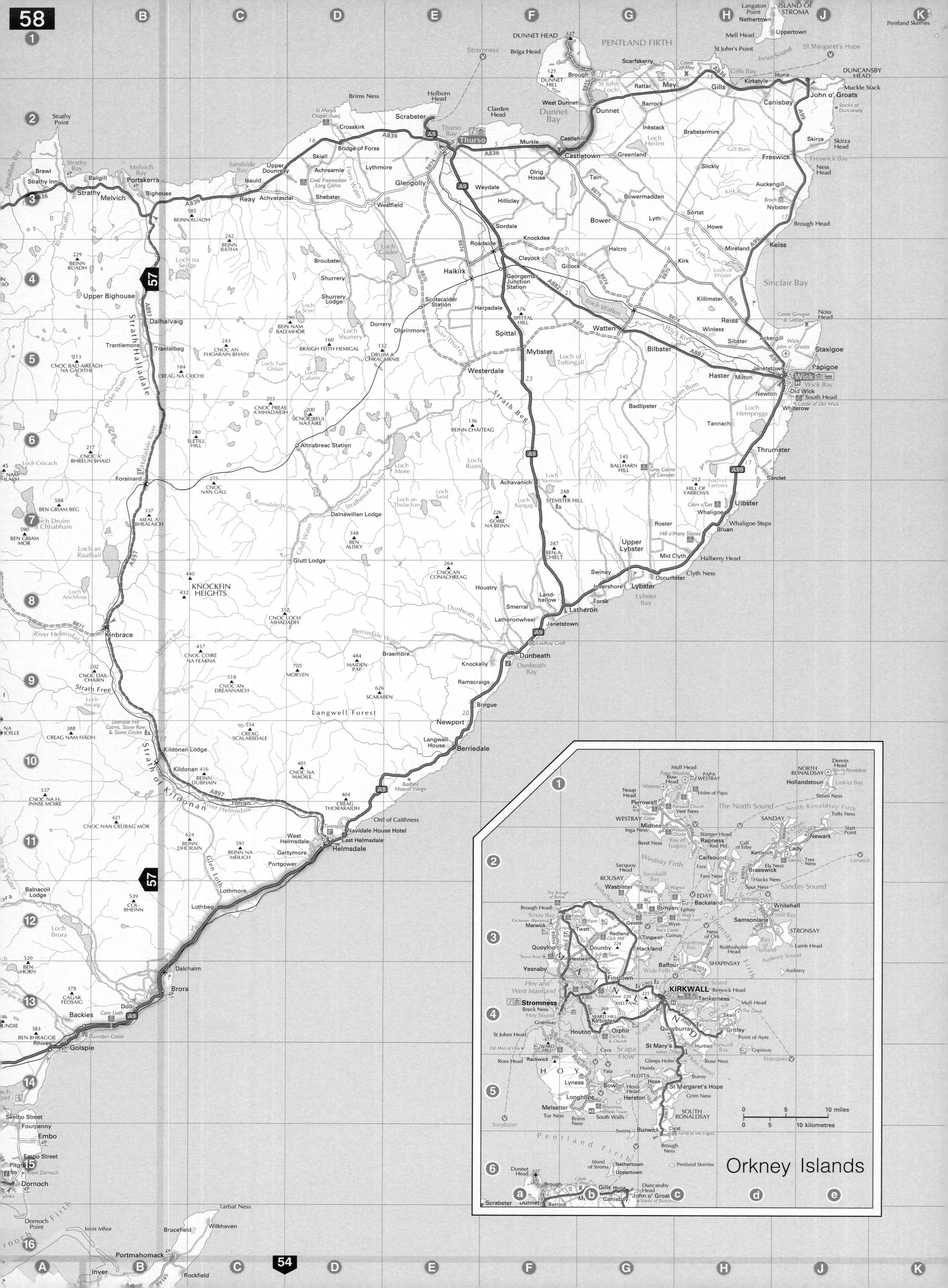
PENTLAND FIRTH
DUNNET HEAD
Dunnet Bay
Thurso
Scrabster
Holborn Head
Brims Ness
Crosskirk
Castletown
Dunnet
Mey
Gills
John o' Groats
DUNCANSBY HEAD
Stacks of Duncansby
Canisbay
Freswick
Keiss
Sinclair Bay
Wick
Staxigoe
Papigoe
Thrumster
Ulbster
Whaligoe
Lybster
Latheron
Dunbeath
Berriedale
Helmsdale
Brora
Golspie
Dornoch
Embo
Dornoch Firth
Tarbat Ness
Portmahomack
Strathy Point
Melvich
Portskerra
Reay
Forsinard
Kinbrace
KNOCKFIN HEIGHTS
Langwell Forest
Strath of Kildonan
Strath Halladale
Halkirk
Georgemas Junction Station
Watten
Loch Watten
Spittal
Mybster
Westerdale
Altnabreac Station
MORVEN
SCARABEN
Orkney Islands
Stromness
KIRKWALL
HOY
Scapa Flow
WESTRAY
SANDAY
STRONSAY
EDAY
ROUSAY
SHAPINSAY
SOUTH RONALDSAY
St Margaret's Hope
PAPA WESTRAY
NORTH RONALDSAY
The North Sound
Westray Firth
Stronsay Firth
Sanday Sound
Pentland Firth
Island of Stroma
Pentland Skerries
10 miles
10 kilometres
A9
A99
A836
A882
A897
57
54

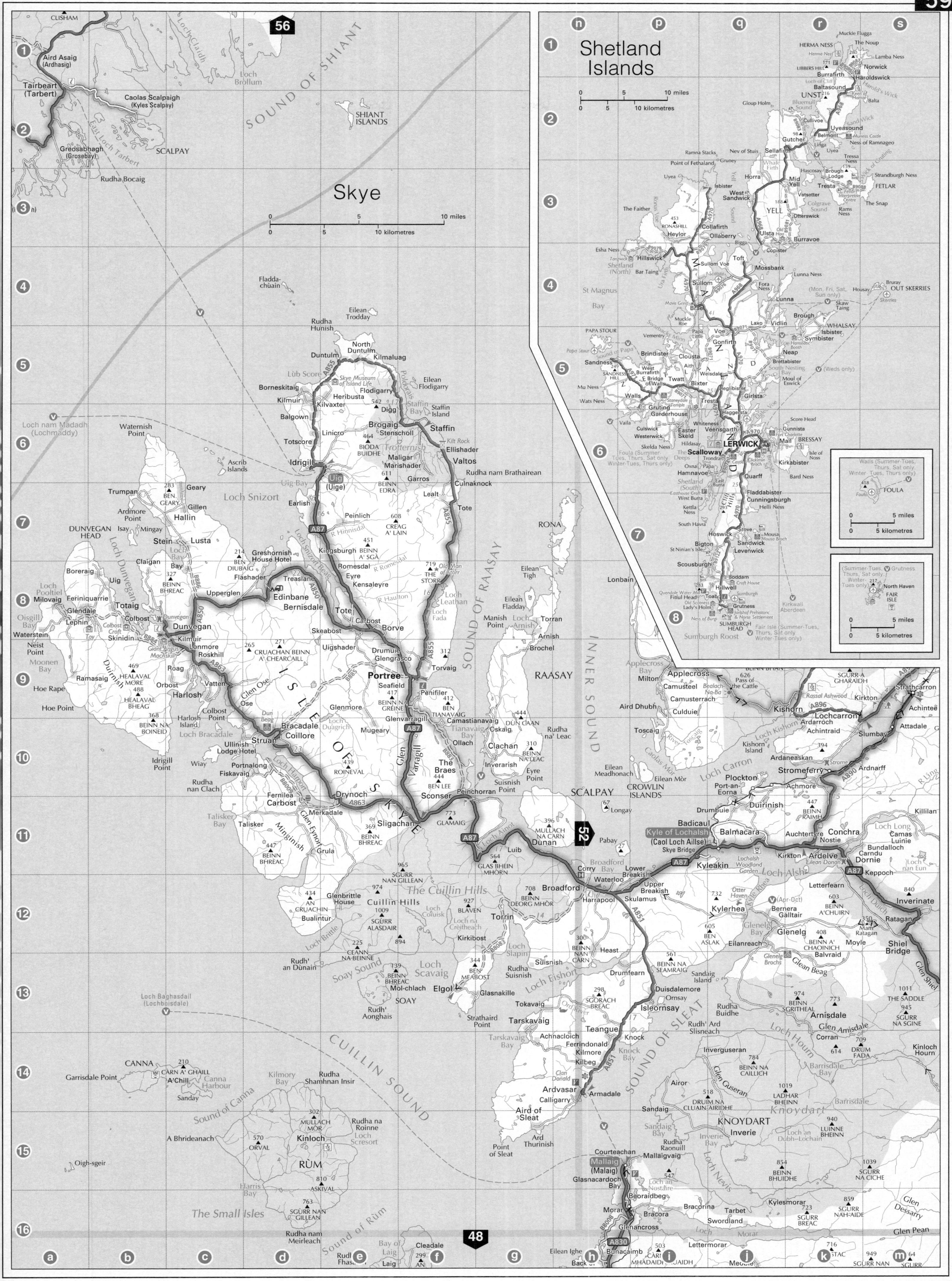

Skye

Shetland Islands

Shetland Islands region

CLISHAM

Aird Asaig (Ardhasig)
Tairbeart (Tarbert)
Caolas Scalpaigh (Kyles Scalpay)
Greosabhagh (Grosebay)
Rudha Bocaig
SCALPAY
SOUND OF SHIANT
SHIANT ISLANDS
Loch Brollum
Loch Claidh

HERMA NESS
The Noup
Muckle Flugga
Burrafirth
Norwick
Haroldswick
UNST
Baltasound
Balta
Uyeasound
Gutcher
Belmont
Ness of Ramnageo
FETLAR
Tresta
Strandburgh Ness
YELL
Mid Yell
Ulsta
Burravoe
OUT SKERRIES
WHALSAY
Symbister
Skaw
BRESSAY
Isle of Noss

LERWICK
Scalloway
Gruting
Garderhouse
Walls
Sandness
PAPA STOUR
Esha Ness
Hillswick
Sullom Voe
Mossbank
Brae
FOULA
St Magnus Bay

Sumburgh Head
SUMBURGH
Grutness
FAIR ISLE
North Haven

Skye

0   5   10 miles
0   5   10 kilometres

North Duntulm
Duntulm
Kilmaluag
Kilmuir
Skye Museum of Island Life
Flodigarry
Eilean Flodigarry
Staffin Island
Staffin
Valtos
Ellishader
Kilt Rock
Brogaig
Stenscholl
Digg
Marishader
Maligar
Lealt
Tote
Rudha nam Brathairean
Culnaknock
Uig (Uige)
Uig Bay
BEINN EDRA
Garros
Peinlich
Earlish
CREAG A' LAIN
Kingsburgh
BEINN A' SGA
Romesdal
Kensaleyre
Old Man of Storr
THE STORR
Loch Leathan
Eilean Tigh
RONA
Eilean Fladday
Brochel
RAASAY
DUN CAAN
SOUND OF RAASAY
INNER SOUND

Waternish Point
Trumpan
Ardmore Point
Hallin
BEN GEARY
Gillen
Stein
Lusta
Loch Snizort
Ascrib Islands
Greshornish House Hotel
BEN DIUBAIG
Edinbane
Bernisdale
Treaslane
Skeabost
Borve
Tote
Carbost
Drynie
Glengrasco
Torvaig
Penifiler
Portree
Seafield
Glenmore
BEINN NA GREINE
Glenvarragill
BEN TIANAVAIG
Camastianavaig
Tianavaig Bay
Oskaig
Ollach
Clachan
Inverarish
BEINN NA'LEAC
Eyre Point
The Braes
BEN LEE
Sconser
Peinchorran
Suishnish Point
SCALPAY
Longay
Pabay
Broadford Bay
Corry
Lower Breakish
Upper Breakish
Skulamus
Waterloo
Broadford
Harrapool
BEINN DEARG MHOR
Torrin
Kirkibost
Loch Slapin
Loch na Creitheach
BLAVEN
BEN MEABOST
Suisnish
Elgol
Glasnakille
Kilmarie
Strathaird Point
Tokavaig
Tarskavaig
Ord
Duisdalemore
Isleornsay
Ornsay
Teangue
Knock
Ferrindonald
Kilmore
Kilbeg
Clan Donald
Armadale
Ardvasar
Calligarry
Aird of Sleat
Point of Sleat
Ard Thurinish

DUNVEGAN HEAD
Geary
Waternish
Claigan
Borreraig
Uig
Loch Dunvegan
Dunvegan
Loch Pooltiel
Milovaig
Feriniquarrie
Glendale
Totaig
Colbost
Skinidin
Kilmuir
Roskhill
Lonmore
Waterstein
Neist Point
Oisgill Bay
Moonen Bay
Ramasaig
HEALAVAL MORE
Roag
Orbost
Vatten
Harlosh
HEALAVAL BHEAG
Hoe Rape
Hoe Point
BEINN NA BOINEID
Harlosh Point
Harlosh Island
Ullinish Lodge Hotel
Idrigill Point
Wiay
Struan
Coillore
Bracadale
Loch Bracadale
Portnalong
Fiskavaig
Rudha nan Clach
Fernilea
Carbost
Talisker
Talisker Bay
Drynoch
Merkadale
Glen Eynort
Sligachan
GLAMAIG
SGURR NAN GILLEAN
Glenbrittle House
Cuillin Hills
THE CUILLIN HILLS
SGURR ALASDAIR
AN CRUACHAN
Bualintur
Loch Coruisk
Loch Scavaig
Soay Sound
SOAY
ISLE OF SKYE
Glen Sligachan
Glen Varragill
Loch Harport
Minginish
BEINN BHREAC
ROINEVAL
CRUACHAN BEINN A' CHEARCAILL
Uigshader
Mugeary
Loch Dubhaig
Dun Beag

Loch nam Madadh (Lochmaddy)

SOUND OF SLEAT
SLEAT
Sandaig Island
Rudha Buidhe
Rudha Slisneach
Inverguseran
Airor
Loch Hourn
KNOYDART
Inverie
Mallaig
Morar
Bracora
Arisaig

APPLECROSS
Applecross
Milton
Camusteel
Camusterrach
Toscaig
Culduie
Aird Dhubh
Pass of the Cattle
Bealach na Ba
Kishorn
Loch Kishorn
Lochcarron
Strathcarron
Achintee
Attadale
Slumbay
Ardarroch
Achintraid
Ardaneaskan
Stromeferry
Loch Carron
Ardnarff
Plockton
Port-an-Eorna
Achmore
Duirinish
Drumbuie
Balmacara
Kyle of Lochalsh (Caol Loch Aillse)
Skye Bridge
Kyleakin
Auchtertyre
Nostie
Conchra
Ardelve
Dornie
Eilean Donan
Kirkton
Letterfearn
Inverinate
Ratagan
Shiel Bridge
Glenelg
Glenelg Bay
Eilanreach
Kylerhea
Moyle
Balvraid
Bernera Galltair
BEN ASLAK
BEINN A' CHUIRN
BEINN A' CHAOINICH
Mam Ratagan
THE SADDLE
SGURR NA SGINE
Glen Shiel
Glen Beag
Arnisdale
Corran
Glen Amisdale
BEINN SGRITHEALL
DRUM FADA
Kinloch Hourn
BEINN NA CAILLICH
LADHAR BHEINN
Barrisdale
LUINNE BHEINN
Loch an Dubh-Lochain
SGURR NA CICHE

CANNA
Garrisdale Point
A'Chill
Canna Harbour
Sanday
A Bhrideanach
Sound of Canna
Kilmory Bay
Rudha Shamhnan Insir
MULLACH MOR
Rudha na Roinne
Kinloch
ORVAL
Loch Scresort
RÙM
ASKIVAL
Harris Bay
SGURR NAN GILLEAN
Rudha nam Meirleach
The Small Isles
Sound of Rùm
Bay of Laig
Cleadale
Laig
CUILLIN SOUND

Loch Baghasdail (Lochboisdale)

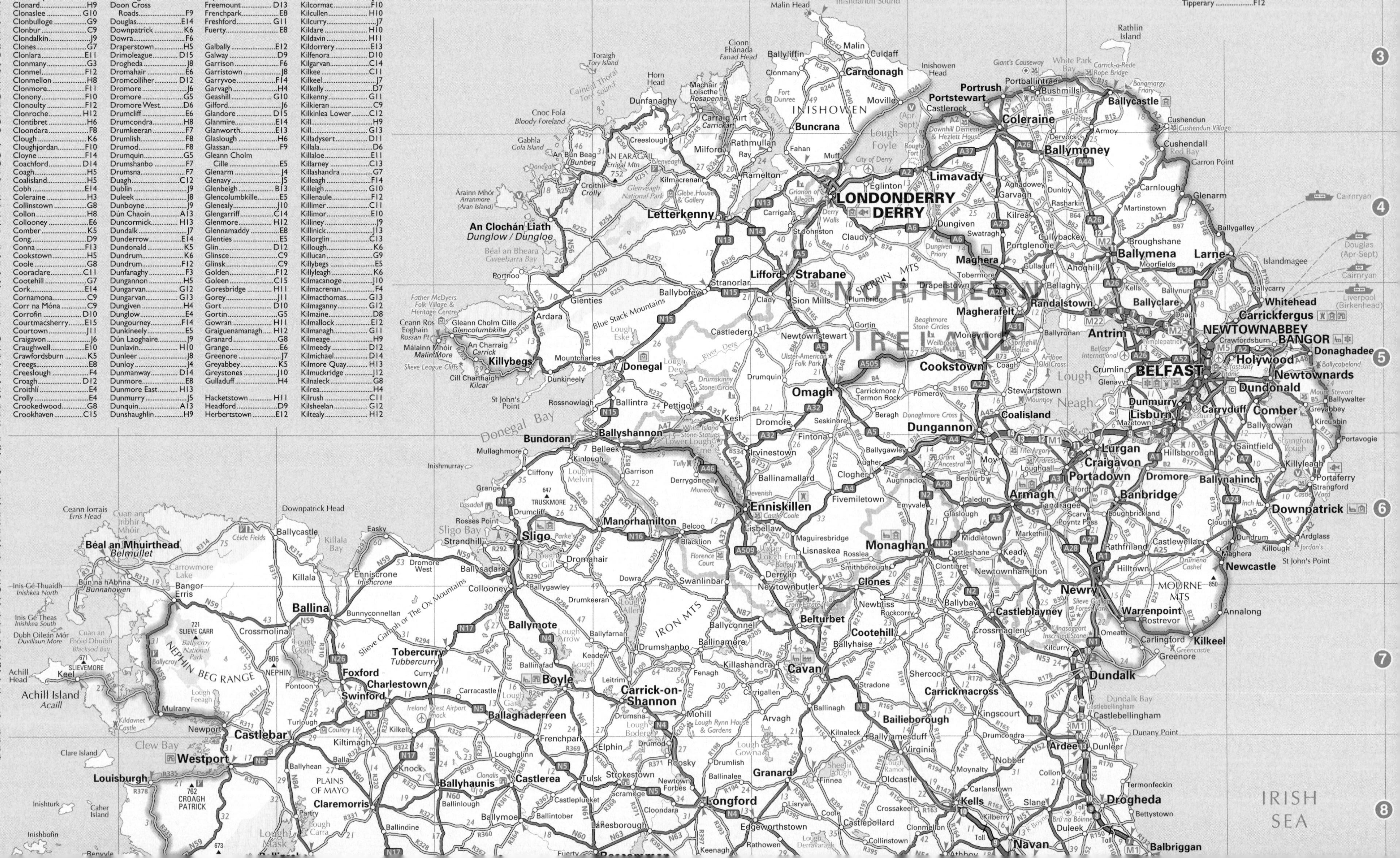

NORTHERN IRELAND
IRISH SEA
LONDONDERRY DERRY
BELFAST
Donegal Bay
Sligo Bay
Clew Bay
Lough Neagh
SPERRIN MTS
MOURNE MTS
IRON MTS
NEPHIN BEG RANGE
Blue Stack Mountains
INISHOWEN
Achill Island
Malin Head
Rathlin Island
Letterkenny
Donegal
Sligo
Ballina
Castlebar
Westport
Enniskillen
Omagh
Strabane
Coleraine
Ballymena
Larne
Antrim
Lisburn
Armagh
Newry
Dundalk
Drogheda
Monaghan
Cavan
Longford
Carrick-on-Shannon
Boyle
Dungannon
Cookstown
Downpatrick
Bangor
Newtownards

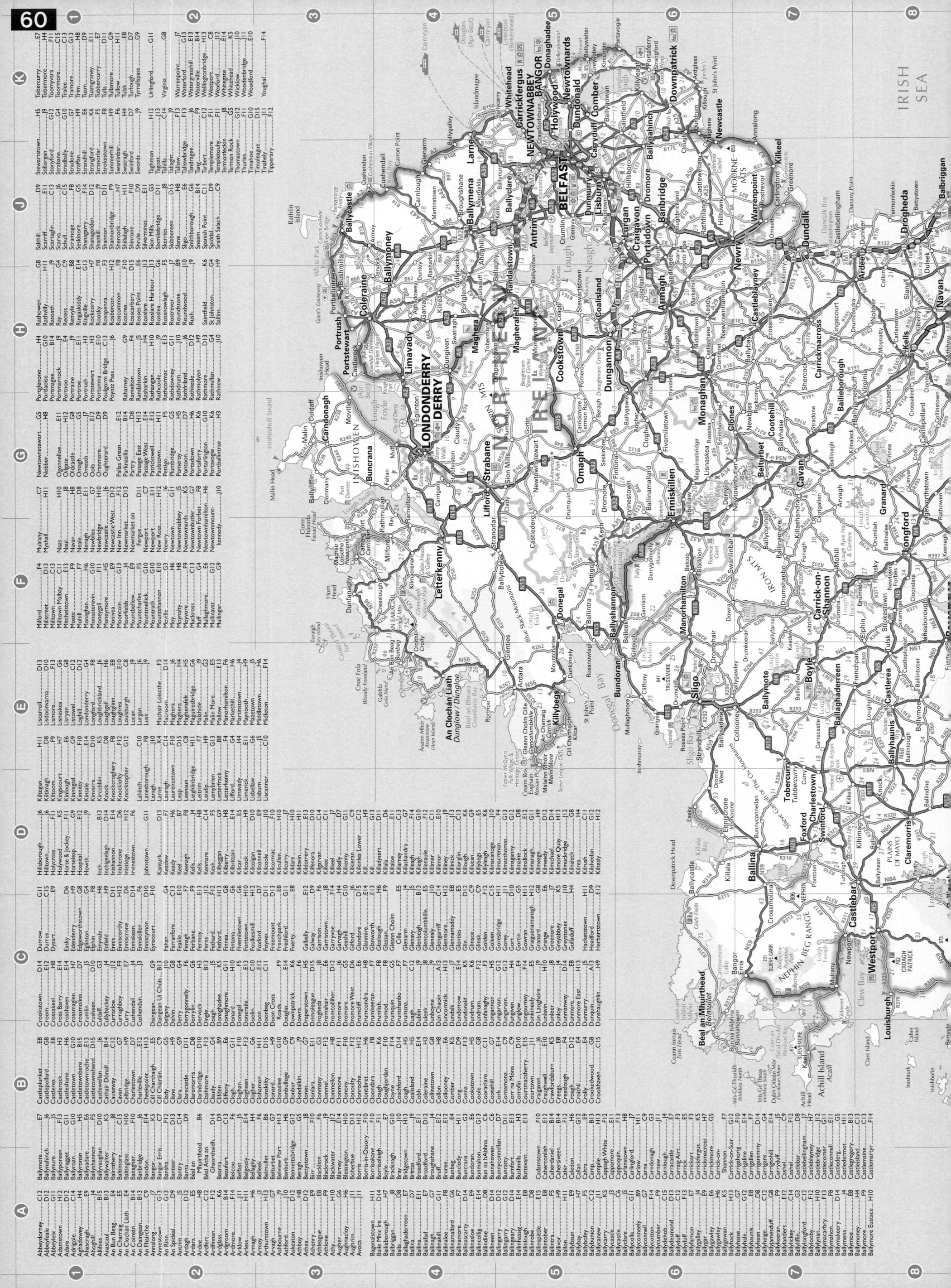

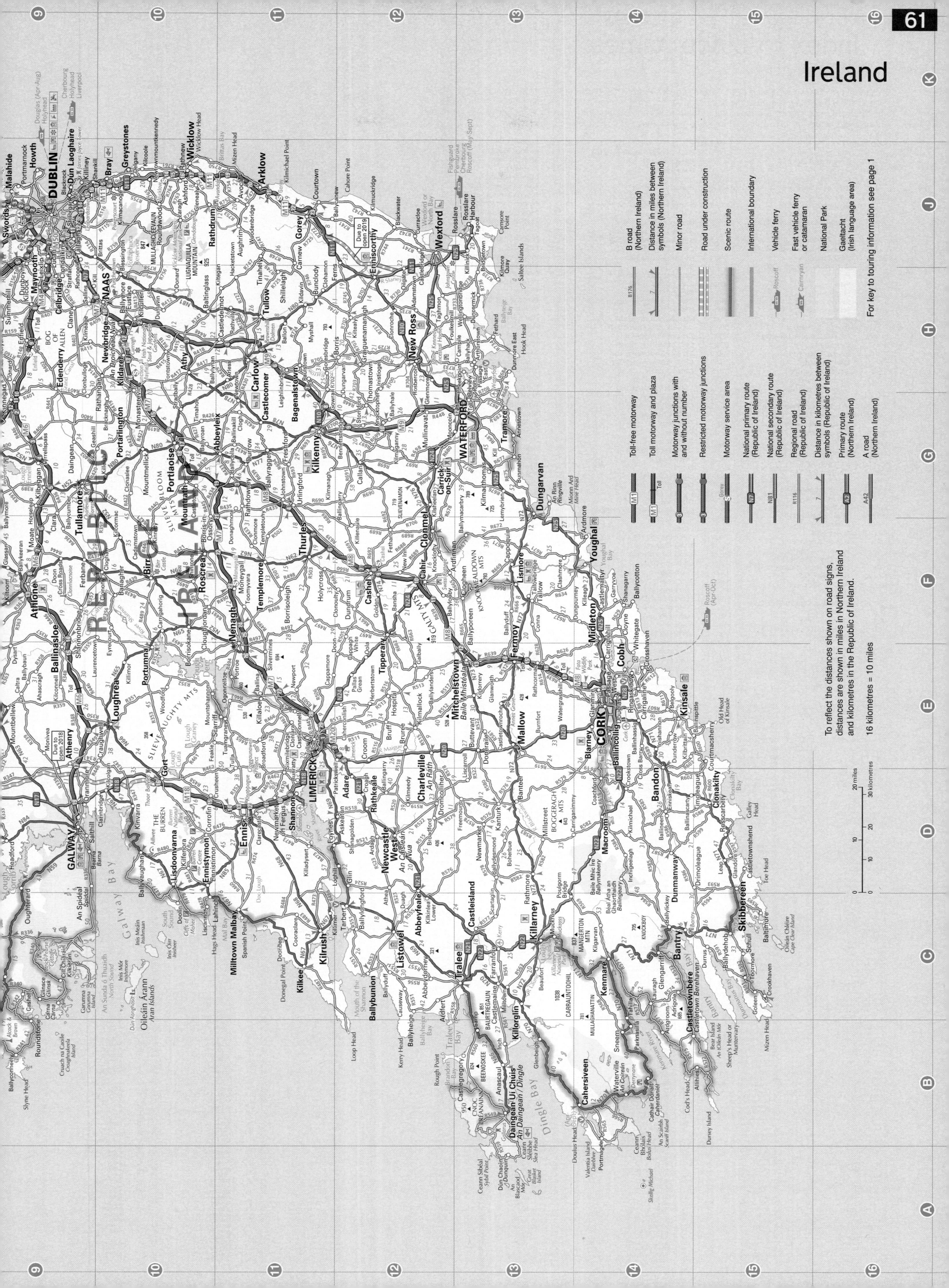

Ireland

Legend

M1	Toll-free motorway
M1 Toll	Toll motorway and plaza
	Motorway junctions with and without number
	Restricted motorway junctions
S	Motorway service area
N7	National primary route (Republic of Ireland)
N81	National secondary route (Republic of Ireland)
R116	Regional road (Republic of Ireland)
7	Distance in kilometres between symbols (Republic of Ireland)
	Primary route (Northern Ireland)
A2	A road (Northern Ireland)
B176	B road (Northern Ireland)
7	Distance in miles between symbols (Northern Ireland)
	Minor road
	Road under construction
	Scenic route
	International boundary
	Vehicle ferry
	Fast vehicle ferry or catamaran
	National Park
	Gaeltacht (Irish language area)

For key to touring information see page 1

To reflect the distances shown on road signs, distances are shown in miles in Northern Ireland and kilometres in the Republic of Ireland.

16 kilometres = 10 miles

Index to place names

This index lists places appearing in the main-map section of the atlas in alphabetical order. The reference following each name gives the atlas page number and grid reference of the square in which the place appears. The map shows counties, unitary authorities and administrative areas, together with a list of the abbreviated name forms used in the index. In addition airports are indexed in blue *italic*.

Scotland

Abers	**Aberdeenshire**
Ag & B	**Argyll and Bute**
Angus	**Angus**
Border	**Scottish Borders**
C Aber	**City of Aberdeen**
C Dund	**City of Dundee**
C Edin	**City of Edinburgh**
C Glas	**City of Glasgow**
Clacks	**Clackmannanshire (1)**
D & G	**Dumfries & Galloway**
E Ayrs	**East Ayrshire**
E Duns	**East Dunbartonshire (2)**
E Loth	**East Lothian**
E Rens	**East Renfrewshire (3)**
Falk	**Falkirk**
Fife	**Fife**
Highld	**Highland**
Inver	**Inverclyde (4)**
Mdloth	**Midlothian (5)**
Moray	**Moray**
N Ayrs	**North Ayrshire**
N Lans	**North Lanarkshire (6)**
Ork	**Orkney Islands**
P & K	**Perth & Kinross**
Rens	**Renfrewshire (7)**
S Ayrs	**South Ayrshire**
S Lans	**South Lanarkshire**
Shet	**Shetland Islands**
Stirlg	**Stirling**
W Duns	**West Dunbartonshire (8)**
W Isls	**Western Isles (Na h-Eileanan an Iar)**
W Loth	**West Lothian**

Wales

Blae G	**Blaenau Gwent (9)**
Brdgnd	**Bridgend (10)**
Caerph	**Caerphilly (11)**
Cardif	**Cardiff**
Carmth	**Carmarthenshire**
Cerdgn	**Ceredigion**
Conwy	**Conwy**
Denbgs	**Denbighshire**
Flints	**Flintshire**
Gwynd	**Gwynedd**
IoA	**Isle of Anglesey**
Mons	**Monmouthshire**
Myr Td	**Merthyr Tydfil (12)**
Neath	**Neath Port Talbot (13)**
Newpt	**Newport (14)**
Pembks	**Pembrokeshire**
Powys	**Powys**
Rhondd	**Rhondda Cynon Taff (15)**
Swans	**Swansea**
Torfn	**Torfaen (16)**
V Glam	**Vale of Glamorgan (17)**
Wrexhm	**Wrexham**

Channel Islands & Isle of Man

Guern	**Guernsey**
Jersey	**Jersey**
IoM	**Isle of Man**

England

BaNES	**Bath & N E Somerset (18)**
Barns	**Barnsley (19)**
Bed	**Bedford**
Birm	**Birmingham**
Bl w D	**Blackburn with Darwen (20)**
Bmouth	**Bournemouth**
Bolton	**Bolton (21)**
Bpool	**Blackpool**
Br & H	**Brighton & Hove (22)**
Br For	**Bracknell Forest (23)**
Bristl	**City of Bristol**
Bucks	**Buckinghamshire**
Bury	**Bury (24)**
C Beds	**Central Bedfordshire**
C Brad	**City of Bradford**
C Derb	**City of Derby**
C KuH	**City of Kingston upon Hull**
C Leic	**City of Leicester**
C Nott	**City of Nottingham**
C Pete	**City of Peterborough**
C Plym	**City of Plymouth**
C Port	**City of Portsmouth**
C Sotn	**City of Southampton**
C Stke	**City of Stoke-on-Trent**
C York	**City of York**
Calder	**Calderdale (25)**
Cambs	**Cambridgeshire**
Ches E	**Cheshire East**
Ches W	**Cheshire West and Chester**
Cnwll	**Cornwall**
Covtry	**Coventry**
Cumb	**Cumbria**
Darltn	**Darlington (26)**
Derbys	**Derbyshire**
Devon	**Devon**
Donc	**Doncaster (27)**
Dorset	**Dorset**
Dudley	**Dudley (28)**
Dur	**Durham**
E R Yk	**East Riding of Yorkshire**
E Susx	**East Sussex**
Essex	**Essex**
Gatesd	**Gateshead (29)**
Gloucs	**Gloucestershire**
Gt Lon	**Greater London**
Halton	**Halton (30)**
Hants	**Hampshire**
Hartpl	**Hartlepool (31)**
Herefs	**Herefordshire**
Herts	**Hertfordshire**
IoS	**Isles of Scilly**
IoW	**Isle of Wight**
Kent	**Kent**
Kirk	**Kirklees (32)**
Knows	**Knowsley (33)**
Lancs	**Lancashire**
Leeds	**Leeds**
Leics	**Leicestershire**
Lincs	**Lincolnshire**
Lpool	**Liverpool**
Luton	**Luton**
M Keyn	**Milton Keynes**
Manch	**Manchester**
Medway	**Medway**
Middsb	**Middlesbrough**
N Linc	**North Lincolnshire**
N Som	**North Somerset (34)**
N Tyne	**North Tyneside (35)**
N u Ty	**Newcastle upon Tyne**
N York	**North Yorkshire**
NE Lin	**North East Lincolnshire**
Nhants	**Northamptonshire**
Norfk	**Norfolk**
Notts	**Nottinghamshire**
Nthumb	**Northumberland**
Oldham	**Oldham (36)**
Oxon	**Oxfordshire**
Poole	**Poole**
R & Cl	**Redcar & Cleveland**
Readg	**Reading**
Rochd	**Rochdale (37)**
Rothm	**Rotherham (38)**
Rutlnd	**Rutland**
S Glos	**South Gloucestershire (39)**
S on T	**Stockton-on-Tees (40)**
S Tyne	**South Tyneside (41)**
Salfd	**Salford (42)**
Sandw	**Sandwell (43)**
Sefton	**Sefton (44)**
Sheff	**Sheffield**
Shrops	**Shropshire**
Slough	**Slough (45)**
Solhll	**Solihull (46)**
Somset	**Somerset**
St Hel	**St Helens (47)**
Staffs	**Staffordshire**
Sthend	**Southend-on-Sea**
Stockp	**Stockport (48)**
Suffk	**Suffolk**
Sundld	**Sunderland**
Surrey	**Surrey**
Swindn	**Swindon**
Tamesd	**Tameside (49)**
Thurr	**Thurrock (50)**
Torbay	**Torbay**
Traffd	**Trafford (51)**
W & M	**Windsor and Maidenhead (52)**
W Berk	**West Berkshire**
W Susx	**West Sussex**
Wakefd	**Wakefield (53)**
Warrtn	**Warrington (54)**
Warwks	**Warwickshire**
Wigan	**Wigan (55)**
Wilts	**Wiltshire**
Wirral	**Wirral (56)**
Wokham	**Wokingham (57)**
Wolves	**Wolverhampton (58)**
Worcs	**Worcestershire**
Wrekin	**Telford & Wrekin (59)**
Wsall	**Walsall (60)**

A

Abbas Combe Somset 7 N7
Abberley Worcs 22 H14
Abberley Common Worcs 22 H14
Abberton Essex 19 M10
Abberton Worcs 15 R1
Abbess Roding Essex 18 F11
Abbeydale Sheff 31 U11
Abbey Dore Herefs 14 H5
Abbey Green Staffs 31 P14
Abbey St Bathans Border 46 K6
Abbeystead Lancs 35 P14
Abbey Town Cumb 39 T10
Abbey Village Lancs 30 J4
Abbey Wood Gt Lon 10 F2
Abbotrule Border 46 H14
Abbots Bickington Devon 4 H8
Abbots Bromley Staffs 23 M5
Abbotsbury Dorset 7 L13
Abbots Deuglie P & K 50 H14
Abbotsham Devon 4 J6
Abbotskerswell Devon 3 Q5
Abbots Langley Herts 17 N10
Abbots Leigh N Som 14 K14
Abbotsley Cambs 25 Q16
Abbots Morton Worcs 23 M16
Abbots Ripton Cambs 25 Q12
Abbot's Salford Warwks 15 S2
Abbots Worthy Hants 8 J6
Abbotts Ann Hants 8 F4
Abbott Street Dorset 7 S11
Abdon Shrops 22 E11
Aberaeron Cerdgn 20 C10
Aberaman Rhondd 14 B10
Aberangell Gwynd 20 H2
Aberarder Highld 53 R10
Aberargie P & K 50 J13
Aberarth Cerdgn 20 C10
Aberavon Neath 13 S12
Abercanaid Myr Td 14 C9
Abercarn Caerph 14 E11
Abercastle Pembks 12 D4
Abercegir Powys 20 H3
Aberchalder Lodge Highld 53 M14
Aberchirder Abers 55 M6
Abercraf Powys 13 T8
Abercregan Neath 13 T10
Abercwmboi Rhondd 14 C10
Abercych Pembks 12 K3
Abercynon Rhondd 14 C11
Aberdalgie P & K 50 H12
Aberdare Rhondd 14 B10
Aberdaron Gwynd 28 B14
Aberdeen C Aber 55 S14
Aberdeen Airport C Aber 55 R13
Aberdour Fife 45 Q3
Aberdulais Neath 13 S10
Aberdyfi Gwynd 20 E4
Aberedw Powys 21 L12
Abereiddy Pembks 12 C5
Abererch Gwynd 28 E12
Aberfan Myr Td 14 C10
Aberfeldy P & K 50 D8
Aberffraw IoA 28 D7
Aberford Leeds 32 C1
Aberfoyle Stirlg 49 U16
Abergavenny Mons 14 F8
Abergele Conwy 29 M5
Abergorlech Carmth 13 P4
Abergwesyn Powys 20 H11
Abergwili Carmth 13 M7
Abergwynfi Neath 13 U11
Abergwyngregyn Gwynd 28 H6
Abergynolwyn Gwynd 20 F3
Aberkenfig Brdgnd 13 U13
Aberlady E Loth 46 F3
Aberlemno Angus 51 P7
Aberllefenni Gwynd 20 G2
Aberllynfi Powys 14 E4
Aberlour, Charlestown of Moray 54 G8
Abermule Powys 21 N5
Abernant Carmth 13 L6
Aber-nant Rhondd 14 B9
Abernethy P & K 50 J13
Abernyte P & K 50 K11
Aberporth Cerdgn 12 K2
Abersoch Gwynd 28 C14
Abersychan Torfn 14 F9
Aberthin V Glam 14 B14
Abertillery Blae G 14 E9
Abertridwr Caerph 14 D12
Abertridwr Powys 29 P15
Aberuthven P & K 50 F13
Aberystwyth Cerdgn 20 D7
Abingdon-on-Thames Oxon 16 E10
Abinger Common Surrey 9 S4
Abinger Hammer Surrey 9 S4
Abington Nhants 24 H15
Abington S Lans 45 L13
Abington Pigotts Cambs 17 R3
Abingworth W Susx 9 S9
Ab Kettleby Leics 24 G5
Ablington Gloucs 15 T9
Abney Derbys 31 S11
Aboyne Abers 55 L15
Abram Wigan 30 J7
Abriachan Highld 53 Q9
Abridge Essex 18 E14
Abronhill N Lans 44 J4
Abson S Glos 15 M14
Abthorpe Nhants 16 G2
Aby Lincs 33 S11
Acaster Malbis C York 37 L16
Acaster Selby N York 32 E1
Accrington Lancs 31 L3
Acha Ag & B 42 e2
Achahoish Ag & B 42 K4
Achalader P & K 50 H8
Achaleven Ag & B 49 L10
Acha Mor W Isls 56 e2
Achanalt Highld 53 L4
Achandunie Highld 53 S3
Achany Highld 57 P13
Acharacle Highld 48 G5
Acharn Highld 48 G7
Acharn P & K 50 C8
Achavanich Highld 58 F7
Achduart Highld 56 G13
Achfary Highld 56 K7
A'Chill Highld 59 c14
Achiltibuie Highld 56 F12
Achina Highld 57 R4
Achinhoan Ag & B 42 K14
Achintee Highld 52 G8
Achintraid Highld 52 E8
Achmelvich Highld 56 G10
Achmore Highld 52 E9
Achmore W Isls 56 e2
Achnacarnin Highld 56 G8
Achnacarry Highld 49 P1
Achnacloich Highld 59 g14
Achnaconeran Highld 53 N12
Achnacroish Ag & B 48 K9
Achnadrish House Ag & B 48 D7
Achnafauld P & K 50 E10
Achnagarron Highld 53 S3
Achnaha Highld 48 D4
Achnahaird Highld 56 F11
Achnahannet Highld 54 C10
Achnairn Highld 57 P11
Achnalea Highld 48 K6
Achnamara Ag & B 42 K2
Achnasheen Highld 52 K5
Achnashellach Lodge Highld 52 G7
Achnastank Moray 54 H9
Achosnich Highld 48 D5
Achranich Highld 48 H8
Achreamie Highld 58 D3
Achriabhach Highld 49 P4
Achriesgill Highld 56 K5
Achtoty Highld 57 Q3
Achurch Nhants 25 M11
Achvaich Highld 57 R15
Achvarasdal Highld 58 C3
Ackergill Highld 58 H5
Acklam Middsb 36 J4
Acklam N York 37 N13
Ackleton Shrops 22 H9
Acklington Nthumb 41 P2
Ackton Wakefd 32 C4
Ackworth Moor Top Wakefd 32 C5
Acle Norfk 27 T7
Acock's Green Birm 23 N11
Acol Kent 11 T4
Acomb C York 36 K15
Acomb Nthumb 40 K7
Aconbury Herefs 14 J4
Acton Ches E 30 J15
Acton Gt Lon 17 Q13
Acton Staffs 22 J2
Acton Suffk 19 L6
Acton Beauchamp Herefs 15 M2
Acton Bridge Ches W 30 J12
Acton Burnell Shrops 22 E8
Acton Green Herefs 15 M2
Acton Park Wrexhm 30 E15
Acton Round Shrops 22 F9
Acton Scott Shrops 21 S5
Acton Trussell Staffs 22 K6
Acton Turville S Glos 15 P13
Adbaston Staffs 22 H4
Adber Dorset 7 L7
Adbolton Notts 24 F2
Adderbury Oxon 16 E4
Adderley Shrops 22 G2
Addiewell W Loth 45 M6
Addingham C Brad 36 C15
Addington Bucks 16 H5
Addington Gt Lon 10 E4
Addington Kent 10 J5
Addiscombe Gt Lon 10 D4
Addlestone Surrey 17 N16
Addlethorpe Lincs 33 U13
Adeyfield Herts 17 N9
Adfa Powys 21 L4
Adforton Herefs 21 R9
Adisham Kent 11 S6
Adlestrop Gloucs 16 A6
Adlingfleet E R Yk 32 J4
Adlington Lancs 30 J5
Admaston Staffs 23 M5
Admaston Wrekin 22 F7
Adpar Cerdgn 12 K3
Adsborough Somset 6 G6
Adscombe Somset 6 E4
Adstock Bucks 16 H5
Adstone Nhants 16 F2
Adversane W Susx 9 S8
Advie Highld 54 E9
Adwick le Street Donc 32 E6
Adwick upon Dearne Donc 32 D7
Ae D & G 39 R4
Ae Bridgend D & G 39 R4
Affleck Abers 55 M8
Affpuddle Dorset 7 P12
Affric Lodge Highld 52 K11
Afon-wen Flints 29 Q6
Afton IoW 8 F14
Agglethorpe N York 36 C9
Aigburth Lpool 30 F10
Aike E R Yk 37 S16
Aiketgate Cumb 40 D11
Aikton Cumb 39 V10
Ailsworth C Pete 25 N9
Ainderby Quernhow N York 36 G10
Ainderby Steeple N York 36 G8
Aingers Green Essex 19 P10
Ainsdale Sefton 30 E6
Ainstable Cumb 40 D11
Ainsworth Bury 31 L6
Ainthorpe N York 37 M5
Aintree Sefton 30 F8
Ainville W Loth 45 P6
Aird Ag & B 48 H16
Aird D & G 38 C8
Aird W Isls 56 f2
Aird a Mhulaidh W Isls 56 d3
Aird Asaig W Isls 56 d4
Aird Dhubh Highld 52 C8
Airdeny Ag & B 49 M11
Aird of Kinloch Ag & B 48 E11
Aird of Sleat Highld 59 g15
Airdrie N Lans 44 J6
Airdriehill N Lans 44 J6
Airds of Kells D & G 39 L7
Aird Uig W Isls 56 d2
Airidh a bhruaich W Isls 56 e3
Airieland D & G 39 M9
Airlie Angus 51 L7
Airmyn E R Yk 32 G3
Airntully P & K 50 H10
Airor Highld 52 C14
Airth Falk 45 L2
Airton N York 35 U13
Aisby Lincs 25 L2
Aisby Lincs 32 J9
Aish Devon 3 N6
Aish Devon 3 Q6
Aisholt Somset 6 F5
Aiskew N York 36 F9
Aislaby N York 37 N9
Aislaby N York 37 P5
Aislaby S on T 36 H5
Aisthorpe Lincs 33 L11
Aith Shet 59 p5
Akeld Nthumb 47 N12
Akeley Bucks 16 H4
Albaston Cnwll 2 J4
Alberbury Shrops 21 Q1
Albourne W Susx 10 C12
Albrighton Shrops 22 D6
Albrighton Shrops 22 J8
Alburgh Norfk 27 R11
Albury Herts 18 D9
Albury Surrey 9 R4
Albury Heath Surrey 9 R4
Alcaig Highld 53 Q5
Alcaston Shrops 21 S6
Alcester Warwks 23 N16
Alcester Lane End Birm 23 M12
Alciston E Susx 10 G14
Alcombe Somset 5 S3
Alconbury Cambs 25 P13
Alconbury Weston Cambs 25 P12
Aldborough N York 36 H12
Aldborough Norfk 27 Q3
Aldbourne Wilts 16 B14
Aldbrough E R Yk 33 Q1
Aldbrough St John N York 36 E5
Aldbury Herts 17 M8
Aldcliffe Lancs 35 N13
Aldclune P & K 50 E5
Aldeburgh Suffk 19 U4
Aldeby Norfk 27 T10
Aldenham Herts 17 P10
Alderbury Wilts 8 D7
Alderford Norfk 27 P6
Alderholt Dorset 8 C10
Alderley Gloucs 15 N11
Alderley Edge Ches E 31 M11
Aldermans Green Covtry 23 R11
Aldermaston W Berk 16 F16
Alderminster Warwks 15 V2
Aldershot Hants 9 P3
Alderton Gloucs 15 R4
Alderton Nhants 16 H2
Alderton Suffk 19 S6
Alderton Wilts 15 P13
Aldfield N York 36 F12
Aldford Ches W 30 F14
Aldgate Rutlnd 25 L8
Aldham Essex 19 L9
Aldham Suffk 19 N6
Aldingbourne W Susx 9 Q11
Aldingham Cumb 34 K11
Aldington Kent 11 Q9
Aldington Worcs 15 S3
Aldington Corner Kent 11 P9
Aldivalloch Moray 54 J10
Aldochlay Ag & B 44 C2
Aldreth Cambs 26 D13
Aldridge Wsall 23 M9
Aldringham Suffk 19 T3
Aldsworth Gloucs 15 T8
Aldunie Moray 54 J10
Aldwark Derbys 31 T15
Aldwark N York 36 J13
Aldwick W Susx 9 P12
Aldwincle Nhants 25 L12
Aldworth W Berk 16 F13
Alexandria W Duns 44 D3
Aley Somset 6 E4
Alfington Devon 6 D11
Alfold Surrey 9 R6
Alfold Crossways Surrey 9 R6
Alford Abers 55 M12
Alford Lincs 33 T12
Alford Somset 7 L5
Alfreton Derbys 32 C15
Alfrick Worcs 15 N1
Alfrick Pound Worcs 15 N1
Alfriston E Susx 10 G14
Algarkirk Lincs 25 Q3
Alhampton Somset 7 M5
Alkborough N Linc 32 K4
Alkham Kent 11 S8
Alkmonton Derbys 23 P2
Allaleigh Devon 3 P7
Allanaquoich Abers 54 E16
Allanbank N Lans 44 K7
Allanton Border 47 M8
Allanton N Lans 44 K7
Allanton S Lans 44 J8
Allaston Gloucs 15 L9
Allbrook Hants 8 H8
All Cannings Wilts 15 S16
Allendale Nthumb 40 J9
Allen End Warwks 23 P9
Allenheads Nthumb 40 J11
Allen's Green Herts 18 D10
Allensmore Herefs 14 J4
Allenton C Derb 23 S3
Aller Devon 5 P6
Aller Somset 6 H6
Allerby Cumb 39 S12
Allercombe Devon 6 C12
Allerford Somset 5 R3
Allerston N York 37 Q10
Allerthorpe E R Yk 37 N15
Allerton C Brad 31 R2
Allerton Highld 53 T4
Allerton Lpool 30 F10
Allerton Bywater Leeds 32 C3
Allerton Mauleverer N York 36 H14
Allesley Covtry 23 R12
Allestree C Derb 23 R2
Allexton Leics 24 J9
Allgreave Ches E 31 P13
Allhallows Medway 11 L2
Alligin Shuas Highld 52 E5
Allington Dorset 6 J12
Allington Lincs 24 J2
Allington Wilts 8 D5
Allington Wilts 15 Q14
Allington Wilts 15 S16
Allithwaite Cumb 35 L11
Alloa Clacks 45 L1
Allonby Cumb 39 S11
Alloway S Ayrs 43 T14
Allowenshay Somset 6 H8
All Stretton Shrops 21 S4
Alltchaorunn Highld 49 P7
Alltwalis Carmth 13 M5
Alltwen Neath 13 R9
Alltyblaca Cerdgn 20 D13
Allweston Dorset 7 M8
Almeley Herefs 21 Q12
Almington Staffs 22 G3
Almondbank P & K 50 G11
Almondbury Kirk 31 S5
Almondsbury S Glos 15 L13
Alne N York 36 J12
Alness Highld 53 S3
Alnham Nthumb 47 N15
Alnmouth Nthumb 47 S15
Alnwick Nthumb 47 R14
Alperton Gt Lon 17 Q13
Alphamstone Essex 18 K7
Alpheton Suffk 18 K5
Alphington Devon 5 R12
Alport Derbys 31 T13
Alpraham Ches E 30 J14
Alresford Essex 19 N10
Alrewas Staffs 23 P6
Alsager Ches E 31 M15
Alsop en le Dale Derbys 31 S15
Alston Cumb 40 G11
Alston Devon 6 G10
Alstone Gloucs 15 R5
Alstonefield Staffs 31 R15
Alston Sutton Somset 6 J2
Alswear Devon 5 N7
Altandhu Highld 56 F11
Altarnun Cnwll 4 F14
Altass Highld 57 N14
Altcreich Ag & B 48 G9
Altgaltraig Ag & B 43 P4
Althorne Essex 19 L13
Althorpe N Linc 32 J6
Altnabreac Station Highld 58 D6
Altnaharra Highld 57 P8
Alton Derbys 32 B13
Alton Hants 9 M5
Alton Staffs 23 M2
Alton Barnes Wilts 15 T16
Alton Pancras Dorset 7 N10
Alton Priors Wilts 15 T16
Altrincham Traffd 31 L10
Altskeith Hotel Stirlg 49 T15
Alva Clacks 50 E16
Alvanley Ches W 30 G12
Alvaston C Derb 23 S3
Alvechurch Worcs 23 M13
Alvecote Warwks 23 Q8
Alvediston Wilts 7 R7
Alveley Shrops 22 H11
Alverdiscott Devon 4 K6
Alverstoke Hants 8 K12
Alverstone IoW 8 K14
Alverthorpe Wakefd 31 U4
Alverton Notts 24 H2
Alves Moray 54 F4
Alvescot Oxon 16 B9
Alveston S Glos 15 L12
Alveston Warwks 23 Q16
Alvingham Lincs 33 R9
Alvington Gloucs 15 L10
Alwalton C Pete 25 N9
Alwinton Nthumb 47 M16
Alwoodley Leeds 31 U1
Alyth P & K 50 K8
Ambergate Derbys 32 B16
Amberley Gloucs 15 P10
Amberley W Susx 9 R9
Amble Nthumb 41 Q1
Amblecote Dudley 22 K11
Ambler Thorn C Brad 31 R3
Ambleside Cumb 35 L6
Ambleston Pembks 12 F6
Ambrosden Oxon 16 G7
Amcotts N Linc 32 J5
Amersham Bucks 17 L10
Amersham Common Bucks 17 M10
Amersham Old Town Bucks 17 L10
Amersham on the Hill Bucks 17 M10
Amesbury Wilts 8 D5
Amhuinnsuidhe W Isls 56 c3
Amington Staffs 23 Q8
Amisfield D & G 39 R5
Amlwch IoA 28 E3
Ammanford Carmth 13 Q8
Amotherby N York 37 N11
Ampfield Hants 8 G8
Ampleforth N York 36 K10
Ampney Crucis Gloucs 15 S10
Ampney St Mary Gloucs 15 T10
Ampney St Peter Gloucs 15 S10
Amport Hants 8 F4
Ampthill C Beds 17 N4
Ampton Suffk 26 K13
Amroth Pembks 12 H9
Amulree P & K 50 E10
Amwell Herts 17 P8
Anaheilt Highld 48 J5
Ancaster Lincs 25 L2
Ancroft Nthumb 47 P9
Ancrum Border 46 H13
Anderby Lincs 33 U12
Andover Hants 8 G4
Andoversford Gloucs 15 S7
Andreas IoM 34 e2
Anerley Gt Lon 10 D3
Anfield Lpool 30 F9
Angarrack Cnwll 1 P11
Angelbank Shrops 22 E13
Angle Pembks 12 D9
Anglesey IoA 28 E5
Angmering W Susx 9 S11
Angram N York 36 K15
Ankerville Highld 53 U2
Anlaby E R Yk 33 M3
Anmer Norfk 26 H4
Anmore Hants 9 L10
Annan D & G 39 U7
Annat Highld 52 F6
Annathill N Lans 44 H5
Anna Valley Hants 8 F4
Annbank S Ayrs 44 D13
Annfield Plain Dur 41 N10
Anniesland C Glas 44 F5
Ansdell Lancs 30 E3
Ansford Somset 7 M5
Ansley Warwks 23 R10
Anslow Staffs 23 P5
Anslow Gate Staffs 23 P5
Anstey Herts 18 D8
Anstey Leics 24 E7
Anstruther Fife 51 Q15
Ansty W Susx 10 D11
Ansty Warwks 23 S11
Ansty Wilts 7 R6
Anthorn Cumb 39 U9
Antingham Norfk 27 R3
An t-Ob W Isls 56 c4
Anton's Gowt Lincs 25 R1
Antony Cnwll 2 J7
Antrobus Ches W 30 K11
Anwick Lincs 33 N16
Anwoth D & G 38 K9
Aperfield Gt Lon 10 E5
Apethorpe Nhants 25 M9
Apley Lincs 33 N12
Apperknowle Derbys 32 C11
Apperley Gloucs 15 P5
Appin Ag & B 49 L8
Appleby N Linc 33 L5
Appleby-in-Westmorland Cumb 35 R3
Appleby Magna Leics 23 R7
Appleby Parva Leics 23 R7
Applecross Highld 52 C7
Appledore Devon 4 J6
Appledore Devon 6 D8
Appledore Kent 11 N10
Appleford Oxon 16 E11
Applegarth Town D & G 39 S4
Appleshaw Hants 8 F4
Appleton Halton 30 H10
Appleton Oxon 16 D10
Appleton Warrtn 30 J10
Appleton-le-Moors N York 37 N9
Appleton-le-Street N York 37 N11
Appleton Roebuck N York 36 K16
Appleton Thorn Warrtn 30 J10
Appleton Wiske N York 36 H6
Appletreehall Border 46 G14
Appletreewick N York 36 C13
Appley Somset 6 D7
Appley Bridge Lancs 30 H6
Apse Heath IoW 8 J14
Apsley End C Beds 17 P5
Apuldram W Susx 9 N11
Arabella Highld 53 U2
Arbirlot Angus 51 Q9
Arboll Highld 54 B1
Arborfield Wokham 16 J15
Arborfield Cross Wokham 16 J15
Arbourthorne Sheff 32 B10
Arbroath Angus 51 R9
Arbuthnott Abers 51 T3
Archddu Carmth 13 M10
Archdeacon Newton Darltn 36 F4
Archencarroch W Duns 44 D3
Archiestown Moray 54 G7
Arclid Green Ches E 31 M14
Ardallie Abers 55 T8
Ardanaiseig Hotel Ag & B 49 N12
Ardaneaskan Highld 52 E9
Ardarroch Highld 52 E8
Ardbeg Ag & B 42 E9
Ardbeg Ag & B 43 P6
Ardbeg Ag & B 43 Q3
Ardcharnich Highld 56 H15
Ardchiavaig Ag & B 48 C13
Ardchonnel Ag & B 49 L14
Ardchullarie More Stirlg 49 V13
Arddarroch Ag & B 43 R1
Arddleen Powys 29 S15
Ardechive Highld 49 P1
Ardeer N Ayrs 43 S10
Ardeley Herts 17 R5
Ardelve Highld 52 F10
Arden Ag & B 44 C3
Ardens Grafton Warwks 15 T1
Ardentallen Ag & B 48 J12
Ardentinny Ag & B 43 R2
Ardentraive Ag & B 43 P4
Ardeonaig Stirlg 50 B10
Ardersier Highld 53 T6
Ardessie Highld 56 G15
Ardfern Ag & B 48 J15
Ardfernal Ag & B 42 G5
Ardgartan Ag & B 49 R15
Ardgay Highld 57 P15
Ardgour Highld 49 M5
Ardgowan Inver 43 R5
Ardhallow Ag & B 43 Q4
Ardhasig W Isls 56 d4
Ardheslaig Highld 52 D5
Ardindrean Highld 56 H15
Ardingly W Susx 10 D10
Ardington Oxon 16 D12
Ardlamont Ag & B 43 N6
Ardleigh Essex 19 N8
Ardleigh Heath Essex 19 N8
Ardler P & K 50 K9
Ardley Oxon 16 F5
Ardlui Ag & B 49 R13
Ardlussa Ag & B 42 H2
Ardmair Highld 56 H14
Ardmaleish Ag & B 43 P5
Ardminish Ag & B 42 H9
Ardmolich Highld 48 H4
Ardmore Ag & B 43 T4
Ardmore Highld 57 R16
Ardnadam Ag & B 43 Q3
Ardnagrask Highld 53 Q6
Ardnarff Highld 52 F9
Ardnastang Highld 48 J6
Ardpatrick Ag & B 42 K7
Ardrishaig Ag & B 43 L2
Ardross Highld 53 R2
Ardrossan N Ayrs 43 R10
Ardsley East Leeds 31 U3
Ardslignish Highld 48 F6
Ardtalla Ag & B 42 F8
Ardtoe Highld 48 F4
Arduaine Ag & B 48 J14
Ardullie Highld 53 R4
Ardvasar Highld 52 B14
Ardvorlich P & K 50 A12
Ardvourlie W Isls 56 d3
Ardwell D & G 38 C11
Ardwick Manch 31 N8
Areley Kings Worcs 22 J13
Arevegaig Highld 48 G4
Arford Hants 9 N6
Argoed Caerph 14 E10
Aribruach W Isls 56 e3
Aridhglas Ag & B 48 B12
Arileod Ag & B 42 d2
Arinagour Ag & B 42 e2
Ariogan Ag & B 48 K11
Arisaig Highld 48 G1
Arisaig House Highld 48 G2
Arkendale N York 36 H13
Arkesden Essex 18 E8
Arkholme Lancs 35 P11
Arkleton D & G 40 B3
Arkley Gt Lon 17 Q11
Arksey Donc 32 E6
Arkwright Town Derbys 32 C12
Arle Gloucs 15 Q6
Arlecdon Cumb 34 G4
Arlesey C Beds 17 Q4
Arleston Wrekin 22 G7
Arley Ches E 30 K11
Arley Warwks 23 Q10
Arlingham Gloucs 15 M8
Arlington Devon 5 M4
Arlington E Susx 10 G14
Armadale Highld 52 B14
Armadale Highld 57 S3
Armadale W Loth 45 L5
Armathwaite Cumb 40 D11
Arminghall Norfk 27 R8
Armitage Staffs 23 M6
Armley Leeds 31 T2
Armscote Warwks 16 A3
Armthorpe Donc 32 F7
Arnabost Ag & B 42 e2
Arncliffe N York 35 U11
Arncroach Fife 51 P15
Arndilly House Moray 54 H7
Arne Dorset 7 R13
Arnesby Leics 24 F10
Arngask P & K 50 H14
Arnisdale Highld 52 E13
Arnish Highld 59 g8
Arniston Mdloth 46 D6
Arnol W Isls 56 e1
Arnold E R Yk 33 N1
Arnold Notts 24 E1
Arnprior Stirlg 44 G1
Arnside Cumb 35 M10
Aros Ag & B 48 F8
Arrad Foot Cumb 34 K10
Arram E R Yk 37 S16
Arran N Ayrs 43 M11
Arrathorne N York 36 E8
Arreton IoW 8 J14
Arrina Highld 52 D5
Arrington Cambs 17 S2
Arrochar Ag & B 49 R15
Arrow Warwks 23 N16
Arscott Shrops 21 R2
Artafallie Highld 53 R6
Arthington Leeds 36 F16
Arthingworth Nhants 24 H12
Arthrath Abers 55 S9
Artrochie Abers 55 T9
Arundel W Susx 9 R10
Asby Cumb 34 G3
Ascog Ag & B 43 Q6
Ascot W & M 17 L15
Ascott-under-Wychwood Oxon 16 B7
Asenby N York 36 H11
Asfordby Leics 24 G6
Asfordby Hill Leics 24 G6
Asgarby Lincs 25 N1
Ash Kent 10 H4
Ash Kent 11 T5
Ash Somset 6 J7
Ash Surrey 9 P3
Ashampstead W Berk 16 F14
Ashbocking Suffk 19 Q4
Ashbourne Derbys 23 P1
Ashbrittle Somset 6 D7
Ashburton Devon 3 P4
Ashbury Devon 4 K11
Ashbury Oxon 16 B12
Ashby N Linc 32 K6
Ashby by Partney Lincs 33 S13
Ashby cum Fenby NE Lin 33 Q7
Ashby de la Launde Lincs 33 M15
Ashby-de-la-Zouch Leics 23 R6

Ashby Folville – Boltonfellend 63

Ashby Folville Leics 24 G7
Ashby Magna Leics 24 E10
Ashby Parva Leics 24 E11
Ashby Puerorum Lincs 33 R12
Ashby St Ledgers Nhants 24 E14
Ashby St Mary Norfk 27 S8
Ashchurch Gloucs 15 Q4
Ashcombe Devon 5 R14
Ashcombe N Som 14 G16
Ashcott Somset 6 J5
Ashdon Essex 18 F6
Ashe Hants 8 J3
Asheldham Essex 19 M13
Ashen Essex 18 J6
Ashendon Bucks 16 H8
Asheridge Bucks 17 L9
Ashfield Stirlg 50 D15
Ashfield cum Thorpe Suffk 19 Q3
Ashfield Green Suffk 27 R13
Ashford Devon 3 N8
Ashford Devon 4 K5
Ashford Kent 11 P8
Ashford Surrey 17 N15
Ashford Bowdler Shrops 22 E14
Ashford Carbonell Shrops 22 E14
Ashford Hill Hants 8 J1
Ashford in the Water Derbys 31 S13
Ashgill S Lans 44 J8
Ash Green Surrey 9 P3
Ash Green Warwks 23 R11
Ashill Devon 6 D9
Ashill Norfk 26 K8
Ashill Somset 6 G8
Ashingdon Essex 18 K14
Ashington Nthumb 41 Q4
Ashington Somset 7 L7
Ashington W Susx 9 S9
Ashkirk Border 46 F13
Ashleworth Gloucs 15 P6
Ashleworth Quay Gloucs 15 P6
Ashley Cambs 18 H3
Ashley Ches E 31 L10
Ashley Devon 5 M9
Ashley Gloucs 15 Q11
Ashley Hants 8 E12
Ashley Hants 8 G6
Ashley Kent 11 T7
Ashley Nhants 24 H10
Ashley Staffs 22 H3
Ashley Wilts 15 P15
Ashley Green Bucks 17 M9
Ash Magna Shrops 22 E2
Ashmansworth Hants 8 G2
Ashmansworthy Devon 4 H8
Ash Mill Devon 5 P7
Ashmore Dorset 7 R8
Ashmore Green W Berk 16 E15
Ashorne Warwks 23 R16
Ashover Derbys 32 B14
Ashow Warwks 23 R14
Ashperton Herefs 15 L3
Ashprington Devon 3 P7
Ash Priors Somset 6 E6
Ashreigney Devon 5 M8
Ash Street Suffk 19 M6
Ashtead Surrey 9 T2
Ash Thomas Devon 5 S9
Ashton Ches W 30 H13
Ashton Cnwll 1 Q13
Ashton Devon 5 Q13
Ashton Herefs 22 E15
Ashton Inver 43 R4
Ashton Nhants 16 J2
Ashton Nhants 25 M11
Ashton Common Wilts 7 Q1
Ashton-in-Makerfield Wigan 30 J8
Ashton Keynes Wilts 15 S11
Ashton under Hill Worcs 15 R4
Ashton-under-Lyne Tamesd 31 P8
Ashurst Hants 8 F10
Ashurst Kent 10 G8
Ashurst Lancs 30 G6
Ashurst W Susx 9 T9
Ashurstwood W Susx 10 E9
Ash Vale Surrey 9 P3
Ashwater Devon 4 H11
Ashwell Herts 17 R3
Ashwell Rutlnd 24 J6
Ashwell End Herts 17 R3
Ashwellthorpe Norfk 27 P9
Ashwick Somset 7 M3
Ashwicken Norfk 26 H6
Askam in Furness Cumb 34 J10
Askern Donc 32 E5
Askerswell Dorset 6 K12
Askett Bucks 16 J9
Askham Cumb 35 N3
Askham Notts 32 H12
Askham Bryan C York 36 K15
Askham Richard C York 36 K15
Asknish Ag & B 43 M2
Askrigg N York 35 U8
Askwith N York 36 E15
Aslackby Lincs 25 N4
Aslacton Norfk 27 P10
Aslockton Notts 24 H2
Aspatria Cumb 39 T11
Aspenden Herts 17 S5
Aspley Guise C Beds 17 L4
Aspley Heath C Beds 17 L4
Aspull Wigan 30 J6
Asselby E R Yk 32 G3
Assington Suffk 19 L7
Assington Green Suffk 18 J5
Astbury Ches E 31 M14
Astcote Nhants 16 H1
Asterby Lincs 33 Q11
Asterley Shrops 21 R3
Asterton Shrops 21 R5
Asthall Oxon 16 B8
Asthall Leigh Oxon 16 B8
Astle Highld 57 R15
Astley Shrops 22 E6
Astley Warwks 23 R10
Astley Wigan 30 K7
Astley Worcs 22 H14
Astley Abbots Shrops 22 G9
Astley Bridge Bolton 31 L6
Astley Cross Worcs 22 J14
Aston Birm 23 N11
Aston Ches E 22 F1
Aston Ches W 30 H11
Aston Derbys 31 S10
Aston Flints 30 E13
Aston Herts 17 R6
Aston Oxon 16 C9
Aston Rothm 32 D10
Aston Shrops 22 E4
Aston Shrops 22 J10
Aston Staffs 22 H2
Aston Staffs 22 K5
Aston Wokham 16 J13
Aston Wrekin 22 F7
Aston Abbotts Bucks 16 K7
Aston Botterell Shrops 22 F11
Aston-by-Stone Staffs 22 K4
Aston Cantlow Warwks 23 N15
Aston Clinton Bucks 16 K8
Aston Crews Herefs 15 M6
Aston End Herts 17 R6
Aston Fields Worcs 23 L14
Aston Flamville Leics 24 D10
Aston Ingham Herefs 15 M6
Aston le Walls Nhants 16 E2
Aston Magna Gloucs 15 U4
Aston Munslow Shrops 22 E11
Aston on Clun Shrops 21 R7
Aston Pigott Shrops 21 Q3
Aston Rogers Shrops 21 Q3
Aston Rowant Oxon 16 H10
Aston Somerville Worcs 15 S4
Aston-sub-Edge Gloucs 15 T3
Aston Tirrold Oxon 16 F12
Aston-upon-Trent Derbys 23 S4
Aston Upthorpe Oxon 16 F12
Astwick C Beds 17 Q4
Astwood M Keyn 17 L2
Astwood Worcs 22 K14
Astwood Bank Worcs 23 M15
Aswarby Lincs 25 M2
Aswardby Lincs 33 S12
Atcham Shrops 22 E7
Athelhampton Dorset 7 P12
Athelington Suffk 27 Q13
Athelney Somset 6 H6
Athelstaneford E Loth 46 G4
Atherington Devon 5 L7
Atherstone Warwks 23 R9
Atherstone on Stour Warwks 15 U2
Atherton Wigan 30 K7
Atlow Derbys 31 T16
Attadale Highld 52 F8
Atterby Lincs 33 L9
Attercliffe Sheff 32 C9
Atterton Leics 23 R9
Attleborough Norfk 27 N9
Attleborough Warwks 23 S10
Attlebridge Norfk 27 P6
Attleton Green Suffk 18 H4
Atwick E R Yk 37 U15
Atworth Wilts 15 P16
Aubourn Lincs 32 K14
Auchbreck Moray 54 G10
Auchedly Abers 55 R9
Auchenblae Abers 51 S3
Auchenbowie Stirlg 44 J2
Auchencairn D & G 39 N10
Auchencairn D & G 39 R4
Auchencairn N Ayrs 43 P12
Auchencrow Border 47 L7
Auchendinny Mdloth 45 R6
Auchengray S Lans 45 M8
Auchenhalrig Moray 54 J4
Auchenheath S Lans 44 J9
Auchenhessnane D & G 39 N2
Auchenlochan Ag & B 43 N5
Auchenmade N Ayrs 44 C9
Auchenmalg D & G 38 E10
Auchentiber N Ayrs 44 C9
Auchindrain Ag & B 49 M15
Auchindrean Highld 52 K1
Auchininna Abers 55 N7
Auchinleck E Ayrs 44 F13
Auchinloch N Lans 44 G5
Auchinstarry N Lans 44 H4
Auchintore Highld 49 N4
Auchiries Abers 55 U8
Auchlean Highld 54 B15
Auchlee Abers 55 R15
Auchleven Abers 55 M11
Auchlochan S Lans 44 J10
Auchlossan Abers 55 M14
Auchlyne Stirlg 49 U11
Auchmillan E Ayrs 44 E12
Auchmithie Angus 51 R8
Auchmuirbridge Fife 50 K15
Auchnacree Angus 51 N5
Auchnagatt Abers 55 S8
Auchnarrow Moray 54 G11
Auchnotteroch D & G 38 B8
Auchroisk Moray 54 H6
Auchterarder P & K 50 F14
Auchteraw Highld 53 M13
Auchterblair Highld 54 C11
Auchtercairn Highld 52 E2
Auchterderran Fife 45 Q1
Auchterhouse Angus 51 L10
Auchterless Abers 55 P8
Auchtermuchty Fife 50 K14
Auchterneed Highld 53 P5
Auchtertool Fife 45 Q2
Auchtertyre Highld 52 E10
Auchtubh Stirlg 49 U12
Auckengill Highld 58 J3
Auckley Donc 32 F7
Audenshaw Tamesd 31 N8
Audlem Ches E 22 G2
Audley Staffs 31 M16
Audley End Essex 18 E7
Audnam Dudley 22 K11
Aughton E R Yk 32 G1
Aughton Lancs 30 F7
Aughton Lancs 35 P12
Aughton Rothm 32 D10
Aughton Wilts 8 E2
Aughton Park Lancs 30 F6
Auldearn Highld 54 C6
Aulden Herefs 21 S11
Auldgirth D & G 39 Q4
Auldhouse S Lans 44 G8
Ault a' chruinn Highld 52 G11
Aultbea Highld 56 D15
Aultgrishin Highld 56 B16
Aultguish Inn Highld 53 M3
Ault Hucknall Derbys 32 D13
Aultmore Moray 54 J6
Aultnagoire Highld 53 Q11
Aultnamain Inn Highld 53 S1
Aunsby Lincs 25 M2
Aust S Glos 14 K12
Austerfield Donc 32 G8
Austrey Warwks 23 R8
Austwick N York 35 S12
Authorpe Lincs 33 S11
Avebury Wilts 15 T15
Aveley Thurr 10 G2
Avening Gloucs 15 Q10
Averham Notts 32 H15
Aveton Gifford Devon 3 N8
Aviemore Highld 54 B12
Avington W Berk 16 C15
Avoch Highld 53 S6
Avon Hants 8 D12
Avonbridge Falk 45 L5
Avon Dassett Warwks 16 D2
Avonmouth Bristl 14 K14
Avonwick Devon 3 N6
Awbridge Hants 8 F8
Awliscombe Devon 6 E10
Awre Gloucs 15 M9
Awsworth Notts 24 D1
Axbridge Somset 6 J2
Axford Hants 8 K4
Axford Wilts 15 V15
Axminster Devon 6 G11
Axmouth Devon 6 F12
Aycliffe Dur 36 F3
Aydon Nthumb 41 L8
Aylburton Gloucs 15 L10
Aylesbeare Devon 5 T12
Aylesbury Bucks 16 K8
Aylesby NE Lin 33 P6
Aylesford Kent 10 K5
Aylesham Kent 11 S6
Aylestone C Leic 24 E9
Aylestone Park C Leic 24 F9
Aylmerton Norfk 27 Q2
Aylsham Norfk 27 Q4
Aylton Herefs 15 L4
Aylworth Gloucs 15 T6
Aymestrey Herefs 21 R9
Aynho Nhants 16 E5
Ayot St Lawrence Herts 17 Q7
Ayr S Ayrs 43 T13
Aysgarth N York 36 B9
Ayshford Devon 6 C8
Ayside Cumb 35 M9
Ayston Rutlnd 24 J9
Ayton Border 47 M7
Azerley N York 36 F11

B

Babbacombe Torbay 3 R5
Babbs Green Herts 18 D11
Babcary Somset 7 L6
Babraham Cambs 18 E5
Babworth Notts 32 G11
Backaland Ork 58 d2
Backfolds Abers 55 T6
Backford Ches W 30 F12
Backies Highld 57 T13
Back of Keppoch Highld 48 G1
Backwell N Som 14 J15
Baconsthorpe Norfk 27 P3
Bacton Herefs 14 G5
Bacton Norfk 27 S3
Bacton Suffk 27 N14
Bacup Lancs 31 N4
Badachro Highld 52 D3
Badbury Swindn 15 U13
Badby Nhants 24 E16
Badcall Highld 56 H7
Badcall Highld 56 J4
Badcaul Highld 56 F15
Baddeley Edge C Stke 31 N16
Baddeley Green C Stke 31 N16
Baddesley Clinton Warwks 23 P13
Baddesley Ensor Warwks 23 Q9
Baddidarrach Highld 56 G10
Baddinsgill Border 45 P8
Badenscoth Abers 55 P8
Badentarbet Highld 56 F12
Badenyon Abers 54 H11
Badger Shrops 22 H9
Badgeworth Gloucs 15 Q7
Badgworth Somset 6 H2
Badicaul Highld 52 D10
Badingham Suffk 27 R14
Badlesmere Kent 11 P6
Badlieu Border 45 N13
Badlipster Highld 58 G6
Badluarach Highld 56 F14
Badninish Highld 57 S14
Badrallach Highld 56 G15
Badsey Worcs 15 S3
Badshot Lea Surrey 9 P4
Badsworth Wakefd 32 D5
Badwell Ash Suffk 27 M14
Bagber Dorset 7 N8
Bagby N York 36 J10
Bag Enderby Lincs 33 R12
Bagendon Gloucs 15 R9
Bagh a Chaisteil W Isls 56 a9
Bagh a Tuath W Isls 56 b8
Bagillt Flints 29 R6
Baginton Warwks 23 R13
Baglan Neath 13 S11
Bagley Shrops 22 C4
Bagley Somset 6 J3
Bagnall Staffs 31 P16
Bagshot Surrey 9 P1
Bagstone S Glos 15 M12
Bagworth Leics 24 D7
Bagwy Llydiart Herefs 14 H6
Baildon C Brad 31 S1
Baildon Green C Brad 31 S1
Baile Ailein W Isls 56 e3
Baile a Mhanaich W Isls 56 b6
Baile Mór Ag & B 48 B12
Baillieston C Glas 44 H6
Bainbridge N York 35 U8
Bainshole Abers 55 M9
Bainton C Pete 25 N8
Bainton E R Yk 37 R15
Baintown Fife 51 L15
Bairnkine Border 46 J14
Bakewell Derbys 31 T13
Bala Gwynd 29 M12
Balallan W Isls 56 e3
Balbeg Highld 53 P9
Balbeggie P & K 50 J11
Balblair Highld 53 Q7
Balblair Highld 53 S4
Balby Donc 32 E7
Balcary D & G 39 N10
Balchraggan Highld 53 Q7
Balchreick Highld 56 J4
Balcombe W Susx 10 D10
Balcomie Links Fife 51 Q14
Baldersby N York 36 G10
Baldersby St James N York 36 G11
Balderstone Lancs 30 J2
Balderton Notts 32 J16
Baldinnie Fife 51 N14
Baldinnies P & K 50 G13
Baldock Herts 17 R4
Baldovie C Dund 51 N10
Baldrine IoM 34 e5
Baldslow E Susx 11 L13
Bale Norfk 27 M3
Baledgarno P & K 50 K11
Balemartine Ag & B 42 b4
Balerno C Edin 45 P6
Balfarg Fife 50 K15
Balfield Angus 51 P4
Balfour Ork 58 c3
Balfron Stirlg 44 F2
Balgaveny Abers 55 N8
Balgonar Fife 45 M1
Balgowan D & G 38 C11
Balgowan Highld 53 R16
Balgown Highld 59 d6
Balgracie D & G 38 B8
Balgray S Lans 45 L13
Balham Gt Lon 10 C3
Balhary P & K 50 K8
Balholmie P & K 50 J10
Baligill Highld 57 T3
Balintore Angus 51 L6
Balintore Highld 54 B2
Balintraid Highld 53 T3
Balivanich W Isls 56 b6
Balkeerie Angus 51 L8
Balkholme E R Yk 32 H3
Ballachulish Highld 49 N6
Ballajora IoM 34 f4
Ballanlay Ag & B 43 P6
Ballantrae S Ayrs 38 C5
Ballasalla IoM 34 c7
Ballater Abers 54 J15
Ballaugh IoM 34 d3
Ballchraggan Highld 53 T2
Ballencrieff E Loth 46 F4
Ballevullin Ag & B 42 b4
Ball Green C Stke 31 N15
Ballidon Derbys 31 S15
Balliekine N Ayrs 43 L10
Balliemore Ag & B 49 N16
Balligmorrie S Ayrs 38 E3
Ballimore Stirlg 49 U13
Ballindalloch Moray 54 F9
Ballindean P & K 50 K11
Ballinger Common Bucks 17 L9
Ballingham Herefs 14 K5
Ballingry Fife 50 J16
Ballinluig P & K 50 F7
Ballinshoe Angus 51 M7
Ballintuim P & K 50 H7
Balloch Highld 53 T7
Balloch N Lans 44 H4
Balloch P & K 50 D12
Balloch S Ayrs 38 F3
Balloch W Duns 44 D3
Balls Cross W Susx 9 Q7
Balls Green E Susx 10 F9
Ballygown Ag & B 48 D9
Ballygrant Ag & B 42 E6
Ballyhaugh Ag & B 42 e2
Balmaclellan D & G 39 L5
Balmae D & G 39 L11
Balmaha Stirlg 44 D2
Balmalcolm Fife 51 L14
Balmangan D & G 39 L11
Balmedie Abers 55 S12
Balmerino Fife 51 M12
Balmichael N Ayrs 43 M11
Balmore E Duns 44 G4
Balmuchy Highld 54 B2
Balmule Fife 45 Q2
Balmullo Fife 51 N12
Balnacoil Lodge Highld 57 S12
Balnacra Highld 52 G7
Balnacroft Abers 54 H16
Balnafoich Highld 53 S9
Balnaguard P & K 50 F7
Balnahard Ag & B 48 C16
Balnahard Ag & B 48 D10
Balnain Highld 53 P10
Balnakeil Highld 57 M2
Balne N York 32 F4
Balquharn P & K 50 G10
Balquhidder Stirlg 49 U12
Balsall Common Solhll 23 Q13
Balsall Heath Birm 23 M11
Balscote Oxon 16 D3
Balsham Cambs 18 F5
Baltasound Shet 59 r2
Baltersan D & G 38 H8
Balthangie Abers 55 Q6
Baltonsborough Somset 6 K5
Balvicar Ag & B 48 H13
Balvraid Highld 52 E12
Balvraid Highld 53 U9
Bamber Bridge Lancs 30 H3
Bamber's Green Essex 18 F9
Bamburgh Nthumb 47 R11
Bamford Derbys 31 S10
Bampton Cumb 35 N4
Bampton Devon 5 R7
Bampton Oxon 16 B9
Bampton Grange Cumb 35 N4
Banavie Highld 49 N3
Banbury Oxon 16 D3
Bancffosfelen Carmth 13 N8
Banchory Abers 55 P15
Banchory-Devenick Abers 55 R14
Bancycapel Carmth 13 M7
Bancyfelin Carmth 13 L7
Bandirran P & K 50 J11
Banff Abers 55 N4
Bangor Gwynd 28 G6
Bangor-on-Dee Wrexhm 22 C1
Bangors Cnwll 4 F11
Banham Norfk 27 N11
Bank Hants 8 F10
Bankend D & G 39 R7
Bankfoot P & K 50 G10
Bankglen E Ayrs 44 F15
Bankhead C Aber 55 R13
Bankhead S Lans 45 M9
Banknock Falk 44 J4
Banks Lancs 30 F4
Bankshill D & G 39 U5
Banningham Norfk 27 Q4
Bannister Green Essex 18 H10
Bannockburn Stirlg 44 J2
Banstead Surrey 10 C5
Bantham Devon 3 M9
Banton N Lans 44 J4
Banwell N Som 6 H1
Bapchild Kent 11 M5
Bapton Wilts 7 S4
Barabhas W Isls 56 e1
Barassie S Ayrs 43 T11
Barbaraville Highld 53 T3
Barbieston S Ayrs 44 D14
Barbon Cumb 35 Q10
Barbrook Devon 5 N3
Barby Nhants 24 E14
Barcaldine Ag & B 49 L9
Barcombe E Susx 10 E12
Barcombe Cross E Susx 10 E12
Barden Park Kent 10 H7
Bardfield End Green Essex 18 G8
Bardfield Saling Essex 18 H9
Bardney Lincs 33 N13
Bardon Leics 24 D7
Bardon Mill Nthumb 40 H8
Bardowie E Duns 44 F5
Bardrainney Inver 43 T5
Bardsea Cumb 34 K11
Bardsey Leeds 36 G16
Bardwell Suffk 27 L13
Bare Lancs 35 M13
Barfad D & G 38 F7
Barford Norfk 27 P7
Barford Warwks 23 Q15
Barford St John Oxon 16 D4
Barford St Martin Wilts 7 T5
Barford St Michael Oxon 16 D5
Barfrestone Kent 11 S7
Bargeddie N Lans 44 H6
Bargoed Caerph 14 D10
Bargrennan D & G 38 G6
Barham Cambs 25 N13
Barham Kent 11 R7
Barham Suffk 19 P5
Bar Hill Cambs 25 S15
Barholm Lincs 25 N7
Barkby Leics 24 F7
Barkby Thorpe Leics 24 F7
Barkestone-le-Vale Leics 24 H3
Barkham Wokham 16 J15
Barking Gt Lon 18 D16
Barking Suffk 19 N4
Barkingside Gt Lon 18 D15
Barking Tye Suffk 19 N5
Barkisland Calder 31 Q4
Barkla Shop Cnwll 1 S9
Barkston Lincs 24 K2
Barkston Ash N York 32 D2
Barkway Herts 17 S4
Barlanark C Glas 44 G6
Barlaston Staffs 22 K2
Barlavington W Susx 9 Q9
Barlborough Derbys 32 D11
Barlby N York 32 F2
Barlestone Leics 23 S8
Barley Herts 18 D7
Barley Lancs 31 M1
Barleythorpe Rutlnd 24 J7
Barling Essex 19 L15
Barlings Lincs 33 M12
Barlochan D & G 39 N9
Barlow Derbys 32 B12
Barlow Gatesd 41 N8
Barlow N York 32 F3
Barmby Moor E R Yk 37 N15
Barmby on the Marsh E R Yk 32 G3
Barmollack Ag & B 42 K9
Barmouth Gwynd 28 H16
Barmpton Darltn 36 G4
Barmston E R Yk 37 U13
Barnacarry Ag & B 43 N1
Barnack C Pete 25 M8
Barnard Castle Dur 36 C4
Barnard Gate Oxon 16 D8
Barnardiston Suffk 18 H5
Barnbarroch D & G 39 P9
Barnburgh Donc 32 D7
Barnby Suffk 27 U10
Barnby Dun Donc 32 F6
Barnby in the Willows Notts 32 J15
Barnby Moor Notts 32 G10
Barncorkrie D & G 38 C12
Barnes Gt Lon 17 Q14
Barnes Street Kent 10 J7
Barnet Gt Lon 17 R11
Barnetby le Wold N Linc 33 M6
Barney Norfk 27 M3
Barnham Suffk 26 K12
Barnham W Susx 9 Q11
Barnham Broom Norfk 27 N7
Barnhead Angus 51 R6
Barnhill C Dund 51 N11
Barnhill Moray 54 F5
Barnhills D & G 38 B7
Barningham Dur 36 C5
Barningham Suffk 27 M12
Barnoldby le Beck NE Lin 33 Q7
Barnoldswick Lancs 35 T15
Barns Green W Susx 9 S7
Barnsley Barns 32 B7
Barnsley Gloucs 15 S9
Barnstaple Devon 5 L5
Barnston Essex 18 G10
Barnston Wirral 30 D10
Barnstone Notts 24 H3
Barnt Green Worcs 23 M13
Barnton C Edin 45 Q4
Barnton Ches W 30 J12
Barnwell All Saints Nhants 25 M11
Barnwell St Andrew Nhants 25 M11
Barnwood Gloucs 15 P7
Barr S Ayrs 38 F3
Barra Airport W Isls 56 b8
Barrachan D & G 38 G10
Barrapoll Ag & B 42 b4
Barrasford Nthumb 40 K6
Barrhead E Rens 44 E7
Barrhill S Ayrs 38 E5
Barrington Cambs 18 D5
Barrington Somset 6 H8
Barripper Cnwll 1 Q11
Barrmill N Ayrs 44 C8
Barrock Highld 58 G2
Barrow Gloucs 15 Q6
Barrow Lancs 31 L1
Barrow Rutlnd 24 K6
Barrow Somset 7 N5
Barrow Suffk 18 J3
Barrowby Lincs 24 K3
Barrowden Rutlnd 25 L9
Barrowford Lancs 31 N1
Barrow Gurney N Som 14 K15
Barrow Haven N Linc 33 M4
Barrow-in-Furness Cumb 34 J12
Barrow Island Cumb 34 J12
Barrow-upon-Humber N Linc 33 M4
Barrow upon Soar Leics 24 E6
Barrow upon Trent Derbys 23 R4
Barry Angus 51 P10
Barry V Glam 14 D15
Barry Island V Glam 14 D15
Barsby Leics 24 G7
Barsham Suffk 27 T10
Barston Solhll 23 P12
Bartestree Herefs 14 K3
Barthol Chapel Abers 55 Q9
Bartholomew Green Essex 18 H10
Barthomley Ches E 31 L15
Bartley Hants 8 F9
Bartley Green Birm 23 L12
Bartlow Cambs 18 F6
Barton Cambs 25 S16
Barton Ches W 30 G15
Barton Gloucs 15 T6
Barton Lancs 30 F6
Barton Lancs 30 H1
Barton N York 36 E5
Barton Oxon 16 F9
Barton Torbay 3 R5
Barton Bendish Norfk 26 H8
Barton End Gloucs 15 P10
Barton Hartshorn Bucks 16 G5
Barton in Fabis Notts 24 E3
Barton in the Beans Leics 23 S8
Barton-le-Clay C Beds 17 N5
Barton-le-Street N York 37 M11
Barton-le-Willows N York 37 M13
Barton Mills Suffk 26 H13
Barton-on-Sea Hants 8 E13
Barton-on-the-Heath Warwks 16 B5
Barton St David Somset 6 K5
Barton Seagrave Nhants 24 K12
Barton Stacey Hants 8 H5
Barton Town Devon 5 N4
Barton Turf Norfk 27 S5
Barton-under-Needwood Staffs 23 P6
Barton-upon-Humber N Linc 33 M4
Barton Waterside N Linc 33 M4
Barvas W Isls 56 e1
Barway Cambs 26 F13
Barwell Leics 24 C9
Barwick Devon 5 L9
Barwick Somset 7 L8
Barwick in Elmet Leeds 32 C1
Baschurch Shrops 22 C5
Bascote Warwks 23 S15
Bashall Eaves Lancs 35 R16
Basildon Essex 18 H15
Basingstoke Hants 8 K3
Baslow Derbys 31 T12
Bason Bridge Somset 6 H3
Bassaleg Newpt 14 F12
Bassendean Border 46 H9
Bassenthwaite Cumb 39 U13
Bassett C Sotn 8 G9
Bassingbourn-cum-Kneesworth Cambs 17 S3
Bassingham Lincs 32 K14
Bassingthorpe Lincs 25 L4
Bassus Green Herts 17 R6
Baston Lincs 25 N6
Bastwick Norfk 27 T6
Batchworth Herts 17 N11
Batcombe Dorset 7 L10
Batcombe Somset 7 M4
Batford Herts 17 P7
Bath BaNES 15 N16
Bathampton BaNES 15 N15
Bathealton Somset 6 D7
Batheaston BaNES 15 N15
Bathford BaNES 15 N15
Bathgate W Loth 45 M5
Bathley Notts 32 H14
Bathpool Cnwll 2 G4
Bathpool Somset 6 F6
Bath Side Essex 19 R8
Bathville W Loth 45 L5
Bathway Somset 7 L2
Batley Kirk 31 T4
Batsford Gloucs 15 U4
Battersby N York 37 L5
Battersea Gt Lon 17 R14
Battisford Tye Suffk 19 N4
Battle E Susx 10 K12
Battle Powys 14 B5
Battledykes Angus 51 N7
Battlesbridge Essex 18 J14
Battleton Somset 5 R6
Baughton Worcs 15 Q3
Baughurst Hants 8 K2
Baulds Abers 55 M16
Baulking Oxon 16 B11
Baumber Lincs 33 P12
Baunton Gloucs 15 S9
Baverstock Wilts 7 S5
Bawburgh Norfk 27 P7
Bawdeswell Norfk 27 N5
Bawdrip Somset 6 H4
Bawdsey Suffk 19 S7
Bawtry Donc 32 F9
Baxenden Lancs 31 L3
Baxterley Warwks 23 Q9
Bay Highld 59 c8
Bayble W Isls 56 f2
Baybridge Hants 8 J8
Baycliff Cumb 34 K11
Baydon Wilts 16 B14
Bayford Herts 17 R9
Bayford Somset 7 N6
Bayhead W Isls 56 b5
Baylham Suffk 19 P5
Baysham Herefs 14 K5
Bayston Hill Shrops 22 D7
Baythorne End Essex 18 H6
Bayton Worcs 22 G13
Bayworth Oxon 16 E10
Beachampton Bucks 16 J4
Beachamwell Norfk 26 J8
Beacon Devon 6 E10
Beacon End Essex 19 L9
Beacon Hill Notts 32 J15
Beacon Hill Surrey 9 P6
Beacon's Bottom Bucks 16 J11
Beaconsfield Bucks 17 L12
Beadlam N York 37 L9
Beadlow C Beds 17 P4
Beadnell Nthumb 47 S12
Beaford Devon 5 L8
Beal N York 32 E3
Beal Nthumb 47 P10
Bealsmill Cnwll 2 H3
Beaminster Dorset 6 K10
Beamish Dur 41 P9
Beamsley N York 36 C15
Beanacre Wilts 15 Q15
Beanley Nthumb 47 Q14
Beardon Devon 4 K13
Beare Green Surrey 9 T5
Bearley Warwks 23 P15
Bearpark Dur 41 P11
Bearsden E Duns 44 F5
Bearsted Kent 11 L6
Bearstone Shrops 22 G2
Bearwood Birm 23 M11
Bearwood Herefs 21 R11
Bearwood Poole 7 T11
Beattock D & G 39 S2
Beauchamp Roding Essex 18 F12
Beaufort Blae G 14 E8
Beaulieu Hants 8 G11
Beauly Highld 53 Q7
Beaumaris IoA 28 H6
Beaumont Cumb 40 B9
Beaumont Essex 19 P9
Beaumont Jersey 3 b3
Beaumont Leys C Leic 24 E7
Beausale Warwks 23 Q13
Beauworth Hants 8 K7
Beaworthy Devon 4 J11
Beazley End Essex 18 H8
Bebington Wirral 30 E10
Beccles Suffk 27 T10
Becconsall Lancs 30 G4
Beckbury Shrops 22 H8
Beckenham Gt Lon 10 E3
Beckermet Cumb 34 F6
Beckfoot Cumb 39 S10
Beckford Worcs 15 R4
Beckhampton Wilts 15 T15
Beckingham Lincs 32 K15
Beckingham Notts 32 H9
Beckington Somset 7 P2
Beckjay Shrops 21 R7
Beckley E Susx 11 L11
Beckley Oxon 16 F8
Beck Row Suffk 26 H12
Beck Side Cumb 34 J10
Beckton Gt Lon 10 F1
Beckwithshaw N York 36 F14
Becontree Gt Lon 18 E15
Bedale N York 36 F9
Bedchester Dorset 7 Q8
Beddau Rhondd 14 C12
Beddgelert Gwynd 28 G10
Beddingham E Susx 10 F14
Beddington Gt Lon 10 D4
Beddington Corner Gt Lon 10 C4
Bedfield Suffk 27 Q14
Bedford Bed 17 N2
Bedhampton Hants 9 L10
Bedingfield Suffk 27 Q14
Bedlam N York 36 F13
Bedlington Nthumb 41 P5
Bedlinog Myr Td 14 D10
Bedminster Bristl 14 K15
Bedminster Down Bristl 14 K15
Bedmond Herts 17 N9
Bednall Staffs 23 L6
Bedrule Border 46 H14
Bedstone Shrops 21 R8
Bedwas Caerph 14 E12
Bedwellty Caerph 14 E10
Bedworth Warwks 23 R11
Beeby Leics 24 G7
Beech Hants 9 L5
Beech Staffs 22 J2
Beech Hill W Berk 16 H16
Beechingstoke Wilts 7 T1
Beedon W Berk 16 E14
Beeford E R Yk 37 T14
Beeley Derbys 31 T13
Beelsby NE Lin 33 P7
Beenham W Berk 16 F15
Beer Devon 6 F12
Beer Somset 6 J6
Beercrocombe Somset 6 G7
Beer Hackett Dorset 7 L9
Beesands Devon 3 P9
Beesby Lincs 33 T11
Beeson Devon 3 P9
Beeston C Beds 17 P2
Beeston Ches W 30 H14
Beeston Leeds 31 U3
Beeston Norfk 27 L6
Beeston Notts 24 E3
Beeston Regis Norfk 27 P2
Beeswing D & G 39 P7
Beetham Cumb 35 N10
Beetham Somset 6 G9
Beetley Norfk 27 M6
Begbroke Oxon 16 E8
Begelly Pembks 12 H9
Beguildy Powys 21 N7
Beighton Norfk 27 T7
Beighton Sheff 32 C10
Beith N Ayrs 44 C8
Bekesbourne Kent 11 R6
Belaugh Norfk 27 R6
Belbroughton Worcs 22 K12
Belchalwell Dorset 7 P9
Belchamp Otten Essex 18 J6
Belchamp St Paul Essex 18 J6
Belchamp Walter Essex 18 K7
Belchford Lincs 33 Q12
Belford Nthumb 47 Q11
Belgrave C Leic 24 F8
Belhaven E Loth 46 J4
Belhelvie Abers 55 S12
Belhinnie Abers 54 K10
Bellabeg Abers 54 J12
Bellanoch Ag & B 42 K1
Bellaty Angus 50 K6
Bell Busk N York 35 U14
Belleau Lincs 33 S11
Bell End Worcs 23 L12
Bellerby N York 36 D8
Belle Vue Cumb 40 B9
Belle Vue Wakefd 32 B4
Bellfield S Lans 44 K11
Bellfield S Lans 45 M13
Bellingdon Bucks 17 L9
Bellingham Nthumb 40 J5
Belloch Ag & B 42 J10
Bellochantuy Ag & B 42 H11
Bell o' th' Hill Ches W 22 E1
Bellshill N Lans 44 H7
Bellside N Lans 44 J7
Bellsquarry W Loth 45 N6
Bells Yew Green E Susx 10 H9
Belluton BaNES 15 L16
Belmaduthy Highld 53 S5
Belmont Bl w D 30 K5
Belmont Gt Lon 10 C5
Belmont S Ayrs 43 T13
Belmont Shet 59 r2
Belnacraig Abers 54 J12
Belper Derbys 23 R1
Belsay Nthumb 41 M5
Belses Border 46 H12
Belsford Devon 3 P6
Belsize Herts 17 N10
Belstead Suffk 19 P6
Belstone Devon 5 M12
Belthorn Lancs 31 L4
Beltinge Kent 11 R4
Beltingham Nthumb 40 H8
Beltoft N Linc 32 J6
Belton Leics 24 D5
Belton Lincs 24 K2
Belton N Linc 32 H6
Belton Norfk 27 U8
Belton Rutlnd 24 J8
Belvedere Gt Lon 10 F2
Belvoir Leics 24 J3
Bembridge IoW 9 L14
Bemerton Wilts 8 C7
Bempton E R Yk 37 U11
Benacre Suffk 27 U11
Benbecula Airport W Isls 56 b6
Benbuie D & G 39 M3
Benderloch Ag & B 48 K9
Benenden Kent 11 L9
Benfieldside Dur 41 M10
Bengeo Herts 17 S8
Bengeworth Worcs 15 S3
Benhall Green Suffk 19 S3
Benhall Street Suffk 19 S3
Benholm Abers 51 T4
Beningbrough N York 36 K14
Benington Herts 17 R6
Benington Lincs 25 S1
Benllech IoA 28 F5
Benmore Ag & B 43 Q3
Bennan N Ayrs 43 N13
Benniworth Lincs 33 P11
Benover Kent 10 J7
Ben Rhydding C Brad 36 D15
Benslie N Ayrs 43 T10
Benson Oxon 16 G11
Benthoul C Aber 55 Q14
Bentley Donc 32 E7
Bentley E R Yk 33 M2
Bentley Hants 9 N4
Bentley Suffk 19 P7
Bentley Warwks 23 Q9
Bentpath D & G 40 A3
Bentwichen Devon 5 N5
Bentworth Hants 9 L5
Benvie Angus 51 L11
Benville Dorset 6 K10
Benwick Cambs 25 R10
Beoley Worcs 23 M14
Beoraidbeg Highld 52 C16
Bepton W Susx 9 P9
Berden Essex 18 E8
Berea Pembks 12 C5
Bere Alston Devon 2 J5
Bere Ferrers Devon 2 J5
Bere Regis Dorset 7 Q11
Bergh Apton Norfk 27 R9
Berinsfield Oxon 16 F11
Berkeley Gloucs 15 M10
Berkhamsted Herts 17 M9
Berkley Somset 7 P3
Berkswell Solhll 23 Q12
Bermondsey Gt Lon 17 S13
Bernera Highld 52 E11
Bernisdale Highld 59 e8
Berrick Prior Oxon 16 G11
Berrick Salome Oxon 16 G11
Berriedale Highld 58 E10
Berrier Cumb 40 B13
Berriew Powys 21 N4
Berrington Shrops 22 E8
Berrington Worcs 22 E14
Berrington Green Worcs 22 E14
Berrow Somset 6 G2
Berrow Green Worcs 22 H16
Berryfields Bucks 16 J7
Berryhillock Moray 55 L5
Berryhillock Moray 55 L6
Berrynarbor Devon 5 L3
Berry Pomeroy Devon 3 Q6
Bersham Wrexhm 30 E16
Bersted W Susx 9 P11
Berwick E Susx 10 G14
Berwick Bassett Wilts 15 T14
Berwick Hill Nthumb 41 N6
Berwick St James Wilts 7 T4
Berwick St John Wilts 7 R7
Berwick St Leonard Wilts 7 R5
Berwick-upon-Tweed Nthumb 47 P8
Bescar Lancs 30 F5
Besford Worcs 15 Q3
Bessacarr Donc 32 F7
Bessingby E R Yk 37 U12
Bessingham Norfk 27 P3
Besthorpe Norfk 27 N9
Besthorpe Notts 32 J13
Bestwood Village Notts 24 E1
Beswick E R Yk 37 R15
Betchworth Surrey 9 U3
Bethel Gwynd 28 F7
Bethel IoA 28 E7
Bethersden Kent 11 M8
Bethesda Gwynd 28 H7
Bethesda Pembks 12 G7
Bethlehem Carmth 13 R6
Bethnal Green Gt Lon 17 S13
Betley Staffs 31 L16
Betsham Kent 10 H3
Betteshanger Kent 11 T6
Bettiscombe Dorset 6 H11
Bettisfield Wrexhm 22 D3
Bettws Newpt 14 F12
Bettws Cedewain Powys 21 M4
Bettws Evan Cerdgn 12 K2
Bettws-Newydd Mons 14 G9
Bettyhill Highld 57 R3
Betws Brdgnd 13 U12
Betws Bledrws Cerdgn 20 E12
Betws Gwerfil Goch Denbgs 29 P10
Betws-y-Coed Conwy 28 K9
Betws-yn-Rhos Conwy 29 M6
Beulah Cerdgn 12 K2
Beulah Powys 20 J12
Bevercotes Notts 32 G12
Beverley E R Yk 33 M1
Beverston Gloucs 15 P11
Bewcastle Cumb 40 E6
Bewdley Worcs 22 H13
Bewerley N York 36 D12
Bewholme E R Yk 37 U15
Bexhill E Susx 10 K14
Bexley Gt Lon 10 F3
Bexleyheath Gt Lon 10 F2
Bexwell Norfk 26 G8
Beyton Suffk 19 L3
Beyton Green Suffk 19 L3
Bhaltos W Isls 56 d2
Bhatarsaigh W Isls 56 a9
Bibury Gloucs 15 T9
Bicester Oxon 16 F6
Bickenhill Solhll 23 P12
Bicker Lincs 25 P2
Bickerstaffe Lancs 30 G7
Bickerton N York 36 J15
Bickford Staffs 22 K6
Bickington Devon 3 P4
Bickington Devon 4 K5
Bickleigh Devon 2 K6
Bickleigh Devon 5 R9
Bickley Ches W 30 H16
Bickley Gt Lon 10 E4
Bickley N York 37 Q8
Bicknacre Essex 18 J13
Bicknoller Somset 6 D4
Bicknor Kent 11 M5
Bicton Shrops 21 P7
Bicton Shrops 22 D6
Bidborough Kent 10 G8
Biddenden Kent 11 L9
Biddenham Bed 17 M2
Biddestone Wilts 15 P14
Biddisham Somset 6 H2
Biddlesden Bucks 16 G3
Biddulph Staffs 31 N14
Biddulph Moor Staffs 31 N14
Bideford Devon 4 J6
Bidford-on-Avon Warwks 15 T1
Bielby E R Yk 37 N16
Bieldside C Aber 55 R14
Bierley IoW 8 J15
Bierton Bucks 16 K7
Big Balcraig D & G 38 G11
Bigbury Devon 3 M8
Bigbury-on-Sea Devon 3 M9
Bigby Lincs 33 M6
Big Carlae D & G 39 L2
Biggar S Lans 45 N10
Biggin Derbys 31 S14
Biggin Hill Gt Lon 10 E5
Biggin Hill Airport Gt Lon 10 E5
Biggleswade C Beds 17 Q3
Bigholms D & G 40 A5
Bighouse Highld 57 U3
Bighton Hants 8 K6
Biglands Cumb 39 U10
Bignor W Susx 9 Q9
Bigrigg Cumb 34 F5
Big Sand Highld 52 D2
Bigton Shet 59 q7
Bilborough C Nott 24 E2
Bilbrook Somset 5 S4
Bilbrough N York 36 K15
Bilbster Highld 58 H5
Bildershaw Dur 36 E3
Bildeston Suffk 19 M5
Billericay Essex 18 G14
Billesdon Leics 24 G8
Billesley Warwks 23 N16
Billingborough Lincs 25 N3
Billinge St Hel 30 H8
Billingford Norfk 27 M5
Billingford Norfk 27 P12
Billingham S on T 36 J3
Billinghay Lincs 33 N15
Billingley Barns 32 C7
Billingshurst W Susx 9 S7
Billingsley Shrops 22 G11
Billington C Beds 17 L6
Billington Lancs 31 L2
Billockby Norfk 27 T7
Billy Row Dur 41 N12
Bilsborrow Lancs 30 H1
Bilsby Lincs 33 T11
Bilsham W Susx 9 Q11
Bilsington Kent 11 P9
Bilsthorpe Notts 32 F14
Bilston Mdloth 45 R6
Bilston Wolves 23 L9
Bilstone Leics 23 R8
Bilton E R Yk 33 P2
Bilton N York 36 G14
Bilton Warwks 24 D13
Bilton-in-Ainsty N York 36 J15
Binbrook Lincs 33 P9
Bincombe Dorset 7 M13
Binegar Somset 7 L3
Binfield Br For 16 K15
Binfield Heath Oxon 16 H14
Bingfield Nthumb 41 L6
Bingham Notts 24 G2
Bingley C Brad 31 R1
Binham Norfk 27 M2
Binley Covtry 23 S12
Binley Hants 8 G3
Binley Woods Warwks 23 S12
Binnegar Dorset 7 Q13
Binniehill Falk 44 K5
Binscombe Surrey 9 Q4
Binstead IoW 8 K13
Binsted Hants 9 M5
Binsted W Susx 9 Q11
Binton Warwks 15 T1
Bintree Norfk 27 M5
Birch Essex 19 L10
Bircham Newton Norfk 26 J3
Bircham Tofts Norfk 26 J3
Birchanger Essex 18 E10
Birch Cross Staffs 23 N4
Bircher Herefs 22 D14
Birchfield Birm 23 M10
Birch Green Essex 19 L10
Birchgrove Cardif 14 E13
Birchgrove Swans 13 R10
Birchgrove W Susx 10 E10
Birchington Kent 11 T4
Birchley Heath Warwks 23 Q10
Birchover Derbys 31 T14
Birch Vale Derbys 31 Q10
Birchwood Lincs 32 K13
Birch Wood Somset 6 F8
Birchwood Warrtn 30 K9
Bircotes Notts 32 F9
Birdbrook Essex 18 H6
Birdforth N York 36 J11
Birdham W Susx 9 N12
Birdingbury Warwks 23 S14
Birdlip Gloucs 15 Q8
Birdsall N York 37 P12
Birds Edge Kirk 31 S6
Birds Green Essex 18 F12
Birdsgreen Shrops 22 H11
Birdsmoorgate Dorset 6 H10
Birdwell Barns 32 B7
Birgham Border 47 L10
Birichin Highld 57 S15
Birkby N York 36 G6
Birkdale Sefton 30 E5
Birkenbog Abers 55 L4
Birkenhead Wirral 30 E9
Birkenhead (Queensway) Tunnel Lpool 30 E9
Birkenhills Abers 55 P7
Birkenshaw Kirk 31 S3
Birkhall Abers 54 J16
Birkhill Angus 51 L10
Birkhill D & G 45 Q14
Birkin N York 32 E3
Birley Herefs 21 S11
Birley Carr Sheff 32 B9
Birling Kent 10 J5
Birlingham Worcs 15 Q3
Birmingham Birm 23 M11
Birmingham Airport Solhll 23 P11
Birnam P & K 50 G9
Birness Abers 55 T9
Birse Abers 55 M15
Birsemore Abers 55 L15
Birstall Kirk 31 T3
Birstall Leics 24 F7
Birstwith N York 36 F13
Birtley Gatesd 41 Q9
Birtley Herefs 21 Q9
Birtley Nthumb 40 J5
Birts Street Worcs 15 N4
Bisbrooke Rutlnd 24 K9
Biscathorpe Lincs 33 Q10
Bisham W & M 16 K12
Bishampton Worcs 15 R1
Bish Mill Devon 5 N6
Bishop Auckland Dur 41 P14
Bishopbridge Lincs 33 M9
Bishopbriggs E Duns 44 G5
Bishop Burton E R Yk 33 L1
Bishop Middleham Dur 41 Q13
Bishopmill Moray 54 G4
Bishop Monkton N York 36 G12
Bishop Norton Lincs 33 L9
Bishopsbourne Kent 11 R6
Bishops Cannings Wilts 15 S16
Bishop's Castle Shrops 21 Q6
Bishop's Caundle Dorset 7 N8
Bishop's Cleeve Gloucs 15 R5
Bishop's Frome Herefs 15 M2
Bishop's Green Essex 18 G10
Bishop's Hull Somset 6 F7
Bishop's Itchington Warwks 23 S16
Bishops Lydeard Somset 6 E6
Bishop's Norton Gloucs 15 P6
Bishop's Nympton Devon 5 P7
Bishop's Offley Staffs 22 H4
Bishop's Stortford Herts 18 E10
Bishop's Sutton Hants 8 K6
Bishop's Tachbrook Warwks 23 R15
Bishop's Tawton Devon 5 L6
Bishopsteignton Devon 3 R4
Bishopstoke Hants 8 H8
Bishopston Swans 13 P12
Bishopstone Bucks 16 J8
Bishopstone E Susx 10 F15
Bishopstone Herefs 21 R13
Bishopstone Kent 11 R4
Bishopstone Swindn 16 A13
Bishopstone Wilts 7 T6
Bishopstrow Wilts 7 Q3
Bishop Sutton BaNES 7 L1
Bishop's Waltham Hants 8 J9
Bishopswood Somset 6 F9
Bishop's Wood Staffs 22 J7
Bishopsworth Bristl 14 K15
Bishop Thornton N York 36 F13
Bishopthorpe C York 37 L15
Bishopton Darltn 36 G3
Bishopton Rens 44 D5
Bishop Wilton E R Yk 37 N14
Bishton Newpt 14 H12
Bishton Staffs 23 M5
Bisley Gloucs 15 Q9
Bisley Surrey 9 Q2
Bissoe Cnwll 1 S11
Bisterne Hants 8 D11
Bitchfield Lincs 25 L4
Bittadon Devon 5 L4
Bittaford Devon 3 M7
Bitterley Shrops 22 E12
Bitterne C Sotn 8 H9
Bitteswell Leics 24 E11
Bitton S Glos 15 M15
Bix Oxon 16 H12
Bixter Shet 59 p5
Blaby Leics 24 E9
Blackadder Border 47 L8
Blackawton Devon 3 P8
Blackborough Devon 6 D9
Blackborough End Norfk 26 G6
Black Bourton Oxon 16 B9
Blackboys E Susx 10 G11
Blackbrook Derbys 32 B16
Blackbrook St Hel 30 H8
Blackbrook Staffs 22 H2
Blackburn Abers 55 Q13
Blackburn Bl w D 30 K3
Blackburn W Loth 45 M6
Black Callerton N u Ty 41 N7
Blackcraig E Ayrs 44 G15
Black Crofts Ag & B 49 L10
Blackdog Abers 55 S12
Black Dog Devon 5 P9
Blackdown Dorset 6 H10
Blacker Hill Barns 32 B7
Blackfen Gt Lon 10 F3
Blackfield Hants 8 H11
Blackford P & K 50 E14
Blackford Somset 6 J3
Blackford Somset 7 M6
Blackfordby Leics 23 R6
Blackhall C Edin 45 Q4
Blackhall Colliery Dur 41 S12
Blackhall Mill Gatesd 41 N9
Blackhaugh Border 46 E10
Blackheath Gt Lon 17 S14
Blackheath Sandw 23 L11
Blackheath Suffk 27 T13
Blackheath Surrey 9 R4
Blackhill Abers 55 U5
Blackhill Abers 55 U8
Blackhill Dur 41 M10
Blackhill of Clackriach Abers 55 S7
Blackhorse Devon 5 S12
Blacklaw D & G 45 N15
Blackley Manch 31 N7
Blacklunans P & K 50 J6
Blackmarstone Herefs 14 J4
Blackmill Brdgnd 13 U12
Blackmoor Hants 9 M6
Blackmoor N Som 14 J16
Blackmoorfoot Kirk 31 R5
Blackmore Essex 18 G13
Blackmore End Essex 18 H8
Blackness Falk 45 N3
Blacknest Hants 9 N5
Black Notley Essex 18 J10
Blacko Lancs 31 N1
Black Pill Swans 13 Q12
Blackpool Bpool 30 E2
Blackpool Devon 3 Q8
Blackpool Airport Lancs 30 E2
Blackridge W Loth 45 L6
Blackrod Bolton 30 J6
Blacksboat Moray 54 F8
Blackshaw D & G 39 S8
Blackshaw Head Calder 31 P3
Blackstone W Susx 10 C12
Black Street Suffk 27 U11
Blackthorn Oxon 16 G7
Blackthorpe Suffk 19 L3
Blacktoft E R Yk 32 J4
Blacktop C Aber 55 R14
Black Torrington Devon 4 K10
Blackwall Derbys 31 T16
Blackwall Tunnel Gt Lon 17 S13
Blackwater Cnwll 1 S10
Blackwater Hants 9 N2
Blackwater IoW 8 J14
Blackwater Somset 6 F8
Blackwaterfoot N Ayrs 43 M12
Blackwell Cumb 40 B10
Blackwell Derbys 31 R12
Blackwell Derbys 32 C14
Blackwell Warwks 16 A3
Blackwell Worcs 23 L13
Blackwood Caerph 14 E10
Blackwood D & G 39 Q4
Blackwood S Lans 44 J9
Blacon Ches W 30 F13
Bladnoch D & G 38 H9
Bladon Oxon 16 D7
Blaenannerch Cerdgn 12 K2
Blaenau Ffestiniog Gwynd 28 J11
Blaenavon Torfn 14 F8
Blaenffos Pembks 12 J4
Blaengarw Brdgnd 13 U11
Blaengwrach Neath 13 T9
Blaengwynfi Neath 13 U10
Blaenpennal Cerdgn 20 E10
Blaenplwyf Cerdgn 20 D8
Blaenporth Cerdgn 12 K2
Blaenrhondda Rhondd 13 U10
Blaenwaun Carmth 12 J5
Blaen-y-Coed Carmth 13 L5
Blaen-y-cwm Rhondd 13 U10
Blagdon N Som 6 K1
Blagdon Somset 6 F8
Blagdon Torbay 3 Q6
Blagdon Hill Somset 6 F8
Blaich Highld 49 M3
Blain Highld 48 G4
Blaina Blae G 14 E9
Blair Atholl P & K 50 E5
Blair Drummond Stirlg 50 C16
Blairgowrie P & K 50 J8
Blairhall Fife 45 M2
Blairingone P & K 50 F16
Blairlogie Stirlg 50 D16
Blairmore Ag & B 43 R3
Blairmore Highld 56 J4
Blair's Ferry Ag & B 43 N5
Blaisdon Gloucs 15 M7
Blakebrook Worcs 22 J13
Blakedown Worcs 22 K12
Blake End Essex 18 H9
Blakemere Ches W 30 H12
Blakemere Herefs 21 Q13
Blakenall Heath Wsall 23 L8
Blakeney Gloucs 15 M9
Blakeney Norfk 27 M2
Blakenhall Ches E 22 H1
Blakenhall Wolves 22 K9
Blakesley Nhants 16 G2
Blanchland Nthumb 40 K10
Blandford Forum Dorset 7 Q10
Blandford St Mary Dorset 7 Q10
Blanefield Stirlg 44 F3
Blankney Lincs 33 M14
Blantyre S Lans 44 H7
Blàr a' Chaorainn Highld 49 N5
Blargie Highld 53 R16
Blarmachfoldach Highld 49 N4
Blaston Leics 24 J9
Blatherwycke Nhants 25 L9
Blawith Cumb 34 K9
Blawquhairn D & G 39 L5
Blaxhall Suffk 19 S4
Blaxton Donc 32 G8
Blaydon Gatesd 41 N8
Bleadney Somset 6 K3
Bleadon N Som 6 H1
Blean Kent 11 Q5
Bleasby Notts 32 G16
Blebocraigs Fife 51 N13
Bleddfa Powys 21 N9
Bledington Gloucs 16 A6
Bledlow Bucks 16 J10
Bledlow Ridge Bucks 16 J10
Blegbie E Loth 46 F6
Blencarn Cumb 40 F13
Blencogo Cumb 39 U10
Blendworth Hants 9 M9
Blennerhasset Cumb 39 T11
Bletchingdon Oxon 16 E7
Bletchingley Surrey 10 D7
Bletchley M Keyn 16 K4
Bletchley Shrops 22 F3
Bletherston Pembks 12 G6
Bletsoe Bed 25 M16
Blewbury Oxon 16 E12
Blickling Norfk 27 Q4
Blidworth Notts 32 F15
Blidworth Bottoms Notts 32 F15
Blindcrake Cumb 39 T13
Blindley Heath Surrey 10 E7
Blisland Cnwll 2 D4
Blissford Hants 8 D9
Bliss Gate Worcs 22 H13
Blisworth Nhants 16 H1
Blithbury Staffs 23 N5
Blockley Gloucs 15 U4
Blofield Norfk 27 S7
Blofield Heath Norfk 27 S7
Blo Norton Norfk 27 M12
Bloomfield Border 46 H13
Blore Staffs 31 R16
Bloxham Oxon 16 D4
Bloxholm Lincs 33 M15
Bloxwich Wsall 23 L8
Bloxworth Dorset 7 Q12
Blubberhouses N York 36 E14
Blue Anchor Somset 5 S4
Blue Bell Hill Kent 10 K5
Blundellsands Sefton 30 E8
Blundeston Suffk 27 V9
Blunham C Beds 17 P2
Blunsdon St Andrew Swindn 15 T12
Bluntington Worcs 22 K13
Bluntisham Cambs 25 R13
Blurton C Stke 22 K2
Blyborough Lincs 32 K9
Blyford Suffk 27 T13
Blymhill Staffs 22 J7
Blyth Notts 32 F10
Blyth Nthumb 41 Q5
Blyth Bridge Border 45 P9
Blythburgh Suffk 27 T13
Blythe Border 46 H8
Blyton Lincs 32 J8
Boarhills Fife 51 P13
Boarhunt Hants 8 K10
Boarstall Bucks 16 G8
Boath Highld 53 R2
Boat of Garten Highld 54 C11
Bobbing Kent 11 M4
Bobbington Staffs 22 J10
Bocking Essex 18 J9
Bocking Churchstreet Essex 18 J9
Boddam Abers 55 V8
Boddam Shet 59 q8
Boddington Gloucs 15 Q6
Bodedern IoA 28 D5
Bodelwyddan Denbgs 29 N6
Bodenham Herefs 14 K2
Bodenham Wilts 8 D7
Bodenham Moor Herefs 14 K2
Bodewryd IoA 28 E3
Bodfari Denbgs 29 P7
Bodffordd IoA 28 E6
Bodfuan Gwynd 28 D12
Bodham Norfk 27 P2
Bodiam E Susx 10 K11
Bodicote Oxon 16 D4
Bodinnick Cnwll 2 E7
Bodle Street Green E Susx 10 J12
Bodmin Cnwll 2 D5
Bodsham Kent 11 Q7
Bodwen Cnwll 2 C6
Bogallan Highld 53 R6
Bogbrae Abers 55 T9
Bogend S Ayrs 44 D11
Boggs Holdings E Loth 46 F5
Boghall Mdloth 45 R6
Boghall W Loth 45 M5
Boghead S Lans 44 J10
Bogmoor Moray 54 J4
Bogmuir Abers 51 R4
Bogniebrae Abers 55 M7
Bognor Regis W Susx 9 Q12
Bogroy Highld 54 B11
Bogue D & G 39 L5
Bohortha Cnwll 1 T12
Bohuntine Highld 49 R2
Bolam Dur 36 E3
Bolberry Devon 3 N9
Boldmere Birm 23 N10
Boldre Hants 8 F12
Boldron Dur 36 C4
Bole Notts 32 H10
Bolehill Derbys 31 U15
Bolham Devon 5 R8
Bolham Water Devon 6 E9
Bolingey Cnwll 1 S9
Bollington Ches E 31 P11
Bolney W Susx 10 C11
Bolnhurst Bed 25 N15
Bolnore W Susx 10 D11
Bolshan Angus 51 Q7
Bolsover Derbys 32 D12
Bolsterstone Sheff 31 T8
Boltby N York 36 J9
Boltenstone Abers 54 K13
Bolton Bolton 31 L6
Bolton Cumb 35 Q3
Bolton E Loth 46 G5
Bolton E R Yk 37 N15
Bolton Nthumb 47 Q14
Bolton Abbey N York 36 C14
Bolton-by-Bowland Lancs 35 S15
Boltonfellend Cumb 40 C7

Castle Hedingham – Cross Hands 65

Castle Hedingham Essex 18 J7
Castlehill Border 45 Q11
Castlehill Highld 58 F2
Castle Hill Suffk 19 P6
Castlehill W Duns 44 C4
Castle Kennedy D & G 38 C9
Castle Lachlan Ag & B 43 N1
Castlemartin Pembks 12 E10
Castlemilk C Glas 44 F7
Castlemorton Worcs 15 N4
Castlemorton Common Worcs 15 N4
Castle O'er D & G 39 U3
Castle Rising Norfk 26 G5
Castleside Dur 41 M10
Castle Stuart Highld 53 T6
Castlethorpe M Keyn 16 J3
Castleton Border 40 D4
Castleton Derbys 31 S10
Castleton N York 37 M5
Castleton Newpt 14 F13
Castleton Rochdl 31 N6
Castletown Highld 58 F2
Castletown IoM 34 c7
Castletown Sundld 41 R9
Castley N York 36 F16
Caston Norfk 27 L9
Castor C Pete 25 N9
Catacol N Ayrs 43 M8
Catcliffe Rothm 32 C9
Catcomb Wilts 15 R14
Catcott Somset 6 H4
Catcott Burtle Somset 6 H4
Caterham Surrey 10 D6
Catfield Norfk 27 S5
Catford Gt Lon 10 E3
Catforth Lancs 30 G2
Cathcart C Glas 44 F7
Cathedine Powys 14 D6
Catherington Hants 9 L9
Catherston Leweston Dorset 6 H12
Catisfield Hants 8 J11
Catlodge Highld 53 R16
Catmere End Essex 18 E7
Catmore W Berk 16 D13
Caton Lancs 35 P13
Caton Green Lancs 35 P12
Catrine E Ayrs 44 F12
Catsfield E Susx 10 K13
Catsgore Somset 6 K6
Catshill Worcs 23 L13
Cattadale Ag & B 42 J15
Cattal N York 36 J14
Cattawade Suffk 19 P8
Catterall Lancs 35 N16
Catterick N York 36 F7
Catterick Bridge N York 36 E7
Catterlen Cumb 40 D13
Catterline Abers 51 U3
Catterton N York 36 J16
Catteshall Surrey 9 Q4
Catthorpe Leics 24 E12
Cattistock Dorset 7 L11
Catton N York 36 G10
Catton Nthumb 40 H9
Catwick E R Yk 37 T16
Catworth Cambs 25 N13
Caudle Green Gloucs 15 Q8
Caulcott Oxon 16 E6
Cauldcots Angus 51 R8
Cauldhame Stirlg 44 G1
Cauldmill Border 46 G14
Cauldon Staffs 31 R16
Cauldwell Derbys 23 Q6
Caulkerbush D & G 39 Q9
Caulside D & G 40 C5
Caundle Marsh Dorset 7 M8
Caunton Notts 32 H14
Causeway End D & G 38 H8
Causeway End Essex 18 H10
Causewayend S Lans 45 N11
Causewayhead Stirlg 44 J1
Causeyend Abers 55 S11
Causey Park Bridge Nthumb 41 N3
Cavendish Suffk 18 J6
Cavenham Suffk 26 J14
Caversfield Oxon 16 F6
Caversham Readg 16 H14
Caverswall Staffs 23 L2
Caverton Mill Border 46 K12
Cawdor Highld 53 U6
Cawood N York 32 E1
Cawsand Cnwll 2 J8
Cawston Norfk 27 P5
Cawthorne Barns 31 U6
Caxton Cambs 25 R16
Caynham Shrops 22 E13
Caythorpe Lincs 32 K16
Caythorpe Notts 24 G1
Cayton N York 37 S9
Ceann a Bhaigh W Isls 56 b5
Ceannacroc Lodge Highld 53 L13
Cearsiadar W Isls 56 e3
Cefn Newpt 14 F12
Cefn-brîth Conwy 29 M10
Cefn-bryn-brain Carmth 13 S8
Cefn Cribwr Brdgnd 13 T13
Cefneithin Carmth 13 P8
Cefngorwydd Powys 20 J13
Cefn-mawr Wrexhm 29 S11
Cefn-y-pant Carmth 12 J6
Cellardyke Fife 51 Q15
Cellarhead Staffs 23 L1
Cemaes IoA 28 D3
Cemmaes Powys 20 H3
Cemmaes Road Powys 20 H3
Cenarth Cerdgn 12 K3
Ceres Fife 51 M14
Cerne Abbas Dorset 7 M10
Cerney Wick Gloucs 15 S11
Cerrigydrudion Conwy 29 N10
Ceunant Gwynd 28 G8
Chaceley Gloucs 15 P5
Chacewater Cnwll 1 S10
Chackmore Bucks 16 H4
Chacombe Nhants 16 E3
Chadbury Worcs 15 S2
Chadderton Oldham 31 N7
Chaddesden C Derb 23 S3
Chaddesley Corbett Worcs 22 K13
Chaddlehanger Devon 2 K3
Chaddleworth W Berk 16 D14
Chadlington Oxon 16 C6
Chadshunt Warwks 16 C1
Chadwell Leics 24 H5
Chadwell Heath Gt Lon 18 E15
Chadwell St Mary Thurr 10 J2
Chadwick Worcs 22 J14
Chadwick End Solhll 23 P13
Chaffcombe Somset 6 H9
Chafford Hundred Thurr 10 H2
Chagford Devon 5 N13
Chailey E Susx 10 E12
Chainhurst Kent 10 K7
Chaldon Surrey 10 D6
Chale IoW 8 H15
Chale Green IoW 8 H15
Chalfont Common Bucks 17 M11
Chalfont St Giles Bucks 17 M11
Chalfont St Peter Bucks 17 M11
Chalford Gloucs 15 Q9
Chalford Wilts 7 Q2
Chalgrove Oxon 16 G10
Chalk Kent 10 J3
Chalkwell Kent 11 M4
Challacombe Devon 5 N4
Challoch D & G 38 G7
Challock Kent 11 P7
Chalton C Beds 17 N6
Chalton Hants 9 M9
Chalvey Slough 17 M13
Chalvington E Susx 10 G13
Chandler's Cross Herts 17 N10
Chandler's Ford Hants 8 H8
Channel Tunnel Terminal Kent 11 R9
Chantry Somset 7 N3
Chantry Suffk 19 P6
Chapel Fife 45 R1
Chapel Allerton Leeds 31 U1
Chapel Allerton Somset 6 J2
Chapel Amble Cnwll 2 C3
Chapel Brampton Nhants 24 H14
Chapel Chorlton Staffs 22 J2
Chapelend Way Essex 18 H7
Chapel-en-le-Frith Derbys 31 Q11
Chapel Green Warwks 24 D15
Chapel Haddlesey N York 32 E3
Chapelhall N Lans 44 J6
Chapel Hill Abers 55 U9
Chapel Hill Lincs 33 P15
Chapel Hill Mons 14 K10
Chapel Hill N York 36 G15
Chapelhope Border 45 Q13
Chapelknowe D & G 40 A6
Chapel Lawn Shrops 21 Q8
Chapel-le-Dale N York 35 R10
Chapel Leigh Somset 6 E6
Chapel of Garioch Abers 55 P11
Chapel Rossan D & G 38 C11
Chapel Row W Berk 16 F15
Chapel St Leonards Lincs 33 U12
Chapel Stile Cumb 35 L6
Chapelton Angus 51 Q8
Chapelton Devon 5 L6
Chapelton S Lans 44 H9
Chapeltown Bl w D 31 L5
Chapeltown Moray 54 G11
Chapeltown Sheff 32 B8
Chapmanslade Wilts 7 P3
Chapmans Well Devon 4 H12
Chapmore End Herts 17 S7
Chappel Essex 19 L9
Chard Somset 6 G9
Chard Junction Somset 6 H10
Chardleigh Green Somset 6 G9
Chardstock Devon 6 G10
Charfield S Glos 15 M11
Charing Kent 11 N7
Charingworth Gloucs 15 U3
Charlbury Oxon 16 C7
Charlcombe BaNES 15 N15
Charlcutt Wilts 15 R14
Charlecote Warwks 23 Q16
Charlemont Sandw 23 M10
Charles Devon 5 N5
Charleston Angus 51 M8
Charlestown C Aber 55 S14
Charlestown C Brad 31 S1
Charlestown Calder 31 P3
Charlestown Cnwll 2 D7
Charlestown Fife 45 N3
Charlestown Highld 52 E2
Charlestown Highld 53 S7
Charlestown Salfd 31 M8
Charlestown of Aberlour Moray 54 G8
Charles Tye Suffk 19 M5
Charlesworth Derbys 31 Q9
Charlinch Somset 6 F4
Charlottetown Fife 51 L14
Charlton Gt Lon 10 E2
Charlton Nhants 16 E4
Charlton Nthumb 40 H4
Charlton Oxon 16 D12
Charlton Somset 6 G6
Charlton Somset 7 M2
Charlton W Susx 9 P9
Charlton Wilts 7 Q7
Charlton Wilts 15 R12
Charlton Worcs 15 R2
Charlton Wrekin 22 F7
Charlton Abbots Gloucs 15 S6
Charlton Adam Somset 6 K6
Charlton All Saints Wilts 8 D8
Charlton Down Dorset 7 M11
Charlton Horethorne Somset 7 M7
Charlton Kings Gloucs 15 R6
Charlton Mackrell Somset 6 K6
Charlton Marshall Dorset 7 Q10
Charlton Musgrove Somset 7 N6
Charlton-on-Otmoor Oxon 16 F7
Charlton on the Hill Dorset 7 Q10
Charlton St Peter Wilts 8 C2
Charlwood Hants 9 L6
Charlwood Surrey 10 C8
Charminster Dorset 7 M12
Charmouth Dorset 6 H12
Charndon Bucks 16 G6
Charney Bassett Oxon 16 C11
Charnock Richard Lancs 30 H5
Charsfield Suffk 19 R4
Charter Alley Hants 8 K2
Charterhall Border 46 K9
Charterhouse Somset 6 K2
Chartershall Stirlg 44 J2
Chartham Kent 11 Q6
Chartham Hatch Kent 11 Q6
Chartridge Bucks 17 L9
Chart Sutton Kent 11 L7
Charvil Wokham 16 J14
Charwelton Nhants 24 E16
Chase Terrace Staffs 23 M7
Chasetown Staffs 23 M7
Chastleton Oxon 16 B5
Chasty Devon 4 H10
Chatburn Lancs 35 S16
Chatcull Staffs 22 H3
Chatham Medway 10 K4
Chatham Green Essex 18 H11
Chathill Nthumb 47 R12
Chattenden Medway 10 K3
Chatteris Cambs 25 S11
Chatterton Lancs 31 M4
Chattisham Suffk 19 N6
Chatto Border 46 K14
Chatton Nthumb 47 P12
Chawleigh Devon 5 N9
Chawton Hants 9 L5
Cheadle Staffs 23 L2
Cheadle Stockp 31 N9
Cheadle Hulme Stockp 31 N10
Cheam Gt Lon 10 C4
Chearsley Bucks 16 H8
Chebsey Staffs 22 J4
Checkendon Oxon 16 G13
Checkley Ches E 22 H1
Checkley Staffs 23 M3
Chedburgh Suffk 18 J4
Cheddar Somset 6 J2
Cheddington Bucks 17 L7
Cheddleton Staffs 31 P15
Cheddon Fitzpaine Somset 6 F6
Chedgrave Norfk 27 S9
Chedington Dorset 6 K10
Chediston Suffk 27 S12
Chedworth Gloucs 15 S8
Chedzoy Somset 6 H4
Cheetham Hill Manch 31 M7
Cheldon Devon 5 N8
Chelford Ches E 31 M12
Chellaston C Derb 23 S4
Chellington Bed 25 L16
Chelmarsh Shrops 22 G11
Chelmondiston Suffk 19 Q7
Chelmorton Derbys 31 R13
Chelmsford Essex 18 H12
Chelmsley Wood Solhll 23 P11
Chelsea Gt Lon 17 R14
Chelsfield Gt Lon 10 F4
Chelsworth Suffk 19 M5
Cheltenham Gloucs 15 R6
Chelveston Nhants 25 L14
Chelvey N Som 14 J15
Chelwood BaNES 15 L16
Chelwood Gate E Susx 10 E10
Cheney Longville Shrops 21 R6
Chenies Bucks 17 M10
Chepstow Mons 14 K11
Cherhill Wilts 15 S15
Cherington Gloucs 15 Q10
Cherington Warwks 16 B4
Cheriton Hants 8 K7
Cheriton Kent 11 R9
Cheriton Pembks 12 F10
Cheriton Swans 13 M11
Cheriton Bishop Devon 5 P12
Cheriton Fitzpaine Devon 5 Q10
Cherrington Wrekin 22 G5
Cherry Burton E R Yk 37 R16
Cherry Hinton Cambs 18 E4
Cherry Orchard Worcs 15 P1
Cherry Willingham Lincs 33 M12
Chertsey Surrey 17 N15
Cheselbourne Dorset 7 N11
Chesham Bucks 17 M10
Chesham Bury 31 M6
Chesham Bois Bucks 17 M10
Cheshunt Herts 17 S10
Cheslyn Hay Staffs 23 L8
Chessetts Wood Warwks 23 P13
Chessington Gt Lon 9 T1
Chester Ches W 30 F13
Chesterblade Somset 7 M4
Chesterfield Derbys 32 C12
Chesterhill Mdloth 46 E6
Chester-le-Street Dur 41 Q10
Chester Moor Dur 41 Q10
Chesters Border 46 H13
Chesters Border 46 H15
Chesterton Cambs 18 E3
Chesterton Cambs 25 N9
Chesterton Gloucs 15 S10
Chesterton Oxon 16 F6
Chesterton Shrops 22 H9
Chesterton Staffs 31 M16
Chesterton Green Warwks 23 R16
Chesterwood Nthumb 40 H8
Chestfield Kent 11 Q4
Cheston Devon 3 N6
Cheswardine Shrops 22 G4
Cheswick Nthumb 47 P9
Chetnole Dorset 7 L9
Chettisham Cambs 26 F11
Chettle Dorset 7 R8
Chetton Shrops 22 G10
Chetwynd Wrekin 22 H5
Chetwynd Aston Wrekin 22 H6
Cheveley Cambs 18 H3
Chevening Kent 10 F5
Chevington Suffk 18 J3
Chevithorne Devon 5 S8
Chew Magna BaNES 14 K16
Chew Stoke BaNES 14 K16
Chewton Keynsham BaNES 15 L15
Chewton Mendip Somset 7 L2
Chicheley M Keyn 17 L2
Chichester W Susx 9 P11
Chickerell Dorset 7 M14
Chicklade Wilts 7 R5
Chidden Hants 9 L9
Chiddingfold Surrey 9 Q6
Chiddingly E Susx 10 G13
Chiddingstone Kent 10 F7
Chiddingstone Causeway Kent 10 G7
Chideock Dorset 6 J12
Chidham W Susx 9 N11
Chidswell Kirk 31 T4
Chieveley W Berk 16 E14
Chignall St James Essex 18 G12
Chignall Smealy Essex 18 G11
Chigwell Essex 18 D14
Chigwell Row Essex 18 E14
Chilbolton Hants 8 G5
Chilcomb Hants 8 J7
Chilcombe Dorset 6 K12
Chilcompton Somset 7 M2
Chilcote Leics 23 Q7
Childer Thornton Ches W 30 F11
Child Okeford Dorset 7 P9
Childrey Oxon 16 C12
Child's Ercall Shrops 22 G5
Childswickham Worcs 15 S4
Childwall Lpool 30 F9
Chilfrome Dorset 7 L11
Chilgrove W Susx 9 N9
Chilham Kent 11 P6
Chillaton Devon 4 J14
Chillenden Kent 11 S6
Chillerton IoW 8 H14
Chillesford Suffk 19 S5
Chillington Devon 3 P9
Chillington Somset 6 H9
Chilmark Wilts 7 R5
Chilmington Green Kent 11 N8
Chilson Oxon 16 C7
Chilsworthy Cnwll 2 J4
Chilsworthy Devon 4 H10
Chilthorne Domer Somset 6 K8
Chilton Bucks 16 H8
Chilton Dur 41 Q13
Chilton Oxon 16 E12
Chilton Candover Hants 8 K5
Chilton Cantelo Somset 7 L7
Chilton Foliat Wilts 16 B15
Chilton Polden Somset 6 H4
Chilton Street Suffk 18 J6
Chilton Trinity Somset 6 G4
Chilwell Notts 24 D3
Chilworth Hants 8 G8
Chilworth Surrey 9 R4
Chimney Oxon 16 C10
Chineham Hants 9 L3
Chingford Gt Lon 17 S11
Chinley Derbys 31 Q10
Chinnor Oxon 16 J10
Chipnall Shrops 22 H4
Chippenham Cambs 26 G14
Chippenham Wilts 15 Q14
Chipperfield Herts 17 N10
Chipping Herts 17 S5
Chipping Lancs 35 Q16
Chipping Campden Gloucs 15 T4
Chipping Norton Oxon 16 B6
Chipping Ongar Essex 18 F13
Chipping Sodbury S Glos 15 M13
Chipping Warden Nhants 16 E2
Chipstable Somset 5 T6
Chipstead Kent 10 G6
Chipstead Surrey 10 C6
Chirbury Shrops 21 P4
Chirk Wrexhm 29 S12
Chirnside Border 47 M7
Chirnsidebridge Border 47 L7
Chirton Wilts 7 T1
Chisbury Wilts 16 B15
Chiselborough Somset 6 J8
Chiseldon Swindn 15 U13
Chiselhampton Oxon 16 F10
Chisholme Border 46 E15
Chislehurst Gt Lon 10 F3
Chislet Kent 11 S4
Chisley Calder 31 Q3
Chiswell Green Herts 17 P9
Chiswick Gt Lon 17 Q14
Chisworth Derbys 31 P9
Chithurst W Susx 9 N8
Chittering Cambs 26 E14
Chitterne Wilts 7 S3
Chittlehamholt Devon 5 M7
Chittlehampton Devon 5 M6
Chittoe Wilts 15 R15
Chivelstone Devon 3 P10
Chivenor Devon 4 K5
Chlenry D & G 38 D8
Chobham Surrey 9 Q1
Cholderton Wilts 8 E5
Cholesbury Bucks 17 L9
Chollerton Nthumb 40 K6
Cholsey Oxon 16 F12
Cholstrey Herefs 21 S10
Chop Gate N York 36 K7
Choppington Nthumb 41 P5
Chopwell Gatesd 41 N9
Chorley Ches E 30 J16
Chorley Lancs 30 J5
Chorley Shrops 22 G11
Chorleywood Herts 17 N10
Chorleywood West Herts 17 M11
Chorlton Ches E 31 L16
Chorlton-cum-Hardy Manch 31 M9
Chorlton Lane Ches W 30 G16
Choulton Shrops 21 R6
Chrishall Essex 18 D7
Chrisswell Inver 43 R4
Christchurch Cambs 26 E9
Christchurch Dorset 8 D13
Christchurch Newpt 14 G12
Christian Malford Wilts 15 R13
Christon N Som 6 H1
Christon Bank Nthumb 47 S13
Christow Devon 5 Q13
Chudleigh Devon 5 Q14
Chudleigh Knighton Devon 3 Q3
Chulmleigh Devon 5 N8
Church Lancs 31 L3
Churcham Gloucs 15 N7
Church Aston Wrekin 22 H6
Church Brampton Nhants 24 G14
Church Broughton Derbys 23 P3
Church Cove Cnwll 1 R16
Church Crookham Hants 9 N3
Churchdown Gloucs 15 Q7
Church Eaton Staffs 22 J6
Church End C Beds 17 Q4
Church End Essex 18 H9
Churchend Essex 19 M14
Church End Gt Lon 17 R12
Church Enstone Oxon 16 C6
Church Fenton N York 32 D2
Churchfield Sandw 23 M10
Church Green Devon 6 E11
Church Hanborough Oxon 16 D8
Church Houses N York 37 M7
Churchill Devon 6 G10
Churchill N Som 6 J1
Churchill Oxon 16 B6
Churchill Worcs 15 Q1
Churchill Worcs 22 K12
Churchinford Somset 6 F9
Church Knowle Dorset 7 R14
Church Langton Leics 24 G10
Church Lawford Warwks 24 D13
Church Leigh Staffs 23 M3
Church Lench Worcs 15 S1
Church Mayfield Staffs 23 P1
Church Minshull Ches E 30 K14
Church Norton W Susx 9 P12
Churchover Warwks 24 D12
Church Preen Shrops 22 E9
Church Pulverbatch Shrops 21 R3
Churchstanton Somset 6 F8
Churchstoke Powys 21 P5
Churchstow Devon 3 N8
Church Stowe Nhants 24 F16
Church Street Kent 10 J3
Church Stretton Shrops 21 S5
Churchtown Cnwll 2 D3
Churchtown Derbys 31 T14
Churchtown IoM 34 e3
Churchtown Lancs 35 N16
Church Village Rhondd 14 C12
Church Warsop Notts 32 E13
Churston Ferrers Torbay 3 R7
Churt Surrey 9 P5
Churton Ches W 30 F15
Churwell Leeds 31 T3
Chwilog Gwynd 28 E12
Chyandour Cnwll 1 N13
Cilcain Flints 29 R7
Cilcennin Cerdgn 20 D10
Cilfrew Neath 13 S10
Cilfynydd Rhondd 14 C11
Cilgerran Pembks 12 J3
Cilmaengwyn Neath 13 S9
Cilmery Powys 20 K12
Cilsan Carmth 13 P6
Ciltalgarth Gwynd 29 M12
Cilycwm Carmth 13 S3
Cimla Neath 13 S11
Cinderford Gloucs 15 L8
Cinder Hill Wolves 22 K10
Cippenham Slough 17 L13
Cirencester Gloucs 15 S10
City Gt Lon 17 S13
City Airport Gt Lon 10 E2
Clabhach Ag & B 42 e2
Clachaig Ag & B 43 Q3
Clachan Ag & B 42 K7
Clachan Ag & B 48 J13
Clachan Ag & B 48 K9
Clachan Highld 59 g10
Clachan-a-Luib W Isls 56 b5
Clachan Mor Ag & B 42 b3
Clachan na Luib W Isls 56 b5
Clachan of Campsie E Duns 44 G4
Clachan-Seil Ag & B 48 J13
Clachnaharry Highld 53 S7
Clachtoll Highld 56 G9
Clackavoid P & K 50 J5
Clackmannan Clacks 45 L1
Clackmannanshire Bridge Fife 45 L2
Clackmarras Moray 54 G5
Clacton-on-Sea Essex 19 Q11
Cladich Ag & B 49 N12
Cladswell Worcs 23 M15
Claggan Highld 48 G8
Claigan Highld 59 b8
Clanfield Hants 9 L9
Clanfield Oxon 16 B10
Clanville Hants 8 F4
Clanville Somset 7 M5
Claonaig Ag & B 43 L7
Clapgate Herts 18 D9
Clapham Bed 17 N1
Clapham Gt Lon 17 R14
Clapham N York 35 R12
Clapham W Susx 9 S11
Clapton Somset 6 J10
Clapton Somset 7 M2
Clapton-in-Gordano N Som 14 J14
Clapton-on-the-Hill Gloucs 15 U7
Claravale Gatesd 41 N8
Clarbeston Pembks 12 G6
Clarbeston Road Pembks 12 F6
Clarborough Notts 32 H10
Clare Suffk 18 J6
Clarebrand D & G 39 N7
Clarencefield D & G 39 S7
Clarilaw Border 46 G14
Clarkston E Rens 44 F7
Clashmore Highld 56 G8
Clashmore Highld 57 S15
Clashnessie Highld 56 G9
Clashnoir Moray 54 G11
Clathy P & K 50 F12
Clathymore P & K 50 G12
Clatt Abers 55 L10
Clatter Powys 20 K5
Clatworthy Somset 6 D6
Claughton Lancs 35 P12
Claughton Lancs 35 P16
Claughton Wirral 30 E9
Claverdon Warwks 23 P14
Claverham N Som 14 J15
Clavering Essex 18 E8
Claverley Shrops 22 H10
Claverton BaNES 15 N16
Clawdd-coch V Glam 14 C14
Clawdd-newydd Denbgs 29 P10
Clawton Devon 4 H11
Claxby Lincs 33 N8
Claxton N York 37 M13
Claxton Norfk 27 S8
Claybrooke Magna Leics 24 D11
Clay Coton Nhants 24 F13
Clay Cross Derbys 32 C14
Claydon Oxon 16 D2
Claydon Suffk 19 P5
Claygate D & G 40 B5
Claygate Kent 10 J8
Claygate Surrey 9 T1
Clayhall Gt Lon 18 D15
Clayhanger Devon 5 S7
Clayhidon Devon 6 E8
Clayhill E Susx 11 L11
Clayock Highld 58 F4
Claypits Gloucs 15 N9
Claypole Lincs 32 J16
Clayton C Brad 31 R2
Clayton Donc 32 D6
Clayton W Susx 10 D13
Clayton-le-Moors Lancs 31 L3
Clayton-le-Woods Lancs 30 H4
Clayton West Kirk 31 T6
Clayworth Notts 32 H10
Cleadale Highld 48 D1
Cleadon S Tyne 41 R8
Clearbrook Devon 2 K5
Clearwell Gloucs 14 K9
Cleasby N York 36 F5
Cleat Ork 58 c6
Cleatlam Dur 36 D4
Cleator Cumb 34 F4
Cleator Moor Cumb 34 F4
Cleckheaton Kirk 31 S3
Cleehill Shrops 22 F13
Cleekhimin N Lans 44 J7
Clee St Margaret Shrops 22 E11
Cleethorpes NE Lin 33 R6
Cleeton St Mary Shrops 22 F12
Cleeve N Som 14 J16
Cleeve Oxon 16 G13
Cleeve Hill Gloucs 15 R5
Cleeve Prior Worcs 15 T2
Cleghornie E Loth 46 H3
Clehonger Herefs 14 J4
Cleish P & K 50 H16
Cleland N Lans 44 J7
Clenamacrie Ag & B 49 L11
Clenchwarton Norfk 26 F5
Clenerty Abers 55 Q5
Clent Worcs 22 K12
Cleobury Mortimer Shrops 22 G13
Cleobury North Shrops 22 F11
Cleongart Ag & B 42 H11
Clephanton Highld 53 U6
Clerkhill D & G 39 V2
Cleuch-head D & G 39 N2
Clevancy Wilts 15 S14
Clevedon N Som 14 H15
Cleveleys Lancs 34 K16
Cleverton Wilts 15 R12
Clewer Somset 6 J2
Cley next the Sea Norfk 27 N1
Cliburn Cumb 40 E14
Cliddesden Hants 8 K3
Cliffe Medway 10 K2
Cliffe N York 32 G2
Cliff End E Susx 11 M13
Cliffe Woods Medway 10 K3
Clifford Herefs 21 P13
Clifford Leeds 36 H16
Clifford Chambers Warwks 15 U1
Clifford's Mesne Gloucs 15 M6
Clifton Bristl 14 K14
Clifton C Beds 17 P4
Clifton C Nott 24 E3
Clifton C York 37 L14
Clifton Calder 31 S4
Clifton Cumb 40 D14
Clifton Derbys 23 P1
Clifton Devon 5 L4
Clifton Donc 32 E8
Clifton Lancs 30 G3
Clifton N York 36 E15
Clifton Oxon 16 E5
Clifton Worcs 15 P2
Clifton Campville Staffs 23 Q7
Clifton Hampden Oxon 16 F11
Clifton Reynes M Keyn 17 L2
Clifton upon Dunsmore Warwks 24 E13
Clifton upon Teme Worcs 22 G15
Cliftonville Kent 11 U3
Climping W Susx 9 R11
Clink Somset 7 P3
Clint N York 36 F13
Clinterty C Aber 55 Q13
Clint Green Norfk 27 M7
Clintmains Border 46 H11
Clippesby Norfk 27 T6
Clipsham Rutlnd 25 L6
Clipston Nhants 24 G12
Clipston Notts 24 F3
Clipstone C Beds 17 L6
Clipstone Notts 32 F14
Clitheroe Lancs 31 L1
Clive Shrops 22 E5
Clixby Lincs 33 N7
Cloatley Wilts 15 R11
Clocaenog Denbgs 29 P9
Clochan Moray 54 J5
Clodock Herefs 14 G5
Clola Abers 55 T7
Clophill C Beds 17 N4
Clopton Nhants 25 M12
Clopton Suffk 19 Q5
Clopton Corner Suffk 19 Q4
Clos du Valle Guern 2 d1
Closeburn D & G 39 P3
Closeburnmill D & G 39 Q3
Closworth Somset 7 L9
Clothall Herts 17 R5
Clotton Ches W 30 H13
Clough Foot Calder 31 N4
Clough Head Calder 31 R4
Cloughton N York 37 R8
Clousta Shet 59 p5
Clova Angus 51 L4
Clovelly Devon 4 G7
Clovenfords Border 46 F11
Clovulin Highld 49 M5
Clowne Derbys 32 D12
Clows Top Worcs 22 G13
Cluanie Inn Highld 52 J13
Cluanie Lodge Highld 52 J13
Clugston D & G 38 G9
Clun Shrops 21 Q7
Clunas Highld 54 B7
Clunbury Shrops 21 R7
Clunderwen Carmth 12 H7
Clune Highld 53 U10
Clunes Highld 49 P1
Clungunford Shrops 21 R7
Clunie P & K 50 H8
Clunton Shrops 21 Q7
Cluny Fife 45 R1
Clutton BaNES 7 M1
Clutton Ches W 30 G15
Clutton Hill BaNES 7 M1
Clydach Mons 14 E8
Clydach Swans 13 R10
Clydach Vale Rhondd 14 B11
Clydebank W Duns 44 E5
Clyffe Pypard Wilts 15 S14
Clynder Ag & B 43 S3
Clyne Neath 13 S10
Clynnog-fawr Gwynd 28 E10
Clyro Powys 21 N13
Clyst Honiton Devon 5 S12
Clyst Hydon Devon 5 S10
Clyst St George Devon 5 S12
Clyst St Lawrence Devon 5 S11
Clyst St Mary Devon 5 S12
Cnoc W Isls 56 f2
Cnwch Coch Cerdgn 20 F8
Coad's Green Cnwll 2 G3
Coalburn S Lans 44 K11
Coalburns Gatesd 41 N8
Coaley Gloucs 15 N10
Coalhill Essex 18 J14
Coalpit Heath S Glos 15 M13
Coal Pool Wsall 23 M9
Coalport Wrekin 22 G8
Coalsnaughton Clacks 45 L1
Coaltown of Balgonie Fife 51 L16
Coaltown of Wemyss Fife 45 S1
Coalville Leics 23 S6
Coanwood Nthumb 40 F9
Coat Somset 6 J7
Coatbridge N Lans 44 H6
Coatdyke N Lans 44 J6
Coate Swindn 15 U13
Coate Wilts 15 S16
Coates Cambs 25 R9
Coates Gloucs 15 R10
Coates Lincs 32 K10
Coates W Susx 9 R9
Cobbaton Devon 5 M6
Coberley Gloucs 15 R7
Cobham Kent 10 J4
Cobham Surrey 9 S2
Cobnash Herefs 21 S10
Cobo Guern 2 c2
Cobridge C Stke 31 N16
Coburby Abers 55 S4
Cockayne Hatley C Beds 17 R2
Cock Bridge Abers 54 G13
Cockburnspath Border 46 K5
Cock Clarks Essex 18 J13
Cockenzie and Port Seton E Loth 46 E4
Cockerham Lancs 35 N15
Cockermouth Cumb 39 T13
Cockernhoe Herts 17 P6
Cockett Swans 13 Q11
Cockfield Dur 36 D3
Cockfield Suffk 19 L4
Cockfosters Gt Lon 17 R11
Cock Green Essex 18 H10
Cocking W Susx 9 P9
Cocking Causeway W Susx 9 P8
Cockington Torbay 3 R5
Cocklake Somset 6 J3
Cockley Cley Norfk 26 J8
Cock Marling E Susx 11 M12
Cockpole Green Wokham 16 J13
Cockshutt Shrops 22 C4
Cockthorpe Norfk 27 M2
Cockwood Devon 5 S14
Cockyard Derbys 31 Q11
Coddenham Suffk 19 P4
Coddington Herefs 15 M3
Coddington Notts 32 J15
Codford St Mary Wilts 7 R4
Codford St Peter Wilts 7 R4
Codicote Herts 17 Q7
Codmore Hill W Susx 9 R8
Codnor Derbys 32 C16
Codrington S Glos 15 M13
Codsall Staffs 22 K8
Codsall Wood Staffs 22 J8
Coedpoeth Wrexhm 30 E16
Coed Talon Flints 30 D14
Coed-y-paen Mons 14 G10
Coffinswell Devon 3 Q5
Cofton Devon 5 S14
Cofton Hackett Worcs 23 L13
Cogan V Glam 14 E15
Cogenhoe Nhants 24 J15
Cogges Oxon 16 C8
Coggeshall Essex 18 K10
Coignafearn Highld 53 S12
Coilacriech Abers 54 H15
Coilantogle Stirlg 49 V15
Coillore Highld 59 d10
Coity Brdgnd 13 U13
Col W Isls 56 f2
Colaboll Highld 57 P12
Colan Cnwll 1 T8
Colaton Raleigh Devon 6 D13
Colbost Highld 59 b8
Colburn N York 36 E7
Colby Cumb 35 Q3
Colby IoM 34 b7
Colchester Essex 19 M9
Cold Ash W Berk 16 E15
Cold Ashby Nhants 24 F13
Cold Ashton S Glos 15 N14
Cold Aston Gloucs 15 T7
Coldbackie Highld 57 Q4
Cold Brayfield M Keyn 17 L1
Coldean Br & H 10 D13
Coldeast Devon 3 P4
Colden Calder 31 P3
Colden Common Hants 8 H8
Cold Hanworth Lincs 33 M10
Coldharbour Surrey 9 T4
Cold Higham Nhants 16 G1
Coldingham Border 47 M6
Cold Kirby N York 36 K9
Coldmeece Staffs 22 J3
Cold Norton Essex 18 K13
Cold Overton Leics 24 J7
Coldred Kent 11 S7
Coldridge Devon 5 N9
Coldstream Border 47 L10
Coldwaltham W Susx 9 R9
Coldwell Herefs 14 H4
Coldwells Abers 55 S8
Cole Somset 7 M5
Colebatch Shrops 21 Q6
Colebrook Devon 5 S10
Colebrooke Devon 5 P11
Coleby Lincs 33 L14
Coleby N Linc 32 K4
Coleford Devon 5 P10
Coleford Gloucs 14 K8
Coleford Somset 7 M3
Colegate End Norfk 27 Q11
Colehill Dorset 7 S10
Coleman's Hatch E Susx 10 F9
Colemere Shrops 22 C3
Colemore Hants 9 L7
Colenden P & K 50 H11
Colerne Wilts 15 P15
Colesbourne Gloucs 15 R8
Coleshill Bucks 17 L11
Coleshill Oxon 15 V11
Coleshill Warwks 23 P10
Coley BaNES 7 L1
Colgate W Susx 10 C9
Colinsburgh Fife 51 N15
Colinton C Edin 45 Q5
Colintraive Ag & B 43 P4
Colkirk Norfk 27 L4
Coll W Isls 56 f2
Collace P & K 50 J10
Collafirth Shet 59 q3
Coll Airport Ag & B 42 d2
Collaton Devon 3 N9
Collaton St Mary Torbay 3 Q6
College of Roseisle Moray 54 F4
College Town Br For 9 P2
Collessie Fife 51 L14
Collier Row Gt Lon 18 E15
Collier's End Herts 17 S7
Collier Street Kent 10 J7
Collieston Abers 55 T10
Collin D & G 39 R6
Collingbourne Ducis Wilts 8 E3
Collingbourne Kingston Wilts 8 E2
Collingham Leeds 36 H16
Collingham Notts 32 J14
Collington Herefs 22 F15
Collingtree Nhants 24 H16
Collins Green Warrtn 30 H9
Colliston Angus 51 Q8
Colliton Devon 6 D10
Collyweston Nhants 25 L8
Colmonell S Ayrs 38 D4
Colmworth Bed 25 N16
Colnabaichin Abers 54 H13
Colnbrook Slough 17 M14
Colne Cambs 25 S13
Colne Lancs 31 N1
Colne Engaine Essex 18 K8
Colney Norfk 27 Q7
Colney Heath Herts 17 Q9
Coln Rogers Gloucs 15 S8
Coln St Aldwyns Gloucs 15 T9
Coln St Dennis Gloucs 15 S8
Colonsay Airport Ag & B 42 D1
Colpy Abers 55 N9
Colquhar Border 45 S10
Colsterworth Lincs 24 K5
Colston Bassett Notts 24 G3
Coltfield Moray 54 E4
Coltishall Norfk 27 R5
Colton Cumb 35 L9
Colton Leeds 32 B2
Colton N York 36 K16
Colton Norfk 27 P7
Colton Staffs 23 M5
Colt's Hill Kent 10 H8
Colvend D & G 39 P9
Colwall Herefs 15 N3
Colwell Nthumb 40 K6
Colwich Staffs 23 M5
Colwinston V Glam 13 U14
Colworth W Susx 9 P11
Colwyn Bay Conwy 29 L5
Colyford Devon 6 F12
Colyton Devon 6 F12
Combe Oxon 16 D7
Combe W Berk 8 G2
Combe Down BaNES 15 N16
Combe Fishacre Devon 3 Q5
Combe Florey Somset 6 E6
Combe Hay BaNES 7 N1
Combeinteignhead Devon 3 R4
Combe Martin Devon 5 L3
Combe Raleigh Devon 6 E10
Comberbach Ches W 30 K11
Comberford Staffs 23 P8
Comberton Cambs 25 S16
Comberton Herefs 22 D14
Combe St Nicholas Somset 6 G9
Combrook Warwks 16 B1
Combs Derbys 31 Q11
Combs Suffk 19 N4
Combs Ford Suffk 19 N4
Combwich Somset 6 F4
Comers Abers 55 N13
Comhampton Worcs 22 J14
Commins Coch Powys 20 H3
Commondale N York 37 M5
Common End Cumb 34 F3
Common Moor Cnwll 2 F4
Compstall Stockp 31 P9
Compstonend D & G 39 L10
Compton Devon 3 Q5
Compton Hants 8 H7
Compton Staffs 22 J11
Compton Surrey 9 Q4
Compton W Berk 16 E13
Compton W Susx 9 M9
Compton Wilts 8 C3
Compton Abbas Dorset 7 Q8
Compton Abdale Gloucs 15 S7
Compton Bassett Wilts 15 S14
Compton Beauchamp Oxon 16 B12
Compton Bishop Somset 6 H2
Compton Chamberlayne Wilts 7 S6
Compton Dando BaNES 15 L16
Compton Dundon Somset 6 K5
Compton Durville Somset 6 J8
Compton Greenfield S Glos 14 K13
Compton Martin BaNES 6 K1
Compton Pauncefoot Somset 7 M6
Compton Valence Dorset 7 L12
Comrie Fife 45 M2
Comrie P & K 50 C12
Conaglen House Highld 49 M4
Conchra Highld 52 F10
Concraigie P & K 50 H8
Conderton Worcs 15 R4
Condicote Gloucs 15 T5
Condorrat N Lans 44 H5
Condover Shrops 22 D8
Coney Hill Gloucs 15 P7
Coneyhurst Common W Susx 9 S8
Coneysthorpe N York 37 M11
Coney Weston Suffk 27 L12
Congerstone Leics 23 S8
Congham Norfk 26 H5
Congleton Ches E 31 N14
Congresbury N Som 14 H16
Conheath D & G 39 R7
Conicavel Moray 54 D6
Coningsby Lincs 33 P14
Conington Cambs 25 P11
Conington Cambs 25 R14
Conisbrough Donc 32 D8
Conisholme Lincs 33 S8
Coniston Cumb 34 K7
Coniston E R Yk 33 N2
Coniston Cold N York 35 U14
Conistone N York 36 B12
Connah's Quay Flints 30 E13
Connel Ag & B 49 L10
Connel Park E Ayrs 44 G14
Connor Downs Cnwll 1 Q11
Conon Bridge Highld 53 Q6
Cononley N York 36 B15
Consall Staffs 31 P16
Consett Dur 41 M10
Constable Burton N York 36 E8
Constable Lee Lancs 31 M4
Constantine Cnwll 1 S13
Constantine Bay Cnwll 1 U5
Contin Highld 53 P5
Conwy Conwy 28 K5
Conyer's Green Suffk 27 L14
Cooden E Susx 10 J14
Cookbury Devon 4 J10
Cookham W & M 17 L12
Cookham Dean W & M 16 K12
Cookham Rise W & M 16 K12
Cookhill Worcs 23 M16
Cookley Suffk 27 S13
Cookley Worcs 22 J12
Cookley Green Oxon 16 H12
Cookney Abers 55 R16
Cook's Green Essex 19 Q10
Cooks Green Suffk 19 M4
Cooksmill Green Essex 18 G12
Coolham W Susx 9 S8
Cooling Medway 10 K2
Coombe Cnwll 2 B7
Coombe Devon 3 R4
Coombe Devon 6 D12
Coombe Gloucs 15 N11
Coombe Hants 9 L8
Coombe Bissett Wilts 8 C7
Coombe Cellars Devon 3 R4
Coombe Hill Gloucs 15 Q6
Coombe Keynes Dorset 7 Q13
Coombe Pafford Torbay 3 R5
Coombes W Susx 9 T10
Coombes-Moor Herefs 21 Q10
Coombeswood Dudley 23 L11
Coopersale Common Essex 18 E13
Copdock Suffk 19 P6
Copford Green Essex 19 L9
Copgrove N York 36 G13
Copister Shet 59 q4
Cople Bed 17 P2
Copley Dur 41 M14
Copmanthorpe C York 36 K15
Copmere End Staffs 22 J4
Copp Lancs 30 F1
Coppenhall Staffs 22 K6
Copperhouse Cnwll 1 P12
Coppingford Cambs 25 P12
Copplestone Devon 5 P10
Coppull Lancs 30 H5
Copsale W Susx 9 T7
Copster Green Lancs 30 K2
Copston Magna Warwks 24 D11
Cop Street Kent 11 T5
Copt Hewick N York 36 G11
Copthorne W Susx 10 D8
Copt Oak Leics 24 D7
Copythorne Hants 8 F9
Corbets Tey Gt Lon 18 F16
Corbière Jersey 3 a3
Corbridge Nthumb 41 L8
Corby Nhants 24 K11
Corby Glen Lincs 25 L5
Cordon N Ayrs 43 N12
Coreley Shrops 22 F13
Corfe Somset 6 F7
Corfe Castle Dorset 7 R14
Corfton Shrops 22 D11
Corgarff Abers 54 H13
Corhampton Hants 8 K8
Corley Warwks 23 R11
Cormuir Angus 51 L5
Cornard Tye Suffk 19 L6
Cornforth Dur 41 Q13
Cornhill Abers 55 M5
Cornhill-on-Tweed Nthumb 47 M10
Cornholme Calder 31 N3
Cornoigmore Ag & B 42 b4
Cornsay Dur 41 N11
Cornsay Colliery Dur 41 N11
Corntown Highld 53 Q5
Corntown V Glam 13 U14
Cornwall Airport Newquay Cnwll 1 U7
Cornwell Oxon 16 B5
Cornwood Devon 3 L6
Cornworthy Devon 3 Q7
Corpach Highld 49 N3
Corpusty Norfk 27 P4
Corrachree Abers 54 K14
Corran Highld 49 M5
Corran Highld 52 E13
Corrie D & G 39 U4
Corrie N Ayrs 43 N10
Corriecravie N Ayrs 43 M13
Corriegills N Ayrs 43 P11
Corriegour Lodge Hotel Highld 53 L16
Corriemoillie Highld 53 N4
Corrimony Highld 53 N10
Corringham Lincs 32 J9
Corringham Thurr 10 J1
Corris Gwynd 20 G2
Corris Uchaf Gwynd 20 G2
Corrow Ag & B 49 P16
Corry Highld 52 B11
Corscombe Devon 5 M11
Corscombe Dorset 6 K10
Corse Gloucs 15 N5
Corse Lawn Gloucs 15 P5
Corsham Wilts 15 P15
Corsindae Abers 55 N13
Corsley Wilts 7 P3
Corsley Heath Wilts 7 P3
Corsock D & G 39 M6
Corston BaNES 15 M16
Corston Wilts 15 Q13
Corstorphine C Edin 45 Q5
Cortachy Angus 51 M6
Corton Suffk 27 V9
Corton Wilts 7 R4
Corton Denham Somset 7 M7
Coruanan Highld 49 N4
Corwen Denbgs 29 P11
Coryton Devon 4 J13
Coryton Thurr 10 K1
Cosby Leics 24 E10
Coseley Dudley 23 L10
Cosgrove Nhants 16 J3
Cosham C Port 9 L11
Cosheston Pembks 12 F9
Coshieville P & K 50 C8
Cossall Notts 24 D2
Cossington Leics 24 F6
Cossington Somset 6 H4
Costessey Norfk 27 Q7
Costock Notts 24 E4
Coston Leics 24 J5
Coston Norfk 27 N8
Cote Oxon 16 C10
Cotebrook Ches W 30 J13
Cotehill Cumb 40 C10
Cotes Leics 24 E5
Cotesbach Leics 24 E12
Cotford St Luke Somset 6 E6
Cotgrave Notts 24 F3
Cothal Abers 55 R12
Cotham Notts 24 H1
Cotherstone Dur 36 B4
Cothill Oxon 16 E10
Cotleigh Devon 6 F10
Cotmanhay Derbys 24 D2
Coton Cambs 25 S15
Coton Nhants 24 G13
Coton Staffs 22 J5
Coton Clanford Staffs 22 K5
Coton Hill Shrops 22 D6
Coton in the Elms Derbys 23 Q6
Cott Devon 3 P6
Cottam Lancs 30 H2
Cottam Notts 32 J11
Cottenham Cambs 26 D14
Cottered Herts 17 S5
Cotteridge Birm 23 M12
Cotterstock Nhants 25 M10
Cottesbrooke Nhants 24 G13
Cottesmore Rutlnd 24 K6
Cottingham E R Yk 33 M2
Cottingham Nhants 24 J10
Cottingley C Brad 31 R1
Cottisford Oxon 16 F5
Cotton Suffk 27 N14
Cottown Abers 55 L10
Cottown Abers 55 Q12
Cottown of Gight Abers 55 Q8
Cotts Devon 2 J5
Coughton Warwks 23 N15
Coulaghailtro Ag & B 42 J6
Coulags Highld 52 G7
Coull Abers 55 L14
Coulport Ag & B 43 R2
Coulsdon Gt Lon 10 D5
Coulston Wilts 7 R2
Coulter S Lans 45 M11
Coulton N York 37 L11
Coultra Fife 51 L12
Cound Shrops 22 E8
Coundon Dur 41 P13
Countersett N York 35 U9
Countess Wear Devon 5 R12
Countesthorpe Leics 24 E9
Countisbury Devon 5 N2
Coupar Angus P & K 50 K9
Coupland Nthumb 47 N11
Cour Ag & B 43 L9
Courteachan Highld 52 C15
Courteenhall Nhants 16 J1
Court Henry Carmth 13 P6
Courtsend Essex 19 M14
Courtway Somset 6 F5
Cousland Mdloth 46 E5
Cousley Wood E Susx 10 J9
Cove Ag & B 43 R3
Cove Border 46 K5
Cove Devon 5 R7
Cove Hants 9 P2
Cove Highld 56 C15
Cove Bay C Aber 55 S14
Covehithe Suffk 27 U12
Coven Staffs 22 K8
Coveney Cambs 26 E12
Covenham St Bartholomew Lincs 33 R8
Covenham St Mary Lincs 33 R9
Coventry Covtry 23 R12
Coventry Airport Warwks 23 R13
Coverack Cnwll 1 S15
Coverack Bridges Cnwll 1 R13
Coverham N York 36 D9
Covington Cambs 25 M14
Covington S Lans 45 M10
Cowan Bridge Lancs 35 Q11
Cowbeech E Susx 10 H12
Cowbit Lincs 25 Q6
Cowbridge V Glam 14 B14
Cowden Kent 10 F8
Cowdenbeath Fife 45 P2
Cowers Lane Derbys 23 R1
Cowes IoW 8 H12
Cowesby N York 36 J8
Cowfold W Susx 10 B11
Cowhill S Glos 15 L11
Cowie Stirlg 44 K2
Cowley Devon 5 R11
Cowley Gloucs 15 R8
Cowley Gt Lon 17 N13
Cowley Oxon 16 F9
Cowling Lancs 30 J5
Cowling N York 36 B16
Cowling N York 36 F9
Cowlinge Suffk 18 H4
Cowpen Nthumb 41 Q5
Cowplain Hants 9 L10
Cowshill Dur 40 J12
Cowslip Green N Som 14 J16
Cowthorpe N York 36 H14
Coxbank Ches E 22 G2
Coxbench Derbys 23 S2
Coxford Cnwll 4 E11
Coxford Norfk 26 K4
Coxheath Kent 10 K6
Coxhoe Dur 41 Q12
Coxley Somset 6 K4
Coxley Wick Somset 6 K3
Coxtie Green Essex 18 F14
Coxwold N York 36 K10
Coychurch Brdgnd 13 U13
Coylton S Ayrs 44 D13
Coylumbridge Highld 54 C13
Coytrahen Brdgnd 13 U12
Crabbs Cross Worcs 23 M14
Crabtree W Susx 10 C11
Crackenthorpe Cumb 35 Q3
Crackington Haven Cnwll 4 E11
Crackley Staffs 31 M16
Crackley Warwks 23 R13
Crackleybank Shrops 22 H7
Cracoe N York 36 B13
Craddock Devon 6 D9
Cradley Dudley 23 L11
Cradley Herefs 15 N2
Cradley Heath Sandw 23 L11
Cradoc Powys 14 C5
Crafthole Cnwll 2 H7
Craggan Highld 54 D10
Craghead Dur 41 P10
Crai Powys 13 U6
Craibstone Moray 55 L5
Craichie Angus 51 P8
Craig Angus 51 R6
Craig Highld 52 H7
Craigbank E Ayrs 44 F15
Craigburn Border 45 Q8
Craigcleuch D & G 40 B4
Craigdam Abers 55 R10
Craigdhu Ag & B 48 J15
Craigearn Abers 55 P12
Craigellachie Moray 54 H7
Craigend P & K 50 H12
Craigend Rens 44 E5
Craigendoran Ag & B 43 S3
Craigends Rens 44 D6
Craighlaw D & G 38 F8
Craighouse Ag & B 42 F6
Craigie P & K 50 H9
Craigie S Ayrs 44 D11
Craigiefold Abers 55 S4
Craigley D & G 39 N9
Craig Llangiwg Neath 13 R9
Craiglockhart C Edin 45 Q5
Craigmillar C Edin 45 R5
Craigneston D & G 39 M4
Craigneuk N Lans 44 J6
Craigneuk N Lans 44 J7
Craignure Ag & B 48 H10
Craigo Angus 51 R5
Craigrothie Fife 51 M14
Craigruie Stirlg 49 U12
Craigton Angus 51 P9
Craigton C Aber 55 Q14
Craigton E Rens 44 E8
Craigton of Airlie Angus 51 L7
Crail Fife 51 Q14
Crailing Border 46 J13
Craiselound N Linc 32 H8
Crakehall N York 36 F8
Crambe N York 37 N13
Cramlington Nthumb 41 Q6
Cramond C Edin 45 Q4
Cramond Bridge C Edin 45 Q4
Cranage Ches E 31 L13
Cranberry Staffs 22 J3
Cranborne Dorset 7 T8
Cranbourne Br For 17 L14
Cranbrook Devon 5 S11
Cranbrook Kent 10 K9
Cranfield C Beds 17 L3
Cranford Gt Lon 17 P14
Cranford St Andrew Nhants 24 K12
Cranford St John Nhants 24 K13
Cranham Gloucs 15 Q8
Crank St Hel 30 H8
Cranleigh Surrey 9 R5
Cranmore Somset 7 M4
Cranoe Leics 24 H9
Cransford Suffk 19 S3
Cranshaws Border 46 J6
Crantock Cnwll 1 S8
Cranwell Lincs 33 M16
Cranwich Norfk 26 J10
Cranworth Norfk 27 M8
Craobh Haven Ag & B 48 J14
Crarae Ag & B 49 M16
Crask Inn Highld 57 N10
Crask of Aigas Highld 53 P8
Craster Nthumb 47 S13
Cratfield Suffk 27 R13
Crathes Abers 55 P15
Crathie Abers 54 G15
Crathie Highld 53 R16
Crathorne N York 36 H5
Craven Arms Shrops 21 R7
Crawcrook Gatesd 41 N8
Crawford S Lans 45 M13
Crawfordjohn S Lans 44 K13
Crawley Hants 8 H6
Crawley Oxon 16 C8
Crawley W Susx 10 C9
Crawley Down W Susx 10 D9
Crawton Abers 51 U3
Cray N York 35 U10
Crayford Gt Lon 10 G3
Crayke N York 36 K12
Crays Hill Essex 18 H15
Creacombe Devon 5 P7
Creagan Inn Ag & B 49 L8
Creag Ghoraidh W Isls 56 b6
Creagorry W Isls 56 b6
Creaguaineach Lodge Highld 49 R4
Creaton Nhants 24 G13
Creca D & G 39 U7
Credenhill Herefs 21 S13
Crediton Devon 5 Q11
Creebank D & G 38 G6
Creebridge D & G 38 H8
Creech Heathfield Somset 6 G6
Creech St Michael Somset 6 G6
Creed Cnwll 2 B8
Creekmouth Gt Lon 10 F1
Creeting St Mary Suffk 19 N4
Creeton Lincs 25 L5
Creetown D & G 38 J9
Cregneash IoM 34 b7
Creich Fife 51 L12
Creigiau Cardif 14 C13
Cremyll Cnwll 2 J7
Cressage Shrops 22 F8
Cressbrook Derbys 31 S12
Cresselly Pembks 12 G9
Cressex Bucks 16 K11
Cressing Essex 18 J10
Cresswell Nthumb 41 Q3
Cresswell Pembks 12 G9
Cresswell Staffs 23 L2
Creswell Derbys 32 E12
Cretingham Suffk 19 Q3
Cretshengan Ag & B 42 J6
Crewe Ches E 30 K15
Crewe-by-Farndon Ches W 30 F15
Crewe Green Ches E 31 L15
Crew Green Powys 29 T16
Crewkerne Somset 6 J9
Crewton C Derb 23 S3
Crianlarich Stirlg 49 S12
Cribyn Cerdgn 20 D12
Criccieth Gwynd 28 F12
Crich Derbys 32 B15
Crichton Mdloth 46 E6
Crick Nhants 24 F13
Crickadarn Powys 21 M13
Cricket St Thomas Somset 6 H9
Crickhowell Powys 14 E7
Cricklade Wilts 15 T11
Cricklewood Gt Lon 17 Q12
Crieff P & K 50 E12
Criggion Powys 29 S16
Crigglestone Wakefd 31 U5
Crimond Abers 55 U5
Crimplesham Norfk 26 G8
Crimscote Warwks 15 V2
Crinaglack Highld 53 P8
Crinan Ag & B 42 K1
Crindledyke N Lans 44 K7
Cringleford Norfk 27 Q8
Crinow Pembks 12 H8
Croachy Highld 53 S10
Crockenhill Kent 10 G4
Crocker End Oxon 16 H12
Crockernwell Devon 5 P12
Crockerton Wilts 7 Q4
Crocketford D & G 39 P6
Crockham Hill Kent 10 F7
Croeserw Neath 13 T11
Croes-goch Pembks 12 D5
Croes-lan Cerdgn 20 B13
Croesor Gwynd 28 H11
Croesyceiliog Carmth 13 M7
Croesyceiliog Torfn 14 G11
Croft Leics 24 D9
Croft Lincs 33 T14
Croft Warrtn 30 J9
Croftamie Stirlg 44 E2
Crofton Wakefd 32 C5
Croft-on-Tees N York 36 F5
Croftown Highld 52 K1
Crofts Moray 54 H6
Crofts of Dipple Moray 54 H5
Crofts of Savoch Abers 55 T5
Crofty Swans 13 P11
Croggan Ag & B 48 H11
Croglin Cumb 40 E11
Croick Highld 57 M15
Cromarty Highld 53 U4
Crombie Fife 45 N3
Cromdale Highld 54 E10
Cromer Herts 17 R5
Cromer Norfk 27 Q2
Cromford Derbys 31 U15
Cromhall S Glos 15 M12
Cromor W Isls 56 e3
Cromwell Notts 32 H14
Cronberry E Ayrs 44 G13
Crondall Hants 9 N4
Cronton Knows 30 G10
Crook Cumb 35 N8
Crook Dur 41 N12
Crookedholm E Ayrs 44 D10
Crookham Nthumb 47 M10
Crookham W Berk 16 F16
Crookham Village Hants 9 N3
Crook Inn Border 45 P12
Crooklands Cumb 35 P9
Crook of Devon P & K 50 G16
Cropredy Oxon 16 E2
Cropston Leics 24 E7
Cropthorne Worcs 15 R3
Cropton N York 37 N9
Cropwell Bishop Notts 24 G3
Cropwell Butler Notts 24 G3
Cros W Isls 56 f1
Crosbost W Isls 56 e3
Crosby Cumb 39 S12
Crosby IoM 34 d5
Crosby N Linc 32 K6
Crosby Sefton 30 E8
Crosby Garret Cumb 35 R5
Crosby Ravensworth Cumb 35 Q4
Croscombe Somset 7 L3
Cross Somset 6 J2
Crossaig Ag & B 43 L8
Crossapol Ag & B 42 b4
Cross Ash Mons 14 H7
Cross-at-Hand Kent 10 K7
Crosscanonby Cumb 39 S12
Crossdale Street Norfk 27 Q2
Cross Flatts C Brad 31 R1
Crossford Fife 45 N2
Crossford S Lans 44 K9
Crossgatehall E Loth 46 E5
Crossgates E Ayrs 44 C9
Crossgates Fife 45 P2
Cross Gates Leeds 32 B2
Crossgates N York 37 S9
Crossgill Lancs 35 P13
Cross Green Leeds 31 U2
Cross Green Suffk 19 L4
Cross Green Suffk 19 M5
Cross Hands Carmth 13 P8

D

E

Crosshands E Ayrs 44 E12
Crosshill Fife 45 Q1
Crosshill S Ayrs 43 T16
Crosshouse E Ayrs 44 E11
Cross Houses Shrops 22 K7
Cross in Hand E Susx 10 T16
Cross Inn Cerdgn 20 G8
Cross Keys Ag & B 43 T13
Crosskeys Caerph 14 E11
Crosskirk Highld 58 D2
Cross Lane IoW 9 P13
Cross Lane Head Shrops 22 K6
Crosslee Rens 44 D6
Crosskirk Highld

Crossmichael D & G

Daccombe Devon 3 R5
Dacre Cumb 40 C14
Dacre N York 36 E13
Dacre Banks N York 36 E13
Daddry Shield Dur 40 J12
Dadford Bucks 16 G4
Dadlington Leics 23 J9
Dagenham Gt Lon 18 E6
Daglingworth Gloucs 15 R9
Dagnall Bucks 17 M7
Dail bho Dheas W Isls 58 G8

Eagland Hill Lancs 35 M16
Eagle Lincs 32 K13
Eaglescliffe Dur & B 41 P3
Eaglesfield Cumb 39 U4
Eaglesfield D & G 44 P8
Eaglesham E Rens 44 F8
Eagley Bolton 35 S4
Eairy IoM 6 c6
Eakring Notts 32 Q6

Ensbury – Great Urswick 67

Ensbury Bmouth 7 T11
Ensdon Shrops 22 C6
Enstone Oxon 16 C6
Enterkinfoot D & G 39 P1
Enville Staffs 22 J11
Eolaigearraidh W Isls 56 b8
Epney Gloucs 15 N8
Epperstone Notts 32 F16
Epping Essex 18 D13
Epping Green Essex 18 D12
Epping Upland Essex 18 D12
Eppleby N York 36 E5
Epsom Surrey 9 U2
Epwell Oxon 16 C3
Epworth N Linc 32 H7
Erbistock Wrexhm 29 T11
Erdington Birm 23 N10
Eridge Green E Susx 10 G9
Erines Ag & B 43 L4
Eriska Ag & B 48 K9
Eriswell Suffk 26 H12
Erith Gt Lon 10 G2
Erlestoke Wilts 7 R2
Ermington Devon 3 M7
Erpingham Norfk 27 Q3
Errogie Highld 53 Q11
Errol P & K 50 K12
Erskine Rens 44 E5
Erskine Bridge Rens 44 E5
Ervie D & G 38 B7
Erwarton Suffk 19 Q8
Erwood Powys 21 M13
Eryholme N York 36 G5
Eryrys Denbgs 29 R9
Escomb Dur 41 N13
Escrick N York 37 L16
Esgairgeiliog Powys 20 G3
Esh Dur 41 P11
Esher Surrey 17 P16
Eshott Nthumb 41 P2
Esh Winning Dur 41 P11
Eskadale Highld 53 P8
Eskbank Mdloth 45 S6
Eskdale Green Cumb 34 H7
Eskdalemuir D & G 39 U2
Esprick Lancs 30 F2
Essendine Rutlnd 25 M7
Essendon Herts 17 R8
Essich Highld 53 S8
Essington Staffs 23 L8
Esslemont Abers 55 S10
Eston R & Cl 36 K4
Etal Nthumb 47 N10
Etchilhampton Wilts 7 S1
Etchingham E Susx 10 J11
Etchinghill Kent 11 R8
Etchinghill Staffs 23 M6
Eton W & M 17 M14
Eton Wick W & M 17 L13
Etruria C Stke 22 J1
Etteridge Highld 53 S16
Ettersgill Dur 40 J13
Ettiley Heath Ches E 31 L14
Ettingshall Wolves 22 K9
Ettington Warwks 16 B2
Etton C Pete 25 N8
Etton E R Yk 37 R16
Ettrick Border 45 R14
Ettrickbridge Border 46 E13
Ettrickhill Border 45 R14
Etwall Derbys 23 Q3
Euston Suffk 27 L12
Euxton Lancs 30 H4
Evanton Highld 53 R4
Evedon Lincs 25 N1
Evelix Highld 57 S15
Evenjobb Powys 21 P10
Evenley Nhants 16 F4
Evenlode Gloucs 15 U5
Evenwood Dur 41 N14
Evercreech Somset 7 M4
Everingham E R Yk 37 P16
Everleigh Wilts 8 D3
Eversholt C Beds 17 M5
Evershot Dorset 7 L10
Eversley Hants 9 M1
Eversley Cross Hants 9 N1
Everthorpe E R Yk 32 K2
Everton C Beds 17 Q2
Everton Hants 8 F13
Everton Lpool 30 E9
Everton Notts 32 G9
Evertown D & G 40 B6
Evesbatch Herefs 15 M2
Evesham Worcs 15 S3
Evington C Leic 24 F8
Ewden Village Sheff 31 T8
Ewell Surrey 10 C5
Ewell Minnis Kent 11 S8
Ewelme Oxon 16 G11
Ewen Gloucs 15 R10
Ewenny V Glam 13 U14
Ewerby Lincs 25 N1
Ewhurst Surrey 9 S5
Ewhurst Green E Susx 11 L11
Ewhurst Green Surrey 9 S5
Ewloe Flints 30 E13
Eworthy Devon 4 J11
Ewshot Hants 9 N3
Ewyas Harold Herefs 14 H5
Exbourne Devon 5 L10
Exbury Hants 8 H12
Exebridge Somset 5 R7
Exelby N York 36 F9
Exeter Devon 5 R12
Exeter Airport Devon 5 S12
Exford Somset 5 Q4
Exfordsgreen Shrops 21 S3
Exhall Warwks 23 N16
Exhall Warwks 23 R11
Exlade Street Oxon 16 G13
Exminster Devon 5 R13
Exmouth Devon 5 S14
Exning Suffk 26 G14
Exton Devon 5 S13
Exton Hants 8 K8
Exton Rutlnd 24 K7
Exton Somset 5 R5
Exwick Devon 5 R12
Eyam Derbys 31 T11
Eydon Nhants 16 F2
Eye C Pete 25 P8
Eye Herefs 22 D15
Eye Suffk 27 P13
Eyemouth Border 47 N6
Eyeworth C Beds 17 R2
Eyhorne Street Kent 11 L6
Eyke Suffk 19 S5
Eynesbury Cambs 25 P15
Eynsford Kent 10 G4
Eynsham Oxon 16 D8
Eype Dorset 6 J12
Eyre Highld 59 e8
Eythorne Kent 11 S7
Eyton Herefs 22 D15
Eyton Shrops 22 D5
Eyton on Severn Shrops 22 E8
Eyton upon the Weald Moors Wrekin 22 F6

F

Faccombe Hants 8 G2
Faceby N York 36 J6
Fachwen Powys 29 P16
Faddiley Ches E 30 J15
Fadmoor N York 37 M8
Faerdre Swans 13 R10
Faifley W Duns 44 E5
Failand N Som 14 K15
Failford S Ayrs 44 E12
Failsworth Oldham 31 N7
Fairbourne Gwynd 20 E2
Fairburn N York 32 D3
Fairfield Derbys 31 Q12
Fairfield Worcs 23 L13
Fairford Gloucs 15 T10
Fairgirth D & G 39 P9
Fair Green Norfk 26 G6
Fairhaven Lancs 30 E3
Fair Isle Airport Shet 59 s8
Fairlands Surrey 9 Q3
Fairlie N Ayrs 43 R8
Fairlight E Susx 11 L13
Fairmile Devon 6 D11
Fairmile Surrey 9 S2
Fairnilee Border 46 F11
Fair Oak Hants 8 J9
Fairoak Staffs 22 H3
Fair Oak Green Hants 9 L2
Fairseat Kent 10 H5
Fairstead Essex 18 J10
Fairstead Norfk 26 G5
Fairwarp E Susx 10 F11
Fairwater Cardif 14 D14
Fairy Cross Devon 4 J7
Fakenham Norfk 27 L4
Fakenham Magna Suffk 27 L13
Fala Mdloth 46 F7
Fala Dam Mdloth 46 F6
Faldingworth Lincs 33 M10
Faldouët Jersey 3 e2
Falfield S Glos 15 M11
Falkenham Suffk 19 R7
Falkirk Falk 45 L3
Falkland Fife 50 K14
Fallburn S Lans 45 M10
Fallin Stirlg 44 K1
Fallodon Nthumb 47 R13
Fallowfield Manch 31 N9
Fallowfield Nthumb 40 K7
Falls of Blarghour Ag & B 49 M13
Falmer E Susx 10 D13
Falmouth Cnwll 1 T12
Falnash Border 46 E16
Falsgrave N York 37 S9
Falstone Nthumb 40 G4
Fanagmore Highld 56 J5
Fancott C Beds 17 M5
Fanellan Highld 53 P8
Fangdale Beck N York 36 K8
Fangfoss E R Yk 37 N14
Fanmore Ag & B 48 C8
Fannich Lodge Highld 53 L4
Fans Border 46 H10
Far Bletchley M Keyn 16 K4
Farcet Cambs 25 P10
Far Cotton Nhants 24 H15
Fareham Hants 8 K11
Far End Cumb 34 K7
Farewell Staffs 23 N7
Faringdon Oxon 16 B11
Farington Lancs 30 H3
Farlam Cumb 40 E9
Farleigh N Som 14 J15
Farleigh Surrey 10 E5
Farleigh Hungerford Somset 7 P1
Farleigh Wallop Hants 8 K4
Farlesthorpe Lincs 33 T12
Farleton Cumb 35 P10
Farleton Lancs 35 P12
Farley Staffs 23 M1
Farley Wilts 8 E7
Farley Green Surrey 9 R4
Farley Hill Wokham 16 J16
Farleys End Gloucs 15 N7
Farlington C Port 9 L11
Farlington N York 37 L12
Farlow Shrops 22 F12
Farmborough BaNES 7 M1
Farmcote Gloucs 15 S5
Farmers Carmth 20 E13
Farmington Gloucs 15 T7
Farmoor Oxon 16 D9
Far Moor Wigan 30 H7
Farmtown Moray 55 L6
Farnborough Gt Lon 10 F4
Farnborough Hants 9 P3
Farnborough W Berk 16 D13
Farnborough Warwks 16 D2
Farnborough Park Hants 9 P3
Farncombe Surrey 9 Q4
Farndish Bed 24 K15
Farndon Ches W 30 F15
Farndon Notts 32 H15
Farnell Angus 51 Q7
Farnham Dorset 7 R8
Farnham Essex 18 E9
Farnham N York 36 G13
Farnham Suffk 19 S3
Farnham Surrey 9 N4
Farnham Common Bucks 17 M12
Farnham Royal Bucks 17 M13
Farningham Kent 10 G4
Farnley Leeds 31 T2
Farnley N York 36 E15
Farnley Tyas Kirk 31 S5
Farnsfield Notts 32 F15
Farnworth Bolton 31 L7
Farnworth Halton 30 H10
Far Oakridge Gloucs 15 Q9
Farr Highld 53 S9
Farr Highld 53 U14
Farr Highld 57 R3
Farraline Highld 53 Q11
Farringdon Devon 5 S12
Farrington Gurney BaNES 7 M2
Far Sawrey Cumb 35 L7
Farthinghoe Nhants 16 F3
Farthingstone Nhants 16 G1
Fartown Kirk 31 S4
Fasnacloich Ag & B 49 M8
Fasnakyle Highld 53 M10
Fassfern Highld 49 M3
Fatfield Sundld 41 Q9
Fauldhouse W Loth 45 L7
Faulkbourne Essex 18 J10
Faulkland Somset 7 N2
Fauls Shrops 22 F3
Faversham Kent 11 P5
Fawdington N York 36 H11
Fawdon N u Ty 41 P7
Fawkham Green Kent 10 H4
Fawler Oxon 16 C7
Fawley Bucks 16 J12
Fawley Hants 8 H11
Fawley W Berk 16 D13
Faxfleet E R Yk 32 J4
Faygate W Susx 10 C9
Fazakerley Lpool 30 F8
Fazeley Staffs 23 P8
Fearby N York 36 E10
Fearn Highld 53 U2
Fearnan P & K 50 C8
Fearnbeg Highld 52 D5
Fearnmore Highld 52 D5
Fearnoch Ag & B 43 M3
Featherstone Staffs 22 K8
Featherstone Wakefd 32 C4
Feckenham Worcs 23 M15
Feering Essex 18 K10
Feetham N York 36 B7
Felbridge Surrey 10 E8
Felbrigg Norfk 27 Q2
Felcourt Surrey 10 E8
Felindre Carmth 13 L4
Felindre Carmth 14 P6
Felindre Powys 21 M7
Felindre Swans 13 Q9
Felindre Farchog Pembks 12 H4
Felingwm Isaf Carmth 13 N6
Felingwm Uchaf Carmth 13 N6
Felixkirk N York 36 J9
Felixstowe Suffk 19 R7
Felling Gatesd 41 Q8
Felmersham Bed 25 L16
Felmingham Norfk 27 Q4
Felpham W Susx 9 Q12
Felsham Suffk 19 L4
Felsted Essex 18 H10
Feltham Gt Lon 17 P14
Felthamhill Surrey 17 N15
Felthorpe Norfk 27 P6
Felton Herefs 14 K2
Felton N Som 14 K16
Felton Nthumb 41 N2
Felton Butler Shrops 22 C6
Feltwell Norfk 26 H10
Fence Lancs 31 M1
Fence Rothm 32 C10
Fencott Oxon 16 F7
Fendike Corner Lincs 33 T14
Fen Ditton Cambs 18 E3
Fen Drayton Cambs 25 R14
Feniscowles Bl w D 30 K3
Feniton Devon 6 D11
Fenn Green Shrops 22 H11
Fenn Street Medway 11 L2
Fenny Bentley Derbys 31 S16
Fenny Bridges Devon 6 D11
Fenny Compton Warwks 16 D1
Fenny Drayton Leics 23 R9
Fenstanton Cambs 25 R14
Fen Street Norfk 27 M9
Fenton Cambs 25 R12
Fenton Cumb 40 D9
Fenton Lincs 32 J11
Fenton Lincs 32 K16
Fenton Notts 32 H10
Fenton Nthumb 47 N11
Fenton Barns E Loth 46 G3
Fenwick Donc 32 F5
Fenwick E Ayrs 44 F9
Fenwick Nthumb 41 M6
Fenwick Nthumb 47 P10
Feock Cnwll 1 T11
Feolin Ferry Ag & B 42 E5
Fergushill N Ayrs 43 T9
Feriniquarrie Highld 59 a8
Fern Angus 51 N6
Ferndale Rhondd 14 B10
Ferndown Dorset 7 T11
Ferness Highld 54 C7
Fernham Oxon 16 B11
Fernhill Heath Worcs 22 K15
Fernhurst W Susx 9 P7
Fernie Fife 51 L13
Ferniegair S Lans 44 H8
Fernilea Highld 59 d10
Fernilee Derbys 31 Q11
Fernwood Notts 32 J16
Ferrensby N York 36 G13
Ferrindonald Highld 52 C13
Ferring W Susx 9 S11
Ferryden Angus 51 S6
Ferryhill Dur 41 Q13
Ferryhill Station Dur 41 Q13
Ferry Point Highld 57 R16
Ferryside Carmth 13 L8
Ferrytown Highld 57 R16
Fersfield Norfk 27 N11
Fersit Highld 49 S3
Feshiebridge Highld 54 B14
Fetcham Surrey 9 T2
Fetterangus Abers 55 T6
Fettercairn Abers 51 R4
Fewston N York 36 E14
Ffairfach Carmth 13 Q6
Ffair Rhos Cerdgn 20 G9
Ffestiniog Gwynd 28 J11
Fforest Carmth 13 P9
Fforest Fach Swans 13 Q11
Ffostrasol Cerdgn 20 B12
Ffrith Flints 30 E15
Ffynnongroyw Flints 29 Q5
Fiag Lodge Highld 57 M9
Fickleshole Surrey 10 E5
Fiddington Somset 6 F4
Fiddleford Dorset 7 P8
Fiddlers Green Cnwll 1 T9
Field Staffs 23 M3
Field Dalling Norfk 27 M2
Field Head Leics 24 D7
Fifehead Magdalen Dorset 7 P7
Fifehead Neville Dorset 7 P9
Fifehead St Quintin Dorset 7 P9
Fife Keith Moray 54 K6
Fifield Oxon 16 A7
Fifield W & M 17 L14
Figheldean Wilts 8 D4
Filby Norfk 27 U7
Filey N York 37 T10
Filgrave M Keyn 16 K2
Filkins Oxon 15 V9
Filleigh Devon 5 M6
Fillingham Lincs 33 L10
Fillongley Warwks 23 Q11
Filton S Glos 15 L13
Fimber E R Yk 37 Q13
Finavon Angus 51 N6
Fincham Norfk 26 H8
Finchampstead Wokham 9 N1
Fincharn Ag & B 48 K15
Finchdean Hants 9 M9
Finchingfield Essex 18 H8
Finchley Gt Lon 17 R11
Findern Derbys 23 R4
Findhorn Moray 54 D4
Findhorn Bridge Highld 53 U10
Findochty Moray 54 K3
Findo Gask P & K 50 G12
Findon Abers 55 S15
Findon W Susx 9 S10
Findon Mains Highld 53 R5
Findrack House Abers 55 M14
Finedon Nhants 24 K13
Fingask P & K 50 J12
Fingest Bucks 16 J11
Finghall N York 36 E8
Fingland D & G 44 J14
Finglesham Kent 11 T6
Fingringhoe Essex 19 M10
Finlarig Stirlg 49 V10
Finmere Oxon 16 G5
Finnart P & K 49 U6
Finningham Suffk 27 N14
Finningley Donc 32 G8
Finsbay W Isls 56 d4
Finstall Worcs 23 L14
Finsthwaite Cumb 35 L9
Finstock Oxon 16 C7
Finstown Ork 58 b4
Fintry Abers 55 P6
Fintry Stirlg 44 G2
Finzean Abers 55 M16
Fionnphort Ag & B 48 B12
Fionnsbhagh W Isls 56 d4
Firbank Cumb 35 Q8
Firbeck Rothm 32 E9
Firby N York 36 F9
Firby N York 37 N12
Firle E Susx 10 F12
Firsby Lincs 33 T14
Fir Tree Dur 41 N13
Fishbourne IoW 8 J13
Fishbourne W Susx 9 N11
Fishburn Dur 41 R13
Fishcross Clacks 45 L1
Fisherford Abers 55 N9
Fisherrow E Loth 46 D5
Fisher's Pond Hants 8 H8
Fisherton Highld 53 T6
Fisherton S Ayrs 43 S14
Fisherton de la Mere Wilts 7 S4
Fishery Estate W & M 17 L13
Fishguard Pembks 12 F4
Fishlake Donc 32 F5
Fishnish Pier Ag & B 48 G9
Fishponds Bristl 15 L14
Fishtoft Lincs 25 R2
Fishtoft Drove Lincs 33 R16
Fiskavaig Highld 59 d10
Fiskerton Lincs 33 M12
Fiskerton Notts 32 H16
Fittleton Wilts 8 D3
Fittleworth W Susx 9 R8
Fitz Shrops 22 D6
Fitzhead Somset 6 D6
Fitzwilliam Wakefd 32 C5
Five Ash Down E Susx 10 F11
Five Ashes E Susx 10 G10
Fivehead Somset 6 H7
Fivelanes Cnwll 4 F14
Five Oak Green Kent 10 J7
Five Oaks Jersey 3 d3
Five Oaks W Susx 9 S7
Five Roads Carmth 13 N9
Flackwell Heath Bucks 17 L12
Fladbury Worcs 15 R2
Fladdabister Shet 59 q6
Flagg Derbys 31 R13
Flamborough E R Yk 37 U12
Flamstead Herts 17 N8
Flamstead End Herts 17 S9
Flansham W Susx 9 Q11
Flanshaw Wakefd 31 U4
Flasby N York 35 U14
Flash Staffs 31 Q13
Flashader Highld 59 d8
Flaunden Herts 17 M10
Flawborough Notts 24 H2
Flawith N York 36 J12
Flax Bourton N Som 14 J15
Flaxby N York 36 H14
Flaxley Gloucs 15 M7
Flaxpool Somset 6 E5
Flaxton N York 37 M13
Fleckney Leics 24 F10
Flecknoe Warwks 24 E15
Fledborough Notts 32 J12
Fleet Dorset 7 M14
Fleet Hants 9 N3
Fleet Lincs 25 S5
Fleet Hargate Lincs 25 S5
Fleetwood Lancs 35 L15
Fleggburgh Norfk 27 T6
Flemingston V Glam 14 B15
Flemington S Lans 44 G7
Flempton Suffk 26 J14
Fletchertown Cumb 39 U11
Fletching E Susx 10 E11
Flexbury Cnwll 4 F9
Flexford Surrey 9 Q3
Flimby Cumb 39 R13
Flimwell E Susx 10 J10
Flint Flints 29 S6
Flintham Notts 24 H1
Flinton E R Yk 33 P2
Flitcham Norfk 26 H4
Flitton C Beds 17 N4
Flitwick C Beds 17 N4
Flixborough N Linc 32 K5
Flixborough Stather N Linc 32 J5
Flixton N York 37 S10
Flixton Suffk 27 R11
Flixton Traffd 31 L9
Flockton Kirk 31 T5
Flockton Green Kirk 31 T5
Flodigarry Highld 59 e5
Flookburgh Cumb 35 L11
Flordon Norfk 27 Q9
Flore Nhants 24 F15
Flowton Suffk 19 N6
Flushing Cnwll 1 T12
Fluxton Devon 6 D12
Flyford Flavell Worcs 23 L16
Fobbing Thurr 18 H16
Fochabers Moray 54 J5
Fochriw Caerph 14 D9
Fockerby N Linc 32 J4
Foddington Somset 7 L6
Foel Powys 20 K2
Foggathorpe E R Yk 32 H1
Fogo Border 46 K8
Fogwatt Moray 54 G5
Foindle Highld 56 J6
Folda Angus 50 J5
Fole Staffs 23 M3
Foleshill Covtry 23 R12
Folke Dorset 7 M8
Folkestone Kent 11 S9
Folkingham Lincs 25 M3
Folkington E Susx 10 G14
Folksworth Cambs 25 N10
Folkton N York 37 S10
Folla Rule Abers 55 P9
Follifoot N York 36 G14
Folly Gate Devon 5 L11
Fonthill Bishop Wilts 7 R5
Fonthill Gifford Wilts 7 R5
Fontmell Magna Dorset 7 Q8
Fontmell Parva Dorset 7 P8
Fontwell W Susx 9 Q10
Foolow Derbys 31 S11
Forbestown Abers 54 J12
Forcett N York 36 E5
Ford Ag & B 48 K15
Ford Bucks 16 J8
Ford Derbys 32 C11
Ford Devon 4 J7
Ford Gloucs 15 T5
Ford Nthumb 47 N10
Ford Somset 6 D6
Ford Staffs 31 Q15
Ford W Susx 9 R11
Ford Wilts 15 P14
Fordcombe Kent 10 G8
Fordell Fife 45 P2
Forden Powys 21 P4
Ford End Essex 18 H10
Forder Green Devon 3 P5
Fordham Cambs 26 G13
Fordham Essex 19 L9
Fordham Norfk 26 G9
Fordingbridge Hants 8 D9
Fordon E R Yk 37 S11
Fordoun Abers 51 S3
Fordstreet Essex 19 L9
Ford Street Somset 6 E8
Fordwich Kent 11 R5
Fordyce Abers 55 M4
Forebridge Staffs 22 K5
Forest Guern 2 c4
Forest Chapel Ches E 31 P12
Forest Gate Gt Lon 18 D16
Forest Green Surrey 9 S5
Forest Hall N Tyne 41 Q7
Forest Hill Gt Lon 10 E3
Forest Hill Oxon 16 F9
Forest Lane Head N York 36 G14
Forest Mill Clacks 45 M1
Forest Row E Susx 10 E9
Forestside W Susx 9 M10
Forfar Angus 51 N7
Forgandenny P & K 50 H13
Forge Hammer Torfn 14 F11
Forgie Moray 54 J6
Forgieside Moray 54 J6
Forgue Abers 55 M7
Formby Sefton 30 E6
Forncett End Norfk 27 P10
Forncett St Mary Norfk 27 P10
Forncett St Peter Norfk 27 P10
Fornham All Saints Suffk 26 K14
Fornham St Martin Suffk 26 K14
Fornighty Highld 54 C6
Forres Moray 54 D5
Forsbrook Staffs 23 L2
Forse Highld 58 G8
Forsinard Highld 57 U7
Fort Augustus Highld 53 N13
Forteviot P & K 50 G13
Forth S Lans 45 L8
Forthampton Gloucs 15 P5
Forth Road Bridge Fife 45 P3
Fortingall P & K 50 C8
Forton Hants 8 G4
Forton Lancs 35 N15
Forton Shrops 22 C6
Forton Somset 6 H9
Forton Staffs 22 H5
Fortrie Abers 55 N7
Fortrose Highld 53 T5
Fortuneswell Dorset 7 M15
Fort William Highld 49 N4
Forty Hill Gt Lon 17 S10
Fosbury Wilts 8 F2
Foscot Oxon 16 B6
Fosdyke Lincs 25 R3
Foss P & K 50 D6
Fossebridge Gloucs 15 S8
Foster Street Essex 18 E12
Foston Derbys 23 P3
Foston Leics 24 F10
Foston Lincs 24 J2
Foston N York 37 M12
Foston on the Wolds E R Yk 37 T14
Fotherby Lincs 33 R9
Fotheringhay Nhants 25 M10
Foula Airport Shet 59 s6
Foulden Border 47 N7
Foulden Norfk 26 J9
Foul End Warwks 23 Q10
Foulridge Lancs 35 U16
Foulsham Norfk 27 N5
Fountainhall Border 46 F8
Four Ashes Suffk 27 M14
Four Crosses Powys 29 S15
Four Elms Kent 10 F7
Four Forks Somset 6 F5
Four Gotes Cambs 26 D6
Four Lanes Cnwll 1 R11
Four Marks Hants 9 L6
Four Mile Bridge IoA 28 C5
Four Oaks Birm 23 N9
Four Oaks Solhll 23 Q12
Fourpenny Highld 57 S15
Four Roads Carmth 13 M8
Fourstones Nthumb 40 J7
Four Throws Kent 10 K10
Fovant Wilts 7 S6
Foveran Abers 55 S11
Fowey Cnwll 2 E7
Fowlhall Kent 10 J7
Fowlis Angus 51 L10
Fowlis Wester P & K 50 F12
Fowlmere Cambs 18 D6
Fownhope Herefs 14 K4
Foxbar Rens 44 D6
Foxcote Somset 7 N2
Foxdale IoM 34 c6
Foxearth Essex 18 K6
Foxfield Cumb 34 J9
Foxhole Cnwll 2 B7
Foxholes N York 37 R11
Foxley Norfk 27 N5
Foxt Staffs 31 Q16
Foxton Cambs 18 D5
Foxton Leics 24 G10
Foxton N York 36 H7
Foxwood Shrops 22 F13
Foy Herefs 15 L5
Foyers Highld 53 P11
Foynesfield Highld 54 B6
Fraddon Cnwll 1 U8
Fradley Staffs 23 P6
Fradswell Staffs 23 L4
Fraisthorpe E R Yk 37 T13
Framfield E Susx 10 F12
Framingham Earl Norfk 27 R8
Framingham Pigot Norfk 27 R8
Framlingham Suffk 19 R3
Frampton Dorset 7 M11
Frampton Lincs 25 R2
Frampton Cotterell S Glos 15 M13
Frampton Mansell Gloucs 15 Q10
Frampton-on-Severn Gloucs 15 N9
Framsden Suffk 19 Q3
Framwellgate Moor Dur 41 Q11
Franche Worcs 22 J12
Frankby Wirral 29 S4
Frankley Worcs 23 L12
Frankton Warwks 23 S14
Frant E Susx 10 H9
Fraserburgh Abers 55 T4
Frating Essex 19 N10
Frating Green Essex 19 N9
Fratton C Port 9 L12
Freathy Cnwll 2 J7
Freckenham Suffk 26 G13
Freckleton Lancs 30 G3
Freeby Leics 24 J5
Freefolk Hants 8 H4
Freeland Oxon 16 D8
Freethorpe Norfk 27 T8
Freethorpe Common Norfk 27 T8
Freiston Lincs 25 S2
Fremington Devon 4 K5
Fremington N York 36 C7
Frenchay S Glos 15 L14
Frenich P & K 50 D6
Frensham Surrey 9 N5
Freshfield Sefton 30 E6
Freshford Wilts 7 P1
Freshwater IoW 8 F14
Fressingfield Suffk 27 R12
Freston Suffk 19 P7
Freswick Highld 58 J2
Fretherne Gloucs 15 M8
Frettenham Norfk 27 R6
Freuchie Fife 51 L15
Freystrop Pembks 12 F8
Friar Park Sandw 23 L10
Friday Bridge Cambs 26 E8
Friday Street Suffk 19 S3
Fridaythorpe E R Yk 37 Q13
Friern Barnet Gt Lon 17 R11
Friesthorpe Lincs 33 M10
Frieston Lincs 24 K1
Frieth Bucks 16 J11
Frilford Oxon 16 D10
Frilsham W Berk 16 F14
Frimley Surrey 9 P2
Frindsbury Medway 10 K3
Fring Norfk 26 H3
Fringford Oxon 16 G5
Frinsted Kent 11 M5
Frinton-on-Sea Essex 19 Q10
Friockheim Angus 51 Q8
Frisby on the Wreake Leics 24 G6
Friskney Lincs 33 T15
Friston E Susx 10 G15
Friston Suffk 19 T3
Fritchley Derbys 32 B15
Fritham Hants 8 E9
Frithelstock Devon 4 J7
Frithelstock Stone Devon 4 J8
Frithville Lincs 33 R16
Frittenden Kent 11 L8
Frittiscombe Devon 3 P9
Fritton Norfk 27 Q10
Fritton Norfk 27 U9
Fritwell Oxon 16 E5
Frizinghall C Brad 31 S2
Frizington Cumb 34 G4
Frocester Gloucs 15 N9
Frodesley Shrops 22 E8
Frodsham Ches W 30 H11
Frogden Border 46 K12
Frog End Cambs 18 D5
Froggatt Derbys 31 T11
Froghall Staffs 23 M1
Frogmore Devon 3 P9
Frognall Lincs 25 P7
Frog Pool Worcs 22 J14
Frogwell Cnwll 2 H5
Frolesworth Leics 24 D10
Frome Somset 7 P3
Frome St Quintin Dorset 7 L10
Fromes Hill Herefs 15 M2
Froncysyllte Denbgs 29 S11
Fron-goch Gwynd 29 M12
Fron Isaf Wrexhm 29 S12
Frosterley Dur 41 L12
Froxfield Wilts 16 B15
Froxfield Green Hants 9 L7
Fryern Hill Hants 8 H8
Fryerning Essex 18 G13
Fuinary Highld 48 F8
Fulbeck Lincs 33 L16
Fulbourn Cambs 18 E4
Fulbrook Oxon 16 B8
Fulflood Hants 8 H7
Fulford C York 37 L15
Fulford Somset 6 F6
Fulford Staffs 23 L2
Fulham Gt Lon 17 R14
Fulking W Susx 10 C13
Fullarton N Ayrs 43 T10
Fuller Street Essex 18 J11
Fullerton Hants 8 G5
Fulletby Lincs 33 Q12
Fullready Warwks 16 B2
Full Sutton E R Yk 37 N14
Fullwood E Ayrs 44 D8
Fulmer Bucks 17 M12
Fulmodeston Norfk 27 M4
Fulnetby Lincs 33 N11
Fulney Lincs 25 Q5
Fulstow Lincs 33 R8
Fulwell Sundld 41 R9
Fulwood Lancs 30 H2
Fulwood Sheff 31 U10
Fundenhall Norfk 27 P9
Funtington W Susx 9 N10
Funtullich P & K 50 C11
Furley Devon 6 G10
Furnace Ag & B 49 M16
Furnace Carmth 13 N10
Furness Vale Derbys 31 Q10
Furneux Pelham Herts 18 D9
Furzley Hants 8 F9
Fyfield Essex 18 F12
Fyfield Hants 8 F4
Fyfield Oxon 16 D10
Fyfield Wilts 8 D2
Fyfield Wilts 15 T15
Fylingthorpe N York 37 Q6
Fyning W Susx 9 N8
Fyvie Abers 55 P8

G

Gabroc Hill E Ayrs 44 D8
Gaddesby Leics 24 G7
Gaddesden Row Herts 17 N8
Gadgirth S Ayrs 44 D13
Gaerllwyd Mons 14 J10
Gaerwen IoA 28 F6
Gailes N Ayrs 43 T11
Gailey Staffs 22 K7
Gainford Dur 36 E4
Gainsborough Lincs 32 J9
Gainsford End Essex 18 H7
Gairloch Highld 52 E2
Gairlochy Highld 49 P2
Gairneybridge P & K 50 H16
Gaitsgill Cumb 40 B11
Galashiels Border 46 F11
Galgate Lancs 35 N14
Galhampton Somset 7 M6
Gallanach Ag & B 48 J11
Gallanachmore Ag & B 48 J11
Gallatown Fife 45 R1
Galleywood Essex 18 H13
Gallovie Highld 49 U1
Gallowfauld Angus 51 N9
Gallowhill P & K 50 J10
Galltair Highld 52 E11
Galmpton Devon 3 N9
Galmpton Torbay 3 Q7
Galphay N York 36 F11
Galston E Ayrs 44 E11
Gamblesby Cumb 40 E12
Gamlingay Cambs 17 Q1
Gamlingay Great Heath Cambs 17 Q1
Gamrie Abers 55 Q4
Gamston Notts 24 F3
Gamston Notts 32 G11
Ganavan Bay Ag & B 48 K10
Ganllwyd Gwynd 28 J14
Gannachy Angus 51 Q4
Ganstead E R Yk 33 N2
Ganthorpe N York 37 M12
Ganton N York 37 R10
Garbity Moray 54 H6
Garboldisham Norfk 27 M11
Garbole Highld 53 T11
Garchory Abers 54 H13
Gardeners Green Wokham 16 K15
Gardenstown Abers 55 Q4
Garden Village Sheff 31 T8
Garderhouse Shet 59 p5
Gare Hill Somset 7 P4
Garelochhead Ag & B 43 R2
Garford Oxon 16 D10
Garforth Leeds 32 C2
Gargrave N York 35 U14
Gargunnock Stirlg 44 H1
Garlic Street Norfk 27 Q11
Garlieston D & G 38 J11
Garlinge Kent 11 T3
Garlinge Green Kent 11 Q6
Garlogie Abers 55 Q14
Garmond Abers 55 Q6
Garmouth Moray 54 H4
Garmston Shrops 22 F8
Garn-Dolbenmaen Gwynd 28 F11
Garnkirk N Lans 44 H5
Garrabost W Isls 56 f2
Garrallan E Ayrs 44 F14
Garras Cnwll 1 R14
Garreg Gwynd 28 H11
Garrigill Cumb 40 G11
Garroch D & G 38 K5
Garrochtrie D & G 38 C12
Garrochty Ag & B 43 P8
Garros Highld 59 f6
Garsdale Head Cumb 35 S8
Garshall Green Staffs 23 L3
Garsington Oxon 16 F10
Garstang Lancs 35 N16
Garston Herts 17 P10
Garston Lpool 30 F10
Gartachossan Ag & B 42 D7
Gartcosh N Lans 44 H5
Garth Powys 20 K12
Garth Wrexhm 29 S11
Garthamlock C Glas 44 G6
Garthmyl Powys 21 N4
Garthorpe Leics 24 J5
Garthorpe N Linc 32 J4
Garth Row Cumb 35 N7
Gartly Abers 55 L9
Gartmore Stirlg 49 U16
Gartness N Lans 44 J6
Gartness Stirlg 44 E2
Gartocharn W Duns 44 D2
Garton-on-the-Wolds E R Yk 37 R13
Gartymore Highld 58 D11
Garva Bridge Highld 53 Q15
Garvald E Loth 46 H5
Garvan Highld 49 L3
Garvard Ag & B 42 D2
Garve Highld 53 N4
Garvestone Norfk 27 M7
Garvock Inver 43 S5
Garway Herefs 14 K6
Garyvard W Isls 56 e3
Gasper Wilts 7 N5
Gastard Wilts 15 Q15
Gasthorpe Norfk 27 M12
Gaston Green Essex 18 E10
Gatcombe IoW 8 H14
Gate Burton Lincs 32 J10
Gateforth N York 32 E3
Gatehead E Ayrs 44 D11
Gate Helmsley N York 37 M14
Gatehouse Nthumb 40 H4
Gatehouse of Fleet D & G 38 K9
Gateley Norfk 27 M5
Gatenby N York 36 G9
Gateshaw Border 46 K13
Gateshead Gatesd 41 P8
Gateside Angus 51 N8
Gateside E Rens 44 E7
Gateside Fife 50 J14
Gateside N Ayrs 44 C8
Gateslack D & G 39 Q2
Gatley Stockp 31 M9
Gattonside Border 46 G11
Gatwick Airport W Susx 10 C8
Gaulby Leics 24 G9
Gauldry Fife 51 M12
Gauldswell P & K 50 K7
Gautby Lincs 33 P12
Gavinton Border 46 K8
Gawcott Bucks 16 H5
Gawsworth Ches E 31 N13
Gawthrop Cumb 35 R9
Gawthwaite Cumb 34 K9
Gaydon Warwks 16 C1
Gayhurst M Keyn 16 K2
Gayle N York 35 T9
Gayles N York 36 D6
Gayton Nhants 16 H1
Gayton Norfk 26 H6
Gayton Staffs 23 L4
Gayton le Marsh Lincs 33 S10
Gayton Thorpe Norfk 26 H6
Gaywood Norfk 26 G5
Gazeley Suffk 18 H3
Gearraidh Bhaird W Isls 56 e3
Geary Highld 59 c7
Gedding Suffk 19 L4
Geddington Nhants 24 K11
Gedling Notts 24 F2
Gedney Lincs 25 S5
Gedney Broadgate Lincs 25 S5
Gedney Drove End Lincs 26 E4
Gedney Dyke Lincs 25 S4
Gedney Hill Lincs 25 R7
Geeston Rutlnd 25 L8
Geldeston Norfk 27 T10
Gellifor Denbgs 29 Q8
Gelligaer Caerph 14 D10
Gellilydan Gwynd 28 J12
Gellinudd Neath 13 R9
Gellyburn P & K 50 H9
Gellywen Carmth 12 K6
Gelston D & G 39 N9
Gelston Lincs 24 K1
Gembling E R Yk 37 T14
Gentleshaw Staffs 23 M7
Georgefield D & G 40 A3
George Green Bucks 17 M13
Georgeham Devon 4 J4
Georgemas Junction Station Highld 58 F4
George Nympton Devon 5 N7
Georth Ork 58 b3
Germansweek Devon 4 J12
Gerrans Cnwll 1 U12
Gerrards Cross Bucks 17 M12
Gerrick R & Cl 37 M5
Gestingthorpe Essex 18 J7
Geuffordd Powys 21 N1
Gidea Park Gt Lon 18 E15
Giffnock E Rens 44 F7
Gifford E Loth 46 G5
Giffordtown Fife 51 L14
Giggleswick N York 35 S13
Gilberdyke E R Yk 32 J3
Gilchriston E Loth 46 F5
Gilcrux Cumb 39 S12
Gildersome Leeds 31 T3
Gildingwells Rothm 32 E10
Gilesgate Moor Dur 41 Q11
Gileston V Glam 14 B15
Gilfach Caerph 14 D10
Gilfach Goch Brdgnd 14 B12
Gilfachrheda Cerdgn 20 B11
Gilgarran Cumb 34 G3
Gillamoor N York 37 M8
Gillen Highld 59 c7
Gillesbie D & G 39 T3
Gilling East N York 37 L10
Gillingham Dorset 7 P6
Gillingham Medway 10 K4
Gillingham Norfk 27 T10
Gilling West N York 36 E6
Gillock Highld 58 G4
Gills Highld 58 H2
Gilmanscleuch Border 46 D13
Gilmerton C Edin 45 R5
Gilmerton P & K 50 E12
Gilmonby Dur 36 B5
Gilmorton Leics 24 E11
Gilsland Nthumb 40 F7
Gilston Border 46 F7
Gilston Herts 18 D11
Gilwern Mons 14 F8
Gimingham Norfk 27 R3
Gipping Suffk 19 N3
Gipsey Bridge Lincs 33 Q16
Girdle Toll N Ayrs 43 T10
Girlsta Shet 59 q5
Girsby N York 36 G5
Girthon D & G 38 K10
Girton Cambs 18 D3
Girton Notts 32 J13
Girvan S Ayrs 38 D2
Gisburn Lancs 35 T15
Gisleham Suffk 27 U11
Gislingham Suffk 27 N13
Gissing Norfk 27 P11
Gittisham Devon 6 E11
Gladestry Powys 21 P11
Gladsmuir E Loth 46 F5
Glais Swans 13 R10
Glaisdale N York 37 N6
Glamis Angus 51 M8
Glanaman Carmth 13 R8
Glandford Norfk 27 N2
Glandwr Pembks 12 J5
Glandyfi Cerdgn 20 F4
Glanllynfi Brdgnd 13 T11
Glan-rhyd Powys 13 S8
Glanton Nthumb 47 Q14
Glanvilles Wootton Dorset 7 M9
Glan-y-don Flints 29 Q5
Glapthorn Nhants 25 M10
Glapwell Derbys 32 D13
Glasbury Powys 14 E4
Glascwm Powys 21 P12
Glasfryn Conwy 29 M10
Glasgow C Glas 44 F6
Glasgow Airport Rens 44 E6
Glasinfryn Gwynd 28 G7
Glasnacardoch Bay Highld 52 C15
Glasnakille Highld 59 g13
Glassford S Lans 44 H9
Glasshouse Gloucs 15 M6
Glasshouses N York 36 E13
Glasson Cumb 39 U8
Glasson Lancs 35 M14
Glassonby Cumb 40 E12
Glasterlaw Angus 51 Q7
Glaston Rutlnd 24 K9
Glastonbury Somset 6 K4
Glatton Cambs 25 N11
Glazebrook Warrtn 30 K9
Glazebury Warrtn 30 K8
Glazeley Shrops 22 G11
Gleaston Cumb 34 K12
Glebe Highld 53 Q12
Gledhow Leeds 31 U1
Gledpark D & G 39 L10
Gledrid Shrops 29 S12
Glemsford Suffk 18 K5
Glenallachie Moray 54 G8
Glenancross Highld 52 C16
Glenaros House Ag & B 48 E8
Glen Auldyn IoM 34 e3
Glenbarr Ag & B 42 H11
Glenbarry Abers 55 M6
Glenbeg Highld 48 F5
Glenbervie Abers 51 S2
Glenboig N Lans 44 H5
Glenborrodale Highld 48 F6
Glenbranter Ag & B 49 N16
Glenbreck Border 45 N13
Glenbrittle House Highld 59 e12
Glenbuck E Ayrs 44 J12
Glencally Angus 51 M5
Glencaple D & G 39 R7
Glencarron Lodge Highld 52 H6
Glencarse P & K 50 J12
Glen Clunie Lodge Abers 50 H2
Glencoe Highld 49 N6
Glencothe Border 45 N12
Glencraig Fife 45 Q1
Glencrosh D & G 39 N4
Glendale Highld 59 a8
Glendaruel Ag & B 43 N3
Glendevon P & K 50 F15
Glendoe Lodge Highld 53 N13
Glendoick P & K 50 K12
Glenduckie Fife 51 L13
Glenegedale Ag & B 42 D8
Glenelg Highld 52 E11
Glenerney Moray 54 D7
Glenfarg P & K 50 J14
Glenfield Leics 24 E8
Glenfinnan Highld 48 K2
Glenfintaig Lodge Highld 49 Q2
Glenfoot P & K 50 J13
Glenfyne Lodge Ag & B 49 Q13
Glengarnock N Ayrs 43 T8
Glengolly Highld 58 E3
Glengorm Castle Ag & B 48 D6
Glengrasco Highld 59 e9
Glenholm Border 45 P11
Glenhoul D & G 39 L4
Glenisla Angus 50 K6
Glenkin Ag & B 43 Q3
Glenkindie Abers 54 K12
Glenlivet Moray 54 F10
Glenlochar D & G 39 M8
Glenlomond P & K 50 J15
Glenluce D & G 38 E9
Glenmassen Ag & B 43 Q2
Glenmavis N Lans 44 J5
Glen Maye IoM 34 b5
Glenmore Highld 59 e9
Glenmore Lodge Highld 54 C13
Glen Nevis House Highld 49 N4
Glenochil Clacks 44 K1
Glen Parva Leics 24 E9
Glenquiech Angus 51 N6
Glenralloch Ag & B 43 L5
Glenridding Cumb 35 M5
Glenrothes Fife 50 K16
Glenshero Lodge Highld 53 Q16
Glenstriven Ag & B 43 P4
Glentham Lincs 33 L9
Glentrool D & G 38 G5
Glen Trool Lodge D & G 38 H5
Glentruim House Highld 53 S15
Glentworth Lincs 32 K10
Glenuig Highld 48 G3
Glenvarragill Highld 59 f9
Glen Vine IoM 34 d5
Glenwhilly D & G 38 D7
Glespin S Lans 44 J12
Glewstone Herefs 14 K6
Glinton C Pete 25 N8
Glooston Leics 24 H9
Glossop Derbys 31 Q9
Gloster Hill Nthumb 47 S16
Gloucester Gloucs 15 P7
Gloucestershire Airport Gloucs 15 Q6
Glusburn N York 36 B16
Glutt Lodge Highld 58 D8
Glympton Oxon 16 D6
Glynarthen Cerdgn 12 K2
Glyn Ceiriog Wrexhm 29 R12
Glyncorrwg Neath 13 T10
Glynde E Susx 10 F13
Glyndyfrdwy Denbgs 29 Q11
Glynneath Neath 13 U9
Glyntawe Powys 13 T7
Glynteg Carmth 13 L4
Gnosall Staffs 22 J5
Gnosall Heath Staffs 22 J5
Goadby Leics 24 H9
Goadby Marwood Leics 24 H4
Goatacre Wilts 15 S14
Goathill Dorset 7 M8
Goathland N York 37 P7
Goathurst Somset 6 F5
Gobowen Shrops 29 S13
Godalming Surrey 9 Q4
Goddard's Green Kent 11 L9
Godmanchester Cambs 25 Q14
Godmanstone Dorset 7 M11
Godmersham Kent 11 P7
Godney Somset 6 K4
Godolphin Cross Cnwll 1 Q13
Godre'r-graig Neath 13 S9
Godshill IoW 8 J15
Godstone Surrey 10 D6
Goetre Mons 14 G9
Goff's Oak Herts 17 S9
Gogar C Edin 45 P5
Goginan Cerdgn 20 F7
Golan Gwynd 28 F11
Golant Cnwll 2 E7
Golberdon Cnwll 2 H4
Golborne Wigan 30 J8
Golcar Kirk 31 R5
Goldcliff Newpt 14 G13
Golden Green Kent 10 H7
Goldenhill C Stke 31 M15
Golden Pot Hants 9 M5
Golders Green Gt Lon 17 Q12
Goldhanger Essex 19 L12
Goldington Bed 17 N2
Goldsborough N York 36 H14
Goldsborough N York 37 P4
Golds Green Sandw 23 L10
Goldsithney Cnwll 1 P13
Goldsworth Park Surrey 9 R2
Goldthorpe Barns 32 D7
Goldworthy Devon 4 H7
Gollanfield Highld 53 U6
Golspie Highld 57 T14
Gomeldon Wilts 8 D6
Gomshall Surrey 9 S4
Gonalston Notts 24 G1
Gonerby Hill Foot Lincs 24 K3
Gonfirth Shet 59 q5
Good Easter Essex 18 G11
Gooderstone Norfk 26 J8
Goodleigh Devon 5 L5
Goodmanham E R Yk 37 Q16
Goodmayes Gt Lon 18 E15
Goodnestone Kent 11 P5
Goodnestone Kent 11 S6
Goodrich Herefs 14 K7
Goodrington Torbay 3 Q6
Goodshaw Lancs 31 M3
Goodwick Pembks 12 E4
Goodworth Clatford Hants 8 G5
Goole E R Yk 32 H4
Goom's Hill Worcs 15 S1
Goonbell Cnwll 1 S10
Goonhavern Cnwll 1 S9
Goonvrea Cnwll 1 R10
Goosecruives Abers 51 S2
Gooseford Devon 5 M12
Goose Green Essex 19 P9
Goose Green S Glos 15 M14
Goosey Oxon 16 C11
Goosnargh Lancs 30 H2
Goostrey Ches E 31 L12
Gordon Border 46 J9
Gordon Arms Hotel Border 45 R12
Gordonstown Abers 55 M5
Gordonstown Abers 55 P8
Gorebridge Mdloth 46 D6
Gorefield Cambs 26 D7
Gores Wilts 8 C2
Gorey Jersey 3 e3
Goring Oxon 16 F13
Goring-by-Sea W Susx 9 S11
Gorleston on Sea Norfk 27 U8
Gorrachie Abers 55 P5
Gorran Churchtown Cnwll 2 C9
Gorran Haven Cnwll 2 C9
Gorsedd Flints 29 Q6
Gorse Hill Swindn 15 T12
Gorseinon Swans 13 P10
Gorsgoch Cerdgn 20 C12
Gorslas Carmth 13 P8
Gorsley Gloucs 15 M6
Gorsley Common Herefs 15 M6
Gorstan Highld 53 N4
Gorsty Hill Staffs 23 N4
Gorten Ag & B 48 H10
Gorthleck Highld 53 P11
Gorton Manch 31 N8
Gosbeck Suffk 19 P4
Gosberton Lincs 25 Q4
Gosfield Essex 18 J8
Gosforth Cumb 34 G6
Gosforth N u Ty 41 P7
Gospel End Staffs 22 K10
Gosport Hants 8 K12
Gossington Gloucs 15 N10
Gotham Notts 24 E4
Gotherington Gloucs 15 R5
Gotton Somset 6 F6
Goudhurst Kent 10 K9
Goulceby Lincs 33 Q11
Gourdas Abers 55 P8
Gourdie C Dund 51 L10
Gourdon Abers 51 T4
Gourock Inver 43 S4
Govan C Glas 44 F6
Goveton Devon 3 N9
Govilon Mons 14 F8
Gowdall E R Yk 32 F4
Gower Highld 53 Q5
Gowerton Swans 13 P11
Gowkhall Fife 45 N2
Goxhill E R Yk 37 U16
Goxhill N Linc 33 N4
Grabhair W Isls 56 e3
Graffham W Susx 9 Q9
Grafham Cambs 25 P14
Grafham Surrey 9 R5
Grafton N York 36 H13
Grafton Oxon 16 B10
Grafton Shrops 22 C6
Grafton Worcs 15 R4
Grafton Flyford Worcs 23 L16
Grafton Regis Nhants 16 J2
Grafton Underwood Nhants 24 K12
Grafty Green Kent 11 M7
Graig Conwy 28 K6
Graigfechan Denbgs 29 Q9
Grain Medway 11 M2
Grainsby Lincs 33 Q8
Grainthorpe Lincs 33 S8
Grampound Cnwll 2 B8
Grampound Road Cnwll 1 U8
Gramsdal W Isls 56 b6
Gramsdale W Isls 56 b6
Granborough Bucks 16 J6
Granby Notts 24 H3
Grandborough Warwks 24 D14
Grand Chemins Jersey 3 d2
Grandes Rocques Guern 2 c2
Grandtully P & K 50 E7
Grange Cumb 34 K4
Grange Medway 11 L4
Grange P & K 50 K12
Grange Crossroads Moray 54 K6
Grange Hall Moray 54 E5
Grangehall S Lans 45 M10
Grange Hill Essex 18 D14
Grangemill Derbys 31 T15
Grange Moor Kirk 31 T5
Grangemouth Falk 45 L3
Grange of Lindores Fife 50 K13
Grange-over-Sands Cumb 35 M10
Grangepans Falk 45 M3
Grange Park Nhants 24 H16
Grangetown R & Cl 36 K3
Grangetown Sundld 41 S9
Gransmoor E R Yk 37 T13
Granston Pembks 12 E4
Grantchester Cambs 18 D4
Grantham Lincs 24 K3
Granton C Edin 45 Q4
Grantown-on-Spey Highld 54 D10
Grantshouse Border 47 L6
Grasby Lincs 33 N7
Grasmere Cumb 35 L6
Grasscroft Oldham 31 P7
Grassendale Lpool 30 F10
Grassington N York 36 B13
Grassmoor Derbys 32 C13
Grassthorpe Notts 32 H13
Grateley Hants 8 E5
Graveley Cambs 25 Q15
Graveley Herts 17 Q5
Gravelly Hill Birm 23 N10
Graveney Kent 11 P5
Gravesend Kent 10 J3
Gravir W Isls 56 e3
Grayingham Lincs 32 K8
Grayrigg Cumb 35 P7
Grays Thurr 10 H2
Grayshott Hants 9 P6
Grayswood Surrey 9 P6
Greasbrough Rothm 32 C8
Greasby Wirral 29 S4
Great Abington Cambs 18 F5
Great Addington Nhants 25 L13
Great Alne Warwks 23 N15
Great Altcar Lancs 30 E7
Great Amwell Herts 17 S8
Great Asby Cumb 35 R5
Great Ashfield Suffk 27 M14
Great Ayton N York 36 K5
Great Baddow Essex 18 H12
Great Badminton S Glos 15 P13
Great Bardfield Essex 18 H8
Great Barford Bed 17 P1
Great Barr Sandw 23 M9
Great Barrington Gloucs 15 U8
Great Barrow Ches W 30 G13
Great Barton Suffk 27 L14
Great Barugh N York 37 N10
Great Bavington Nthumb 41 L5
Great Bealings Suffk 19 Q5
Great Bedwyn Wilts 16 B16
Great Bentley Essex 19 P10
Great Billing Nhants 24 J15
Great Bircham Norfk 26 J3
Great Blakenham Suffk 19 P5
Great Blencow Cumb 40 C13
Great Bolas Wrekin 22 F5
Great Bookham Surrey 9 S3
Great Bourton Oxon 16 D2
Great Bowden Leics 24 H11
Great Bradley Suffk 18 G4
Great Braxted Essex 18 K11
Great Bricett Suffk 19 N5
Great Brickhill Bucks 17 L5
Great Bridgeford Staffs 22 K4
Great Brington Nhants 24 G14
Great Bromley Essex 19 N9
Great Broughton Cumb 39 S13
Great Broughton N York 36 K6
Great Budworth Ches W 30 K11
Great Burdon Darltn 36 G4
Great Burstead Essex 18 H14
Great Busby N York 36 K6
Great Carlton Lincs 33 S10
Great Casterton Rutlnd 25 L7
Great Chalfield Wilts 15 P16
Great Chart Kent 11 N8
Great Chatwell Staffs 22 H6
Great Chell C Stke 31 N15
Great Chesterford Essex 18 E6
Great Cheverell Wilts 7 S2
Great Chishill Cambs 18 D7
Great Clacton Essex 19 Q11
Great Clifton Cumb 39 R13
Great Coates NE Lin 33 Q6
Great Comberton Worcs 15 R3
Great Corby Cumb 40 C9
Great Cornard Suffk 18 K7
Great Cowden E R Yk 37 V16
Great Coxwell Oxon 16 B11
Great Cransley Nhants 24 J13
Great Cressingham Norfk 26 K8
Great Crosthwaite Cumb 34 K3
Great Cubley Derbys 23 P2
Great Dalby Leics 24 H6
Great Denham Bed 17 M2
Great Doddington Nhants 24 K14
Great Dunham Norfk 26 K6
Great Dunmow Essex 18 G10
Great Durnford Wilts 8 C5
Great Easton Essex 18 G9
Great Easton Leics 24 J10
Great Eccleston Lancs 30 G1
Great Ellingham Norfk 27 M9
Great Elm Somset 7 N3
Great Everdon Nhants 24 F16
Great Eversden Cambs 18 S1
Great Fencote N York 36 F8
Great Finborough Suffk 19 M4
Greatford Lincs 25 N7
Great Fransham Norfk 27 L7
Great Gaddesden Herts 17 M8
Greatgate Staffs 23 M2
Great Gidding Cambs 25 N11
Great Givendale E R Yk 37 P14
Great Glemham Suffk 19 S3
Great Glen Leics 24 F9
Great Gonerby Lincs 24 K2
Great Gransden Cambs 25 Q16
Great Green Cambs 17 R3
Great Green Suffk 19 L4
Great Habton N York 37 N11
Great Hale Lincs 25 N2
Great Hallingbury Essex 18 E10
Greatham Hants 9 M7
Greatham Hartpl 41 T14
Greatham W Susx 9 R9
Great Hampden Bucks 16 K10
Great Harrowden Nhants 24 K13
Great Harwood Lancs 31 L2
Great Haseley Oxon 16 G10
Great Hatfield E R Yk 37 U16
Great Haywood Staffs 23 L5
Great Heck N York 32 F4
Great Henny Essex 18 K7
Great Hinton Wilts 7 R1
Great Hockham Norfk 27 L10
Great Holland Essex 19 Q10
Great Hollands Br For 16 K15
Great Horkesley Essex 19 M8
Great Hormead Herts 18 D8
Great Horton C Brad 31 S2
Great Horwood Bucks 16 J5
Great Houghton Barns 32 C6
Great Houghton Nhants 24 H15
Great Hucklow Derbys 31 S11
Great Kelk E R Yk 37 T14
Great Kimble Bucks 16 K9
Great Kingshill Bucks 16 K10
Great Langdale Cumb 34 K6
Great Langton N York 36 F7
Great Leighs Essex 18 H10
Great Limber Lincs 33 N6
Great Linford M Keyn 16 K3
Great Livermere Suffk 26 K13
Great Longstone Derbys 31 S12
Great Lumley Dur 41 Q10
Great Malvern Worcs 15 N2
Great Maplestead Essex 18 J8
Great Marton Bpool 30 E2
Great Massingham Norfk 26 J5
Great Milton Oxon 16 G9
Great Missenden Bucks 17 L10
Great Mitton Lancs 31 L1
Great Mongeham Kent 11 T6
Great Moulton Norfk 27 P10
Great Musgrave Cumb 35 S5
Great Ness Shrops 22 C6
Great Notley Essex 18 J10
Great Oak Mons 14 H8
Great Oakley Essex 19 Q9
Great Oakley Nhants 24 J11
Great Offley Herts 17 P5
Great Ormside Cumb 35 R4
Great Orton Cumb 40 A9
Great Ouseburn N York 36 J13
Great Oxendon Nhants 24 H11
Great Park N u Ty 41 P7
Great Parndon Essex 18 D12
Great Paxton Cambs 25 P15
Great Plumpton Lancs 30 F2
Great Plumstead Norfk 27 R7
Great Ponton Lincs 24 K4
Great Preston Leeds 32 C3
Great Raveley Cambs 25 Q12
Great Rissington Gloucs 15 U7
Great Rollright Oxon 16 C5
Great Ryburgh Norfk 27 L4
Great Ryton Shrops 22 D8
Great Saling Essex 18 H9
Great Salkeld Cumb 40 E12
Great Sampford Essex 18 G7
Great Saughall Ches W 30 F13
Great Shefford W Berk 16 C14
Great Shelford Cambs 18 E5
Great Smeaton N York 36 G6
Great Snoring Norfk 27 L3
Great Somerford Wilts 15 R13
Great Soudley Shrops 22 H4
Great Stainton Darltn 36 G3
Great Stambridge Essex 19 L15
Great Staughton Cambs 25 N15
Great Steeping Lincs 33 S13
Great Stoke S Glos 15 L13
Greatstone-on-Sea Kent 11 Q11
Great Strickland Cumb 35 P3
Great Stukeley Cambs 25 P13
Great Sturton Lincs 33 P11
Great Swinburne Nthumb 40 K6
Great Tew Oxon 16 D5
Great Tey Essex 19 L9
Great Thurlow Suffk 18 H5
Great Torrington Devon 4 K7
Great Tosson Nthumb 41 L2
Great Totham Essex 18 K11
Great Totham Essex 18 K11
Great Urswick Cumb 34 K11

68 Great Wakering – Horton

Great Wakering Essex 19 L15
Great Waldingfield Suffk 19 L6
Great Walsingham Norfk 27 L3
Great Waltham Essex 18 H11
Great Warley Essex 18 F15
Great Washbourne Gloucs 15 R4
Great Weeke Devon 5 N13
Great Wenham Suffk 19 N7
Great Whittington Nthumb 41 L7
Great Wigborough Essex 19 M11
Great Wilbraham Cambs 18 F4
Great Wishford Wilts 7 T5
Great Witcombe Gloucs 15 Q7
Great Witley Worcs 22 H14
Great Wolford Warwks 16 B4
Greatworth Nhants 16 F3
Great Wratting Suffk 18 H5
Great Wymondley Herts 17 Q5
Great Wyrley Staffs 23 L7
Great Yarmouth Norfk 27 U7
Great Yeldham Essex 18 J7
Greenburn W Loth 45 L7
Green End Herts 17 S4
Green End Herts 17 S6
Greenfield Ag & B 43 S2
Greenfield C Beds 17 N4
Greenfield Flints 29 R5
Greenfield Highld 52 K15
Greenfield Oldham 31 P7
Greenford Gt Lon 17 P13
Greengairs N Lans 44 J5
Greengates C Brad 31 S1
Greenham Somset 6 D7
Green Hammerton N York 36 J14
Greenhaugh Nthumb 40 H4
Greenhead Nthumb 40 F8
Green Heath Staffs 23 L7
Greenhill D & G 39 S5
Greenhill Falk 44 K4
Greenhill Kent 11 R4
Greenhill S Lans 45 L11
Greenhithe Kent 10 H3
Greenholm E Ayrs 44 F10
Greenhouse Border 46 G13
Greenhow Hill N York 36 D13
Greenland Highld 58 G2
Greenland Sheff 32 C9
Greenlaw Border 46 K9
Greenlea D & G 39 R6
Greenloaning P & K 50 D14
Greenmount Bury 31 L5
Greenock Inver 43 S4
Greenodd Cumb 34 K10
Green Ore Somset 7 L2
Green Quarter Cumb 35 N6
Greenshields S Lans 45 M9
Greenside Gatesd 41 N8
Greenside Kirk 31 S5
Greens Norton Nhants 16 G2
Greenstead Green Essex 18 K9
Green Street Herts 17 Q10
Green Street Herts 18 D10
Green Street Green Kent 10 H3
Green Tye Herts 18 D10
Greenway Somset 6 G7
Greenwich Gt Lon 17 S14
Greet Gloucs 15 S5
Greete Shrops 22 E13
Greetham Lincs 33 R12
Greetham Rutlnd 24 K6
Greetland Calder 31 R4
Greinton Somset 6 J5
Grenaby IoM 34 c7
Grendon Nhants 24 K15
Grendon Warwks 23 Q9
Grendon Underwood Bucks 16 H7
Grenoside Sheff 32 B9
Greosabhagh W Isls 56 d4
Gresford Wrexhm 30 E15
Gresham Norfk 27 P2
Greshornish House Hotel Highld 59 d8
Gressenhall Norfk 27 M6
Gressenhall Green Norfk 27 M6
Gressingham Lancs 35 P12
Greta Bridge Dur 36 C5
Gretna D & G 40 A7
Gretna Green D & G 40 A7
Gretton Gloucs 15 R5
Gretton Nhants 24 K10
Gretton Shrops 22 E9
Grewelthorpe N York 36 F11
Greyrigg D & G 39 S4
Greys Green Oxon 16 H13
Greysouthen Cumb 39 S14
Greystoke Cumb 40 C13
Greystone Angus 51 P9
Greywell Hants 9 M3
Griff Warwks 23 R11
Griffithstown Torfn 14 F10
Grimeford Village Lancs 30 J5
Grimesthorpe Sheff 32 B9
Grimethorpe Barns 32 C6
Grimley Worcs 22 J15
Grimmet S Ayrs 43 T15
Grimoldby Lincs 33 S10
Grimpo Shrops 29 T14
Grimsargh Lancs 30 J2
Grimsby NE Lin 33 Q6
Grimscote Nhants 16 G1
Grimscott Cnwll 4 G10
Grimshader W Isls 56 e2
Grimsthorpe Lincs 25 M5
Grimston Leics 24 G5
Grimston Norfk 26 H5
Grimstone Dorset 7 M12
Grimstone End Suffk 27 L14
Grindale E R Yk 37 T11
Grindleford Derbys 31 T11
Grindleton Lancs 35 S16
Grindley Brook Shrops 22 E2
Grindlow Derbys 31 S11
Grindon Staffs 31 R15
Gringley on the Hill Notts 32 H9
Grinsdale Cumb 40 B9
Grinshill Shrops 22 E5
Grinton N York 36 C7
Griomaisiader W Isls 56 e2
Griomsaigh W Isls 56 b6
Grishipoll Ag & B 42 e2
Gristhorpe N York 37 T10
Griston Norfk 27 L9
Gritley Ork 58 d4
Grittenham Wilts 15 S13
Grittleton Wilts 15 P13
Grizebeck Cumb 34 J9
Grizedale Cumb 35 L8
Groby Leics 24 E8
Groes Conwy 29 N8
Groes-faen Rhondd 14 C13
Groeslon Gwynd 28 F9
Groes-Wen Caerph 14 D12
Grogarry W Isls 56 b7
Grogport Ag & B 42 K9
Groigearraidh W Isls 56 b7
Gronant Flints 29 P5
Groombridge E Susx 10 G9
Grosebay W Isls 56 d4
Grosmont Mons 14 H6
Grosmont N York 37 P6
Groton Suffk 19 M6
Grouville Jersey 3 e3
Grove Notts 32 H11
Grove Oxon 16 D11
Grove Green Kent 10 K6
Grove Park Gt Lon 10 E3
Grovesend Swans 13 P10
Gruinard Highld 56 E15
Gruinart Ag & B 42 C6
Grula Highld 59 d11
Gruline Ag & B 48 E9
Grundisburgh Suffk 19 Q5
Gruting Shet 59 p5
Grutness Shet 59 q8
Gualachulain Highld 49 N8
Guardbridge Fife 51 N13
Guarlford Worcs 15 P2
Guay P & K 50 G8
Guernsey Guern 2 c3
Guernsey Airport Guern 2 c3
Guestling Green E Susx 11 L13
Guestling Thorn E Susx 11 L12
Guestwick Norfk 27 N4
Guide Bridge Tamesd 31 P8
Guilden Morden Cambs 17 R3
Guilden Sutton Ches W 30 G13
Guildford Surrey 9 R3
Guildtown P & K 50 H10
Guilsborough Nhants 24 G13
Guilsfield Powys 21 N2
Guiltreehill S Ayrs 44 C15
Guineaford Devon 5 L4
Guisborough R & Cl 37 L4
Guiseley Leeds 36 E16
Guist Norfk 27 M5
Guiting Power Gloucs 15 T6
Gullane E Loth 46 F3
Gulval Cnwll 1 N13
Gulworthy Devon 2 J4
Gumfreston Pembks 12 H10
Gumley Leics 24 G10
Gunby Lincs 24 K5
Gunby Lincs 33 T13
Gundleton Hants 8 K6
Gun Hill E Susx 10 G12
Gunn Devon 5 M5
Gunnerside N York 35 U7
Gunnerton Nthumb 40 K6
Gunness N Linc 32 J6
Gunnislake Cnwll 2 J4
Gunnista Shet 59 r6
Gunthorpe N Linc 32 J8
Gunthorpe Norfk 27 M3
Gunthorpe Notts 24 G1
Gunwalloe Cnwll 1 Q14
Gurnard IoW 8 H12
Gurney Slade Somset 7 M3
Gurnos Powys 13 S8
Gussage All Saints Dorset 7 S9
Gussage St Andrew Dorset 7 R8
Gussage St Michael Dorset 7 S9
Guston Kent 11 T8
Gutcher Shet 59 r2
Guthrie Angus 51 Q7
Guyhirn Cambs 25 S8
Guyzance Nthumb 41 P1
Gwaenysgor Flints 29 P5
Gwalchmai IoA 28 E6
Gwaun-Cae-Gurwen Carmth 13 R8
Gweek Cnwll 1 R13
Gwenddwr Powys 21 L13
Gwennap Cnwll 1 S11
Gwernaffield Flints 29 R7
Gwernesney Mons 14 H10
Gwernogle Carmth 13 P4
Gwernymynydd Flints 29 R8
Gwespyr Flints 29 Q5
Gwinear Cnwll 1 Q12
Gwithian Cnwll 1 P11
Gwyddelwern Denbgs 29 P10
Gwyddgrug Carmth 13 N4
Gwytherin Conwy 29 L8

H

Habberley Shrops 21 R3
Habberley Worcs 22 J12
Habergham Lancs 31 M2
Habertoft Lincs 33 T13
Habrough NE Lin 33 N5
Hacconby Lincs 25 N5
Haceby Lincs 25 M3
Hacheston Suffk 19 R3
Hackbridge Gt Lon 10 C4
Hackenthorpe Sheff 32 C10
Hackford Norfk 27 N8
Hackforth N York 36 F8
Hackland Ork 58 b3
Hackleton Nhants 24 J16
Hacklinge Kent 11 T6
Hackness N York 37 R8
Hackney Gt Lon 17 S12
Hackthorn Lincs 33 L10
Hackthorpe Cumb 35 P3
Hadden Border 47 L11
Haddenham Bucks 16 H8
Haddenham Cambs 26 E13
Haddington E Loth 46 G4
Haddington Lincs 32 K14
Haddiscoe Norfk 27 T9
Haddo Abers 55 Q8
Haddon Cambs 25 N10
Hadfield Derbys 31 Q8
Hadham Ford Herts 18 D10
Hadleigh Essex 18 J15
Hadleigh Suffk 19 M6
Hadley Worcs 22 J15
Hadley Wrekin 22 G7
Hadley End Staffs 23 N5
Hadley Wood Gt Lon 17 R10
Hadlow Kent 10 H7
Hadlow Down E Susx 10 G11
Hadnall Shrops 22 E5
Hadstock Essex 18 F6
Hadzor Worcs 22 K15
Haggersta Shet 59 q6
Haggerston Nthumb 47 P9
Haggs Falk 44 J4
Hagley Herefs 14 K3
Hagley Worcs 22 K12
Hagworthingham Lincs 33 R13
Haile Cumb 34 G5
Hailey Oxon 16 C8
Hailsham E Susx 10 H13
Hail Weston Cambs 25 P15
Hainault Gt Lon 18 D15
Hainford Norfk 27 Q6
Hainton Lincs 33 P10
Haisthorpe E R Yk 37 T12
Hakin Pembks 12 E9
Halam Notts 32 G15
Halbeath Fife 45 P2
Halberton Devon 5 S9
Halcro Highld 58 G4
Hale Cumb 35 N10
Hale Halton 30 G10
Hale Hants 8 D9
Hale Surrey 9 N4
Hale Traffd 31 L10
Halebarns Traffd 31 M10
Hales Norfk 27 S9
Hales Staffs 22 G3
Halesowen Dudley 23 L11
Hales Place Kent 11 R5
Hale Street Kent 10 J7
Halesworth Suffk 27 S12
Halewood Knows 30 G10
Halford Devon 3 P4
Halford Warwks 16 B2
Halfpenny Green Staffs 22 J10
Halfway House Shrops 21 Q2
Halfway Houses Kent 11 N3
Halifax Calder 31 R3
Halket E Ayrs 44 D8
Halkirk Highld 58 E4
Halkyn Flints 29 R6
Hall E Rens 44 D8
Halland E Susx 10 F12
Hallaton Leics 24 H9
Hallatrow BaNES 7 M1
Hallbankgate Cumb 40 E9
Hall Dunnerdale Cumb 34 J7
Hallen S Glos 14 K13
Hallgarth Dur 41 Q11
Hall Glen Falk 45 L4
Hall Green Birm 23 N12
Hallin Highld 59 c7
Halling Medway 10 J4
Hallington Lincs 33 R10
Hallington Nthumb 41 L6
Halliwell Bolton 30 K6
Halloughton Notts 32 G15
Hallow Worcs 22 J16
Hall's Green Herts 17 R5
Hallyne Border 45 Q10
Halmore Gloucs 15 M10
Halnaker W Susx 9 P10
Halsall Lancs 30 F6
Halse Nhants 16 F3
Halse Somset 6 E6
Halsetown Cnwll 1 N11
Halsham E R Yk 33 Q3
Halstead Essex 18 J8
Halstead Kent 10 F5
Halstead Leics 24 H8
Halstock Dorset 6 K9
Haltham Lincs 33 Q14
Halton Bucks 16 K8
Halton Halton 30 H11
Halton Lancs 35 N13
Halton Leeds 32 B2
Halton Nthumb 41 L7
Halton Wrexhm 29 S12
Halton East N York 36 C14
Halton Gill N York 35 T11
Halton Holegate Lincs 33 S13
Halton Lea Gate Nthumb 40 F9
Halton Shields Nthumb 41 L7
Halton West N York 35 T14
Haltwhistle Nthumb 40 G8
Halvergate Norfk 27 T8
Halwell Devon 3 P7
Halwill Devon 4 J11
Halwill Junction Devon 4 J11
Ham Devon 6 F10
Ham Gloucs 15 M10
Ham Gt Lon 17 Q15
Ham Kent 11 T6
Ham Somset 6 G7
Ham Wilts 8 F1
Hambleden Bucks 16 J12
Hambledon Hants 9 L9
Hambledon Surrey 9 Q5
Hamble-le-Rice Hants 8 H10
Hambleton Lancs 35 L16
Hambleton N York 32 E3
Hambridge Somset 6 H7
Hambrook W Susx 9 N10
Hameringham Lincs 33 R13
Hamerton Cambs 25 N12
Ham Green Worcs 23 M15
Hamilton S Lans 44 H7
Hamlet Dorset 7 L9
Hammersmith Gt Lon 17 Q13
Hammerwich Staffs 23 M8
Hammoon Dorset 7 P8
Hamnavoe Shet 59 q6
Hampden Park E Susx 10 H15
Hampnett Gloucs 15 T7
Hampole Donc 32 D6
Hampreston Dorset 7 T11
Hampstead Gt Lon 17 R12
Hampstead Norreys W Berk 16 E14
Hampsthwaite N York 36 F13
Hampton C Pete 25 P10
Hampton Gt Lon 17 P15
Hampton Kent 11 R4
Hampton Shrops 22 H11
Hampton Swindn 15 U11
Hampton Worcs 15 S3
Hampton Bishop Herefs 14 K4
Hampton Heath Ches W 30 H16
Hampton-in-Arden Solhll 23 P12
Hampton Lovett Worcs 22 K14
Hampton Lucy Warwks 23 Q16
Hampton Magna Warwks 23 Q14
Hampton Poyle Oxon 16 E7
Hampton Wick Gt Lon 17 Q15
Hamptworth Wilts 8 E8
Hamsey E Susx 10 E13
Hamstall Ridware Staffs 23 N6
Hamstead Birm 23 M10
Hamstead Marshall W Berk 16 D16
Hamsterley Dur 41 M9
Hamsterley Dur 41 N13
Hamstreet Kent 11 P9
Ham Street Somset 7 L5
Hamworthy Poole 7 S12
Hanbury Staffs 23 P4
Hanbury Worcs 23 L14
Hanchurch Staffs 22 J2
Hand and Pen Devon 6 C11
Handbridge Ches W 30 F13
Handcross W Susx 10 C10
Handforth Ches E 31 N10
Handley Ches W 30 G14
Handley Derbys 32 C14
Handsworth Birm 23 M10
Handsworth Sheff 32 C10
Hanford C Stke 22 K2
Hanging Heaton Kirk 31 T4
Hanging Houghton Nhants 24 H13
Hanging Langford Wilts 7 S5
Hangleton Br & H 10 C14
Hanham S Glos 15 L14
Hankelow Ches E 22 G1
Hankerton Wilts 15 R11
Hanley C Stke 22 K1
Hanley Castle Worcs 15 P3
Hanley Child Worcs 22 F14
Hanley Swan Worcs 15 P3
Hanley William Worcs 22 G14
Hanlith N York 35 U13
Hanmer Wrexhm 22 D2
Hannaford Devon 5 L6
Hannington Hants 8 J2
Hannington Nhants 24 J14
Hannington Swindn 15 U11
Hannington Wick Swindn 15 U11
Hanslope M Keyn 16 J2
Hanthorpe Lincs 25 N5
Hanwell Gt Lon 17 P13
Hanwell Oxon 16 D3
Hanwood Shrops 21 S2
Hanworth Gt Lon 17 P15
Hanworth Norfk 27 Q3
Happendon S Lans 44 K11
Happisburgh Norfk 27 S4
Happisburgh Common Norfk 27 S4
Hapsford Ches W 30 G12
Hapton Lancs 31 M2
Hapton Norfk 27 Q9
Harberton Devon 3 P6
Harbertonford Devon 3 P7
Harbledown Kent 11 Q5
Harborne Birm 23 M11
Harborough Magna Warwks 24 D12
Harbottle Nthumb 47 N16
Harbourneford Devon 3 N6
Harbury Warwks 23 S15
Harby Leics 24 H4
Harby Notts 32 K12
Harcombe Devon 5 Q14
Harcombe Devon 6 E12
Harcombe Bottom Devon 6 G11
Harden C Brad 31 R1
Harden Wsall 23 M9
Hardenhuish Wilts 15 Q14
Hardgate Abers 55 Q14
Hardgate D & G 39 N7
Hardgate W Duns 44 E5
Hardham W Susx 9 R9
Hardingham Norfk 27 N8
Hardingstone Nhants 24 H16
Hardington Somset 7 N2
Hardington Mandeville Somset 6 K9
Hardington Marsh Somset 6 K9
Hardington Moor Somset 6 K9
Hardisworthy Devon 4 F7
Hardley Hants 8 H11
Hardley Street Norfk 27 S9
Hardraw N York 35 T8
Hardstoft Derbys 32 C14
Hardway Hants 8 K11
Hardway Somset 7 N5
Hardwick Bucks 16 J7
Hardwick Cambs 25 S15
Hardwick Nhants 24 J14
Hardwick Norfk 27 Q10
Hardwick Oxon 16 C9
Hardwick Oxon 16 F5
Hardwick Wsall 23 M9
Hardwicke Gloucs 15 N8
Hardwicke Gloucs 15 Q5
Hardy's Green Essex 19 L10
Hare Croft C Brad 31 R2
Harefield Gt Lon 17 N11
Hare Green Essex 19 N9
Hare Hatch Wokham 16 J14
Harehill Derbys 23 P3
Harehills Leeds 32 B2
Harelaw Border 46 G13
Harelaw D & G 40 C5
Harescombe Gloucs 15 P8
Haresfield Gloucs 15 P8
Harestock Hants 8 H6
Hare Street Essex 18 D12
Hare Street Herts 18 D8
Harewood Leeds 36 G16
Harewood End Herefs 14 K5
Harford Devon 3 M6
Hargrave Ches W 30 G14
Hargrave Nhants 25 M14
Hargrave Suffk 18 J3
Harkstead Suffk 19 Q8
Harlaston Staffs 23 P7
Harlaxton Lincs 24 K3
Harlech Gwynd 28 G13
Harlescott Shrops 22 D6
Harlesden Gt Lon 17 Q13
Harlesthorpe Derbys 32 D11
Harleston Devon 3 P8
Harleston Norfk 27 R11
Harleston Suffk 19 M3
Harlestone Nhants 24 G15
Harle Syke Lancs 31 N2
Harley Rothm 32 B8
Harley Shrops 22 F8
Harlington C Beds 17 N5
Harlington Donc 32 D7
Harlington Gt Lon 17 N14
Harlosh Highld 59 c9
Harlow Essex 18 D11
Harlow Hill Nthumb 41 M7
Harlthorpe E R Yk 32 H1
Harlton Cambs 18 C5
Harlyn Cnwll 1 U5
Harman's Cross Dorset 7 S14
Harmby N York 36 D8
Harmer Green Herts 17 R7
Harmer Hill Shrops 22 D5
Harmston Lincs 33 L14
Harnage Shrops 22 E8
Harnhill Gloucs 15 S10
Harold Hill Gt Lon 18 F14
Haroldston West Pembks 12 D7
Haroldswick Shet 59 r1
Harold Wood Gt Lon 18 F15
Harome N York 37 L10
Harpenden Herts 17 P8
Harpford Devon 6 D12
Harpham E R Yk 37 T13
Harpley Norfk 26 J4
Harpley Worcs 22 G15
Harpole Nhants 24 G15
Harpsdale Highld 58 E4
Harpswell Lincs 32 K9
Harpurhey Manch 31 N7
Harraby Cumb 40 C9
Harracott Devon 5 L6
Harrapool Highld 52 C11
Harrietfield P & K 50 F11
Harrietsham Kent 11 M6
Harringay Gt Lon 17 S12
Harrington Cumb 39 R14
Harrington Lincs 33 R12
Harrington Nhants 24 H12
Harringworth Nhants 24 K9
Harrogate N York 36 G14
Harrold Bed 25 L16
Harrow Gt Lon 17 P12
Harrowbarrow Cnwll 2 J4
Harrowgate Village Darltn 36 F4
Harrow Green Suffk 18 K4
Harrow on the Hill Gt Lon 17 P12
Harrow Weald Gt Lon 17 P11
Harston Cambs 18 D5
Harston Leics 24 J4
Harswell E R Yk 32 J1
Hart Hartpl 41 S13
Hartburn Nthumb 41 M4
Hartburn S on T 36 H4
Hartest Suffk 18 K5
Hartfield E Susx 10 F9
Hartford Cambs 25 Q13
Hartford Ches W 30 J12
Hartfordbridge Hants 9 M2
Hartford End Essex 18 H10
Hartforth N York 36 E6
Hartgrove Dorset 7 Q8
Harthill Ches W 30 G15
Harthill N Lans 45 L6
Harthill Rothm 32 D11
Hartington Derbys 31 R14
Hartland Devon 4 G7
Hartland Quay Devon 4 F7
Hartlebury Worcs 22 J13
Hartlepool Hartpl 41 T13
Hartley Cumb 35 S5
Hartley Kent 10 H4
Hartley Kent 10 K9
Hartley Wespall Hants 9 L2
Hartley Wintney Hants 9 M2
Hartlip Kent 11 L4
Harton N York 37 M13
Harton S Tyne 41 R8
Hartpury Gloucs 15 N6
Hartshead Kirk 31 S4
Hartshill C Stke 22 J1
Hartshill Warwks 23 R10
Hartshorne Derbys 23 R5
Hartwell Nhants 16 J2
Hartwith N York 36 E13
Hartwood N Lans 44 K7
Hartwoodmyres Border 46 F12
Harvel Kent 10 J4
Harvington Worcs 15 S2
Harvington Worcs 22 K13
Harwell Notts 32 G9
Harwell Oxon 16 E12
Harwich Essex 19 R8
Harwood Dale N York 37 R7
Harworth Notts 32 F9
Hasbury Dudley 23 L12
Hascombe Surrey 9 R5
Haselbech Nhants 24 G12
Haselbury Plucknett Somset 6 J9
Haseley Warwks 23 Q14
Haselor Warwks 23 N16
Hasfield Gloucs 15 P5
Haskayne Lancs 30 F6
Hasketon Suffk 19 R5
Haslemere Surrey 9 P6
Haslingden Lancs 31 M4
Haslingfield Cambs 18 D5
Haslington Ches E 31 L15
Hassingham Norfk 27 S8
Hassocks W Susx 10 D12
Hassop Derbys 31 T12
Haster Highld 58 H5
Hastingleigh Kent 11 Q7
Hastings E Susx 11 L13
Hastingwood Essex 18 E12
Hastoe Herts 17 L8
Haswell Dur 41 R11
Haswell Plough Dur 41 R11
Hatch Beauchamp Somset 6 G7
Hatch End Gt Lon 17 P11
Hatchmere Ches W 30 H12
Hatcliffe NE Lin 33 P7
Hatfield Donc 32 G6
Hatfield Herefs 22 F15
Hatfield Herts 17 Q8
Hatfield Broad Oak Essex 18 F10
Hatfield Heath Essex 18 E11
Hatfield Peverel Essex 18 J11
Hatfield Woodhouse Donc 32 G6
Hatford Oxon 16 C11
Hatherden Hants 8 F3
Hatherleigh Devon 5 L10
Hathern Leics 24 D5
Hatherop Gloucs 15 T9
Hathersage Derbys 31 T11
Hathersage Booths Derbys 31 T11
Hatherton Ches E 22 G1
Hatherton Staffs 23 L7
Hatley St George Cambs 17 R2
Hatt Cnwll 2 J6
Hattersley Tamesd 31 P8
Hatton Abers 55 T9
Hatton Angus 51 N9
Hatton Derbys 23 P4
Hatton Gt Lon 17 N14
Hatton Lincs 33 P11
Hatton Shrops 21 S5
Hatton Warrtn 30 J10
Hatton Warwks 23 Q14
Hatton of Fintray Abers 55 Q12
Haugh E Ayrs 44 E12
Haugham Lincs 33 R11
Haughhead E Duns 44 G4
Haughley Suffk 19 M3
Haughley Green Suffk 19 M3
Haugh of Glass Moray 54 K8
Haugh of Urr D & G 39 N7
Haughs of Kinnaird Angus 51 R6
Haughton Ches E 30 J15
Haughton Shrops 22 C4
Haughton Staffs 22 J5
Haughton le Skerne Darltn 36 G4
Haultwick Herts 17 S6
Haunton Staffs 23 Q7
Hauxton Cambs 18 D5
Havant Hants 9 M11
Havenstreet IoW 8 J13
Havercroft Wakefd 32 C5
Haverfordwest Pembks 12 E7
Haverhill Suffk 18 G6
Haverigg Cumb 34 H10
Havering-atte-Bower Gt Lon 18 E14
Haversham M Keyn 16 K3
Haverthwaite Cumb 35 L9
Havyat N Som 14 J16
Hawarden Flints 30 E13
Hawbush Green Essex 18 J10
Hawen Cerdgn 20 A13
Hawes N York 35 T8
Hawe's Green Norfk 27 Q9
Hawford Worcs 22 J15
Hawick Border 46 G14
Hawkchurch Devon 6 H11
Hawkedon Suffk 18 J4
Hawkeridge Wilts 7 Q2
Hawkesbury S Glos 15 N12
Hawkesbury Upton S Glos 15 N12
Hawkhurst Kent 10 K10
Hawkinge Kent 11 S8
Hawkley Hants 9 M7
Hawkridge Somset 5 Q6
Hawkshead Cumb 35 L7
Hawkshead Hill Cumb 35 L7
Hawksland S Lans 44 K10
Hawkstone Shrops 22 F4
Hawkswick N York 36 B12
Hawksworth Leeds 31 S1
Hawksworth Notts 24 H2
Hawkwell Essex 18 K15
Hawley Hants 9 P2
Hawling Gloucs 15 S6
Hawnby N York 36 K8
Haworth C Brad 31 Q1
Hawstead Suffk 18 K3
Hawthorn Dur 41 S11
Hawthorn Hill Lincs 33 P15
Hawton Notts 32 H16
Haxby C York 37 L14
Haxey N Linc 32 H8
Haydock St Hel 30 H8
Haydon Bridge Nthumb 40 J8
Haydon Wick Swindn 15 T12
Hayes Gt Lon 10 E4
Hayes Gt Lon 17 N13
Hayes End Gt Lon 17 N13
Hayfield Ag & B 49 N12
Hayfield Derbys 31 Q10
Hayhillock Angus 51 P9
Hayle Cnwll 1 P12
Hayley Green Dudley 23 L12
Hayne Devon 5 P13
Haynes (Church End) C Beds 17 N3
Haynes (Northwood End) C Beds 17 N3
Haynes (Silver End) C Beds 17 P3
Haynes (West End) C Beds 17 N3
Hay-on-Wye Powys 21 P13
Hayscastle Pembks 12 E6
Hayscastle Cross Pembks 12 E6
Hay Street Herts 18 D9
Hayton Cumb 39 S11
Hayton Cumb 40 D9
Hayton E R Yk 37 P16
Hayton Notts 32 G10
Haytor Vale Devon 3 P3
Haytown Devon 4 H8
Haywards Heath W Susx 10 D11
Haywood Donc 32 E5
Hazelbank S Lans 44 K9
Hazelbury Bryan Dorset 7 N9
Hazeleigh Essex 18 K13
Hazel Grove Stockp 31 N10
Hazelton Walls Fife 51 L12
Hazelwood Derbys 23 R1
Hazlemere Bucks 17 L11
Hazlerigg N u Ty 41 P7
Hazleton Gloucs 15 S7
Heacham Norfk 26 H3
Headbourne Worthy Hants 8 H6
Headcorn Kent 11 L8
Headingley Leeds 31 U2
Headington Oxon 16 F9
Headlam Dur 36 E4
Headlesscross N Lans 45 L7
Headless Cross Worcs 23 M14
Headley Hants 8 J1
Headley Hants 9 N6
Headley Surrey 9 T3
Headley Down Hants 9 N6
Headon Notts 32 H11
Heads Nook Cumb 40 D9
Heage Derbys 32 B16
Healaugh N York 36 B7
Healaugh N York 36 J15
Heald Green Stockp 31 M10
Heale Somset 6 F7
Heale Somset 6 H6
Healey N York 36 E10
Healeyfield Dur 41 M10
Healing NE Lin 33 P6
Heamoor Cnwll 1 N13
Heanor Derbys 23 S1
Heanton Punchardon Devon 4 K5
Heapham Lincs 32 K10
Heasley Mill Devon 5 N5
Heast Highld 52 C12
Heath Derbys 32 D13
Heath Wakefd 32 B4
Heath and Reach C Beds 17 L5
Heathcote Derbys 31 S14
Heather Leics 23 S7
Heathfield E Susx 10 H11
Heathfield Somset 6 E6
Heath Green Worcs 23 M13
Heath Hall D & G 39 R5
Heath Hayes & Wimblebury Staffs 23 M7
Heath Hill Shrops 22 H6
Heathrow Airport Gt Lon 17 N14
Heathton Shrops 22 J10
Heath Town Wolves 22 K9
Heatley Warrtn 30 K9
Heaton C Brad 31 R2
Heaton N u Ty 41 Q7
Heaton Staffs 31 P14
Heaton Chapel Stockp 31 N9
Heaton Mersey Stockp 31 N9
Heaton Norris Stockp 31 N9
Heaton's Bridge Lancs 30 F6
Heaverham Kent 10 G5
Heavitree Devon 5 R12
Hebburn S Tyne 41 Q8
Hebden N York 36 C13
Hebden Bridge Calder 31 P3
Hebing End Herts 17 R6
Hebron Carmth 12 J5
Hebron Nthumb 41 P4
Heckfield Hants 9 M2
Heckfield Green Suffk 27 Q13
Heckfordbridge Essex 19 L10
Heckington Lincs 25 N1
Heckmondwike Kirk 31 T4
Heddington Wilts 15 R15
Heddon-on-the-Wall Nthumb 41 N7
Hedenham Norfk 27 R10
Hedge End Hants 8 H9
Hedgerley Bucks 17 M12
Hedging Somset 6 G6
Hedley on the Hill Nthumb 41 M9
Hednesford Staffs 23 L7
Hedon E R Yk 33 P3
Hedsor Bucks 17 L12
Heeley Sheff 32 B10
Heglibister Shet 59 q5
Heighington Darltn 36 F3
Heighington Lincs 33 M13
Heightington Worcs 22 H13
Heiton Border 46 K12
Hele Devon 4 K3
Hele Devon 5 S10
Helensburgh Ag & B 43 S3
Helenton S Ayrs 44 D12
Helford Cnwll 1 S13
Helford Passage Cnwll 1 S13
Helhoughton Norfk 26 K4
Helions Bumpstead Essex 18 G6
Helland Cnwll 2 D4
Hellescott Cnwll 4 G12
Hellesdon Norfk 27 Q7
Hellidon Nhants 24 E16
Hellifield N York 35 T14
Hellingly E Susx 10 H13
Helmdon Nhants 16 F3
Helme Kirk 31 R6
Helmingham Suffk 19 Q4
Helmsdale Highld 58 D11
Helmshore Lancs 31 M4
Helmsley N York 37 L9
Helperby N York 36 H12
Helperthorpe N York 37 R12
Helpringham Lincs 25 N2
Helpston C Pete 25 N8
Helsby Ches W 30 G12
Helston Cnwll 1 R13
Helstone Cnwll 4 D14
Helton Cumb 35 N3
Hemel Hempstead Herts 17 N9
Hemerdon Devon 3 L6
Hemingbrough N York 32 G3
Hemingby Lincs 33 Q12
Hemingford Abbots Cambs 25 Q13
Hemingford Grey Cambs 25 Q14
Hemingstone Suffk 19 P4
Hemington Leics 24 D4
Hemington Nhants 25 N11
Hemington Somset 7 N2
Hemley Suffk 19 R6
Hemlington Middsb 36 J4
Hempnall Norfk 27 Q10
Hempnall Green Norfk 27 R10
Hempriggs Moray 54 E4
Hempstead Essex 18 G7
Hempstead Medway 11 L4
Hempstead Norfk 27 P3
Hempstead Norfk 27 T4
Hempton Norfk 27 L4
Hempton Oxon 16 D5
Hemsby Norfk 27 U6
Hemswell Lincs 32 K9
Hemswell Cliff Lincs 33 L9
Hemsworth Wakefd 32 C5
Hemyock Devon 6 E8
Henbury Bristl 14 K13
Hendon Gt Lon 17 Q12
Hendon Sundld 41 S9
Hendy Carmth 13 P9
Henfield W Susx 10 B12
Hengoed Caerph 14 D11
Hengoed Powys 21 N11
Hengrave Suffk 26 K14
Henham Essex 18 F9
Heniarth Powys 21 M2
Henlade Somset 6 G7
Henley Dorset 7 N10
Henley Somset 6 J5
Henley Suffk 19 P5
Henley W Susx 9 P7
Henley-in-Arden Warwks 23 P14
Henley-on-Thames Oxon 16 J13
Henley's Down E Susx 10 K13
Henllan Cerdgn 20 A14
Henllan Denbgs 29 N7
Henllys Torfn 14 F11
Henlow C Beds 17 Q4
Hennock Devon 5 Q14
Henny Street Essex 18 K7
Henryd Conwy 28 K6
Henry's Moat (Castell Hendre) Pembks 12 G5
Hensall N York 32 F4
Henshaw Nthumb 40 G8
Hensingham Cumb 34 F4
Henstead Suffk 27 U11
Hensting Hants 8 H8
Henstridge Somset 7 N7
Henstridge Ash Somset 7 N7
Henton Oxon 16 J10
Henton Somset 6 K3
Henwick Worcs 22 J16
Henwood Cnwll 2 G4
Heol-y-Cyw Brdgnd 13 U13
Hepple Nthumb 41 L2
Hepscott Nthumb 41 P4
Heptonstall Calder 31 P3
Hepworth Kirk 31 S6
Hepworth Suffk 27 M13
Herbrandston Pembks 12 D9
Hereford Herefs 14 J3
Hereson Kent 11 U4
Heribusta Highld 59 e5
Heriot Border 46 E8
Hermiston C Edin 45 Q5
Hermitage Border 40 D3
Hermitage Dorset 7 M10
Hermitage W Berk 16 E14
Hermon Carmth 13 L5
Hermon Pembks 12 J5
Herne Kent 11 R4
Herne Bay Kent 11 R4
Herne Hill Gt Lon 17 S14
Herne Pound Kent 10 J6
Hernhill Kent 11 P5
Herodsfoot Cnwll 2 F6
Heronsford S Ayrs 38 D5
Herriard Hants 9 L4
Herringfleet Suffk 27 U9
Herringswell Suffk 26 H14
Herringthorpe Rothm 32 D9
Herrington Sundld 41 R10
Hersden Kent 11 R5
Hersham Surrey 17 P16
Herstmonceux E Susx 10 H13
Herston Ork 58 c5
Hertford Herts 17 S8
Hertford Heath Herts 17 S8
Hertingfordbury Herts 17 R8
Hesketh Bank Lancs 30 G4
Hesketh Lane Lancs 30 J1
Hesket Newmarket Cumb 40 B12
Hesleden Dur 41 S12
Heslington C York 37 L15
Hessay C York 36 K14
Hessenford Cnwll 2 G6
Hessett Suffk 19 L3
Hessle E R Yk 33 M3
Hessle Wakefd 32 C5
Hest Bank Lancs 35 N12
Heston Gt Lon 17 P14
Hestwall Ork 58 b3
Heswall Wirral 30 D11
Hethe Oxon 16 F5
Hethersett Norfk 27 P8
Hethersgill Cumb 40 D7
Hett Dur 41 Q12
Hetton N York 36 B13
Hetton-le-Hole Sundld 41 R10
Heugh Nthumb 41 M6
Heughhead Abers 54 J13
Heugh Head Border 47 M6
Heveningham Suffk 27 S13
Hever Kent 10 F7
Heversham Cumb 35 N9
Hevingham Norfk 27 Q5
Hewas Water Cnwll 2 B8
Hewelsfield Gloucs 14 K10
Hewish Somset 6 J9
Hewood Dorset 6 H10
Hexham Nthumb 40 K8
Hextable Kent 10 G3
Hexthorpe Donc 32 E7
Hexton Herts 17 P5
Hexworthy Cnwll 4 H14
Hexworthy Devon 3 M4
Heybridge Essex 18 G13
Heybridge Essex 18 K12
Heybrook Bay Devon 2 K8
Heydon Cambs 18 D7
Heydon Norfk 27 P4
Heydour Lincs 25 L2
Heylipoll Ag & B 42 b4
Heylor Shet 59 p3
Heysham Lancs 35 M13
Heyshott W Susx 9 P9
Heytesbury Wilts 7 R4
Heythrop Oxon 16 C5
Heywood Rochdl 31 N6
Heywood Wilts 7 Q2
Hibaldstow N Linc 33 L7
Hickleton Donc 32 D7
Hickling Norfk 27 T5
Hickling Notts 24 G4
Hickling Green Norfk 27 T5
Hickstead W Susx 10 C12
Hidcote Bartrim Gloucs 15 U3
Hidcote Boyce Gloucs 15 U3
High Ackworth Wakefd 32 C5
Higham Barns 31 U6
Higham Derbys 32 C14
Higham Kent 10 H7
Higham Kent 10 J3
Higham Lancs 31 M2
Higham Suffk 19 N7
Higham Suffk 26 J14
Higham Ferrers Nhants 25 L14
Higham Gobion C Beds 17 P5
Higham Hill Gt Lon 17 S12
Higham on the Hill Leics 23 S9
Highampton Devon 4 K10
Highams Park Gt Lon 18 C15
High Ardwell D & G 38 C11
High Auldgirth D & G 39 Q4
High Bankhill Cumb 40 E11
High Beach Essex 18 D14
High Bentham N York 35 Q12
High Bickington Devon 5 L7
High Biggins Cumb 35 Q10
High Blantyre S Lans 44 H7
High Bonnybridge Falk 44 K4
High Bray Devon 5 N5
Highbridge Somset 6 G3
Highbrook W Susx 10 E10
High Brooms Kent 10 H8
Highburton Kirk 31 S5
Highbury Gt Lon 17 S12
Highbury Somset 7 M3
High Casterton Cumb 35 Q10
High Catton E R Yk 37 M14
Highclere Hants 8 H2
Highcliffe Dorset 8 E13
High Coniscliffe Darltn 36 E4
High Crosby Cumb 40 C8
High Cross E Ayrs 44 D9
High Cross Hants 9 M7
High Cross Herts 17 S7
High Cross Warwks 23 P14
High Drummore D & G 38 D12
High Easter Essex 18 G11
High Ellington N York 36 E9
Higher Ansty Dorset 7 P10
Higher Bartle Lancs 30 H2
Higher Bockhampton Dorset 7 N12
Higher Brixham Torbay 3 R7
High Ercall Wrekin 22 F6
Higher Chillington Somset 6 H9
Higher Folds Wigan 30 K8
Higher Gabwell Devon 3 R5
Higher Heysham Lancs 35 M13
Higher Irlam Salfd 31 L8
Higher Kinnerton Flints 30 E14
Higher Muddiford Devon 5 L4
Higher Penwortham Lancs 30 H3
Higher Prestacott Devon 4 H11
Higher Town Cnwll 1 T10
Higher Town Cnwll 2 C6
Higher Town IoS 1 b1
Higher Walton Lancs 30 J3
Higher Walton Warrtn 30 J10
Higher Wambrook Somset 6 G9
Higher Waterston Dorset 7 N11
Higher Wheelton Lancs 30 J4
Higher Whitley Ches W 30 J11
Higher Wincham Ches W 30 K11
Higher Wraxhall Dorset 7 L10
Higher Wych Ches W 22 D2
High Etherley Dur 41 N14
Highfield Gatesd 41 N9
Highfield N Ayrs 43 S8
High Garrett Essex 18 J9
Highgate Gt Lon 17 R12
High Grantley N York 36 F12
High Green Norfk 27 P10
High Green Norfk 27 P8
High Green Sheff 32 B8
High Halden Kent 11 M9
High Halstow Medway 10 K3
High Ham Somset 6 J6
High Harrington Cumb 39 R14
High Harrogate N York 36 G14
High Hatton Shrops 22 F5
High Hauxley Nthumb 41 Q1
High Hawsker N York 37 Q5
High Hesket Cumb 40 C11
High Hoyland Barns 31 T6
High Hurstwood E Susx 10 F11
High Hutton N York 37 N12
High Ireby Cumb 39 U12
High Kilburn N York 36 K10
High Lands Dur 41 N14
Highlane Derbys 32 C11
High Lane Stockp 31 P10
High Lanes Cnwll 1 P12
Highleadon Gloucs 15 N6
High Legh Ches E 30 K10
Highleigh W Susx 9 N12
High Leven S on T 36 J5
Highley Shrops 22 H11
High Littleton BaNES 7 M1
High Lorton Cumb 39 T14
High Marnham Notts 32 J12
High Melton Donc 32 D7
High Mickley Nthumb 41 M8
Highmoor Oxon 16 H12
Highmoor Cross Oxon 16 H13
Highnam Gloucs 15 N7
High Newport Sundld 41 R9
High Newton Cumb 35 M10
High Nibthwaite Cumb 34 K8
High Offley Staffs 22 H4
High Ongar Essex 18 F13
High Onn Staffs 22 J6
High Park Corner Essex 19 N10
High Pennyvenie E Ayrs 44 E15
High Roding Essex 18 G10
High Salvington W Susx 9 S11
High Spen Gatesd 41 N9
Highsted Kent 11 M5
High Street Cnwll 2 C7
Highstreet Kent 11 Q5
Highstreet Green Surrey 9 Q6
Hightae D & G 39 S5
Highter's Heath Birm 23 N12
Hightown Sefton 30 E7
Hightown Green Suffk 19 M4
High Toynton Lincs 33 Q13
High Valleyfield Fife 45 M2
Highweek Devon 3 Q4
Highwood Essex 18 G13
Highwood Hill Gt Lon 17 Q11
Highworth Swindn 15 U11
High Wray Cumb 35 L7
High Wych Herts 18 E11
High Wycombe Bucks 16 K11
Hilborough Norfk 26 K9
Hilcott Wilts 8 C2
Hildenborough Kent 10 G7
Hilden Park Kent 10 H7
Hildersham Cambs 18 F5
Hilderstone Staffs 23 L3
Hilderthorpe E R Yk 37 U12
Hilgay Norfk 26 G9
Hill S Glos 15 L11
Hill Warwks 24 D14
Hillam N York 32 D3
Hill Brow Hants 9 N7
Hillbutts Dorset 7 S10
Hill Chorlton Staffs 22 J2
Hillcliffiane Derbys 23 Q1
Hill Common Somset 6 E6
Hilldyke Lincs 25 R1
Hill End Fife 45 N1
Hillend Fife 45 P3
Hill End Gloucs 15 Q4
Hillend Mdloth 45 R6
Hillend N Lans 44 K6
Hillesden Bucks 16 H5
Hillesley Gloucs 15 N12
Hillfarrance Somset 6 E7
Hill Green Kent 11 L5
Hillhead Abers 55 M9
Hill Head Hants 8 J11
Hillhead S Lans 45 M10
Hillhead of Cocklaw Abers 55 U7
Hilliclay Highld 58 F3
Hillingdon Gt Lon 17 N13
Hillington C Glas 44 E6
Hillington Norfk 26 H5
Hillmorton Warwks 24 E13
Hill of Beath Fife 45 P2
Hill of Fearn Highld 53 U2
Hillowton D & G 39 N8
Hill Ridware Staffs 23 N6
Hillside Abers 55 S15
Hillside Angus 51 R6
Hill Side Kirk 31 S5
Hills Town Derbys 32 D13
Hillstreet Hants 8 F9
Hillswick Shet 59 p4
Hill Top Sandw 23 L10
Hill Top Wakefd 32 B5
Hillwell Shet 59 q8
Hilmarton Wilts 15 S14
Hilperton Wilts 7 Q1
Hilsea C Port 9 L11
Hilston E R Yk 33 Q2
Hilton Border 47 M8
Hilton Cambs 25 Q14
Hilton Cumb 35 R3
Hilton Derbys 23 Q4
Hilton Dorset 7 P10
Hilton Dur 36 E3
Hilton Highld 54 B2
Hilton S on T 36 J5
Hilton Shrops 22 H9
Himbleton Worcs 23 L15
Himley Staffs 22 K10
Hincaster Cumb 35 N9
Hinchley Wood Surrey 17 P16
Hinckley Leics 23 S10
Hinderclay Suffk 27 M13
Hinderwell N York 37 N4
Hindhead Surrey 9 P6
Hindhead Tunnel Surrey 9 P6
Hindley Wigan 30 J7
Hindlip Worcs 22 K15
Hindolveston Norfk 27 N4
Hindon Wilts 7 R5
Hindringham Norfk 27 M3
Hingham Norfk 27 M8
Hinstock Shrops 22 G4
Hintlesham Suffk 19 N6
Hinton Herefs 14 G4
Hinton S Glos 15 N14
Hinton Shrops 21 R2
Hinton Ampner Hants 8 K7
Hinton Blewett BaNES 7 L1
Hinton Charterhouse BaNES 7 P1
Hinton-in-the-Hedges Nhants 16 F4
Hinton Martell Dorset 7 S10
Hinton on the Green Worcs 15 S3
Hinton Parva Swindn 15 V13
Hinton St George Somset 6 J9
Hinton St Mary Dorset 7 P8
Hinton Waldrist Oxon 16 C10
Hints Staffs 23 P8
Hinwick Bed 24 K15
Hinxhill Kent 11 P8
Hinxton Cambs 18 E6
Hinxworth Herts 17 Q3
Hipperholme Calder 31 R3
Hipswell N York 36 E7
Hirn Abers 55 P15
Hirnant Powys 29 P14
Hirst Nthumb 41 Q4
Hirst Courtney N York 32 F4
Hirwaun Rhondd 14 B9
Hiscott Devon 5 L6
Histon Cambs 18 D3
Hitcham Suffk 19 M5
Hitcham Causeway Suffk 19 M5
Hitcham Street Suffk 19 M5
Hitchin Herts 17 Q5
Hither Green Gt Lon 10 E3
Hittisleigh Devon 5 N11
Hive E R Yk 32 J3
Hixon Staffs 23 L5
Hoaden Kent 11 S5
Hoar Cross Staffs 23 N5
Hoarwithy Herefs 14 K5
Hoath Kent 11 R4
Hobarris Shrops 21 Q7
Hobkirk Border 46 H15
Hobson Dur 41 N9
Hoby Leics 24 G6
Hockering Norfk 27 N7
Hockerton Notts 32 G15
Hockley Essex 18 K14
Hockley Heath Solhll 23 P13
Hockliffe C Beds 17 M6
Hockwold cum Wilton Norfk 26 H11
Hockworthy Devon 5 T7
Hoddesdon Herts 17 S9
Hoddlesden Bl w D 31 L4
Hoddom Cross D & G 39 T6
Hoddom Mains D & G 39 T6
Hodgeston Pembks 12 G10
Hodnet Shrops 22 F4
Hodsock Notts 32 F10
Hodsoll Street Kent 10 H5
Hodson Swindn 15 U13
Hodthorpe Derbys 32 E11
Hoe Norfk 27 M6
Hogben's Hill Kent 11 P6
Hoggeston Bucks 16 J6
Hoggrill's End Warwks 23 Q10
Hoghton Lancs 30 J3
Hognaston Derbys 31 T16
Hogsthorpe Lincs 33 U12
Holbeach Lincs 25 R5
Holbeach Bank Lincs 25 R4
Holbeach Clough Lincs 25 R4
Holbeach Drove Lincs 25 R7
Holbeach Hurn Lincs 25 S4
Holbeach St Johns Lincs 25 R6
Holbeach St Mark's Lincs 25 S4
Holbeach St Matthew Lincs 25 S3
Holbeck Notts 32 E12
Holberrow Green Worcs 23 M15
Holbeton Devon 3 M8
Holborn Gt Lon 17 R13
Holbrook Derbys 23 R1
Holbrook Suffk 19 P7
Holbrooks Covtry 23 R12
Holbury Hants 8 H11
Holcombe Devon 3 R4
Holcombe Somset 7 M3
Holcombe Rogus Devon 6 D8
Holcot Nhants 24 H14
Holden Lancs 35 S15
Holdenby Nhants 24 G14
Holder's Green Essex 18 G8
Holdgate Shrops 22 E10
Holdingham Lincs 25 M1
Holditch Dorset 6 H10
Holemoor Devon 4 J10
Holford Somset 6 E4
Holgate C York 36 K15
Holker Cumb 35 L10
Holkham Norfk 27 L2
Hollacombe Devon 4 H10
Holland Fen Lincs 33 Q16
Holland-on-Sea Essex 19 Q10
Hollandstoun Ork 58 e1
Hollee D & G 39 V7
Hollesley Suffk 19 S6
Hollicombe Torbay 3 R6
Hollingbourne Kent 11 L6
Hollingbury Br & H 10 D14
Hollingdon Bucks 16 K5
Hollington Derbys 23 Q2
Hollington Staffs 23 M2
Hollingworth Tamesd 31 Q8
Hollinsclough Staffs 31 Q13
Hollins End Sheff 32 C10
Hollins Green Warrtn 30 K9
Hollinswood Wrekin 22 G7
Hollocombe Devon 5 M9
Holloway Derbys 31 U15
Holloway Gt Lon 17 R12
Hollowell Nhants 24 G13
Hollowmoor Heath Ches W 30 G13
Hollows D & G 40 B5
Hollybush Caerph 14 E9
Hollybush E Ayrs 44 D14
Hollybush Herefs 15 N4
Hollym E R Yk 33 R3
Holmbridge Kirk 31 R6
Holmbury St Mary Surrey 9 S4
Holmbush Cnwll 2 D7
Holmcroft Staffs 22 K5
Holme Cambs 25 P11
Holme Cumb 35 N10
Holme Kirk 31 R7
Holme N York 36 G10
Holme Notts 32 J14
Holme Chapel Lancs 31 N3
Holme Hale Norfk 26 K7
Holme Lacy Herefs 14 K4
Holme Marsh Herefs 21 Q11
Holme next the Sea Norfk 26 H2
Holme on the Wolds E R Yk 37 R16
Holme Pierrepont Notts 24 F2
Holmer Herefs 14 J3
Holmer Green Bucks 17 L10
Holme St Cuthbert Cumb 39 S11
Holmes Chapel Ches E 31 L13
Holmesfield Derbys 31 U11
Holmeswood Lancs 30 G5
Holmethorpe Surrey 10 C6
Holme upon Spalding Moor E R Yk 32 J1
Holmewood Derbys 32 C13
Holmfirth Kirk 31 S6
Holmhead E Ayrs 44 F13
Holmpton E R Yk 33 R4
Holmrook Cumb 34 G7
Holmside Dur 41 P10
Holne Devon 3 N4
Holnicote Somset 5 R3
Holsworthy Devon 4 H10
Holsworthy Beacon Devon 4 H9
Holt Dorset 7 S10
Holt Norfk 27 N2
Holt Wilts 15 P16
Holt Worcs 22 J15
Holt Wrexhm 30 F15
Holtby C York 37 M14
Holt End Worcs 23 M14
Holt Heath Worcs 22 J15
Holton Oxon 16 F9
Holton Somset 7 M6
Holton Suffk 27 T12
Holton cum Beckering Lincs 33 N11
Holton le Clay Lincs 33 Q7
Holton le Moor Lincs 33 M8
Holton St Mary Suffk 19 N7
Holwell Dorset 7 N9
Holwell Herts 17 P4
Holwell Leics 24 H5
Holwell Oxon 15 V8
Holwick Dur 40 K14
Holybourne Hants 9 M5
Holyhead IoA 28 C5
Holy Island Nthumb 47 Q10
Holy Island Nthumb 47 Q9
Holymoorside Derbys 32 B13
Holyport W & M 17 L14
Holystone Nthumb 40 K1
Holytown N Lans 44 J7
Holywell C Beds 17 M7
Holywell Cambs 25 R14
Holywell Cnwll 1 S8
Holywell Dorset 7 L10
Holywell Flints 29 R6
Holywell Green Calder 31 R4
Holywell Lake Somset 6 D7
Holywell Row Suffk 26 H12
Holywood D & G 39 Q5
Holywood Village D & G 39 Q5
Homer Shrops 22 F8
Homer Green Sefton 30 E7
Homersfield Suffk 27 R11
Homington Wilts 8 C7
Honeybourne Worcs 15 T3
Honeychurch Devon 5 M10
Honeystreet Wilts 15 T16
Honey Tye Suffk 19 L7
Honiley Warwks 23 Q13
Honing Norfk 27 S4
Honingham Norfk 27 P7
Honington Lincs 24 K2
Honington Suffk 27 L13
Honington Warwks 16 B3
Honiton Devon 6 E11
Honley Kirk 31 R6
Hooe C Plym 2 K7
Hooe E Susx 10 J13
Hoo Green Ches E 31 L10
Hoohill Bpool 30 E1
Hook E R Yk 32 H3
Hook Gt Lon 17 Q16
Hook Hants 9 M3
Hook Pembks 12 F8
Hook Wilts 15 S12
Hooke Dorset 6 K11
Hook Green Kent 10 J9
Hook Norton Oxon 16 C4
Hookway Devon 5 Q11
Hooley Surrey 10 C6
Hoo St Werburgh Medway 10 K3
Hooton Levitt Rothm 32 E9
Hooton Pagnell Donc 32 D6
Hooton Roberts Rothm 32 D8
Hope Derbys 31 S10
Hope Devon 3 M9
Hope Flints 30 E14
Hope Staffs 31 R15
Hope Bagot Shrops 22 F13
Hope Bowdler Shrops 22 D10
Hopehouse Border 45 R14
Hopeman Moray 54 F3
Hope Mansell Herefs 15 L7
Hopesay Shrops 21 R7
Hope under Dinmore Herefs 14 J1
Hopgrove C York 37 L14
Hopperton N York 36 H14
Hopstone Shrops 22 H10
Hopton Derbys 31 T15
Hopton Staffs 23 L4
Hopton Suffk 27 M12
Hopton Cangeford Shrops 22 E12
Hopton Castle Shrops 21 Q7
Hoptonheath Shrops 21 R7
Hopton on Sea Norfk 27 V9
Hopton Wafers Shrops 22 F13
Hopwas Staffs 23 P8
Hopwood Worcs 23 M13
Horam E Susx 10 H12
Horbling Lincs 25 N3
Horbury Wakefd 31 U5
Horden Dur 41 S12
Hordle Hants 8 E12
Hordley Shrops 22 C4
Horfield Bristl 15 L14
Horham Suffk 27 Q13
Horkesley Heath Essex 19 M8
Horkstow N Linc 33 L5
Horley Oxon 16 D3
Horley Surrey 10 C8
Hornblotton Green Somset 7 L5
Hornby Lancs 35 P12
Hornby N York 36 E8
Hornby N York 36 G6
Horncastle Lincs 33 Q13
Hornchurch Gt Lon 18 F15
Horncliffe Nthumb 47 N8
Horndean Border 47 M8
Horndean Hants 9 L9
Horndon Devon 4 K14
Horndon on the Hill Thurr 10 J1
Horne Surrey 10 D8
Horner Somset 5 R3
Horning Norfk 27 S6
Horninghold Leics 24 J9
Horninglow Staffs 23 Q5
Horningsea Cambs 18 E3
Horningsham Wilts 7 P4
Horningtoft Norfk 27 L5
Horns Cross Devon 4 H7
Hornsea E R Yk 37 U15
Hornsey Gt Lon 17 R12
Hornton Oxon 16 D3
Horra Shet 59 q3
Horrabridge Devon 2 K4
Horringer Suffk 18 K3
Horrocksford Lancs 35 S16
Horsebridge Devon 2 J4
Horsebridge E Susx 10 H13
Horsebridge Hants 8 F7
Horsehay Wrekin 22 G7
Horseheath Cambs 18 G5
Horsehouse N York 36 C10
Horsell Surrey 9 Q2
Horseman's Green Wrexhm 22 D2
Horsey Norfk 27 U5
Horsey Somset 6 G4
Horsford Norfk 27 Q6
Horsforth Leeds 31 T1
Horsham W Susx 9 T6
Horsham Worcs 22 H16
Horsham St Faith Norfk 27 Q6
Horsington Lincs 33 P13
Horsington Somset 7 N7
Horsley Derbys 23 S1
Horsley Gloucs 15 P10
Horsley Nthumb 40 J2
Horsley Nthumb 41 M8
Horsleycross Street Essex 19 P8
Horsleyhill Border 46 G13
Horsley Woodhouse Derbys 23 S1
Horsmonden Kent 10 J8
Horspath Oxon 16 F9
Horstead Norfk 27 R5
Horsted Keynes W Susx 10 E10
Horton Bucks 17 L7
Horton Dorset 7 S9
Horton Lancs 35 T15
Horton Nhants 16 K1

Horton – Leadburn 69

Horton S Glos 15 N12
Horton Somset 6 G8
Horton Staffs 31 P15
Horton Swans 13 N12
Horton W & M 17 M14
Horton Wilts 15 S16
Horton Wrekin 22 G6
Horton-cum-Studley Oxon 16 F8
Horton Green Ches W 30 G16
Horton-in-Ribblesdale N York 35 S11
Horton Kirby Kent 10 G4
Horwich Bolton 30 J6
Horwood Devon 4 K6
Hoscote Border 46 E15
Hose Leics 24 H4
Hosh P & K 50 D12
Hoswick Shet 59 q7
Hotham E R Yk 32 K2
Hothfield Kent 11 N8
Hoton Leics 24 E5
Hough Ches E 30 K16
Hougham Lincs 24 K1
Hough Green Halton 30 G10
Hough-on-the-Hill Lincs 24 K1
Houghton Cambs 25 Q13
Houghton Hants 8 F6
Houghton Pembks 12 F9
Houghton W Susx 9 R10
Houghton Conquest C Beds 17 N3
Houghton Green E Susx 11 M11
Houghton-le-Spring Sundld 41 R10
Houghton on the Hill Leics 24 G8
Houghton Regis C Beds 17 M6
Houghton St Giles Norfk 27 L3
Hound Green Hants 9 M2
Houndslow Border 46 H9
Houndwood Border 47 L6
Hounslow Gt Lon 17 P14
Househill Highld 54 B6
Houses Hill Kirk 31 S5
Housieside Abers 55 R10
Houston Rens 44 D6
Houstry Highld 58 F8
Houton Ork 58 b4
Hove Br & H 10 C14
Hoveringham Notts 24 G1
Hoveton Norfk 27 R6
Hovingham N York 37 M11
How Caple Herefs 15 L5
Howden E R Yk 32 H3
Howden-le-Wear Dur 41 N13
Howe Highld 58 H3
Howe N York 36 G10
Howe Norfk 27 R9
Howe Green Essex 18 J13
Howegreen Essex 18 K13
Howell Lincs 25 N1
Howe of Teuchar Abers 55 Q7
Howes D & G 39 U7
Howe Street Essex 18 H11
Howe Street Essex 18 H8
Howey Powys 21 L11
Howgate Cumb 34 F3
Howgate Mdloth 45 R7
Howick Nthumb 47 S14
Howlett End Essex 18 F8
Howley Somset 6 G9
How Mill Cumb 40 D9
Howmore W Isls 56 b7
Hownam Border 46 K13
Howsham N Linc 33 M7
Howsham N York 37 N13
Howtel Nthumb 47 M11
How Wood Herts 17 P9
Howwood Rens 44 D7
Hoxa Ork 58 c5
Hoxne Suffk 27 Q12
Hoylake Wirral 29 R3
Hoyland Nether Barns 32 B7
Hoyland Swaine Barns 31 T7
Hubberston Pembks 12 E9
Huby N York 36 F15
Huby N York 36 K12
Hucclecote Gloucs 15 P7
Hucking Kent 11 L5
Hucknall Notts 32 E16
Huddersfield Kirk 31 S5
Huddington Worcs 23 L16
Hudswell N York 36 D7
Huggate E R Yk 37 Q14
Hughenden Valley Bucks 16 K10
Hughley Shrops 22 E9
Hugh Town IoS 1 b2
Huish Devon 4 K9
Huish Wilts 15 T16
Huish Champflower Somset 6 C6
Huish Episcopi Somset 6 J6
Huisinis W Isls 56 c3
Hulcott Bucks 16 K7
Hulham Devon 5 S13
Hulland Derbys 23 Q1
Hulland Ward Derbys 23 Q1
Hullavington Wilts 15 Q13
Hullbridge Essex 18 J14
Hull, Kingston upon C KuH 33 N3
Hulme Manch 31 M8
Hulme Staffs 22 K1
Hulme Warrtn 30 J9
Hulme End Staffs 31 R14
Hulme Walfield Ches E 31 M13
Hulverstone IoW 8 G14
Hulver Street Suffk 27 U11
Humber Bridge N Linc 33 M4
Humberside Airport N Linc 33 N6
Humberston NE Lin 33 R7
Humberstone C Leic 24 F8
Humbie E Loth 46 F6
Humbleton E R Yk 33 P2
Humby Lincs 25 L3
Hume Border 46 J10
Humshaugh Nthumb 40 K7
Huna Highld 58 J2
Huncote Leics 24 E9
Hundalee Border 46 J14
Hunderthwaite Dur 36 B3
Hundleby Lincs 33 S13
Hundleton Pembks 12 F10
Hundon Suffk 18 H5
Hundred House Powys 21 M11
Hungarton Leics 24 G8
Hungerford Somset 6 C4
Hungerford W Berk 16 C15
Hungerford Newtown W Berk 16 C15
Hungerstone Herefs 14 J4
Hunmanby N York 37 T10
Hunningham Warwks 23 S14
Hunsbury Hill Nhants 24 H16
Hunsdon Herts 18 D11
Hunsingore N York 36 H14
Hunslet Leeds 31 U3
Hunsonby Cumb 40 E12
Hunstanton Norfk 26 G2
Hunstanworth Dur 40 K10
Hunsterson Ches E 22 G1
Hunston Suffk 27 M14
Hunston W Susx 9 P11
Hunstrete BaNES 15 L16
Hunsworth Kirk 31 S3
Hunter's Quay Ag & B 43 R4
Huntham Somset 6 H6
Hunthill Lodge Angus 51 N4
Huntingdon Cambs 25 Q13
Huntingfield Suffk 27 S13
Huntington C York 37 L14
Huntington Ches W 30 F13
Huntington E Loth 46 F4
Huntington Herefs 21 P11
Huntington Staffs 23 L7
Huntley Gloucs 15 M7
Huntly Abers 55 L8
Hunton Kent 10 K7
Hunton N York 36 E8
Huntscott Somset 5 R3
Huntsham Devon 5 S7
Huntshaw Devon 4 K7
Huntspill Somset 6 G3
Huntstile Somset 6 G5
Huntworth Somset 6 G5
Hunwick Dur 41 N13
Hunworth Norfk 27 N3
Hurdcott Wilts 8 D6
Hurdsfield Ches E 31 P12
Hurley W & M 16 K13
Hurley Warwks 23 Q9
Hurley Common Warwks 23 Q9
Hurlford E Ayrs 44 D11
Hurn Dorset 8 C12
Hursley Hants 8 H7
Hurst Wokham 16 J14
Hurstbourne Priors Hants 8 H4
Hurstbourne Tarrant Hants 8 G3
Hurst Green E Susx 10 K10
Hurst Green Essex 19 N10
Hurst Green Lancs 30 K1
Hurst Green Surrey 10 E7
Hurst Hill Dudley 22 K10
Hurstpierpoint W Susx 10 C12
Hurstwood Lancs 31 N2
Hurtiso Ork 58 C4
Hurworth-on-Tees Darltn 36 F5
Hurworth Place Darltn 36 F5
Husbands Bosworth Leics 24 F11
Husborne Crawley C Beds 17 M4
Husthwaite N York 36 K11
Huthwaite Notts 32 D14
Huttoft Lincs 33 T11
Hutton Border 47 M8
Hutton E R Yk 37 S14
Hutton Essex 18 G14
Hutton Lancs 30 G3
Hutton N Som 6 H1
Hutton Buscel N York 37 R9
Hutton Conyers N York 36 G11
Hutton Cranswick E R Yk 37 S15
Hutton End Cumb 40 C12
Hutton Henry Dur 41 S12
Hutton-le-Hole N York 37 M8
Hutton Lowcross R & Cl 37 L4
Hutton Magna Dur 36 D5
Hutton Roof Cumb 35 P10
Hutton Roof Cumb 40 B13
Hutton Rudby N York 36 J6
Hutton Sessay N York 36 J11
Hutton Wandesley N York 36 J15
Huxham Devon 5 R11
Huxley Ches W 30 H14
Huyton Knows 30 G9
Hycemoor Cumb 34 G8
Hyde Tamesd 31 P8
Hyde Heath Bucks 17 L10
Hyde Lea Staffs 22 K5
Hyndford Bridge S Lans 45 L10
Hynish Ag & B 42 b5
Hyssington Powys 21 Q5
Hythe Essex 19 M9
Hythe Hants 8 G10
Hythe Kent 11 R9
Hythe End W & M 17 M14

I

Ibberton Dorset 7 P9
Ible Derbys 31 T15
Ibsley Hants 8 D10
Ibstock Leics 23 S7
Ibstone Bucks 16 J11
Ibthorpe Hants 8 G3
Iburndale N York 37 Q6
Ibworth Hants 8 K3
Ichrachan Ag & B 49 M11
Ickburgh Norfk 26 J9
Ickenham Gt Lon 17 N12
Ickford Bucks 16 G9
Ickham Kent 11 S5
Ickleford Herts 17 Q5
Icklesham E Susx 11 M12
Ickleton Cambs 18 E6
Icklingham Suffk 26 J13
Ickornshaw N York 36 B16
Ickwell Green C Beds 17 P2
Icomb Gloucs 15 U6
Idbury Oxon 15 V7
Iddesleigh Devon 5 L9
Ide Devon 5 R12
Ideford Devon 3 Q3
Ide Hill Kent 10 F6
Iden E Susx 11 M11
Iden Green Kent 10 K9
Iden Green Kent 11 L10
Idle C Brad 31 S1
Idless Cnwll 1 T10
Idlicote Warwks 16 B3
Idmiston Wilts 8 D5
Idole Carmth 13 M7
Idridgehay Derbys 31 U16
Idrigill Highld 59 d6
Idstone Oxon 16 B13
Iffley Oxon 16 E9
Ifield W Susx 10 C9
Ifold W Susx 9 R6
Iford Bmouth 8 C13
Iford E Susx 10 E14
Ifton Mons 14 J12
Ightfield Shrops 22 F2
Ightham Kent 10 H6
Ilam Staffs 31 R16
Ilchester Somset 6 K7
Ilderton Nthumb 47 P13
Ilford Gt Lon 18 D15
Ilford Somset 6 H8
Ilfracombe Devon 4 K3
Ilkeston Derbys 24 D2
Ilketshall St Andrew Suffk 27 S11
Ilketshall St Margaret Suffk 27 S11
Ilkley C Brad 36 D15
Illand Cnwll 2 G3
Illey Dudley 23 L12
Illogan Cnwll 1 R11
Illston on the Hill Leics 24 G9
Ilmer Bucks 16 J9
Ilmington Warwks 15 U3
Ilminster Somset 6 H8
Ilsington Devon 3 P3
Ilston Swans 13 P12
Ilton N York 36 E10
Ilton Somset 6 H8
Imachar N Ayrs 43 L10
Immingham NE Lin 33 P5
Immingham Dock NE Lin 33 P5
Impington Cambs 18 D3
Ince Ches W 30 G11
Ince Blundell Sefton 30 E7
Ince-in-Makerfield Wigan 30 J7
Inchbae Lodge Hotel Highld 53 N3
Inchbare Angus 51 Q5
Inchberry Moray 54 H6
Incheril Highld 52 H4
Inchinnan Rens 44 E5
Inchlaggan Highld 52 K14
Inchmichael P & K 50 K12
Inchnacardoch Hotel Highld 53 N13
Inchnadamph Highld 56 K10
Inchture P & K 50 K11
Inchvuilt Highld 53 L8
Inchyra P & K 50 J12
Indian Queens Cnwll 1 U8
Ingatestone Essex 18 G13
Ingbirchworth Barns 31 T7
Ingestre Staffs 23 L5
Ingham Lincs 33 L10
Ingham Norfk 27 T4
Ingham Suffk 26 K14
Ingham Corner Norfk 27 T4
Ingleby Derbys 23 R4
Ingleby Arncliffe N York 36 J7
Ingleby Barwick S on T 36 J4
Ingleby Greenhow N York 36 K6
Ingleigh Green Devon 5 L9
Inglesbatch BaNES 15 M16
Inglesham Swindn 15 U10
Ingleston D & G 39 R8
Ingleton Dur 36 E3
Ingleton N York 35 R11
Inglewhite Lancs 30 H1
Ingoe Nthumb 41 L6
Ingol Lancs 30 H2
Ingoldisthorpe Norfk 26 H3
Ingoldmells Lincs 33 U13
Ingoldsby Lincs 25 L4
Ingram Nthumb 47 P14
Ingrave Essex 18 G15
Ingrow C Brad 31 Q1
Ings Cumb 35 M7
Ingst S Glos 14 K12
Ingthorpe Rutlnd 25 L7
Ingworth Norfk 27 Q4
Inkberrow Worcs 23 M16
Inkhorn Abers 55 S8
Inkpen W Berk 16 C16
Inkstack Highld 58 G2
Innellan Ag & B 43 Q5
Innerleithen Border 45 S11
Innerleven Fife 51 M16
Innermessan D & G 38 C8
Innerwick E Loth 46 K4
Innesmill Moray 54 H4
Insch Abers 55 N10
Insh Highld 53 U14
Inskip Lancs 30 G1
Instow Devon 4 K6
Intake Sheff 32 C10
Inver Abers 54 G16
Inver Highld 54 B1
Inver P & K 50 G9
Inverailort Highld 48 H2
Inveralligin Highld 52 E5
Inverallochy Abers 55 T4
Inveran Highld 57 P14
Inveraray Ag & B 49 N14
Inverarish Highld 59 g10
Inverarity Angus 51 N8
Inverarnan Stirlg 49 R13
Inverasdale Highld 56 D16
Inverbeg Ag & B 49 S16
Inverbervie Abers 51 T4
Inverboyndie Abers 55 N4
Invercreran House Hotel Ag & B 49 M8
Inverdruie Highld 54 B13
Inveresk E Loth 46 D5
Inveresragan Ag & B 49 M10
Inverey Abers 50 H1
Inverfarigaig Highld 53 Q11
Inverfolla Ag & B 49 L8
Invergarry Highld 53 M14
Invergeldie P & K 50 C11
Invergloy Highld 49 Q1
Invergordon Highld 53 S3
Invergowrie P & K 51 L11
Inverguseran Highld 52 D13
Inverhadden P & K 50 B6
Inverherive Hotel Stirlg 49 S11
Inverie Highld 52 D15
Inverinan Ag & B 49 M13
Inverinate Highld 52 F11
Inverkeilor Angus 51 R8
Inverkeithing Fife 45 P3
Inverkeithny Abers 55 N7
Inverkip Inver 43 R5
Inverkirkaig Highld 56 G10
Inverlael Highld 56 J16
Inverlair Highld 49 R3
Inverliever Lodge Ag & B 48 K15
Inverlochy Ag & B 49 P11
Invermark Angus 51 N2
Invermoriston Highld 53 N12
Invernaver Highld 57 R4
Inverness Highld 53 S7
Inverness Airport Highld 53 T6
Invernoaden Ag & B 49 N16
Inveroran Hotel Ag & B 49 R9
Inverquharity Angus 51 M6
Inverquhomery Abers 55 T7
Inverroy Highld 49 Q2
Inversanda Highld 49 L6
Invershiel Highld 52 G11
Invershin Highld 57 P14
Invershore Highld 58 G8
Inversnaid Hotel Stirlg 49 R14
Inverugie Abers 55 U7
Inveruglas Ag & B 49 R14
Inveruglass Highld 53 U15
Inverurie Abers 55 Q11
Inwardleigh Devon 5 L11
Inworth Essex 18 K10
Iping W Susx 9 P8
iPort Logistics Park Donc 32 F8
Ipplepen Devon 3 Q5
Ipsden Oxon 16 G12
Ipstones Staffs 31 Q16
Ipswich Suffk 19 P6
Irby Wirral 29 S4
Irby in the Marsh Lincs 33 T14
Irby upon Humber NE Lin 33 P7
Irchester Nhants 24 K14
Ireby Cumb 39 U12
Ireby Lancs 35 Q11
Ireleth Cumb 34 J10
Ireshopeburn Dur 40 J12
Irlam Salfd 31 L8
Irnham Lincs 25 M4
Iron Acton S Glos 15 M13
Ironbridge Wrekin 22 G8
Ironmacannie D & G 39 L6
Ironville Derbys 32 C15
Irstead Norfk 27 S5
Irthington Cumb 40 D8
Irthlingborough Nhants 25 L14
Irton N York 37 R9
Irvine N Ayrs 43 T10
Isauld Highld 58 C3
Isbister Shet 59 q3
Isbister Shet 59 r5
Isfield E Susx 10 F12
Isham Nhants 24 K13
Isington Hants 9 M5
Islay Airport Ag & B 42 D8
Isle Abbotts Somset 6 H7
Isle Brewers Somset 6 H7
Isleham Cambs 26 G13
Isle of Dogs Gt Lon 17 S13
Isle of Man IoM 34 d4
Isle of Man Ronaldsway Airport IoM 34 c7
Isle of Sheppey Kent 11 N3
Isle of Skye Highld 59 e10
Isle of Whithorn D & G 38 J12
Isle of Wight IoW 8 J14
Isleornsay Highld 52 C13
Isles of Scilly St Mary's Airport IoS 1 b2
Islesteps D & G 39 Q6
Isleworth Gt Lon 17 P14
Isley Walton Leics 23 S5
Islibhig W Isls 56 c2
Islington Gt Lon 17 S13
Islip Nhants 25 L12
Islip Oxon 16 E8
Islivig W Isls 56 c2
Isombridge Wrekin 22 F6
Itchen Abbas Hants 8 J6
Itchen Stoke Hants 8 J6
Itchingfield W Susx 9 S7
Itteringham Norfk 27 P4
Itton Mons 14 J11
Itton Common Mons 14 J11
Ivegill Cumb 40 C11
Iver Bucks 17 N13
Iver Heath Bucks 17 M13
Iveston Dur 41 N10
Ivinghoe Bucks 17 L7
Ivinghoe Aston Bucks 17 L7
Ivington Herefs 21 S11
Ivybridge Devon 3 M7
Ivychurch Kent 11 P10
Ivy Hatch Kent 10 H6
Iwade Kent 11 M4
Iwerne Courtney Dorset 7 Q9
Iwerne Minster Dorset 7 Q8
Ixworth Suffk 27 L14
Ixworth Thorpe Suffk 27 L13

J

Jack-in-the-Green Devon 5 S11
Jackton S Lans 44 F8
Jacobstow Cnwll 4 F11
Jacobstowe Devon 5 L10
Jameston Pembks 12 G10
Jamestown Highld 53 P5
Jamestown W Duns 44 D3
Janetstown Highld 58 F8
Janetstown Highld 58 H5
Jardine Hall D & G 39 S4
Jarrow S Tyne 41 Q8
Jasper's Green Essex 18 H9
Jawcraig Falk 44 K4
Jaywick Essex 19 P11
Jedburgh Border 46 J13
Jeffreyston Pembks 12 G9
Jemimaville Highld 53 T4
Jerbourg Guern 2 d4
Jersey Jersey 3 c2
Jersey Airport Jersey 3 b2
Jesmond N u Ty 41 P7
Jevington E Susx 10 G15
Jockey End Herts 17 N8
Johnby Cumb 40 C13
John Lennon Airport Lpool 30 G10
John o' Groats Highld 58 J2
Johnshaven Abers 51 T5
Johnston Pembks 12 E8
Johnstone D & G 39 U2
Johnstone Rens 44 D6
Johnstonebridge D & G 39 S3
Johnstown Carmth 13 M7
Johnstown Wrexhm 29 S11
Joppa C Edin 45 S5
Joppa Cerdgn 20 D9
Joppa S Ayrs 44 D13
Jordanston Pembks 12 E5
Joyden's Wood Kent 10 G3
Juniper Nthumb 40 K9
Juniper Green C Edin 45 Q5
Jurby IoM 34 d2

K

Kaber Cumb 35 S5
Kaimend S Lans 45 M9
Kames Ag & B 43 N5
Kames E Ayrs 44 H12
Kea Cnwll 1 T11
Keadby N Linc 32 J6
Keal Cotes Lincs 33 R14
Kearsley Bolton 31 L7
Kearsney Kent 11 T8
Kearstwick Cumb 35 Q10
Kedington Suffk 18 H6
Kedleston Derbys 23 R2
Keelby Lincs 33 P6
Keele Staffs 22 J1
Keelham C Brad 31 R2
Keeston Pembks 12 E7
Keevil Wilts 7 R1
Kegworth Leics 24 D4
Kehelland Cnwll 1 Q11
Keig Abers 55 M11
Keighley C Brad 36 C16
Keilarsbrae Clacks 45 L1
Keillour P & K 50 F11
Keiloch Abers 54 F16
Keils Ag & B 42 F5
Keinton Mandeville Somset 6 K6
Keir Mill D & G 39 P3
Keisley Cumb 35 R3
Keiss Highld 58 H4
Keith Moray 54 K6
Keithick P & K 50 J9
Keithock Angus 51 Q5
Keithtown Highld 53 Q5
Kelbrook Lancs 35 U16
Kelby Lincs 25 L2
Keld N York 35 U7
Kelfield N York 32 F1
Kelham Notts 32 H15
Kelhead D & G 39 T7
Kellamergh Lancs 30 F3
Kellas Angus 51 N10
Kellas Moray 54 F6
Kellaton Devon 3 P9
Kelling Norfk 27 N2
Kellington N York 32 E4
Kelloe Dur 41 R12
Kelloholm D & G 44 H15
Kelly Devon 4 J14
Kelmarsh Nhants 24 H12
Kelmscott Oxon 16 B10
Kelsale Suffk 27 T14
Kelsall Ches W 30 H13
Kelshall Herts 17 S4
Kelsick Cumb 39 U10
Kelso Border 46 K11
Kelstedge Derbys 32 B14
Kelstern Lincs 33 Q9
Kelston BaNES 15 M15
Keltneyburn P & K 50 C8
Kelton D & G 39 R7
Kelty Fife 45 P1
Kelvedon Essex 18 K10
Kelvedon Hatch Essex 18 F13
Kelynack Cnwll 1 M13
Kemback Fife 51 M13
Kemberton Shrops 22 H8
Kemble Gloucs 15 R10
Kemerton Worcs 15 R4
Kemeys Commander Mons 14 G9
Kemnay Abers 55 P12
Kempley Gloucs 15 M5
Kempley Green Gloucs 15 M5
Kempsey Worcs 15 P2
Kempsford Gloucs 15 U11
Kempshott Hants 8 K3
Kempston Bed 17 N2
Kempton Shrops 21 Q7
Kemp Town Br & H 10 D14
Kemsing Kent 10 G5
Kenardington Kent 11 N10
Kenchester Herefs 21 R13
Kencot Oxon 16 B9
Kendal Cumb 35 N8
Kenfig Brdgnd 13 S13
Kenilworth Warwks 23 Q13
Kenley Gt Lon 10 D5
Kenley Shrops 22 E9
Kenmore Highld 52 D5
Kenmore P & K 50 C8
Kenn Devon 5 R13
Kenn N Som 14 H15
Kennacraig Ag & B 43 L6
Kennerleigh Devon 5 P9
Kennessee Green Sefton 30 F7
Kennet Clacks 45 L2
Kennethmont Abers 55 L10
Kennett Cambs 26 H14
Kennford Devon 5 R13
Kenninghall Norfk 27 N11
Kennington Kent 11 P7
Kennington Oxon 16 E10
Kennoway Fife 51 L15
Kenny Somset 6 G8
Kenny Hill Suffk 26 G12
Kennythorpe N York 37 N12
Kenovay Ag & B 42 b4
Kensaleyre Highld 59 e8
Kensington Gt Lon 17 R13
Kensworth Common C Beds 17 N7
Kentallen Highld 49 M6
Kentchurch Herefs 14 H6
Kentford Suffk 26 H14
Kentisbeare Devon 6 D9
Kentisbury Devon 5 M3
Kentish Town Gt Lon 17 R12
Kentmere Cumb 35 M6
Kenton Devon 5 R13
Kenton Gt Lon 17 Q12
Kenton N u Ty 41 P7
Kenton Suffk 27 Q14
Kenton Bankfoot N u Ty 41 P7
Kentra Highld 48 G4
Kent's Green Gloucs 15 N6
Kent's Oak Hants 8 F8
Kenwyn Cnwll 1 T10
Keoldale Highld 57 L3
Keppoch Highld 52 F11
Kepwick N York 36 J8
Keresley Covtry 23 R11
Kerris Cnwll 1 N13
Kerry Powys 21 M5
Kerrycroy Ag & B 43 Q6
Kersall Notts 32 G14
Kersbrook Devon 6 D13
Kersey Suffk 19 M6
Kershader W Isls 56 e3
Kerswell Devon 6 D10
Kerswell Green Worcs 15 P2
Kesgrave Suffk 19 Q6
Kessingland Suffk 27 U11
Kestle Cnwll 2 C8
Kestle Mill Cnwll 1 T8
Keston Gt Lon 10 E4
Keswick Cumb 34 K3
Keswick Norfk 27 Q8
Kettering Nhants 24 J12
Ketteringham Norfk 27 P8
Kettins P & K 50 K9
Kettlebaston Suffk 19 M5
Kettlebridge Fife 51 L14
Kettlebrook Staffs 23 P8
Kettleburgh Suffk 19 R3
Kettleholm D & G 39 T6
Kettleshulme Ches E 31 P11
Kettlesing N York 36 E14
Kettlesing Bottom N York 36 E14
Kettlestone Norfk 27 M3
Kettlethorpe Lincs 32 J12
Kettletoft Ork 58 d2
Kettlewell N York 36 B11
Ketton Rutlnd 25 L8
Kew Gt Lon 17 Q14
Kewstoke N Som 14 G16
Kexby C York 37 M15
Kexby Lincs 32 K10
Key Green Ches E 31 N14
Keyham Leics 24 G8
Keyhaven Hants 8 F13
Keyingham E R Yk 33 Q3
Keymer W Susx 10 D12
Keynsham BaNES 15 L15
Keysoe Bed 25 M15
Keysoe Row Bed 25 M15
Keyston Cambs 25 M13
Keyworth Notts 24 F4
Kibblesworth Gatesd 41 P9
Kibworth Beauchamp Leics 24 G10
Kibworth Harcourt Leics 24 G10
Kidbrooke Gt Lon 10 E2
Kidderminster Worcs 22 J13
Kidlington Oxon 16 E8
Kidmore End Oxon 16 H13
Kidsdale D & G 38 H12
Kidsgrove Staffs 31 M15
Kidwelly Carmth 13 M9
Kiel Crofts Ag & B 48 K9
Kielder Nthumb 40 F3
Kiells Ag & B 42 E5
Kilbarchan Rens 44 D6
Kilbeg Highld 52 C14
Kilberry Ag & B 42 J6
Kilbirnie N Ayrs 43 S8
Kilbride Ag & B 42 J3
Kilbride Ag & B 43 P5
Kilbuiack Moray 54 E5
Kilburn Derbys 23 S1
Kilburn Gt Lon 17 R13
Kilburn N York 36 J10
Kilby Leics 24 F9
Kilchamaig Ag & B 42 K7
Kilchattan Ag & B 42 D1
Kilchattan Ag & B 43 P8
Kilcheran Ag & B 48 J9
Kilchoan Highld 48 E5
Kilchoman Ag & B 42 B6
Kilchrenan Ag & B 49 M12
Kilconquhar Fife 51 N15
Kilcot Gloucs 15 M6
Kilcoy Highld 53 R6
Kilcreggan Ag & B 43 R3
Kildale N York 37 L5
Kildalloig Ag & B 42 K13
Kildary Highld 53 T2
Kildavaig Ag & B 43 N6
Kildavanan Ag & B 43 N6
Kildonan Highld 58 B10
Kildonan N Ayrs 43 P13
Kildonan Lodge Highld 58 B10
Kildonnan Highld 48 E2
Kildrochet House D & G 38 C9
Kildrummy Abers 54 K12
Kildwick N York 36 B16
Kilfinan Ag & B 43 M4
Kilfinnan Highld 53 L15
Kilgetty Pembks 12 H9
Kilgrammie S Ayrs 38 E2
Kilgwrrwg Common Mons 14 J10
Kilham E R Yk 37 S13
Kilkenneth Ag & B 42 a4
Kilkenzie Ag & B 42 H12
Kilkerran Ag & B 42 J13
Kilkhampton Cnwll 4 G9
Killamarsh Derbys 32 D11
Killay Swans 13 Q11
Killearn Stirlg 44 E2
Killen Highld 53 S5
Killerby Darltn 36 E3
Killerton Devon 5 S11
Killichonan P & K 49 U6
Killiechonate Highld 49 Q2
Killiechronan Ag & B 48 E9
Killiecrankie P & K 50 E5
Killilan Highld 52 G10
Killimster Highld 58 H4
Killin Stirlg 49 V10
Killinghall N York 36 F14
Killington Cumb 35 Q9
Killingworth N Tyne 41 Q7
Killochyett Border 46 F9
Kilmacolm Inver 44 C5
Kilmahog Stirlg 50 A14
Kilmahumaig Ag & B 42 K1
Kilmaluag Highld 59 e5
Kilmany Fife 51 M12
Kilmarnock E Ayrs 44 D10
Kilmartin Ag & B 48 J16
Kilmaurs E Ayrs 44 D10
Kilmelford Ag & B 48 K14
Kilmersdon Somset 7 N2
Kilmeston Hants 8 K7
Kilmichael Ag & B 42 J13
Kilmichael Glassary Ag & B 43 L1
Kilmichael of Inverlussa Ag & B 42 K2
Kilmington Devon 6 G11
Kilmington Wilts 7 P5
Kilmington Common Wilts 7 P5
Kilmington Street Wilts 7 P5
Kilmorack Highld 53 P7
Kilmore Ag & B 48 K11
Kilmore Highld 52 C13
Kilmory Ag & B 42 J4
Kilmory Highld 48 E4
Kilmory N Ayrs 43 N13
Kilmuir Highld 53 S6
Kilmuir Highld 53 T3
Kilmuir Highld 59 c9
Kilmuir Highld 59 d5
Kilmun Ag & B 43 R3
Kilnave Ag & B 42 C5
Kilncadzow S Lans 45 L9
Kilndown Kent 10 J9
Kilninver Ag & B 48 J12
Kilnsea E R Yk 33 S5
Kilnsey N York 36 B12
Kilnwick E R Yk 37 R15
Kiloran Ag & B 48 C16
Kilpatrick N Ayrs 43 M12
Kilpeck Herefs 14 J5
Kilpin E R Yk 32 H3
Kilrenny Fife 51 Q15
Kilsby Nhants 24 E13
Kilspindie P & K 50 K11
Kilstay D & G 38 D12
Kilsyth N Lans 44 H4
Kiltarlity Highld 53 Q8
Kilton R & Cl 37 M4
Kilton Thorpe R & Cl 37 M4
Kilvaxter Highld 59 d6
Kilve Somset 6 E4
Kilvington Notts 24 H2
Kilwinning N Ayrs 43 S9
Kimberley Norfk 27 N8
Kimberley Notts 24 D1
Kimberworth Rothm 32 C9
Kimblesworth Dur 41 P11
Kimbolton Cambs 25 N14
Kimbolton Herefs 22 E15
Kimcote Leics 24 E11
Kimmeridge Dorset 7 R14
Kimpton Hants 8 E4
Kimpton Herts 17 Q7
Kinbrace Highld 57 T8
Kinbuck Stirlg 50 D15
Kincaple Fife 51 N13
Kincardine Fife 45 L2
Kincardine Highld 57 Q15
Kincardine Bridge Fife 45 L2
Kincardine O'Neil Abers 55 M15
Kinclaven P & K 50 J9
Kincorth C Aber 55 S14
Kincorth House Moray 54 D5
Kincraig Highld 53 U14
Kincraigie P & K 50 F8
Kindallachan P & K 50 F7
Kinerarach Ag & B 42 H8
Kineton Gloucs 15 T6
Kineton Warwks 16 C2
Kinfauns P & K 50 J12
Kingarth Ag & B 43 P7
Kingcausie Abers 55 R15
Kingcoed Mons 14 H9
Kingerby Lincs 33 M9
Kingham Oxon 16 B6
Kingholm Quay D & G 39 R6
Kinghorn Fife 45 R2
Kinglassie Fife 50 K16
Kingoldrum Angus 51 L7
Kingoodie P & K 51 L11
Kingsand Cnwll 2 J8
Kingsbarns Fife 51 Q14
Kingsbridge Devon 3 N9
Kingsbridge Somset 5 S4
King's Bromley Staffs 23 N6
Kingsburgh Highld 59 e7
Kingsbury Gt Lon 17 Q12
Kingsbury Warwks 23 P9
Kingsbury Episcopi Somset 6 J7
King's Caple Herefs 14 K5
Kingsclere Hants 8 J2
King's Cliffe Nhants 25 L9
Kings Clipstone Notts 32 F13
Kingscote Gloucs 15 P11
Kingscott Devon 5 L8
King's Coughton Warwks 23 N15
Kingscross N Ayrs 43 P12
Kingsdon Somset 6 K6
Kingsdown Kent 11 U7
Kingsdown Swindn 15 U12
Kingsdown Wilts 15 P15
Kingseat Fife 45 P2
Kingsey Bucks 16 H9
Kingsfold W Susx 9 T6
Kingsford C Aber 55 R14
Kingsford E Ayrs 44 D9
Kingsgate Kent 11 U3
Kingshall Street Suffk 19 L3
King's Heath Birm 23 M12
Kings Hill Kent 10 J6
King's Hill Wsall 23 L9
Kings House Hotel Highld 49 Q7
Kingshouse Hotel Stirlg 49 V12
Kingshurst Solhll 23 P11
Kingskerswell Devon 3 Q5
Kingskettle Fife 51 L14
Kingsland Herefs 21 S10
Kingsland IoA 28 C5
Kings Langley Herts 17 N9
Kingsley Ches W 30 H12
Kingsley Hants 9 N5
Kingsley Staffs 23 M1
Kingsley Green W Susx 9 P7
Kingsley Park Nhants 24 H15
King's Lynn Norfk 26 G5
Kings Meaburn Cumb 35 Q3
King's Mills Guern 2 c3
Kingsmuir Angus 51 N8
Kings Muir Border 45 R10
Kingsmuir Fife 51 P14
Kingsnorth Kent 11 P8
King's Norton Birm 23 M12
King's Norton Leics 24 G9
Kings Nympton Devon 5 N7
King's Pyon Herefs 21 S12
Kings Ripton Cambs 25 Q13
King's Somborne Hants 8 G6
King's Stag Dorset 7 N9
King's Stanley Gloucs 15 P9
King's Sutton Nhants 16 E4
Kingstanding Birm 23 M10
Kingsteignton Devon 3 Q4
Kingsthorne Herefs 14 J5
Kingsthorpe Nhants 24 H15
Kingston Cambs 25 R16
Kingston Cnwll 2 H3
Kingston Devon 3 M8
Kingston Dorset 7 N9
Kingston Dorset 7 R14
Kingston E Loth 46 G3
Kingston IoW 8 H15
Kingston Kent 11 R6
Kingston Bagpuize Oxon 16 D10
Kingston Blount Oxon 16 H10
Kingston Deverill Wilts 7 Q5
Kingstone Herefs 14 H4
Kingstone Somset 6 H8
Kingstone Staffs 23 M4
Kingston Lisle Oxon 16 C12
Kingston near Lewes E Susx 10 E13
Kingston on Soar Notts 24 D4
Kingston on Spey Moray 54 H4
Kingston Russell Dorset 7 L12
Kingston St Mary Somset 6 F6
Kingston Seymour N Som 14 H15
Kingston upon Hull C KuH 33 N3
Kingston upon Thames Gt Lon 17 Q15
King's Walden Herts 17 P6
Kingswear Devon 3 Q7
Kingswells C Aber 55 R14
Kings Weston Bristl 14 K14
Kingswinford Dudley 22 K11
Kingswood Bucks 16 H7
Kingswood Gloucs 15 N11
Kingswood S Glos 15 L14
Kingswood Somset 6 D4
Kingswood Surrey 10 C6
Kingswood Warwks 23 P13
Kingswood Common Staffs 22 J8
Kings Worthy Hants 8 H6
Kingthorpe Lincs 33 N12
Kington Herefs 21 P11
Kington S Glos 15 L11
Kington Worcs 23 L16
Kington Langley Wilts 15 Q14
Kington Magna Dorset 7 P7
Kington St Michael Wilts 15 Q14
Kingussie Highld 53 T14
Kingweston Somset 6 K6
Kinharrachie Abers 55 S10
Kinharvie D & G 39 Q7
Kinkell Bridge P & K 50 F13
Kinknockie Abers 55 T8
Kinleith C Edin 45 Q6
Kinlet Shrops 22 G12
Kinloch Highld 57 L8
Kinloch Highld 57 P5
Kinloch Highld 59 e15
Kinloch P & K 50 J8
Kinlochard Stirlg 49 T15
Kinlochbervie Highld 56 J4
Kinlocheil Highld 49 L3
Kinlochewe Highld 52 H4
Kinloch Hourn Highld 52 G13
Kinlochlaggan Highld 49 U1
Kinlochleven Highld 49 P6
Kinlochmoidart Highld 48 H4
Kinlochnanuagh Highld 48 H2
Kinloch Rannoch P & K 50 B6
Kinloss Moray 54 E4
Kinmel Bay Conwy 29 N5
Kinmuck Abers 55 Q11
Kinmundy Abers 55 R12
Kinnabus Ag & B 42 C10
Kinnadie Abers 55 S8
Kinnaird P & K 50 F6
Kinneff Abers 51 T3
Kinnelhead D & G 39 R2
Kinnell Angus 51 Q7
Kinnerley Shrops 29 T15
Kinnersley Herefs 21 Q12
Kinnersley Worcs 15 Q3
Kinnerton Powys 21 P10
Kinnesswood P & K 50 J15
Kinnordy Angus 51 M7
Kinoulton Notts 24 G4
Kinross P & K 50 H15
Kinrossie P & K 50 J10
Kinsham Herefs 21 Q10
Kinsham Worcs 15 Q4
Kinsley Wakefd 32 C5
Kinson Bmouth 7 T11
Kintbury W Berk 16 C15
Kintessack Moray 54 D5
Kintillo P & K 50 H13
Kinton Herefs 21 R8
Kinton Shrops 29 T15
Kintore Abers 55 Q12
Kintour Ag & B 42 E8
Kintra Ag & B 42 D9
Kintra Ag & B 48 B12
Kintraw Ag & B 48 J15
Kinveachy Highld 54 B12
Kinver Staffs 22 J11
Kippax Leeds 32 C3
Kippen Stirlg 44 G1
Kippford D & G 39 P9
Kipping's Cross Kent 10 J8
Kirbister Ork 58 b4
Kirby Bedon Norfk 27 R8
Kirby Bellars Leics 24 G6
Kirby Cane Norfk 27 S10
Kirby Cross Essex 19 Q10
Kirby Grindalythe N York 37 Q12
Kirby Hill N York 36 D6
Kirby Hill N York 36 H12
Kirby Knowle N York 36 J9
Kirby-le-Soken Essex 19 Q10
Kirby Misperton N York 37 N10
Kirby Muxloe Leics 24 E8
Kirby Underdale E R Yk 37 P14
Kirby Wiske N York 36 H9
Kirdford W Susx 9 R7
Kirk Highld 58 G4
Kirkabister Shet 59 q6
Kirkandrews D & G 38 K10
Kirkandrews upon Eden Cumb 40 B9
Kirkbampton Cumb 40 A9
Kirkbean D & G 39 R9
Kirk Bramwith Donc 32 F6
Kirkbride Cumb 39 U9
Kirkbuddo Angus 51 P9
Kirkburn Border 45 R10
Kirkburn E R Yk 37 R14
Kirkburton Kirk 31 S6
Kirkby Knows 30 F8
Kirkby Lincs 33 M9
Kirkby N York 36 K6
Kirkby Fleetham N York 36 F8
Kirkby Green Lincs 33 N15
Kirkby-in-Ashfield Notts 32 D15
Kirkby-in-Furness Cumb 34 J10
Kirkby la Thorpe Lincs 25 N1
Kirkby Lonsdale Cumb 35 Q10
Kirkby Malham N York 35 U13
Kirkby Mallory Leics 24 D9
Kirkby Malzeard N York 36 F11
Kirkbymoorside N York 37 M9
Kirkby on Bain Lincs 33 Q14
Kirkby Overblow N York 36 G15
Kirkby Stephen Cumb 35 S5
Kirkby Thore Cumb 40 F14
Kirkby Underwood Lincs 25 M4
Kirkby Wharf N York 32 D1
Kirkcaldy Fife 45 R1
Kirkcambeck Cumb 40 D7
Kirkchrist D & G 39 L10
Kirkcolm D & G 38 B7
Kirkconnel D & G 44 H15
Kirkconnell D & G 39 R7
Kirkcowan D & G 38 F8
Kirkcudbright D & G 39 L10
Kirkdale Lpool 30 E9
Kirk Deighton N York 36 H15
Kirk Ella E R Yk 33 M3
Kirkfieldbank S Lans 44 K9
Kirkgunzeon D & G 39 P7
Kirk Hallam Derbys 24 D2
Kirkham Lancs 30 F2
Kirkham N York 37 N12
Kirkhamgate Wakefd 31 U4
Kirk Hammerton N York 36 J14
Kirkhaugh Nthumb 40 G10
Kirkheaton Kirk 31 S5
Kirkheaton Nthumb 41 L6
Kirkhill Highld 53 Q7
Kirkhope S Lans 45 M16
Kirkibost Highld 59 g12
Kirkinch P & K 51 L8
Kirkinner D & G 38 H10
Kirkintilloch E Duns 44 G4
Kirk Ireton Derbys 31 T16
Kirkland Cumb 34 G4
Kirkland D & G 39 N3
Kirkland D & G 39 R4
Kirkland D & G 44 H14
Kirk Langley Derbys 23 Q2
Kirkleatham R & Cl 37 L3
Kirklevington S on T 36 H5
Kirkley Suffk 27 V10
Kirklington N York 36 G10
Kirklington Notts 32 G15
Kirklinton Cumb 40 C7
Kirkliston C Edin 45 P4
Kirkmabreck D & G 38 J9
Kirkmaiden D & G 38 D12
Kirk Merrington Dur 41 Q13
Kirk Michael IoM 34 C4
Kirkmichael P & K 50 H6
Kirkmichael S Ayrs 43 T15
Kirkmuirhill S Lans 44 J10
Kirknewton Nthumb 47 M12
Kirknewton W Loth 45 P6
Kirkney Abers 55 L9
Kirk of Shotts N Lans 44 K6
Kirkoswald Cumb 40 E12
Kirkoswald S Ayrs 43 R15
Kirkpatrick D & G 39 Q3
Kirkpatrick Durham D & G 39 N7
Kirkpatrick-Fleming D & G 39 V7
Kirk Sandall Donc 32 F6
Kirksanton Cumb 34 H10
Kirk Smeaton N York 32 E5
Kirkstall Leeds 31 T2
Kirkstead Lincs 33 P14
Kirkstile Abers 55 L9
Kirkstile D & G 40 B3
Kirkstyle Highld 58 H2
Kirkthorpe Wakefd 32 B4
Kirkton Abers 55 N10
Kirkton D & G 39 R5
Kirkton Fife 51 M12
Kirkton Highld 52 E10
Kirkton Highld 52 F8
Kirkton P & K 50 F13
Kirkton Manor Border 45 Q10
Kirkton of Airlie Angus 51 L7
Kirkton of Auchterhouse Angus 51 L9
Kirkton of Barevan Highld 53 U7
Kirkton of Collace P & K 50 J10
Kirkton of Glenbuchat Abers 54 J12
Kirkton of Logie Buchan Abers 55 T10
Kirkton of Maryculter Abers 55 R15
Kirkton of Menmuir Angus 51 P5
Kirkton of Monikie Angus 51 P9
Kirkton of Rayne Abers 55 N10
Kirkton of Skene Abers 55 Q13
Kirkton of Strathmartine Angus 51 M10
Kirkton of Tealing Angus 51 M9
Kirkton of Tough Abers 55 M12
Kirktown Abers 55 T4
Kirktown Abers 55 U6
Kirktown of Alvah Abers 55 N5
Kirktown of Bourtie Abers 55 Q10
Kirktown of Fetteresso Abers 51 T2
Kirktown of Mortlach Moray 54 H8
Kirktown of Slains Abers 55 T10
Kirkurd Border 45 P9
Kirkwall Ork 58 c4
Kirkwall Airport Ork 58 c4
Kirkwhelpington Nthumb 41 L4
Kirk Yetholm Border 47 L12
Kirmington N Linc 33 N6
Kirmond le Mire Lincs 33 P9
Kirn Ag & B 43 R4
Kirriemuir Angus 51 M7
Kirstead Green Norfk 27 R9
Kirtlebridge D & G 39 U6
Kirtling Cambs 18 H4
Kirtling Green Cambs 18 H4
Kirtlington Oxon 16 E7
Kirtomy Highld 57 S3
Kirton Lincs 25 R2
Kirton Notts 32 G13
Kirton Suffk 19 R7
Kirtonhill W Duns 44 D4
Kirton in Lindsey N Linc 32 K8
Kirwaugh D & G 38 H9
Kishorn Highld 52 E8
Kislingbury Nhants 24 G15
Kittisford Somset 6 D7
Kitt's Green Birm 23 P11
Kittybrewster C Aber 55 S13
Kivernoll Herefs 14 J5
Kiveton Park Rothm 32 D10
Knaith Lincs 32 J10
Knap Corner Dorset 7 P7
Knaphill Surrey 9 Q2
Knapp Somset 6 G6
Knapton C York 36 K15
Knapton N York 37 Q11
Knapton Norfk 27 R3
Knapwell Cambs 25 R15
Knaresborough N York 36 G14
Knarsdale Nthumb 40 F9
Knaven Abers 55 R8
Knayton N York 36 H9
Knebworth Herts 17 R7
Knedlington E R Yk 32 H3
Kneesall Notts 32 G13
Kneeton Notts 24 G1
Knelston Swans 13 N12
Knenhall Staffs 22 K3
Knightcote Warwks 16 D1
Knightley Staffs 22 J5
Knighton C Leic 24 F9
Knighton Dorset 7 L9
Knighton Powys 21 P8
Knighton Somset 6 E3
Knighton Staffs 22 H2
Knighton Staffs 22 H4
Knighton on Teme Worcs 22 F14
Knightwick Worcs 22 H16
Knill Herefs 21 P10
Knipton Leics 24 J4
Kniveton Derbys 31 S16
Knock Cumb 40 F14
Knock Highld 52 C13
Knock Moray 55 L6
Knock W Isls 56 f2
Knockally Highld 58 F9
Knockan Highld 56 J12
Knockando Moray 54 F8
Knockbain Highld 53 Q8
Knockbain Highld 53 R5
Knock Castle N Ayrs 43 R6
Knockdee Highld 58 F4
Knockdow Ag & B 43 Q5
Knockdown Wilts 15 P12
Knockeen S Ayrs 38 F3
Knockenkelly N Ayrs 43 P12
Knockentiber E Ayrs 44 D10
Knockholt Kent 10 F5
Knockholt Pound Kent 10 F5
Knockin Shrops 29 T14
Knockinlaw E Ayrs 44 D10
Knocknain D & G 38 A8
Knockrome Ag & B 42 G5
Knocksharry IoM 34 c4
Knocksheen D & G 38 K5
Knockvennie Smithy D & G 39 N7
Knodishall Suffk 19 T3
Knodishall Common Suffk 19 T3
Knole Somset 6 K7
Knolls Green Ches E 31 M11
Knolton Wrexhm 22 C2
Knook Wilts 7 R4
Knossington Leics 24 J7
Knott End-on-Sea Lancs 35 L15
Knotting Bed 25 L15
Knotting Green Bed 25 L15
Knottingley Wakefd 32 D4
Knotty Ash Lpool 30 F9
Knowbury Shrops 22 E13
Knowe D & G 38 F7
Knowehead D & G 38 K3
Knoweside S Ayrs 43 S14
Knowle Bristl 15 L15
Knowle Devon 4 K4
Knowle Devon 5 P10
Knowle Devon 5 S9
Knowle Devon 6 D13
Knowle Shrops 22 F13
Knowle Solhll 23 P13
Knowle Somset 5 R4
Knowlefield Cumb 40 B9
Knowle Green Lancs 30 J1
Knowle St Giles Somset 6 H9
Knowl Hill W & M 16 K13
Knowsley Knows 30 G8
Knowstone Devon 5 Q7
Knox Bridge Kent 11 L8
Knucklas Powys 21 P8
Knuston Nhants 24 K14
Knutsford Ches E 31 L11
Krumlin Calder 31 Q5
Kuggar Cnwll 1 R15
Kyleakin Highld 52 D10
Kyle of Lochalsh Highld 52 D10
Kylerhea Highld 52 D11
Kylesku Highld 56 J8
Kylesmorar Highld 52 E16
Kyles Scalpay W Isls 56 d4
Kylestrome Highld 56 J8
Kynnersley Wrekin 22 G6
Kyrewood Worcs 22 F14

L

Lacasaigh W Isls 56 e3
Lacasdal W Isls 56 f2
Laceby NE Lin 33 P7
Lacey Green Bucks 16 K10
Lach Dennis Ches W 30 K12
Lackford Suffk 26 J14
Lackford Green Suffk 26 J13
Lacock Wilts 15 Q15
Ladbroke Warwks 23 S15
Laddingford Kent 10 J7
Ladock Cnwll 1 U9
Lady Ork 58 d2
Ladybank Fife 51 L14
Ladygill S Lans 45 L12
Lady Hall Cumb 34 J9
Ladykirk Border 47 M9
Ladywood Birm 23 M11
Ladywood Worcs 22 K15
La Fontenelle Guern 2 e1
Lag D & G 39 P4
Laga Highld 48 G6
Lagavulin Ag & B 42 E9
Lagg N Ayrs 43 M13
Laggan Highld 53 M15
Laggan Highld 53 R16
Lagganlia Highld 54 B14
La Grève de Lecq Jersey 3 b1
Laid Highld 57 M4
Laide Highld 56 E15
Laig Highld 48 D1
Laigh Clunch E Ayrs 44 E9
Laigh Fenwick E Ayrs 44 E10
Laigh Glenmuir E Ayrs 44 G13
Laighstonehall S Lans 44 H8
Laindon Essex 18 H15
Lairg Highld 57 P12
Laisterdyke C Brad 31 S2
Lake IoW 8 K14
Lake Wilts 8 C5
Lakenheath Suffk 26 H12
Lakesend Norfk 26 E9
Laleston Brdgnd 13 T13
Lamarsh Essex 19 L7
Lamas Norfk 27 R5
Lambden Border 46 K9
Lamberhurst Kent 10 J9
Lamberhurst Down Kent 10 J9
Lamberton Border 47 N7
Lambeth Gt Lon 17 R13
Lambfair Green Suffk 18 H4
Lambley Notts 24 F1
Lambley Nthumb 40 F9
Lambourn W Berk 16 C13
Lambourne End Essex 18 E14
Lambs Green W Susx 10 C9
Lamerton Devon 2 J3
Lamesley Gatesd 41 P9
Lamington S Lans 45 M11
Lamlash N Ayrs 43 N11
Lamonby Cumb 40 C12
Lamorna Cnwll 1 N14
Lamorran Cnwll 1 U11
Lampeter Cerdgn 20 D12
Lampeter Velfrey Pembks 12 H8
Lamphey Pembks 12 F10
Lamplugh Cumb 34 G3
Lamport Nhants 24 H13
Lamyatt Somset 7 M5
Lanark S Lans 44 K9
Lancaster Lancs 35 N13
Lanchester Dur 41 N11
Lancing W Susx 9 T11
L'Ancresse Guern 2 d1
Landbeach Cambs 26 E14
Landcross Devon 4 J7
Landerberry Abers 55 P14
Landford Wilts 8 E8
Land-hallow Highld 58 F8
Landimore Swans 13 N11
Landkey Devon 5 L6
Landore Swans 13 Q11
Landrake Cnwll 2 H6
Land's End Airport Cnwll 1 M13
Landulph Cnwll 2 J6
Lane Cnwll 1 T8
Laneast Cnwll 4 F13
Lane End Bucks 16 J11
Lane End Wilts 7 P3
Lane Ends Derbys 23 Q3
Laneham Notts 32 J11
Lane Head Dur 36 D5
Lanehead Dur 40 J11
Lane Head Wsall 23 L9
Langaller Somset 6 G6
Langar Notts 24 G3
Langbank Rens 44 C5
Langbar N York 36 D15
Langcliffe N York 35 T12
Langdale End N York 37 Q8
Langdown Hants 8 G10
Langdyke Fife 51 L15
Langenhoe Essex 19 M10
Langford C Beds 17 Q3
Langford Devon 5 S10
Langford Essex 18 K12
Langford Notts 32 J14
Langford Oxon 16 B9
Langford Budville Somset 6 D7
Langham Essex 19 M8
Langham Norfk 27 M2
Langham Rutlnd 24 J7
Langham Suffk 27 M14
Langho Lancs 30 K2
Langholm D & G 40 B4
Langlee Border 46 G11
Langley Hants 8 H11
Langley Herts 17 Q6
Langley Kent 11 L6
Langley Nthumb 40 H8
Langley Slough 17 M13
Langley Somset 6 D6
Langley W Susx 9 N7
Langley Warwks 23 P15
Langley Burrell Wilts 15 Q14
Langley Green Essex 18 K10
Langley Marsh Somset 6 D6
Langley Park Dur 41 P11
Langley Street Norfk 27 S8
Langley Upper Green Essex 18 D8
Langney E Susx 10 H14
Langold Notts 32 E10
Langore Cnwll 4 G13
Langport Somset 6 J6
Langrick Lincs 33 Q16
Langridge BaNES 15 N15
Langrigg Cumb 39 T11
Langrish Hants 9 L8
Langsett Barns 31 T8
Langside P & K 50 D13
Langstone Hants 9 M11
Langthorne N York 36 F8
Langthorpe N York 36 H12
Langthwaite N York 36 B6
Langtoft E R Yk 37 R12
Langtoft Lincs 25 N7
Langton Dur 36 E4
Langton Lincs 33 Q13
Langton Lincs 33 S12
Langton N York 37 N12
Langton by Wragby Lincs 33 N11
Langton Green Kent 10 G8
Langton Herring Dorset 7 L14
Langton Matravers Dorset 7 S14
Langtree Devon 4 J8
Langwathby Cumb 40 E13
Langwell House Highld 58 E10
Langwith Derbys 32 E13
Langwith Junction Derbys 32 E13
Langworth Lincs 33 M11
Lanivet Cnwll 2 D5
Lanlivery Cnwll 2 D6
Lanner Cnwll 1 R11
Lanreath Cnwll 2 E7
Lansallos Cnwll 2 E7
Lanteglos Cnwll 4 D14
Lanteglos Highway Cnwll 2 E7
Lanton Border 46 H13
Lanton Nthumb 47 N11
Lapford Devon 5 N9
Laphroaig Ag & B 42 D9
Lapley Staffs 22 K7
Lapworth Warwks 23 P13
Larachbeg Highld 48 G8
Larbert Falk 44 K3
Largie Abers 55 M9
Largiemore Ag & B 43 M2
Largoward Fife 51 N14
Largs N Ayrs 43 R7
Largybeg N Ayrs 43 P13
Largymore N Ayrs 43 P13
Larkfield Inver 43 R4
Larkfield Kent 10 J5
Larkhall S Lans 44 J8
Larkhill Wilts 8 C4
Larling Norfk 27 M11
La Rocque Jersey 3 e4
Lartington Dur 36 B4
Lasham Hants 9 L5
Lasswade Mdloth 45 R6
Lastingham N York 37 M8
Latchford Warrtn 30 J10
Latchingdon Essex 18 K13
Latchley Cnwll 2 J4
Lathbury M Keyn 16 K3
Latheron Highld 58 F8
Latheronwheel Highld 58 F8
Lathones Fife 51 N14
Latimer Bucks 17 M10
Latteridge S Glos 15 M12
Lattiford Somset 7 N6
Latton Wilts 15 T11
Lauder Border 46 G9
Laugharne Carmth 12 K8
Laughterton Lincs 32 J12
Laughton E Susx 10 F13
Laughton Leics 24 G11
Laughton Lincs 25 M4
Laughton Lincs 32 J8
Laughton-en-le-Morthen Rothm 32 E10
Launcells Cnwll 4 F10
Launceston Cnwll 4 H13
Launton Oxon 16 G6
Laurencekirk Abers 51 S4
Laurieston D & G 39 L8
Laurieston Falk 45 L4
Lavendon M Keyn 17 L1
Lavenham Suffk 19 L5
Lavernock V Glam 14 E15
Laversdale Cumb 40 D8
Laverstock Wilts 8 D7
Laverstoke Hants 8 H4
Laverton Gloucs 15 S4
Laverton N York 36 E11
Laverton Somset 7 P2
La Villette Guern 2 d3
Lavister Wrexhm 30 F14
Law S Lans 44 K8
Lawers P & K 50 B9
Lawford Essex 19 N8
Lawford Somset 6 E5
Law Hill S Lans 44 K8
Lawhitton Cnwll 4 H14
Lawkland N York 35 S12
Lawrenny Pembks 12 F9
Lawshall Suffk 18 K4
Laxay W Isls 56 e3
Laxdale W Isls 56 f2
Laxey IoM 34 e5
Laxfield Suffk 27 R13
Laxford Bridge Highld 56 J6
Laxo Shet 59 q5
Laxton E R Yk 32 H3
Laxton Nhants 25 L9
Laxton Notts 32 G13
Laycock C Brad 31 Q1
Layer Breton Essex 19 L10
Layer-de-la-Haye Essex 19 M10
Layer Marney Essex 19 L10
Layham Suffk 19 M7
Laymore Dorset 6 H10
Laytham E R Yk 32 H1
Lazonby Cumb 40 E12
Lea Derbys 31 U15
Lea Herefs 15 L6
Lea Lincs 32 J10
Lea Shrops 21 Q6
Lea Wilts 15 R12
Leachkin Highld 53 R7
Leadburn Border 45 Q7

March – North Brentor 71

March S Lans 45 M14
Marcham Oxon 16 D10
Marchamley Shrops 22 F4
Marchington Staffs 23 N4
Marchros Gwynd 28 D14
Marchwiel Wrexhm 29 T10
Marchwood Hants 8 G10
Marcross V Glam 13 U15
Marden Herefs 14 K2
Marden Kent 10 K8
Marden Wilts 7 T1
Marden Thorn Kent 10 K8
Mardy Mons 14 G7
Mareham le Fen Lincs 33 Q14
Mareham on the Hill Lincs 33 Q13
Marehill W Susx 9 R9
Maresfield E Susx 10 F11
Marfleet C KuH 33 N3
Marford Wrexhm 30 F15
Margam Neath 13 S12
Margaret Marsh Dorset 7 P8
Margaretting Essex 18 G13
Margaretting Tye Essex 18 H13
Margate Kent 11 U3
Margnaheglish N Ayrs 43 P11
Margrie D & G 38 K10
Margrove Park R & Cl 37 L4
Marham Norfk 26 H7
Marhamchurch Cnwll 4 F10
Marholm C Pete 25 N8
Mariansleigh Devon 5 N7
Marine Town Kent 11 M3
Marionburgh Abers 55 P14
Marishader Highld 59 f6
Maristow Devon 2 K5
Marjoriebanks D & G 39 S5
Mark Somset 6 H3
Markbeech Kent 10 F8
Markby Lincs 33 T11
Mark Cross E Susx 10 H10
Market Bosworth Leics 23 S8
Market Deeping Lincs 25 N7
Market Drayton Shrops 22 G3
Market Harborough Leics 24 H11
Market Lavington Wilts 7 S2
Market Overton Rutlnd 24 K6
Market Rasen Lincs 33 N9
Market Stainton Lincs 33 Q11
Market Warsop Notts 32 E13
Market Weighton E R Yk 32 K1
Market Weston Suffk 27 M12
Markfield Leics 24 D7
Markham Caerph 14 E10
Markham Moor Notts 32 G12
Markinch Fife 51 L15
Markington N York 36 F12
Markle E Loth 46 H4
Marksbury BaNES 15 M16
Marks Tey Essex 19 L9
Markyate Herts 17 N7
Marlborough Wilts 15 U15
Marlcliff Warwks 15 T2
Marldon Devon 3 Q5
Marlesford Suffk 19 S4
Marlingford Norfk 27 P7
Marloes Pembks 12 C9
Marlow Bucks 16 K12
Marlow Bottom Bucks 16 K12
Marlpit Hill Kent 10 F7
Marnhull Dorset 7 P8
Marple Stockp 31 P9
Marr Donc 32 D7
Marrick N York 36 C7
Marsden Kirk 31 Q6
Marsden S Tyne 41 R8
Marshalswick Herts 17 P9
Marsham Norfk 27 Q5
Marsh Baldon Oxon 16 F10
Marshborough Kent 11 T5
Marshbrook Shrops 21 S5
Marshchapel Lincs 33 R8
Marsh Farm Luton 17 N6
Marshfield Newpt 14 F13
Marshfield S Glos 15 N14
Marshgate Cnwll 4 E12
Marsh Gibbon Bucks 16 G6
Marsh Green Devon 5 T12
Marsh Green Kent 10 F8
Marshland St James Norfk 26 E7
Marsh Lane Derbys 32 C11
Marsh Street Somset 5 S3
Marshwood Dorset 6 H11
Marske N York 36 D7
Marske-by-the-Sea R & Cl 37 L3
Marston Herefs 21 Q11
Marston Lincs 24 K2
Marston Oxon 16 E8
Marston Staffs 22 K4
Marston Wilts 7 R1
Marston Green Solhll 23 P11
Marston Magna Somset 7 L7
Marston Meysey Wilts 15 T10
Marston Montgomery Derbys 23 N3
Marston Moretaine C Beds 17 M3
Marston on Dove Derbys 23 Q4
Marston St Lawrence Nhants 16 F3
Marston Trussell Nhants 24 G11
Marstow Herefs 14 K7
Marsworth Bucks 17 L8
Marten Wilts 8 F2
Martham Norfk 27 T6
Martin Hants 7 T7
Martin Kent 11 T7
Martin Lincs 33 N14
Martinhoe Devon 5 M3
Martin Hussingtree Worcs 22 K15
Martinstown Dorset 7 M12
Martlesham Suffk 19 R6
Martlesham Heath Suffk 19 R6
Martletwy Pembks 12 G8
Martley Worcs 22 H15
Martock Somset 6 J7
Marton Ches E 31 M13
Marton E R Yk 33 P1
Marton Lincs 32 J11
Marton Middsb 36 J4
Marton N York 36 H13
Marton N York 37 N9
Marton Shrops 21 P3
Marton Warwks 23 S14
Marton-le-Moor N York 36 G12
Martyr Worthy Hants 8 J6
Marwick Ork 58 a3
Marwood Devon 5 L4
Marybank Highld 53 P6
Maryburgh Highld 53 Q5
Marygold Border 47 L7
Maryhill C Glas 44 F5
Marykirk Abers 51 R5
Marylebone Gt Lon 17 R13
Marylebone Wigan 30 J6
Marypark Moray 54 F8
Maryport Cumb 39 R12
Maryport D & G 38 D13
Marystow Devon 4 J13
Mary Tavy Devon 4 K14
Maryton Angus 51 R6
Marywell Abers 55 M15
Marywell Abers 55 S15
Marywell Angus 51 R8
Masham N York 36 E10
Masongill N York 35 Q11
Mastin Moor Derbys 32 D12
Matching Green Essex 18 F11
Matching Tye Essex 18 E11
Matfen Nthumb 41 L7
Matfield Kent 10 J8
Mathern Mons 14 K11
Mathon Herefs 15 N2
Mathry Pembks 12 D5
Matlask Norfk 27 P3
Matlock Derbys 31 U14
Matlock Bath Derbys 31 U14
Matson Gloucs 15 P7
Mattersey Notts 32 G9
Mattingley Hants 9 M2
Mattishall Norfk 27 N7
Mattishall Burgh Norfk 27 N7
Mauchline E Ayrs 44 E12
Maud Abers 55 S7
Maufant Jersey 3 d2
Maugersbury Gloucs 15 U6
Maughold IoM 34 f3
Mauld Highld 53 N8
Maulden C Beds 17 N4
Maulds Meaburn Cumb 35 Q4
Maunby N York 36 G9
Maundown Somset 6 D6
Mautby Norfk 27 U7
Mavesyn Ridware Staffs 23 N6
Mavis Enderby Lincs 33 R13
Mawbray Cumb 39 S11
Mawdesley Lancs 30 G5
Mawdlam Brdgnd 13 S13
Mawgan Cnwll 1 R14
Mawgan Porth Cnwll 1 T7
Mawla Cnwll 1 R10
Mawnan Cnwll 1 S13
Mawnan Smith Cnwll 1 S13
Mawsley Nhants 24 J13
Maxey C Pete 25 N7
Maxstoke Warwks 23 Q11
Maxton Border 46 H12
Maxton Kent 11 T8
Maxwell Town D & G 39 Q6
Maxworthy Cnwll 4 G12
May Bank Staffs 22 J1
Maybole S Ayrs 43 S15
Maybury Surrey 9 R2
Mayfield E Susx 10 H10
Mayfield Mdloth 46 D6
Mayfield Staffs 23 P1
Mayford Surrey 9 R2
May Hill Gloucs 15 M7
Mayland Essex 19 L13
Maylandsea Essex 19 L13
Maynard's Green E Susx 10 H12
Maypole Birm 23 M12
Maypole Green Norfk 27 T9
Maypole Green Suffk 19 L4
Meadgate BaNES 7 M1
Meadle Bucks 16 J9
Meadowfield Dur 41 P12
Meadwell Devon 4 J14
Meanwood Leeds 31 U1
Meare Somset 6 J4
Meare Green Somset 6 G7
Meare Green Somset 6 H6
Mearns E Rens 44 F8
Mears Ashby Nhants 24 J14
Measham Leics 23 R7
Meathop Cumb 35 M10
Meavy Devon 3 L5
Medbourne Leics 24 H10
Meddon Devon 4 G8
Meden Vale Notts 32 E13
Medmenham Bucks 16 J12
Medomsley Dur 41 N9
Medstead Hants 9 L5
Meerbrook Staffs 31 P14
Meesden Herts 18 D8
Meeth Devon 5 L9
Meeting House Hill Norfk 27 R4
Meidrim Carmth 12 K7
Meifod Powys 21 M2
Meigle P & K 51 L8
Meikle Carco D & G 44 J14
Meikle Earnock S Lans 44 H8
Meikle Kilmory Ag & B 43 P7
Meikle Obney P & K 50 G10
Meikleour P & K 50 J9
Meikle Wartle Abers 55 P10
Meinciau Carmth 13 N8
Meir C Stke 22 K2
Melbourn Cambs 17 S3
Melbourne Derbys 23 S5
Melbourne E R Yk 37 N16
Melbury Abbas Dorset 7 Q7
Melbury Bubb Dorset 7 L10
Melbury Osmond Dorset 7 L9
Melchbourne Bed 25 M14
Melcombe Bingham Dorset 7 N10
Meldon Devon 5 L12
Meldon Nthumb 41 N5
Meldreth Cambs 17 S2
Meldrum Stirlg 50 C16
Melfort Ag & B 48 J13
Meliden Denbgs 29 P5
Melin-y-wig Denbgs 29 P10
Melkinthorpe Cumb 40 E14
Melkridge Nthumb 40 G8
Melksham Wilts 15 Q16
Melling Lancs 35 P11
Melling Sefton 30 F8
Mellis Suffk 27 N13
Mellon Charles Highld 56 D15
Mellon Udrigle Highld 56 E14
Mellor Lancs 30 K3
Mellor Stockp 31 P9
Mellor Brook Lancs 30 J2
Mells Somset 7 N3
Melmerby Cumb 40 E12
Melmerby N York 36 C9
Melmerby N York 36 G11
Melness Highld 57 P3
Melplash Dorset 6 K11
Melrose Border 46 G11
Melsetter Ork 58 b5
Melsonby N York 36 E5
Meltham Kirk 31 R6
Melton E R Yk 33 L3
Melton Suffk 19 R5
Melton Constable Norfk 27 N3
Melton Mowbray Leics 24 H6
Melton Ross N Linc 33 M6
Melvaig Highld 56 B16
Melverley Shrops 29 T15
Melvich Highld 57 T3
Membury Devon 6 G10
Memsie Abers 55 S4
Memus Angus 51 N6
Menai Bridge IoA 28 G6
Mendham Suffk 27 R12
Mendlesham Suffk 27 P14
Mendlesham Green Suffk 19 N3
Menheniot Cnwll 2 G6
Mennock D & G 44 J15
Menston C Brad 36 E16
Menstrie Clacks 50 D16
Mentmore Bucks 17 L7
Meoble Highld 48 J1
Meole Brace Shrops 22 D7
Meonstoke Hants 8 K8
Meopham Kent 10 H4
Mepal Cambs 26 D12
Meppershall C Beds 17 P4
Mere Ches E 31 L11
Mere Wilts 7 P5
Mere Brow Lancs 30 F5
Mereclough Lancs 31 N3
Mere Green Birm 23 N9
Mereworth Kent 10 J6
Meriden Solhll 23 Q12
Merkadale Highld 59 d11
Merley Poole 7 S11
Merrion Pembks 12 E10
Merriott Somset 6 J9
Merrow Surrey 9 R3
Merry Hill Herts 17 P11
Merryhill Wolves 22 K9
Merrymeet Cnwll 2 G5
Mersey Crossing Halton 30 H10
Mersham Kent 11 P8
Merstham Surrey 10 C6
Merston W Susx 9 P11
Merstone IoW 8 J14
Merthyr Cynog Powys 14 B4
Merthyr Mawr Brdgnd 13 U14
Merthyr Tydfil Myr Td 14 C9
Merthyr Vale Myr Td 14 C10
Merton Devon 4 K9
Merton Gt Lon 10 C3
Merton Norfk 27 L9
Merton Oxon 16 F7
Meshaw Devon 5 P7
Messing Essex 19 L10
Messingham N Linc 32 K7
Metfield Suffk 27 R12
Metherell Cnwll 2 J4
Metheringham Lincs 33 M14
Methil Fife 51 M16
Methilhill Fife 51 M16
Methlick Abers 55 R8
Methven P & K 50 G11
Methwold Norfk 26 H10
Methwold Hythe Norfk 26 H10
Mettingham Suffk 27 S10
Metton Norfk 27 Q3
Mevagissey Cnwll 2 C9
Mexborough Donc 32 D8
Mey Highld 58 H2
Meyllteyrn Gwynd 28 B13
Meysey Hampton Gloucs 15 T10
Miabhig W Isls 56 d2
Miavaig W Isls 56 d2
Michaelchurch Herefs 14 K6
Michaelchurch Escley Herefs 14 G4
Michaelstone-y-Fedw Newpt 14 F13
Michaelston-le-Pit V Glam 14 D14
Michaelstow Cnwll 2 D3
Micheldever Hants 8 J5
Micheldever Station Hants 8 J5
Michelmersh Hants 8 F7
Mickfield Suffk 19 P3
Micklebring Donc 32 E8
Mickleby N York 37 P5
Micklefield Leeds 32 C2
Mickleham Surrey 9 T3
Mickleover C Derb 23 R3
Mickleton Dur 36 B3
Mickleton Gloucs 15 U3
Mickletown Leeds 32 C3
Mickle Trafford Ches W 30 G13
Mickley N York 36 F10
Mickley Square Nthumb 41 M8
Mid Ardlaw Abers 55 S4
Midbea Ork 58 c2
Mid Beltie Abers 55 N14
Mid Calder W Loth 45 N5
Mid Clyth Highld 58 H7
Mid Culbeuchly Abers 55 N4
Middle Aston Oxon 16 E6
Middle Barton Oxon 16 D6
Middlebie D & G 39 U6
Middlebridge P & K 50 E5
Middle Chinnock Somset 6 J8
Middle Claydon Bucks 16 H6
Middleham N York 36 D9
Middle Handley Derbys 32 C11
Middlehill Wilts 15 P15
Middlehope Shrops 22 D11
Middle Kames Ag & B 43 M2
Middle Littleton Worcs 15 T2
Middlemarsh Dorset 7 M9
Middle Mayfield Staffs 23 N1
Middle Rasen Lincs 33 N9
Middle Rocombe Devon 3 R4
Middlesbrough Middsb 36 J4
Middleshaw Cumb 35 P9
Middlesmoor N York 36 D11
Middle Stoke Medway 11 L2
Middlestone Dur 41 P13
Middlestown Wakefd 31 T5
Middlethird Border 46 J9
Middleton Ag & B 42 a4
Middleton Derbys 31 S14
Middleton Derbys 31 T15
Middleton Essex 18 K7
Middleton Hants 8 H4
Middleton Herefs 22 E14
Middleton Leeds 31 U3
Middleton N York 36 D15
Middleton N York 37 N9
Middleton Nhants 24 J10
Middleton Norfk 26 G6
Middleton Nthumb 41 M4
Middleton P & K 50 H15
Middleton Rochdl 31 N7
Middleton Shrops 22 E12
Middleton Suffk 27 T14
Middleton Swans 13 M12
Middleton Warwks 23 P9
Middleton Cheney Nhants 16 E3
Middleton-in-Teesdale Dur 40 K14
Middleton Moor Suffk 27 T14
Middleton One Row Darltn 36 G5
Middleton-on-Sea W Susx 9 Q12
Middleton on the Hill Herefs 22 E14
Middleton on the Wolds E R Yk 37 R15
Middleton Park C Aber 55 S13
Middleton Quernhow N York 36 G10
Middleton St George Darltn 36 G5
Middleton Scriven Shrops 22 G11
Middleton Stoney Oxon 16 F6
Middleton Tyas N York 36 E6
Middle Town IoS 1 b2
Middletown Powys 21 Q2
Middle Tysoe Warwks 16 C3
Middle Wallop Hants 8 F5
Middlewich Ches E 30 K13
Middle Winterslow Wilts 8 E6
Middlewood Cnwll 2 G4
Middle Woodford Wilts 8 C6
Middlewood Green Suffk 19 N3
Middleyard E Ayrs 44 E11
Middlezoy Somset 6 H5
Midford BaNES 15 N16
Midgham W Berk 16 F15
Midgley Calder 31 Q3
Midgley Wakefd 31 T5
Midhopestones Sheff 31 T8
Midhurst W Susx 9 P8
Mid Lavant W Susx 9 P10
Midlem Border 46 G12
Mid Mains Highld 53 N8
Midpark Ag & B 43 N7
Midsomer Norton BaNES 7 M2
Midtown Highld 57 P3
Mid Yell Shet 59 r3
Migvie Abers 54 K14
Milborne Port Somset 7 M8
Milborne St Andrew Dorset 7 P11
Milborne Wick Somset 7 M7
Milbourne Nthumb 41 N6
Milbourne Wilts 15 R12
Milburn Cumb 40 F13
Milbury Heath S Glos 15 M12
Milby N York 36 H12
Milcombe Oxon 16 D4
Milden Suffk 19 L6
Mildenhall Suffk 26 H13
Mildenhall Wilts 15 U15
Mileham Norfk 27 L5
Mile Oak Br & H 10 C14
Milesmark Fife 45 N2
Miles Platting Manch 31 N8
Mile Town Kent 11 M3
Milfield Nthumb 47 N11
Milford Derbys 23 R1
Milford Devon 4 F7
Milford Staffs 23 L5
Milford Surrey 9 Q5
Milford Haven Pembks 12 E9
Milford on Sea Hants 8 F13
Milkwall Gloucs 14 K8
Milland W Susx 9 N7
Mill Bank Calder 31 Q4
Millbreck Abers 55 T7
Millbridge Surrey 9 N5
Millbrook C Beds 17 M4
Millbrook C Sotn 8 G9
Millbrook Cnwll 2 J7
Millbrook Jersey 3 c3
Mill Brow Stockp 31 P9
Millbuie Abers 55 Q13
Millbuie Highld 53 Q6
Millcorner E Susx 11 L11
Millcraig Highld 53 S3
Milldale Staffs 31 R15
Mill End Bucks 16 J12
Mill End Herts 17 S5
Millerhill Mdloth 45 S5
Miller's Dale Derbys 31 S12
Millerston C Glas 44 G5
Mill Green Cambs 18 G6
Mill Green Essex 18 G13
Mill Green Lincs 25 P5
Mill Green Suffk 19 L6
Mill Green Suffk 19 M4
Mill Green Suffk 19 P3
Millhalf Herefs 21 P12
Millheugh S Lans 44 J8
Mill Hill Gt Lon 17 Q11
Millhouse Ag & B 43 M5
Millhousebridge D & G 39 S4
Millhouse Green Barns 31 T7
Millhouses Sheff 32 B10
Milliken Park Rens 44 D6
Millington E R Yk 37 P15
Millmeece Staffs 22 J3
Mill of Drummond P & K 50 D13
Mill of Haldane W Duns 44 D3
Millom Cumb 34 H10
Millport N Ayrs 43 Q8
Mill Street Suffk 27 N13
Millthrop Cumb 35 Q8
Milltimber C Aber 55 R14
Milltown Abers 54 G13
Milltown Abers 54 K12
Milltown D & G 40 B6
Milltown Devon 5 L4
Milltown of Auchindoun Moray 54 J8
Milltown of Campfield Abers 55 N15
Milltown of Edinvillie Moray 54 G8
Milltown of Learney Abers 55 N14
Milnathort P & K 50 H15
Milngavie E Duns 44 F4
Milnrow Rochdl 31 N5
Milnthorpe Cumb 35 N10
Milovaig Highld 59 a8
Milson Shrops 22 F13
Milstead Kent 11 M5
Milston Wilts 8 D4
Milthorpe Nhants 16 F2
Milton C Stke 31 N16
Milton Cambs 18 E3
Milton Cumb 40 E8
Milton D & G 38 E9
Milton D & G 39 P7
Milton Derbys 23 R4
Milton Highld 52 C7
Milton Highld 53 P10
Milton Highld 53 R6
Milton Highld 53 T2
Milton Highld 58 H5
Milton Inver 44 C5
Milton Kent 10 J3
Milton Moray 54 F11
Milton Moray 55 L4
Milton N Som 14 G16
Milton Notts 32 G12
Milton Oxon 16 D4
Milton Oxon 16 E11
Milton P & K 50 H6
Milton Pembks 12 G9
Milton Somset 6 J7
Milton Stirlg 49 U15
Milton W Duns 44 D4
Milton Abbas Dorset 7 P10
Milton Abbot Devon 4 J14
Milton Bridge Mdloth 45 R6
Milton Bryan C Beds 17 M5
Milton Clevedon Somset 7 M5
Milton Combe Devon 2 K5
Milton Damerel Devon 4 H9
Milton Ernest Bed 25 L16
Milton Green Ches W 30 G14
Milton Hill Oxon 16 E12
Milton Keynes M Keyn 16 K4
Milton Lilbourne Wilts 8 D2
Milton Malsor Nhants 24 H16
Milton Morenish P & K 50 A10
Milton of Auchinhove Abers 55 L14
Milton of Balgonie Fife 51 L16
Milton of Buchanan Stirlg 44 D2
Milton of Campsie E Duns 44 G4
Milton of Leys Highld 53 S8
Milton of Murtle C Aber 55 R14
Milton of Tullich Abers 54 J15
Milton on Stour Dorset 7 P6
Milton Regis Kent 11 M4
Milton-under-Wychwood Oxon 16 B7
Milverton Somset 6 E6
Milverton Warwks 23 R14
Milwich Staffs 23 L3
Minard Ag & B 43 N1
Minchinhampton Gloucs 15 Q10
Minehead Somset 5 S3
Minera Wrexhm 30 D15
Minety Wilts 15 S11
Minffordd Gwynd 28 G12
Mingarrypark Highld 48 G4
Miningsby Lincs 33 R13
Minions Cnwll 2 G4
Minishant S Ayrs 43 T14
Minllyn Gwynd 20 H1
Minnigaff D & G 38 H7
Minnonie Abers 55 Q5
Minskip N York 36 H13
Minstead Hants 8 E10
Minsted W Susx 9 P8
Minster Kent 11 N3
Minster Kent 11 T4
Minsterley Shrops 21 R3
Minster Lovell Oxon 16 C8
Minsterworth Gloucs 15 N7
Minterne Magna Dorset 7 M10
Minting Lincs 33 P12
Mintlaw Abers 55 T7
Minto Border 46 G13
Minton Shrops 21 R5
Mirehouse Cumb 34 F4
Mireland Highld 58 H4
Mirfield Kirk 31 S4
Miserden Gloucs 15 Q8
Miskin Rhondd 14 C13
Misson Notts 32 G8
Misterton Leics 24 E11
Misterton Notts 32 H8
Misterton Somset 6 J9
Mistley Essex 19 P8
Mitcham Gt Lon 10 C4
Mitcheldean Gloucs 15 M7
Mitchell Cnwll 1 T9
Mitchellslacks D & G 39 Q3
Mitchel Troy Mons 14 J8
Mitford Nthumb 41 N4
Mithian Cnwll 1 S9
Mixbury Oxon 16 G4
Mobberley Ches E 31 M11
Mobberley Staffs 23 L2
Mochdre Powys 21 L6
Mochrum D & G 38 G11
Mockbeggar Kent 10 J7
Mockerkin Cumb 34 G3
Modbury Devon 3 M7
Moddershall Staffs 22 K3
Moelfre IoA 28 F4
Moelfre Powys 29 R14
Moffat D & G 45 N16
Moggerhanger C Beds 17 P2
Moira Leics 23 R6
Molash Kent 11 P6
Mol-chlach Highld 59 e13
Mold Flints 29 R8
Moldgreen Kirk 31 S5
Molehill Green Essex 18 F9
Molescroft E R Yk 33 M1
Molesworth Cambs 25 M13
Molland Devon 5 P6
Mollington Ches W 30 F12
Mollington Oxon 16 D2
Mollinsburn N Lans 44 H5
Mondynes Abers 51 S3
Monewden Suffk 19 Q4
Moneydie P & K 50 G11
Moniaive D & G 39 N3
Monifieth Angus 51 N10
Monikie Angus 51 P9
Monimail Fife 51 L13
Monken Hadley Gt Lon 17 R10
Monk Fryston N York 32 D3
Monkhide Herefs 15 L3
Monkhill Cumb 40 B9
Monkhopton Shrops 22 F10
Monkland Herefs 21 S11
Monkleigh Devon 4 J7
Monknash V Glam 13 U15
Monkokehampton Devon 5 L10
Monkseaton N Tyne 41 R6
Monks Eleigh Suffk 19 M5
Monk's Gate W Susx 9 T7
Monks Heath Ches E 31 M12
Monk Sherborne Hants 8 K2
Monksilver Somset 6 D4
Monks Kirby Warwks 24 D11
Monk Soham Suffk 27 Q14
Monks Risborough Bucks 16 J9
Monksthorpe Lincs 33 T13
Monk Street Essex 18 G8
Monkswood Mons 14 G9
Monkton Devon 6 E10
Monkton Kent 11 T4
Monkton S Ayrs 44 C12
Monkton S Tyne 41 Q8
Monkton Combe BaNES 15 N16
Monkton Deverill Wilts 7 Q5
Monkton Farleigh Wilts 15 P16
Monkton Heathfield Somset 6 F6
Monkton Wyld Dorset 6 H11
Monkwearmouth Sundld 41 R9
Monkwood Hants 9 L7
Monmore Green Wolves 22 K9
Monmouth Mons 14 J8
Monnington on Wye Herefs 21 R13
Monreith D & G 38 G12
Montacute Somset 6 K8
Montford Shrops 21 R1
Montford Bridge Shrops 22 C6
Montgarrie Abers 55 M12
Montgomery Powys 21 N4
Montrose Angus 51 S6
Mont Saint Guern 2 b3
Monxton Hants 8 F4
Monyash Derbys 31 S13
Monymusk Abers 55 N12
Monzie P & K 50 E12
Moodiesburn N Lans 44 H5
Moonzie Fife 51 L13
Moor Allerton Leeds 31 U1
Moorby Lincs 33 Q13
Moor Crichel Dorset 7 S9
Moordown Bmouth 7 T11
Moore Halton 30 J10
Moor End Calder 31 Q3
Moorends Donc 32 G5
Moorhead C Brad 31 R1
Moorhouse Cumb 40 A9
Moorhouse Notts 32 H13
Moorhouse Bank Surrey 10 E6
Moorlinch Somset 6 H5
Moor Monkton N York 36 J14
Moorsholm R & Cl 37 M4
Moorside Dorset 7 P7
Moor Street Birm 23 L12
Moorswater Cnwll 2 F5
Moorthorpe Wakefd 32 D6
Moortown Leeds 31 U1
Moortown Lincs 33 M8
Morangie Highld 53 T1
Morar Highld 52 C16
Morborne Cambs 25 N10
Morchard Bishop Devon 5 P9
Morcombelake Dorset 6 H12
Morcott Rutlnd 24 K9
Morda Shrops 29 S14
Morden Dorset 7 R11
Morden Gt Lon 10 C4
Mordiford Herefs 14 K4
Mordon Dur 41 Q14
More Shrops 21 Q5
Morebath Devon 5 R7
Morebattle Border 46 K12
Morecambe Lancs 35 M13
Moredon Swindn 15 T12
Morefield Highld 56 H14
Morehall Kent 11 R9
Moreleigh Devon 3 P7
Morenish P & K 50 A10
Morestead Hants 8 J7
Moreton Dorset 7 P12
Moreton Essex 18 F12
Moreton Herefs 22 D15
Moreton Oxon 16 H9
Moreton Wirral 29 S3
Moreton Corbet Shrops 22 E5
Moretonhampstead Devon 5 P13
Moreton-in-Marsh Gloucs 15 U5
Moreton Jeffries Herefs 15 L2
Moreton Morrell Warwks 23 R16
Moreton on Lugg Herefs 14 J2
Moreton Pinkney Nhants 16 F2
Moreton Say Shrops 22 F3
Moreton Valence Gloucs 15 N8
Morfa Nefyn Gwynd 28 C12
Morham E Loth 46 G5
Morland Cumb 35 P3
Morley Ches E 31 M10
Morley Derbys 23 S2
Morley Leeds 31 T3
Morley Green Ches E 31 M11
Morley St Botolph Norfk 27 N9
Morningside C Edin 45 R5
Morningside N Lans 44 K7
Morningthorpe Norfk 27 Q10
Morpeth Nthumb 41 P4
Morphie Abers 51 S5
Morrey Staffs 23 N6
Morriston Swans 13 Q10
Morston Norfk 27 M2
Mortehoe Devon 4 J3
Morthen Rothm 32 D9
Mortimer W Berk 16 G16
Mortimer West End Hants 8 K1
Mortlake Gt Lon 17 Q14
Morton Cumb 40 B9
Morton Derbys 32 C14
Morton Lincs 25 N5
Morton Lincs 32 J9
Morton Notts 32 G16
Morton Shrops 29 S14
Morton-on-Swale N York 36 G8
Morton on the Hill Norfk 27 P6
Morvah Cnwll 1 M12
Morvich Highld 52 G11
Morville Shrops 22 G10
Morwenstow Cnwll 4 F8
Mosborough Sheff 32 C11
Moscow E Ayrs 44 E10
Moseley Birm 23 M11
Moseley Wolves 23 L9
Moseley Worcs 22 J15
Moss Ag & B 42 b4
Moss Donc 32 F5
Mossat Abers 54 K11
Mossbank Shet 59 q4
Moss Bank St Hel 30 H8
Mossbay Cumb 39 R14
Mossblown S Ayrs 44 D12
Mossburnford Border 46 J14
Mossdale D & G 39 L7
Mossdale E Ayrs 38 J1
Moss Edge Lancs 35 M16
Mossend N Lans 44 J7
Mossley Tamesd 31 P7
Mosspaul Hotel Border 40 B2
Moss-side Highld 54 B6
Mosstodloch Moray 54 H5
Mossyard D & G 38 K10
Mossy Lea Lancs 30 H6
Mosterton Dorset 6 J10
Moston Manch 31 N7
Mostyn Flints 29 Q5
Motcombe Dorset 7 Q6
Mothecombe Devon 3 M8
Motherby Cumb 40 C14
Motherwell N Lans 44 J7
Motspur Park Gt Lon 10 C4
Mottingham Gt Lon 10 E3
Mottisfont Hants 8 F7
Mottistone IoW 8 G14
Mottram in Longdendale Tamesd 31 P8
Mottram St Andrew Ches E 31 N11
Mouldsworth Ches W 30 H12
Moulin P & K 50 F6
Moulsecoomb Br & H 10 D14
Moulsford Oxon 16 F13
Moulsoe M Keyn 17 L3
Moultavie Highld 53 R3
Moulton Ches W 30 K13
Moulton Lincs 25 R5
Moulton N York 36 F6
Moulton Nhants 24 H14
Moulton Suffk 18 H3
Moulton V Glam 14 C15
Moulton Chapel Lincs 25 Q6
Moulton St Mary Norfk 27 T7
Moulton Seas End Lincs 25 R4
Mount Cnwll 2 E5
Mountain C Brad 31 R2
Mountain Ash Rhondd 14 C10
Mountain Cross Border 45 P9
Mount Ambrose Cnwll 1 R11
Mount Bures Essex 19 L8
Mountfield E Susx 10 K12
Mountgerald House Highld 53 Q5
Mount Hawke Cnwll 1 R10
Mountjoy Cnwll 1 U8
Mount Lothian Mdloth 45 R7
Mountnessing Essex 18 G14
Mounton Mons 14 J11
Mount Pleasant Derbys 32 B16
Mount Pleasant Suffk 18 H5
Mountsorrel Leics 24 E6
Mount Tabor Calder 31 Q3
Mousehole Cnwll 1 N13
Mouswald D & G 39 S6
Mow Cop Ches E 31 M15
Mowhaugh Border 47 L13
Mowmacre Hill C Leic 24 E7
Mowsley Leics 24 F11
Moy Highld 49 T2
Moy Highld 53 T9
Moyle Highld 52 F12
Moylegrove Pembks 12 H3
Muasdale Ag & B 42 J10
Muchalls Abers 55 R16
Much Birch Herefs 14 J5
Much Cowarne Herefs 15 L2
Much Dewchurch Herefs 14 J5
Muchelney Somset 6 J7
Muchelney Ham Somset 6 J7
Much Hadham Herts 18 D10
Much Hoole Lancs 30 G4
Muchlarnick Cnwll 2 F7
Much Marcle Herefs 15 L5
Much Wenlock Shrops 22 F9
Mucklestone Staffs 22 G3
Muckton Lincs 33 S11
Muddiford Devon 5 L4
Muddles Green E Susx 10 G13
Mudeford Dorset 8 D13
Mudford Somset 7 L7
Mudford Sock Somset 7 L8
Mugdock Stirlg 44 F4
Mugeary Highld 59 e10
Mugginton Derbys 23 Q2
Muirden Abers 55 P6
Muirdrum Angus 51 P10
Muiresk Abers 55 N7
Muirhead Angus 51 L10
Muirhead Fife 51 L15
Muirhead N Lans 44 H5
Muirkirk E Ayrs 44 H12
Muirmill Stirlg 44 H3
Muir of Fowlis Abers 55 M13
Muir of Miltonduff Moray 54 F5
Muir of Ord Highld 53 Q6
Muirshearlich Highld 49 P2
Muirtack Abers 55 T8
Muirton P & K 50 E14
Muirton Mains Highld 53 P6
Muirton of Ardblair P & K 50 J9
Muker N York 35 U7
Mulbarton Norfk 27 Q9
Mulben Moray 54 J6
Mullion Cnwll 1 R15
Mullion Cove Cnwll 1 R15
Mumby Lincs 33 U12
Munderfield Row Herefs 15 L1
Munderfield Stocks Herefs 15 L2
Mundesley Norfk 27 R3
Mundford Norfk 26 J10
Mundham Norfk 27 S9
Mundon Hill Essex 18 K13
Mungrisdale Cumb 40 B13
Munlochy Highld 53 S6
Munnoch N Ayrs 43 S9
Munsley Herefs 15 M3
Munslow Shrops 22 E11
Murchington Devon 5 N13
Murcott Oxon 16 F7
Murkle Highld 58 F2
Murlaggan Highld 52 H16
Murroes Angus 51 N10
Murrow Cambs 25 S7
Mursley Bucks 16 K5
Murthill Angus 51 N6
Murthly P & K 50 H9
Murton C York 37 L14
Murton Cumb 35 R3
Murton Dur 41 R11
Murton N Tyne 41 Q7
Murton Nthumb 47 N9
Musbury Devon 6 G11
Musselburgh E Loth 46 D5
Muston Leics 24 J2
Muston N York 37 T10
Muswell Hill Gt Lon 17 R12
Mutehill D & G 39 M10
Mutford Suffk 27 U11
Muthill P & K 50 E13
Mybster Highld 58 F5
Myddfai Carmth 13 S5
Myddle Shrops 22 D5
Mydroilyn Cerdgn 20 C11
Mylor Cnwll 1 T12
Mylor Bridge Cnwll 1 T12
Mynachlog ddu Pembks 12 H5
Mynydd-bach Mons 14 J11
Mynydd-Bach Swans 13 Q10
Mynyddgarreg Carmth 13 M9
Mynydd Isa Flints 29 S8
Myrebird Abers 55 P15
Myredykes Border 40 E2
Mytchett Surrey 9 P3
Mytholm Calder 31 P3
Mytholmroyd Calder 31 Q3
Myton-on-Swale N York 36 H12

N

Naast Highld 52 E1
Na Buirgh W Isls 56 c4
Naburn C York 37 L16
Nackington Kent 11 R6
Nacton Suffk 19 Q7
Nafferton E R Yk 37 S13
Nailsbourne Somset 6 F6
Nailsea N Som 14 J15
Nailstone Leics 23 S8
Nailsworth Gloucs 15 P10
Nairn Highld 54 B5
Nannerch Flints 29 Q7
Nanpantan Leics 24 D6
Nanpean Cnwll 2 B7
Nanstallon Cnwll 2 D5
Nanternis Cerdgn 20 B11
Nantgaredig Carmth 13 N6
Nantglyn Denbgs 29 N8
Nantmel Powys 21 L9
Nantmor Gwynd 28 H11
Nant Peris Gwynd 28 H9
Nantwich Ches E 30 K15
Nantyglo Blae G 14 E8
Nant-y-moel Brdgnd 13 U11
Naphill Bucks 16 K10
Napton on the Hill Warwks 24 D15
Narberth Pembks 12 H7
Narborough Leics 24 E9
Narborough Norfk 26 J7
Nasareth Gwynd 28 F10
Naseby Nhants 24 G12
Nash Bucks 16 J4
Nash Newpt 14 G13
Nash Shrops 22 F13
Nassington Nhants 25 M9
Nateby Cumb 35 S6
Nateby Lancs 35 N16
Natland Cumb 35 N9
Naughton Suffk 19 M5
Naunton Gloucs 15 T6
Naunton Worcs 15 Q3
Naunton Beauchamp Worcs 15 R1
Navenby Lincs 33 L14
Navestock Essex 18 F14
Navestock Side Essex 18 F14
Navidale House Hotel Highld 58 D11
Navity Highld 53 T4
Nawton N York 37 L9
Nayland Suffk 19 M8
Nazeing Essex 18 D12
Neap Shet 59 r5
Near Cotton Staffs 23 M1
Near Sawrey Cumb 35 L7
Neasden Gt Lon 17 Q12
Neasham Darltn 36 G5
Neath Neath 13 S10
Neatham Hants 9 M5
Neatishead Norfk 27 S5
Nebo Cerdgn 20 D10
Nebo Conwy 29 L9
Nebo Gwynd 28 F10
Nebo IoA 28 F3
Necton Norfk 26 K7
Nedd Highld 56 H8
Nedging Suffk 19 M5
Nedging Tye Suffk 19 M5
Needham Norfk 27 Q12
Needham Market Suffk 19 N4
Needingworth Cambs 25 R13
Neen Savage Shrops 22 G12
Neen Sollars Shrops 22 G13
Neenton Shrops 22 F11
Nefyn Gwynd 28 C12
Neilston E Rens 44 E7
Nelson Caerph 14 D11
Nelson Lancs 31 N1
Nemphlar S Lans 44 K9
Nempnett Thrubwell BaNES 6 K1
Nenthead Cumb 40 H11
Nenthorn Border 46 J10
Nercwys Flints 29 R8
Nereabolls Ag & B 42 B7
Nerston S Lans 44 G7
Nesbit Nthumb 47 N11
Nesfield N York 36 D15
Nesscliffe Shrops 22 C6
Neston Ches W 30 E11
Neston Wilts 15 P15
Netchwood Shrops 22 F10
Nether Alderley Ches E 31 M11
Netheravon Wilts 8 D4
Nether Blainslie Border 46 G9
Netherbrae Abers 55 Q5
Nether Broughton Leics 24 G4
Netherburn S Lans 44 J9
Netherbury Dorset 6 J11
Netherby N York 36 G15
Nether Cerne Dorset 7 M11
Nethercleuch D & G 39 T4
Nether Compton Dorset 7 L8
Nether Crimond Abers 55 Q11
Nether Dallachy Moray 54 J4
Netherend Gloucs 15 L10
Netherfield E Susx 10 J12
Netherfield Notts 24 F2
Nether Fingland S Lans 45 L15
Netherhampton Wilts 8 C7
Nether Handwick Angus 51 M9
Nether Haugh Rothm 32 C8
Netherhay Dorset 6 J10
Nether Headon Notts 32 H11
Nether Heage Derbys 32 B16
Nether Heyford Nhants 24 G16
Nether Howcleugh S Lans 45 N14
Nether Kellet Lancs 35 N12
Nether Kinmundy Abers 55 T7
Nether Langwith Notts 32 E12
Netherlaw D & G 39 M11
Netherley Abers 55 R16
Nethermill D & G 39 S4
Nethermuir Abers 55 R7
Netherne-on-the-Hill Surrey 10 D6
Netheroyd Hill Kirk 31 S4
Nether Padley Derbys 31 T11
Netherplace E Rens 44 E7
Nether Poppleton C York 36 K14
Netherseal Derbys 23 Q7
Nether Silton N York 36 J8
Nether Stowey Somset 6 E4
Netherthong Kirk 31 R6
Netherton Angus 51 P6
Netherton Devon 3 Q4
Netherton Dudley 23 L11
Netherton Kirk 31 R5
Netherton N Lans 44 J8
Netherton Nthumb 47 N15
Netherton P & K 50 J7
Netherton Sefton 30 E8
Netherton Stirlg 44 F3
Netherton Wakefd 31 U5
Nethertown Cumb 34 F6
Nethertown Highld 58 H1
Nethertown Staffs 23 N6
Netherurd Border 45 P9
Nether Wallop Hants 8 F6
Nether Wasdale Cumb 34 H6
Nether Westcote Gloucs 15 U7
Nether Whitacre Warwks 23 Q10
Nether Whitecleuch S Lans 44 K13
Nether Winchendon Bucks 16 H8
Netherwitton Nthumb 41 M3
Nethy Bridge Highld 54 D11
Netley Hants 8 H10
Netley Marsh Hants 8 F9
Nettlebed Oxon 16 H12
Nettlebridge Somset 7 M3
Nettlecombe Dorset 6 K11
Nettleden Herts 17 M8
Nettleham Lincs 33 L12
Nettlestead Kent 10 J6
Nettlestead Green Kent 10 J7
Nettlestone IoW 8 K13
Nettlesworth Dur 41 P10
Nettleton Lincs 33 N8
Nettleton Wilts 15 P13
Netton Wilts 8 C6
Nevern Pembks 12 G3
Nevill Holt Leics 24 J10
New Abbey D & G 39 Q7
New Aberdour Abers 55 R4
New Addington Gt Lon 10 E5
Newall Leeds 36 E16
New Alresford Hants 8 K6
New Alyth P & K 50 K8
Newark Ork 58 e2
Newark-on-Trent Notts 32 H15
Newarthill N Lans 44 J7
New Ash Green Kent 10 H4
New Balderton Notts 32 J15
New Barn Kent 10 H4
New Barnet Gt Lon 17 R11
Newbattle Mdloth 45 S6
New Bewick Nthumb 47 P13
Newbie D & G 39 T8
Newbiggin Cumb 40 C14
Newbiggin Cumb 40 E10
Newbiggin Cumb 40 F14
Newbiggin Dur 40 K14
Newbiggin N York 36 B9
Newbiggin-by-the-Sea Nthumb 41 Q4
Newbigging Angus 51 L9
Newbigging Angus 51 M10
Newbigging Angus 51 P10
Newbigging S Lans 45 M9
Newbiggin-on-Lune Cumb 35 R6
New Bilton Warwks 24 D13
Newbold Derbys 32 B12
Newbold on Avon Warwks 24 D12
Newbold on Stour Warwks 16 B2
Newbold Pacey Warwks 23 R16
Newbold Verdon Leics 24 D8
New Bolingbroke Lincs 33 R15
Newborough C Pete 25 P8
Newborough IoA 28 E7
Newborough Staffs 23 N5
New Boultham Lincs 33 L12
Newbourne Suffk 19 R6
New Bradwell M Keyn 16 K3
New Brampton Derbys 32 B12
New Brancepeth Dur 41 P12
Newbridge C Edin 45 P5
Newbridge Caerph 14 E10
Newbridge Cnwll 1 M13
Newbridge D & G 39 Q5
Newbridge Hants 8 F9
Newbridge IoW 8 G14
Newbridge Green Worcs 15 P3
Newbridge-on-Wye Powys 21 L11
New Brighton Wirral 30 E9
Newbrough Nthumb 40 J7
New Buckenham Norfk 27 N10
Newbuildings Devon 5 P10
Newburgh Abers 55 S5
Newburgh Abers 55 T10
Newburgh Fife 50 K13
Newburgh Lancs 30 G6
Newburgh Priory N York 36 K11
Newburn N u Ty 41 N8
Newbury Somset 7 N2
Newbury W Berk 16 E15
Newbury Park Gt Lon 18 D15
Newby Cumb 35 P3
Newby Lancs 35 T16
Newby N York 35 R12
Newby N York 36 J5
Newby Bridge Cumb 35 L9
Newby East Cumb 40 D9
New Byth Abers 55 Q6
Newby West Cumb 40 B9
Newcastle Mons 14 J7
Newcastle Shrops 21 P7
Newcastle Airport Nthumb 41 N7
Newcastle Emlyn Carmth 12 K3
Newcastleton Border 40 D4
Newcastle-under-Lyme Staffs 22 J1
Newcastle upon Tyne N u Ty 41 P8
Newchapel Pembks 12 J3
Newchapel Surrey 10 E8
Newchurch IoW 8 J14
Newchurch Kent 11 P10
Newchurch Mons 14 J10
Newchurch Powys 21 N12
Newchurch Staffs 23 N5
New Costessey Norfk 27 Q7
Newcraighall C Edin 45 S5
New Crofton Wakefd 32 C5
New Cross Gt Lon 17 S14
New Cross Somset 6 J7
New Cumnock E Ayrs 44 G14
New Deer Abers 55 R7
New Denham Bucks 17 N12
Newdigate Surrey 9 T5
New Duston Nhants 24 G15
New Earswick C York 37 L14
New Edlington Donc 32 E8
New Elgin Moray 54 G5
New Ellerby E R Yk 33 P1
Newell Green Br For 16 K15
New Eltham Gt Lon 10 F3
New End Worcs 23 M15
Newenden Kent 11 L10
New England C Pete 25 P9
Newent Gloucs 15 M6
New Ferry Wirral 30 E10
Newfield Dur 41 P13
Newfield Highld 53 T2
New Fletton C Pete 25 P9
Newgale Pembks 12 D6
New Galloway D & G 39 L6
Newgate Street Herts 17 R9
New Gilston Fife 51 N14
New Grimsby IoS 1 b1
Newhall Ches E 22 F1
New Hartley Nthumb 41 Q6
Newhaven C Edin 45 R4
Newhaven E Susx 10 F15
New Haw Surrey 9 R1
New Hedges Pembks 12 H10
New Holland N Linc 33 M4
Newholm N York 37 P5
New Houghton Derbys 32 D13
New Houghton Norfk 26 J4
Newhouse N Lans 44 J6
New Hutton Cumb 35 P8
Newick E Susx 10 E11
Newington Kent 11 M4
Newington Kent 11 R9
Newington Oxon 16 G10
New Inn Carmth 13 N4
New Inn Torfn 14 G10
New Invention Shrops 21 P8
New Lakenham Norfk 27 Q8
New Lanark S Lans 44 K10
Newland C KuH 33 M2
Newland Gloucs 14 K8
Newland N York 32 G3
Newland Somset 5 Q4
Newland Worcs 15 N2
Newlandrig Mdloth 46 E6
Newlands Border 40 D3
Newlands Nthumb 41 M9
Newlands of Dundurcas Moray 54 H6
New Langholm D & G 40 B4
New Leake Lincs 33 S15
New Leeds Abers 55 T6
New Lodge Barns 32 B6
New Longton Lancs 30 H3
New Luce D & G 38 D8
Newlyn Cnwll 1 N13
Newmachar Abers 55 R11
Newmains N Lans 44 K7
New Malden Gt Lon 10 B4
Newman's Green Suffk 19 L6
Newmarket Suffk 18 G3
Newmarket W Isls 56 e2
New Marske R & Cl 37 L3
New Marston Oxon 16 E9
New Mill Abers 51 R2
New Mill Border 46 F15
New Mill Cnwll 1 N12
New Mill Kirk 31 S6
Newmill Moray 54 K6
Newmillerdam Wakefd 32 B5
Newmill of Inshewan Angus 51 M6
Newmills C Edin 45 P6
New Mills Derbys 31 Q10
Newmills Fife 45 M2
Newmills Mons 14 J9
New Mills Powys 21 M4
Newmiln P & K 50 H11
Newmilns E Ayrs 44 F10
New Milton Hants 8 E12
New Mistley Essex 19 P8
New Moat Pembks 12 G6
Newney Green Essex 18 G12
Newnham Hants 9 L3
Newnham Herts 17 R4
Newnham Kent 11 N5
Newnham Nhants 24 E15
Newnham Worcs 22 F14
Newnham on Severn Gloucs 15 M8
New Ollerton Notts 32 G13
New Oscott Birm 23 N10
New Pitsligo Abers 55 R5
Newport Cnwll 4 H13
Newport E R Yk 32 K3
Newport Essex 18 E8
Newport Gloucs 15 M10
Newport Highld 58 E10
Newport IoW 8 J13
Newport Newpt 14 G12
Newport Pembks 12 G3
Newport Wrekin 22 H6
Newport-on-Tay Fife 51 M11
Newport Pagnell M Keyn 16 K3
New Prestwick S Ayrs 43 T13
New Quay Cerdgn 20 B10
Newquay Cnwll 1 T8
New Rackheath Norfk 27 R7
New Radnor Powys 21 N10
New Ridley Nthumb 41 M9
New Romney Kent 11 P11
New Rossington Donc 32 F8
New Sauchie Clacks 45 L1
Newseat Abers 55 P9
Newsham Lancs 30 H2
Newsham N York 36 D5
Newsham N York 36 H9
Newsham Nthumb 41 R6
New Sharlston Wakefd 32 C4
Newsholme E R Yk 32 G3
New Silksworth Sundld 41 R10
Newsome Kirk 31 S5
New Somerby Lincs 24 K3
Newstead Border 46 G11
Newstead Notts 32 E15
Newstead Nthumb 47 R12
New Stevenston N Lans 44 J7
Newthorpe Notts 24 D1
New Thundersley Essex 18 J15
Newton Ag & B 49 M16
Newton Border 46 H13
Newton Brdgnd 13 T14
Newton C Beds 17 Q3
Newton Cambs 18 D5
Newton Cambs 26 D6
Newton Ches W 30 F13
Newton Ches W 30 H14
Newton Cumb 34 J11
Newton Derbys 32 C14
Newton Herefs 14 G5
Newton Herefs 14 J1
Newton Highld 53 R6
Newton Highld 53 T4
Newton Highld 53 T7
Newton Highld 58 H5
Newton Lincs 25 M3
Newton Mdloth 45 S5
Newton Moray 54 F4
Newton Moray 54 H4
Newton Nhants 24 K11
Newton Norfk 26 K6
Newton Notts 24 G2
Newton Nthumb 41 L8
Newton S Lans 44 H7
Newton S Lans 45 L11
Newton Sandw 23 M10
Newton Staffs 23 M5
Newton Suffk 19 L7
Newton W Loth 45 N4
Newton Warwks 24 E12
Newton Abbot Devon 3 Q4
Newton Arlosh Cumb 39 U9
Newton Aycliffe Dur 41 Q14
Newton Bewley Hartpl 41 S14
Newton Blossomville M Keyn 17 L1
Newton Bromswold Nhants 25 L14
Newton Burgoland Leics 23 S7
Newton-by-the-Sea Nthumb 47 S12
Newton by Toft Lincs 33 M10
Newton Ferrers Devon 3 L8
Newton Ferry W Isls 56 c5
Newton Flotman Norfk 27 Q9
Newtongrange Mdloth 46 D6
Newton Green Mons 14 K11
Newton Harcourt Leics 24 F9
Newton Heath Manch 31 N7
Newtonhill Abers 55 R16
Newton-in-Bowland Lancs 35 R15
Newton Kyme N York 36 J16
Newton-le-Willows N York 36 E8
Newton-le-Willows St Hel 30 J8
Newtonloan Mdloth 46 D6
Newton Longville Bucks 16 K5
Newton Mearns E Rens 44 F7
Newtonmill Angus 51 Q5
Newtonmore Highld 53 S15
Newton Morrell N York 36 F5
Newton of Balcanquhal P & K 50 J14
Newton of Balcormo Fife 51 P15
Newton-on-Ouse N York 36 J13
Newton-on-Rawcliffe N York 37 P8
Newton-on-the-Moor Nthumb 47 R16
Newton on Trent Lincs 32 J12
Newton Poppleford Devon 6 D12
Newton Purcell Oxon 16 G5
Newton Regis Warwks 23 Q8
Newton Reigny Cumb 40 D13
Newton St Cyres Devon 5 Q11
Newton St Faith Norfk 27 Q6
Newton St Loe BaNES 15 M16
Newton St Petrock Devon 4 J9
Newton Solney Derbys 23 Q4
Newton Stacey Hants 8 G5
Newton Stewart D & G 38 H8
Newton Tony Wilts 8 E5
Newton Tracey Devon 4 K6
Newton under Roseberry R & Cl 36 K5
Newton upon Derwent E R Yk 37 M15
Newton Valence Hants 9 M6
Newton Wamphray D & G 39 S3
Newton with Scales Lancs 30 G3
Newtown Cumb 39 S10
Newtown Cumb 40 D8
Newtown D & G 44 J15
Newtown Devon 5 P7
Newtown Devon 6 D11
New Town Dorset 7 R8
New Town Dorset 7 S8
New Town E Susx 10 F11
Newtown Gloucs 15 M10
Newtown Hants 8 K9
Newtown Herefs 15 L3
Newtown Herefs 15 L5
Newtown Highld 53 M14
Newtown IoW 8 G13
Newtown Nthumb 47 P12
Newtown Poole 7 S12
Newtown Powys 21 M5
Newtown Shrops 22 D4
Newtown Somset 6 G9
Newtown Staffs 31 N14
Newtown Wigan 30 H7
Newtown Worcs 22 K16
Newtown Linford Leics 24 E7
Newtown of Beltrees Rens 44 C7
Newtown St Boswells Border 46 H11
New Tredegar Caerph 14 D9
New Trows S Lans 44 J10
Newtyle Angus 51 L9
New Walsoken Cambs 26 E7
New Waltham NE Lin 33 Q7
New Winton E Loth 46 E5
Newyork Ag & B 49 L14
New York Lincs 33 Q15
New York N Tyne 41 Q7
Neyland Pembks 12 F9
Nicholashayne Devon 6 D8
Nicholaston Swans 13 N12
Nidd N York 36 G13
Nigg C Aber 55 S14
Nigg Highld 53 U3
Nigg Ferry Highld 53 T3
Ninebanks Nthumb 40 H10
Nine Elms Swindn 15 T12
Ninfield E Susx 10 J13
Ningwood IoW 8 G13
Nisbet Border 46 J12
Nisbet Hill Border 47 L8
Niton IoW 8 J15
Nitshill C Glas 44 E7
Nocton Lincs 33 M13
Noke Oxon 16 F8
Nolton Pembks 12 D7
Nolton Haven Pembks 12 D7
No Man's Heath Ches W 30 H16
No Man's Heath Warwks 23 Q7
Nomansland Devon 5 Q8
Nomansland Wilts 8 E9
Noneley Shrops 22 D4
Nonington Kent 11 S6
Nook Cumb 35 P10
Norbiton Gt Lon 17 Q15
Norbury Ches E 22 E1
Norbury Derbys 23 N2
Norbury Gt Lon 10 D3
Norbury Shrops 21 Q5
Norbury Staffs 22 H5
Norchard Worcs 22 J14
Nordelph Norfk 26 F9
Nordley Shrops 22 G9
Norham Nthumb 47 M9
Norley Ches W 30 J12
Norleywood Hants 8 G12
Normanby Lincs 33 L10
Normanby N Linc 32 K5
Normanby N York 37 N10
Normanby R & Cl 36 K4
Normanby le Wold Lincs 33 N8
Normandy Surrey 9 Q3
Norman's Green Devon 6 D10
Normanton C Derb 23 R3
Normanton Leics 24 J2
Normanton Notts 32 G15
Normanton Wakefd 32 C4
Normanton le Heath Leics 23 S7
Normanton on Cliffe Lincs 25 L1
Normanton on Soar Notts 24 E5
Normanton on the Wolds Notts 24 F3
Normanton on Trent Notts 32 H13
Norris Green Lpool 30 F8
Norris Hill Leics 23 R6
Norristhorpe Kirk 31 T4
Northall Bucks 17 L7
Northallerton N York 36 G8
Northam C Sotn 8 H10
Northam Devon 4 J6
Northampton Nhants 24 H15
Northampton Worcs 22 J14
North Anston Rothm 32 E10
North Ascot Br For 17 L15
North Aston Oxon 16 E5
Northaw Herts 17 R10
Northay Somset 6 G9
North Baddesley Hants 8 G8
North Ballachulish Highld 49 M6
North Barrow Somset 7 L6
North Barsham Norfk 27 L3
North Benfleet Essex 18 J15
North Berwick E Loth 46 G3
North Boarhunt Hants 8 K10
Northborough C Pete 25 N7
Northbourne Kent 11 T6
North Bovey Devon 5 N13
North Bradley Wilts 7 Q2
North Brentor Devon 4 K14

72 North Brewham – Quenington

North Brewham Somset 7 N5
Northbrook Hants 8 J5
North Buckland Devon 4 K4
North Burlingham Norfk 27 S7
North Cadbury Somset 7 M6
North Carlton Lincs 33 L11
North Carlton Notts 32 F10
North Cave E R Yk 32 K2
North Cerney Gloucs 15 S9
North Chailey E Susx 10 E11
Northchapel W Susx 9 Q7
North Charford Hants 8 D8
North Charlton Nthumb 47 R13
North Cheam Gt Lon 10 C4
North Cheriton Somset 7 M6
North Chideock Dorset 6 J12
Northchurch Herts 17 M8
North Cliffe E R Yk 32 K2
North Clifton Notts 32 J12
North Cockerington Lincs 33 S9
North Connel Ag & B 48 K10
North Cornelly Brdgnd 13 T13
North Cotes Lincs 33 R8
Northcott Devon 4 H12
Northcourt Oxon 16 E10
North Cove Suffk 27 U10
North Cowton N York 36 F6
North Crawley M Keyn 17 L3
North Creake Norfk 26 K2
North Curry Somset 6 G6
North Dalton E R Yk 37 Q15
North Deighton N York 36 H15
Northdown Kent 11 U3
North Duffield N York 32 G1
North Duntulm Highld 59 e5
North Elmham Norfk 27 M5
North Elmsall Wakefd 32 D6
North End C Port 9 L11
North End Essex 18 G10
North End Hants 8 C9
North End Nhants 25 L14
North End W Susx 9 Q11
Northend Warwks 16 D1
Northenden Manch 31 M9
North Erradale Highld 52 D1
North Evington C Leic 24 F8
North Fambridge Essex 18 K14
North Ferriby E R Yk 33 L3
Northfield Birm 23 M12
Northfield C Aber 55 R13
Northfield E R Yk 33 M3
Northfields Lincs 25 M7
Northfleet Kent 10 H3
North Frodingham E R Yk 37 T14
North Gorley Hants 8 D10
North Green Suffk 19 R3
North Greetwell Lincs 33 L12
North Grimston N York 37 P12
North Grimston N York 37 P12
North Haven Shet 59 s8
North Hill Cnwll 2 G3
North Hillingdon Gt Lon 17 N12
North Hinksey Village Oxon 16 E9
North Holmwood Surrey 9 T4
North Huish Devon 3 N7
North Hykeham Lincs 32 K13
Northiam E Susx 11 L11
Northill C Beds 17 P2
Northington Hants 8 K5
North Kelsey Lincs 33 M7
North Kessock Highld 53 S7
North Killingholme N Linc 33 N5
North Kilvington N York 36 H9
North Kilworth Leics 24 F11
North Kyme Lincs 33 N15
North Landing E R Yk 37 V11
Northlands Lincs 33 R15
Northleach Gloucs 15 T8
North Lee Bucks 16 K8
Northleigh Devon 6 F11
North Leigh Oxon 16 D8
North Leverton with Habblesthorpe Notts 32 H11
Northlew Devon 4 K11
North Littleton Worcs 15 S2
North Lopham Norfk 27 N12
North Luffenham Rutlnd 24 K8
North Marden W Susx 9 N9
North Marston Bucks 16 J6
North Middleton Mdloth 46 E7
North Millbrex Abers 55 Q7
North Milmain D & G 38 C10
North Molton Devon 5 N6
Northmoor Oxon 16 D9
North Moreton Oxon 16 F12
Northmuir Angus 51 M7
North Mundham W Susx 9 P11
North Muskham Notts 32 H14
North Newbald E R Yk 32 K2
North Newington Oxon 16 D3
North Newnton Wilts 8 C2
North Newton Somset 6 G6
Northney Hants 9 M11
North Nibley Gloucs 15 N11
Northolt Gt Lon 17 P13
Northop Flints 29 S7
Northop Hall Flints 30 D13
North Ormesby Middsb 36 J3
North Ormsby Lincs 33 Q9
Northorpe Kirk 31 T4
Northorpe Lincs 25 P3
Northorpe Lincs 32 K8
North Otterington N York 36 G8
North Owersby Lincs 33 M8
Northowram Calder 31 R3
North Perrott Somset 6 J9
North Petherton Somset 6 G5
North Petherwin Cnwll 4 G12
North Pickenham Norfk 26 K8
North Piddle Worcs 15 R1
North Poorton Dorset 6 K11
Northport Dorset 7 R13
North Queensferry Fife 45 P3
North Rauceby Lincs 25 M1
Northrepps Norfk 27 R2
North Reston Lincs 33 S10
North Rigton N York 36 F15
North Rode Ches E 31 N13
North Ronaldsay Airport Ork 58 e1
North Runcton Norfk 26 G6
North Scarle Lincs 32 J13
North Shian Ag & B 48 K9
North Shields N Tyne 41 R7
North Shoebury Sthend 19 L15
North Shore Bpool 30 E1
North Side C Pete 25 Q9
North Somercotes Lincs 33 S8
North Stainley N York 36 F11
North Stifford Thurr 10 H2
North Stoke BaNES 15 M15
North Stoke Oxon 16 G12
North Stoke W Susx 9 R10
North Street Kent 11 P5
North Street W Berk 16 G15
North Sunderland Nthumb 47 R11
North Tamerton Cnwll 4 G11
North Tawton Devon 5 M10
North Third Stirlg 44 J2
North Thoresby Lincs 33 Q8
Northton W Isls 56 C4
North Town Devon 4 K9
North Town Somset 7 L4
North Town W & M 17 L13
North Tuddenham Norfk 27 N6
North Walsham Norfk 27 R4
North Waltham Hants 8 J4
North Warnborough Hants 9 M3
North Weald Bassett Essex 18 E13
North Wheatley Notts 32 H10
Northwich Ches W 30 K12
Northwick Worcs 22 J16
North Widcombe BaNES 7 L1
North Willingham Lincs 33 P9
North Wingfield Derbys 32 C13
North Witham Lincs 24 K5
Northwold Norfk 26 J9
Northwood C Stke 31 N16
Northwood Gt Lon 17 N11
Northwood IoW 8 H13
Northwood Shrops 22 D3
Northwood Green Gloucs 15 M7
North Wootton Dorset 7 M8
North Wootton Norfk 26 G5
North Wootton Somset 7 L4
North Wraxall Wilts 15 P14
Norton Donc 32 E5
Norton E Susx 10 F15
Norton Gloucs 15 P6
Norton Halton 30 H11
Norton Nhants 24 F15
Norton Notts 32 E12
Norton Powys 21 Q9
Norton S on T 36 J3
Norton Shrops 22 H9
Norton Suffk 27 L14
Norton W Susx 9 Q11
Norton Wilts 15 Q13
Norton Worcs 15 Q2
Norton Worcs 15 S2
Norton Bavant Wilts 7 R4
Norton Bridge Staffs 22 K4
Norton Canes Staffs 23 M7
Norton Canon Herefs 21 R12
Norton Disney Lincs 32 K14
Norton Fitzwarren Somset 6 F6
Norton Green IoW 8 F14
Norton Hawkfield BaNES 15 L16
Norton Heath Essex 18 F12
Norton in Hales Shrops 22 G2
Norton in the Moors C Stke 31 N15
Norton-Juxta-Twycross Leics 23 R8
Norton-le-Clay N York 36 H11
Norton Lindsey Warwks 23 Q15
Norton Little Green Suffk 27 M14
Norton Malreward BaNES 15 L16
Norton-on-Derwent N York 37 N11
Norton St Philip Somset 7 P1
Norton Subcourse Norfk 27 T9
Norton sub Hamdon Somset 6 J8
Norwell Notts 32 H14
Norwell Woodhouse Notts 32 H14
Norwich Norfk 27 Q7
Norwich Airport Norfk 27 Q7
Norwick Shet 59 s1
Norwood Clacks 44 K1
Norwood Green Gt Lon 17 P13
Norwood Hill Surrey 10 C8
Norwoodside Cambs 25 S9
Noss Mayo Devon 3 L8
Nosterfield N York 36 F10
Nostie Highld 52 E10
Notgrove Gloucs 15 T7
Nottage Brdgnd 13 T14
Nottingham C Nott 24 E2
Notton Wakefd 32 B5
Notton Wilts 15 Q15
Noutard's Green Worcs 22 J14
Nuffield Oxon 16 G12
Nunburnholme E R Yk 37 P15
Nuneaton Warwks 23 R10
Nunhead Gt Lon 17 S14
Nun Monkton N York 36 J14
Nunney Somset 7 N3
Nunnington N York 37 M10
Nunsthorpe NE Lin 33 Q6
Nunthorpe C York 37 L15
Nunthorpe Middsb 36 K4
Nunthorpe Village Middsb 36 K5
Nunton Wilts 8 D7
Nunwick N York 36 G11
Nursling Hants 8 G9
Nutbourne W Susx 9 M11
Nutbourne W Susx 9 S8
Nutfield Surrey 10 D7
Nuthall Notts 24 E2
Nuthampstead Herts 18 D8
Nuthurst W Susx 9 T7
Nutley E Susx 10 F10
Nuttall Bury 31 M5
Nybster Highld 58 J3
Nyetimber W Susx 9 P12
Nyewood W Susx 9 N8
Nymet Rowland Devon 5 N9
Nymet Tracey Devon 5 N11
Nympsfield Gloucs 15 N10
Nynehead Somset 6 E7
Nyton W Susx 9 Q11

O

Oadby Leics 24 F9
Oad Street Kent 11 M5
Oakamoor Staffs 23 M1
Oakbank W Loth 45 N6
Oak Cross Devon 5 L11
Oakdale Caerph 14 E10
Oake Somset 6 E7
Oaken Staffs 22 J8
Oakenclough Lancs 35 P15
Oakengates Wrekin 22 G7
Oakenshaw Dur 41 P12
Oakenshaw Kirk 31 S3
Oakford Cerdgn 20 C11
Oakford Devon 5 R7
Oakham Rutlnd 24 J7
Oakhanger Hants 9 M6
Oakhill Somset 7 M3
Oakington Cambs 25 S15
Oakle Street Gloucs 15 N7
Oakley Bed 17 M1
Oakley Bucks 16 G8
Oakley Fife 45 M2
Oakley Hants 8 K3
Oakley Suffk 27 P12
Oakridge Lynch Gloucs 15 Q9
Oaksey Wilts 15 R11
Oakthorpe Leics 23 R7
Oakwood C Derb 23 S2
Oakworth C Brad 31 Q1
Oare Kent 11 P4
Oare Somset 5 P3
Oare Wilts 15 U16
Oasby Lincs 25 L2
Oath Somset 6 H6
Oathlaw Angus 51 N6
Oatlands Park Surrey 17 N16
Oban Ag & B 48 K11
Oban Airport Ag & B 48 K10
Obley Shrops 21 Q7
Obney P & K 50 G10
Oborne Dorset 7 M8
Occold Suffk 27 P13
Occumster Highld 58 G8
Ochiltree E Ayrs 44 E13
Ockbrook Derbys 23 S3
Ocker Hill Sandw 23 L10
Ockham Surrey 9 S2
Ockle Highld 48 E4
Ockley Surrey 9 T5
Ocle Pychard Herefs 15 L2
Odcombe Somset 6 K8
Odd Down BaNES 15 N16
Oddingley Worcs 22 K15
Oddington Gloucs 15 U6
Oddington Oxon 16 F7
Odell Bed 25 L16
Odiham Hants 9 M3
Odsal C Brad 31 S3
Odsey Cambs 17 R4
Odstock Wilts 8 D7
Odstone Leics 23 S7
Offchurch Warwks 23 R14
Offenham Worcs 15 S2
Offerton Stockp 31 N9
Offham E Susx 10 E13
Offham Kent 10 J5
Offham W Susx 9 R10
Offord Cluny Cambs 25 P14
Offord D'Arcy Cambs 25 P14
Offton Suffk 19 N5
Offwell Devon 6 F11
Ogbourne Maizey Wilts 15 U15
Ogbourne St Andrew Wilts 15 U14
Ogbourne St George Wilts 15 U14
Ogle Nthumb 41 N5
Oglet Lpool 30 G11
Ogmore V Glam 13 U14
Ogmore-by-Sea V Glam 13 T14
Ogmore Vale Brdgnd 13 U12
Okeford Fitzpaine Dorset 7 P9
Okehampton Devon 5 L11
Oker Side Derbys 31 T14
Okewood Hill Surrey 9 S5
Old Nhants 24 H13
Old Aberdeen C Aber 55 S13
Old Alresford Hants 8 K6
Oldany Highld 56 G8
Old Auchenbrack D & G 39 M2
Old Basford C Nott 24 E2
Old Basing Hants 9 L3
Old Beetley Norfk 27 M6
Oldberrow Warwks 23 N14
Old Bewick Nthumb 47 P13
Old Bolingbroke Lincs 33 R13
Old Bramhope Leeds 36 F16
Old Brampton Derbys 32 B12
Old Bridge of Urr D & G 39 N7
Old Buckenham Norfk 27 N10
Old Burghclere Hants 8 H2
Oldbury Sandw 23 L11
Oldbury Shrops 22 G10
Oldbury Warwks 23 R10
Oldbury-on-Severn S Glos 15 L11
Oldbury on the Hill Gloucs 15 P12
Old Byland N York 36 K9
Old Cantley Donc 32 F7
Oldcastle Mons 14 G6
Old Catton Norfk 27 Q7
Old Clee NE Lin 33 Q6
Old Cleeve Somset 5 T4
Old Colwyn Conwy 29 L5
Oldcotes Notts 32 F9
Old Dailly S Ayrs 38 E2
Old Dalby Leics 24 G5
Old Deer Abers 55 S7
Old Edlington Donc 32 E8
Old Ellerby E R Yk 33 P1
Old Felixstowe Suffk 19 S7
Oldfield Worcs 22 J14
Old Fletton C Pete 25 P9
Oldford Somset 7 P2
Old Forge Herefs 14 K7
Old Grimsby IoS 1 b1
Old Hall Green Herts 17 S6
Oldham Oldham 31 N7
Oldhamstocks E Loth 46 K5
Old Harlow Essex 18 E11
Old Hunstanton Norfk 26 H2
Old Hurst Cambs 25 R12
Old Hutton Cumb 35 P9
Old Kilpatrick W Duns 44 E5
Old Knebworth Herts 17 Q7
Old Lakenham Norfk 27 Q8
Oldland S Glos 15 M15
Old Langho Lancs 30 K2
Old Leake Lincs 33 S16
Old Malton N York 37 N11
Oldmeldrum Abers 55 Q10
Oldmill Cnwll 2 H4
Old Milverton Warwks 23 R14
Oldmixon N Som 6 H1
Old Newton Suffk 19 N3
Old Portlethen Abers 55 S15
Old Radford C Nott 24 E2
Old Radnor Powys 21 P11
Old Rayne Abers 55 N10
Old Romney Kent 11 P11
Old Shoreham W Susx 9 U11
Oldshoremore Highld 56 J4
Old Sodbury S Glos 15 N13
Old Somerby Lincs 25 L3
Oldstead N York 36 K10
Old Stratford Nhants 16 J3
Old Struan P & K 50 D5
Old Swinford Dudley 22 K11
Old Thirsk N York 36 H10
Old Town Cumb 35 P10
Old Town E Susx 10 H15
Old Town IoS 1 b2
Old Trafford Traffd 31 M8
Oldwall Cumb 40 D8
Oldwalls Swans 13 N11
Old Warden C Beds 17 P3
Old Weston Cambs 25 N12
Old Wick Highld 58 J5
Old Windsor W & M 17 M14
Old Wives Lees Kent 11 Q6
Old Woking Surrey 9 R2
Olgrinmore Highld 58 E5
Olive Green Staffs 23 N6
Oliver's Battery Hants 8 H7
Ollaberry Shet 59 q3
Ollach Highld 59 f10
Ollerton Ches E 31 L11
Ollerton Notts 32 F13
Ollerton Shrops 22 F5
Olney M Keyn 17 L1
Olrig House Highld 58 F3
Olton Solhll 23 N12
Olveston S Glos 15 L12
Ombersley Worcs 22 J15
Ompton Notts 32 G13
Onchan IoM 34 e6
Onecote Staffs 31 Q15
Onibury Shrops 21 S7
Onich Highld 49 M6
Onllwyn Neath 13 T8
Onneley Staffs 22 H2
Onslow Green Essex 18 G10
Onslow Village Surrey 9 Q3
Onston Ches W 30 J12
Opinan Highld 52 D3
Orbliston Moray 54 H5
Orbost Highld 59 c9
Orby Lincs 33 T13
Orchard Portman Somset 6 F7
Orcheston Wilts 7 T3
Orcop Herefs 14 J6
Orcop Hill Herefs 14 J5
Ord Abers 55 M5
Ordhead Abers 55 N13
Ordie Abers 54 K14
Ordiequish Moray 54 H5
Ordsall Notts 32 G11
Ore E Susx 11 L13
Orford Suffk 19 T5
Orford Warrtn 30 J9
Organford Dorset 7 R12
Orkney Islands Ork 58 c4
Orlestone Kent 11 N9
Orleton Herefs 22 D14
Orleton Worcs 22 G14
Orlingbury Nhants 24 J13
Ormesby R & Cl 36 K4
Ormesby St Margaret Norfk 27 U6
Ormesby St Michael Norfk 27 U6
Ormiscaig Highld 56 D15
Ormiston E Loth 46 E5
Ormsaigmore Highld 48 D5
Ormsary Ag & B 42 J5
Ormskirk Lancs 30 F6
Oronsay Ag & B 42 D2
Orphir Ork 58 b4
Orpington Gt Lon 10 F4
Orrell Sefton 30 E8
Orrell Wigan 30 H7
Orroland D & G 39 N11
Orsett Thurr 10 H1
Orslow Staffs 22 J6
Orston Notts 24 H2
Orton Cumb 35 Q5
Orton Nhants 24 J12
Orton Staffs 22 K9
Orton Longueville C Pete 25 P9
Orton-on-the-Hill Leics 23 R8
Orton Waterville C Pete 25 N9
Orwell Cambs 17 S2
Osbaldeston Lancs 30 K2
Osbaldwick C York 37 L15
Osbaston Leics 23 S8
Osbaston Shrops 29 T14
Osbournby Lincs 25 M2
Oscroft Ches W 30 H13
Ose Highld 59 c9
Osgathorpe Leics 23 S6
Osgodby Lincs 33 M9
Osgodby N York 32 F2
Osgodby N York 37 S9
Oskaig Highld 59 g10
Oskamull Ag & B 48 D9
Osmaston Derbys 23 P2
Osmington Dorset 7 N13
Osmington Mills Dorset 7 N14
Osmondthorpe Leeds 32 B2
Osmotherley N York 36 J7
Osney Oxon 16 E9
Ospringe Kent 11 P5
Ossett Wakefd 31 T4
Ossington Notts 32 H13
Osterley Gt Lon 17 P14
Oswaldkirk N York 37 L10
Oswaldtwistle Lancs 31 L3
Oswestry Shrops 29 S13
Otford Kent 10 G5
Otham Kent 11 L6
Othery Somset 6 H5
Otley Leeds 36 E16
Otley Suffk 19 Q4
Otterbourne Hants 8 H8
Otterburn N York 35 T14
Otterburn Nthumb 40 J3
Otter Ferry Ag & B 43 M3
Otterham Cnwll 4 E12
Otterhampton Somset 6 F4
Otternish W Isls 56 c5
Ottershaw Surrey 17 M16
Otterswick Shet 59 r3
Otterton Devon 6 D13
Ottery St Mary Devon 6 D11
Ottinge Kent 11 R8
Ottringham E R Yk 33 Q4
Oughterside Cumb 39 T12
Oughtibridge Sheff 31 U9
Oughtrington Warrtn 30 K10
Oulston N York 36 K11
Oulton Cumb 39 U10
Oulton Norfk 27 P4
Oulton Staffs 22 K3
Oulton Suffk 27 U10
Oulton Broad Suffk 27 U10
Oulton Street Norfk 27 P4
Oundle Nhants 25 M11
Ounsdale Staffs 22 K10
Ousby Cumb 40 E13
Ousden Suffk 18 H3
Ousefleet E R Yk 32 J4
Ouston Dur 41 P9
Outgate Cumb 35 L7
Outhgill Cumb 35 S6
Outhill Warwks 23 N14
Outlane Kirk 31 R5
Out Rawcliffe Lancs 30 F1
Outwell Norfk 26 E8
Outwood Surrey 10 D7
Outwoods Staffs 22 H6
Ouzlewell Green Leeds 32 B3
Over Cambs 25 S14
Overbury Worcs 15 R4
Overcombe Dorset 7 N14
Over Compton Dorset 7 L8
Over Haddon Derbys 31 S13
Over Kellet Lancs 35 N12
Over Kiddington Oxon 16 D6
Overleigh Somset 6 K5
Over Norton Oxon 16 B5
Over Peover Ches E 31 L12
Overpool Ches W 30 F11
Overscaig Hotel Highld 57 M10
Overseal Derbys 23 R6
Over Silton N York 36 J8
Oversland Kent 11 P5
Overstone Nhants 24 H14
Over Stowey Somset 6 E4
Overstrand Norfk 27 R2
Over Stratton Somset 6 J8
Overthorpe Nhants 16 E3
Overton C Aber 55 R12
Overton Hants 8 J3
Overton Lancs 35 M14
Overton N York 36 K14
Overton Shrops 22 D13
Overton Swans 13 N12
Overton Wakefd 31 T5
Overton Wrexhm 29 T11
Overtown N Lans 44 J8
Over Wallop Hants 8 F5
Over Whitacre Warwks 23 Q10
Over Worton Oxon 16 D5
Oving Bucks 16 J6
Oving W Susx 9 P11
Ovingdean Br & H 10 D14
Ovingham Nthumb 41 M8
Ovington Dur 36 D4
Ovington Essex 18 J6
Ovington Hants 8 J6
Ovington Norfk 27 L8
Ovington Nthumb 41 M8
Ower Hants 8 F9
Owermoigne Dorset 7 P13
Owlerton Sheff 32 B9
Owlsmoor Br For 9 N1
Owlswick Bucks 16 J9
Owmby Lincs 33 L10
Owmby Lincs 33 M7
Owslebury Hants 8 J8
Owston Donc 32 E6
Owston Leics 24 H7
Owston Ferry N Linc 32 J8
Owstwick E R Yk 33 Q2
Owthorne E R Yk 33 R3
Owthorpe Notts 24 G3
Owton Manor Hartpl 41 T13
Oxborough Norfk 26 H8
Oxcombe Lincs 33 R11
Oxenholme Cumb 35 P8
Oxenhope C Brad 31 Q2
Oxen Park Cumb 35 L9
Oxenpill Somset 6 J4
Oxenton Gloucs 15 R5
Oxenwood Wilts 8 F2
Oxford Oxon 16 E9
Oxford Airport Oxon 16 E7
Oxhey Herts 17 P11
Oxhill Warwks 16 B2
Oxley Wolves 22 K8
Oxley Green Essex 19 L11
Oxlode Cambs 26 E11
Oxnam Border 46 J14
Oxnead Norfk 27 Q5
Oxshott Surrey 9 T2
Oxspring Barns 31 T7
Oxted Surrey 10 E6
Oxton Border 46 F8
Oxton N York 36 J16
Oxton Notts 32 F16
Oxton Wirral 30 E10
Oxwich Swans 13 N12
Oxwich Green Swans 13 N12
Oykel Bridge Hotel Highld 57 L13
Oyne Abers 55 N10
Oystermouth Swans 13 Q12

P

Pabail W Isls 56 f2
Packington Leics 23 R6
Packmoor C Stke 31 N15
Padanaram Angus 51 M7
Padbury Bucks 16 H5
Paddington Gt Lon 17 R13
Paddlesworth Kent 10 J5
Paddlesworth Kent 11 R8
Paddock Wood Kent 10 J8
Padiham Lancs 31 M2
Padside N York 36 E13
Padstow Cnwll 2 B4
Padworth W Berk 16 G15
Pagham W Susx 9 P12
Paglesham Essex 19 L14
Paignton Torbay 3 Q6
Pailton Warwks 24 D12
Painscastle Powys 21 N13
Painshawfield Nthumb 41 M8
Painsthorpe E R Yk 37 P14
Painswick Gloucs 15 P8
Painter's Forstal Kent 11 N5
Paisley Rens 44 E6
Pakefield Suffk 27 V10
Pakenham Suffk 27 L14
Paley Street W & M 16 K14
Palfrey Wsall 23 M9
Palgrave Suffk 27 P12
Pallington Dorset 7 P12
Palmerston E Ayrs 44 E13
Palnackie D & G 39 N9
Palnure D & G 38 H8
Palterton Derbys 32 D13
Pamber End Hants 8 K2
Pamber Green Hants 8 K2
Pamber Heath Hants 8 K1
Pamington Gloucs 15 Q4
Pamphill Dorset 7 S11
Pampisford Cambs 18 E5
Panbride Angus 51 P10
Pancrasweek Devon 4 G10
Pandy Mons 14 G6
Pandy Tudur Conwy 29 L8
Panfield Essex 18 H9
Pangbourne W Berk 16 G14
Pangdean W Susx 10 D13
Pannal N York 36 G15
Pannal Ash N York 36 F14
Pannanich Wells Hotel Abers 54 J15
Pant Shrops 29 S14
Pantasaph Flints 29 Q6
Pant-ffrwyth Brdgnd 13 U13
Pant Glas Gwynd 28 F10
Pantglas Powys 20 G4
Panton Lincs 33 P11
Pant-y-dwr Powys 20 K8
Pant-y-mwyn Flints 29 R8
Panxworth Norfk 27 S7
Papa Stour Airport Shet 59 n5
Papa Westray Airport Ork 58 c1
Papcastle Cumb 39 S13
Papigoe Highld 58 J5
Papple E Loth 46 H5
Papplewick Notts 32 E16
Papworth Everard Cambs 25 Q15
Papworth St Agnes Cambs 25 Q15
Par Cnwll 2 D7
Parbold Lancs 30 G6
Parbrook Somset 7 L5
Parc Gwynd 29 L13
Parc Seymour Newpt 14 H11
Pardshaw Cumb 39 S14
Parham Suffk 19 R3
Park D & G 39 Q3
Park Nthumb 40 F8
Park Corner Oxon 16 H12
Parkend Gloucs 15 L9
Parkers Green Kent 10 H7
Park Farm Kent 11 P8
Parkgate Ches W 30 D11
Parkgate D & G 39 R4
Park Gate Hants 8 J10
Park Gate Leeds 31 S1
Parkgate Surrey 9 T4
Parkhall W Duns 44 E5
Parkham Devon 4 H7
Parkmill Swans 13 P12
Park Royal Gt Lon 17 Q13
Parkside Dur 41 S10
Parkside N Lans 44 J7
Parkstone Poole 7 S12
Park Street Herts 17 P9
Parracombe Devon 5 M3
Parson Drove Cambs 25 S7
Parson's Heath Essex 19 M9
Partick C Glas 44 F5
Partington Traffd 31 L9
Partney Lincs 33 S13
Parton Cumb 34 F3
Partridge Green W Susx 9 T8
Parwich Derbys 31 S15
Passenham Nhants 16 J3
Paston Norfk 27 S3
Patcham Br & H 10 D13
Patching W Susx 9 S10
Patchway S Glos 15 L13
Pateley Bridge N York 36 D12
Pathhead Fife 45 R1
Pathhead Mdloth 46 E6
Path of Condie P & K 50 H14
Patna E Ayrs 44 D15
Patney Wilts 7 T1
Patrick IoM 34 b5
Patrick Brompton N York 36 E8
Patricroft Salfd 31 L8
Patrington E R Yk 33 R4
Patrington Haven E R Yk 33 R4
Patrixbourne Kent 11 R6
Patterdale Cumb 35 M4
Pattingham Staffs 22 J9
Pattishall Nhants 16 G1
Pattiswick Green Essex 18 K9
Paul Cnwll 1 N13
Paulerspury Nhants 16 H2
Paull E R Yk 33 P3
Paul's Dene Wilts 8 D6
Paulton BaNES 7 M1
Pauperhaugh Nthumb 41 M2
Pavenham Bed 25 L16
Pawlett Somset 6 G4
Paxford Gloucs 15 U4
Paxton Border 47 N8
Payhembury Devon 6 D10
Paythorne Lancs 35 T15
Peacehaven E Susx 10 E15
Peak Forest Derbys 31 R11
Peakirk C Pete 25 P8
Peasedown St John BaNES 7 N1
Peaseland Green Norfk 27 N6
Peasemore W Berk 16 D14
Peasenhall Suffk 27 S14
Pease Pottage W Susx 10 C9
Peaslake Surrey 9 S4
Peasley Cross St Hel 30 H9
Peasmarsh E Susx 11 M11
Peathill Abers 55 S4
Peat Inn Fife 51 N14
Peatling Magna Leics 24 F10
Peatling Parva Leics 24 F10
Pebmarsh Essex 18 K8
Pebworth Worcs 15 T2
Pecket Well Calder 31 P3
Peckforton Ches E 30 H15
Peckham Gt Lon 17 S14
Peckleton Leics 24 D9
Pedlinge Kent 11 Q9
Pedmore Dudley 22 K12
Pedwell Somset 6 J5
Peebles Border 45 R10
Peel IoM 34 b5
Peene Kent 11 R9
Pegsdon C Beds 17 P5
Pegswood Nthumb 41 P4
Pegwell Kent 11 U4
Peinchorran Highld 59 f10
Peinlich Highld 59 e7
Peldon Essex 19 M10
Pelsall Wsall 23 M8
Pelton Dur 41 P10
Pelynt Cnwll 2 F7
Pemberton Carmth 13 P10
Pemberton Wigan 30 H7
Pembrey Carmth 13 M10
Pembridge Herefs 21 R11
Pembroke Pembks 12 F10
Pembroke Dock Pembks 12 F9
Pembury Kent 10 H8
Pen-allt Herefs 14 K5
Penallt Mons 14 K8
Penally Pembks 12 H10
Penarth V Glam 14 E15
Pen-bont Rhydybeddau Cerdgn 20 F6
Penbryn Cerdgn 12 K1
Pencader Carmth 13 M4
Pencaitland E Loth 46 F5
Pencarnisiog IoA 28 D6
Pencarreg Carmth 20 D13
Pencelli Powys 14 D6
Penclawdd Swans 13 P11
Pencoed Brdgnd 14 B13
Pencombe Herefs 15 L1
Pencraig Herefs 14 K7
Pencraig Powys 29 P14
Pendeen Cnwll 1 M12
Penderyn Rhondd 13 U9
Pendine Carmth 12 J9
Pendlebury Salfd 31 M7
Pendleton Lancs 31 L1
Pendock Worcs 15 N5
Pendoggett Cnwll 4 C14
Pendomer Somset 6 K9
Pendoylan V Glam 14 C14
Penegoes Powys 20 G4
Pen-ffordd Pembks 12 G6
Pengam Caerph 14 D10
Pengam Cardif 14 E14
Penge Gt Lon 10 D3
Pengelly Cnwll 4 D13
Penhallow Cnwll 1 S9
Penhalvean Cnwll 1 R11
Penhill Swindn 15 T12
Penhow Newpt 14 H11
Penicuik Mdloth 45 Q7
Penifiler Highld 59 f9
Peninver Ag & B 42 K13
Penistone Barns 31 T7
Penkill S Ayrs 38 E2
Penkridge Staffs 22 K6
Penley Wrexhm 22 C2
Penllyn V Glam 14 B14
Penmachno Conwy 28 K10
Penmaen Caerph 14 E10
Penmaen Swans 13 P12
Penmaenmawr Conwy 28 J6
Penmaenpool Gwynd 28 J15
Penmark V Glam 14 C15
Penmynydd IoA 28 F6
Pennal Gwynd 20 F4
Pennan Abers 55 R4
Pennant Powys 20 J4
Pennerley Shrops 21 Q4
Pennington Cumb 34 K10
Pennorth Powys 14 D6
Penn Street Bucks 17 L11
Penny Bridge Cumb 34 K10
Pennycross Ag & B 48 E11
Pennyghael Ag & B 48 E11
Pennyglen S Ayrs 43 S15
Pennymoor Devon 5 Q9
Pennywell Sundld 41 R9
Penparc Cerdgn 12 J2
Penperlleni Mons 14 G9
Penpoll Cnwll 2 E7
Penponds Cnwll 1 Q11
Penpont D & G 39 P3
Pen-rhiw Pembks 12 K3
Penrhiwceiber Rhondd 14 C10
Pen Rhiwfawr Neath 13 S8
Penrhiwllan Cerdgn 20 A13
Penrhiw-pal Cerdgn 20 A13
Penrhos Gwynd 28 D13
Penrhos Mons 14 H8
Penrhyn Bay Conwy 29 L5
Penrhyn-coch Cerdgn 20 E6
Penrhyndeudraeth Gwynd 28 H12
Penrice Swans 13 N12
Penrioch N Ayrs 43 L9
Penrith Cumb 40 D13
Penrose Cnwll 1 U6
Penruddock Cumb 40 C14
Penryn Cnwll 1 S12
Pensarn Conwy 29 M5
Pensax Worcs 22 G14
Penselwood Somset 7 N5
Pensford BaNES 15 L16
Pensham Worcs 15 Q3
Penshaw Sundld 41 Q10
Penshurst Kent 10 G8
Pensilva Cnwll 2 G4
Pensnett Dudley 22 K10
Pentewan Cnwll 2 C8
Pentir Gwynd 28 G7
Pentire Cnwll 1 S8
Pentlow Essex 18 J6
Pentney Norfk 26 H6
Pentonbridge Cumb 40 C6
Penton Mewsey Hants 8 F4
Pentraeth IoA 28 F5
Pentre Mons 14 H10
Pentre Rhondd 14 B11
Pentre Shrops 29 T15
Pentrebach Myr Td 14 C9
Pentre-bach Powys 13 U5
Pentre Berw IoA 28 F6
Pentrecelyn Denbgs 29 Q9
Pentre-celyn Powys 20 J3
Pentre-chwyth Swans 13 R11
Pentre-cwrt Carmth 13 M4
Pentredwr Denbgs 29 R10
Pentrefelin Gwynd 28 G12
Pentrefoelas Conwy 29 L10
Pentregat Cerdgn 20 A12
Pentre-Gwenlais Carmth 13 Q7
Pentre Hodrey Shrops 21 Q8
Pentre Llanrhaeadr Denbgs 29 P8
Pentre Meyrick V Glam 14 B14
Pentre-tafarn-y-fedw Conwy 29 L8
Pentrich Derbys 32 C15
Pentridge Dorset 7 S8
Pen-twyn Mons 14 K8
Pentwynmaur Caerph 14 E11
Pentyrch Cardif 14 D13
Penwithick Cnwll 2 C7
Penybanc Carmth 13 Q6
Penybont Powys 21 M10
Pen-y-bont Powys 29 R14
Pen-y-bont-fawr Powys 29 P14
Pen-y-bryn Pembks 12 J3
Penycae Wrexhm 29 S11
Pen-y-clawdd Mons 14 J9
Pen-y-coedcae Rhondd 14 C12
Penycwn Pembks 12 D6
Pen-y-felin Flints 29 Q7
Penyffordd Flints 30 E14
Pen-y-Garnedd Powys 29 Q14
Pen-y-graig Gwynd 28 B13
Penygraig Rhondd 14 B11
Penygroes Carmth 13 P8
Penygroes Gwynd 28 F9
Pen-y-Mynydd Carmth 13 N9
Penymynydd Flints 30 E14
Penysarn IoA 28 F3
Pen-y-stryt Denbgs 29 R10
Penywaun Rhondd 14 B9
Penzance Cnwll 1 N13
Peopleton Worcs 15 Q2
Peplow Shrops 22 F5
Perceton N Ayrs 44 C10
Percyhorner Abers 55 S4
Perham Down Wilts 8 E4
Periton Somset 5 R3
Perivale Gt Lon 17 P13
Perkins Village Devon 5 S12
Perlethorpe Notts 32 F12
Perranarworthal Cnwll 1 S11
Perranporth Cnwll 1 S9
Perranuthnoe Cnwll 1 P13
Perranwell Cnwll 1 S11
Perranzabuloe Cnwll 1 S9
Perry Birm 23 M10
Perry Barr Birm 23 M10
Perry Green Wilts 15 R12
Pershall Staffs 22 J4
Pershore Worcs 15 R2
Pertenhall Bed 25 M14
Perth P & K 50 H12
Perthy Shrops 29 T13
Perton Herefs 15 L3
Perton Staffs 22 J9
Peterborough C Pete 25 P9
Peterchurch Herefs 14 G4
Peterculter C Aber 55 R14
Peterhead Abers 55 V7
Peterlee Dur 41 S12
Petersfield Hants 9 M8
Peter's Green Herts 17 P7
Petersham Gt Lon 17 Q14
Peters Marland Devon 4 K8
Peterstone Wentlooge Newpt 14 F13
Peterston-super-Ely V Glam 14 C14
Peterstow Herefs 14 K6
Peter Tavy Devon 2 K3
Petham Kent 11 Q6
Petherwin Gate Cnwll 4 G12
Petrockstow Devon 4 K9
Pett E Susx 11 M13
Pettaugh Suffk 19 P3
Petterden Angus 51 M9
Pettinain S Lans 45 L10
Pettistree Suffk 19 R4
Petton Devon 5 S7
Petts Wood Gt Lon 10 F4
Pettycur Fife 45 R2
Pettymuk Abers 55 R11
Petworth W Susx 9 Q8
Pevensey E Susx 10 J14
Pevensey Bay E Susx 10 J14
Pewsey Wilts 8 D2
Phepson Worcs 23 L15
Philham Devon 4 G7
Philiphaugh Border 46 F12
Phillack Cnwll 1 P11
Philleigh Cnwll 1 T11
Philpstoun W Loth 45 N4
Phoenix Green Hants 9 M2
Phones Highld 53 S16
Pibsbury Somset 6 J6
Pickburn Donc 32 D6
Pickering N York 37 N9
Picket Twenty Hants 8 G4
Pickford Covtry 23 Q12
Pickhill N York 36 G9
Picklescott Shrops 21 R4
Pickmere Ches E 30 K11
Pickney Somset 6 F6
Pickwell Leics 24 H7
Pickworth Lincs 25 M3
Pickworth Rutlnd 25 L6
Picton Ches W 30 G12
Picton N York 36 H6
Piddinghoe E Susx 10 F14
Piddington Nhants 16 J1
Piddington Oxon 16 G7
Piddlehinton Dorset 7 N11
Piddletrenthide Dorset 7 N11
Pidley Cambs 25 R12
Piercebridge Darltn 36 E4
Pierowall Ork 58 C1
Pilgrims Hatch Essex 18 F14
Pilham Lincs 32 J9
Pillaton Cnwll 2 H5
Pillerton Hersey Warwks 16 B2
Pillerton Priors Warwks 16 B2
Pilley Barns 32 B7
Pilley Hants 8 F12
Pilling Lancs 35 M15
Pilning S Glos 14 K12
Pilsbury Derbys 31 R14
Pilsdon Dorset 6 J11
Pilsley Derbys 31 T12
Pilsley Derbys 32 C14
Pilson Green Norfk 27 S6
Piltdown E Susx 10 F11
Pilton Devon 5 L5
Pilton Nhants 25 M11
Pilton Rutlnd 24 K8
Pilton Somset 7 L4
Pimlico Herts 17 N9
Pimperne Dorset 7 R9
Pinchbeck Lincs 25 Q4
Pin Green Herts 17 R6
Pinhoe Devon 5 R12
Pinley Green Warwks 23 P14
Pinminnoch S Ayrs 38 E3
Pinmore S Ayrs 38 E3
Pinn Devon 6 D13
Pinner Gt Lon 17 P12
Pinner Green Gt Lon 17 P12
Pinvin Worcs 15 R2
Pinwherry S Ayrs 38 E4
Pinxton Derbys 32 D15
Pipe and Lyde Herefs 14 J3
Pipe Aston Herefs 21 S8
Pipe Gate Shrops 22 H2
Piperhill Highld 54 B6
Pipewell Nhants 24 J11
Pirbright Surrey 9 Q2
Pirnie Border 46 J12
Pirnmill N Ayrs 43 L9
Pirton Herts 17 P5
Pishill Oxon 16 H12
Pistyll Gwynd 28 D11
Pitagowan P & K 50 D5
Pitblae Abers 55 S4
Pitcairngreen P & K 50 G11
Pitcalnie Highld 53 U3
Pitcaple Abers 55 P10
Pitcarity Angus 51 L5
Pitchcombe Gloucs 15 P9
Pitchcott Bucks 16 J7
Pitchford Shrops 22 E8
Pitch Green Bucks 16 J9
Pitchroy Moray 54 F8
Pitcombe Somset 7 M5
Pitcox E Loth 46 J4
Pitfichie Abers 55 N12
Pitglassie Abers 55 N7
Pitgrudy Highld 57 S15
Pitlessie Fife 51 L14
Pitlochry P & K 50 F6
Pitmachie Abers 55 N10
Pitmain Highld 53 T15
Pitmedden Abers 55 R10
Pitminster Somset 6 F7
Pitmuies Angus 51 P8
Pitmunie Abers 55 N12
Pitney Somset 6 J6
Pitroddie P & K 50 K12
Pitscottie Fife 51 M14
Pitsea Essex 18 H15
Pitsford Nhants 24 H14
Pitstone Bucks 17 L7
Pittarrow Abers 51 S3
Pittenweem Fife 51 P15
Pitteuchar Fife 51 L16
Pittington Dur 41 Q11
Pittodrie House Hotel Abers 55 N11
Pitton Wilts 8 E6
Pittulie Abers 55 S4
Pity Me Dur 41 Q11
Pixham Surrey 9 T3
Plains N Lans 44 J6
Plaish Shrops 22 E9
Plaistow Gt Lon 10 E1
Plaistow W Susx 9 R7
Plaitford Hants 8 E8
Plawsworth Dur 41 Q10
Plaxtol Kent 10 H6
Playden E Susx 11 M11
Playford Suffk 19 Q5
Play Hatch Oxon 16 H14
Playing Place Cnwll 1 T11
Playley Green Gloucs 15 N5
Plealey Shrops 21 R3
Plean Stirlg 44 K2
Pleasance Fife 50 K14
Pleasington Bl w D 30 K3
Pleasley Derbys 32 D13
Plemstall Ches W 30 G12
Pleshey Essex 18 G11
Plockton Highld 52 E9
Plowden Shrops 21 R6
Pluckley Kent 11 M7
Pluckley Thorne Kent 11 M8
Plumbland Cumb 39 T12
Plumley Ches E 31 L12
Plumpton Cumb 40 D12
Plumpton E Susx 10 E13
Plumpton Nhants 16 F2
Plumpton Green E Susx 10 E12
Plumstead Gt Lon 10 F2
Plumstead Norfk 27 P3
Plumtree Notts 24 F3
Plungar Leics 24 H3
Plurenden Kent 11 N9
Plush Dorset 7 N10
Plwmp Cerdgn 20 A12
Plymouth C Plym 2 K7
Plymouth Airport C Plym 2 K6
Plympton C Plym 3 L7
Plymstock C Plym 2 K7
Plymtree Devon 6 D10
Pockley N York 37 L9
Pocklington E R Yk 37 P15
Podimore Somset 6 K7
Podington Bed 24 K15
Podmore Staffs 22 H3
Pointon Lincs 25 N3
Pokesdown Bmouth 8 C13
Polbain Highld 56 F12
Polbathic Cnwll 2 H7
Polbeth W Loth 45 M6
Polebrook Nhants 25 M11
Polegate E Susx 10 H14
Polesworth Warwks 23 Q8
Polglass Highld 56 G12
Polgooth Cnwll 2 C8
Polgown D & G 39 M1
Poling W Susx 9 R11
Poling Corner W Susx 9 R11
Polkerris Cnwll 2 D7
Pollington E R Yk 32 F4
Polloch Highld 48 J4
Pollokshaws C Glas 44 F7
Pollokshields C Glas 44 F6
Polmassick Cnwll 2 C8
Polmont Falk 45 L4
Polnish Highld 48 H2
Polperro Cnwll 2 F7
Polruan Cnwll 2 E8
Polstead Suffk 19 M7
Poltalloch Ag & B 48 J16
Poltimore Devon 5 S11
Polton Mdloth 45 R6
Polwarth Border 46 K8
Polyphant Cnwll 4 G14
Polzeath Cnwll 2 B3
Pomathorn Mdloth 45 R7
Pondersbridge Cambs 25 Q10
Ponders End Gt Lon 17 S11
Ponsanooth Cnwll 1 S12
Ponsworthy Devon 3 N4
Pontantwn Carmth 13 M8
Pontardawe Neath 13 R9
Pontarddulais Swans 13 P9
Pont-ar-gothi Carmth 13 N6
Pontarsais Carmth 13 M5
Pontblyddyn Flints 30 D14
Pontefract Wakefd 32 D4
Ponteland Nthumb 41 N6
Ponterwyd Cerdgn 20 G7
Pontesbury Shrops 21 R3
Pontesford Shrops 21 R3
Pontfadog Wrexhm 29 R12
Pontfaen Pembks 12 F4
Pont-faen Powys 14 B4
Pontgarreg Cerdgn 20 A11
Ponthenry Carmth 13 N8
Ponthir Torfn 14 G11
Ponthirwaun Cerdgn 12 K3
Pontllanfraith Caerph 14 E11
Pontlliw Swans 13 Q10
Pontlottyn Caerph 14 D9
Pontlyfni Gwynd 28 E10
Pontnêddféchan Neath 13 U9
Pontnewydd Torfn 14 F11
Pontrhydfendigaid Cerdgn 20 G9
Pont-rhyd-y-fen Neath 13 S11
Pontrhydygroes Cerdgn 20 G8
Pontrilas Herefs 14 H5
Pont Robert Powys 21 M2
Pontshaen Cerdgn 20 B13
Pontsticill Myr Td 14 C8
Pontwelly Carmth 20 B14
Pontyates Carmth 13 N9
Pontyberem Carmth 13 N8
Pontybodkin Flints 30 D14
Pontyclun Rhondd 14 C13
Pontycymer Brdgnd 13 U11
Pont-y-pant Conwy 28 K9
Pontypool Torfn 14 F10
Pontypridd Rhondd 14 C12
Pontywaun Caerph 14 E11
Pool Cnwll 1 R11
Pool Leeds 36 F16
Poole Poole 7 S12
Poole Keynes Gloucs 15 R11
Poolewe Highld 52 E1
Pooley Bridge Cumb 40 C14
Poolfold Staffs 31 N14
Poolhill Gloucs 15 M5
Pool of Muckhart Clacks 50 G16
Pool Street Essex 18 J7
Poplar Gt Lon 17 S13
Porchfield IoW 8 H13
Poringland Norfk 27 R8
Porkellis Cnwll 1 R12
Porlock Somset 5 Q3
Porlock Weir Somset 5 Q3
Portachoillan Ag & B 42 K7
Port-an-Eorna Highld 52 D9
Port Appin Ag & B 48 K8
Port Askaig Ag & B 42 E5
Portavadie Ag & B 43 M5
Port Bannatyne Ag & B 43 P6
Portbury N Som 14 J14
Port Carlisle Cumb 39 U8
Port Charlotte Ag & B 42 C7
Portchester Hants 8 K11
Port Driseach Ag & B 43 N4
Port Ellen Ag & B 42 D9
Port Elphinstone Abers 55 Q11
Portencalzie D & G 38 B7
Portencross N Ayrs 43 R9
Port Erin IoM 34 b7
Portesham Dorset 7 L13
Portessie Moray 54 K4
Port Eynon Swans 13 N12
Portfield Gate Pembks 12 E7
Portgate Devon 4 J13
Port Gaverne Cnwll 4 C14
Port Glasgow Inver 43 T4
Portgordon Moray 54 J4
Portgower Highld 58 D11
Porth Cnwll 1 T7
Porth Rhondd 14 C11
Porthallow Cnwll 1 S14
Porthallow Cnwll 2 F7
Porthcawl Brdgnd 13 T14
Porthcothan Cnwll 1 T6
Porthcurno Cnwll 1 M14
Port Henderson Highld 52 D3
Porthgain Pembks 12 D5
Porthgwarra Cnwll 1 L14
Porthill Staffs 31 M16
Porthkerry V Glam 14 C15
Porthleven Cnwll 1 Q13
Porthmadog Gwynd 28 G12
Porth Navas Cnwll 1 S13
Porthoustock Cnwll 1 T14
Porthpean Cnwll 2 C8
Porthtowan Cnwll 1 R10
Porthyrhyd Carmth 13 N7
Portincaple Ag & B 43 R1
Portington E R Yk 32 H2
Portinnisherrich Ag & B 49 L14
Portinscale Cumb 34 K3
Port Isaac Cnwll 4 C14
Portishead N Som 14 J14
Portknockie Moray 55 L3
Portland Dorset 7 M15
Portlethen Abers 55 S15
Portling D & G 39 P9
Portloe Cnwll 2 B9
Port Logan D & G 38 C12
Portmahomack Highld 58 B16
Portmellon Cnwll 2 C9
Port Mor Highld 48 D3
Portnacroish Ag & B 49 L8
Portnaguran W Isls 56 f2
Portnahaven Ag & B 42 A8
Portnalong Highld 59 d10
Port nan Giuran W Isls 56 f2
Port nan Long W Isls 56 c5
Port Nis W Isls 56 f1
Portobello C Edin 45 R4
Portobello Wolves 23 L9
Port of Menteith Stirlg 49 V15
Port of Ness W Isls 56 f1
Porton Wilts 8 D6
Portpatrick D & G 38 B9
Port Quin Cnwll 4 C14
Port Ramsay Ag & B 48 K8
Portreath Cnwll 1 Q10
Portree Highld 59 f9
Port St Mary IoM 34 b7
Portscatho Cnwll 1 U12
Portsea C Port 8 K12
Portskerra Highld 57 T3
Portskewett Mons 14 J12
Portslade Br & H 10 C14
Portslade-by-Sea Br & H 10 C14
Portslogan D & G 38 B9
Portsmouth C Port 9 L12
Portsmouth Calder 31 N3
Port Soderick IoM 34 d6
Portsonachan Hotel Ag & B 49 M12
Portsoy Abers 55 M4
Port Sunlight Wirral 30 E10
Portswood C Sotn 8 H9
Port Talbot Neath 13 S12
Portuairk Highld 48 D4
Portway Sandw 23 L11
Portway Worcs 23 N13
Port Wemyss Ag & B 42 A8
Port William D & G 38 G11
Portwrinkle Cnwll 2 H7
Portyerrock D & G 38 J12
Poslingford Suffk 18 J5
Posso Border 45 Q11
Postbridge Devon 5 M14
Postcombe Oxon 16 H10
Postling Kent 11 R8
Postwick Norfk 27 R7
Potarch Abers 55 M15
Potten End Herts 17 M8
Potter Brompton N York 37 R10
Potterhanworth Lincs 33 M13
Potterhanworth Booths Lincs 33 M13
Potter Heigham Norfk 27 T5
Potterne Wilts 7 S1
Potterne Wick Wilts 7 S1
Potters Bar Herts 17 R10
Potters Crouch Herts 17 P9
Potters Green Covtry 23 S12
Potters Marston Leics 24 D9
Potterspury Nhants 16 J3
Potter Street Essex 18 E12
Potterton Abers 55 S12
Potto N York 36 J6
Potton C Beds 17 Q2
Pott Shrigley Ches E 31 P11
Poughill Cnwll 4 F9
Poughill Devon 5 Q9
Poulner Hants 8 D11
Poulshot Wilts 7 R1
Poulton Gloucs 15 T10
Poulton Wirral 30 E9
Poulton-le-Fylde Lancs 30 E1
Poundbury Dorset 7 M12
Poundffald Swans 13 P11
Pound Green E Susx 10 G11
Pound Green Suffk 18 H4
Pound Hill W Susx 10 D9
Poundon Bucks 16 G6
Poundsgate Devon 3 N4
Poundstock Cnwll 4 F11
Pouton D & G 38 H11
Povey Cross Surrey 10 C8
Powburn Nthumb 47 P14
Powderham Devon 5 S13
Powerstock Dorset 6 K11
Powfoot D & G 39 T8
Powick Worcs 15 P1
Powmill P & K 50 G16
Poxwell Dorset 7 N13
Poyle Slough 17 N14
Poynings W Susx 10 C13
Poyntington Dorset 7 M7
Poynton Ches E 31 N10
Poynton Green Wrekin 22 E6
Praa Sands Cnwll 1 P13
Praze-an-Beeble Cnwll 1 Q12
Prees Shrops 22 E3
Preesall Lancs 35 L15
Prees Green Shrops 22 E4
Prees Heath Shrops 22 E2
Prees Higher Heath Shrops 22 E3
Pren-gwyn Cerdgn 20 B13
Prenteg Gwynd 28 G11
Prescot Knows 30 G9
Prescott Devon 6 D8
Presnerb Angus 50 J5
Prestatyn Denbgs 29 P5
Prestbury Ches E 31 N11
Prestbury Gloucs 15 R6
Presteigne Powys 21 Q10
Prestleigh Somset 7 M4
Preston Border 47 L7
Preston Br & H 10 D14
Preston Devon 3 Q4
Preston Dorset 7 N13
Preston E R Yk 33 P3
Preston Gloucs 15 S10
Preston Herts 17 Q6
Preston Kent 11 P5
Preston Kent 11 S5
Preston Lancs 30 H3
Preston Nthumb 47 R12
Preston Rutlnd 24 J8
Preston Somset 6 D5
Preston Torbay 3 Q6
Preston Wilts 15 S14
Preston Bagot Warwks 23 P14
Preston Bissett Bucks 16 G5
Preston Bowyer Somset 6 E6
Preston Brockhurst Shrops 22 E5
Preston Brook Halton 30 H11
Preston Candover Hants 8 K5
Preston Capes Nhants 16 F1
Preston Green Warwks 23 P14
Preston Gubbals Shrops 22 D5
Preston on Stour Warwks 15 U2
Preston on the Hill Halton 30 J11
Preston on Wye Herefs 21 R13
Prestonpans E Loth 46 E4
Preston Patrick Cumb 35 P9
Preston Plucknett Somset 6 K8
Preston St Mary Suffk 19 L5
Preston-under-Scar N York 36 C8
Preston upon the Weald Moors Wrekin 22 G6
Preston Wynne Herefs 14 K2
Prestwich Bury 31 M7
Prestwick S Ayrs 44 C12
Prestwick Airport S Ayrs 44 C12
Prestwood Bucks 16 K10
Prickwillow Cambs 26 F12
Priddy Somset 6 K2
Priest Hutton Lancs 35 N11
Priestland E Ayrs 44 F10
Priest Weston Shrops 21 P4
Primrosehill Border 46 K7
Primrose Hill Dudley 23 L11
Primsidemill Border 47 L12
Princes Risborough Bucks 16 J9
Princethorpe Warwks 23 S14
Princetown Devon 3 L4
Priors Hardwick Warwks 24 D16
Priorslee Wrekin 22 G7
Priors Marston Warwks 24 D16
Priors Norton Gloucs 15 P6
Priston BaNES 7 N1
Prittlewell Sthend 18 K15
Privett Hants 9 L7
Prixford Devon 5 L5
Probus Cnwll 1 U10
Prora E Loth 46 G3
Prospect Cumb 39 T12
Prospidnick Cnwll 1 Q13
Protstonhill Abers 55 Q4
Prudhoe Nthumb 41 M8
Publow BaNES 15 L16
Puckeridge Herts 17 T6
Puckington Somset 6 H8
Pucklechurch S Glos 15 M14
Puddington Ches W 30 E12
Puddington Devon 5 Q9
Puddletown Dorset 7 N12
Pudsey Leeds 31 T2
Pulborough W Susx 9 R8
Pulford Ches W 30 F14
Pulham Dorset 7 N9
Pulham Market Norfk 27 Q11
Pulham St Mary Norfk 27 Q11
Pulloxhill C Beds 17 N4
Pulverbatch Shrops 21 R3
Pumpherston W Loth 45 N5
Pumsaint Carmth 20 F14
Puncheston Pembks 12 F5
Puncknowle Dorset 6 K13
Punnett's Town E Susx 10 H11
Purbrook Hants 9 L10
Purfleet Thurr 10 G2
Puriton Somset 6 G4
Purleigh Essex 18 K13
Purley Gt Lon 10 D5
Purley W Berk 16 G14
Purse Caundle Dorset 7 N8
Purtington Somset 6 H9
Purton Gloucs 15 M9
Purton Gloucs 15 M9
Purton Wilts 15 T12
Purton Stoke Wilts 15 T11
Pury End Nhants 16 H3
Pusey Oxon 16 C10
Putley Herefs 15 L4
Putley Green Herefs 15 L4
Putney Gt Lon 17 Q14
Puttenham Surrey 9 Q4
Puxley Nhants 16 J3
Puxton N Som 14 H16
Pwll Carmth 13 N10
Pwll-glâs Denbgs 29 Q9
Pwllgloyw Powys 14 C4
Pwllheli Gwynd 28 D12
Pwllmeyric Mons 14 K11
Pwll Trap Carmth 12 K7
Pwll-y-glaw Neath 13 S11
Pye Bridge Derbys 32 C15
Pyecombe W Susx 10 C13
Pyle Brdgnd 13 T13
Pyleigh Somset 6 E6
Pylle Somset 7 L4
Pymoor Cambs 26 E11
Pymore Dorset 6 J12
Pyrford Surrey 9 R2
Pyrton Oxon 16 H11
Pytchley Nhants 24 J13
Pyworthy Devon 4 G10

Q

Quadring Lincs 25 P3
Quadring Eaudike Lincs 25 Q3
Quainton Bucks 16 J7
Quarff Shet 59 q6
Quarley Hants 8 E4
Quarndon Derbys 23 R2
Quarrier's Village Inver 44 C6
Quarrington Lincs 25 M1
Quarrington Hill Dur 41 R12
Quarry Bank Dudley 22 K11
Quarrywood Moray 54 F4
Quarter N Ayrs 43 R6
Quarter S Lans 44 H8
Quatford Shrops 22 H10
Quatt Shrops 22 H11
Quebec Dur 41 N11
Quedgeley Gloucs 15 P8
Queen Adelaide Cambs 26 F12
Queen Camel Somset 7 L7
Queen Charlton BaNES 15 L15
Queenhill Worcs 15 P4
Queen Oak Dorset 7 P6
Queen's Bower IoW 8 K14
Queensbury C Brad 31 R3
Queensferry Flints 30 E13
Queensferry Crossing Fife 45 P3
Queenslie C Glas 44 G6
Queen's Park Bed 17 N2
Queenzieburn N Lans 44 H4
Quendon Essex 18 E8
Queniborough Leics 24 F7
Quenington Gloucs 15 T9

Column 1

Tarporley Ches W 30 H14
Tarrant Crawford Dorset 7 R10
Tarrant Gunville Dorset 7 R9
Tarrant Hinton Dorset 7 R9
Tarrant Keyneston Dorset 7 R10
Tarrant Launceston Dorset 7 R9
Tarrant Monkton Dorset 7 R9
Tarrant Rawston Dorset 7 R10
Tarrant Rushton Dorset 7 R10
Tarring Neville E Susx 10 F14
Tarrington Herefs 15 L3
Tarskavaig Highld 59 J13
Tarves Abers 55 R9
Tarvin Ches W 30 G13
Tasburgh Norfk 23 P5
Tasley Shrops 23 P5
Tathwell Lincs 33 R10
Tatsfield Surrey 10 E6
Tattenhall Ches W 30 G14
Tatterford Norfk 26 K4
Tattershall Lincs 33 P14
Tattershall Thorpe Lincs 33 P14
Tattingstone Suffk 19 P7
Tattingstone White Horse Suffk 19 P7
Tatworth Somset 6 G10
Tauchers Moray 54 F6
Taunton Somset 6 F9
Taverham Norfk 27 P6
Taverspite Pembks 12 J8
Tavistock Devon 3 K4
Taw Green Devon 5 M11
Tawstock Devon 5 L6
Taxal Derbys 31 Q11
Tay Bridge C Dund 51 M1
Taychreggan Hotel Ag & B 49 M12
Tayinloan Ag & B 42 J9
Taynton Gloucs 15 M6
Taynton Oxon 15 V8
Taynuilt Ag & B 49 M11
Tayport Fife 51 N11
Tayvallich Ag & B 42 J2
Tealby Lincs 33 M3
Tealing Angus 51 M9
Team Valley Gatesd 41 P8
Teangue Highld 52 G13
Teanord Highld 53 S4
Tebay Cumb 35 Q6
Tebworth C Beds 7 M6
Tedburn St Mary Devon 5 R5
Teddington Gloucs 15 R5
Teddington Gt Lon 17 P15
Tedstone Delamere Herefs 22 G15
Tedstone Wafer Herefs 22 G15
Teeton Nhants 24 G14
Teffont Evias Wilts 7 S3
Teffont Magna Wilts 7 S3
Tegryn Pembks 12 J5
Teigh Rutlnd 24 J6
Teigngrace Devon 3 R4
Teignmouth Devon 5 R4
Teindside Border 46 F15
Teirford Wrekin 22 G7
Tellisford Somset 7 P2
Telscombe E Susx 10 E14
Tempar P & K 50 B6
Templand D & G 46 F5
Temple Cnwll 2 E4
Temple Mdloth 45 S7
Temple Bar Cerdgn 20 D11
Temple Cloud BaNES 7 P2
Templecombe Somset 7 N7
Temple Grafton Warwks 23 F7
Temple Guiting Gloucs 15 T5
Temple Hirst N York 32 F4
Temple Normanton Derbys 32 C13
Temple Sowerby Cumb 5 Q8
Templeton Devon 5 Q8
Templeton Pembks 12 J8
Templetown Dur 41 M10
Tempsford C Beds 17 P1
Tenbury Wells Worcs 22 F14
Tenby Pembks 12 H10
Tendring Essex 19 P9
Tendring Green Essex 19 P9
Ten Mile Bank Norfk 26 F9
Tenterden Kent 11 N4
Terling Essex 18 H1
Ternhill Shrops 22 F3
Terregles D & G 9 V14
Terrington N York 37 M12
Terrington St Clement Norfk 26 F6
Terrington St John Norfk 26 F6
Teston Kent 10 J6
Testwood Hants 8 G9
Tetbury Gloucs 15 Q11
Tetbury Upton Gloucs 22 C5
Tetchill Shrops 22 C3
Tetcott Devon 4 H11
Tetford Lincs 33 P12
Tetney Lincs 33 R7
Tetsworth Oxon 16 H10
Tettenhall Wolves 22 K9
Tettenhall Wood Wolves 32 D14
Teversal Notts 32 D14
Teversham Cambs 18 E4
Teviothead Border 46 F16
Tewin Herts 17 R8
Tewkesbury Gloucs 15 Q5
Teynham Kent 11 N5
Thackley C Brad 31 S1
Thainstone Abers 55 Q12
Thakeham W Susx 9 S9
Thame Oxon 16 H9
Thames Ditton Surrey 17 P15
Thamesmead Medway 11 M4
Thamington Kent 11 N5
Thankerton S Lans 45 M10
Tharston Norfk 27 Q10
Thatcham W Berk 18 G18
Thaxted Essex 18 G15
Theakston N York 36 K5
Thealby N Linc 32 K3
Theale Somset 6 L5
Theale W Berk 16 G15
Thearne E R Yk 33 M2
The Beeches Gloucs 15 S10
Theberton Suffk 27 T14
The Braes Highld 59 F10
The Brunt E Loth 46 J4
The Bungalow IoM 34 e4
The Burf Worcs 22 J7
The Butts Gloucs 6 C10
The City Bucks 16 H10
The Common Wilts 8 E6
Theddingworth Leics 24 C11
Theddlethorpe All Saints Lincs 33 T10
Theddlethorpe St Helen Lincs 33 T8
The Den N Ayrs 43 T8
The Forstal Kent 11 P8
The Green Cumb 34 J9
The Green Essex 18 J10
The Green N York 37 N16
The Green Wilts 37 T13
The Headland Hartpl 41 T13
The Hill Cumb 34 J9
The Lee Bucks 17 L9
The Linen IoM 34 d2
The Lochs Moray 54 H4
Thelnetham Suffk 27 M12
The Lochs Moray 54 H4
Thelveton Norfk 27 K5
Thelwall Warrtn 30 N10
Themelthorpe Norfk 27 N6
The Middles Dur 41 M10
The Moor Kent 10 K10
The Mumbles Swans 13 Q12
The Murray S Lans 44 H4
The Neuk Abers 55 E3
Therfield Herts 17 S4
The Ross P & K 50 G2
The Spring Warwks 5 L4
The Stocks Kent 11 M10
The Strand Wilts 7 T3
The Thrift Herts 26 B8
Theydon Bois Essex 18 D13
Thickwood Wilts 15 P14
Thimbleby Lincs 33 U10
Thimbleby N York 36 J5
Thingwall Wirral 30 J9
Thirlby N York 36 J9
Thirlestane Border 46 J9
Thirn N York 36 E9
Thirsk N York 36 E9
Thistleton Lancs 40 D9
Thistleton Rutlnd 24 J6
Thistley Green Suffk 18 P13
Thixendale N York 37 N9
Thockrington Nthumb 40 K5
Tholomas Drove Cambs 26 M9
Tholthorpe N York 55 M12
Thomastown Abers 55 M9
Thompson Norfk 27 M9
Thongsbridge Kirk 36 B9
Thoralby N York 36 J9
Thoresway Lincs 33 P8
Thorganby Lincs 33 P8
Thorganby N York 37 T10
Thorgill N York 37 M12
Thorington Suffk 27 T13
Thorington Street Suffk 18 P13
Thorlby N York 39 B14
Thorley Herts 18 B1
Thorley Street IoW 8 E13

Column 2

Thornaby-on-Tees S on T 36 J4
Thornage Norfk 27 N3
Thornborough Bucks 16 H4
Thornborough N York 36 F10
Thornbury C Brad 31 S2
Thornbury Devon 4 J9
Thornbury Herefs 22 D15
Thornbury S Glos 15 L12
Thornby Nhants 24 Q11
Thorncombe Dorset 6 H10
Thorncombe Street Surrey 9 Q13
Thorncote Green C Beds 17 R10
Thorncross IoW 8 F12
Thorndon Suffk 27 P14
Thorndon Cross Devon 4 K12
Thorne Donc 32 G5
Thorner Leeds 32 C1
Thorne St Margaret Somset 6 D7
Thorney C Pete 26 D7
Thorney Notts 32 Q8
Thorney Somset 6 Q8
Thorney Hill Hants 8 D12
Thornfalcon Somset 6 F2
Thornford Dorset 7 L9
Thorngrafton Nthumb 40 H9
Thorngumbald E R Yk 33 R2
Thornham Norfk 26 B2
Thornham Magna Suffk 27 P13
Thornham Parva Suffk 27 P13
Thornhaugh C Pete 25 P9
Thornhill C Sotn 31 C1
Thornhill Cumb 34 F6
Thornhill D & G 39 P3
Thornhill Derbys 31 J8
Thornhill Kirk 31 T1
Thornhill Stirlg 50 B16
Thornhills Calder 50 B16
Thornholme E R Yk 37 Q10
Thornicombe Dorset 7 Q10
Thornington Nthumb 47 M11
Thornley Dur 41 M12
Thornley Dur 41 P4
Thornliebank E Rens 44 F7
Thorns Suffk 18 H4
Thornsett Derbys 31 L6
Thornthwaite Cumb 34 L16
Thornthwaite N York 36 J9
Thornton Angus 51 M8
Thornton Bucks 16 J4
Thornton C Brad 31 R2
Thornton E R Yk 37 N16
Thornton Fife 51 S13
Thornton Lancs 35 L16
Thornton Leics 24 D7
Thornton Lincs 33 M9
Thornton Middsb 41 Q5
Thornton Nthumb 47 M9
Thornton Pembks 13 L35
Thornton Curtis N Linc 33 M5
Thornton Garden of Rest Sefton 44 E7
Thornton Heath Gt Lon 10 D4
Thornton Hough Wirral 30 J10
Thornton-in-Craven N York 35 U15
Thornton in Lonsdale N York 35 N11
Thornton-le-Beans N York 36 H8
Thornton-le-Clay N York 37 M12
Thornton-le-Dale N York 37 P9
Thornton le Moor Lincs 33 M8
Thornton-le-Moor N York 36 H9
Thornton-le-Moors Ches W 30 G12
Thornton-le-Street N York 35 E9
Thornton Rust N York 35 K4
Thornton Steward N York 36 E9
Thornton Watlass N York 36 E9
Thornydykes Border 46 H9
Thornythwaite Cumb 35 H2
Thoroton Notts 32 B7
Thorp Arch Leeds 32 H16
Thorpe Derbys 31 R15
Thorpe E R Yk 31 N8
Thorpe N York 35 B13
Thorpe Notts 32 H16
Thorpe Surrey 17 M15
Thorpe Abbotts Norfk 27 Q12
Thorpe Arnold Leics 24 H5
Thorpe Audlin Wakefd 32 D5
Thorpe Bassett N York 37 P11
Thorpe Bay Sthend 19 U9
Thorpe by Water Rutlnd 24 K9
Thorpe Common Suffk 19 N7
Thorpe Constantine Staffs 23 Q7
Thorpe End Norfk 27 R7
Thorpe Green Essex 19 U9
Thorpe Green Suffk 19 U9
Thorpe Hesley Rothm 32 C8
Thorpe in Balne Donc 32 F6
Thorpe Langton Leics 24 H10
Thorpe le Soken Essex 19 U9
Thorpe-le-Street E R Yk 37 P16
Thorpe Malsor Nhants 24 K10
Thorpe Mandeville Nhants 16 E3
Thorpe Market Norfk 27 N3
Thorpe Marriot Norfk 27 P6
Thorpe Morieux Suffk 19 L3
Thorpeness Suffk 27 R7
Thorpe on the Hill Lincs 32 K9
Thorpe St Andrew Norfk 27 R7
Thorpe St Peter Lincs 33 T14
Thorpe Salvin Rothm 32 E11
Thorpe Satchville Leics 24 J7
Thorpe Thewles S on T 36 H4
Thorpe Tilney Lincs 33 N15
Thorpe Underwood Nhants 37 R7
Thorpe Waterville Nhants 25 M2
Thorpe Willoughby N York 32 E2
Thorrington Essex 19 N10
Thorverton Devon 5 N6
Thrandeston Suffk 27 M12
Thrapston Nhants 25 N16
Threapland Cumb 16 G15
Threapwood Ches W 22 M2
Threave S Ayrs 44 M2
Three Bridges W Susx 10 G4
Three Chimneys Kent 11 K6
Three Cocks Powys 14 E4
Three Crosses Swans 13 P11
Three Cups Corner E Susx 10 H12
Threekingham Lincs 25 N3
Three Leg Cross E Susx 10 G13
Three Legged Cross Dorset 7 T10
Three Mile Cross Wokham 16 H15
Threemilestone Cnwll 1 M5
Three Oaks E Susx 11 L12
Threlkeld Cumb 40 H8
Threshers Bush Essex 18 E12
Threshfield N York 36 B13
Thrigby Norfk 27 M5
Thringstone Leics 24 L5
Thrintoft N York 36 E8
Thriplow Cambs 18 N2
Throckenholt Lincs 26 B7
Throcking Herts 17 S4
Throckley N u Ty 41 N2
Throckmorton Worcs 15 R2
Throop Bmouth 8 C12
Thropton Nthumb 47 L12
Throsk Stirlg 50 d2
Throughgate D & G 39 M4
Throwleigh Devon 5 M12
Throwley Forstal Kent 11 N3
Thrumpton Notts 24 H3
Thrumster Highld 58 H6
Thrunscoe NE Lin 25 P9
Thrupp Gloucs 15 P9
Thrupp Oxon 24 D9
Thruxton Hants 8 F4
Thrybergh Rothm 32 C8
Thulston Derbys 24 J5
Thundersley Essex 18 G11
Thurcaston Leics 24 E7
Thurcroft Rothm 32 D8
Thurgarton Norfk 27 N3
Thurgarton Notts 24 B2
Thurgoland Barns 36 J16
Thurlaston Leics 24 D9
Thurlaston Warwks 24 L13
Thurlbear Somset 6 G7
Thurlby Lincs 25 P8
Thurlby Lincs 32 K11
Thurleigh Bed 25 M16
Thurlestone Devon 5 L12
Thurloxton Somset 6 G6
Thurlstone Barns 31 S1
Thurlton Norfk 27 M5
Thurlwood Ches E 22 F2
Thurmaston Leics 24 F7
Thurnby Leics 24 F7
Thurne Norfk 27 M5
Thurnham Kent 11 L5
Thurning Nhants 25 N4
Thurning Norfk 27 M4
Thurnscoe Barns 32 D6
Thursby Cumb 40 A5
Thursford Norfk 27 M3
Thursley Surrey 9 Q13
Thurso Highld 58 D3
Thurstaston Wirral 30 E2
Thurston Suffk 18 E2
Thurston Clough Oldham 31 A9
Thurstonfield Cumb 40 A7
Thurstonland Kirk 31 A9
Thurton Norfk 27 Q1
Thurvaston Derbys 31 N7
Thuxton Norfk 27 L4
Thwaite N York 35 J4
Thwaite Suffk 27 P4
Thwaite Head Cumb 35 L8

Column 3

Thwaite St Mary Norfk 27 S10
Thwing E R Yk 37 S12
Tibbermore P & K 50 G12
Tibberton Gloucs 15 N6
Tibberton Worcs 22 B15
Tibberton Wrekin 27 P10
Tibenham Norfk 27 R14
Tibshelf Derbys 32 C13
Tibthorpe E R Yk 37 R14
Ticehurst E Susx 10 J10
Tichborne Hants 8 K7
Tickencote Rutlnd 25 L7
Tickenham N Som 14 J15
Tickford E R Yk 32 F9
Tickhill Donc 32 G6
Ticklerton Shrops 22 H3
Ticknall Derbys 23 R5
Tickton E R Yk 37 M1
Tidbury Green Solhll 36 F2
Tidcombe Wilts 46 F2
Tiddington Oxon 16 G10
Tiddington Warwks 23 P16
Tidebrook E Susx 10 H10
Tideford Cnwll 2 J9
Tideford Cross Cnwll 14 K11
Tideswell Derbys 31 J8
Tidmarsh W Berk 16 B4
Tidmington Warwks 15 P2
Tidworth Wilts 8 E4
Tiers Cross Pembks 16 H2
Tiffield Nhants 23 U3
Tigerton Angus 51 P5
Tigh a Ghearraidh W Isls 56 D5
Tigharry W Isls 56 b5
Tighnabruaich Ag & B 43 N5
Tigley Devon 5 R8
Tilbrook Cambs 25 M14
Tilbury Thurr 10 H7
Tile Cross Birm 23 P11
Tile Hill Covtry 23 Q12
Tilehurst Readg 16 G14
Tilford Surrey 9 P4
Tilgate W Susx 10 F3
Tilham Street Somset 7 L5
Tillicoultry Clacks 50 E16
Tillietudlem S Lans 44 J9
Tillingham Essex 19 S13
Tillington Herefs 22 G8
Tillington W Susx 9 Q8
Tillington Common Herefs 21 S13
Tillybirloch Abers 55 N13
Tillyfourie Abers 55 N13
Tillygreig Abers 55 R11
Tillyrie P & K 50 H15
Tilmanstone Kent 11 T6
Tilney All Saints Norfk 26 F6
Tilney High End Norfk 26 F6
Tilney St Lawrence Norfk 26 F6
Tilshead Wilts 8 E14
Tilstock Shrops 22 E2
Tilston Ches W 30 C16
Tilstone Fearnall Ches W 30 H14
Tilsworth C Beds 17 M6
Tilton on the Hill Leics 24 H8
Titlups End Gloucs 15 H9
Timberland Lincs 33 N14
Timbersbrook Ches E 31 N14
Timberscombe Somset 5 R6
Timble N York 36 E14
Timpanheck D & G 40 K2
Timperley Traffd 31 M9
Timsbury BaNES 7 M1
Timsbury Hants 8 F8
Timsgearraidh W Isls 56 d2
Timworth Suffk 27 S14
Timworth Green Suffk 26 K14
Tincleton Dorset 26 P12
Tindale Cumb 40 H2
Tingewick Bucks 16 G15
Tingrith C Beds 17 M5
Tingwall Airport Shet 59 s6
Tinhay Devon 4 J13
Tinsley Sheff 32 C8
Tinsley Green W Susx 10 C8
Tintagel Cnwll 4 D13
Tintern Parva Mons 14 K10
Tintinhull Somset 7 N2
Tintwistle Derbys 31 L6
Tinwald D & G 39 R5
Tinwell Rutlnd 24 L8
Tipton Sandw 23 C1
Tipton Green Sandw 23 C1
Tipton St John Devon 6 D12
Tiptree Essex 19 L11
Tiptree Heath Essex 18 H1
Tirabad Powys 20 J13
Tiree Airport Ag & B 48 D11
Tiretigam Ag & B 42 J6
Tirley Gloucs 15 P5
Tiroran Ag & B 48 G11
Tirphil Caerph 14 D9
Tirril Cumb 40 D9
Tisbury Wilts 7 R6
Tisman's Common W Susx 10 D13
Tissington Derbys 31 S15
Titchberry Devon 4 H7
Titchfield Hants 8 H3
Titchmarsh Nhants 25 M12
Titchwell Norfk 26 J2
Tithby Notts 24 G3
Titley Herefs 14 B9
Titsey Surrey 10 G6
Titson Cnwll 4 E11
Tittensor Staffs 22 K2
Titteshall Staffs 32 G2
Titton Worcs 22 J14
Tiverton Ches W 30 H14
Tiverton Devon 5 R6
Tivetshall St Margaret Norfk 27 Q11
Tivetshall St Mary Norfk 27 P11
Tixall Staffs 23 L5
Tixover Rutlnd 24 L7
Toab Shet 59 d8
Tobermory Ag & B 48 E7
Toberonochy Ag & B 48 H14
Tobha Mor W Isls 56 b7
Tocher Abers 55 P9
Tochieneal Moray 55 L5
Tockenham Wilts 15 M5
Tockholes Bl w D 35 K4
Tockington S Glos 15 L11
Tockwith N York 36 J15
Todber Dorset 7 P7
Toddington C Beds 17 M5
Toddington Gloucs 15 R4
Todenham Gloucs 15 V4
Todhills Angus 51 M9
Todmorden Calder 31 P4
Todwick Rothm 32 D10
Toft Cambs 25 R16
Toft Lincs 25 P8
Toft Shet 59 Q4
Toft Hill Dur 41 N14
Toft Monks Norfk 27 N10
Toft next Newton Lincs 33 M10
Toftrees Norfk 27 L4
Togston Nthumb 41 P2
Tokavaig Highld 52 F6
Tokers Green Oxon 16 H4
Tolastadh W Isls 56 e1
Toll N York 56 F2
Tollard Royal Wilts 6 D5
Toll Bar Donc 32 E6
Toller Fratrum Dorset 7 L5
Toller Porcorum Dorset 7 L5
Tollerton N York 24 F3
Tollerton Notts 24 F3
Tollesbury Essex 19 J2
Tolleshunt D'Arcy Essex 19 L11
Tolleshunt Knights Essex 19 L11
Tolleshunt Major Essex 19 L11
Tolpuddle Dorset 7 P12
Tolsta W Isls 56 F1
Tolworth Gt Lon 17 U15
Tomatin Highld 53 S3
Tomchrasky Highld 52 K10
Tomdoun Highld 52 M10
Tomich Highld 53 S5
Tomich Highld 53 S3
Tomich Highld 54 M5
Tomintoul Moray 54 J12
Tomnacross Highld 53 Q8
Tomnavoulin Moray 54 B10
Tonbridge Kent 10 G7
Tondu Brdgnd 13 U12
Tonedale Somset 6 E11
Tong C Brad 31 T3
Tong Kent 11 N3
Tong Shrops 22 Q1
Tonge Leics 24 C5
Tong Green Kent 11 N3
Tongham Surrey 9 P4
Tongland D & G 9 P4
Tong Norton Shrops 22 G1
Tongue Highld 57 R3
Tongwynlais Cardif 14 D11
Tonmawr Neath 13 U11
Tonna Neath 13 U11
Tonwell Herts 17 T9
Tonypandy Rhondd 14 C10
Tonyrefail Rhondd 14 D11
Toot Baldon Oxon 16 F9
Toot Hill Essex 18 F10
Topcliffe N York 36 H6
Topcroft Norfk 27 R8
Topcroft Street Norfk 27 R8
Toppesfield Essex 18 H6
Toppings Bolton 31 M6
Toprow Norfk 27 Q5
Topsham Devon 6 C12
Torbeg N Ayrs 43 R8

Column 4

Torboll Highld 57 S14
Torbreck Highld 53 S8
Torbryan Devon 5 R8
Torcastle Highld 49 P5
Torcross Devon 3 P9
Tore Highld 53 R6
Torksey Lincs 32 J11
Tormarton S Glos 15 R6
Tormore N Ayrs 43 R8
Tornagrain Highld 53 T6
Tornaveen Abers 55 M11
Toronto Dur 41 P13
Torpenhow Cumb 40 K5
Torphichen W Loth 45 M14
Torphins Abers 55 M12
Torpoint Cnwll 2 K9
Torquay Torbay 3 R5
Torr Devon 3 P6
Torran Highld 59 F9
Torrance E Duns 44 G4
Torranyard N Ayrs 44 C9
Torridon Highld 52 F5
Torridon House Highld 52 F5
Torrin Highld 59 G12
Torrisdale Ag & B 42 C9
Torrisdale Highld 57 N4
Torrisholme Lancs 35 P13
Torrobull Highld 57 P13
Torry C Aber 55 S13
Torryburn Fife 45 N2
Torthorwald D & G 39 R5
Tortington W Susx 9 R11
Tortworth S Glos 15 M12
Torvaig Highld 59 F9
Torver Cumb 23 U10
Torwood Falk 45 M2
Torwoodlee Border 46 F10
Torworth Notts 32 B10
Toscaig Highld 52 C8
Toseland Cambs 25 Q15
Tosside Lancs 35 M11
Tostock Suffk 27 S14
Totaig Highld 59 b8
Tote Highld 59 d8
Tote Highld 59 e8
Totland IoW 8 E14
Totley Sheff 31 U11
Totnes Devon 3 P6
Toton Notts 24 C9
Totronald Ag & B 48 D7
Totscore Highld 59 d6
Tottenham Gt Lon 17 R11
Tottenhill Norfk 26 F7
Totteridge Gt Lon 17 R12
Totternhoe C Beds 17 M7
Tottington Bury 31 M5
Totton Hants 8 F8
Toulvaddie Highld 54 B8
Tovil Kent 10 J6
Toward Ag & B 43 Q5
Toward Quay Ag & B 43 Q5
Towcester Nhants 16 E3
Towednack Cnwll 1 H11
Towersey Oxon 16 H9
Towie Abers 54 K12
Tow Law Dur 41 N13
Town End Cambs 26 C9
Townend W Duns 44 D4
Townhead Barns 36 G4
Townhead D & G 39 R4
Townhead of Greenlaw D & G 39 M8
Townhill Fife 45 P2
Town Littleworth E Susx 10 E12
Towns End Hants 16 G11
Townsend Somset 6 J2
Townshend Cnwll 1 H11
Town Street Suffk 26 C9
Town Yetholm Border 47 L12
Towthorpe C York 37 Q11
Towthorpe E R Yk 37 P11
Towton N York 36 A16
Towyn Conwy 29 N5
Toxteth Lpool 30 F10
Toynton All Saints Lincs 33 T14
Toy's Hill Kent 10 R2
Trabboch E Ayrs 44 D13
Trabbochburn E Ayrs 44 E13
Tradespark Highld 54 M5
Trafford Park Traffd 31 M8
Traigh House Highld 51 B5
Trallong Powys 14 B5
Tranent E Loth 46 D5
Tranmere Wirral 30 E10
Trantelbeg Highld 57 U6
Trantlemore Highld 57 U6
Tranwell Nthumb 47 P12
Trapp Carmth 13 V9
Traprain E Loth 46 H4
Trapshill W Berk 8 G4
Traquair Border 45 S11
Trawden Lancs 35 N2
Trawscoed Cerdgn 20 C5
Trawsfynydd Gwynd 28 J12
Trealaw Rhondd 14 B11
Treales Lancs 35 C2
Trearddur Bay IoA 28 C5
Treaslane Highld 59 b8
Trebanog Rhondd 1 S5
Trebanos Neath 14 A8
Trebartha Cnwll 2 H3
Trebarwith Cnwll 4 D13
Trebetherick Cnwll 3 N1
Treborough Somset 5 S5
Trebullett Cnwll 3 J5
Treburley Cnwll 3 J5
Trebyan Cnwll 2 P15
Trecastle Powys 13 T4
Trecwn Pembks 12 G5
Trecynon Rhondd 14 C9
Tredaule Cnwll 4 E14
Tredavoe Cnwll 1 B9
Tredegar Blae G 14 D8
Tredington Gloucs 15 R5
Tredington Warwks 15 B3
Tredinnick Cnwll 2 K11
Treen Cnwll 1 B9
Treeton Rothm 32 C10
Trefasser Pembks 12 E6
Trefecca Powys 14 D3
Trefeglwys Powys 20 G3
Trefenter Cerdgn 20 M9
Treffgarne Pembks 12 D6
Treffgarne Owen Pembks 12 D6
Trefforest Rhondd 14 C11
Trefilan Cerdgn 20 C12
Trefin Pembks 12 D5
Trefnant Denbgs 29 J2 (wait)

Trefnant Denbgs 29 T9
Trefonen Shrops 29 D11
Trefor Gwynd 28 K8
Trefor IoA 28 D7
Treforest Rhondd 14 C11
Trefriw Conwy 29 K8
Tregadillett Cnwll 4 G13
Tre-gagle Mons 14 K8
Tregaian IoA 28 J2
Tregare Mons 14 J7
Tregarne Cnwll 1 L5
Tregaron Cerdgn 20 M9
Tregarth Gwynd 28 J2
Tregeare Cnwll 4 E14
Tregeiriog Wrexhm 29 R13
Tregele IoA 28 D7
Tregidden Cnwll 1 L5
Treglemais Pembks 12 D5
Tregole Cnwll 4 E11
Tregonetha Cnwll 2 H2
Tregony Cnwll 1 M5
Tregoodwell Cnwll 4 E14
Tregorrick Cnwll 2 H7
Tregoyd Powys 14 E3
Tregunnon Cnwll 4 E14
Tregurrian Cnwll 2 H4
Tregynon Powys 20 C2
Trehafod Rhondd 14 C11
Treharris Myr Td 14 D10
Treherbert Rhondd 14 B9
Trehemborne Cnwll 2 H4
Trekenner Cnwll 3 J5
Treknow Cnwll 4 D13
Trelaverock Cnwll 2 H7
Trelech Carmth 12 K4
Treleddyd-fawr Pembks 12 C5
Trelewis Myr Td 14 D10
Treligga Cnwll 4 D13
Trelights Cnwll 3 N1
Trelill Cnwll 2 P15
Trelinnoe Cnwll 4 G13
Trelissick Cnwll 1 K6
Trelleck Mons 14 K8
Trelleck Grange Mons 14 J9
Trelogan Flints 29 J2
Trelystan Powys 22 C1
Tremadog Gwynd 28 K8
Tremail Cnwll 4 E14
Tremain Cerdgn 20 F10
Tremaine Cnwll 4 G14
Tremar Cnwll 2 H5
Trematon Cnwll 2 J8
Tremeirchion Denbgs 29 T9
Trenance Cnwll 2 H4
Trenance Cnwll 2 H7
Trenarren Cnwll 2 H7
Trench Wrekin 22 G1
Trench Green Oxon 16 H4
Trendeal Cnwll 2 G4
Trendrine Cnwll 1 H11
Treneglos Cnwll 4 F14
Trenewan Cnwll 2 H9
Trenewth Cnwll 4 C14
Trengune Cnwll 4 E11
Trent Dorset 7 P7
Trentham C Stke 22 K3
Trentishoe Devon 5 N2
Trent Vale C Stke 22 K3
Trentworthy Devon 4 H9
Treoes V Glam 13 V12
Treorchy Rhondd 14 B9
Trequite Cnwll 4 C14
Tre'r-ddol Cerdgn 20 M4
Trerhyngyll V Glam 14 B12
Trerulefoot Cnwll 2 J9
Tresaith Cerdgn 20 E10
Trescott Staffs 22 K9
Trescowe Cnwll 1 P10
Tresean Cnwll 2 M4
Tresham Gloucs 15 N11
Tresillian Cnwll 1 M5
Treskinnick Cross Cnwll 4 F11
Tresmeer Cnwll 4 F14
Tresparrett Cnwll 4 F11
Tressait P & K 50 E5
Tresta Shet 59 d5
Tresta Shet 59 u8
Treswell Notts 32 J11
Tre Taliesin Cerdgn 20 M4
Trethevey Cnwll 4 D13
Trethewey Cnwll 1 B9
Trethomas Caerph 14 D11
Trethurgy Cnwll 2 H7
Tretio Pembks 12 C5
Tretire Herefs 14 J6
Tretower Powys 14 E4
Treuddyn Flints 29 T13
Trevalga Cnwll 4 D13
Trevanson Cnwll 3 N1
Trevarrack Cnwll 1 B8
Trevarren Cnwll 2 H4
Trevarrian Cnwll 2 H4
Trevarrick Cnwll 2 G7
Trevaughan Carmth 12 H7
Trevaughan Carmth 12 K7
Tre-vaughan Carmth 12 K7
Trevellas Downs Cnwll 2 M4
Trevelmond Cnwll 2 H6
Treveor Cnwll 2 G7
Treverva Cnwll 1 K4
Trevescan Cnwll 1 L14
Treviscoe Cnwll 2 P7
Trevone Cnwll 3 N5
Trewalder Cnwll 2 D14
Trewarmett Cnwll 4 D13
Trewen Cnwll 4 F13
Trewennack Cnwll 1 J4
Trewern Powys 22 B9
Trewetha Cnwll 2 C7
Trewint Cnwll 4 F14
Trewithian Cnwll 1 M5
Trewoon Cnwll 2 G7
Treworga Cnwll 1 M5
Treyarnon Cnwll 2 H4
Treyford W Susx 9 R9
Trickett's Cross Dorset 8 B10
Triermain Cumb 48 J13
Triffleton Pembks 12 G6
Trillacott Cnwll 4 G14
Trimdon Dur 41 R12
Trimdon Colliery Dur 41 R12
Trimdon Grange Dur 41 R12
Trimingham Norfk 27 N2
Trimley Lower Street Suffk 19 N8
Trimley St Martin Suffk 19 P8
Trimley St Mary Suffk 19 R7
Trimsaran Carmth 13 R9
Trimstone Devon 5 K4
Trinafour P & K 50 C5
Trinant Caerph 14 E8
Tring Herts 17 M8
Tringford Herts 17 M8
Trinity Angus 51 Q6
Trinity Jersey 7 c1
Trinity Gask P & K 50 F11
Triscombe Somset 6 E5
Trislaig Highld 49 N4
Trispen Cnwll 1 T9
Tritlington Nthumb 41 P3
Trochrie P & K 50 G8
Troedrhiwfuwch Caerph 14 D8
Troedyrhiw Myr Td 14 C10
Troon Cnwll 1 J4
Troon S Ayrs 43 T11
Tropical World Leeds 31 U14
Trosaraidh W Isls 56 b9
Trossachs Stirlg 49 U14
Trossachs Pier Stirlg 49 U14
Troston Suffk 27 S14
Troswell Cnwll 4 F11
Trottiscliffe Kent 10 K6
Trotton W Susx 9 R9
Troutbeck Cumb 35 M6
Troutbeck Bridge Cumb 35 M6
Troway Derbys 31 U11
Trowbridge Wilts 7 Q1
Trowell Notts 24 C4
Trowle Common Wilts 7 Q1
Trowse Newton Norfk 27 R8
Troydoxhill Norfk 27 N3
Trudoxhill Somset 7 N4
Trull Somset 6 F2
Trumfleet Donc 32 F6
Trumpan Highld 59 b7
Trumpet Herefs 15 L3
Trumpington Cambs 18 P1
Trumpsgreen Surrey 16 N8
Trunch Norfk 27 N2
Truro Cnwll 1 T10
Trusham Devon 5 R5
Trusley Derbys 23 S5
Trusthorpe Lincs 33 U10
Trysull Staffs 22 J4
Tubney Oxon 16 D10
Tuckenhay Devon 5 Q8
Tuckhill Shrops 22 G4
Tuckingmill Cnwll 1 R11
Tuckingmill Wilts 7 T13
Tuckton Bmouth 8 C9
Tuddenham Suffk 19 N5
Tuddenham Suffk 18 D13
Tudeley Kent 10 G7
Tudhoe Dur 41 P12
Tudweiliog Gwynd 28 C8
Tuffley Gloucs 15 C2
Tufton Hants 8 H3
Tufton Pembks 12 G5
Tugby Leics 24 H9
Tugford Shrops 22 H4
Tughall Nthumb 47 T14
Tullibardine P & K 50 E11
Tullibody Clacks 44 K1
Tullich Abers 54 G14
Tullich Highld 54 C7
Tulliemet P & K 50 G7
Tulloch Abers 55 N11
Tullochgorm Ag & B 42 K2
Tulloch Station Highld 49 S2
Tullymurdoch P & K 50 J6
Tullynessle Abers 55 M11
Tumble Carmth 13 U7
Tumby Lincs 33 Q15
Tumby Woodside Lincs 33 Q15
Tummel Bridge P & K 50 C6
Tunbridge Wells Kent 10 H8
Tunga W Isls 56 e1
Tunley BaNES 7 M2
Tunstall E R Yk 33 R2
Tunstall Kent 11 L5
Tunstall Lancs 35 N11
Tunstall N York 36 E7
Tunstall Norfk 27 R8
Tunstall Staffs 22 A4
Tunstall Staffs 23 L4
Tunstall Suffk 19 R2
Tunstall Sundld 41 R10
Tunstead Derbys 31 U11
Tunstead Norfk 27 R6
Tunstead Milton Derbys 31 Q11
Turgis Green Hants 9 Q2
Turkdean Gloucs 15 U10
Tur Langton Leics 24 G10
Turleigh Wilts 7 P1
Turnastone Herefs 21 R16
Turnberry S Ayrs 43 R16
Turnchapel C Plym 3 M7
Turnditch Derbys 23 P4
Turner Green Lancs 35 C2
Turner's Hill W Susx 10 D4
Turners Puddle Dorset 7 P9
Turnford Herts 18 N7
Turnhouse C Edin 45 Q4
Turnworth Dorset 7 P9
Turriff Abers 55 P6
Turton Bottoms Bl w D 31 T1
Turves Cambs 26 C11
Turvey Bed 25 M16
Turville Bucks 16 H12
Turville Heath Bucks 16 H11
Turweston Bucks 16 F4
Tushielaw Inn Border 45 R16
Tutbury Staffs 23 S4
Tutnall Worcs 27 C4
Tutshill Gloucs 14 K11
Tuttington Norfk 27 N4
Tutwell Cnwll 3 J5
Tuxford Notts 32 H12
Twatt Ork 59 b5
Twatt Shet 59 d5
Twechar E Duns 44 H4
Tweedbank Border 46 G11
Tweedmouth Nthumb 47 N4
Tweedsmuir Border 45 P13
Twelveheads Cnwll 1 S5
Twemlow Green Ches E 31 S11
Twenty Lincs 25 Q11
Twerton BaNES 15 N16
Twickenham Gt Lon 17 P14
Twigworth Gloucs 15 Q5
Twineham W Susx 10 C12
Twinhoe BaNES 7 P2
Twinstead Essex 18 H6
Twitchen Devon 5 R6
Twitchen Shrops 22 E14
Two Dales Derbys 31 S13
Two Gates Staffs 24 C7
Two Mile Oak Cross Devon 5 R8
Two Waters Herts 17 N7
Twycross Leics 24 C7
Twyford Bucks 16 G5
Twyford Hants 8 H7
Twyford Leics 24 H7
Twyford Lincs 24 J6
Twyford Norfk 27 M4
Twyford Wokham 16 H4
Twyford Common Herefs 14 J6
Twyn-carno Caerph 14 D8
Twynholm D & G 49 P11
Twyning Green Gloucs 15 R4
Twynllanan Carmth 14 A6
Twyn-yr-Odyn V Glam 14 C12
Twywell Nhants 25 L4
Tyberton Herefs 21 S15
Tycroes Carmth 13 V8
Tycrwyn Powys 29 Q15
Tydd Gote Lincs 26 D7
Tydd St Giles Cambs 26 D7
Tydd St Mary Lincs 26 D7
Tye Green Essex 18 B5
Tyersal C Brad 31 T3
Tyldesley Wigan 30 M4
Tyler Hill Kent 11 L5
Tylers Green Bucks 16 J11
Tylorstown Rhondd 14 C10
Tylwch Powys 20 H4
Tyndrum Stirlg 49 S11

Ty'n-dwr Denbgs 29 P10
Tyne Tunnel S Tyne 41 T7
Tyneham Dorset 7 P12
Tynemouth N Tyne 41 T7
Tyn-y-coedcae Caerph 14 D11
Tyningham E Loth 46 H3
Tyn-y-Groes Conwy 29 N8
Tyn Rhos Powys 28 K4
Tyringham M Keyn 25 L11
Tyseley Birm 23 N11
Tythegston Brdgnd 13 T12
Tytherington Ches E 31 N11
Tytherington S Glos 15 M12
Tytherington Somset 15 R14
Tytherington Wilts 15 R14
Tytherleigh Devon 6 H11
Tytherton Lucas Wilts 15 R14
Tywardreath Cnwll 2 H7
Tywardreath Highway Cnwll 2 H7
Tywyn Gwynd 20 E4

U

Ubbeston Green Suffk 27 S13
Ubley BaNES 6 K1
Uckfield E Susx 10 F12
Uckinghall Worcs 15 Q3
Uckington Gloucs 15 N6
Uckington Shrops 22 D1
Uddingston S Lans 44 H4
Uddington S Lans 44 K11
Udimore E Susx 11 M12
Udny Green Abers 55 R9
Udny Station Abers 55 R9
Uffc.ulme Devon 6 D7
Uffington Lincs 25 Q16 (?)
Uffington Oxon 15 Q10
Uffington Shrops 22 B12
Ufford C Pete 25 N7
Ufford Suffk 19 P2
Ufton Warwks 23 S13
Ufton Nervet W Berk 16 G14
Ugadale Ag & B 42 K2
Ugborough Devon 5 N9
Uggeshall Suffk 27 T10
Ugglebarnby N York 37 T10
Ughill Sheff 31 T7
Ugley Essex 18 E10
Ugley Green Essex 18 E10
Ugthorpe N York 37 N5
Uig Ag & B 48 J8
Uig Highld 59 D6
Uig Highld 59 e6
Uig W Isls 56 d2
Uig W Isls 59 D6
Uisken Ag & B 48 G13
Ulbster Highld 58 H7
Ulceby Lincs 33 T11
Ulceby N Linc 33 N5
Ulceby Skitter N Linc 33 N5
Ulcombe Kent 11 N6
Uldale Cumb 40 K5
Uley Gloucs 15 N10
Ulgham Nthumb 41 P3
Ullapool Highld 56 H5
Ullenhall Warwks 23 N14
Ulleskelf N York 32 E1
Ullesthorpe Leics 24 D11
Ulley Rothm 32 D10
Ullingswick Herefs 22 H1
Ullinish Lodge Hotel Highld 59 d10
Ullock Cumb 34 L16
Ulpha Cumb 34 J8
Ulrome E R Yk 37 S11
Ulsta Shet 59 u5
Ulverley Green Solhll 23 N12
Ulverston Cumb 34 K10
Ulwell Dorset 8 D11
Ulwell Dorset 7 S12 (?)
Umberleigh Devon 5 N6
Unapool Highld 57 J8
Underbarrow Cumb 35 N8
Under Burnmouth Border 40 C5
Undercliffe C Brad 31 S2
Underdale Shrops 22 C4
Underriver Kent 10 G6
Underwood Notts 24 C3
Undy Mons 14 K11
Union Mills IoM 34 d6
Unstone Derbys 32 C13
Unstone Green Derbys 32 C13 (?)
Unthank Cumb 41 L4
Upavon Wilts 8 D3
Upchurch Kent 11 L4
Upcott Devon 5 S8
Up Exe Devon 6 C11
Upgate Norfk 27 P6
Uphall Dorset 7 N4
Uphall W Loth 45 M4
Uphall Station W Loth 45 M4
Upham Devon 5 S10
Upham Hants 8 H8
Uphampton Herefs 21 R10
Uphampton Worcs 22 J14
Uphill N Som 6 J2
Up Holland Lancs 30 H7
Uplawmoor E Rens 44 E7
Upleadon Gloucs 15 N4
Upleatham R & Cl 37 L4
Uplees Kent 11 M4
Uploders Dorset 7 L5
Uplowman Devon 5 C8
Uplyme Devon 6 G12
Up Marden W Susx 9 R9
Upminster Gt Lon 18 D11
Up Mudford Somset 7 P7 (?)
Up Nately Hants 9 Q2
Upottery Devon 6 F11
Upper Affcot Shrops 21 S6
Upper Arley Worcs 22 J15
Upper Arncott Oxon 16 H8
Upper Astrop Nhants 16 F4
Upper Basildon W Berk 16 F14
Upper Batley Kirk 31 T16
Upper Beeding W Susx 10 B10 (?)
Upper Benefield Nhants 25 L3
Upper Bentley Worcs 23 C4
Upper Bighouse Highld 57 U4
Upper Boat Rhondd 14 D11
Upper Boddington Nhants 24 B16
Upper Brailes Warwks 16 B3
Upper Breakish Highld 52 G3
Upper Broadheath Worcs 22 J16
Upper Broughton Notts 24 H4
Upper Buckenhill Herefs 15 M3
Upper Bucklebury W Berk 16 F15
Upper Burgate Hants 8 D9
Upperby Cumb 40 B4
Upper Caldecote C Beds 17 Q3
Upper Canada N Som 6 L2
Upper Catesby Nhants 24 B16
Upper Chapel Powys 14 D2
Upper Cheddon Somset 6 F9
Upper Chicksgrove Wilts 7 R6
Upper Chute Wilts 8 F3
Upper Clapton Gt Lon 17 S12
Upper Clatford Hants 8 G4
Upper Coberley Gloucs 15 V5 (?)
Upper Cound Shrops 22 E8
Upper Cumberworth Kirk 31 S1
Upper Dallachy Moray 54 F3
Upper Dean Bed 25 L4
Upper Denby Kirk 31 S1
Upper Dicker E Susx 10 G13
Upper Dounreay Highld 58 B3
Upper Dovercourt Essex 19 U8
Upper Drumbane Stirlg 36 B15
Upper Dunsforth N York 37 L7
Upper Eashing Surrey 9 P2
Upper Eathie Highld 54 A4
Upper Egleton Herefs 15 L3
Upper Elkstone Staffs 31 S15
Upper Ellastone Staffs 23 N2
Upper Farmcote Shrops 15 V6 (?)
Upper Farringdon Hants 9 U3
Upper Framilode Gloucs 15 N6
Upper Froyle Hants 9 N5
Upper Godney Somset 6 L4
Upper Gravenhurst C Beds 17 P4
Upper Green W Berk 8 G4
Upper Grove Common Herefs 14 K6
Upper Hackney Derbys 31 S13
Upper Hale Surrey 9 P3
Upper Halliford Surrey 17 N15
Upper Hambleton Rutlnd 24 K7
Upper Hardres Court Kent 11 M5
Upper Hartfield E Susx 11 Q5
Upper Hatherley Gloucs 15 M6
Upper Heaton Kirk 31 T16
Upper Helmsley N York 37 M14
Upper Hergest Herefs 21 G11
Upper Heyford Nhants 24 E15
Upper Heyford Oxon 24 D9
Upper Hill Herefs 21 L10
Upper Hockenden Kent 10 S8
Upper Hopton Kirk 31 T16
Upper Howsell Worcs 15 N2
Upper Hulme Staffs 31 S14
Upper Ifold Surrey 10 E3
Upper Inglesham Swindn 15 U11
Upper Killay Swans 13 P11
Upper Kinchrackine Ag & B 49 P11
Upper Knockando Moray 54 F7
Upper Lambourn W Berk 8 G5
Upper Landywood Staffs 23 L8
Upper Langford N Som 6 L2
Upper Langwith Derbys 32 D13
Upper Largo Fife 51 N12
Upper Leigh Staffs 23 L4
Upper Lochton Abers 55 N15
Upper Longdon Staffs 23 M6
Upper & Lower Stondon C Beds 17 P4
Upper Ludstone Shrops 22 J7
Upper Lybster Highld 58 G7
Upper Lydbrook Gloucs 15 R9
Upper Lye Herefs 21 R9
Uppermill Oldham 31 A9
Upper Milton Worcs 22 H13
Upper Minety Wilts 15 R11
Upper Mulben Moray 54 F4
Upper Netchwood Shrops 22 F10
Upper Nobut Staffs 23 L4
Upper Norwood W Susx 9 S5
Upper Poppleton C York 37 M13
Upper Quinton Warwks 23 F7
Upper Ratley Hants 8 F8
Upper Rissington Gloucs 15 U7
Upper Rochford Worcs 22 F14
Upper Ruscoe D & G 38 F8
Upper Sapey Herefs 22 G15
Upper Seagry Wilts 15 R13
Upper Shelton C Beds 25 M3
Upper Sheringham Norfk 27 M2
Upper Skelmorlie N Ayrs 43 R5
Upper Slaughter Gloucs 15 U6
Upper Soudley Gloucs 15 R7
Upper Standen Kent 11 R8
Upper Stoke Norfk 27 R8
Upper Stowe Nhants 24 D15
Upper Street Hants 8 D9
Upper Street Norfk 27 R7
Upper Street Norfk 27 R6
Upper Street Suffk 18 G6
Upper Sundon C Beds 17 M5
Upper Swell Gloucs 15 U5
Upper Tasburgh Norfk 27 M9
Upper Tean Staffs 23 L4
Upperthong Kirk 31 A9
Upper Threapwood Ches W 22 M2
Upperton W Susx 9 Q8
Upper Town Derbys 31 S13
Upper Town Dur 41 L12
Upper Town Herefs 21 S11
Upper Town N Som 15 L14
Upper Town Suffk 18 E11
Upper Tysoe Warwks 16 B3
Upper Ufford Suffk 19 P2
Upper Upham Wilts 8 H6 (?)
Upper Upnor Medway 10 K4
Upper Victoria Angus 51 N12
Upper Vobster Somset 7 N4
Upper Wardington Oxon 16 E2
Upper Weald M Keyn 16 H3
Upper Weedon Nhants 24 D15
Upper Welland Worcs 15 N2
Upper Wellingham E Susx 10 F13
Upper Weston BaNES 15 N16 (?)
Upper Weybread Suffk 27 Q12
Upper Wield Hants 9 R3
Upper Winchendon Bucks 16 G8
Upper Woodford Wilts 8 C5
Upper Wraxall Wilts 15 P14
Uppingham Rutlnd 24 J9
Uppington Shrops 22 F2 (?)
Upsall N York 36 H9
Upshire Essex 18 D8 (?)
Up Somborne Hants 8 F7
Upstreet Kent 11 S4
Up Sydling Dorset 7 N4
Upton Bucks 16 H8
Upton C Pete 25 P12
Upton Cambs 25 P13
Upton Ches W 30 G13
Upton Cnwll 3 C4 (?)
Upton Cnwll 4 N9
Upton Cumb 40 N6 (?)
Upton Devon 5 S10
Upton Devon 5 R12
Upton Dorset 8 N10 (?)
Upton Dorset 8 S12 (?)
Upton E R Yk 37 G10 (?)
Upton Halton 30 H9 (?)
Upton Hants 8 G4
Upton Hants 8 G10 (?)
Upton Leics 24 C9
Upton Lincs 32 J10
Upton Norfk 27 R6
Upton Notts 24 B1
Upton Notts 32 H12
Upton Oxon 16 D11 (?)
Upton Pembks 12 H9
Upton Slough 17 M13
Upton Somset 5 S10
Upton Somset 6 J9 (?)
Upton Wakefd 32 D5
Upton Warwks 23 P16 (?)
Upton Wilts 7 T4
Upton Wirral 30 D10
Upton Bishop Herefs 15 L5
Upton Cheyney S Glos 15 N16
Upton Cressett Shrops 22 G10
Upton Crews Herefs 15 L5
Upton Cross Cnwll 4 L4 (?)
Upton End C Beds 17 P4
Upton Grey Hants 9 R4
Upton Heath Ches W 30 G13
Upton Hellions Devon 5 R11
Upton Lovell Wilts 7 S2
Upton Magna Shrops 22 E2
Upton Noble Somset 7 N4
Upton Pyne Devon 5 R11
Upton St Leonards Gloucs 15 R7
Upton Scudamore Wilts 7 T3
Upton Snodsbury Worcs 15 R1
Upton-upon-Severn Worcs 15 N2 (?)
Upton Warren Worcs 22 K4 (?)
Upwaltham W Susx 9 R8
Upware Cambs 26 Q12 (?)
Upwell Norfk 26 E12 (?)
Upwey Dorset 7 R12
Upwick Green Herts 18 C3 (?)
Upwood Cambs 26 B16 (?)
Urchfont Wilts 8 C2 (?)
Urmston Traffd 31 L8
Urquhart Moray 54 H4
Urra N York 36 E6
Urray Highld 53 Q6
Ushaw Moor Dur 41 R10
Usk Mons 14 H10
Usselby Lincs 33 M4
Usworth Sundld 41 R10 (?)
Utkinton Ches W 30 H13
Utley C Brad 31 K4 (?)
Uton Devon 5 R11
Utterby Lincs 33 S8
Uttoxeter Staffs 23 L3
Uxbridge Gt Lon 17 N12
Uyeasound Shet 59 v2
Uzmaston Pembks 12 F8

V

Vale Guern 7 d2
Valley IoA 28 C5
Valtos Highld 59 F6
Valtos W Isls 56 d2
Vange Essex 18 B11 (?)
Vatsetter Shet 59 r3
Vaynor Myr Td 14 C8
Veensgarth Shet 59 d8 (?)
Velindre Powys 14 E4 (?)
Venngreen Devon 4 J9 (?)
Venn Ottery Devon 6 D12
Ventnor IoW 8 G15 (?)
Venton Devon 5 L9 (?)
Vernham Dean Hants 8 F2
Vernham Street Hants 8 F2
Vernolds Common Shrops 7 T9 (?)
Veryan Cnwll 1 U11 (?)
Vickerstown Cumb 34 J2 (?)
Victoria Cnwll 2 G6 (?)
Vidlin Shet 59 u6
Viewfield Moray 54 H3
Viewpark N Lans 44 H5
Vigo Kent 10 N5 (?)
Village de Putron Guern 7 c2
Vines Cross E Susx 10 H12
Virginia Water Surrey 17 M15 (?)
Virginstow Devon 4 J13 (?)
Vobster Somset 7 N3
Voe Shet 59 u7 (?)
Vowchurch Herefs 14 G4

W

Waberthwaite Cumb 34 H8
Wackerfield Dur 36 D3
Wacton Norfk 27 Q10
Wadborough Worcs 15 Q2
Waddesdon Bucks 16 J8
Waddeton Devon 5 C3 (?)
Waddingham Lincs 33 L5
Waddington Lancs 35 L13
Waddington Lincs 32 K14
Wadebridge Cnwll 3 N1
Wadeford Somset 6 H11
Wadenhoe Nhants 25 L3
Wadesmill Herts 17 T9 (?)
Wadhurst E Susx 10 H10
Wadshelf Derbys 31 U12
Wadworth Donc 32 G6
Wainfelin Torfn 14 E8 (?)
Wainfleet All Saints Lincs 33 T14
Wainhouse Corner Cnwll 4 E11
Wainscott Medway 10 K3 (?)
Wainstalls Calder 31 S2 (?)
Waitby Cumb 35 Q5 (?)
Waithe Lincs 33 P8 (?)
Wakefield Wakefd 32 B4
Wake Green Birm 23 C13 (?)
Wakerley Nhants 25 L9
Wakes Colne Essex 19 L9 (?)
Walberswick Suffk 27 T14
Walberton W Susx 9 R9
Walbottle N u Ty 41 M7 (?)
Walbut D & G 39 M7 (?)
Walby Cumb 40 A7 (?)
Walcombe Somset 6 M4 (?)
Walcot Lincs 25 Q11 (?)
Walcot Lincs 32 K3 (?)
Walcot Shrops 22 K11 (?)
Walcot Swindn 16 F15 (?)
Walcot Warwks 23 F7 (?)
Walcot Green Norfk 27 P11 (?)
Walcote Leics 24 D11 (?)
Walcott Lincs 33 N14 (?)
Walcott Norfk 27 R4 (?)
Walden N York 35 S9 (?)
Walden Stubbs N York 32 E4 (?)
Walderslade Medway 10 K4 (?)
Walderton W Susx 9 R9 (?)
Walditch Dorset 7 L6 (?)
Waldley Derbys 23 P10 (?)
Waldridge Dur 41 R10 (?)
Waldringfield Suffk 19 P3 (?)
Waldron E Susx 10 R10 (?)
Wales Rothm 32 D10 (?)
Wales Somset 6 P10 (?)
Walesby Lincs 33 M9 (?)
Walesby Notts 32 G12 (?)
Walford Herefs 14 K6 (?)
Walford Herefs 21 R9 (?)
Walford Shrops 22 C9 (?)
Walford Heath Shrops 22 C9 (?)
Walgherton Ches E 22 F3 (?)
Walgrave Nhants 25 J13 (?)
Walkden Salfd 31 L7 (?)
Walker N u Ty 41 S7 (?)
Walker Fold Lancs 35 L13 (?)
Walkeringham Notts 32 J9 (?)
Walkerith Lincs 32 J8 (?)
Walkern Herts 17 S7 (?)
Walker's Heath Birm 23 M12 (?)
Walkerville N York 36 F6 (?)
Walkford BCP 8 C12 (?)
Walkhampton Devon 5 N9 (?)
Walkington E R Yk 37 C10 (?)
Walk Mill Lancs 35 C2 (?)
Walkwood Worcs 23 C4 (?)
Wall Nthumb 40 K6 (?)
Wall Staffs 23 M6 (?)
Wallacetown S Ayrs 43 T11 (?)
Wallacetown S Ayrs 43 T13 (?)
Wallands Park E Susx 10 F13 (?)
Wallasey Wirral 30 E9 (?)
Wallasey (Kingsway) Wirral 30 E9 (?)
Wall Heath Dudley 22 J15 (?)
Wallingford Oxon 16 G12 (?)
Wallington Gt Lon 17 R16 (?)
Wallington Hants 8 H3 (?)
Wallington Herts 17 R5 (?)
Wallis Pembks 12 G5 (?)
Wallisdown Poole 8 B10 (?)
Walliswood Surrey 10 E3 (?)
Walls Shet 59 d7 (?)
Wallsend N Tyne 41 T7 (?)
Wallthwaite Cumb 40 H8 (?)
Wall under Heywood Shrops 22 H2 (?)
Wallyford E Loth 46 D5 (?)
Walmer Kent 11 U6 (?)
Walmer Bridge Lancs 35 C4 (?)
Walmersley Bury 31 M5 (?)
Walmestone Kent 11 S4 (?)
Walmley Birm 23 P9 (?)
Walney Ash Birm 23 N12 (?)
Walpole Somset 6 H2 (?)
Walpole Suffk 27 S13 (?)
Walpole Cross Keys Norfk 26 E6 (?)
Walpole Highway Norfk 26 E6 (?)

Column 8

Walpole St Andrew Norfk 26 E6
Walpole St Peter Norfk 26 E6
Walsall Wsall 23 M9
Walsden Calder 31 P4
Walsgrave on Sowe Covtry 23 S12
Walsham le Willows Suffk 18 M13 (?)
Walshford N York 36 H14
Walsoken Norfk 26 E7
Walston S Lans 45 M9
Walsworth Herts 17 Q5 (?)
Walter's Ash Bucks 16 K10 (?)
Waltham Kent 11 L6
Waltham NE Lin 33 P7 (?)
Waltham Abbey Essex 18 C13 (?)
Waltham Chase Hants 8 H9 (?)
Waltham Cross Herts 17 S10 (?)
Waltham on the Wolds Leics 24 J6
Waltham St Lawrence W & M 16 K14 (?)
Walthamstow Gt Lon 17 S12 (?)
Walton Cumb 40 D8 (?)
Walton Derbys 32 B13 (?)
Walton Leeds 36 N16 (?)
Walton Leics 24 F11 (?)
Walton M Keyn 16 P10 (?)
Walton Powys 21 L5 (?)
Walton Somset 6 J5 (?)
Walton Suffk 19 R7 (?)
Walton W Susx 9 R9 (?)
Walton Wakefd 32 B5 (?)
Walton Wrekin 22 G8 (?)
Walton Cardiff Gloucs 15 R4 (?)
Walton East Pembks 12 G6 (?)
Walton Highway Norfk 26 E7 (?)
Walton-in-Gordano N Som 14 H14 (?)
Walton-le-Dale Lancs 30 H3 (?)
Walton-on-the-Hill Staffs 23 L5 (?)
Walton on the Hill Surrey 10 C6 (?)
Walton-on-the-Naze Essex 19 R9 (?)
Walton on the Wolds Leics 24 F6 (?)
Walton-on-Trent Derbys 23 S6 (?)
Walton Park N Som 14 H14 (?)
Walton West Pembks 12 D8 (?)
Walworth Darltn 36 F4 (?)
Walworth Gt Lon 17 S14 (?)
Walwyn's Castle Pembks 12 D8
Wambrook Somset 6 H11 (?)
Wanborough Surrey 9 P3 (?)
Wanborough Swindn 15 U13 (?)
Wandsworth Gt Lon 17 R14 (?)
Wangford Suffk 27 T13 (?)
Wanlockhead D & G 44 K14 (?)
Wannock E Susx 10 H14 (?)
Wansford C Pete 25 M9 (?)
Wansford E R Yk 37 R10 (?)
Wanshurst Green Kent 10 K7 (?)
Wanstead Gt Lon 17 S12 (?)
Wanstrow Somset 7 N4 (?)
Wanswell Gloucs 15 M10 (?)
Wantage Oxon 16 D13 (?)
Wapley S Glos 15 S14 (?)
Wappenbury Warwks 23 S14 (?)
Wappenham Nhants 16 E3 (?)
Warbleton E Susx 10 H12 (?)
Warborough Oxon 16 G12 (?)
Warboys Cambs 26 B16 (?)
Warbreck Bpool 30 E1 (?)
Warbstow Cnwll 4 F13 (?)
Warburton Traffd 30 K9 (?)
Warcop Cumb 35 Q5 (?)
Ward End Birm 23 P9 (?)
Warden Nthumb 40 K6 (?)
Wardington Oxon 16 N2 (?)
Wardle Ches E 30 H13 (?)
Wardle Rochd 31 Q5 (?)
Wardley Gatesd 41 S7 (?)
Wardley Rutlnd 24 K9 (?)
Wardlow Derbys 31 J8 (?)
Wardy Hill Cambs 26 B12 (?)
Ware Herts 17 T9 (?)
Wareham Dorset 7 R13 (?)
Warehorne Kent 11 N4 (?)
Warenford Nthumb 47 M7 (?)
Wareside Herts 18 D11 (?)
Waresley Cambs 17 N1 (?)
Warfield Br For 16 K15 (?)
Warfleet Devon 5 Q8 (?)
Wargrave Wokham 16 K14 (?)
Warham Norfk 27 M2 (?)
Wark Nthumb 40 L10 (?)
Wark Nthumb 47 M7 (?)
Warkleigh Devon 5 M7 (?)
Warkton Nhants 25 K4 (?)
Warkworth Nhants 16 E2 (?)
Warkworth Nthumb 41 P3 (?)
Warlaby N York 36 S8 (?)
Warleggan Cnwll 2 H3 (?)
Warley Town Calder 31 S2 (?)
Warlingham Surrey 10 E6 (?)
Warmfield Wakefd 32 B4 (?)
Warmingham Ches E 30 K14 (?)
Warmington Nhants 25 M11 (?)
Warmington Warwks 16 N2 (?)
Warminster Wilts 7 T3 (?)
Warmley S Glos 15 R5 (?)
Warmsworth Donc 32 E7 (?)
Warmwell Dorset 7 R13 (?)
Warnford Hants 8 K8 (?)
Warnham W Susx 10 K3 (?)
Warningcamp W Susx 9 R10 (?)
Warninglid W Susx 10 C11 (?)
Warren Ches E 31 N11 (?)
Warren Pembks 12 E10 (?)
Warrenhill S Lans 45 M11 (?)
Warren Row W & M 16 K13 (?)
Warren Street Kent 11 M1 (?)
Warrington M Keyn 25 L10 (?)
Warrington Warrtn 30 N10 (?)
Warriston C Edin 45 N4 (?)
Warsash Hants 8 H5 (?)
Warslow Staffs 31 S14 (?)
Warsop Vale Notts 32 D13 (?)
Warter E R Yk 37 P16 (?)
Warthermarske N York 36 R9 (?)
Warthill N York 37 M14 (?)
Wartling E Susx 10 H14 (?)
Wartnaby Leics 24 J5 (?)
Warton Lancs 35 D4 (?)
Warton Lancs 35 N11 (?)
Warton Nthumb 47 L12 (?)
Warton Warwks 23 N11 (?)
Warwick Warwks 23 Q14 (?)
Warwick Bridge Cumb 40 B7 (?)
Wasbister Ork 59 b5 (?)
Wasdale Head Cumb 34 K4 (?)
Washaway Cnwll 2 C7 (?)
Washbourne Devon 5 P9 (?)
Washbrook Suffk 19 P4 (?)
Washfield Devon 5 S10 (?)
Washford Somset 6 D4 (?)
Washford Pyne Devon 5 R9 (?)
Washingborough Lincs 32 K13 (?)
Washington Sundld 41 R9 (?)
Washington W Susx 9 S10 (?)
Washwood Heath Birm 23 P9 (?)
Wasperton Warwks 23 Q15 (?)
Wass N York 36 K10 (?)
Watchet Somset 6 D4 (?)
Watchfield Oxon 15 U11 (?)
Watchgate Cumb 35 P5 (?)
Water Devon 5 R12 (?)
Waterbeach Cambs 18 P13 (?)
Waterbeck D & G 40 U6 (?)
Waterden Norfk 27 K2 (?)
Waterfall Staffs 31 S15 (?)
Waterfoot Ag & B 42 J2 (?)
Waterfoot E Rens 44 G7 (?)
Waterford Herts 17 T9 (?)
Waterhead Cumb 35 N2 (?)
Waterheads Border 45 R8 (?)
Waterhouses Staffs 31 S15 (?)
Wateringbury Kent 10 K6 (?)
Waterloo Cnwll 4 L4 (?)
Waterloo Derbys 32 B14 (?)
Waterloo Herefs 21 S11 (?)
Waterloo N Lans 45 L8 (?)
Waterloo P & K 50 G9 (?)
Waterloo Pembks 12 G10 (?)
Waterloo Poole 8 B10 (?)
Waterloo Sefton 30 F8 (?)
Waterlooville Hants 9 S9 (?)
Water Newton Cambs 25 P10 (?)
Water Orton Warwks 23 P9 (?)
Waterperry Oxon 16 G9 (?)
Waterrow Somset 6 D5 (?)
Watersfield W Susx 9 R9 (?)
Waterside Bucks 17 L9 (?)
Waterside E Ayrs 44 H5 (?)
Waterside E Ayrs 43 T13 (?)
Waterside E Duns 44 H4 (?)
Waterstock Oxon 16 G9 (?)
Waterston Pembks 12 E9 (?)
Water Stratford Bucks 16 G4 (?)
Waters Upton Wrekin 22 F11 (?)
Watford Herts 17 P11 (?)
Watford Nhants 24 E15 (?)
Wath N York 36 R9 (?)
Wath N York 37 L7 (?)
Wath upon Dearne Rothm 32 C7 (?)
Watlington Norfk 26 F7 (?)
Watlington Oxon 16 H11 (?)
Watten Highld 58 F5 (?)
Wattisfield Suffk 18 M13 (?)
Wattisham Suffk 18 L4 (?)
Watton Dorset 7 L6 (?)
Watton E R Yk 37 M1 (?)
Watton Norfk 26 H11 (?)
Watton-at-Stone Herts 17 R7 (?)
Wattston N Lans 44 H3 (?)
Wattstown Rhondd 14 C10 (?)
Wattsville Caerph 14 E11

Place	County	Page	Grid
Waulkmill	Abers	55	N16
Waunarlwydd	Swans	13	Q11
Waunfawr	Cerdgn	20	E7
Waunfawr	Gwynd	28	F8
Wavendon	M Keyn	17	L4
Waverbridge	Cumb	39	U10
Waverton	Ches W	39	Q11
Waverton	Cumb	33	N2
Wawne	E R Yk	33	N2
Waxham	Norfk	6	H10
Wayford	Somset	6	D4
Waytown	Dorset	7	Q9
Weacombe	Somset	8	D4
Weald	Oxon	16	B10
Wealdstone	Gt Lon	17	P12
Weardley	Leeds	58	F16
Weare	Somset	4	J12
Weare Giffard	Devon	4	K7
Wearhead	Dur	40	J12
Weasenham All Saints	Norfk	6	J6
Weasenham St Peter	Norfk	26	K5
Weaste	Salfd	31	M8
Weatheroak Hill	Worcs	23	R4
Weaverham	Ches W	30	R11
Weaverthorpe	N York	37	R11
Webheath	Worcs	23	R10
Wedderlairs	Abers	55	R9
Weddington	Warwks	23	N8
Wedhampton	Wilts	7	J1
Wedmore	Somset	6	J3
Wednesbury	Sandw	23	L9
Wednesfield	Wolves	23	K8
Weedon	Bucks	16	J7
Weedon Bec	Nhants	24	F15
Weedon Lois	Nhants	24	B10
Weeford	Staffs	23	N8
Weeke	Hants	24	K12
Weethley	Warwks	24	F11
Week St Mary	Cnwll	4	R4
Weel	E R Yk	33	T10
Weeley	Essex	19	P10
Weeley Heath	Essex	19	D1
Weem	P & K	50	D1
Weethley	Warwks	24	M16
Weeting	Norfk	6	G3
Weeton	E R Yk	33	R4
Weeton	Lancs	31	F15
Weeton	N York	31	T1
Weetwood Leeds	Leeds	58	N3
Weir	Lancs	25	D3
Weir Quay	Devon	5	N7
Weisdale	Shet	59	q5
Welborne	Norfk	27	L5
Welbourn	Lincs	33	S2
Welburn	N York	37	H6
Welbury	N York	37	L2
Welby	Lincs	25	R9
Welcombe	Devon	4	M8
Weldon	Nhants	24	K10
Welford	Nhants	24	B2
Welford	W Berk	16	D14
Welford-on-Avon Warwks	Warwks	15	T1
Welham	Leics	24	J4
Welham	Notts	32	Q11
Welham Green	Herts	17	Q9
Well	Hants	9	T3
Well	Lincs	33	T12
Well	N York	31	N1
Welland	Worcs	15	N3
Wellbank	Angus	51	N1
Wellesbourne Warwks	Warwks	23	Q15
Well Head	Herts	17	Q5
Wellhouse	W Berk	17	L2
Welling	Gt Lon	10	B6
Wellingborough Nhants	Nhants	26	K5
Wellingore	Lincs	33	L15
Wellington	Cumb	14	J2
Wellington	Herefs	22	G7
Wellington	Somset	15	M3
Wellington	Wrekin	7	N1
Wellington Heath Herefs	Herefs	8	G14
Wellow	BaNES	32	C13
Wellow	IoW	6	K8
Wellow	Notts	27	Q10
Wells	Somset	50	E10
Wells-next-the-Sea	Norfk	37	L12
Wellstye Green	Essex	45	N2
Welltree	F & K	26	E10
Wellwood	Fife	23	P13
Welney	Norfk	14	N5
Welshampton Shrops	Shrops	33	B11
Welsh Frankton	Shrops	40	P12
Welsh Newton	Herefs	32	F2
Welshpool	Powys	33	S4
Welsh St Donats V Glam	V Glam	14	J6
Welton	Cumb	24	E7
Welton	E R Yk	19	R9
Welton	Lincs	33	Q5
Welton	Nhants	33	R13
Welton le Marsh Lincs	Lincs	33	R4
Welton le Wold Lincs	Lincs	17	P14
Welwick	E R Yk	35	T4
Welwyn	Herts	17		
Welwyn Garden City Herts	Herts	17	Q8
Wem	Shrops	22	G4
Wembdon	Somset	6	G4
Wembley	Gt Lon	17	Q12
Wembury	Devon	3	M9
Wembworthy	Devon	4	R5
Wemyss Bay	Inver	16	P6
Wenallt	Cerdgn	21	D5
Wendens Ambo Essex	Essex	17	F7
Wendlebury	Oxon	14	J7
Wendling	Norfk	17	S2
Wendover	Bucks	27	T13
Wendron	Cnwll	1	R13
Wendy	Cambs	29	S1
Wenhaston	Suffk	30	D8
Wennington Cambs	Cambs	10	G2
Wennington Gt Lon	Gt Lon	31	T14
Wensley	Derbys	36	D8
Wensley	N York	26	D5
Wentbridge	Wakefd	22	G7
Wentnor	Shrops	26	E12
Wentworth Cambs	Cambs	57	G5
Wentworth Rothm	Rothm	14	D14
Wenvoe	V Glam	21	R12
Weobley	Herefs	9	R10
Wepham	W Susx	6	C8
Wereham	Norfk	49	P2
Werrington C Pete	C Pete	4	H13
Werrington	Cnwll	30	E9
Wervin	Ches W	32	B15
Wesham	Lancs	8	E8
Wessington Derbys	Derbys	26	A6
West Acre	Norfk	55	R9
West Alvington Devon	Devon	18	K3
West Anstey Somset	Somset	33	G12
West Ashby Lincs	Lincs	9	N10
West Ashling W Susx	W Susx	8	H3
West Ashton	Wilts	47	N9
West Auckland	Dur	6	K8
West Ayton	N York	55	S7
West Bagborough Somset	Somset	55	H10
West Bank	Halton	30	H11
West Barkwith Lincs	Lincs	57	P5
West Barns	E Loth	46	J2
West Barsham Norfk	Norfk	6	H12
West Bay	Dorset	27	J6
West Beckham Norfk	Norfk	6	G10
West Bedfont Surrey	Surrey	15	N3
Westbere	Kent	19	L9
West Bergholt Essex	Essex	26	H6
West Bexington Dorset	Dorset	10	C14
West Bilney Norfk	Norfk	21	R8
West Blatchington Br & H	Br & H	27	R5
West Boldon S Tyne	S Tyne	35	H11
Westborough Lincs	Lincs	7	T12
Westbourne Bmouth	Bmouth	5	M10
Westbourne W Susx	W Susx	31	S3
West Bowling C Brad	C Brad	27	L7
West Bradenham Norfk	Norfk	31	T13
West Bradford Lancs	Lancs	6	F6
West Bradley Somset	Somset	7	T10
West Bretton Wakefd	Wakefd	24	E3
West Bridgford Notts	Notts	11	R9
West Bromwich Sandw	Sandw	11	D14
Westbrook Kent	Kent	5		
Westbrook W Berk	W Berk	12	P6
West Buckland Devon	Devon	6	E7
West Buckland Somset	Somset	55	Q25
West Burrafirth Shet	Shet	26	G2
West Burton N York	N York	16	C4
Westbury Bucks	Bucks	7	Q2
Westbury Shrops	Shrops			
Westbury Wilts	Wilts	7	Q2
Westbury Leigh Wilts	Wilts	14	M8
Westbury-on-Severn Gloucs	Gloucs	14	K14
Westbury-on-Trym Bristl	Bristl			
Westbury-sub-Mendip Somset	Somset			
West Butterwick N Linc	N Linc	32	D5
Westby Lancs	Lancs	30	F2
West Byfleet Surrey	Surrey	9	S9
West Cairngaan D & G	D & G	38	D13
West Caister Norfk	Norfk	27	T5
West Calder W Loth	W Loth	45	M6
West Camel	Somset	7	Q11
West Chaldon Dorset	Dorset	16	C12
West Challow Oxon	Oxon	9	S9
West Charleton Devon	Devon	3		
West Chinnock Somset	Somset	6	J8
West Clandon Surrey	Surrey	9	J8
West Cliffe Kent	Kent	11	R7
Westcliff-on-Sea Sthend	Sthend	18	K16
West Coker Dorset	Dorset	6	N4

Place	County	Page	Grid
West Compton	Somset	7	L4
West Compton Abbas Dorset	Dorset	7	L12
Westcote	Gloucs	15	P4
Westcote Barton Oxon	Oxon	16	D6
Westcott	Bucks	16	H7
Westcott	Devon	5	S10
Westcott	Surrey	10	T4
West Cottingwith N York	N York	37	M16
Westcourt	Wilts	15	U16
West Cowick E R Yk	E R Yk	32	A2
West Cross Swans	Swans	13	Q12
West Curthwaite Cumb	Cumb	40	A10
Westdean E Susx	E Susx	10	U15
West Dean W Susx	W Susx	9	P9
West Dean Wilts	Wilts	9	E4
West Deeping Lincs	Lincs	25	N7
West Derby Lpool	Lpool	30	K7
West Dereham Norfk	Norfk	26	K8
West Down Devon	Devon	4	K4
Westdowns Cnwll	Cnwll	4	D13
West Drayton Gt Lon	Gt Lon	17	P7
West Drayton Notts	Notts	32	G12
West Dunnet Highld	Highld	58	G2
West Ella E R Yk	E R Yk	33	L5
West End	Bed	17	M1
West End	Hants	8	H9
West End	N Som	14	J15
West End	Norfk	27	U7
West End	Surrey	17	U7
West End	Wilts	17	P16
West End Green Hants	Hants	9	L1
Wester Aberchalder Highld	Highld	53	Q11
Westerdale Highld	Highld	58	E5
Westerdale N York	N York	37	M6
Westerfield Suffk	Suffk	19	Q5
Westergate W Susx	W Susx	9	M2
Westerham Kent	Kent	10	F6
Westerhope N u Ty	N u Ty	41	P7
Westerland Devon	Devon	3	S6
Westerleigh S Glos	S Glos	15	M13
Western Isles W Is	W Is	56	d4
Wester Ochiltree W Loth	W Loth			
Wester Pitkierie Fife	Fife	51	P15
Westerton of Rossie Angus	Angus	51	R7
Westerwick Shet	Shet	59	p7
West Farleigh Kent	Kent	10	J6
West Farndon Nhants	Nhants	28	G6
West Felton Shrops	Shrops	29	T14
Westfield	BaNES	7	M2
Westfield	Cumb	39	R14
Westfield	E Susx	12	E12
Westfield	Highld	58	D4
Westfield	N Lans	44	H5
Westfield	Norfk	25	L2
Westfields of Rattray P & K.	P & K	50	J8
Westgate	Dur	40	J8
Westgate	N Linc	32	H6
Westgate-on-Sea Kent	Kent	11	T3
West Grafton	Wilts	15	M2
West Green Hants	Hants	9	D7
West Grimstead Wilts	Wilts	8	J3
West Grinstead W Susx	W Susx	10	T8
West Haddlesey N York	N York	32	E3
West Haddon Nhants	Nhants	24	F13
West Hagbourne Oxon	Oxon	16	E12
West Hagley Worcs	Worcs	23	S1
Westhall	Suffk	27	S11
West Hallam Derbys	Derbys	23	S2
West Ham Gt Lon	Gt Lon	18	D16
Westham	E Susx	10	H2
Westham	Somset	6	K3
West Ham Gt Lon	Gt Lon	24	N4
Westhampnett W Susx	W Susx	9	P11
West Handley Derbys	Derbys	32	T4
West Hanney Oxon	Oxon	16	D11
West Hanningfield Essex	Essex	18	H13
West Harnham Wilts	Wilts	8	C7
West Harptree BaNES	BaNES	7	L1
West Harting W Susx	W Susx	9	B6
West Hatch Wilts	Wilts	7	R6
West Haven Angus	Angus	51	Q10
West Heath Birm	Birm	6	J4
West Helmsdale Highld	Highld	58	F11
West Hendred Oxon	Oxon	16	D12
West Heslerton N York	N York	37	J13
West Hewish N Som	N Som	14	K3
Westhide	Herefs	14	K3
West Hill Devon	Devon	5	S6
West Hoathly W Susx	W Susx	10	E10
West Holme Dorset	Dorset	7	U13
Westhope	Herefs	21	S12
Westhope	Shrops	21	S6
West Horndon Essex	Essex	18	F11
West Horrington Somset	Somset	15	J8
West Horsley Surrey	Surrey	7	L3
West Hougham Kent	Kent	11	N8
Westhoughton Bolton	Bolton	35	R11
Westhouses Lincs	Lincs	35	R14
West Howe Bmouth	Bmouth	7	T11
Westhumble Surrey	Surrey			
West Huntingtower P & K.	P & K	50	H12
West Huntspill	Somset	6	G3
West Hythe Kent	Kent	11	L9
West Ilsley W Berk	W Berk	16	E13
West Itchenor W Susx	W Susx	9	N11
West Kennett Wilts	Wilts	15	L15
West Kilbride N Ayrs	N Ayrs	43	R9
West Kingsdown Kent	Kent	10	A4
West Kington Wilts	Wilts	15	P14
West Knoyle Wilts	Wilts	7	Q5
Westlake Devon	Devon	3	J8
West Lambrook Somset	Somset	6	J8
West Langdon Kent	Kent	11	T7
West Lavington W Susx	W Susx	9	P8
West Lavington Wilts	Wilts	7	P1
West Layton N York	N York	36	K6
Westleigh	Devon	4	K6
West Leake Notts	Notts	24	A4
Westleigh	Devon	6	K4
Westleton Suffk	Suffk	27	T14
West Lexham Norfk	Norfk	6	K3
Westley Suffk	Suffk	18	K3
Westley Waterless Cambs	Cambs	18	G4
West Lilling N York	N York	37	L12
Westlington Bucks	Bucks	16	J8
West Linton Border	Border	45	P8
West Littleton S Glos	S Glos	15	N14
West Lockinge Oxon	Oxon	16	D12
West Lulworth Dorset	Dorset	7	U13
West Lutton N York	N York	37	P12
West Lydford	Somset	6	H2
West Lyng	Somset	26	G5
West Malling	Kent	10	B3
West Malvern Worcs	Worcs	15	N3
West Marden W Susx	W Susx	9	M8
West Markham Notts	Notts	33	N4
Westmarsh Kent	Kent	11	S5
West Marsh NE Lin	NE Lin	33	Q8
West Marton N York	N York	31	S9
West Melbury Dorset	Dorset	7	Q7
West Meon Hants	Hants	9	T5
West Mersea Essex	Essex	19	M11
Westmeston E Susx	E Susx	10	M8
Westmill	Herts	17	T7
West Milton Dorset	Dorset	6	K11
Westminster Gt Lon	Gt Lon	17	P13
West Molesey Surrey	Surrey	17	P15
West Monkton	Somset	6	F6
West Moors Dorset	Dorset	7	T10
West Morden Dorset	Dorset	7	T10
West Morriston Border	Border	46	H10
West Mudford Somset	Somset	6	H2
West Ness N York	N York	37	M10
West Newton Cumb	Cumb	39	L3
West Newton E R Yk	E R Yk	33	S4
West Newton Norfk	Norfk	26	H4
West Newton Somset	Somset	6		
West Norwood Gt Lon	Gt Lon	10	D3
Westoe S Tyne	S Tyne	41	M8
West Ogwell Devon	Devon	3	S6
Weston	BaNES	15	M15
Weston	Ches E	31	L1
Weston	Halton	30	H4
Weston	Hants	9	M6
Weston	Herts	17	S6
Weston	Lincs	25	N5
Weston	N York	31	Q4
Weston	Notts	32	H13
Weston	Shrops	29	N7
Weston	Shrops	22	H5
Weston	Staffs	23	L4
Weston	W Berk	12	C3
Weston Beggard Herefs	Herefs	15	P12
Westonbirt	Gloucs	15	N4
Weston by Welland Nhants	Nhants			
Weston Colville Cambs	Cambs	18	G4
Weston Corbett Hants	Hants	9	Q5
Weston Coyney C Stke	C Stke	22	H3
Weston Favell Nhants	Nhants	24	H15
Westoning	C Beds	17	N5

Place	County	Page	Grid
Weston-in-Gordano N Som	N Som	14	J14
Weston Jones Staffs	Staffs	22	H5
Weston Longville Norfk	Norfk	27	P6
Weston Lullingfields Shrops	Shrops			
Weston-on-the-Green Oxon	Oxon	16	F7
Weston Patrick Hants	Hants	9	L4
Weston Rhyn Shrops	Shrops	29	S12
Weston-sub-Edge Gloucs	Gloucs	15	T3
Weston-super-Mare N Som	N Som	14	G16
Weston Turville Bucks	Bucks	16	K8
Weston-under-Lizard Staffs	Staffs	22	J7
Weston under Penyard Herefs	Herefs	15	L6
Weston-under-Redcastle Shrops	Shrops	22	E4
Weston under Wetherley Warwks	Warwks	23	S14
Westonwick Keyset Shrops	Shrops	21	P7
Weston Underwood Derbys	Derbys	23	Q2
Weston Underwood M Keyn	M Keyn	16	K2
Westow N York	N York	14	J14
West Orchard Dorset	Dorset	6	H5
West Overton Wilts	Wilts	15	T15
West Park Abers	Abers	55	Q15
West Parley Dorset	Dorset	7	T11
West Peckham Kent	Kent	10	J10
West Pelton Dur	Dur	41	P10
West Pennard Somset	Somset	6	K4
West Pentire Cnwll	Cnwll	1	S8
West Perry Cambs	Cambs	25	N14
West Porlock Somset	Somset	5	H7
Westport Somset	Somset	6	K3
West Putford Devon	Devon	4	J9
West Quantoxhead Somset	Somset	6	D4
West Rainton Dur	Dur	41	Q11
West Rasen Lincs	Lincs	33	M9
Westray Airport Ork	Ork	58	c1
West Raynham Norfk	Norfk	6	J6
Westrigg W Loth	W Loth	45	L6
Westrop Swindn	Swindn	15	U11
West Rounton N York	N York	36	H6
West Row Suffk	Suffk	18	H13
West Rudham Norfk	Norfk	26	K4
West Runton Norfk	Norfk	27	Q2
Westruther Border	Border	46	H11
Westry Cambs	Cambs	25	S9
West Saltoun E Loth	E Loth	46	F6
West Sandford Devon	Devon	6	D5
West Sandwick Shet	Shet	59	s4
West Scrafton N York	N York	36	C9
West Stafford Dorset	Dorset	7	P12
West Stockwith Notts	Notts	32	H6
West Stoke W Susx	W Susx	9	N10
West Stour Dorset	Dorset	7	N5
West Stourmouth Kent	Kent	11	S5
West Stow Suffk	Suffk	26	J13
West Stowell Wilts	Wilts	15	T16
West Street Suffk	Suffk	27	M13
West Tanfield N York	N York	36	E10
West Taphouse Cnwll	Cnwll	2	E8
West Tarbert Ag & B	Ag & B	43	L5
West Tarring W Susx	W Susx	9	S11
West Thirston Nthumb	Nthumb	41	N1
West Thorney W Susx	W Susx	9	M11
West Thorpe Notts	Notts	24	F5
West Thurrock Thurr	Thurr	10	H2
West Tilbury Thurr	Thurr	10	G2
West Tisted Hants	Hants	9	S4
West Torrington Lincs	Lincs	33	N11
West Town Hants	Hants	9	M12
West Town N Som	N Som	14	H4
West Tytherley Hants	Hants	8	H3
West Walton Norfk	Norfk	26	E6
Westward Cumb	Cumb	39	V11
Westward Ho! Devon	Devon	4	H7
Westwell Kent	Kent	11	N7
Westwell Oxon	Oxon	15	U8
Westwell Leacon Kent	Kent	11	N7
West Wellow Hants	Hants	8	F8
West Wembury Devon	Devon	2	K4
West Wemyss Fife	Fife	45	S1
Westwick Cambs	Cambs	26	D14
West Wickham Cambs	Cambs	18	G4
West Wickham Gt Lon	Gt Lon	10	E4
West Williamston Pembks	Pembks	12	G9
West Winch Norfk	Norfk	26	G6
West Winterslow Wilts	Wilts	8	H2
West Wittering W Susx	W Susx	9	M12
West Witton N York	N York	36	C9
Westwood Devon	Devon	5	S11
Westwood Kent	Kent	11	U5
Westwood Wilts	Wilts	7	P1
West Woodburn Nthumb	Nthumb	40	G1
Westwoodside N Linc	N Linc	32	H6
West Worldham Hants	Hants	9	M6
West Worthing W Susx	W Susx	9	S11
West Wratting Cambs	Cambs	18	G5
Wetheral Cumb	Cumb	40	C15
Wetherby Leeds	Leeds	36	H15
Wetherden Suffk	Suffk	18	M3
Wetheringsett Suffk	Suffk	27	P14
Wethersfield Essex	Essex	18	H1
Wethersta Shet	Shet	59	q5
Wetherup Street Suffk	Suffk	19	R1
Wetley Rocks Staffs	Staffs	31	P16
Wettenhall Ches E	Ches E	30	D14
Wetton Staffs	Staffs	31	M1
Wetwang E R Yk	E R Yk	37	Q13
Wetwood Staffs	Staffs	22	H4
Wexcombe Wilts	Wilts	8	P2
Wexbourne North	North	47	Q12
Weybourne Norfk	Norfk	27	P2
Weybread Suffk	Suffk	27	R12
Weybread Street Suffk	Suffk	27	R12
Weybridge Surrey	Surrey	10	C11
Weycroft Devon	Devon	6	G11
Weydale Highld	Highld	58	F3
Weyhill Hants	Hants	8	M4
Weymouth Dorset	Dorset	7	N14
Whaddon Bucks	Bucks	16	J4
Whaddon Cambs	Cambs	17	S1
Whaddon Gloucs	Gloucs	15	P8
Whaddon Wilts	Wilts	15	Q16
Whaddon Wilts	Wilts	8	G3
Whaley Derbys	Derbys	32	D11
Whaley Bridge Derbys	Derbys	31	E12
Whaley Thorns Derbys	Derbys	32	E12
Whaligoe Highld	Highld	58	G8
Whalley Lancs	Lancs	31	L2
Whalton Nthumb	Nthumb	41	N5
Whaplode Lincs	Lincs	25	N6
Whaplode Drove Lincs	Lincs	25	N9
Wharf Warwks	Warwks	16	D1
Wharfe N York	N York	35	S12
Wharles Lancs	Lancs	30	G2
Wharley End C Beds	C Beds	17	L3
Wharncliffe Side Sheff	Sheff	31	L8
Wharram-le-Street N York	N York	37	P12
Wharton Herefs	Herefs	22	D16
Whashton N York	N York	36	D6
Whasset Cumb	Cumb	35	N10
Whatcote Warwks	Warwks	16	Q3
Whateley Warwks	Warwks	23	L8
Whatfield Suffk	Suffk	19	M9
Whatley Somset	Somset	6	K8
Whatley Somset	Somset	7	N4
Whatlington E Susx	E Susx	11	U8
Whatsole Street Kent	Kent	11	N7
Whatstandwell Derbys	Derbys	32	J8
Whatton Notts	Notts	24	H2
Whauphill D & G	D & G	38	H10
Whaw N York	N York	31	L6
Wheatacre Norfk	Norfk	27	S10
Wheathampstead Herts	Herts	17	Q8
Wheatley Hants	Hants	9	U3
Wheatley Oxon	Oxon	16	G6
Wheatley Hills Donc	Donc	32	E6
Wheaton Aston Staffs	Staffs	22	J8
Wheddon Cross Somset	Somset	5	R4
Wheelock Ches E	Ches E	31	J1
Wheelton Lancs	Lancs	31	Q6
Wheldrake C York	C York	37	M16
Whelford Gloucs	Gloucs	15	U8
Whelpley Hill Bucks	Bucks	17	E8
Whempstead Herts	Herts	17	S8
Whenby N York	N York	37	U8
Wherstead Suffk	Suffk	19	P4
Wherwell Hants	Hants	8	K4
Wheston Derbys	Derbys	31	L12
Whetsted Kent	Kent	10	J7
Whetstone Leics	Leics	24	F16
Whicham Cumb	Cumb	34	K1
Whichford Warwks	Warwks	16	N5
Whickham Gatesd	Gatesd	41	N6
Whiddon Down Devon	Devon	5	N12
Whigstreet Angus	Angus	51	N2
Whilton Nhants	Nhants	24	F14
Whimple Devon	Devon	5	C11
Whimpwell Green Norfk	Norfk	27	T6
Whinburgh Norfk	Norfk	6	E8
Whinnie Liggate D & G	D & G	39	M10
Whinnyfold Abers	Abers	55	T8
Whippingham IoW	IoW	9	J11
Whipsnade C Beds	C Beds	17	N7
Whipton Devon	Devon	5	U9
Whisby Lincs	Lincs	33	L9
Whissendine Rutlnd	Rutlnd	25	N5
Whissonsett Norfk	Norfk	27	L5
Whistlefield Inn Ag & B	Ag & B	43	R6
Whistley Green Wokham	Wokham	16	B10
Whiston Knows	Knows	30	K8
Whiston Nhants	Nhants	25	S14
Whiston Rothm	Rothm	32	Q8
Whiston Staffs	Staffs	22	K8

Place	County	Page	Grid
Whiston Staffs	Staffs	23	M1
Whitbeck Cumb	Cumb	34	H9
Whitbourne Herefs	Herefs	22	G1
Whitburn S Tyne	S Tyne	41	S8
Whitburn W Loth	W Loth	45	L6
Whitby Ches W	Ches W	30	K7
Whitby N York	N York	37	L15
Whitchester Border	Border	40	G6
Whitchurch BaNES	BaNES	15	L15
Whitchurch Bucks	Bucks	16	J7
Whitchurch Cardif	Cardif	14	D15
Whitchurch Devon	Devon	5	C4
Whitchurch Hants	Hants	8	H4
Whitchurch Herefs	Herefs	14	K3
Whitchurch Oxon	Oxon	16	G14
Whitchurch Pembks	Pembks	12	C6
Whitchurch Shrops	Shrops	22	E2
Whitchurch Canonicorum Dorset	Dorset	6	H11
Whitchurch Hill Oxon	Oxon	16	G13
Whitcombe Dorset	Dorset	7	N13
Whitcot Shrops	Shrops	21	R5
Whiteacre Heath Warwks	Warwks	23	P10
White Ball Somset	Somset	35	M3
Whitebridge Highld	Highld	53	P12
Whitebrook Mons	Mons	14	P10
Whitebushes Surrey	Surrey	10	C7
Whitecairns Abers	Abers	55	S12
Whitechapel Gt Lon	Gt Lon	17	S13
White Chapel Lancs	Lancs	30	H1
Whitecliffe Gloucs	Gloucs	14	K8
White Colne Essex	Essex	18	K8
White Cross Cnwll	Cnwll	1	R14
Whitecross Falk	Falk	45	M4
Whiteface Highld	Highld	57	R15
Whitefarland N Ayrs	N Ayrs	43	S13
Whitefaulds S Ayrs	S Ayrs	43	S15
Whitefield Bury	Bury	31	M7
Whitefield Somset	Somset	6	D6
Whiteford Abers	Abers	55	P10
Whitegate Ches W	Ches W	30	J13
Whitehall Ork	Ork	58	f3
Whitehaven Cumb	Cumb	34	F4
Whitehills Abers	Abers	9	N6
Whitehouse Abers	Abers	55	N4
Whitehouse Ag & B	Ag & B	43	L6
Whitehouse Common Birm	Birm	23	L9
Whitekirk E Loth	E Loth	46	H3
White Lackington Dorset	Dorset	7	N11
Whitelackington Somset	Somset	6	H8
White Ladies Aston Worcs	Worcs	15	Q1
Whiteleaf Bucks	Bucks	16	K9
Whiteley Hants	Hants	8	J10
Whiteley Bank IoW	IoW	9	J15
Whiteley Green Surrey	Surrey	10	E2
Whitemire Moray	Moray	54	C6
Whitemoor C Nott	C Nott	24	E2
Whitemoor Cnwll	Cnwll	2	C6
Whiteness Shet	Shet	59	q6
White Notley Essex	Essex	18	J10
Whiteparish Wilts	Wilts	8	H3
White Pit Lincs	Lincs	33	S11
Whiterashes Abers	Abers	55	R10
White Roding Essex	Essex	18	F11
Whiterow Highld	Highld	58	J6
Whiterow Moray	Moray	54	D5
Whitesmith E Susx	E Susx	10	C15
Whitestaunton Somset	Somset	6	G9
Whitestone Cross Devon	Devon	5	Q12
White Waltham W & M	W & M	16	K14
Whiteway BaNES	BaNES	15	M8
Whitewell Lancs	Lancs	31	K1
Whitfield C Dund	C Dund	51	N10
Whitfield Kent	Kent	11	T7
Whitfield Nthumb	Nthumb	40	H9
Whitfield S Glos	S Glos	15	M11
Whitford Devon	Devon	6	F6
Whitford Flints	Flints	30	B6
Whitgift E R Yk	E R Yk	32	J4
Whitgreave Staffs	Staffs	22	K4
Whithorn D & G	D & G	38	H10
Whiting Bay N Ayrs	N Ayrs	43	P12
Whitkirk Leeds	Leeds	32	B2
Whitland Carmth	Carmth	13	J7
Whitlaw Border	Border	46	B14
Whitletts S Ayrs	S Ayrs	44	C15
Whitley N York	N York	32	E4
Whitley Readg	Readg	16	J15
Whitley Sheff	Sheff	32	B8
Whitley Wilts	Wilts	15	P15
Whitley Bay N Tyne	N Tyne	41	S5
Whitley Chapel Nthumb	Nthumb	40	J9
Whitley Lower Kirk	Kirk	31	T5
Whitminster Gloucs	Gloucs	15	N9
Whitmore Staffs	Staffs	22	J2
Whitnage Devon	Devon	5	B8
Whitnash Warwks	Warwks	23	R15
Whitney-on-Wye Herefs	Herefs	21	R5
Whitsbury Hants	Hants	8	C8
Whitsome Border	Border	47	M8
Whitson Newpt	Newpt	14	H13
Whitstable Kent	Kent	11	Q4
Whitstone Cnwll	Cnwll	4	G12
Whittingham Nthumb	Nthumb	47	P15
Whittingslow Shrops	Shrops	21	S6
Whittington Derbys	Derbys	31	C12
Whittington Gloucs	Gloucs	15	R6
Whittington Lancs	Lancs	35	S1
Whittington Norfk	Norfk	26	G2
Whittington Shrops	Shrops	30	G1
Whittington Staffs	Staffs	22	P7
Whittington Staffs	Staffs	23	R9
Whittington Warwks	Warwks	23	N8
Whittington Worcs	Worcs	15	T9
Whittle-le-Woods Lancs	Lancs	30	K2
Whittlesey Cambs	Cambs	25	K2
Whittlesford Cambs	Cambs	18	Q4
Whitton N Linc	N Linc	32	J2
Whitton Powys	Powys	21	P9
Whitton S on T	S on T	41	M2
Whitton Shrops	Shrops	22	C11
Whittonstall Nthumb	Nthumb	41	R11
Whitway Hants	Hants	8	E1
Whitwell Derbys	Derbys	32	E11
Whitwell Herts	Herts	17	R8
Whitwell IoW	IoW	9	S13
Whitwell N York	N York	36	D6
Whitwell Rutlnd	Rutlnd	24	K7
Whitwell-on-the-Hill N York	N York	37	M5
Whitwick Leics	Leics	23	N6
Whitwood Wakefd	Wakefd	32	E3
Whitworth Lancs	Lancs	31	E5
Whixall Shrops	Shrops	22	E5
Whixley N York	N York	36	H14
Whorlton Dur	Dur	36	K6
Whyle Herefs	Herefs	22	E15
Whyteleafe Surrey	Surrey	10	D5
Wibsey C Brad	C Brad	31	D1
Wibtoft Warwks	Warwks	24	D15
Wichenford Worcs	Worcs	22	H15
Wichling Kent	Kent	11	M6
Wick Bmouth	Bmouth	8	D13
Wick Highld	Highld	58	J5
Wick S Glos	S Glos	15	M14
Wick V Glam	V Glam	14	K7
Wick W Susx	W Susx	9	R11
Wick Worcs	Worcs	15	R2
Wicken Cambs	Cambs	18	E5
Wicken Nhants	Nhants	16	J4
Wicken Bonhunt Essex	Essex	18	E8
Wickenby Lincs	Lincs	33	N10
Wicken Green Village Norfk	Norfk	26	K3
Wickersley Rothm	Rothm	32	D9
Wicker Street Green Suffk	Suffk	19	M6
Wickford Essex	Essex	18	J14
Wickham Hants	Hants	8	H11
Wickham W Berk	W Berk	16	D15
Wickham Bishops Essex	Essex	18	K11
Wickhambreaux Kent	Kent	23	P1
Wickhambrook Suffk	Suffk	18	K9
Wickhamford Worcs	Worcs	15	S3
Wickham Green Suffk	Suffk	19	N1
Wickham Market Suffk	Suffk	19	R4
Wickhampton Norfk	Norfk	6	U3
Wickham St Paul Essex	Essex	18	K7
Wickham Skeith Suffk	Suffk	27	N14
Wickham Street Suffk	Suffk			

Place	County	Page	Grid
Wiggenhall St Germans Norfk	Norfk	26	F6
Wiggenhall St Mary Magdalen Norfk	Norfk	26	F6
Wiggenhall St Mary the Virgin Norfk	Norfk	27	L14
Wigginton Herts	Herts	17	L8
Wigginton Oxon	Oxon	16	D4
Wigginton Shrops	Shrops	29	S14
Wigginton Staffs	Staffs	23	M8
Wiggonby Cumb	Cumb	40	A10
Wighill N York	N York	36	H15
Wighton Norfk	Norfk	22	R9
Wigley Hants	Hants	8	H4
Wigmore Herefs	Herefs	21	P9
Wigmore Medway	Medway	11	L4
Wigsley Notts	Notts	32	M12
Wigsthorpe Nhants	Nhants	25	M12
Wigston Leics	Leics	24	F16
Wigston Fields Leics	Leics	24	F9
Wigston Parva Leics	Leics	24	D16
Wigthorpe Notts	Notts	32	Q3
Wigtoft Lincs	Lincs	25	Q3
Wigton Cumb	Cumb	39	V10
Wigtown D & G	D & G	38	G5
Wike Leeds	Leeds	36	G16
Wilbarston Nhants	Nhants	24	J3
Wilberfoss E R Yk	E R Yk	37	N15
Wilburton Cambs	Cambs	26	D7
Wilby Nhants	Nhants	24	J14
Wilby Norfk	Norfk	27	Q13
Wilby Suffk	Suffk	27	T12
Wilcot Wilts	Wilts	15	T16
Wilcott Shrops	Shrops	29	P14
Wilddaughterlands Ches E	Ches E	31	P13
Wilden Bed	Bed	25	N16
Wilden Worcs	Worcs	22	J13
Wildmanbridge S Lans	S Lans	45	J8
Wildmoor Worcs	Worcs	23	J4
Wildsworth Lincs	Lincs	32	J8
Willand Devon	Devon	6	C12
Willaston Ches E	Ches E	30	K15
Willaston Ches W	Ches W	30	L11
Willen M Keyn	M Keyn	24	J4
Willenhall Covtry	Covtry	23	R13
Willenhall Wsall	Wsall	23	K8
Willerby E R Yk	E R Yk	37	N10
Willerby N York	N York	37	Q10
Willersey Gloucs	Gloucs	21	Q12
Willersley Herefs	Herefs	15	T4
Willesborough Kent	Kent	11	N8
Willesborough Lees Kent	Kent	11	P8
Willesden Gt Lon	Gt Lon	17	P12
Willesley Wilts	Wilts	15	L15
Willett Somset	Somset	6	D5
Willey Shrops	Shrops	22	D8
Willey Warwks	Warwks	24	E10
Willey Green Surrey	Surrey	9	S2
Williamscot Oxon	Oxon	16	N11
Willian Herts	Herts	17	G5
Willingale Essex	Essex	6	H14
Willingdon E Susx	E Susx	10	S14
Willingham Cambs	Cambs	26	D11
Willingham by Stow Lincs	Lincs	32	K10
Willington Bed	Bed	25	Q12
Willington Derbys	Derbys	23	Q4
Willington Dur	Dur	41	P13
Willington Kent	Kent	10	J5
Willington Warwks	Warwks	16	H3
Willington Corner Ches W	Ches W	30	M8
Willitoft E R Yk	E R Yk	32	H2
Willoughby Lincs	Lincs	33	S12
Willoughby Warwks	Warwks	24	E14
Willoughby-on-the-Wolds Notts	Notts	24	F5
Willoughby Waterleys Leics	Leics	32	E9
Willoughton Lincs	Lincs	32	H10
Willows Green Essex	Essex	18	H10
Willtown Somset	Somset	6	K4
Wilmcote Warwks	Warwks	23	P16
Wilmington Devon	Devon	6	F6
Wilmington E Susx	E Susx	10	G16
Wilmington Kent	Kent	10	F2
Wilmslow Ches E	Ches E	31	M11
Wilpshire Lancs	Lancs	31	L3
Wilsden C Brad	C Brad	31	J4
Wilsford Lincs	Lincs	25	R9
Wilsford Wilts	Wilts	8	C5
Wilsford Wilts	Wilts	8	C2
Wilshaw Kirk	Kirk	36	E14
Wilsill N York	N York	36	F9
Wilson Leics	Leics	24	C5
Wilson S Lans	S Lans	45	L8
Wilsthorpe Lincs	Lincs	25	N7
Wilstone Herts	Herts	16	N6
Wilton Herefs	Herefs	37	P10
Wilton N York	N York	37	P10
Wilton R & Cl	R & Cl	36	K3
Wilton Wilts	Wilts	8	E1
Wilton Wilts	Wilts	8	T1
Wilton Dean Border	Border	46	F14
Wimbish Green Essex	Essex	17	L4
Wimblebury Staffs	Staffs	23	S11
Wimbledon Gt Lon	Gt Lon	17	S11
Wimblington Cambs	Cambs	16	K2
Wimboldsley Ches W	Ches W	30	K14
Wimborne Minster Dorset	Dorset	7	S11
Wimborne St Giles Dorset	Dorset	26	S8
Wimpole Cambs	Cambs	17	S2
Wimpstone Warwks	Warwks	15	U2
Wincanton Somset	Somset	7	N6
Winchburgh W Loth	W Loth	45	N4
Winchcombe Gloucs	Gloucs	15	M12
Winchelsea E Susx	E Susx	11	M12
Winchester Hants	Hants	9	N4
Winchet Hill Kent	Kent	10	K8
Winchfield Hants	Hants	9	S2
Winchmore Hill Bucks	Bucks	17	L11
Winchmore Hill Gt Lon	Gt Lon	17	R11
Wincle Ches E	Ches E	31	R1
Wincobank Sheff	Sheff	32	M7
Windermere Cumb	Cumb	35	M1
Winderton Warwks	Warwks	16	M7
Windhill Highld	Highld	53	S5
Windlesham Surrey	Surrey	9	L5
Windmill Cnwll	Cnwll	1	U5
Windsham Surrey	Surrey	10	Q5
Windsor W & M	W & M	16	J5
Windsoredge Gloucs	Gloucs	15	U5
Windsor Green Suffk	Suffk	51	C16
Windygates Fife	Fife	41	M9
Wineham W Susx	W Susx	10	L6
Winestead E R Yk	E R Yk	33	N4
Winfarthing Norfk	Norfk	8	J14
Winford IoW	IoW	9	J4
Winford N Som	N Som	14	K16
Winforton Herefs	Herefs	21	R8
Winfrith Newburgh Dorset	Dorset	7	P13
Wing Bucks	Bucks	16	K6
Wing Rutlnd	Rutlnd	24	K8
Wingate Dur	Dur	41	R12
Wingerworth Derbys	Derbys	32	C12
Wingfield C Beds	C Beds	17	M6
Wingfield Suffk	Suffk	27	R12
Wingfield Wilts	Wilts	7	P1
Wingham Kent	Kent	11	Q4
Wingmore Kent	Kent	11	N7
Wingrave Bucks	Bucks	16	K7
Winkburn Notts	Notts	32	C14
Winkfield Br For	Br For	17	L15
Winkfield Row Br For	Br For	17	L15
Winkhill Staffs	Staffs	31	N1
Winkleigh Devon	Devon	4	N5
Winksley N York	N York	36	F11
Winlaton Gatesd	Gatesd	41	N8
Winless Highld	Highld	58	H5
Winmarleigh Lancs	Lancs	31	H5
Winnersh Wokham	Wokham	16	H15
Winscales Cumb	Cumb	39	R13
Winscombe N Som	N Som	14	K4
Winsford Ches W	Ches W	30	H3
Winsford Somset	Somset	4	K3
Winsham Somset	Somset	6	H4
Winshill Staffs	Staffs	23	Q6
Winshwen Swans	Swans	8	R11
Winskill Cumb	Cumb	40	H16
Winsley Wilts	Wilts	15	N16
Winslow Bucks	Bucks	16	K5
Winson Gloucs	Gloucs	15	U7
Winston Dur	Dur	36	M8
Winston Suffk	Suffk	19	Q1
Winstone Gloucs	Gloucs	15	L6
Winswell Devon	Devon	5	C16
Winterborne Came Dorset	Dorset	7	N13
Winterborne Clenston Dorset	Dorset	7	P10
Winterborne Houghton Dorset	Dorset	7	U9
Winterborne Kingston Dorset	Dorset	7	Q11
Winterborne Monkton Dorset	Dorset	7	M13
Winterborne Stickland Dorset	Dorset	7	Q10
Winterborne Zelston Dorset	Dorset	7	U11
Winterbourne S Glos	S Glos	15	L13
Winterbourne W Berk	W Berk	16	D14

Place	County	Page	Grid
Winterbourne Abbas Dorset	Dorset	7	L12
Winterbourne Bassett Wilts	Wilts	15	T14
Winterbourne Dauntsey Wilts	Wilts	8	D6
Winterbourne Earls Wilts	Wilts	8	D6
Winterbourne Gunner Wilts	Wilts	8	D6
Winterbourne Monkton Wilts	Wilts	15	T15
Winterbourne Steepleton Dorset	Dorset	7	M12
Winterbourne Stoke Wilts	Wilts	8		
Winterbourn N York	N York	35	U13
Winteringham N Linc	N Linc	33	L3
Winterley Ches E	Ches E	31	M1
Wintersett Wakefd	Wakefd	31	E6
Winterslow Wilts	Wilts	8	H2
Winterton N Linc	N Linc	33	P12
Winterton-on-Sea Norfk	Norfk	27	U6
Winthorpe Notts	Notts	32	J15
Winton Bmouth	Bmouth	7	T12
Winton Cumb	Cumb	40	D1
Wintringham N York	N York	37	L11
Winwick Cambs	Cambs	25	N12
Winwick Nhants	Nhants	24	F13
Winwick Warrtn	Warrtn	30	J10
Wirksworth Derbys	Derbys	23	U1
Wirswall Ches E	Ches E	22	E3
Wisbech Cambs	Cambs	25	N10
Wisbech St Mary Cambs	Cambs	26	D7
Wisborough Green W Susx	W Susx	9	R7
Wiseman's Bridge Pembks	Pembks	12	H9
Wiseton Notts	Notts	32	G9
Wishaw N Lans	N Lans	45	J7
Wishaw Warwks	Warwks	31	L16
Wispington Lincs	Lincs	33	P12
Wissenden Kent	Kent	11	R6
Wissett Suffk	Suffk	27	T12
Wistanstow Shrops	Shrops	21	R6
Wistanswick Shrops	Shrops	30	K15
Wistaston Ches E	Ches E	30	K15
Wistaston Green Ches E	Ches E	30	C16
Wiston Pembks	Pembks	12	H7
Wiston S Lans	S Lans	45	L11
Wiston W Susx	W Susx	10	T9
Wistow Cambs	Cambs	26	B13
Wistow N York	N York	32	F2
Wiswell Lancs	Lancs	31	L1
Witcham Cambs	Cambs	26	C11
Witchampton Dorset	Dorset	26	E12
Witchford Cambs	Cambs	18	E12
Witcombe Somset	Somset	6	H3
Witham Essex	Essex	18	K11
Witham Friary Somset	Somset	7	K9
Witham on the Hill Lincs	Lincs	25	M6
Withcall Lincs	Lincs	32	M6
Withdean Br & H	Br & H	10	L14
Witherenden Hill E Susx	E Susx	10	J11
Witheridge Devon	Devon	5	P9
Witherley Leics	Leics	23	S11
Withern Lincs	Lincs	33	S11
Withernsea E R Yk	E R Yk	33	R3
Withernwick E R Yk	E R Yk	33	R3
Withersdale Street Suffk	Suffk	27	R12
Withersfield Suffk	Suffk	35	M9
Witherslack Cumb	Cumb	35	M9
Withiel Cnwll	Cnwll	2	C5
Withiel Florey Somset	Somset	5	C5
Withington Gloucs	Gloucs	15	S11
Withington Herefs	Herefs	14	J4
Withington Manch	Manch	31	M9
Withington Shrops	Shrops	23	E8
Withleigh Devon	Devon	5	R9
Withybrook Warwks	Warwks	33	T11
Withycombe Somset	Somset	5	T9
Withyham E Susx	E Susx	10	P9
Withywood Bristl	Bristl	14	K15
Witley Surrey	Surrey	9	Q5
Witnesham Suffk	Suffk	19	Q5
Witney Oxon	Oxon	16	B7
Wittering C Pete	C Pete	25	M10
Wittersham Kent	Kent	11	M10
Witton Birm	Birm	23	Q4
Witton Gilbert Dur	Dur	41	P11
Witton le Wear Dur	Dur	41	H10
Witton Park Dur	Dur	41	N4
Wiveliscombe Somset	Somset	6	L5
Wivelrod Hants	Hants	9	L5
Wivelsfield E Susx	E Susx	10	L13
Wivelsfield Green E Susx	E Susx	10	D12
Wivenhoe Essex	Essex	19	N2
Wiveton Norfk	Norfk	19	T1
Wix Essex	Essex	19	P7
Wixams Bed	Bed	18	F3
Wixford Warwks	Warwks	15	T1
Wixoe Suffk	Suffk	18	F1
Woburn C Beds	C Beds	17	L4
Woburn Sands M Keyn	M Keyn	17	L4
Woking Surrey	Surrey	9	S2
Wokingham Wokham	Wokham	16	S11
Woldingham Surrey	Surrey	10	S11
Wold Newton E R Yk	E R Yk	37	S9
Wold Newton NE Lin	NE Lin	33	Q8
Wolfclyde S Lans	S Lans	45	M11
Wolferton Norfk	Norfk	26	K4
Wolfhill P & K	P & K	50	J9
Wolf's Castle Pembks	Pembks	12	F6
Wollaston Dudley	Dudley	23	K4
Wollaston Nhants	Nhants	24	K15
Wollaston Shrops	Shrops	15	M12
Wollaton C Nott	C Nott	24	E2
Wollerton Shrops	Shrops	22	E2
Wollescote Dudley	Dudley	23	K4
Wolseley Bridge Staffs	Staffs	23	M5
Wolsingham Dur	Dur	31	M16
Wolstanton Staffs	Staffs	31	M16
Wolston Warwks	Warwks	24	E10
Wolvercote Oxon	Oxon	16	E6
Wolverhampton Wolverhampton Airport Staffs	Staffs	22	J10
Wolverley Shrops	Shrops	22	J3
Wolverley Worcs	Worcs	16	J3
Wolverton Hants	Hants	8	F2
Wolverton Kent	Kent	8	P3
Wolverton M Keyn	M Keyn	24	J5
Wolverton Warwks	Warwks	16	J2
Wolvesnewton Mons	Mons	14	H9
Wolvey Warwks	Warwks	24	D11
Wolviston S on T	S on T	41	M9
Wombleton N York	N York	37	M10
Wombourne Staffs	Staffs	22	K2
Wombwell Barns	Barns	32	N5
Womersley N York	N York	32	F4
Wonersh Surrey	Surrey	9	R2
Wonford Devon	Devon	5	R2
Wonston Dorset	Dorset	7	P10
Wonston Hants	Hants	8	J13
Wooburn Bucks	Bucks	17	L12
Wooburn Green Bucks	Bucks	17	M12
Woodacott Devon	Devon	4	D2
Woodall Rothm	Rothm	32	D11
Woodbastwick Norfk	Norfk	27	N6
Wood Bevington Warwks	Warwks	15	S1
Woodborough Notts	Notts	32	F16
Woodborough Wilts	Wilts	8	B2
Woodbridge Dorset	Dorset	7	N8
Woodbridge Suffk	Suffk	19	P2
Woodbury Devon	Devon	5	S13
Woodbury Salterton Devon	Devon			
Woodchester Gloucs	Gloucs	15	S12
Woodchurch Kent	Kent	11	L8
Woodcombe Somset	Somset	5	U3
Woodcote Gt Lon	Gt Lon	10	E3
Woodcote Oxon	Oxon	16	G13
Woodcote Wrekin	Wrekin	22	G8
Woodcroft Gloucs	Gloucs	14	H9
Woodcutts Dorset	Dorset	7	R6
Wood Dalling Norfk	Norfk	6	D10
Woodditton Cambs	Cambs	18	G5
Woodeaton Oxon	Oxon	16	G6
Wood End Bed	Bed	25	M14
Wood End Gt Lon	Gt Lon	17	S14
Wood Enderby Lincs	Lincs	33	Q13
Woodend Highld	Highld	48	J5
Woodend Nhants	Nhants	16	B10
Woodend Staffs	Staffs	23	P7
Woodend W Susx	W Susx	9	M9
Wood End Warwks	Warwks	23	P13
Woodend Green Essex	Essex	18	E8
Wood Enderby Lincs	Lincs	33	Q13
Woodfalls Wilts	Wilts	8	G3
Woodford Gloucs	Gloucs	15	N5
Woodford Gt Lon	Gt Lon	17	S12
Woodford Nhants	Nhants	25	L14
Woodford Green Gt Lon	Gt Lon	17	S12
Woodford Halse Nhants	Nhants	16	H6
Woodford Wells Gt Lon	Gt Lon	17		
Woodgate Birm	Birm	23	J4
Woodgate Devon	Devon	5	C4
Woodgate Norfk	Norfk	27	L7
Woodgate W Susx	W Susx	9	N10
Woodgate Worcs	Worcs	23	S13
Wood Green Gt Lon	Gt Lon	17	R4
Woodhall Herts	Herts	17	Q7

Place	County	Page	Grid
Woodham Mortimer Essex	Essex	18	J12
Woodham Walter Essex	Essex	18	J12
Wood Hayes Wolves	Wolves	23	L8
Woodhead Abers	Abers	55	Q8
Woodhill Shrops	Shrops	22	H3
Woodhill Somset	Somset	6	K11
Woodhorn Nthumb	Nthumb	41	Q4
Woodhouse Cumb	Cumb	35	M9
Woodhouse Leeds	Leeds	35	P1
Woodhouse Sheff	Sheff	32	C10
Woodhouse Wakefd	Wakefd	32	C2
Woodhouse Eaves Leics	Leics	24	E6
Woodhouselee Mdloth	Mdloth	45	P6
Woodhouses Oldham	Oldham	31	N7
Woodhouses Staffs	Staffs	23	P6
Woodhurst Cambs	Cambs	25	R13
Woodingdean Br & H	Br & H	10	L14
Woodkirk Leeds	Leeds	31	T3
Woodland Abers	Abers	55	R11
Woodland Devon	Devon	5	M7
Woodland Dur	Dur	41	L4
Woodland S Ayrs	S Ayrs	38	D4
Woodlands Dorset	Dorset	7	T8
Woodlands Donc	Donc	32	E6
Woodlands Hants	Hants	8	G8
Woodlands N York	N York	36	E16
Woodlands Park W & M	W & M	16	K13
Woodleigh Devon	Devon	3	N10
Woodmancote Gloucs	Gloucs	15	R5
Woodmancote Gloucs	Gloucs	15	R8
Woodmancote Gloucs	Gloucs	15	M9
Woodmancote W Susx	W Susx	10	C12
Woodmancote Hants	Hants	9	M5
Woodmancott Hants	Hants	9	Q4
Woodmansey E R Yk	E R Yk	33	M1
Woodmansgreen W Susx	W Susx	9	P7
Woodmansterne Surrey	Surrey	10	S4
Woodmanton Devon	Devon	5	S13
Woodnesborough Kent	Kent	11	S5
Wood Norton Norfk	Norfk	27	M4
Woodplumpton Lancs	Lancs	30	K2
Woodrising Norfk	Norfk	27	L8
Wood's Corner E Susx	E Susx	10	J12
Woodseaves Staffs	Staffs	22	J4
Woodsetts Rothm	Rothm	32	E10
Woodside Br For	Br For	17	L15
Woodside Cumb	Cumb	50	J9
Woodside P & K	P & K	50	J9
Woodstock Oxon	Oxon	16	D7
Woodston C Pete	C Pete	25	L9
Wood Street Village Surrey	Surrey	9	Q3
Woodton Norfk	Norfk	27	R10
Woodtown Devon	Devon	4	J7
Woodvale Sefton	Sefton	30	H5
Woodville Derbys	Derbys	23	M5
Woodwall Green Staffs	Staffs	22	H3
Woody Bay Devon	Devon	4	M2
Woofferton Shrops	Shrops	22	E14
Wookey Somset	Somset	6	K3
Wookey Hole Somset	Somset	6	K3
Wool Dorset	Dorset	7	U13
Woolacombe Devon	Devon	4	J3
Woolage Green Kent	Kent	11	P7
Woolaston Gloucs	Gloucs	14	K10
Woolavington Somset	Somset	6	L10
Woolbeding W Susx	W Susx	9	P7
Wooler Nthumb	Nthumb	47	N12
Woolfardisworthy Devon	Devon	5	R11
Woolfords S Lans	S Lans	45	M8
Woolhampton W Berk	W Berk	16	F15
Woolhope Herefs	Herefs	15	P13
Woolland Dorset	Dorset	7	T9
Woolley BaNES	BaNES	15	N15
Woolley Cambs	Cambs	25	M15
Woolley Wakefd	Wakefd	31	R9
Woolmere Green Worcs	Worcs	23	N13
Woolmer Green Herts	Herts	17	S8
Woolpit Suffk	Suffk	19	M3
Woolscott Warwks	Warwks	24	S4
Woolstaston Shrops	Shrops	21	S5
Woolsthorpe Lincs	Lincs	24	K5
Woolsthorpe-by-Colsterworth Lincs	Lincs	24	K5
Woolston C Sotn	C Sotn	8	H10
Woolston Somset	Somset	29	T14
Woolston Somset	Somset	7	M6
Woolston Shrops	Shrops	21	N4
Woolston Warrtn	Warrtn	30	R10
Woolstone Gloucs	Gloucs	15	K4
Woolstone M Keyn	M Keyn	24	K4
Woolstone Oxon	Oxon	15	B12
Woolton Lpool	Lpool	30	J9
Woolton Hill Hants	Hants	16	E15
Woolverstone Suffk	Suffk	27	Q7
Woolverton Somset	Somset	7	P2
Woolwich Gt Lon	Gt Lon	10	D2
Woore Shrops	Shrops	30	F2
Wootten Green Suffk	Suffk	27	Q13
Wootton Bed	Bed	17	L1
Wootton IoW	IoW	9	R11
Wootton Kent	Kent	11	P7
Wootton N Linc	N Linc	33	L3
Wootton Nhants	Nhants	16	H1
Wootton Oxon	Oxon	16	C6
Wootton Oxon	Oxon	16	E6
Wootton Shrops	Shrops	22	F9
Wootton Staffs	Staffs	22	H5
Wootton Bassett Wilts	Wilts	15	T12
Wootton Bridge IoW	IoW	9	R11
Wootton Courtenay Somset	Somset	5	R4
Wootton Fitzpaine Dorset	Dorset	6	K6
Wootton Rivers Wilts	Wilts	8	B1
Wootton St Lawrence Hants	Hants	8	K4
Wootton Wawen Warwks	Warwks	23	P15
Worcester Worcs	Worcs	22	G1
Worcester Park Gt Lon	Gt Lon	10	C3
Wordsley Dudley	Dudley	22	K11
Worfield Shrops	Shrops	22	E8
Workington Cumb	Cumb	39	R13
Worksop Notts	Notts	32	E11
Worlaby N Linc	N Linc	33	L5
Worlds End W Susx	W Susx	10	L9
Worleston Ches E	Ches E	30	C16
Worlingham Suffk	Suffk	27	S10
Worlington Suffk	Suffk	18	H13
Worlingworth Suffk	Suffk	27	Q13
Wormbridge Herefs	Herefs	14	K2
Wormegay Norfk	Norfk	26	G6
Wormelow Tump Herefs	Herefs	14	J2
Wormhill Derbys	Derbys	31	K12
Wormingford Essex	Essex	19	L6
Worminghall Bucks	Bucks	16	G6
Wormington Gloucs	Gloucs	15	S3
Wormit Fife	Fife	51	M11
Wormleighton Warwks	Warwks	16	J2
Wormley Herts	Herts	17	S10
Wormley Surrey	Surrey	9	R5
Wormshill Kent	Kent	11	L5
Wormsley Herefs	Herefs	21	R12
Worplesdon Surrey	Surrey	9	R2
Worrall Sheff	Sheff	32	L8
Worsbrough Barns	Barns	32	N5
Worsbrough Bridge Barns	Barns	32	B7
Worsbrough Dale Barns	Barns	32	B7
Worsley Salfd	Salfd	31	L8
Worstead Norfk	Norfk	27	Q5
Worsthorne Lancs	Lancs	31	S4
Worston Lancs	Lancs	35	U3
Worth Kent	Kent	11	T5
Worth Somset	Somset	6	K2
Worth W Susx	W Susx	10	D9
Wortham Suffk	Suffk	27	L13
Worthen Shrops	Shrops	20	G12
Worthenbury Wrexhm	Wrexhm	22	C3
Worthing Norfk	Norfk	26	M7
Worthing W Susx	W Susx	9	S11
Worthington Leics	Leics	24	C5
Wortley Barns	Barns	32	M8
Wortley Leeds	Leeds	31	N3
Worton N York	N York	36	B8
Worton Wilts	Wilts	7	M1
Wortwell Norfk	Norfk	27	R11
Wotton Surrey	Surrey	10	T4
Wotton-under-Edge Gloucs	Gloucs	15	M9
Wotton Underwood Bucks	Bucks	16	H7
Woughton on the Green M Keyn	M Keyn	24	K4
Wouldham Kent	Kent	10	H3
Wrabness Essex	Essex	19	Q6
Wrafton Devon	Devon	4	K6
Wragby Lincs	Lincs	33	N11
Wragby Wakefd	Wakefd	31	S5
Wrangaton Devon	Devon	3	Q7
Wrangle Lincs	Lincs	33	S16
Wrangway Somset	Somset	6	E13
Wrantage Somset	Somset	6	K12
Wrawby N Linc	N Linc	33	M6
Wraxall N Som	N Som	14	K14
Wraxall Somset	Somset	7	L8
Wray Lancs	Lancs	35	U6
Wraysbury W & M	W & M	17	M14
Wrayton Lancs	Lancs	35	U6
Wrea Green Lancs	Lancs	30	G3
Wreay Cumb	Cumb	40	C10

Place	County	Page	Grid
Wrekenton Gatesd	Gatesd	41	Q9
Wrelton N York	N York	37	M9
Wrenbury Ches E	Ches E	22	F1
Wreningham Norfk	Norfk	27	P9
Wrentham Suffk	Suffk	27	U12
Wrenthorpe Wakefd	Wakefd	31	K3
Wressle E R Yk	E R Yk	32	H2
Wressle N Linc	N Linc	33	L6
Wrestlingworth C Beds	C Beds	17	S3
Wretton Norfk	Norfk	26	H9
Wrexham Wrexhm	Wrexhm	30	E16
Wrexham Industrial Estate Wrexhm	Wrexhm	30	F16
Wribbenhall Worcs	Worcs	22	H13
Wrinehill Staffs	Staffs	22	H1
Wrington N Som	N Som	14	K4
Writtle Essex	Essex	18	H12
Wrockwardine Wrekin	Wrekin	22	H12
Wroot N Linc	N Linc	32	H5
Wroxall IoW	IoW	8	J15
Wroxall Warwks	Warwks	23	R13
Wroxeter Shrops	Shrops	21	K3
Wroxham Norfk	Norfk	27	Q6
Wroxton Oxon	Oxon	16	D5
Wyaston Derbys	Derbys	23	R3
Wyberton East Lincs	Lincs	25	S3
Wyboston Bed	Bed	25	Q9
Wybunbury Ches E	Ches E	30	K16
Wychbold Worcs	Worcs	23	K14
Wychnor Staffs	Staffs	23	P6
Wyck Rissington Gloucs	Gloucs	15	P5
Wyck Hants	Hants	9	D4
Wycliffe Dur	Dur	36	K6
Wycoller Lancs	Lancs			
Wycomb Leics	Leics	24	H5
Wycombe Marsh Bucks	Bucks	17	L11
Wyddial Herts	Herts	17	T5
Wye Kent	Kent	11	P7
Wyke C Brad	C Brad	31	S3
Wyke Champflower Somset	Somset	7	M5
Wyken Covtry	Covtry	23	R9
Wyken Shrops	Shrops	22	S12
Wyke Regis Dorset	Dorset	7	P14
Wykey Shrops	Shrops	29	C5
Wylam Nthumb	Nthumb	41	M8
Wylde Green Birm	Birm	23	N10
Wyllie Caerph	Caerph	14	F8
Wylye Wilts	Wilts	8	A5
Wymeswold Leics	Leics	24	F5
Wymington Bed	Bed	25	L15
Wymondham Leics	Leics	24	J6
Wymondham Norfk	Norfk	27	N8
Wynford Eagle Dorset	Dorset	7	L12
Wyre Piddle Worcs	Worcs	15	R2
Wysall Notts	Notts	24	F4
Wythall Worcs	Worcs	23	N13
Wytham Oxon	Oxon	16	E9
Wythenshawe Manch	Manch	31	M10
Wyton Cambs	Cambs	25	Q13
Wyverstone Suffk	Suffk	27	M7
Wyverstone Street Suffk	Suffk	27	N14

Y

Place	County	Page	Grid
Yaddlethorpe N Linc	N Linc	32	K6
Yafforth N York	N York	36	U6
Yalberton Torbay	Torbay	3	B6
Yalding Kent	Kent	10	J7
Yanwath Cumb	Cumb	40	D14
Yanworth Gloucs	Gloucs	15	R6
Yapham E R Yk	E R Yk	37	N15
Yapton W Susx	W Susx	9	Q11
Yarborough N Som	N Som	3	R9
Yarburgh Lincs	Lincs	33	R9
Yarcombe Devon	Devon	6	F9
Yard Devon	Devon	5	R7
Yardley Birm	Birm	23	M4
Yardley Gobion Nhants	Nhants	16	J3
Yardley Hastings Nhants	Nhants	24	J16
Yardley Wood Birm	Birm	23	N12
Yarkhill Herefs	Herefs	15	L3
Yarley Somset	Somset	6	K3
Yarlington Somset	Somset	7	M5
Yarm S on T	S on T	36	H5
Yarmouth IoW	IoW	8	K11
Yarnbrook Wilts	Wilts	7	Q2
Yarnfield Staffs	Staffs	22	J4
Yarnscombe Devon	Devon	4	L7
Yarnton Oxon	Oxon	29	T14
Yarpole Herefs	Herefs	21	S11
Yarrow Border	Border	46	E12
Yarrow Feus Border	Border	46	E12
Yarrowford Border	Border	46	E12
Yarwell Nhants	Nhants	25	M9
Yate S Glos	S Glos	15	L13
Yateley Hants	Hants	9	N2
Yatesbury Wilts	Wilts	15	S15
Yattendon W Berk	W Berk	16	F14
Yatton Herefs	Herefs	21	H16
Yatton N Som	N Som	14	K4
Yatton Keynell Wilts	Wilts	15	N7
Yaverland IoW	IoW	9	R12
Yaxham Norfk	Norfk	27	M7
Yaxley Cambs	Cambs	25	P3
Yazor Herefs	Herefs	21	R13
Yeading Gt Lon	Gt Lon	17	P11
Yeadon Leeds	Leeds	31	S1
Yealand Conyers Lancs	Lancs	35	M11
Yealand Redmayne Lancs	Lancs			
Yealmpton Devon	Devon	35	M11
Yearsley N York	N York	3	L1
Yeaton Shrops	Shrops	36	K11
Yeaveley Derbys	Derbys	23	N11
Yeavering Nthumb	Nthumb	47	N12
Yedingham N York	N York	37	O15
Yelford Oxon	Oxon	16	Q9
Yelland Devon	Devon	4	K5
Yelling Cambs	Cambs	25	Q16
Yelvertoft Nhants	Nhants	24	E2
Yelverton Devon	Devon	2	K7
Yelverton Norfk	Norfk	27	R9
Yenston Somset	Somset	7	N7
Yeoford Devon	Devon	5	P11
Yeolmbridge Cnwll	Cnwll	4	K8
Yeo Vale Devon	Devon	4	K6
Yeovil Somset	Somset	7	L8
Yeovil Marsh Somset	Somset	6	J3
Yeovilton Somset	Somset	6	D3
Yesnaby Ork	Ork	58	b5
Yetminster Dorset	Dorset	7	L9
Yettington Devon	Devon	6	D8
Yetts o' Muckhart Clacks	Clacks	50	G15
Yew Tree Sandw	Sandw			
Y Felinheli Gwynd	Gwynd	28	H7
Y Ferwig Cerdgn	Cerdgn	20	C1
Y Ffor Gwynd	Gwynd	28	F5
Y Gyffylliog Denbgs	Denbgs	29	P9
Yielden Bed	Bed	25	N13
Yieldshields S Lans	S Lans	45	L8
Yiewsley Gt Lon	Gt Lon	17	N13
Y Maerdy Conwy	Conwy	29	N11
Ynysboeth Rhondd	Rhondd	14	C11
Ynysddu Caerph	Caerph	14	F9
Ynyshir Rhondd	Rhondd	14	C11
Yockleton Shrops	Shrops	21	J2
Yokefleet E R Yk	E R Yk	32	K4
Yoker C Glas	C Glas	44	E5
York C York	C York	37	L15
Yorkletts Kent	Kent	11	M5
Yorkley Gloucs	Gloucs	15	L8
York Town Surrey	Surrey	9	N2
Youlgreave Derbys	Derbys	31	S13
Youlton N York	N York	36	J12
Yoxall Staffs	Staffs	23	L8
Yoxford Suffk	Suffk	27	S14
Y Rhiw Gwynd	Gwynd	28	D8
Ysbyty Ifan Conwy	Conwy	29	P10
Ysbyty Ystwyth Cerdgn	Cerdgn	20	Q6
Ystalyfera Neath	Neath	26	C5
Ystrad Rhondd	Rhondd	14	B11
Ystrad Aeron Cerdgn	Cerdgn	20	J9
Ystradfellte Powys	Powys	14	D5
Ystradgynlais Powys	Powys	26	B5
Ystrad Meurig Cerdgn	Cerdgn	20	J12
Ystrad Mynach Caerph	Caerph	14	F8
Ythanbank Abers	Abers	55	R9
Ythsie Abers	Abers	55	R10

Z

Place	County	Page	Grid
Zeal Monachorum Devon	Devon	5	N10
Zeals Wilts	Wilts	7	P5
Zelah Cnwll	Cnwll	1	U5
Zennor Cnwll	Cnwll	1	M11
Zouch Notts	Notts	24	D5